# Introductory Statistical Methods

# THE DUXBURY SERIES IN STATISTICS AND DECISION SCIENCES

*Applications, Basics, and Computing of Exploratory Data Analysis*, Velleman and Hoaglin
*Applied Regression Analysis and Other Multivariable Methods*, Second Edition,
   Kleinbaum, Kupper, and Muller
*Classical and Modern Regression with Applications*, Myers
*A Course in Business Statistics*, Second Edition, Mendenhall
*Elementary Statistics for Business*, Second Edition, Johnson and Siskin
*Elementary Statistics*, Fifth Edition, Johnson
*Elementary Survey Sampling*, Third Edition, Scheaffer, Mendenhall, and Ott
*Essential Business Statistics: A Minitab Framework*, Bond and Scott
*Fundamental Statistics for Human Services and Social Work*, Krishef
*Fundamental Statistics for the Behavioral Sciences*, Howell
*Fundamentals of Biostatistics*, Second Edition, Rosner
*Fundamentals of Statistics in the Biological, Medical, and Health Sciences*, Runyon
*Introduction to Contemporary Statistical Methods*, Second Edition, Koopmans
*Introduction to Probability and Mathematical Statistics*, Bain and Engelhardt
*Introduction to Probability and Statistics*, Seventh Edition, Mendenhall
*An Introduction to Statistical Methods and Data Analysis*, Third Edition, Ott
*Introductory Statistical Methods: An Integrated Approach Using Minitab*, Groeneveld
*Introductory Statistics for Management and Economics*, Second Edition, Kenkel
*Linear Statistical Models: An Applied Approach*, Bowerman, O'Connell, and Dickey
*Management Science: An Introduction*, Davis, McKeown, and Rakes
*Mathematical Statistics with Applications*, Third Edition, Mendenhall, Scheaffer, and Wackerly
*Minitab Handbook*, Second Edition, Ryan, Joiner, and Ryan
*Minitab Handbook for Business and Economics*, Miller
*Operations Research: Applications and Algorithms*, Winston
*Probability Modeling and Computer Simulation*, Matloff
*Probability and Statistics for Engineers*, Second Edition, Scheaffer and McClave
*Probability and Statistics for Modern Engineering*, Lapin
*Quantitative Management: An Introduction*, Second Edition, Anderson and Lievano
*Quantitative Models for Management*, Second Edition, Davis and McKeown
*Statistical Experiments Using BASIC*, Dowdy
*Statistical Methods for Psychology*, Second Edition, Howell
*Statistical Thinking for Behavioral Scientists*, Hildebrand
*Statistical Thinking for Managers*, Second Edition, Hildebrand and Ott
*Statistics for Management and Economics*, Fifth Edition, Mendenhall, Reinmuth, Beaver,
   and Duhan
*Statistics: A Tool for the Social Sciences*, Fourth Edition, Ott, Larson, and Mendenhall
*Time Series Analysis*, Cryer
*Time Series Forecasting: Unified Concepts and Computer Implementation*, Second
   Edition, Bowerman and O'Connell
*Understanding Statistics*, Fourth Edition, Ott and Mendenhall

# Introductory Statistical Methods

## An Integrated Approach Using Minitab

Richard A. Groeneveld
Iowa State University

PWS–KENT Publishing Company
BOSTON

# PWS–KENT
## Publishing Company

20 Park Plaza
Boston, Massachusetts 02116

*QA*
*276*
*.4*
*G76*
*1988*

**LIBRARY OF CONGRESS**
Library of Congress Cataloging-in-Publication Data

Groeneveld, Richard A.
    Introductory statistical methods: an integrated approach using
Minitab  /  Richard A. Groeneveld.
        p.   cm.
    Includes index.
    ISBN 0-534-91486-1
    1. Statistics—Data processing.   2. Minitab (Computer system)
I. Title.
QA276.4.G76 1988
519.5—dc19                                                      88-10221
                                                                      CIP

Printed in the United States of America

88 89 90 91 92—10 9 8 7 6 5 4 3 2 1

*Sponsoring Editor*: Michael Payne
*Production Coordinator*: Robine Andrau
*Production*: Lifland et al., Bookmakers
*Interior Design*: Ellie Connolly
*Cover Design*: Robine Andrau
*Typesetting*: The Alden Press Ltd
*Cover Printing*: New England Book Components, Inc.
*Printing and Binding*: Arcata Graphics/Halliday

To my wife, Valerie

# Preface

*Introductory Statistical Methods* is a text for an introductory course in statistics. Two years of secondary school algebra provide an adequate mathematical background. Courses for which this book is appropriate are currently being given in college at the sophomore level, although there is good evidence that such courses will appear at an earlier educational level in the future. The text is not limited to any particular educational or professional field of interest; the basic statistical principles described can be broadly applied. I believe that a concentration on basic principles provides an essential foundation for understanding statistics and a good basis for applying more advanced statistical methods in specific fields.

Three features of this text merit special mention. *First*, data from contemporary real-life situations are used throughout in examples to stimulate interest in statistical ideas and methods. Similar data sets are also used in many of the exercises. These examples and exercises using real data from published sources are, I feel, implicitly more interesting than those involving artificial data, even if the reader (like the author) is not familiar with all the areas of application. *Second*, emphasis is placed on those statistical methods concerned with explaining the relationship between variables. The aim here is to illustrate the important role statistics plays in the scientific method. This emphasis is particularly clear in the chapters on two-sample problems, the analysis of variance, simple linear regression, and multiple regression. *Third*, actual computer printouts are frequently used to introduce, illustrate, and emphasize statistical analyses and ideas.

It seems clear that in the future most statistical computations will be carried out by means of computerized statistical packages. Such packages are rapidly becoming widely available on a commercial basis to academic, business, and government users. Those most commonly used include BMDP, Minitab, SAS, and SPSS. At the introductory level, the Minitab system seems most helpful as a teaching device. It is "user friendly," allowing individuals with relatively little training to carry out substantial statistical computations. It is capable of producing graphical displays illustrating statistical properties of data sets. It has sufficient simulation power to provide data sets and, more importantly, to illustrate the meaning of statistical ideas such as the Central Limit Theorem, confidence coefficients, elementary probabilistic concepts, and type I and II errors. The details of the use of Minitab are given in the *Minitab Student Handbook* by Thomas A. Ryan, Brian L. Joiner, and Barbara F. Ryan. Experience has shown, however, that college students can attain reasonable proficiency in the use of Minitab simply by learning elementary Minitab commands and then practicing at local computer facilities. (In this regard, it is recommended that students save data sets that are introduced in the exercises, as they may be used in subsequent exercises.) Appendix B describes all the elementary Minitab commands needed to understand this text and complete the exercises. I believe that only by using modern computing technology will students become aware of the important role statistics plays in a technological society.

## Organization of the Text

After an introduction to statistics in Chapter 1, Chapter 2 presents elementary graphical and statistical methods used to organize, display, and summarize the information in a sample. The aim of Chapter 2 is to introduce methods that are currently in use in descriptive statistics. Chapter 3 presents an overview of the mathematical discipline of probability. Some knowledge of probability is necessary in order to understand statistical methods and their justification. Chapter 4 introduces discrete and continuous random variables, observations of which provide the raw data used in inference. Special attention is given to the standard normal distribution.

In Chapters 5 and 6 the fundamental inferential statistical ideas of estimation and testing hypotheses are introduced. These inferential methods are first considered in the large-sample context, with the normal distribution serving as the theoretical basis for carrying out such methods. The computer is used to clarify the concepts of confidence intervals and tests of hypotheses. Chapter 7 concerns tests based on small samples under the assumption of a normal population.

In the remaining chapters important practical statistical methods are introduced. Comparisons of populations are considered in Chapter 8, which discusses the comparisons of the locations (or centers) of two populations and of two population proportions. In Chapter 9, attention is directed to categorical, or enumerative, data. Methods of testing the independence of two variables are considered in this chapter. Statistical methods of verifying or rejecting distributional assumptions are also discussed.

In Chapter 10 the basic ideas of simple linear regression are introduced. The importance of regression models in explaining and predicting the relationship between two variables is emphasized. In Chapter 11 the simple linear regression model is extended to the multiple regression model, which permits a statistical description of complex relationships. Both the strengths and the limitations of the multiple regression model as a forecasting tool are examined. Finally, Chapter 12 provides an introduction to the analysis of variance.

## Acknowledgments

Completion of this text would not have been possible without the assistance and counsel of many individuals. First I must thank PWS–KENT editor Michael Payne for his encouragement and recommendations for revisions that transformed the initial manuscript into its present form. My thanks go also to Aleksandra Hall and Sharon Shepard for typing the initial manuscript and the following drafts cheerfully and accurately. And I am grateful to Quica Ostrander and particularly to Sally Lifland, who did excellent copyediting work on the final manuscript.

I would like to thank the following reviewers for their helpful comments: Patricia M. Buchanan, Pennsylvania State University; Anne M. Burns, C. W. Post College, Long Island University; Dennis D. Cox, University of Illinois, Urbana; Larry Haugh, University of Vermont; David Lund, University of Wisconsin, Eau Claire; W. Robert Stephenson, Iowa State University; Robert B. Stewart, Jr., Oakland University; Virginia Taylor, University of Lowell; William K. Tomhave, Concordia College; and Paul F. Velleman, Cornell University.

I am indebted to the staffs of the University of Pennsylvania and the Iowa State University computing centers for providing the computer time and support that allowed me to generate the Minitab computer output and programs in this text. The *Minitab Student Handbook*, Second Edition, written by Barbara Ryan, Brian L. Joiner, and Thomas A. Ryan, Jr., was an invaluable resource. I would particularly like to thank Thomas A. Ryan, Jr., who made Release 5.1 of Minitab available for me to use on the National Advanced System AS/9160 at Iowa State University. I also thank Professor David K. Hildebrand of the University of Pennsylvania and Professor William Q. Meeker of Iowa State University for their assistance and encouragement.

Most of all, I thank my family for their help and support during the preparation of this text.

R.G.

# Contents

# Chapter 1

# What Is Statistics?

## 1.1

**Introduction**    Statistical descriptions and statistical reasoning are no further away than the morning newspaper or the evening news on television. This is particularly obvious during the fall of an election year in the United States, as is illustrated by two front-page articles in the Sunday edition of *The New York Times* for October 31, 1982, two days before the November election. The first was headlined:

> **Both Parties View Election as a Test of Reagan Policies**
>
> **Economy Aids Democrats**
>
> **Late Shift in Voter Sentiment Hints at Large G.O.P. Loss in the House Tuesday**

The second was headlined:

> **Poll Finds Popularity of President Modifying Impact of Jobless Issue**

## Table 1.1

**The New York Times/CBS News Poll: Congressional Preferences in the Election**

*"If the 1982 election for U.S. House of Representatives were being held today, would you vote for the Republican candidate or the Democratic candidate in your district? If other or undecided, which way do you lean as of today—toward the Republican candidate or toward the Democratic candidate?"*

### Support Broken Down by Subgroups of Those Polled

|  | Prefer Republican | Prefer Democrat |
|---|---|---|
| *Total* | 39% | 51% |
| *Sex* | | |
| Male | 41 | 51 |
| Female | 35 | 53 |
| *Race* | | |
| White | 41 | 48 |
| Black | 6 | 85 |
| *Political Philosophy* | | |
| Conservative | 50 | 39 |
| Moderate | 37 | 53 |
| Liberal | 20 | 73 |
| *Education* | | |
| Less than high school | 24 | 62 |
| High school graduate | 39 | 52 |
| Some college | 43 | 46 |
| College graduate or more | 44 | 49 |
| *Annual Income* | | |
| Less than $20,000 | 28 | 62 |
| $20,000–$40,000 | 44 | 46 |
| More than $40,000 | 53 | 42 |
| *Union Membership in Household* | 24 | 62 |
| *Family Financial Situation* | | |
| Worse than a year ago | 24 | 64 |
| Same as a year ago | 37 | 51 |
| Better than a year ago | 59 | 37 |

Poll based on a probable electorate derived from a total sample of 2,111, of which 1,437 said they were registered voters. Those with no opinion are not shown. The poll was conducted Oct. 23–27.

*Source:* Copyright © 1982 by the New York Times Company. Reprinted by permission.

Both stories used polls to justify their conclusions. In fact, most of the conclusions were based on data from the same *New York Times*/CBS News Poll, summarized in Table 1.1. The headlines, however, suggest the two different ways the pre–election day polls were interpreted.

The first story reported the results of the three polls as evidence supporting its predictions.

---

The major national public opinion polls uniformly found voter preference running in favor of Democratic candidates. The *New York Times*/CBS News Poll put the Democratic edge at 51 percent to 39 percent. The Gallup Poll found respondents favoring Democrats by 55 percent to 45 percent, and the Harris Poll showed a 52 to 40 percent advantage for Democrats.

---

The article stated that Democratic leaders expected a gain of about thirty seats in the House of Representatives. Additionally, analysts in both parties agreed that only an unexpected landslide vote would shift control of the Senate to the Democrats, and there seemed to be little evidence for such a landslide.

The second story pointed out that although the polls indicated that an increase in House seats for the Democrats was likely, the magnitude of the gain was uncertain for several reasons. The first was that the conversion of national vote percentages into the sum of results in individual House of Representatives races is an uncertain art. The second was that last-minute shifts in voting have been common in recent U.S. elections. The third was that President Reagan's own standing with the electorate had improved in the *New York Times*/CBS Poll from a 43/44 percent approval/disapproval rating in September to a 46/43 percent rating in October.

**political polls**  How are such **political polls** carried out? The *New York Times*/CBS Poll was based on telephone interviews with 2111 adults in the 48 continental states. Of this total, 1437 said that they were registered voters. In an effort to determine whether a respondent would be likely to vote, pollsters asked questions dealing with voter registration, residency, and past voting history. Questions concerning voting preference were reported in terms of a "probable electorate." The respondents were asked, "If the 1982 election for the U.S. House of Representatives were being held today, would you vote for the Republican candidate or the Democratic candidate in your district?" A breakdown of the responses by subgroups is given in Table 1.1. Can a telephone sample of 1437 registered voters adequately reflect the voting intentions of the U.S. electorate? How accurate are such polls? The first *New York Times* story stated, "In theory, it can be said that in 19 cases out of 20 the results based on the entire sample differ by no more than 3 percentage points from what would have been obtained by interviewing all adult Americans." How can such a statement be justified?

This example is instructive because it illustrates several aspects of statistical practice. First, a need is identified for information about characteristics of a large population. In this case the population could be defined as the population of adult U.S. citizens likely to vote. The characteristics of interest are various political opinions and voting intentions of this population. Second, because cost, time constraints, and various other considerations make it impossible to survey the entire population, a small group is selected from the population. Third, the characteristics of the sampled group are carefully tabulated and summarized. Fourth, these characteristics are interpreted with respect to the population as a whole. We have described two such interpretations which, although similar, highlight different issues. This type of reasoning, from partial information to the whole, is called **inferential reasoning**. Finally, a measure of the accuracy of such inference is made. Most statistical studies include the five steps mentioned here in some form.

inferential reasoning

The above example helps to answer the question "What is statistics?" Statistics is a body of knowledge used in situations where, first, the available data are incomplete, and second, inference is to be made about the characteristics of a larger population on the basis of these **incomplete data**. The methods used to make inference should satisfy some criteria of efficiency or effectiveness. These characteristics suggest the following definitions.

incomplete data

---

**Definition 1.1** ━━━━━━━━━━━━━━━━━━━━━━━━━━━━━━━━━━━━━━

population

A **population** is the totality of all possible elements of interest in an investigation.

---

**Definition 1.2** ━━━━━━━━━━━━━━━━━━━━━━━━━━━━━━━━━━━━━━

sample

A **sample** is the set of all elements of a population that have been observed.

---

**Definition 1.3** ━━━━━━━━━━━━━━━━━━━━━━━━━━━━━━━━━━━━━━

statistics

**Statistics** is a body of knowledge dealing with the collection, summarization, and presentation of the data as a basis for inference. Statistics is essentially concerned with how justifiable conclusions can be made on the basis of necessarily incomplete information.

---

There is an important difference between political polls and most other statistical studies in that the behavior of interest in political polls can eventually be observed. Many predictions made about the probable voting behavior of voters in 1982 were found to be substantially correct. The Democratic Party achieved a gain of 26 seats in the U.S. House of Representatives, increasing their seats from 241 to 267. The Republican majority of 54 Republican Senators to 46 Democratic Senators remained unchanged, with both parties having offsetting gains and losses. The general swing of the electorate toward the Democrats was most clearly demonstrated by an increase of seven governorships. This increase changed the split in governorships from 27/23 Democratic/Republican to 34/16. The sample of only 2111 adults (1437 registered voters), plus an intelligent analysis, did quite well in forecasting voting behavior in the 1982 U.S. election.

Of the two *New York Times* articles, the first better predicted the essential outcome of the elections. The second author's warnings of a possible misreading of the poll data do not seem to have been necessary in this particular election. The fact that different individuals drew different inferences from the same data, however, underlines the idea that the data do not, in general, "speak for themselves." Judicious and informed interpretation is required for successful application of inferential techniques.

What is striking about modern statistical practice is how many fields make use of statistical ideas and methods. Biometricians are experts in the application of statistics in biology. Econometricians use **economic statistics** in their forecasts of economic behavior. Psychometricians use statistical means of describing individual behavior. Statistical reasoning is used in fields as diverse as anthropology, engineering, history, and the law.

In medicine, the use of statistical methods is well advanced. Large medical centers such as the Mayo Clinic have departments of **medical statistics**. Statisticians assist in the design of experiments to determine which of two or more medical treatments is most effective. Pharmaceutical companies employ statisticians to design experiments to determine the effectiveness of drugs, and then to analyze the resulting data. Analyses of such data are used to request approval from the U.S. Food and Drug Administration for permission to market a new drug.

Many important economic indices, such as the Consumer Price Index (CPI) published by the Bureau of Labor Statistics and the monthly estimate of the percent unemployed published by the Commerce Department (U.S. Census Bureau), are prepared from sample data. These indices have an important economic and political impact on the society. Social Security payments, for example, are adjusted by a formula based on the CPI. Many other such indices are used in industry in making decisions about future plans for production and employment.

In industrial production, **industrial statistics** plays an important role in the area referred to as quality control or quality assurance. Production lines are sampled in order to determine whether a process is producing units satisfactorily (according to some measurement). If a process is found to be "out of control," it is stopped and adjusted. In an associated application, statistical reasoning is used in reliability theory to estimate the chance that a component will perform long enough to complete its intended function.

Statistical means are used to forecast future performance of people in jobs and in college. Scholastic Aptitude Test (SAT) scores and high school rank are considered to be good predictors of how individuals will perform academically in college.

The list of ways in which the discipline of statistics affects us all goes on and on. Hence it is important for every educated citizen to be aware of some of the basic concepts of this discipline. The basic ideas and methods used in statistical analysis

*economic statistics*

*medical statistics*

*industrial statistics*

are described in this text. Examples demonstrate the pervasiveness of statistics in a modern technological society.

## 1.2
## Probability and Statistics

*probability*

In order to understand statistical practice, one must be aware of the distinction between the roles of probability and statistics. **Probability** is a mathematical discipline, the aim of which is to describe random or chance experiments. A chance event is one whose outcome cannot be predicted in advance. An example of such an experiment is a baseball player's turn at bat. It cannot be predicted in advance whether a player will get a hit or make an out. Nevertheless, baseball fans use the players' batting averages as an indication of the likelihood of a player's getting a hit. A player's batting average is

$$\text{BA} = \frac{n_H}{n}$$

*relative frequency*

where $n$ represents the number of "at bats" for a player and $n_H$ represents the number of hits during those at bats. In other words, the **relative frequency** of a hit during a season constitutes the player's seasonal batting average.

The seasonal batting averages for two famous baseball players are presented in Figures 1.1 and 1.2. In Figure 1.1, Lou Gehrig's batting averages are plotted on the vertical axis versus time (1925–1938) on the horizontal axis. Only seasons in which Gehrig had at least 300 at bats are plotted. Gehrig's lifetime batting average of 0.340 is also graphed in Figure 1.1. There is substantial variation in the seasonal averages, particularly near the beginning of his career. In Figure 1.2, Willie Stargell's season batting averages are plotted from 1963 to 1979. His lifetime average was 0.282. Again, only seasons in which Stargell had at least 300 at

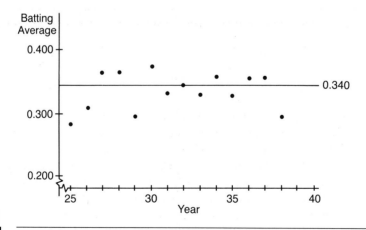

**Figure 1.1**

Lou Gehrig's Batting Averages

*Source: The Baseball Encyclopedia* (New York: Macmillan, 1985), p. 944.

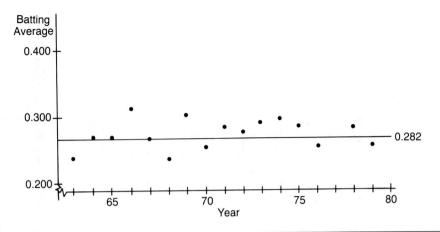

**Figure 1.2**

**Willie Stargell's Batting Averages**

*Source: The Baseball Encyclopedia* (New York: Macmillan, 1985), pp. 1422–23.

bats are included. There is substantial variation in these averages also, again particularly near the beginning of his career.

One can observe a regularity in these two graphs—that is, a tendency for the seasonal batting averages to cluster near a constant. (The constant is not the same in the two cases. A baseball fan would refer to Lou Gehrig as a "three-forty" hitter and to Willie Stargell as a "two-eighty-two" hitter.) Of course the at bats for the players are not repetitions of the same experiment on each occasion. The opposing pitchers differ, the games are played in different ball parks, the umpires are different, and the hitters themselves change as they become older. Nevertheless, it is the regularity of the yearly batting averages on which a baseball fan focuses.

---

**Definition 1.4** ▬▬▬▬▬▬▬▬▬▬▬▬▬▬▬▬▬▬▬▬▬▬▬▬▬

**Probability** is an axiomatic system that makes theoretically exact the idea of stable long-run frequencies.

---

Definition 1.4 is referred to as the frequentist interpretation of probability. In this definition, probabilities are interpreted as long-run relative frequencies. Thus a theoretical "three hundred" hitter would be described as one who has exactly three chances in every ten at bats of getting a hit. Alternatively, one can interpret probabilities as subjective values. For example, a person might state, "The chance of my getting an A in this course is 1 in 3." As the course is only taken once, this evaluation of the chance of a future event is subjective. The frequentist viewpoint will be used in this text.

From a relatively small number of assumptions, called axioms, which are introduced in Chapter 3, the substantial mathematical discipline of probability has emerged. Developed mostly within the last three centuries, it is quite young in relation to other mathematical disciplines such as algebra or geometry. Probability has as its aim the description of uncertain or chance phenomena. The empirical basis for probability is the stability of long-run relative frequencies.

Probability theory is important in almost all phases of a statistical study. It is used to justify the method employed to select the sample. It provides the theoretical basis for the interferential leap from sample to population. Probability is important in describing the sense in which inference is accurate or reliable. As such it can be thought of as the theoretical basis for inferential reasoning.

## 1.3
## The Role of the Computer in This Text

statistical computing package

Minitab

user friendly

It seems clear that from now on most statistical computations will be done via **statistical computing packages**. These are groups of statistical programs made available to users such as businesses, government agencies, and universities on a commercial basis. The most widely used of these packages currently are the BMDP, Minitab, SAS, and SPSS systems. The existence of organizations which continually update and improve such packaged programs is essential to effective statistical computing. In the author's view, the best of these packages for an introductory statistics course is, for several reasons, the **Minitab** system. First, the package may be used with either a batch-processing system or an interactive system. Second, experience has shown that with a relatively small amount of instruction, individuals with even a modest mathematical background can become effective users of a fairly powerful group of statistical programs. The Minitab system has been designed, in the words of the trade, to be "**user friendly**." The capabilities and limitations of users rather than those of the computer were paramount in the minds of the developers of this system. Third, the use of Minitab here will provide the basis for the use of Minitab as it evolves in the future and for learning to use other packages as well.

There are three important ways in which the computer can be of valuable assistance in an introductory statistics course. First, it provides a means of performing routine but tedious computations correctly, saving countless hours of computation with desk calculators and reducing the number of arithmetical errors. Second, the use of various editing, graphing, and table formatting commands permits visual displays of characteristics of a data set, which greatly aid in statistical analysis. Experienced statistical consultants always urge their clients to "look at the data." Third, the simulation capacity of the computer permits the selection of samples and the demonstration of statistical concepts in ways not previously possible.

Exhibit 1.1 is a Minitab list of the 25 largest cities in the United States according to the 1980 census. The columns list (from left to right) the 1980 rank by population, the city name, the 1980 population, the 1970 rank by population, and the percentage change from 1970 to 1980. (The reader is not now expected to be able to write the Minitab statements required to produce the output given.) The

**Exhibit 1.1**

```
MTB > NOTE POPULATION OF 25 LARGEST CITIES IN 1980

MTB > FPRINT C1-C9
 MTB > (5X,F3.0,1X,5A4,F10.0,2X,F4.0,F9.1)

    1980      CITY              1980POP   1970    PERCHG

        1. NEW YORK CITY       7071030.    1.    -10.4
        2. CHICAGO             3005072.    2.    -10.8
        3. LOS ANGELES         2966763.    3.      5.5
        4. PHILADELPHIA        1688210.    4.    -13.4
        5. HOUSTON             1594086.    6.     29.2
        6. DETROIT             1203339.    5.    -20.5
        7. DALLAS               904078.    8.      7.1
        8. SAN DIEGO            875504.   14.     25.5
        9. PHOENIX              789704.   20.     35.2
       10. BALTIMORE            786775.    7.    -13.1
       11. SAN ANTONIO          785410.   15.     20.1
       12. INDIANAPOLIS         700807.   11.     -4.9
       13. SAN FRANCISCO        678974.   13.     -5.1
       14. MEMPHIS              646356.   17.      3.6
       15. WASHINGTON,D.C.      637651.    9.    -15.7
       16. SAN JOSE             636550.   29.     38.4
       17. MILWAUKEE            636212.   12.    -11.3
       18. CLEVELAND            573822.   10.    -23.6
       19. COLUMBUS             564871.   21.      4.6
       20. BOSTON               562994.   16.    -12.2
       21. NEW ORLEANS          557482.   19.     -6.1
       22. JACKSONVILLE         540898.   26.      7.3
       23. SEATTLE              493846.   22.     -7.0
       24. DENVER               491396.   24.     -4.5
       25. NASHVILLE-DAVIDSON   455651.   32.      7.0

MTB > NAME C7 '1980POP'

MTB > MEAN '1980POP'
    MEAN    =     1193899

MTB > MEDIAN '1980POP'
    MEDIAN =      678974
```

computer was asked to compute the average population size and the median
population (the population of the city ranking thirteenth) of the 25 cities. These
values are, respectively, 1,193,899 and 678,974. Exhibit 1.2, a list of these cities by
percentage gain during the 1970–1980 decade, illustrates the value of being able to
manipulate data sets. This listing shows quite clearly what was happening to the
urban population of the United States during the decade. Of the ten cities with the
greatest population declines by percentage, eight were in the industrial Northeast
or Midwest (Washington, D.C. and Seattle, Washington were the other two). Of
the ten cities with the greatest population gains, eight were in the Sun Belt
(Nashville-Davidson, Tennessee and Columbus, Ohio were the others). Again,
this example is meant only to illustrate the usefulness of the package program.
Elementary Minitab commands are described in detail in Appendix B.

Exhibit 1.2

```
MTB > NOTE LIST OF 25 CITIES BY PERCENTAGE GAIN 1970-1980

MTB > SORT C9 CARRYING C1-C8 IN C9,C1-C8

MTB > FPRINT C1-C9
 MTB > (5X,F3.0,1X,5A4,F10.0,2X,F4.0,F9.1)

    1980      CITY                   1980POP  1970    PERCHG

       18. CLEVELAND               573822.   10.    -23.6
        6. DETROIT                1203339.    5.    -20.5
       15. WASHINGTON,D.C.          637651.    9.    -15.7
        4. PHILADELPHIA           1688210.    4.    -13.4
       10. BALTIMORE                786775.    7.    -13.1
       20. BOSTON                   562994.   16.    -12.2
       17. MILWAUKEE                636212.   12.    -11.3
        2. CHICAGO                 3005072.    2.    -10.8
        1. NEW YORK CITY          7071030.    1.    -10.4
       23. SEATTLE                  493846.   22.     -7.0
       21. NEW ORLEANS              557482.   19.     -6.1
       13. SAN FRANCISCO            678974.   13.     -5.1
       12. INDIANAPOLIS             700807.   11.     -4.9
       24. DENVER                   491396.   24.     -4.5
       14. MEMPHIS                  646356.   17.      3.6
       19. COLUMBUS                 564871.   21.      4.6
        3. LOS ANGELES            2966763.    3.      5.5
       25. NASHVILLE-DAVIDSON       455651.   32.      7.0
        7. DALLAS                   904078.    8.      7.1
       22. JACKSONVILLE             540898.   26.      7.3
       11. SAN ANTONIO              785410.   15.     20.1
        8. SAN DIEGO                875504.   14.     25.5
        5. HOUSTON                 1594086.    6.     29.2
        9. PHOENIX                  789704.   20.     35.2
       16. SAN JOSE                 636550.   29.     38.4
```

## Summary

There are five basic steps common to most statistical studies:

1   A need for information concerning a large population is determined.
2   Because cost, time limitations, or other considerations make it impossible to examine each element of the population, a subset of the population, referred to as a sample, is selected.
3   Numerical characteristics of the subset are summarized.
4   Estimates concerning characteristics of the population as a whole are made from the sample information.
5   Measures of the efficiency or effectiveness of inferential procedures are included to justify inference from the sample to the population.

The importance of the use of statistical reasoning and statistical methods in real-world situations is undeniable. One is almost always faced with limited information, and statistical procedures play an extremely important role in any field in which decisions must be made in the face of uncertainty.

The distinction between probability and statistics is a fundamental one. Whereas probability, a mathematical discipline important in its own right, aims at describing chance events, statistics aims at providing justifiable procedures for inference. Probability is crucial to the user of statistical methods because it provides a theoretical justification for the validity of these methods. The view of probability adopted here is the frequentist view that probabilities are the theoretical counterparts of stable long-run relative frequencies.

The role of the computer as a computational, graphical, and educational device in statistics is becoming clearly recognized. For a text at this level, the Minitab statistical package is one of the most accessible and versatile available. Exhibits 1.1 and 1.2 demonstrated how Minitab can be used to illustrate population trends. Minitab will be used similarly throughout the text to explain and develop statistical ideas and to implement statistical methods.

## Key Words

economic statistics

incomplete data

industrial statistics

inferential reasoning

medical statistics

Minitab

political polls

population

probability

relative frequency

sample

statistical computing package

statistics

"user friendly"

# Chapter 2

# Summarizing Data

**Introduction**  How should a sample be chosen? How should data be summarized? This chapter introduces issues in the selection and description of a set of numerical observations. Graphical, tabular, and statistical methods used to summarize the properties of a set of measurements are presented.

It is easy to think of examples of sets of measurements. Consider, for example,

**1**  the current yields of fifty stocks selected from the major U.S. stock exchanges;

**2**  the number of home runs hit in a season by American League batters who had a batting average of at least 0.300;

**3**  the amount of time in minutes spent at the checkout counter by each of the customers at a supermarket on a Friday evening from 6:00 P.M to 9:00 P.M.

A mere listing of such a set of numbers is difficult to interpret. The longer the list of numbers, the more difficult interpretation becomes. Hence methods are needed to summarize the information in a set of numerical observations.

Frequently, a set of numerical measurements of a single attribute is obtained from a much larger group of values. As stated in Definition 1.2, the set of elements actually observed is called a sample. The set of observed measurements of an attribute of each of the sampled elements is the raw material of a statistical investigation. The goal of statistical analysis is to reason from the properties of the observed measurements made on the sampled elements to the properties of the population. If the sample is not typical of the population, this inductive type of reasoning can lead to erroneous statements about the population. Hence a sample should be obtained in a way that makes it likely that the sample is representative of the population from which it has been obtained.

Once the information has been collected, it must be summarized. The aim of summarization is to describe a few major characteristics of the sampled values. Important characteristics are **location**, **variability**, and **skewness**. Location is described by a point or number about which the values of an attribute are centered. Variability means the spread of the measurements about the center. A class with an average examination grade of 70, but with all grades between 60 and 80, is quite different from a class with an average of 70 but with several scores below 50 and several above 90. Skewness is a property of measurements that are bunched on one side of center and tailed out on the other side. A set of sampled values is said to be skewed to the right if most of the sample values cluster about a central point, but there are also a small number of unusually large observations. Sampled incomes of professional golfers might be skewed in this way.

*location*
*variability*
*skewness*

## Example 2.1

Consider a sample of 50 stocks, selected from a population of 900 stocks of the largest companies in the United States. The sampled data appear in Table 2.1. Measurements were recorded on two attributes. The first attribute is the yield of each stock in 1981, which is the indicated annual dividend divided by the year-end price of the stock and multiplied by 100. The second attribute is the percentage change in price of each stock from the end of 1980 to the end of 1981. Many

## Table 2.1

**Data on Yield and Percentage Price Change in 1981**

| Stock | Yield (%) | Price Change (%) |
|-------|-----------|------------------|
| 1. American Hoist & Derrick | 6.890 | −20.000 |
| 2. American Telephone & Telegraph | 9.090 | 24.000 |
| 3. Amsted Industries | 7.090 | −19.000 |
| 4. Anderson Clayton | 4.620 | 26.000 |
| 5. Arkla | 0.800 | 4.000 |
| 6. Arrow Electronics | 2.180 | −37.000 |
| 7. Associated Dry Goods | 6.960 | 6.000 |
| 8. Bally Manufacturing | 0.320 | 39.000 |
| 9. Centex | 0.930 | −37.000 |
| 10. Chrysler | 0.0 | −10.000 |
| 11. Clark Equipment | 8.000 | −14.000 |
| 12. Coca-Cola | 6.510 | 7.000 |
| 13. Delta Air Lines | 1.910 | −11.000 |
| 14. Detroit Bank | 8.420 | 13.000 |
| 15. Fieldcrest Mills | 8.160 | −1.000 |
| 16. First Interstate Bancorp | 5.230 | 11.000 |
| 17. Hewlett-Packard | 0.508 | −7.000 |
| 18. Hoover | 10.530 | −25.000 |
| 19. Houston Natural Gas | 3.490 | −20.000 |
| 20. International Harvester | 0.0 | −68.000 |

**Table 2.1**

(cont.)

**Data on Yield and Percentage Price Change in 1981**

| Stock | Yield (%) | Price Change (%) |
|---|---|---|
| 21. JWT Group | 5.970 | − 10.000 |
| 22. Joy Manufacturing | 3.880 | − 2.000 |
| 23. Lonestar Industries | 6.610 | − 13.000 |
| 24. MGM Grand Hotels | 5.180 | 6.000 |
| 25. Mapco | 5.310 | − 19.000 |
| 26. Marine Midland Banks | 5.150 | 39.000 |
| 27. Michigan National | 6.320 | 21.000 |
| 28. Mitchell Energy & Development | 1.070 | − 43.000 |
| 29. Moore McCormack Resources | 3.150 | − 9.000 |
| 30. Occidental Petroleum | 9.800 | − 26.000 |
| 31. Olin | 5.050 | 19.000 |
| 32. PSA | 3.020 | − 19.000 |
| 33. Pacific Gas & Electric | 12.580 | 9.000 |
| 34. Parker Drilling | 0.740 | − 37.000 |
| 35. Peabody International | 2.420 | − 85.000 |
| 36. Peoples Energy | 7.610 | − 19.000 |
| 37. Ponderosa | 2.580 | 49.000 |
| 38. Potlatch | 4.570 | − 14.000 |
| 39. RLC | 6.170 | − 37.000 |
| 40. Roadway Express | 3.810 | 5.000 |
| 41. Robertson (H. H.) | 4.090 | 54.000 |
| 42. Rolm | 0.0 | − 29.000 |
| 43. Signode | 5.630 | − 5.000 |
| 44. Square D | 5.410 | 45.000 |
| 45. Syntex | 2.710 | − 18.000 |
| 46. Texas Instruments | 2.610 | − 36.000 |
| 47. Transway International | 7.740 | − 11.000 |
| 48. Tyco Labs | 5.740 | − 45.000 |
| 49. USF&G | 7.110 | 6.000 |
| 50. Zenith Radio | 5.450 | − 44.000 |

*Source:* Sample selected from data for 900 stocks in *Business Week*, December 28, 1981, pp. 109–125.

questions come to mind about these variables. Would the average dividend of these 50 stocks represent a good estimate of the average yield for the population of 900 stocks? How was the average price change influenced by the two large percentage changes for International Harvester and Peabody International? Do stocks with high yields tend to decrease less proportionately during a generally down market than do low-yield stocks?

Answers to these questions are taken up in later chapters. Here we focus on the selection of a sample, on graphical and tabular methods of displaying the characteristics of a sample, and on numerical measures of location and variation.

## 2.2
## Choosing a Sample from a Population

The idea of a population as the set of all possible elements of interest in an investigation was presented in Definition 1.1. A population need not be animate; all packages of a breakfast food produced at a given factory on a given day constitute a population. A population may be a theoretical one as well. Consider a navigator who is measuring the angle the star Betelgeuse makes with the horizon at a given time, place, and date. Although it is not observable, the set of all possible angles the navigator might observe is a population according to Definition 1.1. Further, a population may be either finite or infinite. Consider the selection of a number from the interval of real numbers $0 \leqslant x \leqslant 1$. This set of numbers, the population in this case, is infinite. Any actual sample will, of course, consist of only **infinite population** a finite number of values from this **infinite population**. Although this example may seem somewhat theoretical, it has, in fact, many practical applications. In contrast, the population of stocks from which the sample in Table 2.1 was selected—an alphabetical listing of 900 of the largest U.S. corporations listed in the year-end **finite population** edition of *Business Week* for 1981—is a **finite population** because it is possible to list all the elements in the population. The technical name for such a list is a frame.

---

**Definition 2.1** ▬▬▬▬▬▬▬▬▬▬▬▬▬▬▬▬▬▬▬▬▬▬▬▬▬▬▬▬▬▬▬▬

**frame**

A **frame** is a list of all the elements of a finite population.

---

In many practical situations the list used as a frame will not be fully accurate. A student directory published by a university is often used as a frame for the current student population. In many cases the list is inaccurate because some students have left the university, others have enrolled at the university, and some names have been erroneously included or excluded from the directory. Nevertheless, such a directory can be useful as a frame for a population of individuals. Because the frame used may not accurately describe the population intended to be sampled, two types of populations are defined.

---

**Definition 2.2** ▬▬▬▬▬▬▬▬▬▬▬▬▬▬▬▬▬▬▬▬▬▬▬▬▬▬▬▬▬▬▬▬

**target population**

The **target population** is the population about which we wish to make inference.

---

**Definition 2.3** ▬▬▬▬▬▬▬▬▬▬▬▬▬▬▬▬▬▬▬▬▬▬▬▬▬▬▬▬▬▬▬▬

**sampled population**

The **sampled population** is the set from which the sample has actually been selected.

---

In situations where researchers wish to select a sample from *all* adult individuals living in a certain town, the telephone directory is often used as a frame. There are, however, both individuals without telephones and individuals who do not have their telephone number listed. There may also be telephone numbers listed for individuals who are not adults. The target population here is all adult individuals in the town, whereas the sampled population is all individuals with listed telephone numbers. There have been many cases in which the sampled population has been incorrectly identified as the target population. The target population, for example, might be all women living in a city. A telephone survey made during the hours of 8:00 A.M. and 5:00 P.M., however, would have as a sampled population those women in the city with telephones who were at home during these hours. Such a survey would certainly underrepresent working women, who are part of the target population. Although this difference between the target population and sampled population is quite obvious, in other situations more subtle biases in a sampling plan may also lead to samples that are not representative of the target population. For this reason we will consider first a sampling method designed to produce samples likely to be representative of the population from which these samples came.

## Random Sampling

The method of selection used to obtain the sample of 50 stocks in Table 2.1 from the frame of 900 stocks listed in *Business Week* is called simple random sampling.

---

**Definition 2.4** ■

simple random sample

A **simple random sample** of size $n$ from a finite population of size $N$ is a sample chosen in such a way that all possible samples of size $n$ have equal probability of being selected.

---

The technique used to achieve a simple random sample of stocks was as follows. Each of the stocks listed was given a number from 1 to 900. The frame had the following form:

| No. | Stock | Yield | Percent Price Change (1981) |
|---|---|---|---|
| 1 | ACF Industries | 7.17 | − 16 |
| 2 | AM International | 0.00 | − 68 |
| . | . | . | . |
| . | . | . | . |
| . | . | . | . |
| 899 | Zenith Radio | 5.45 | − 44 |
| 900 | Zurn Industries | 4.53 | 41 |

Once each of the stocks had been assigned a number, a simple random sample was obtained by successively selecting 50 numbers from the integers 1, 2, . . . , 900. This process was carried out in such a way that at each selection each of the 900 integers had an equal chance of being chosen. The 50 stocks corresponding to the integers selected comprised the sample given in Table 2.1.

## Minitab Random Integer Generator

Minitab provides a convenient means of selecting a random sample from a finite population. Appendix B provides a description of the Minitab commands that are used in this text and how they are implemented. Your instructor can provide information about how to run Minitab programs at your local computing facilities.

**RANDOM**        Minitab uses the **RANDOM** command to generate a sequence of random integers chosen from the set of integers from 1 to $N$, where the value of $N$ is a number chosen by the user. At each selection, each of the $N$ integers has an equal chance of being chosen. Exhibit 2.1 shows the commands required to obtain a set of 55 integers randomly selected from the integers from 1 to 900, as well as the integers selected. The number of integers to be printed out was specified as 55, to allow for possible duplications. In fact, only one number—646—is repeated.

**Exhibit 2.1**    **Fifty-Five Random Integers from 1 to 900**

```
MTB > BASE = 1000
MTB > RANDOM 55 INTEGERS IN C1;
SUBC> INTEGER A = 1 B = 900.
MTB > PRINT C1
C1
    262     152     491      55     399     218     550     117     738     313
    646     211     803     263     524     742     138     168     467     893
    440     439     311     225     135      91     283     695     448     554
    341      64      23     804     388     428     402     351     216     856
     62     794     437     553     707     697     539     331     148     201
    646     727     354       1     506
```

The sample is then made up of those items corresponding to the numbers selected. Thus stocks numbered 262, 152, 491, . . . , would be included in the sample. (Note: A set of random numbers different from that given in Exhibit 2.1 was used to select the sample in Table 2.1.) This method of sampling permits the selection of a random sample from a finite population for which a frame exists. With the above procedure, each group of 50 items has an equal chance of being selected.

## Other Sampling Methods

There are many situations in which one wishes to use a random sample, but circumstances beyond the control of the investigator make it impossible to obtain such a sample. There may be no frame listing the elements of the population. Or practical considerations such as cost and time may prevent generation of a frame although it is theoretically possible to obtain one. In these situations other methods must be used. First we will consider judgment sampling.

---

**Definition 2.5** ▬▬▬▬▬▬▬▬▬▬▬▬▬▬▬▬▬▬▬▬▬▬▬▬▬▬▬▬▬▬▬▬

judgment sample

A **judgment sample** is one for which judgment is used in order to choose a "representative sample."

---

An example of a judgment sample is one made up of certain precincts in a city that are selected for observation on election night. The election results in these "bellwether" precincts are used to make a rapid prediction of an election outcome. Although judgment sampling has been used effectively, there are two major difficulties with it. The first is that the judgment may be erroneous and thus yield a sample not representative of the intended target population. Second, the use of statistical analysis to make statements about the precision of estimation is in general not justified for judgment samples. The use of judgment samples inflicts the judgment of one or a few individuals on the selected sample. Whether a sample chosen in this way is "representative" will always be open to challenge. The magnitude of errors based on judgment samples may be substantial.

As its name implies, convenience sampling occurs when the more available, or convenient, elements are selected from a population for study.

---

**Definition 2.6** ▬▬▬▬▬▬▬▬▬▬▬▬▬▬▬▬▬▬▬▬▬▬▬▬▬▬▬▬▬▬▬▬

convenience sample

A **convenience sample** is one selected because of the ease of obtaining the sample.

---

An example of convenience sampling is the brief interviewing of individuals by a reporter at a busy city intersection. It is quite clear that the target population, perhaps adult residents of a metropolitan area, may not be very well represented by a sample obtained in this way. For example, clerical workers might be greatly overrepresented. Another example of convenience sampling is having television viewers answer a "yes/no" question by calling one number for a "yes" and another for a "no." One obvious sampling bias results from the cost of such calls to the viewers. Clearly it is difficult to define the sampled population when this self-selected method of sampling is used.

We consider one further sampling procedure. Although it has some aspects of a random sample, systematic random sampling does not yield a simple random sample. It is often used, however, because of its technical simplicity. Assume a finite population is of size $N$ and a sample of size $n = N/k$ is desired.

---

**Definition 2.7** ▄▄▄▄▄▄▄▄▄▄▄▄▄▄▄▄▄▄▄▄▄▄▄▄▄▄▄▄▄▄▄▄▄▄▄▄▄▄▄▄

systematic random sample

A **systematic random sample** for a finite population is one for which one element is selected at random from the first $k$ elements listed in the frame, and thereafter every $k$th element is selected.

---

For a finite population of size $N = kn$, where $n$ is the required sample size, sample selection is achieved as follows. An integer is chosen randomly from the first $k$ integers $1, 2, \ldots, k$. If we call this element $i$, then the elements in the systematic sample are those numbered $i, i + k, i + 2k, i + 3k, \ldots, i + (n - 1)k$. For example, suppose a finite population has $N = 2800$ elements and a sample of size $n = 400$ is required. Here $N = 2800 = k(400) = 7(400) = kn$. A random integer, $i$, from 1 to $k = 7$ is chosen, say 2. The elements in the sample are numbered $2, 9, 16, 23, \ldots, 2795$.

This sampling method has the virtue of being easy to understand, so it can be easily learned and implemented. It is particularly attractive for selecting items from a file of documents (such as business invoices numbered from 1 to $N$ for a particular year). The difficulty with systematic sampling, however, is that there may be a periodic characteristic of the population listing that is reflected in the sample, but is not typical of the population as a whole.

Suppose license plates have two letters identifying the county followed by six numbers (e.g., AB-123429). Assume the plates are issued in increasing numerical order (i.e., beginning with AB-000001), with the exception that "vanity plates" ending in 00 are issued for a fee to those ordering them. Suppose we sample 2000 licenses in a county that has issued $N = 100,000 = 50(2000) = kn$ plates. The selection of a starting value from $1, 2, \ldots, 50$ of $i = 50$ will yield a sample in which every other license ends in 00; vanity plate holders will be overrepresented in this case. If, on the other hand, $i = 21$ is selected, no license number in this sample will end in 00; they all will end with 1. The vanity plate holders will not be represented in the sample at all in this case. The danger of hidden periodic bias is an ever-present one in systematic sampling, and it can lead to samples that are not representative of the population.

Because of the limitations of judgment sampling and convenience sampling, our samples will generally be selected using methods similar to those used to select our sample of stocks. There are times, however, when one is forced to use judgment or even convenience samples. In these cases one must be careful to define accurately the target population and the sampled population. Also, the potential biases in these types of samples should be clearly understood and stated in any summary of conclusions made from the analysis of such samples.

**2.1**   **a.** Choose a novel of 300–500 pages and use the RANDOM command to take a simple random sample of 50 pages.
   **b.** Count the number of times conjunctions (and, or, nor, for, so, yet, while, but) appear on each sampled page. To some degree, a large number of conjunctions indicates complex writing. Save this data set for later problems.

**2.2**   **a.** Using the RANDOM command, select a random sample of 40 pages from a city telephone directory of at least 200 pages. Your library should have one you can use if the local directory does not have 200 pages.
   **b.** For the first page selected, count the number of surnames ending in an A, I, or O.
   **c.** Do you think that most large cities would tend to produce roughly an equal percentage of such surnames? Explain.

**2.3**   The following table gives a list of the 50 states and some information from the 1970 and 1980 censuses about the population of the 50 states and of the United States as a whole. The numerical data will be used in later problems.
   **a.** Number the states from 1 to 50. Select a random sample of 10 of the 50 states using RANDOM.
   **b.** Consider the sample of the states numbered 5, 10, 15, . . . , 50. Assuming the integer 5 was chosen at random from 1, 2, 3, 4, 5, what was the sampling method used? What are the values of $N$, $k$, and $n$?
   **c.** Suppose an individual selected the six New England states and the four Middle Atlantic states of Delaware, New Jersey, New York, and Pennsylvania as a sample of size ten of the 50 states. Does this sample appear to be a random sample? What type of sampling method might produce such a sample?

| State | Percentage Change (1970–1980) | Population per Square Mile |
|---|---|---|
| Alabama | 12.9 | 76.7 |
| Alaska | 32.4 | 0.7 |
| Arizona | 53.1 | 24.0 |
| Arkansas | 18.8 | 44.0 |
| California | 18.5 | 151.4 |
| Colorado | 30.7 | 27.8 |
| Connecticut | 2.5 | 639.2 |
| Delaware | 8.6 | 300.3 |
| Florida | 43.4 | 180.1 |
| Georgia | 19.1 | 94.1 |
| Hawaii | 25.3 | 150.2 |
| Idaho | 32.4 | 11.4 |
| Illinois | 2.8 | 202.5 |
| Indiana | 5.7 | 152.1 |
| Iowa | 3.1 | 52.5 |
| Kansas | 5.1 | 28.9 |
| Kentucky | 13.7 | 92.3 |
| Louisiana | 15.3 | 93.6 |
| Maine | 13.2 | 36.4 |
| Maryland | 7.5 | 426.3 |
| Massachusetts | 0.8 | 733.1 | (cont.) |

| | | |
|---|---|---|
| Michigan | 4.2 | 162.95 |
| Minnesota | 7.1 | 51.4 |
| Mississippi | 13.7 | 53.3 |
| Missouri | 5.1 | 71.3 |
| Montana | 13.3 | 5.4 |
| Nebraska | 5.7 | 20.5 |
| Nevada | 63.5 | 7.3 |
| New Hampshire | 24.8 | 102.0 |
| New Jersey | 2.7 | 979.2 |
| New Mexico | 27.8 | 10.7 |
| New York | − 3.8 | 367.1 |
| North Carolina | 15.5 | 120.4 |
| North Dakota | 5.6 | 9.4 |
| Ohio | 1.3 | 263.5 |
| Oklahoma | 18.2 | 44.0 |
| Oregon | 25.9 | 27.4 |
| Pennsylvania | 0.6 | 263.9 |
| Rhode Island | − 0.3 | 902.9 |
| South Carolina | 20.4 | 103.2 |
| South Dakota | 3.6 | 9.1 |
| Tennessee | 16.9 | 111.1 |
| Texas | 27.1 | 54.3 |
| Utah | 37.9 | 17.8 |
| Vermont | 15.0 | 55.1 |
| Virginia | 14.9 | 134.4 |
| Washington | 21.0 | 62.0 |
| West Virginia | 11.8 | 81.0 |
| Wisconsin | 6.5 | 86.4 |
| Wyoming | 41.6 | 4.8 |
| U.S. | 10.9 | 62.7 |

*Source:* U.S. Bureau of the Census.

**2.4** In order to estimate the percentage of bass among the fish in a lake, a catch of fish is made at a central location on each of 30 consecutive days. The percentage of bass among the 3000 fish caught in the 30-day period is used to estimate the unknown percentage. Does this sampling plan appear to be a good one? Why or why not?

**2.5** Every school-age child in 4 of 25 elementary schools in a school district is asked to state the number of children in his or her family in elementary school. The intention of the investigator is to find a good estimate of the average number of elementary-school-age children per family. What is the target population in this case? What is the sampled population?

## 2.3
## Graphical Displays of Data

Like tabular methods, graphical methods are techniques for summarizing the information in a sample of measurements on a single variable. The end product, however, is in graphical rather than a numerical form—a picture of the data set.

**Exhibit 2.2**

```
MTB > NOTE LISTING OF STOCK DATA BY YIELD
MTB > NAME C1 'STK'  C10 'YIELD' C11 'PERCHG'
MTB > SORT C10 CARRY C1 C11 PUT IN C10 C1 C11
MTB > PRINT C1 C10 C11
 ROW   STK   YIELD  PERCHG

   1    42    0.00    -29
   2    20    0.00    -68
   3    10    0.00    -10
   4     8    0.32     39
   5    17    0.58     -7
   6    34    0.74    -37
   7     5    0.80      4
   8     9    0.93    -37
   9    28    1.07    -43
  10    13    1.91    -11
  11     6    2.18    -37
  12    35    2.42    -85
  13    37    2.58     49
  14    46    2.61    -36
  15    45    2.71    -18
  16    32    3.02    -19
  17    29    3.15     -9
  18    19    3.49    -20
  19    40    3.81      5
  20    22    3.88     -2
  21    41    4.09     54
  22    38    4.57    -14
  23     4    4.62     26
  24    31    5.05     19
  25    26    5.15     39
  26    24    5.18      6
  27    16    5.23     11
  28    25    5.31    -19
  29    44    5.41     45
  30    50    5.45    -44
  31    43    5.63     -5
  32    48    5.74    -45
  33    21    5.97    -10
  34    39    6.17    -37
  35    27    6.32     21
  36    12    6.51      7
  37    23    6.61    -13
  38     1    6.89    -20
  39     7    6.96      6
  40     3    7.09    -19
  41    49    7.11      6
  42    36    7.61    -19
  43    47    7.74    -11
  44    11    8.00    -14
  45    15    8.16     -1
  46    14    8.42     13
  47     2    9.09     24
  48    30    9.80    -26
  49    18   10.53    -25
  50    33   12.58      9
```

## Histograms

histogram

Of the various graphical methods available, a **histogram** is probably the best known and most widely used. A histogram is a vertical bar graph that indicates the numbers of the observations in a sample that fall into intervals displayed on the horizontal axis.

SORT

As a first example, let us consider the yields of the 50 selected stocks in Table 2.1. Minitab has a simple command **SORT** that arranges the numerical observations in columns on a worksheet in numerical order from the smallest to the largest. In Exhibit 2.2 the SORT command has been used to order the 50 values for stock yield from smallest to largest. The yield values are in column C10. Columns C1 and C11 have been sorted in the same way as column C10. Column C1 contains the initial alphabetical position of each stock. Column C11 contains the percentage changes. To obtain the ordered listing in Exhibit 2.2, only the

NAME, PRINT

**NAME, PRINT**, and SORT commands are needed.

class intervals

The data on yields can now be summarized in a table called a frequency table. We see from Exhibit 2.2 that the minimum yield is 0.0 and the maximum yield is 12.58. Each observation is to be assigned to one of $k$ nonoverlapping **class intervals** that must cover the range 0.0 to 12.58. We will choose to use $k = 7$ intervals. (Conventions for determining $k$ will be explained later in this section.) The *width* of each class must equal at least the quantity (Maximum − Minimum)$/k = 12.58/7 = 1.80$. In order to use convenient numerical values, we will round the class width up to 2. (To ensure that all of the observations are covered, the class width must always be rounded up, not down.) The seven classes we will use are given in Table 2.2. The endpoints of these seven classes are 0–2, 2–4, 4–6, 6–8, 8–10, 10–12, and 12–14, respectively. We will use the convention that an observation falling on an endpoint will be assigned to the class with the larger midpoint. This convention explains the inclusion of the left-hand endpoint and exclusion of the right-hand endpoint in the intervals of Table 2.2.

## Table 2.2

**Frequency Table for Yield Data**

| Interval Number | Endpoints | Midpoint, $v_i$ | Frequency, $F_i$ | Cumulative Frequency, $CF_i$ |
|---|---|---|---|---|
| 1 | $0 \leqslant x < 2$ | 1 | 10 | 10 |
| 2 | $2 \leqslant x < 4$ | 3 | 10 | 20 |
| 3 | $4 \leqslant x < 6$ | 5 | 13 | 33 |
| 4 | $6 \leqslant x < 8$ | 7 | 10 | 43 |
| 5 | $8 \leqslant x < 10$ | 9 | 5 | 48 |
| 6 | $10 \leqslant x < 12$ | 11 | 1 | 49 |
| 7 | $12 \leqslant x < 14$ | 13 | 1 | 50 |

For each interval in a frequency table, there is a column for endpoints, midpoints, frequencies, and cumulative frequencies. The midpoints are denoted $v_1$, $v_2, \ldots, v_k$ and are the averages of the endpoints of the respective intervals. The **frequency** column gives the number of observations that fall into each interval. These frequencies are denoted $F_1, F_2, \ldots, F_k$, where $F_1$ is the number of observations assigned to the first interval, $F_2$ the number assigned to the second interval, and so forth. We must have

$$F_1 + F_2 + \cdots + F_k = n \qquad\qquad\qquad \textbf{2.1}$$

**cumulative frequency**  where $n$ is the total number of observations in the data set. The **cumulative frequency** column gives the total number of observations up to (but not including) the right endpoint of the interval in question.

In the frequency table for the stock yield data (Table 2.2), we observe that 10 of the 50 stocks had a yield greater than or equal to 0 but less than 2 percent. Hence $F_1 = 10$. There were $F_5 = 5$ stocks with yields of at least 8 but less than 10 percent. Similarly, the cumulative frequency for class three, denoted $CF_3$, was 33. Thus 33 of the 50 stocks had a yield between 0 and 6 percent (including 0 but excluding 6 percent). The information in a frequency table is sufficient to construct a histogram of the data.

The following are standard symbols for denoting quantities used in constructing a histogram.

$n$   The total number of observations

$c$   The width of a class interval

$k$   The number of class intervals

$v_i$   The midpoint of the $i$th interval

$F_i$   The number of measurements in the sample falling into the interval numbered $i$

$CF_i$   The number of observations falling into the $i$th class or a previous class

In this case, $c = 2$, $k = 7$, $n = 50$, and the last three columns of Table 2.2 give the midpoints, frequencies, and cumulative frequencies.

The values of the midpoint of the first interval $v_1$, the class interval $c$, and the number of classes $k$ completely determine the partitioning of the horizontal axis of the histogram into classes. A histogram is simply a bar graph in which a vertical bar is constructed for each interval. The height of the vertical bar for the $i$th interval is $F_i$, the number of observations in the corresponding class. A histogram for the yields of the 50 stocks, which displays the frequencies in the individual classes through bar heights, is given in Figure 2.1.

Various conventions are used for determining the value of $k$, the number of classes, as a function of the sample size $n$. One of these is to find intervals between two successive powers of 2 of the form $2^{k-1} < i \leqslant 2^k$. In our example these intervals are (1,2], (2,4], (4,8], (8,16], and so forth. The unique interval of this form that contains the sample size $n$ is found, and the exponent of 2 at the right-hand endpoint is used to determine $k$. In the case being considered, $32 = 2^5 < n = 50 \leqslant 64 = 2^6$. Hence the rule yields $k = 6$. The rule serves only as a rough

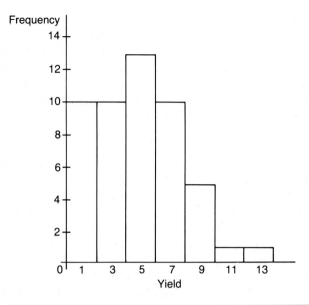

**Figure 2.1**

Histogram of Yields of 50 Stocks

guideline. Note that we have used seven intervals in our histogram of stock yields. An additional convention used in the construction of a histogram is to call the endpoints of an interval the class boundaries. The successive class boundaries for the yield data are 0, 2, 4, 6, 8, 10, 12, and 14. The vertical bars for the histogram are drawn at these boundaries, as shown in Figure 2.1.

Sometimes we may want to construct a relative frequency histogram instead of a frequency histogram. This type of histogram is the same as a frequency histogram, except that the frequencies $F_i$ are replaced by $f_i = F_i/n$, $i = 1$, $2, \ldots, k$. The value $f_i$ represents the proportion of the observations in the $i$th class. For the yield data we have

$$f_1 = f_2 = \frac{10}{50} = 0.2 \qquad f_3 = \frac{13}{50} = 0.26 \qquad f_4 = \frac{10}{50} = 0.2$$

$$f_5 = \frac{5}{50} = 0.1 \qquad f_6 = f_7 = \frac{1}{50} = 0.02$$

Because the frequencies $F_i$ add up to $n$, the relative frequencies add up to 1. That is,

$$f_1 + f_2 + \cdots + f_k = 1 \qquad\qquad \textbf{2.2}$$

A relative frequency histogram for the yield data of Table 2.2 is presented in Figure 2.2. In this figure the height of the bar for a particular class gives the proportion of the sampled observations in that class and thus, in a sense, indicates the relative importance of that class.

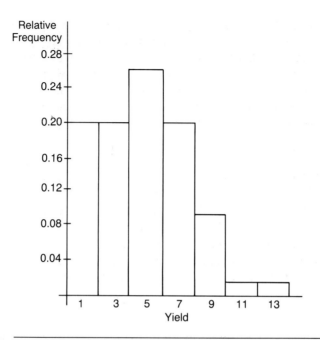

**Figure 2.2**

**Relative Frequency Histogram of Yields of 50 Stocks**

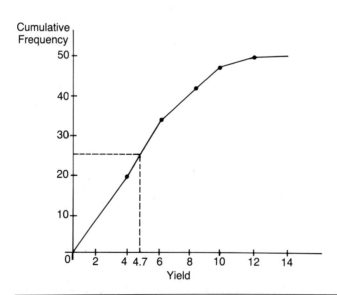

**Figure 2.3**

**Ogive of Yield Data for 50 Stocks**

A graphical display of the last column of the frequency table, cumulative frequency, is also useful. The cumulative frequency is plotted on the vertical axis against the right-hand boundaries of the classes. So that the resulting curve is not left "hanging," the value of zero on the vertical axis is plotted at the left-hand boundary of the first class on the horizontal axis. The points for adjacent classes are then joined by line segments. The resulting curve is called an **ogive** or a cumulative frequency curve. The ogive for the stock-yield data is plotted in Figure 2.3.

**ogive**

## Minitab Histograms and Ogives

Minitab can be used to obtain histograms and ogives. The data on the stock yields have been **SET** in column 10 of Exhibit 2.3. We can easily use the **HISTOGRAM** command to produce a histogram for which $v_1$, $c$, and $k$ are determined by the statistical package. The package selects $v_1 = 0$, $c = 1$, and $k = 14$. Alternatively we can input any values of $v_1$ and $c$ we choose, and a

**SET**

**HISTOGRAM**

**Exhibit 2.3**

```
MTB > HISTOGRAM C10

Histogram of YIELD   N = 50

Midpoint   Count
       0       4   ****
       1       5   *****
       2       3   ***
       3       6   ******
       4       3   ***
       5       9   *********
       6       5   *****
       7       6   ******
       8       5   *****
       9       1   *
      10       1   *
      11       1   *
      12       0
      13       1   *

MTB > HISTOGRAM C10;
SUBC> START = 1;
SUBC> INCREMENT = 2.

Histogram of YIELD   N = 50

Midpoint   Count
    1.00      10   **********
    3.00      10   **********
    5.00      13   *************
    7.00      10   **********
    9.00       5   *****
   11.00       1   *
   13.00       1   *
```

histogram will be constructed using our chosen values. Here we will choose $v_1 = 1$ and $c = 2$, as in Figure 2.1. Minitab adheres to the convention of including the left-hand endpoint and not the right. The two histograms are displayed in Exhibit 2.3. The bars extend horizontally rather than vertically, but the information provided is the same, as may be readily seen by comparing Figure 2.1 with the second histogram in Exhibit 2.3.

The histogram, whether constructed by hand or by Minitab, provides visual information about the way in which the numerical observations of a sample attribute are distributed. Frequently a large number of the observations are found in several central classes. As shown in Exhibit 2.3, 33 of the 50 stock yields are found in the classes with midpoints 3, 5, and 7. Frequently there are declining numbers of observations in the classes at increasing distance from the central classes. For the stock-yield data, this is true of the classes with midpoints 9, 11, and 13 (i.e., the classes with midpoints larger than the central classes). There are, however, ten observations in the first class, which equals the numbers in classes two and four. This data set, with a longer "tail" to the right than to the left, is described as skewed to the right. The skewness is moderate in this case.

PLOT    The Minitab command **PLOT** can be used to construct an ogive by plotting the ordered values on the horizontal axis against the integers 1, 2, . . . , $n$ on the vertical axis. The ogive for the stock-yield data appears in the Minitab output in Exhibit 2.4.

**Exhibit 2.4**

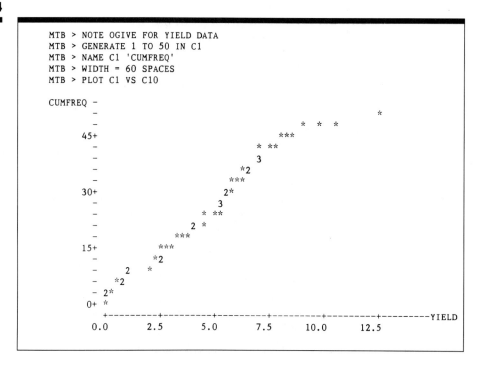

### Stem-and-Leaf Displays

stem-and-leaf
display

Another graphical method that can be used to display the observations of a sample is a **stem-and-leaf display**. This technique is one of a number of recently developed statistical methods used to explore data. Collectively these methods are called Exploratory Data Analysis (EDA). In a stem-and-leaf display the first digits of the numerical data from a sample are used to construct the display structure, which permits the retrieval of individual values.

## Example 2.2

The following are 32 scores on a statistics exam:

69 57 83 82 99 75 58 78 66 61 71 70 68 70 65 86
65 64 47 68 93 66 51 80 61 80 62 61 63 62 89 84

The stem-and-leaf display for this sample is

```
4|7
5|7 8 1
6|9 6 1 8 5 5 4 8 6 1 2 1 3 2
7|5 8 1 0 0
8|3 2 6 0 0 9 4
9|9 3
```

The first digit in each line represents the stem, and the remaining digits on a line are called the leaves. The observations 57, 58, and 51 in Example 2.2 produced the line 5 7 8 1 in the stem-and-leaf display.

### Minitab Stem-and-Leaf Displays

STEM-AND-LEAF

It is very easy to generate a stem-and-leaf display for the numerical observations in a Minitab column. The simple command **STEM-AND-LEAF** produces such a display for a single data set. The Minitab stem-and-leaf display for the stock-yield data is given in Exhibit 2.5. Minitab prints the numbers on each leaf in increasing order. Clearly, this display is very similar to the first histogram in Exhibit 2.3 constructed for these data by Minitab.

The left column gives cumulative frequency values from both "ends" of the distribution. Thus the value 15 on the third line of the output means that there are 15 observations in the first three classes. The value 4 on the tenth line means that there are 4 observations in the last four classes. The class containing the middle observation by magnitude (for $n$ = odd) or the average of the two middle observations (for $n$ = even) is called the "middle class." In this case, $(5.15 + 5.18)/2 = 5.165$ defines the middle class. The middle class is labeled with (10), the

2.3 **GRAPHICAL DISPLAYS OF DATA**    **29**

**Exhibit 2.5**

```
MTB > NOTE STEM-AND-LEAF PLOT FOR STOCK YIELDS
MTB > PRINT C10
YIELD
    0.00    0.00    0.00    0.32    0.58    0.74    0.80    0.93
    1.07    1.91    2.18    2.42    2.58    2.61    2.71    3.02
    3.15    3.49    3.81    3.88    4.09    4.57    4.62    5.05
    5.15    5.18    5.23    5.31    5.41    5.45    5.63    5.74
    5.97    6.17    6.32    6.51    6.61    6.89    6.96    7.09
    7.11    7.61    7.74    8.00    8.16    8.42    9.09    9.80
   10.53   12.58

MTB > STEM-AND-LEAF C10

Stem-and-leaf of YIELD       N  = 50
Leaf Unit = 0.10

     8    0 00035789
    10    1 09
    15    2 14567
    20    3 01488
    23    4 056
   (10)   5 0112344679
    17    6 135689
    11    7 0167
     7    8 014
     4    9 08
     2   10 5
     1   11
     1   12 5
```

number of observations in that class. The second column gives the stem values (in this case, the first digits of the percentage values). The remaining numbers on a line constitute the "leaf," as described before. The units of the leaf values are given by the number called the "leaf unit." In this case the leaf unit is 0.1, or one-tenth of a percentage point.

The frequency table for the stock-yield data in Table 2.2 showed that a large number of observations tended to cluster in a few intervals. The histogram for this data set visually confirms this clustering. Additionally, the histogram display gives a visual and numerical indication of the "center" of the observations. This center is called the modal class.

---

**Definition 2.8** ▰▰▰▰▰▰▰▰▰▰▰▰▰▰▰▰▰▰▰▰▰▰▰▰▰▰▰

modal class

The **modal class** for data represented by a histogram is the class or classes with the greatest frequency.

---

If there is only one modal class, its midpoint can be used as a measure of location. In the stock-yield example, this value, which we call $M$, is equal to 5. The stock yields are roughly centered at a 5 percent annual dividend.

If the values in a sample are ordered by magnitude, it is informative to identify percentiles—the observations in the sample having a specific percentage of observations less than or equal to them.

---

**Definition 2.9** ▄▄▄▄▄▄▄▄▄▄▄▄▄▄▄▄▄▄▄▄▄▄▄▄▄▄▄▄▄▄▄▄▄▄▄▄▄

percentile

The $p$th **percentile** of a sample is the observation in the sample having $p$ percent of the sample observations less than or equal to it by magnitude.

---

The stock yields in Exhibit 2.5 are ordered by magnitude. There are 5 observations that are less than or equal to the value 0.58; thus that value is the 10th percentile for these yields. The observation 0.58 is the 10th percentile because $5/50 = 1/10$ (or ten percent) of the 50 sampled observations are less than or equal to 0.58 in magnitude. Similarly, because there are 30 observations that are less than or equal to the value 5.45, that value is the 60th percentile for these yields. The 50th percentile is particularly important as the value indicating the center or location of the sample. The 25th and 75th percentiles give information about the variability of the sample.

The ogive can be used to estimate the 50th percentile of the sample. We draw a horizontal line from the cumulative frequency equal to $n/2$ on the vertical axis and find the point of intersection with the ogive. The abscissa (horizontal coordinate) of this point approximates the 50th percentile of the sample. In this case, as Figure 2.3 shows, this value (which we denote $\tilde{m}$) equals about 4.7. Roughly 50 percent of the yields are less than or equal to an annual dividend of 4.7 percent. If $n$ is odd, $(n + 1)/2$ should be used instead of $n/2$.

## Exercises 2.3

**2.6** Construct a frequency table and a histogram for the number of conjunctions observed on each of the 50 pages sampled in exercise 2.1.

**2.7** The following are the weights of a random sample of $n = 50$ women to the nearest pound.

115 128 147 120 126 121 126 126 136 133 128 140 136 127 134 120 128 131
133 127 130 138 125 129 128 128 135 128 136 137 115 118 129 120 127 141
124 133 134 116 132 131 138 131 132 126 128 109 127 142

**a.** Construct a histogram of these observations using the classes $108.5 \leqslant w < 115.5$, $115.5 \leqslant w < 122.5$, $122.5 \leqslant w < 129.5$, $129.5 \leqslant w < 136.5$, $136.5 \leqslant w < 143.5$, and $143.5 \leqslant w < 150.5$.
**b.** What are the values of $v_1$, $c$, and $k$?
**c.** Which class is the modal class in part a?
**d.** Use the HISTOGRAM command in Minitab to construct a histogram of these observations.
**e.** Use the HISTOGRAM command in Minitab with the values of $v_1$, $c$, and $k$ in part b to create a histogram of these observations.

**2.8** The scores below are exam grades of 45 students in an accounting class.

53 63 54 65 64 76 74 61 59 53 71 78 89 67 54 63 74 75 68 74 81 76 77 61
64 55 74 68 68 74 64 78 79 82 73 94 88 73 72 80 77 93 57 81 71

**a.** Use Minitab to construct a histogram for these data with $v_1 = 51$, $c = 7$, and $k = 7$.

**b.** Use the STEM-AND-LEAF command in Minitab to construct a stem-and-leaf display for these data.

**c.** Are the general shapes of the graphs in parts a and b the same? How would you describe this shape?

**d.** Construct an ogive for these data using Minitab. Estimate the fiftieth percentile of this sample using the ogive.

**2.9** Below are data on the average paid circulation of 69 leading U.S. and Canadian magazines during the last half of 1981, in thousands of magazines.[1]

| Magazine | Circulation | Magazine | Circulation |
|---|---|---|---|
| AARP News Bulletin | 6763 | Marvel Comics | 10,518 |
| American Legion Mag. | 2599 | Mechanix Illustrated | 1626 |
| Better Homes and Gardens | 8053 | Modern Maturity | 6749 |
| Bon Appetit | 1190 | Mother Earth News | 1044 |
| Boys' Life | 1463 | National Enquirer | 5051 |
| Changing Times | 1408 | National Geographic | 10,711 |
| Chatelaine | 1034 | Nation's Business | 1266 |
| Cosmopolitan | 2837 | Newsweek | 2964 |
| DC Comics | 5638 | New Woman | 1252 |
| Discovery | 1005 | 1001 Decorating Ideas | 1106 |
| Ebony | 1288 | Organic Gardening | 1336 |
| Elks Magazine | 1652 | Outdoor Life | 1734 |
| Family Circle | 7530 | Parents | 1516 |
| Family Handyman | 1018 | Penthouse | 4331 |
| Farm Journal | 1221 | People Weekly | 2500 |
| Field and Stream | 2022 | Playboy | 5011 |
| Glamour | 1936 | Popular Mechanics | 1677 |
| Globe | 1803 | Popular Science | 1933 |
| Golf Digest | 1016 | Prevention | 2429 |
| Good Housekeeping | 5291 | Psychology Today | 1171 |
| House and Garden | 1126 | Reader's Digest | 17,899 |
| Hustler | 1421 | Reader's Digest (Canada) | 1288 |
| Ladies' Home Journal | 5601 | Redbook | 4354 |
| Life | 1338 | Scholastic Mag. | 3397 |
| McCall's | 6218 | Senior Scholastic | 2529 |
| Mademoiselle | 1097 | Seventeen | 1553 |

---

[1]Throughout this text, data sets will be selected from various sources, to indicate the wide application of statistics. Although the discussions of the data sets often do not focus on the same issues as did the authors' original articles, the data sets have been chosen because they are useful for displaying statistical ideas or methods.

| Magazine | Circulation | Magazine | Circulation |
|---|---|---|---|
| Smithsonian | 1905 | True Story | 1433 |
| Southern Living | 1783 | TV Guide | 17,982 |
| Sport | 1223 | U.S. News & World Report | 2056 |
| Sports Illustrated | 2266 | Us | 1103 |
| Star, The | 3509 | V.F.W. Magazine | 1845 |
| Sunset | 1417 | Vogue | 1101 |
| Teen | 1059 | Woman's Day | 7748 |
| Time | 4359 | Workbasket, The | 1472 |
| Today's Education | 1652 | | |

*Source:* Audit Bureau of Circulations. Publishers' statements for the period 7/1/81 to 12/31/81.

a. Use Minitab to make a histogram for these data using 9 classes, with $v_1 = 1000$ and $c = 2000$. Which class is the modal class? What is the value of $M$ for these data?

b. Use Minitab to make another histogram for these data with $v_1 = 1500$ and $c = 1000$. Which class is the modal class in this case? What is the value of $M$? How would you describe the general shape of the histogram?

c. Which of the two histograms appears to provide a better description of this data set? Why?

d. Using the information from the Minitab output in part b, make a frequency table for these data, as in Table 2.2.

e. Plot by hand an ogive for these data using this frequency table, and estimate the location of the sample by finding the circulation corresponding to the $(69 + 1)/2 = 35$th observation.

**2.10** Following are the weights of 25 randomly sampled nominal 1-pound containers of a chemical additive:

0.9473 0.9775 0.9964 1.0077 1.0182 0.9655 0.9788 0.9974 1.0084 1.0225 0.9703

0.9861 1.0002 1.0102 1.0248 0.9757 0.9887 1.0016 1.0132 1.0306 0.9770 0.9958

1.0058 1.0173 1.0396

*Source:* G. S. Hahn and S. S. Shapiro, *Statistical Models in Engineering* (New York: John Wiley and Sons, 1967), p. 258.

a. How many classes are suggested by the $2^{k-1} < n \leqslant 2^k$ rule?

b. Construct a histogram for these data using $v_1 = 0.95$ and $c = 0.02$, by hand or by Minitab.

c. What is the general shape of this histogram, and how does it differ from that of the preceding exercise?

d. Construct a stem-and-leaf display for this data set using Minitab.

**2.11** a. Use Minitab to construct a histogram for the data on percentage change in population given in exercise 2.3. Use the first midpoint value $v_1 = -5$ with interval $c = 10$.

b. Find the modal class and the value of $M$.

**2.12** Find the number of classes recommended by the $2^{k-1} < n \leqslant 2^k$ rule for $n = 48, 208, 658,$ and $1000$.

**2.13** The following data give the numbers of pages in 25 introductory statistics texts.

253 335 345 356 378 407 427 451 451 496 505 519 536 589 594 598 605 606
637 666 687 689 743 789 790

**a.** Construct a histogram by hand, using $v_1 = 250$ and $c = 100$.
**b.** Plot an ogive for these data.
**c.** Estimate the "middle" of this sample by finding the number of pages corresponding to the $(25 + 1)/2 = $ 13th observation.
**d.** Construct a stem-and-leaf display for these data.

**2.14** In a test run to study the properties of a sugar-packaging machine, a random sample of 2.5-pound bags was taken. The net weights in ounces of the sampled items are given below.

42.2 40.2 42.7 40.5 38.4 42.0 39.8 39.1 39.7 38.4 39.4 40.0 38.3 42.2 41.6 40.9
39.7 37.2 38.9 41.3 40.6 41.9 39.4 39.1 40.0 41.7 39.3 39.1 38.9 39.8 40.5 41.1
40.0 42.6 41.5 37.6 39.4 37.4 39.8 38.5 38.7 40.3 40.3 40.1 40.4 39.2 41.1 39.6

**a.** Use Minitab to plot a histogram for these data.
**b.** Use Minitab to plot an ogive for these data.
**c.** Use the output in parts a and b to estimate the "middle" of this sample.
**d.** Why would it be better for the production manager of this firm *not* to set the filling level for this machine at 40 ounces even though the bags are supposed to contain 2.5 pounds?

**2.15** The annual rainfall (in mm) in 34 cities in El Salvador was presented in an article by Bradley Efron entitled "Regression and ANOVA with Zero-One Data: Measures of Residual Variation," which appeared in the *Journal of the American Statistical Association* 73 (1978): 113–121. These values were as follows:

1735 1936 2000 1973 1750 1800 1750 2077 1920 1800 2050 1830 1650 2200
2000 1770 1920 1770 2240 1620 1756 1650 2250 1796 1890 1871 2063 2100
1918 1834 1780 1900 1976 2296

**a.** Make a histogram of this data set using the HISTOGRAM command in Minitab.
**b.** Make a stem-and-leaf display of this data set using the STEM command in Minitab.
**c.** Plot an ogive of this data set using Minitab and estimate the 50th percentile of this data set based on the computer output.
**d.** Using the Minitab displays in parts a, b, and c, indicate the direction of skewness for this data set.

## 2.4

## Statistical Measures of Location

In the previous section we considered graphical methods of summarizing the information in a sample. Here we focus on numerical methods of data summarization. The first aim is to define a numerical measure of location. Before we look at the definitions of various measures of location, we need a technical definition of the term "statistic."

**Definition 2.10** ▬▬▬▬▬▬▬▬▬▬▬▬▬▬▬▬▬▬▬▬▬▬▬▬▬

A **statistic** is a function of the observations in a sample, which we denote $x_1$, $x_2, \ldots, x_n$.

## The Sample Mean

The most widely used measure of location is the sample average or sample mean.

**Definition 2.11** ▬▬▬▬▬▬▬▬▬▬▬▬▬▬▬▬▬▬▬▬▬▬▬▬▬

The **sample mean** is defined to be[2]

$$\bar{x} = \sum_{i=1}^{n} \frac{x_i}{n}$$

# Example 2.3

Consider the number of children observed in a random sample of ten families:

3 0 4 2 1 2 2 1 4 3

For these data, $\bar{x} = 22/10 = 2.2$. Here the value of the sample mean is a value that cannot be observed within the sample, as the number of children in a family must be an integer.

To understand the sense in which $\bar{x}$ is a measure of location, consider the deviations from the mean: $x_1 - \bar{x}$, $x_2 - \bar{x}, \ldots, x_n - \bar{x}$. These are the signed distances of the observations from the mean. Figure 2.4 shows the first two of these differences for the sample in Example 2.3. Values less than $\bar{x}$ yield negative distances, and values greater than $\bar{x}$ produce positive distances. The sample mean is the only point that can be chosen such that the sum of these signed distances is zero. It is easy to see that $\bar{x}$ has this property, as

$$\sum_{i=1}^{n} (x_i - \bar{x}) = \sum_{i=1}^{n} x_i - n\bar{x}$$

---

[2] Appendix A contains a discussion of summation notation.

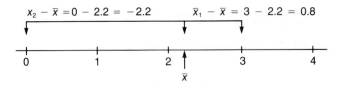

$$x_2 - \bar{x} = 0 - 2.2 = -2.2 \qquad \bar{x}_1 - \bar{x} = 3 - 2.2 = 0.8$$

**Figure 2.4**

**Deviations from the Mean**

The latter expression equals zero if $\sum_{i=1}^{n} x_i = n\bar{x}$, which is equivalent to $\bar{x} = \sum_{i=1}^{n} x_i/n$, the definition of $\bar{x}$. It is also straightforward to show that if $\sum_{i=1}^{n} (x_i - a) = 0$, then $a = \bar{x}$. The value $\bar{x}$ serves as a fulcrum for the observations in a sample. If, as shown in Figure 2.5, 1-pound weights were placed at each observation in the sample in Example 2.3, the value $\bar{x}$ would be the point at which a fulcrum would have to be placed in order for the weights to just balance the beam.

Two properties of the sample mean are worth noting. First, if the same constant $b$ is added to each element in a data set, then the mean of these new observations is changed by the amount $b$ also. For example, it is intuitively clear that if the weight of each person in a sample is increased by 10 pounds then the average weight is also increased by 10 pounds. A formal proof goes as follows: Let $y_i = x_i + b$ for $i = 1, 2, \ldots, n$.

$$\bar{y} = \sum_{i=1}^{n} \frac{y_i}{n} = \sum_{i=1}^{n} \frac{(x_i + b)}{n} = \sum_{i=1}^{n} \frac{x_i}{n} + \frac{nb}{n} = \bar{x} + b$$

Second, if each number in a data set is multiplied by a constant $c$, then the average of the new data set is $c$ times the average of the original data set. Thus if $y_i = cx_i$ for $i = 1, 2, \ldots, n$, then $\bar{y} = c\bar{x}$. You will be asked to demonstrate this fact in one of the exercises.

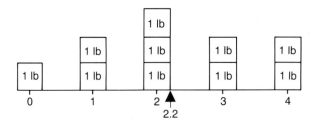

**Figure 2.5**

**Balancing Property of the Mean**

CHAPTER 2  **SUMMARIZING DATA**

## The Sample Median

Another widely used statistic is the sample median.

---

**Definition 2.12** ━━━━━━━━━━━━━━━━━━━━━━━━━━━━━━━━

sample median

The **sample median** $\hat{m}$ for a sample of size $n$, where $n$ is an odd number, is the middle observation among the sampled observations ordered by magnitude. If $n$ is even, then the median is the average of the two central values.

---

The ordered numbers of children in the ten families considered in Example 2.3 are

$$0 \quad 1 \quad 1 \quad 2 \quad \boxed{2 \quad 2} \quad 3 \quad 3 \quad 4 \quad 4$$

Hence $\hat{m} = (2 + 2)/2 = 2$. The median is a measure of location in the sense that at least one-half of the sampled values are less than or equal to the median and at least one-half of the sampled values are greater than or equal to the median. In the case considered above, six of ten observations are less than or equal to $\hat{m} = 2$, and seven of ten observations are greater than or equal to $\hat{m} = 2$. The ordered observations in a sample are denoted by $x_{(1)} \leqslant x_{(2)} \leqslant \cdots \leqslant x_{(n)}$. That is, the smallest observation is denoted $x_{(1)}$, the next smallest is denoted $x_{(2)}$, and so forth, up to the largest, which is denoted $x_{(n)}$. Hence in Example 2.3, $x_1 = 3$ but $x_{(1)} = 0$, $x_2 = 0$ but $x_{(2)} = 1$, $x_3 = 4$ but $x_{(3)} = 1, \ldots, x_{10} = 3$ but $x_{(10)} = 4$. A technical expression for the median of a sample of size $n$ is

$$\hat{m} = \begin{cases} x_{(n+1)/2} & \text{if } n \text{ is odd} \\ [x_{(n/2)} + x_{(n/2)+1}]/2 & \text{if } n \text{ is even} \end{cases}$$

As $n = 10$ is even, for the numbers of children in the ten families we have

$$\hat{m} = \frac{[x_{(5)} + x_{(6)}]}{2} = \frac{(2 + 2)}{2} = 2$$

as before.

## The Sample Mode

A third statistic occasionally used as a measure of location of a sample is the mode.

---

**Definition 2.13** ━━━━━━━━━━━━━━━━━━━━━━━━━━━━━━━━

sample mode

The **sample mode** $M$ is the value or values occurring most frequently in the sample.

---

For Example 2.3, we have $M = 2$, as three of the ten families have two children and no other number occurs more than twice.

### Minitab Calculation of the Sample Mean and Median

**MEAN**
**MEDIAN**

Minitab has very simple but useful commands for calculating $\bar{x}$ and $\hat{m}$. The commands **MEAN** and **MEDIAN** can be used to compute these statistics for the sample data in a single column. Exhibit 2.6 shows the output when these two statistics were computed for the data in Table 2.1 on both stock yield and percentage price change. The 50 observations of yield are in column C10, and the observations of percentage price change are in column C11.

**Exhibit 2.6**

```
MTB > NOTE YIELD DATA FOR 50 STOCKS
MTB > SET C10
C10
    0.00    0.00    0.00    0.32    .   .   .

MTB > NAME C10 'YIELD'
MTB > MEAN C10
    MEAN    =      4.7838
MTB > MEDIAN C10
    MEDIAN =      5.1650
MTB > NOTE PERCENTAGE CHANGE DATA FOR 50 STOCKS
MTB > SET C11
C11
   -29    -10    -68    39    .   .   .

MTB > NAME C11 'PCTCHG'
MTB > MEAN C11
    MEAN    =     -8.1400
MTB > MEDIAN C11
    MEDIAN =     -10.500
```

As the Minitab output in Exhibit 2.6 shows, the average yield is $\bar{x} = 4.7838$. The median value (namely, the average of the 25th and 26th values of yields by magnitude) is $\hat{m} = 5.165$. The values of these statistical measures can be compared with the rough measures of location found in the preceding section: the midpoint of the modal class given by $M = 5$ and the estimate of the 50th percentile of 4.7 obtained from the ogive shown in Figure 2.3. These rough estimates of location are not too far from the calculated statistics $\bar{x}$ and $\hat{m}$.

We now consider a second data set in an attempt to answer the natural question "Which of these statistical measures is the best measure of location?" The data sets present the number of at bats, runs, hits, home runs, and runs batted in and the batting averages for all players in the major leagues in 1980 who batted 0.300 or better. Exhibit 2.7 gives the information for the American League, and Exhibit 2.8 for the National League.

**Exhibit 2.7**

```
MTB > NOTE DATA FOR AMERICAN LEAGUE BATTERS 1980
MTB > NOTE   AB,RUNS,HITS,HOMERS,RBIS,BA
MTB > FPRINT C1-C10
MTB > (1X,F5.0,2X,2A4,A3,3X,F4.0,3X,F5.0,3X,F4.0,3X,F3.0,3X,F4.0,3X,F8.3)
   1.   BRETT       449.    87.   175.   24.   118.    0.390
   2.   COOPER      622.    96.   219.   25.   122.    0.352
   3.   DILONE      528.    87.   180.    0.    40.    0.341
   4.   RIVERS      630.    96.   210.    7.    60.    0.333
   5.   CAREW       540.    74.   179.    3.    59.    0.331
   6.   BELL        489.    76.   161.   17.    83.    0.329
   7.   WILSON      705.   134.   230.    3.    50.    0.326
   8.   STAPLETON   449.    61.   144.    7.    45.    0.321
   9.   BUMBRY      641.   117.   205.    9.    53.    0.320
  10.   OLIVER      656.    96.   209.   19.   117.    0.319
  11.   HASSEY      390.    42.   124.    8.    65.    0.318
  12.   WATSON      469.    62.   144.   13.    68.    0.307
  13.   WATHAN      453.    57.   138.    6.    58.    0.305
  14.   MOLITOR     450.    81.   137.    9.    37.    0.304
  15.   OGLIVIE     592.    94.   180.   41.   117.    0.304
  16.   HARGROVE    589.    86.   179.   11.    85.    0.304
  17.   HENDERSON   591.   111.   179.    9.    53.    0.303
  18.   SINGLETON   579.    84.   175.   24.   103.    0.302
  19.   CASTINO     546.    67.   165.   13.    64.    0.302
  20.   MURRAY      620.   100.   187.   32.   115.    0.302
  21.   LYNN        415.    67.   125.   12.    61.    0.301
  22.   WOODS       373.    54.   112.   15.    47.    0.300
  23.   BOCHTE      520.    62.   156.   13.    78.    0.300
  24.   STAUB       340.    42.   102.    9.    55.    0.300
  25.   JACKSON     514.    94.   154.   41.   111.    0.300
```

*Source:* Unofficial statistics for 1980–81 as reported in *The Information Please Almanac* (Boston: Houghton Mifflin, 1982), p. 919.

There is no simple answer to the question stated above. The sample mean is generally considered to be appropriate if a sample has a histogram that is generally bell-shaped with a modal class near the center of the histogram. Exhibit 2.9 presents the histograms for all six attributes mentioned above for the combined data in Exhibits 2.7 and 2.8. The sample means and medians are calculated for each attribute. The histogram for runs is roughly bell-shaped. In this case the mean and the median are not very different; Minitab calculates $\bar{x} = 76.795$ and $\hat{m} = 77$. For symmetric data, the mean and the median are generally similar. The other histograms are not very symmetric in shape.

For histograms of skewed data, the median is generally the preferred measure of location. If the sample is skewed to the right, the histogram will have a "short tail" to the left and a "long tail" to the right. Typically for such samples we have

$$\text{Mode} = M < \text{Median} = \hat{m} < \text{Mean} = \bar{x}$$

This relationship holds true for home runs, for which $M = 5$ or $10 < \hat{m} = 11 < \bar{x} = 13.409$. A few large values, such as the 41 home runs by Ben Oglivie and Reggie Jackson, have the effect of increasing $\bar{x}$, whereas such disparate values do not affect the median. The histogram for batting averages is similarly skewed, whereas the histograms for at bats and hits are skewed to the left. For samples

**Exhibit 2.8**

```
MTB > NOTE DATA FOR NATIONAL LEAGUE BATTERS 1980
MTB > NOTE   AB,RUNS,HITS,HOMERS,RBIS,BA
MTB > FPRINT C11-C20
MTB > (1X,F5.0,2X,2A4,A3,3X,F4.0,3X,F5.0,3X,F4.0,3X,F3.0,3X,F4.0,3X,F8.3)
   1.   L.SMITH      298.    69.   101.    3.    20.    0.339
   2.   EASLER       393.    66.   133.   21.    74.    0.338
   3.   LACY         278.    45.    93.    7.    33.    0.335
   4.   BUCKNER      578.    69.   187.   10.    68.    0.324
   5.   R.SMITH      311.    47.   100.   15.    55.    0.322
   6.   HERNANDEZ    595.   111.   191.   16.    99.    0.321
   7.   TEMPLETON    504.    83.   161.    4.    43.    0.319
   8.   VALENTINE    311.    40.    99.   13.    67.    0.318
   9.   MCBRIDE      554.    68.   171.    9.    87.    0.309
  10.   CEDENO       499.    70.   154.   10.    73.    0.309
  11.   DAWSON       577.    96.   178.   17.    87.    0.308
  12.   JOHNSTONE    251.    31.    77.    2.    20.    0.307
  13.   GARVEY       658.    78.   200.   26.   106.    0.304
  14.   OBERKFELL    422.    58.   128.    3.    47.    0.303
  15.   SIMMONS      495.    84.   150.   21.    98.    0.303
  16.   COLLINS      551.    94.   167.    3.    34.    0.303
  17.   HENDRICK     572.    73.   173.   25.   109.    0.302
  18.   CRUZ         612.    79.   185.   11.    91.    0.302
  19.   RICHARDS     642.    91.   193.    4.    41.    0.301
```

*Source:* Unofficial statistics for 1980–81 as reported in *The Information Please Almanac* (Boston: Houghton Mifflin, 1982), p. 919.

**Exhibit 2.9**

```
MTB > MEAN C5                          MTB > MEAN C6
   MEAN    =      505.70                  MEAN    =      76.795
MTB > MEDIAN C5                        MTB > MEDIAN C6
   MEDIAN =    · 524.00                   MEDIAN =      77.000
MTB > HISTOGRAM C5                     MTB > HISTOGRAM C6

Histogram of AB   N = 44              Histogram of RUNS   N = 44

Midpoint  Count                       Midpoint  Count
     250      1  *                          30      1  *
     300      4  ****                        40      3  ***
     350      2  **                          50      3  ***
     400      4  ****                        60      5  *****
     450      5  *****                        70      9  *********
     500      6  ******                       80      7  *******
     550      6  ******                       90      7  *******
     600     10  **********                  100      5  *****
     650      5  *****                       110      2  **
     700      1  *                           120      1  *
                                             130      1  *
```

```
MTB > MEAN C7                              MTB > MEAN C8
    MEAN    =        159.32                    MEAN    =        13.409
MTB > MEDIAN C7                            MTB > MEDIAN C8
    MEDIAN =         166.00                    MEDIAN =         11.000
MTB > HISTOGRAM C7                         MTB > HISTOGRAM C8

Histogram of HITS    N = 44               Histogram of HOMERS   N = 44

Midpoint   Count                          Midpoint   Count
      80       1   *                              0       2   **
     100       5   *****                          5      11   ***********
     120       4   ****                          10      11   ***********
     140       5   *****                         15       9   *********
     160       8   ********                      20       3   ***
     180      13   *************                 25       5   *****
     200       5   *****                         30       1   *
     220       2   **                            35       0
     240       1   *                             40       2   **




MTB > MEAN C9                              MTB > MEAN C10
    MEAN    =        70.818                    MEAN    =        0.31548
MTB > MEDIAN C9                            MTB > MEDIAN C10
    MEDIAN =         66.000                    MEDIAN =         0.30750
MTB > HISTOGRAM C9                         MTB > HISTOGRAM C10

Histogram of RBIS    N = 44               Histogram of BA    N = 44

Midpoint   Count                          Midpoint   Count
      20       2   **                          0.30      19   ********************
      30       2   **                          0.31       6   ******
      40       4   ****                        0.32       9   *********
      50       6   ******                      0.33       4   ****
      60       7   *******                     0.34       4   ****
      70       6   ******                      0.35       1   *
      80       2   **                          0.36       0
      90       4   ****                        0.37       0
     100       3   ***                         0.38       0
     110       3   ***                         0.39       1   *
     120       5   *****
```

skewed to the left, typically,

$$\bar{x} < \hat{m} < M$$

as in the latter two cases. For skewed data the median is generally the preferred measure of location, as it yields a value more nearly typical of the observed values than does the mean or the mode. In the histogram for runs batted in, the observations appear to be neither symmetric nor skewed. In such cases it is probably best to present the mean, the median, and the histogram to describe the data adequately.

The mode is rarely used as a measure of location except in cases where a small number of values of an attribute can be observed. A possible example is the numbers of children in ten families. Because a housebuilder cannot build a house for a fraction of a child, the mode, $M = 2$, may be a better measure of location than the mean, $\bar{x} = 2.2$. Similarly, if a class is graded on only a three-point scale, where 2 represents excellent, 1 represents pass, and 0 represents fail, the best summary measure of class performance might well be the modal value $M$.

In the exercises below you will be asked to use Minitab to calculate the median and the mean for several sets of data. Only with knowledge of the histogram can you make a reasonable decision about whether the median or the mean is the better statistical measure of location for a given data set. Remember that data sets are frequently skewed and that the median is an appropriate measure of location for such data.

## Exercises 2.4

**2.16** Using the data on the weights of the 50 women from exercise 2.7, calculate the mean and the median using the commands MEAN and MEDIAN. Which of these measures of location would you prefer for these data? Why?

**2.17** Use the appropriate Minitab commands to find the mean and the median of the exam-score data in exercise 2.8. What is the relationship between $\bar{x}$ and $\hat{m}$ for this data set? Which type of skewness does this relationship suggest?

**2.18** **a.** Using the commands MEAN and MEDIAN, calculate the mean and the median of the data on the circulation of 69 magazines in exercise 2.9. Which of these measures of location appears to be better? Why?

    **b.** Is the relationship between the mean and the median what you would expect? Explain.

    **c.** Find the average circulation for the 67 magazines that remain after deletion of *Readers Digest* and *TV Guide*. Is the change in the value of $\bar{x}$ substantial?

    **d.** Find the value of the median of the 67 circulations in part c. Is the change very large in relation to the change in the mean?

**2.19** **a.** Find the mean and the median of the 25 weights of containers of chemical additives given in exercise 2.10. Which measure of location would you prefer for this data set? Why?

    **b.** What is the relationship between $\bar{x}$ and $\hat{m}$ for this data set?

**2.20** **a.** For the sample giving the numbers of pages in 25 statistics texts in exercise 2.13, calculate $\bar{x}$ and $\hat{m}$ without using the computer.

    **b.** Is the relationship between the mean and the median what you would expect from the histogram for these data? Explain.

**2.21** Using Minitab, find the mean and the median of the weights of the sugar bags in exercise 2.14. Also find the mode. Which measure of location is preferred?

**2.22** **a.** Add 10 to the value of each observation in the data set of exercise 2.14. A simple Minitab command will accomplish this task.

    **b.** Find the average of the new data set.

    **c.** Has the mean increased by 10?

**2.23** Given observations $x_1, x_2, \ldots, x_n$ and the relationship $y_i = cx_i$ for a constant $c$, show that $\bar{y} = c\bar{x}$.

**2.24** Using the result of exercise 2.23 and the fact that "pounds = ounces/16," find the average weight in pounds of the sugar bags in exercise 2.21.

**2.25** The results of this section and the previous exercise imply that if $y_i = ax_i + b$, $i = 1, \ldots, n$, then $\bar{y} = a\bar{x} + b$. Letting $y$ represent Fahrenheit temperature in degrees and $x$ represent Centigrade temperature in degrees, we have $y = (9/5)x + 32$. Find the average temperature in Fahrenheit of 10,000 Centigrade temperatures that average 20.

**2.26** If the average high temperature in August is 86 degrees Fahrenheit, what is the average high temperature in Centigrade?

**2.27** The output below gives the lengths of time in minutes spent at checkout counters by 50 customers sampled randomly from 6:00 P.M. to 9:00 P.M. on a Friday evening.

10.41 17.79 3.99 3.94 5.59 2.35 18.94 21.78 2.71 69.61 12.44 12.48 8.59

6.65 45.95 14.96 13.98 1.33 16.94 1.09 4.59 5.85 4.36 6.97 11.10 5.43

4.25 10.34 4.49 2.68 19.67 5.94 18.53 1.99 37.71 13.33 2.37 21.10 13.01

6.45 10.08 13.30 5.00 0.62 3.32 2.28 7.38 15.42 40.83 19.86

**a.** Use the MEAN and MEDIAN commands with these data.
**b.** Make a histogram of these data.
**c.** Which measure of location would you prefer? Why?

**2.28 a.** For the data set in exercise 2.1, use Minitab to find the mean and the median number of conjunctions appearing on the 50 selected pages.
**b.** Use Minitab to make a histogram of the numerical values in part a. Would you prefer the mean or the median as a location measure?

**2.29** Suppose a sample of 25 men yields 21 with no winning lottery tickets during a given month, 3 with one winning ticket, and 1 with two winning tickets. Which measure of location is appropriate to describe the typical number of winning tickets a man in this group has during the month? What is the value of this measure?

**2.30 a.** For the data on rainfall in 34 cities in El Salvador given in exercise 2.15, use Minitab and the output from the HISTOGRAM command to find the values of the mode, median, and mean.
**b.** Are the measures of location in part a in the order suggested by the skewness of this data set?
**c.** Which location measure would you use for this data set?

## 2.5
## Statistical Measures of Variability

As mentioned in Section 2.1, two samples may have the same mean (i.e., location) but at the same time may differ substantially because one sample is more variable or "spread out" than the other. As a real-world example of this phenomenon, consider Table 2.3, which gives the average daily maximum and minimum temperatures (Fahrenheit) for San Francisco, California and Washington, D.C. in 1980.

The average daily maximum and minimum temperatures for these two cities differ on an annual basis by no more than 2.5 degrees. However, most people would prefer to live in San Francisco if climate were the only consideration, because the temperature fluctuations are less extreme there. The average July

## Table 2.3

**Average Temperatures**

| Month | Average Daily Maximum | Average Daily Minimum |
|---|---|---|
| *San Francisco* | | |
| January | 57.0 | 44.0 |
| April | 64.7 | 47.0 |
| July | 71.9 | 54.1 |
| October | 71.9 | 50.4 |
| Annual | 65.6 | 48.6 |
| *Washington, D.C.* | | |
| January | 43.4 | 31.0 |
| April | 69.6 | 50.6 |
| July | 91.0 | 73.6 |
| October | 68.6 | 51.2 |
| Annual | 68.1 | 50.9 |

*Sources:* Department of Commerce, National Oceanic and Atmospheric Administration Environmental Services, as reported in *The Information Please Almanac* (Boston: Houghton Mifflin, 1982), p. 424.

maximum in the nation's capital was 91.0, whereas that in San Francisco was 71.9. The average January low in Washington was 31.0, whereas in San Francisco it was 44.0. In Washington, D.C., the average annual highs and lows would appear to indicate a moderate climate, but these yearly averages do not reflect the pronounced seasonal fluctuations in temperatures.

## The Range

Taking $x_1, x_2, \ldots, x_n$ to be the observations in a sample, we now consider several statistics used to reflect the variability of the sample. The first of these statistics, the range, has been used already in the construction of a frequency table.

---

**Definition 2.14**

range

The **range** $R$ of a sample is the difference between the largest and the smallest value in the sample:

$$R = x_{(n)} - x_{(1)}$$

---

For the sample of the numbers of children in ten randomly chosen families,

3 0 4 2 1 2 2 1 4 3

the range is $R = 4 - 0 = 4$.

An advantage of the range is that it is very easy to calculate. This advantage is less important today than it used to be, however, because of the power of modern computers to make complex calculations easily. On other grounds the range $R$ is not a very satisfactory measure of the variation of a sample. The most important of these is that the value of $R$ tends to grow with the sample size $n$. Suppose that the sample size above had been 1000 instead of 10. In all likelihood one family with a large number of children would have been selected. If the largest family had 10 children and at least one family was childless, the range would have been $R = 10 - 0 = 10$, which is 2.5 times the value for the sample of size 10. The tendency of the range to increase as $n$ increases is not a desirable property. Just as one expects the mean to stabilize as $n$ increases, one hopes that the measure of variation will stabilize. Stability can be achieved by considering measures of variability based on the deviations from the mean, $x_1 - \bar{x}, x_2 - \bar{x}, \ldots, x_n - \bar{x}$.

## Mean Deviation

The mean deviation is one of several statistics used to measure variability, all of which are functions of the deviations from the mean.

---

**mean deviation**

**Definition 2.15** ◼━━━━━━━━━━━━━━━━━━━━━━━━━━━━━━

The **mean deviation** of a sample, MD, is the average absolute deviation of the observations in a sample from the sample mean:

$$\text{MD} = \sum_{i=1}^{n} \frac{|x_i - \bar{x}|}{n}$$

---

For the sample of numbers of children, $\bar{x} = 2.2$ and

$$
\begin{aligned}
\text{MD} = \{&|3 - 2.2| + |0 - 2.2| + |4 - 2.2| + |2 - 2.2| + |1 - 2.2| \\
+ &|2 - 2.2| + |2 - 2.2| + |1 - 2.2| + |4 - 2.2| \\
+ &|3 - 2.2|\}/10 = 1.04
\end{aligned}
$$

The absolute value function is awkward in a mathematical sense. It also proves to be inadequate for inference concerning the variability of normally distributed attributes. (Normally distributed attributes are an important class of variables that will be discussed in Chapter 4.) Because of these limitations of the absolute value function, we make use of an alternative measure of variation called the variance.

## Variance

The statistic that is most commonly used as measure of variability is the sample variance.

---

**Definition 2.16**

*variance*

The sample **variance** $s^2$ is given by

$$s^2 = \sum_{i=1}^{n} \frac{(x_i - \bar{x})^2}{(n - 1)}$$

---

The sample variance is almost the average of the $n$ squared deviations from the mean. If the divisor in Definition 2.15 were $n$ instead of $n - 1$, it would be exactly this average. (The reason for the choice of $n - 1$ will be explained in Chapter 7.) For large $n$, however, the use of $n - 1$ instead of $n$ will make little difference. Using the same data as we did for the range and the mean deviation, we find

$$s^2 = \{(0.8)^2 + (-2.2)^2 + (1.8)^2 + (-0.2)^2 + (-1.2)^2 + (-0.2)^2$$

$$+ (-0.2)^2 + (-1.2)^2 + (1.8)^2 + (0.8)^2\}/9 = \frac{15.6}{9} = 1.7333$$

## Standard Deviation

The units of the sample variance are not the same as those of the original values, but rather the square of the original units. For this reason (and others), we define a final measure of variability, the standard deviation.

---

**Definition 2.17**

*standard deviation*

The sample **standard deviation** $s$ is the positive square root of the variance $s^2$.

---

For the data of Example 2.3, the value of the standard deviation is $s = \sqrt{1.7333} = 1.3166$. In Example 2.4, comparison of two samples with the same mean is used to illustrate how the sample standard deviation $s$ reflects variability.

## Example 2.4

Observations of the amount of money (to the nearest dollar) in the pockets of five randomly selected faculty members and five randomly selected students are given in Table 2.4. Although the average number of dollars in the students' and faculty members' pockets is $9.00, the number of dollars in the faculty members' pockets

**Table 2.4**

Two Data Sets with Equal Means but Different Variances

| | | Sample 1 | | | Sample 2 | |
|---|---|---|---|---|---|---|
| $i$ | $x_i$ | $x_i - \bar{x}$ | $(x_i - \bar{x})^2$ | $x_i$ | $x_i - \bar{x}$ | $(x_i - \bar{x})^2$ |
| 1 | 1 | $-8$ | 64 | 7 | $-2$ | 4 |
| 2 | 8 | $-1$ | 1 | 8 | $-1$ | 1 |
| 3 | 9 | 0 | 0 | 9 | 0 | 0 |
| 4 | 11 | 2 | 4 | 10 | 1 | 1 |
| 5 | 16 | 7 | 49 | 11 | 2 | 4 |
| Totals | 45 | 0 | 118 | 45 | 0 | 10 |

$$\bar{x}_1 = 9 \qquad\qquad \bar{x}_2 = 9$$
$$s_1^2 = \frac{118}{4} = 29.5 \qquad\qquad s_2^2 = \frac{10}{4} = 2.5$$
$$s_1 = \sqrt{29.5} = 5.43 \qquad\qquad s_2 = \sqrt{2.5} = 1.58$$

is clearly more variable. This difference is reflected by a standard deviation of $5.43 for the faculty sample and of $1.58 for the students.

Putting off for the moment an interpretation of the sample variance $s^2$ and the sample standard deviation $s$, we will consider some properties of the variance and the standard deviation.

**1**  The units of the sample variance are the units of the original observations squared. Thus in sample 1 of Table 2.4, the variance is 29.5 (dollars)$^2$. The standard deviation has the original units.

**2**  Adding the same constant to each value in the sample will not change the variance of a sample. If each faculty member in Example 2.4 were given $10.00, then his or her pocket money would increase by $10, but the mean of the sample would also increase by $10. Thus the deviation from the mean for each faculty member would remain the same, leaving $s^2$ and $s$ unchanged.

**3**  If every element in a sample is multiplied by $c$, the variance is multiplied by $c^2$ and the standard deviation by $|c|$.

## Minitab Calculation of the Standard Deviation

**STANDARD DEVIATION**  Two very simple Minitab commands can be used to obtain the standard deviation of a column of data. The first command, **STANDARD DEVIATION**, was used with the yield and percentage change data for the sample of 50 stocks in

Example 2.1. We find the output

```
MTB > NOTE YIELD DATA FOR 50 STOCKS
MTB > STANDARD DEVIATION C10
   ST.DEV. =      2.9823
MTB > NOTE PERCENTAGE CHANGE DATA FOR 50 STOCKS
MTB > STANDARD DEVIATION C11
   ST.DEV. =      28.571
```

which shows that the standard deviation of the yield of the 50 stocks is 2.98 percentage points. Similarly, the standard deviation of the percentage change of these stocks is 28.57 percentage points.

**DESCRIBE**      The **DESCRIBE** command causes a number of statistics to be computed for the observations in a column of the Minitab worksheet. It has been used with the baseball data of Exhibits 2.7 and 2.8. The statistics calculated by this command are (for each column) the number of observations, the sample mean, the sample median, the 5 percent trimmed mean, the standard deviation, the standard error of the mean, the minimum value, the maximum value, and the first and third quartiles. The 5 percent trimmed mean will be discussed in Chapter 5. The standard error of the mean, which is defined to be $s/\sqrt{n}$, is important in statistical estimation. The first and third quartiles and the median divide the sample into four equal parts. The precise definitions of these quartiles are given in Appendix B. The output from DESCRIBE is given for the American League batters in Exhibit 2.10 and for National League batters in Exhibit 2.11.

**Exhibit 2.10**    **American League Batters**

```
    MTB > DESCRIBE C5-C10

                N      MEAN    MEDIAN    TRMEAN     STDEV    SEMEAN
    AB         25     526.0     528.0     526.3      96.5      19.3
    RUNS       25     81.08     84.00     80.48     22.75      4.55
    HITS       25    166.76    175.00    166.83     33.55      6.71
    HOMERS     25     14.80     12.00     14.30     10.94      2.19
    RBIS       25     74.56     64.00     74.13     28.15      5.63
    BA         25   0.31656   0.30500   0.31409   0.02128   0.00426

                MIN       MAX        Q1        Q3
    AB        340.0     705.0     449.5     606.0
    RUNS      42.00    134.00     62.00     96.00
    HITS     102.00    230.00    141.00    183.50
    HOMERS     0.00     41.00      7.50     21.50
    RBIS      37.00    122.00     53.00    107.00
    BA      0.30000   0.39000   0.30200   0.32750
```

The DESCRIBE command has been used with the number of at bats, runs, hits, home runs, runs batted in, and the batting average for the over-0.300 hitters in both leagues. Comparison of the data for the two leagues yields some interesting

**Exhibit 2.11**    National League Batters

```
MTB > DESCRIBE C15-C20

                   N      MEAN    MEDIAN    TRMEAN    STDEV    SEMEAN
      AB-N        19     479.0     504.0     481.9    133.8      30.7
      RUNS-N      19     71.16     70.00     71.18    20.56      4.72
      HITS-N      19    149.53    161.00    150.82    39.20      8.99
      HOMERS-N    19     11.58     10.00     11.29     7.78      1.78
      RBIS-N      19     65.89     68.00     66.06    29.03      6.66
      AVE-N       19   0.31405   0.30900   0.31335  0.01280   0.00294

                 MIN       MAX        Q1        Q3
      AB-N       251.0     658.0     311.0     578.0
      RUNS-N     31.00    111.00     58.00     84.00
      HITS-N     77.00    200.00    101.00    185.00
      HOMERS-N    2.00     26.00      4.00     17.00
      RBIS-N     20.00    109.00     41.00     91.00
      AVE-N    0.30100   0.33900   0.30300   0.32200
```

information. The mean numbers for each of these variables are higher in the American League than in the National League, but the standard deviations for American League batters and National League batters are not very different for several variables, including runs, hits, and runs batted in. This comparison is suggestive of some of the statistical comparisons we will be making between two groups in Chapter 8.

## Boxplots

boxplot

quartile

One graphical technique from Exploratory Data Analysis that was not discussed in Section 2.3 is the **boxplot**. The boxplot is useful in giving information about the spread of observations in a data set. With this technique the observations are ordered and displayed horizontally. The values in the sample that represent the first quartile, the median, and the third quartile are important in such a display. The first **quartile** is the observation that is greater than or equal to approximately one-fourth of the observations in the data set. The third quartile is the observation that is less than or equal to approximately one-fourth of the observations in the data set. In EDA these values are referred to as the upper and lower hinges. The values between the upper and lower hinge, the "middle half" of the data set, are represented by a box. The median, which is plotted with a plus sign, will in all cases fall in the box.

The H-spread of a data set is the distance between the quartiles—i.e., the difference between the upper hinge and the lower hinge. Two additional values are used in a boxplot to indicate the spread of a data set. These are inner fences, which are at the lower hinge less 1.5 times the H-spread and at the upper hinge plus 1.5 times the H-spread. Dashed "whiskers" run from the hinges to the most extreme values still within the inner fences. The outer fences are at the lower hinge minus three times the H-spread and at the upper hinge plus three times the H-spread.

Values less than the lower inner fence or greater than the upper inner fence, but within the outer fences, are plotted with an asterisk and should be considered to be potential extreme values. Values below the lower outer fence or above the upper outer fence are plotted with a zero and are definitely extreme values.

### Minitab Boxplots

BOXPLOT    Boxplots are easily constructed using the Minitab command **BOXPLOT**. Consider the data from Table 2.1 again, on the yields and the percentage price change for the 50 selected stocks. Boxplots for each data set are given in Exhibit 2.12. The moderate right skewness of the yields is shown by the long whisker to the right. The percentage change data are fairly symmetric (with the median of −10.5 having been previously calculated). There is one extreme observation in the latter data set, which is indicated by an asterisk. From Table 2.1 we know that this value is −85 percent, the 1981 percentage price decline of Peabody International.

**Exhibit 2.12**

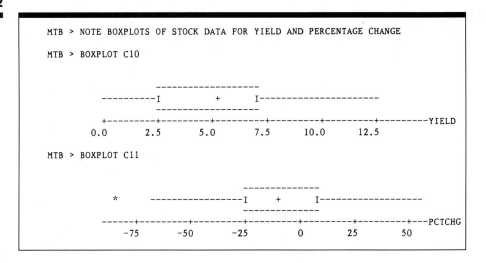

### Exercises 2.5

**2.31** The following observations represent the number of student conduct cases reported at a major university during a two-year period.

| Classification | Year 1 | Year 2 |
|---|---|---|
| Freshmen | 66 | 67 |
| Sophomore | 44 | 27 |
| Junior | 42 | 39 |
| Senior | 40 | 42 |
| Graduate Student | 11 | 11 |

a. Find the mean of the five observations for both years.
b. Find the range, the variance, and the standard deviation for each of the two groups of five observations.

**2.32** a. Use the Minitab command DESCRIBE to find the standard deviation of the data on the weights of 50 women given in exercise 2.7.
b. Use the Minitab command BOXPLOT to produce a boxplot for these observations.
c. Does the boxplot indicate a fairly symmetric distribution of these weights about the mean?

**2.33** a. Use the DESCRIBE command to find the standard deviation of the exam scores in exercise 2.8.
b. Use the Minitab command BOXPLOT to produce a boxplot for these observations. Do these observations appear to be symmetric about the mean?

**2.34** The following data set gives the life expectancy at birth for citizens of European countries in the late 1970s.

| | Life Expectancy at Birth | |
| Country | Male ($x_i$) | Female ($y_i$) |
| --- | --- | --- |
| Albania | 69.0 | 69.0 |
| Austria | 68.1 | 75.1 |
| Belgium | 68.6 | 75.1 |
| Czechoslovakia | 67.0 | 74.1 |
| Denmark | 71.3 | 77.4 |
| Finland | 68.5 | 77.1 |
| France | 69.9 | 78.0 |
| Germany, East | 68.8 | 74.7 |
| Germany, West | 69.0 | 75.6 |
| Greece | 70.1 | 73.6 |
| Hungary | 66.7 | 73.6 |
| Iceland | 73.4 | 79.3 |
| Italy | 67.0 | 73.1 |
| Netherlands, The | 71.9 | 78.5 |
| Norway | 72.3 | 78.7 |
| Poland | 67.4 | 75.1 |
| Romania | 67.4 | 72.1 |
| Spain | 70.4 | 76.2 |
| Sweden | 72.5 | 78.7 |
| Switzerland | 70.3 | 76.2 |
| United Kingdom | 69.8 | 75.9 |
| Yugoslavia | 67.6 | 72.6 |

*Source: Britannica Book of the Year* (1982).

a. Use Minitab to find the mean life expectancy for the 22 countries for males. Find the standard deviation and the variance of these life expectancies.
b. Do the same for females.
c. Create boxplots for both data sets using Minitab.

**d.** Create a new variable, the difference between male and female life expectancies in each country (female minus male), and use Minitab to find the mean, the standard deviation, and the variance of this variable.

**e.** Is the average in part d equal to $\bar{y} - \bar{x}$?

**f.** Is the variance in part d equal to $s_y^2 - s_x^2$?

**2.35** Find the variance and the standard deviation of the numbers of pages in the 25 statistics texts in exercise 2.13.

**2.36** A sample of 16 "1-pound" packages of butter has a mean weight of 16.16 ounces with a standard deviation of 0.32 ounce. Find the value of the mean and the standard deviation of these weights in pounds.

**2.37** Using the data in exercise 2.14, which are measured in ounces, use Minitab to create the variable $y_i = x_i/16$ for $i = 1, 2, \ldots, 48$. Verify that $s_y = s_x/16$ by finding $s_x$ and $s_y$.

**2.38** **a.** Using Minitab, create a boxplot for the data on checkout counter times in exercise 2.27.

**b.** Do these data appear to be skewed? In which direction?

**c.** Does the boxplot point out any extreme observations? If so, which ones?

**2.39** Use the data of exercise 2.15 concerning the rainfall in 34 cities in El Salvador.

**a.** Compute the values of the mean and standard deviation of this data set using the DESCRIBE command.

**b.** Use the Minitab command BOXPLOT with this data set. What is the direction of skewness indicated by this plot?

**2.40** The lengths in inches of 64 bluegill sunfish captured for tagging are presented in an article by Sanford Weisburg entitled "A Linear Model Approach to Backcalculation of Fish Length," which appeared in the *Journal of the American Statistical Association* 81 (1986): 922–929. The values are as follows:

 81   97   97  102  102  104  112  112  119  120  122  124  127  130  130  130  150  130
140  140  140  130  130  130  127  137  142  145  140  160  160  140  140  160  140  160
150  160  170  132  132  147  147  152  152  155  157  160  168  170  170  170  150  170
170  150  180  180  168  170  170  172  180  170

**a.** Use the DESCRIBE command to find the median and first and third quartiles of this data set.

**b.** What are the values of $\bar{x}$ and $s$ for these data?

**c.** Make a boxplot for these lengths. Are there any values that are not within the inner fences? If so, which ones? What is the direction of skewness indicated by the boxplot?

**2.41** Data on the time until death (in days) for 58 mice in an untreated group in a series of radiation experiments are presented below [from Gregg E. Dinse, "Nonparametric Prevalence and Mortality Estimators for Annual Experiments with Incomplete Cause-of-death Data," *Journal of the American Statistical Association* 81 (1986): 328–336].

231 444 468 473 527 550  593  600  610  650 655 660 715 720 752  785 832

838 859 891 896 904 931  952  998  559  595 596 603 765 783 794  811 856

870 883 897 975 978 991 1005 1023 1026 1053 593 735 816 848 850 1046 500

591 713 751 778 784 786  796

**a.** Use the DESCRIBE command to find $\bar{x}$ and $s$ for this data set. What are the units of $\bar{x}$? of $s$?

**b.** Make a boxplot for this data set using Minitab. What is the indicated direction of skewness?

**c.** Is the order of the mode, median, and mean what you would expect based on the direction of skewness determined in part b? (Use the HISTOGRAM command.)

**2.42** The January 12, 1987 issue of *Forbes* magazine gave the following data on the five-year return on equity for 19 north central banks.

| Bank | Return on Equity (%) |
|------|---------------------|
| Banc One | 18.9 |
| Boatmen's Banc Shares | 16.8 |
| First of America Bank | 15.6 |
| Marshall and Ilsley | 15.2 |
| Huntington Bcshs | 14.5 |
| Mercantile Bancorp | 14.4 |
| First Bank System | 13.5 |
| National City | 13.5 |
| First Wisconsin | 12.4 |
| Society | 12.4 |
| NBD Bancorp | 11.5 |
| Commerce Bcshs | 11.4 |
| Comerica | 10.8 |
| AmeriTrust | 10.7 |
| Manufacturers Natl | 10.4 |
| Norwest | 9.6 |
| Centerre Bancorp | 9.1 |
| Northern Trust | 8.4 |
| Michigan National | 5.2 |

**a.** Use the DESCRIBE command to find $\bar{x}$ and $s$ for this data set.

**b.** Make a boxplot and histogram for this data set using Minitab. What is the indicated direction of skewness, if any?

**c.** *Forbes* uses the median as a location measure. Do you agree with this choice?

**Summary** The basic notion of this chapter is that numbers do not "speak for themselves" but must be organized and summarized to permit a description of a sample and, subsequently, to allow inference to the characteristics of the population from which the sample was drawn.

There are several methods of sampling from a population, including random sampling, judgment sampling, convenience sampling, and systematic sampling. The preferred method is random sampling, but for reasons of conservation of energy, time, or money, the other types are often used in practice.

A frequency table is the basic tabular method of summarizing the information in a sample. A histogram, based on the information in the frequency table, is a useful graphical summary of the numerical values of an attribute observed in a sample. An ogive, a plot of the ordered sample values versus their cumulative frequency, is useful in providing rough estimates of sample percentiles.

Two important characteristics of a sample of measurements are location and variation. Several statistics (i.e., computations based on these measurements) are used to express information about location and variability. The mean, the median, and the mode are popular measures of location. The choice of an appropriate location measure depends on the general distribution of the sample. For skewed data the median is generally preferred; for bell-shaped or symmetric samples the mean is preferred. Statistics used to measure variability are the range, the mean deviation, variance, and the standard deviation. The sample standard deviation is the measure most often used in practice.

Minitab is very useful for calculating statistics and constructing graphical displays. The stem-and-leaf plot and the boxplot give some initial information about the properties of a data set. The Minitab command DESCRIBE gives ten useful statistics for a sample.

## Key Words

| | |
|---|---|
| boxplot | quartile |
| class interval | range |
| convenience sample | sample mean |
| cumulative frequency | sample median |
| finite population | sample mode |
| frame | sampled population |
| frequency | simple random sample |
| histogram | skewness |
| infinite population | standard deviation |
| judgment sample | statistic |
| location | stem-and-leaf display |
| mean deviation | systematic random sample |
| modal class | target population |
| ogive | variability |
| percentile | variance |

## Minitab Commands

| | | |
|---|---|---|
| BOXPLOT | NAME | SORT |
| DESCRIBE | PLOT | STANDARD |
| HISTOGRAM | PRINT | DEVIATION |
| MEAN | RANDOM | STEM-AND-LEAF |
| MEDIAN | SET | |

# Chapter 3

# Elementary Probability

Most people have an intuitive idea of what is meant by the probability of an event. A fair coin, when tossed, is thought to have equal likelihood of coming up heads or tails. Colloquially, we say that there is one chance in two of a head's occurring on a single toss. Intuitively we assume that if a coin is tossed a large number of times, the proportion of times a head will occur is about one-half. Suppose a real coin were tossed 5000 times and a total of 2532 heads were observed. In that case the **relative frequency** of heads would be $2532/5000 = 0.5064$. The author once simulated the tossing of a fair coin 1,000,000 times (using a computer) and observed 500,671 heads. In this case the relative frequency of heads was $500,671/1,000,000 = 0.500671$. This relative frequency is quite close to 0.5. Our intuition suggests that the relative frequency of heads is likely to be closer to 0.5 for a large number of tosses than for a small number of tosses, as in fact is true in the two cases described here.

*relative frequency*

Similarly, in games of chance played with dice, we assume that each of the faces, numbered 1, 2, 3, 4, 5, and 6, has an equal chance of appearing on the throw of a fair die. That is, we think of 1/6 as the "correct" proportion of times that a fair die "should" show a 5, for example, over a large number of tosses. Probability is the branch of mathematics that describes theoretically the intuitive notion of the stability of long-run relative frequencies.

To emphasize the idea of the stability of long-run relative frequencies of repeated experiments, let us consider an "experiment" that occurs each year in

**Table 3.1**

**Live Births by Sex**

| Year | Male | Female | Proportion Male |
|------|------|--------|-----------------|
| 1970 | 1,915,378 | 1,816,008 | 0.5133 |
| 1971 | 1,822,910 | 1,733,060 | 0.5126 |
| 1972 | 1,669,927 | 1,588,484 | 0.5125 |
| 1973 | 1,608,326 | 1,528,639 | 0.5127 |
| 1974 | 1,622,114 | 1,537,844 | 0.5133 |
| 1975 | 1,613,135 | 1,531,063 | 0.5131 |
| 1976 | 1,624,436 | 1,543,352 | 0.5128 |
| 1977 | 1,705,916 | 1,620,716 | 0.5128 |
| 1978 | 1,709,394 | 1,623,885 | 0.5128 |
| Total | 15,291,536 | 14,523,051 | 0.5129 |

*Source:* Department of Health and Human Services, National Center for Health Statistics, as reported in *The Information Please Almanac* (Boston: Houghton Mifflin, 1982), p. 752.

the United States between 3 and 4 million times. The "experiment" is having a child. The possible outcomes are the birth of a girl and the birth of a boy. Table 3.1 lists the number of male and female births for each of the years from 1970 to 1978. The proportion of male births in the United States appears to be very stable —about 0.513. For example, in 1970 the relative frequency of male births (the number of male births divided by the total number of births for that year) equaled 1,915,378/3,731,386, or 0.5133 to four-decimal-place accuracy. This example differs from the coin tossing example in that the outcomes of a male birth and a female birth are not equally likely. Still, however, the relative frequency of an outcome (e.g., a male birth) of the chance experiment tends to be a constant when the number of trials of the experiment becomes large.

Table 3.2 provides another example of the stability of long-run frequencies. This table of vital statistics presents the death rates from 1951 to 1970 in the United States, as collected by the United States Bureau of the Census. Over this period of time the overall annual death rate of the white population was quite stable at about 9.4 deaths per 1000 population, or a relative frequency of 0.0094. The death rates for white males and white females were also quite stable over this perioid, but they were by no means the same. The rates for females yield a median of 8.0 deaths per 1000 or a relative frequency of 0.008, whereas the rates for males yield a median of 10.9 deaths per 1000 or a relative frequency of 0.0109 over this period. This example once again emphasizes that in many situations the relative frequencies of the outcomes of chance experiments repeated a large number of times appear to be quite stable. It is this aspect of the "real world" that is described mathematically by the discipline of probability.

In Section 3.2 we consider three elementary definitions required to understand basic concepts of probability—definitions of an experiment with a random outcome, an outcome space, and a probability assignment. In Section 3.3 the technical ideas of an event and the probability of an event are introduced. Ways

**Table 3.2**

**Death Rate for White Population (Number of Deaths per 1000 Population)**

| Year | Both Sexes | Male | Female |
|------|------------|------|--------|
| 1951 | 9.5 | 11.0 | 8.0 |
| 52 | 9.4 | 11.0 | 8.0 |
| 53 | 9.4 | 11.0 | 8.0 |
| 54 | 9.1 | 10.6 | 7.6 |
| 55 | 9.2 | 10.7 | 7.8 |
| 56 | 9.3 | 10.8 | 7.8 |
| 57 | 9.5 | 11.0 | 8.0 |
| 58 | 9.4 | 10.9 | 8.0 |
| 59 | 9.3 | 10.8 | 7.9 |
| 1960 | 9.5 | 11.0 | 8.0 |
| 61 | 9.3 | 10.7 | 7.8 |
| 62 | 9.4 | 10.8 | 8.0 |
| 63 | 9.5 | 11.0 | 8.1 |
| 64 | 9.4 | 10.8 | 8.0 |
| 65 | 9.4 | 10.8 | 8.0 |
| 66 | 9.5 | 10.9 | 8.1 |
| 67 | 9.4 | 10.8 | 8.0 |
| 68 | 9.6 | 11.1 | 8.2 |
| 69 | 9.5 | 10.9 | 8.2 |
| 1970 | 9.5 | 10.9 | 8.1 |
| Median 1951–70 | 9.4 | 10.9 | 8.0 |

*Source:* Vital Statistics of the United States, 1982, Volume II —Mortality Part A, National Center for Health Statistics (1986), p. 1.

of forming new events by combining other events are discussed in this section, as are techniques for computing the probabilities of these new events. In Section 3.4 elementary ideas about the algebra of probability are discussed. In Section 3.5 the important idea of probabilistic independence is presented. The binomial distribution, based on the idea of independence, is introduced and explained using examples.

## 3.2
## Basic Concepts in Probability

A fundamental idea in probability is that of an experiment whose outcome is random.

**experiment**

---

**Definition 3.1**

A theoretical **experiment** is a trial for which the outcome is random—that is, not predictable in advance through knowledge of the experimental conditions.

---

The word "theoretical" is used in the definition above because we are considering an idealization of a real-world experiment. We toss a theoretical fair coin or fair die. Corresponding real-world experiments occur naturally in everyday life. A worker goes to a manufacturing job every day intending not to have an accident. Each working day, however, may be considered to be a trial on which an accident occurs or does not occur. The theoretical and mathematical description of all experiments whose outcomes cannot be predicted in advance is the topic of probability theory.

In defining theoretical experiments, we generally concentrate not on a single outcome of an experiment, but on the set of all possible outcomes.

---

**Definition 3.2** ▰▰▰▰▰▰▰▰▰▰▰▰▰▰▰▰▰▰▰▰▰▰▰▰

outcome space

The **outcome space** $S$ for a theoretical experiment is the set of all possible outcomes of the experiment.

---

For the experiment of having a child, we define the outcome space $S$ to have two outcomes:

$$S = \{\text{Female, Male}\}$$

For the experiment of tossing a die, we define $S$ to have six outcomes:

$$S = \{1, 2, 3, 4, 5, 6\}$$

We saw in Chapter 2 that the RANDOM command in Minitab can be used to select an integer from 1 to $k$, where $k$ may have any positive integral value we choose. The theoretical sample space corresponding to this experiment would be

$$S = \{1, 2, 3, \ldots, k\}$$

In the example in which a sample of stocks was selected, the value of $k$ was chosen to be 900. The RANDOM command simulates repeated selections of an integer from 1 to $k$ in such a way that each such integer has an "equal chance" of being chosen at each selection.

Now we make precise the idea of a probability assignment to an outcome space. A finite outcome space $S$ is composed of $k$ possible outcomes. In the case of the sex of a child, of course, $k = 2$, and in the case of tossing a die, $k = 6$. We write $S$ as follows:

$$S = \{e_1, e_2, \ldots, e_k\}$$

By $e_1, e_2, \ldots, e_k$ we mean the first, second, $\ldots$, $k$th possible outcomes of a theoretical experiment.

## Definition 3.3

A finite outcome space $S$ is given a **probability assignment** by giving to each outcome a number, $P(e_1),\ P(e_2), \ldots, P(e_k)$, satisfying the following conditions:

**a.** $0 \leqslant P(e_i) \leqslant 1$ for $i = 1, 2, \ldots, k$

**b.** $\sum_{i=1}^{k} P(e_i) = 1$

For the birth example we might make the following probability assignment:

$$P(\text{Female}) = \frac{1}{2} \qquad P(\text{Male}) = \frac{1}{2}$$

This assignment satisfies the requirements of Definition 3.3. It is not the only acceptable probability assignment, however. The following assignment would be more "realistic":

$$P(\text{Female}) = 0.487 \qquad P(\text{Male}) = 0.513$$

Properties 3.3(a) and 3.3(b) of a probability assignment have been chosen to reflect the corresponding properties of relative frequencies. For example, for the 5000 tosses of a fair coin in Section 3.1, the proportions of heads and tails, $f_H = 2532/5000 = 0.5064$ and $f_T = 2468/5000 = 0.4936$, clearly satisfy the conditions

$$0 \leqslant f_H \leqslant 1 \qquad 0 \leqslant f_T \leqslant 1 \qquad f_H + f_T = 1$$

In a theoretical probability assignment to an outcome space $S$, probabilities are the abstract correspondents of relative frequencies and are assigned algebraic properties analogous to those of relative frequencies.

## Definition 3.4

The term **simulation** describes a computer's capacity to repeat a theoretical experiment and describe its outcome.

The Minitab package has the power to simulate a theoretical experiment repeatedly and to summarize the outcomes accurately and very rapidly. The simulation capacity of Minitab is useful for illustrating the increasing stability of relative frequencies as the number of trials of an experiment increases. The Minitab command RANDOM with a simple subcommand, BINOMIAL, simulates the outcome of an experiment in which $n$ trials are made, with probability of success $p$ at each trial. For example, in the coin-tossing experiment of Section 3.1, $n = 5000$, $p = 1/2$, and the number of observed successes was 2532. The relative frequency of heads, $2532/5000 = 0.5064$, approximates the theoretical value of $1/2$. The usefulness of the computer lies in the fact that it never tires of tossing coins or performing other more complex and interesting simulations. The entire experiment of $n$ trials may be repeated many times.

## Example 3.1

TALLY

Consider the experiment of tossing a fair coin 20 times and counting the number of heads obtained. Exhibit 3.1 shows the output obtained when the command RANDOM was used to repeat the experiment 50 times. There were 7 heads in the first experiment, 10 heads in the second, and so forth, with 13 heads observed in the 50th experiment. The output from the **TALLY** command gives a frequency table for these 50 values, each of which represents the number of heads in 20 tosses of a fair coin. It shows that in 1 of the 50 experiments 5 heads were observed, in 4 of the 50 experiments 7 heads were observed, and so forth. The relative frequency of the outcomes 5, 6, . . . , 16 heads can be obtained by dividing the observed frequencies by the number of times the experiment was repeated. Hence, $f(5) = 1/50 = 0.02$, $f(7) = 4/50 = 0.08, . . . , f(16) = 1/50 = 0.02$. Note that the relative frequencies of 8, 9, 10, 11, and 12 heads are 0.16, 0.16, 0.12, 0.14, and 0.18, respectively. Although the relative frequency of exactly 10 heads in the 20 tosses was only 0.12, values near $(1/2)(20) = 10$ heads had high relative frequencies. The total relative frequency of outcomes between 8 and 12 heads is $0.16 + 0.16 + 0.12 + 0.14 + 0.18 = 0.76$. Thus it is likely that the number of heads in 20 trials will be close to 10; extreme values such as 0, 1, or 2 heads or 18, 19, or 20 heads are very unlikely. In fact, there were no such outcomes in this simulation.

## Exhibit 3.1

```
MTB > NOTE SIMULATION OF RELATIVE FREQUENCIES
MTB > NOTE OBS IN A COLUMN ARE THE NUMBER OF HEADS IN N TOSSES
MTB > BASE = 100
MTB > RANDOM 50 OBSERVATIONS C1;
SUBC> BINOMIAL N = 20 P = 0.5.
MTB > PRINT C1
C1
    7    10     8     9    12    10    14     9     8     8    14
   11     8    12    13     9    14    12     8    12    11     9
   12     7    10    11     9     9    12    10     8    16     7
    7    12     9    13    10    11     9    10    11     8    11
   12    12     5    11     8    13

MTB > TALLY C1

     C1  COUNT
      5      1
      7      4
      8      8
      9      8
     10      6
     11      7
     12      9
     13      3
     14      3
     16      1
     N=     50
```

**Exhibit 3.2**

```
MTB > RANDOM 50 OBSERVATIONS IN C2;
SUBC> BINOMIAL N = 50 P = 0.5.
MTB > TALLY C2

       C2   COUNT
       16     1
       19     1
       20     1
       21     2
       22     6
       23     6
       24    10
       25     6
       26     3
       27     5
       28     1
       29     4
       30     3
       32     1
       N=    50

MTB > PRINT C2
C2
    23    23    24    26    24    25    27    22    30    24    24
    22    25    24    21    20    23    24    24    23    28    22
    29    29    22    22    27    26    25    23    30    27    24
    16    22    21    25    24    25    19    29    27    29    32
    24    30    27    25    23    26


MTB > RANDOM 50 OBSERVATIONS IN C3;
SUBC> BINOMIAL N = 100 P = 0.5.
MTB > TALLY C3

       C3   COUNT
       39     1
       41     1
       42     2
       43     3
       44     5
       45     3
       46     3
       47     1
       48     6
       49     4
       50     3
       51     4
       53     4
       54     2
       55     2
       57     1
       58     1
       60     1
       62     1
       63     1
       64     1
       N=    50

MTB > PRINT C3
C3
    53    53    64    43    46    49    49    47    58    55    43
    42    43    63    48    44    57    41    53    46    50    60
    48    42    51    51    55    45    49    54    39    50    45
    48    44    54    44    45    48    46    49    48    62    53
    51    48    51    50    44    44
```

　　　The **BASE** command used in Exhibit 3.1 permits the same simulated values to be obtained in subsequent executions of the program. This capacity of Minitab is useful for checking programs. Let us consider tossing the coin 50 times and 100 times. The Minitab output for 50 repetitions of 50 and 100 tosses is shown in Exhibit 3.2. (See page 61.)

　　　Note that the range of the number of heads observed is $16 - 5 = 11$ for 20 tosses, $32 - 16 = 16$ for 50 tosses, and $64 - 39 = 25$ for 100 tosses. In the absolute sense, the "spread" of the number of heads observed increases with the number of tosses. If the difference between the largest and smallest *relative frequencies* is computed for the three cases, however, we get $16/20 - 5/20 = 11/20 = 0.55$, $32/50 - 16/50 = 16/50 = 0.32$, and $64/100 - 39/100 = 25/100 = 0.25$ for $n = 20$, 50, and 100 tosses, respectively. The "spread," or variability, of the relative frequencies decreases with increasing values of $n$.

　　　The tendency for the relative frequency to stabilize close to the *theoretical value* of $p = 0.5$ as $n$ increases is seen most clearly in plots of the relative frequency of heads. In Exhibit 3.3 relative frequencies of heads for 20, 50, and 100 tosses are plotted against the trial number on the horizontal axis. For 20 tosses (the first part of Exhibit 3.3), the relative frequency is $7/20 = 0.35$ in the first experiment, $10/20 = 0.50$ in the second, and so forth, ending with $13/20 = 0.65$ in the fiftieth experiment. The relative frequencies are centered roughly about 0.5 in each case, but the second and third parts of Exhibit 3.3 show that the variability of the relative

**Exhibit 3.3**

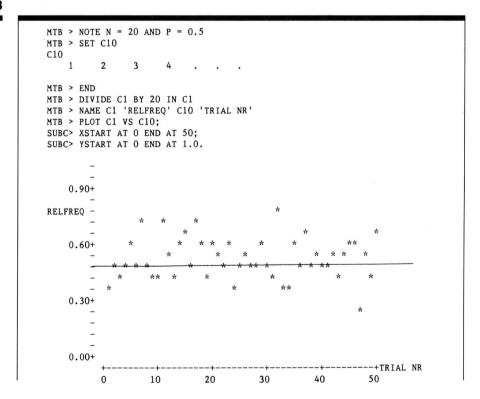

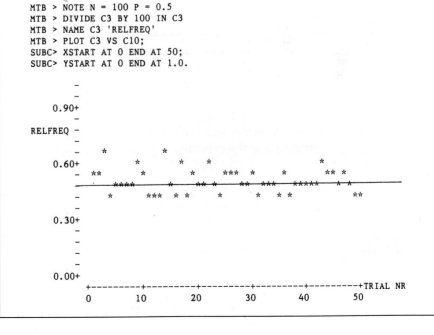

```
MTB > NOTE N = 50 P = 0.5
MTB > DIVIDE C2 BY 50 IN C2
MTB > NAME C2 'RELFREQ'
MTB > PLOT C2 VS C10;
SUBC> XSTART AT 0 END AT 50;
SUBC> YSTART AT 0 END AT 1.0.
```

```
MTB > NOTE N = 100 P = 0.5
MTB > DIVIDE C3 BY 100 IN C3
MTB > NAME C3 'RELFREQ'
MTB > PLOT C3 VS C10;
SUBC> XSTART AT 0 END AT 50;
SUBC> YSTART AT 0 END AT 1.0.
```

frequencies about 0.5 decreases as the sample size increases. (Note that the horizontal lines for $p = 0.5$ have been drawn through the asterisks representing 0.5 in Exhibit 3.3. These asterisks are a little higher than the vertical scale would indicate because of the inaccuracy of computer plotting.)

Another example of the use of RANDOM is presented in Example 3.2, to emphasize the idea that probabilities are the theoretical correspondents of long-run relative frequencies.

## Example 3.2

Consider the number of females in a family with three children. The number of females can be thought of as the number of successes in $n = 3$ trials for which the probability of success at each trial is $p = 1/2$. (In this case the probability of a female or male birth is considered to be equally likely.) The result of the experiment at each trial is the number of females in the family. Only four outcomes are possible, and the corresponding outcome space is

$$S = \{0, 1, 2, 3\}$$

When the RANDOM command was used to repeat this experiment (having three children) 400 times, the output (Exhibit 3.4) gave the following relative frequencies:

$$f(0) = \frac{56}{400} = 0.140 \qquad f(1) = \frac{145}{400} = 0.3625$$

$$f(2) = \frac{147}{400} = 0.3675 \qquad f(3) = \frac{52}{400} = 0.130$$

Obviously these relative frequencies are not tending to the same constant. The outcomes of one and two females are much more frequent than the outcomes of zero and three females. We will see later in this chapter that a reasonable probability assignment to $S$ in this case is $P(0) = P(3) = 0.125$ and $P(1) = P(2) = 0.375$. These theoretical probabilities are reasonably consistent with the observed relative frequencies. The point here is that probabilities can be thought of as the theoretical correspondents of relative frequencies as the number of repetitions of the experiment (400 in this case) becomes arbitrarily large.

We will consider two more examples of probability assignments to theoretical outcome spaces.

## Example 3.3

Assume RANDOM is used to select an integer at random from 1, 2, . . . , 8. The outcome space is

$$S = \{1, 2, 3, 4, 5, 6, 7, 8\}$$

**Exhibit 3.4**

```
MTB > NOTE SIMULATION OF NUMBER OF FEMALES IN 3 CHILD FAMILY
MTB > NOTE OBSERVATIONS ARE THE NUMBER OF FEMALES IN 400 FAMILIES
MTB > BASE = 1000
MTB > RANDOM 400 OBSERVATIONS IN C1;
SUBC> BINOMIAL N = 3 P = 0.5.
MTB > HISTOGRAM C1

Histogram of C1    N = 400
Each * represents 5 obs.

Midpoint    Count
        0      56   ************
        1     145   ****************************
        2     147   *****************************
        3      52   ***********

MTB > NOTE RELATIVE FREQUENCY OF 0,1,2,3
MTB > INDICATOR FOR C1, PUT IN C2-C5
MTB > MEAN C2
   MEAN     =      0.14000
MTB > MEAN C3
   MEAN     =      0.36250
MTB > MEAN C4
   MEAN     =      0.36750
MTB > MEAN C5
   MEAN     =      0.13000
```

As each outcome is equally likely, we have $P(1) = P(2) = \cdots = P(8)$. Let this common probability be called $p$. From part b of Definition 3.3, we know that

$$p + p + \cdots + p = 8p = 1$$

so the common probability is clearly $p = 1/8$. A simulation of 1000 observations from this distribution yielded the following:

```
MTB > BASE = 1000
MTB > RANDOM 1000 INTEGERS IN C1;
SUBC> INTEGER A = 1 B = 8.
MTB > TALLY C1;
SUBC> ALL.
```

| C1 | COUNT | CUMCNT | PERCENT | CUMPCT |
|----|-------|--------|---------|--------|
| 1 | 124 | 124 | 12.40 | 12.40 |
| 2 | 130 | 254 | 13.00 | 25.40 |
| 3 | 105 | 359 | 10.50 | 35.90 |
| 4 | 135 | 494 | 13.50 | 49.40 |
| 5 | 131 | 625 | 13.10 | 62.50 |
| 6 | 122 | 747 | 12.20 | 74.70 |
| 7 | 129 | 876 | 12.90 | 87.60 |
| 8 | 124 | 1000 | 12.40 | 100.00 |
| N= | 1000 | | | |

Note that the values of the relative frequencies of 1, 2, . . . , 8 are given by the TALLY command (as percentages). These values are all estimates of the common probability $1/8 = 0.125$ (or 12.5 percent).

It is frequently the case that each outcome of $S$ is given equal probability, so that in this case

$$P(e_1) \;=\; P(e_2) = \cdots = P(e_k) = \frac{1}{k}$$

The probability of each of the $k$ outcomes is $1/k$ when each outcome is equally likely. This probability assignment clearly satisfies the properties of Definition 3.3. Such a probability assignment to $S$ is called an equiprobable assignment.

It is not necessary that the probabilities be equal for each outcome, however. We will now consider another example in which the probabilities of the various outcomes differ.

## Example 3.4

Assume a symmetrical cube has one face numbered 1, two faces numbered 2, and three faces numbered 3. The outcome space for the experiment of tossing the cube and observing the number that faces up is

$$S \;=\; \{1, 2, 3\}$$

Clearly, $P(2) = 2P(1)$ and $P(3) = 3P(1)$ are reasonable assumptions, because a 2 is "twice as likely" as a 1 and a 3 is "three times as likely" as a 1. By Definition 3.3, these assumptions imply

$$P(1) + P(2) + P(3) \;=\; P(1) + 2P(1) + 3P(1) \;=\; 6P(1) \;=\; 1$$

Hence $P(1) = 1/6, P(2) = 2P(1) = 2/6 = 1/3$, and $P(3) = 3P(1) = 3/6 = 1/2$. This assignment of probabilities satisfies the conditions of Definition 3.3, but the outcomes do not have equal probability.

## Exercises 3.2

**3.1**  In 1979 the U.S. Bureau of the Census provided the following information about the numbers of persons in families in the United States:

| Size of Family | Number of Families (thousands) |
|---|---|
| 2 persons | 22,913 |
| 3 persons | 13,332 |
| 4 persons | 12,180 |
| 5 persons | 5,871 |
| 6 persons | 2,439 |
| 7 persons or more | 1,691 |
| Total families | 58,426 |

**a.** Find the relative frequencies of families of the indicated sizes.
**b.** Verify that the sum of these relative frequencies is 1.
**c.** What proportion of the families have four or fewer members?

**3.2.**  A fair cube has two faces numbered 1, two faces numbered 2, and two faces numbered 3. Define a reasonable probability model for the outcome of a toss of such a cube.

**3.3** Working days are defined to be Monday through Friday. We wish to make a probability assignment to $S = \{M, T, W, Th, F\}$, assigning to each day a probability equal to the "likelihood" that a worker will be absent on that day. Monday and Friday are to be given twice the probability of either Tuesday or Thursday, which in turn are to be given twice the probability of Wednesday. Find the required probabilities. These probabilities can be thought of as giving the long-run relative frequency that a worker will be absent on the given day of the week, assuming an absence occurs. *Hint:* Let $P(W) = c$. Find the probabilities of the other days in terms of $c$.

**3.4** **a.** During his career in the NBA, Rick Barry made 90 percent of his foul shots. Use the Minitab command RANDOM to simulate the number of successes in 25 games if he shoots 20 foul shots in each game.
   **b.** Simulate the number of successes in 25 weeks if he shoots 100 foul shots each week.
   **c.** For the data in parts a and b, PLOT the relative frequency of success on the vertical axis and the trial numbers 1, 2, . . . , 25 on the horizontal axis. Is the variability of the relative frequencies in these two plots as you expected? Explain.

**3.5** Let $S = \{1, 2, 3, 4, 5\}$. Assign a probability measure to the elements of $S$ so that $P(k)$ is directly proportional to $k$ [i.e., $P(k) = ck$ for some constant $c$ for $k = 1, 2, 3, 4, 5$]. Find the value of $c$, using the fact that the sum of the probabilities is 1, and then find the individual probabilities for $k = 1, 2, 3, 4$, and 5.

**3.6** Consider the outcome space
$$S = \{1, 2, 3, 4\}$$
   **a.** Assume that the probability of each outcome is inversely proportional to the indicated number. That is, $P(k) = c/k$ for a constant $c$. Find the constant $c$.
   **b.** Find the values of $P(k)$ for $k = 1, 2, 3, 4$.

**3.7** **a.** A fair coin is tossed once, with either a head or a tail resulting. Define an outcome space for this experiment, where an outcome indicates the number of heads observed.
   **b.** A fair coin is tossed twice and the results of both tosses are recorded. Define an outcome space for this experiment, where an outcome indicates the number of heads observed.
   **c.** Use Minitab to simulate the number of heads in 400 tosses of two fair coins, by twice using the RANDOM command with the subcommand INTEGER A = 0 B = 1. Put the outcomes from the RANDOM commands in C1 and C2, and then add C1 and C2 in C3. Use the TALLY command with the numbers in C3. Do the outcomes of 0, 1, and 2 heads seem equally likely?

**3.8** The following data set gives the reservoir water capacity in millions of cubic meters for 70 of the world's highest dams:

| | | | | | | | | | |
|---|---|---|---|---|---|---|---|---|---|
| 11,700 | 10,400 | 401 | 1,100 | 169 | 1,660 | 24,670 | 31,300 | 815 | 182 |
| 4,299 | 2,780 | 9,868 | 36,703 | 106 | 880 | 182 | 33,305 | 141,852 | 19,500 |
| 2,837 | 88 | 31,000 | 3,340 | 2,649 | 2,900 | 200 | 1,184 | 2,960 | 199 |
| 932 | 1,603 | 5,615 | 70,309 | 230 | 205 | 255 | 4,000 | 227 | 2,504 |
| 65 | 4,278 | 1,460 | 64,000 | 2,000 | 11,795 | 465 | 4,750 | 1,170 | 3,020 |
| 921 | 1,696 | 910 | 270 | 41 | 601 | 10 | 51 | 327 | 240 |
| 123 | 76 | 13,462 | 4,674 | 100 | 139 | 183 | 100 | 187 | 678 |

*Source:* Department of Interior, Bureau of Reclamation, as reported in *The Information Please Almanac* (Boston: Houghton Mifflin, 1982), p. 318.

**a.** Make a histogram of the left-most digits of these numbers (e.g., 4,299 is recorded as a 4).

**b.** Here $S = \{1, 2, 3, 4, 5, 6, 7, 8, 9\}$. Does a model assigning equal probability to the digits seem appropriate? Why or why not?

**3.9** As exercise 3.8 indicates, assigning equal probability to the points in an outcome space is not always appropriate. Give several examples in which equal probability assignments would appear appropriate for at least four outcomes in $S$.

**3.10** Use RANDOM in Minitab with the subcommand BINOMIAL to complete the following simulations:

**a.** Find the number of hits made by a batter with a 0.250 average in 4 at bats per game over a 100-game season. Here $n = 4$ and $p = 0.25$.

**b.** Find the number of hits made by a batter with a 0.400 average in 4 at bats per game over a 100-game season. Use the TALLY command to find the relative frequencies of 0, 1, 2, 3, and 4 hits in the 100 games for each of the batters in parts a and b. Do these relative frequencies suggest equal likelihood of the outcomes 0, 1, 2, 3, and 4 in either part a or part b?

## 3.3

## Probability of Events

In this section we will consider further properties of a probability assignment to an outcome space $S$. The focus will continue to be on outcome spaces with a finite number of outcomes. First, however, we must define the terms "event" and "probability of an event."

---

**Definition 3.5** ▬▬▬▬▬▬▬▬▬▬▬▬▬▬▬▬▬▬▬▬▬▬▬

event

An **event** $E$ is a subset of $S$.

---

**Definition 3.6** ▬▬▬▬▬▬▬▬▬▬▬▬▬▬▬▬▬▬▬▬▬▬

probability

The **probability** of an event, $P(E)$, is the sum of the probabilities for all those outcomes in $E$.

---

As $E$ is a subset of $S$, we must have $P(E) \leqslant P(S) = 1$.

## Example 3.5

Consider the best-of-seven-game World Series in baseball. The number of games played in the series will be the outcome observed. The outcome space for this experiment is

$$S = \{4, 5, 6, 7\}$$

**Table 3.3**

| World Series Games, 1903–1986 | |
| --- | --- |
| Games Played | Number of Series |
| 4 | 13 |
| 5 | 19 |
| 6 | 17 |
| 7 | 30 |
| Total | 79 |

*Source:* Adapted from *The Information Please Almanac* (Boston: Houghton Mifflin, 1986), pp. 930–932.

Let us now define several events—i.e., subsets of this outcome space.

$E_1$ = exactly 4 games are played
= {4}

$E_2$ = an odd number of games are played
= {5, 7}

$E_3$ = at least 5 games are played
= {5, 6, 7}

$E_4$ = no more than 6 games are played
= {4, 5, 6}

It is easy to see that the events $E_1$, $E_2$, $E_3$, and $E_4$ defined verbally above are in fact the indicated subsets of $S$.

Data on the number of games played in the 79 seven-game World Series played from 1903 to 1986 are presented in Table 3.3. Without any further information it seems plausible to define the probabilities of a 4-, 5-, 6-, or 7-game series by their observed relative frequencies. Hence, we let $P(4) = 13/79$, $P(5) = 19/79$, $P(6) = 17/79$, and $P(7) = 30/79$. The probability of any event can now be found by using Definition 3.6. For example, the probability of a 4-game series is $P(E_1) = 13/79$, and probability of an odd number of games is $P(E_2) = P(5) + P(7) = 49/79$. Similarly, the probability of at least a 5-game series is $P(E_3) = 66/79$, and the probability of no more than 6 games is $P(E_4) = 49/79$.

Suppose we are given two events of $S$, say $A$ and $B$. Three new events can then be defined in terms of the outcomes in $A$ and $B$.

---

**Definition 3.7** ■■■■■■■■■■■■■■■■■■■■■■■■■■■■■■■■■■

union

The **union** of $A$ and $B$, $A \cup B$, is the event composed of the outcomes of $A$, of $B$, or of both.

---

The union, intersection, and complement are most clearly visualized by means of a graphical device called a Venn diagram. In a Venn diagram the space $S$ is indicated by a rectangle and events are depicted as subsets of the rectangle. In Figure 3.1 the events $A$ and $B$ are indicated as subsets of $S$. The union $A \cup B$ is represented by those points in $A$ or $B$ (including the points in both $A$ and $B$); the shaded area of Figure 3.1 is the union of $A$ and $B$. The intersection $A \cap B$ is represented by those points common to $A$ and $B$; the shaded area of Figure 3.2 is the intersection of $A$ and $B$. The complement of $A$ is those points in $S$ but not in $A$; the complement $\bar{A}$ is represented by the shaded area in Figure 3.3.

For our World Series example, we have

$$
\begin{aligned}
E_1 \cup E_2 &= \{4, 5, 7\} \\
E_3 \cap E_4 &= \{5, 6\} \\
\bar{E}_1 &= \{5, 6, 7\} \\
\bar{E}_4 &= \{7\}
\end{aligned}
$$

The event $A \cup B$ means "$A$ or $B$," where "or" is defined inclusively as one or the other or both. Thus $E_1 \cup E_2$ consists of World Series that are completed in either four games or an odd number of games. The event $A \cap B$ means "$A$ and $B$." Hence, $E_3 \cap E_4$ consists of World Series that are completed in at least five games and in no more than six games. The event $\bar{A}$ means "not $A$." Hence, $\bar{E}_1$ contains those World Series that do not end in four games. Similarly, $\bar{E}_4$ contains those series that end in more than six games—i.e., seven games.

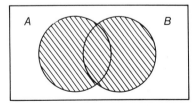

**Figure 3.1** ━━━━━━━━━━━━━━━━━━━━━━━━━━━━━━━━━━━━━━━━━━━━━━━━━━━━━━━━━━━━━━━━━━━━━━━━━━━━

**The Union of _A_ and _B_**

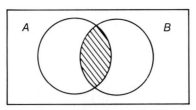

**Figure 3.2**

The Intersection of *A* and *B*

We also can compute

$$P(E_1 \cup E_2) \;=\; P(4) + P(5) + P(7) \;=\; \frac{13}{79} + \frac{19}{79} + \frac{30}{79} \;=\; \frac{62}{79}$$

Similarly,

$$P(E_3 \cap E_4) \;=\; P(5) + P(6) \;=\; \frac{19}{79} + \frac{17}{79} \;=\; \frac{36}{79}$$

and

$$P(\bar{E}_1) \;=\; P(5) + P(6) + P(7) \;=\; \frac{66}{79}$$

Finally,

$$P(\bar{E}_4) \;=\; P(7) \;=\; \frac{30}{79}$$

Frequently, as mentioned above, it is reasonable to assign equal probability to each point in the sample space. For example, a fair die with outcome space $S = \{1, 2, 3, 4, 5, 6\}$ quite naturally would be given the probability assignment $P(i) = 1/6$ for $i = 1, 2, 3, 4, 5, 6$. As previous examples indicate, however, such a probability assignment is not by any means the only appropriate one for an outcome space. For example, exercise 3.1 suggests that in assigning probabilities

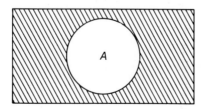

**Figure 3.3**

The Complement of *A*

to family sizes, it is reasonable to assign decreasing probabilities to families as their size increases.

## Example 3.6

As another example of a probability assignment to an outcome space, consider tossing two regular tetrahedra, one red and one green, each with faces numbered 1, 2, 3, and 4. (A regular tetrahedron is a solid with four faces that are congruent equilateral triangles.) The outcome observed will be the two numbers that fall face downward.

A natural sample space has the sixteen outcomes indicated in Figure 3.4. The outcome (2, 4) means that a 2 is downward on the red tetrahedron and a 4 is downward on the green. In this case it is reasonable to assign each outcome an equal probability of 1/16. Events of interest are the sums of the values falling face downward. It is easy to see that the possible sums are 2 through 8. The events with a sum of 3 are circled in Figure 3.4; the events with a sum of 3 are the points (1, 2) and (2, 1). The probabilities of various events are easily found to be as follows:

| Event | Sum | Probability |
|-------|-----|-------------|
| $S_2$ | 2 | 1/16 = 0.0625 |
| $S_3$ | 3 | 2/16 = 0.125 |
| $S_4$ | 4 | 3/16 = 0.1875 |
| $S_5$ | 5 | 4/16 = 0.25 |
| $S_6$ | 6 | 3/16 = 0.1875 |
| $S_7$ | 7 | 2/16 = 0.125 |
| $S_8$ | 8 | 1/16 = 0.0625 |

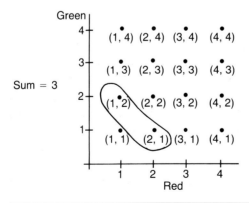

## Figure 3.4

**Outcome Space for Two Tetrahedra**

The sum of 5 has the largest probability (namely, 4/16), and the sums of 2 and 8 have the smallest probabilities (namely, 1/16 for each). As each point of $S$ falls into one and only one of these subsets, the sum of these probabilities must be equal to 1, which is indeed the case.

The probabilities of other events can be found by referring to Figure 3.4. For example, define $A$, $B$, and $C$ as follows:

$A$ = The sum of the two tetrahedra is odd.

$B$ = The sum of the two tetrahedra is prime.

$C$ = The sum of the two tetrahedra is evenly divisible by 3.

The points that represent events $A$, $B$, and $C$ are given below.

$A$ = {(1, 2), (2, 1), (1, 4), (2, 3), (3, 2), (4, 1), (3, 4), (4, 3)}

$B$ = {(1, 1), (1, 2), (2, 1), (1, 4), (2, 3), (3, 2), (4, 1), (3, 4), (4, 3)}

$C$ = {(1, 2), (2, 1), (2, 4), (3, 3), (4, 2)}

Thus we have $P(A) = 8/16 = 1/2$, $P(B) = 9/16$, and $P(C) = 5/16$.

All possible pairwise unions of $A$, $B$, and $C$ are as follows.

$A \cup B$ = $B$

$A \cup C$ = {(1, 2), (2, 1), (1, 4), (2, 3), (3, 2), (4, 1), (2, 4), (3, 3), (4, 2), (3, 4), (4, 3)}

$B \cup C$ = {(1, 1), (1, 2), (2, 1), (1, 4), (2, 3), (3, 2), (4, 1), (2, 4), (3, 3), (4, 2), (3, 4), (4, 3)}

Hence $P(A \cup B) = P(B) = 9/16$, $P(A \cup C) = 11/16$, and $P(B \cup C) = 12/16 = 3/4$. Similarly, for intersections we have

$A \cap B$ = $A$

$A \cap C$ = {(1, 2), (2, 1)}

$B \cap C$ = {(1, 2), (2, 1)}

Hence $P(A \cap B) = P(A) = 1/2$, $P(A \cap C) = 2/16 = 1/8$, and $P(B \cap C) = 2/16 = 1/8$. For the complements we have

$\bar{A}$ = {(1, 1), (1, 3), (2, 2), (3, 1), (2, 4), (3, 3), (4, 2), (4, 4)}

$\bar{B}$ = {(1, 3), (2, 2), (3, 1), (2, 4), (3, 3), (4, 2), (4, 4)}

$\bar{C}$ = {(1, 1), (1, 3), (2, 2), (3, 1), (1, 4), (2, 3), (3, 2), (4, 1), (3, 4), (4, 3), (4, 4)}

and $P(\bar{A}) = 8/16 = 1/2 = 1 - P(A)$, $P(\bar{B}) = 7/16 = 1 - P(B)$, and $P(\bar{C}) = 11/16 = 1 - P(C)$.

## Example 3.7

The Minitab system has a useful subcommand DISCRETE (used with RANDOM) that permits random observations to be obtained from a finite sample space $S = \{e_1, e_2, \ldots, e_k\}$, where the probabilities $P(e_i)$, $i = 1, 2, \ldots, k$, are assumed to be known. Consider the World Series example introduced earlier. It takes a long time to observe actual World Series, but the computer can simulate the outcomes of many such series in a brief period of time. Given the probabilities 13/79, 19/79, 17/79, and 30/79 of four-, five-, six-, and seven-game series, respectively, RANDOM was used to generate the outcomes of 1000 such simulated series, which are presented in Exhibit 3.5. The relative frequencies of four-, five-, six-, and seven-game series in the 1000 simulated series are 0.166, 0.238, 0.213, and 0.383, respectively; these are approximations of the theoretical probabilities 13/79, 19/79, 17/79, and 30/79, which to four decimal places are 0.1646, 0.2405, 0.2152, and 0.3797,

**Exhibit 3.5**

```
MTB > NOTE SIMULATION OF NUMBER OF GAMES PLAYED IN 1000 WORLD SERIES
MTB > SET C1
C1
     4     5     6     7

MTB > END
MTB > SET C2
C2
   0.1646   0.2405   0.2152   0.3797

MTB > END
MTB > BASE = 1000
MTB > RANDOM 1000 OBSERVATIONS IN C3;
SUBC> DISCRETE C1 C2.
MTB > HISTOGRAM C3

Histogram of C3   N = 1000
Each * represents 10 obs.

Midpoint    Count
       4      166   *****************
       5      238   ************************
       6      213   **********************
       7      383   ****************************************

MTB > INDICATOR FOR C3, PUT IN C4-C7

MTB > NOTE RELATIVE FREQUENCY OF 4,5,6,7 GAMES
MTB > MEAN C4
    MEAN    =      0.16600
MTB > MEAN C5
    MEAN    =      0.23800
MTB > MEAN C6
    MEAN    =      0.21300
MTB > MEAN  C7
    MEAN    =      0.38300
MTB > NOTE AVERAGE SERIES LENGTH
MTB > MEAN C3
    MEAN    =      5.8130
```

respectively. The relative frequencies were calculated using the **INDICATOR** command. Again, the theoretical probabilities should be thought of as the limiting values of the relative frequencies as the number of series simulated becomes very large, just as in the previous section the theoretical probability 0.5 of obtaining a head on a toss of a fair coin was approximated by the relative frequency of heads.

## Example 3.8

As a second example of the use of the DISCRETE subcommand, Minitab was used to simulate the tossing of the red and green tetrahedra described in Example 3.6. Specifically, Minitab was used to simulate the sum of the two values resulting from the tossing of the two tetrahedra. One thousand observations of tosses of such "dice" were generated in C3 and C4. The sums of C3 and C4 shown in Exhibit 3.6 correspond to 1000 observations of the tossing of the two tetrahedra. The relative frequencies of the sums 2 through 8 can be obtained from the histogram of C5 by dividing the indicated frequencies by 1000.

| Sum | 2 | 3 | 4 | 5 | 6 | 7 | 8 |
|---|---|---|---|---|---|---|---|
| Relative Frequency | 0.056 | 0.135 | 0.191 | 0.254 | 0.170 | 0.127 | 0.067 |
| Probabilities | 0.0625 | 0.125 | 0.1875 | 0.25 | 0.1875 | 0.125 | 0.0625 |

## Exhibit 3.6

```
MTB > NOTE SIMULATION OF THE SUM OF TWO FAIR TETRAHEDRA
MTB > SET C1
C1
    1    2    3    4

MTB > END
MTB > SET C2
C2
   0.25   0.25   0.25   0.25

MTB > END
MTB > BASE = 2000
MTB > RANDOM 1000 OBSERVATIONS IN C3;
SUBC> DISCRETE C1 C2.
MTB > RANDOM 1000 OBSERVATIONS IN C4;
SUBC> DISCRETE C1 C2.
MTB > ADD C3 TO C4 IN C5
MTB > HISTOGRAM C5

Histogram of C5   N = 1000
Each * represents 10 obs.

Midpoint    Count
       2       56   ******
       3      135   **************
       4      191   ********************
       5      254   **************************
       6      170   *****************
       7      127   *************
       8       67   *******
```

Compare these relative frequencies with the corresponding theoretical probabilities given earlier. The closeness of these relative frequencies to the corresponding probabilities emphasizes again the interpretation of probabilities of events as stable long-run frequencies.

## Exercises 3.3

**3.11** Consider the fair die of exercise 3.2 with two faces numbered 1, two numbered 2, and two numbered 3, Use $S = \{1, 2, 3\}$ with an appropriate probability measure. Three events are defined: $E_1$ is the set of even outcomes, $E_2$ the set of odd outcomes, and $E_3$ the set of outcomes evenly divisible by 3. Using Definition 3.6, find $P(E_1)$, $P(E_2)$, and $P(E_3)$.

**3.12** Use the following probability assignment for the number of games played in a best-of-seven-game series: $P(4) = 1/8$; $P(5) = 1/4$; $P(6) = P(7) = 5/16$. Find the probabilities of the events $E_1$, $E_2$, $E_3$, and $E_4$ as defined in Example 3.5.

**3.13** In exercise 3.5 the integers in the outcome space

$$S = \{1, 2, 3, 4, 5\}$$

were assigned probabilities directly proportional to the outcomes [i.e., $P(k) = ck$ for a constant $c$]. Define the events $E_1$, $E_2$, and $E_3$ as follows:

$E_1 = $ The outcome is an odd integer.

$E_2 = $ The outcome exceeds 2.

$E_3 = $ The outcome is less than 5.

**a.** Find the elements in $E_1$, $E_2$, and $E_3$.
**b.** Using the probability assignments in exercise 3.5, find $P(E_1)$, $P(E_2)$, and $P(E_3)$.
**c.** Find the elements of $E_1 \cup E_2$, $E_1 \cup E_3$, and $E_2 \cup E_3$. Find the elements of $E_1 \cap E_2$, $E_1 \cap E_3$, and $E_2 \cap E_3$.
**d.** Using the probability assignment in part b, find the probabilities of the unions and intersections identified in part c.
**e.** Using the probability assignment in part b, find $P(\bar{E}_1)$, $P(\bar{E}_2)$, and $P(\bar{E}_3)$.

**3.14** Assume that a freshman class has 1000 students. Let $A$ represent the subset of these students taking an English course and let $B$ represent the subset taking a mathematics course. There are 700 students in subset $A$ and 500 students in subset $B$. Of the 1000 students, there are 100 who are taking neither an English course nor a mathematics course.

**a.** Let $n(E)$ represent the number of elements in a set $E$. It can be shown that

$$n(A \cup B) = n(A) + n(B) - n(A \cap B)$$

Find $n(A \cap B)$ for the subsets $A$ and $B$ defined above.
**b.** Construct a Venn diagram indicating the values of $n(A \cap \bar{B})$, $n(\bar{A} \cap B)$, and $n(\bar{A} \cap \bar{B})$.
**c.** Assume that each student has equal probability of being selected. Find $P(A \cup B)$, $P(A \cap B)$, $P(\bar{A})$, and $P(\bar{B})$.

**3.15** In Example 3.3 equal probability was assigned to the integers from 1 to 8. Define events $E_1$, $E_2$, and $E_3$ as follows:

$E_1$ = The outcome is even.

$E_2$ = The outcome is a prime number.

$E_3$ = The outcome is divisible by 4.

**a.** Find the elements of $E_1$, $E_2$, and $E_3$.

**b.** Find the elements of $E_1 \cap E_2$, $E_1 \cap E_3$, and $E_2 \cap E_3$.

**c.** What probabilities should be assigned to the intersections in part b?

**3.16** From 1933 to 1981 there were 51 All-Star baseball games played. The margin of victory for all of these games is given below.

| Winning Margin (Runs) | Frequency |
|---|---|
| 1 | 17 |
| 2 | 14 |
| 3 | 5 |
| 4 | 5 |
| 5 | 4 |
| 6 | 5 |
| . | 0 |
| . | 0 |
| . | 0 |
| 12 | 1 |
| Total | 51 |

*Source:* Adapted from major league All-Star Game records, as reported in *The Information Please Almanac* (Boston: Houghton Mifflin, 1982), p. 910.

**a.** Using the relative frequencies as probabilities, find the probabilities that the winning margin is at least two runs, at most two runs, and exactly two runs.

**b.** Find the probability that the winning margin is an odd number and the probability that it is an even number.

**3.17** Use the probability assignment to $S$ = {M, T, W, Th, F} from exercise 3.3 to find the probability of $E_1$ = {M, F}, $E_2$ = {T, Th}, $E_1 \cup E_2$, and $E_1 \cap E_2$.

**3.18** Consider the outcome space $S$ = {2, 3, 4, 5, 6, 7, 8, 9, 10, 11}. Assign equal probability to each element of this space. The following events are defined:

$E_1$ = The outcome is even.

$E_2$ = The outcome is a prime number.

$E_3$ = The outcome is evenly divisible by 3.

**a.** Find $P(E_1)$, $P(E_2)$, and $P(E_3)$.

**b.** Find the following:

   **i.** $P(\bar{E_1})$       **v.** $P(E_1 \cap E_2)$

   **ii.** $P(E_1 \cup E_2)$    **vi.** $P(E_1 \cap E_3)$

   **iii.** $P(E_1 \cup E_3)$    **vii.** $P(E_2 \cap E_3)$

   **iv.** $P(E_2 \cup E_3)$    **viii.** $P[(E_1 \cap E_2) \cap E_3]$

**3.19** A letter is sent from New York to Denver. Let the outcome space $S = \{2, 3, 4, 5, 6\}$ be the number of days it takes for the letter to be delivered. Assume $P(2) = 1/10$, $P(3) = 2/10$, $P(4) = 3/10$, $P(5) = 3/10$, and $P(6) = 1/10$.

**a.** Let $E_1$ be the event that the letter is delivered in at most four days; let $E_2$ be the event that the letter requires at least four days for delivery; let $E_3$ be the event that it takes more than four days to deliver the letter. Find $P(E_1)$, $P(E_2)$, and $P(E_3)$.

**b.** Find the following probabilities:

   **i.** $P(E_1 \cup E_2)$     **iv.** $P(E_1 \cap E_3)$

   **ii.** $P(E_1 \cap E_2)$     **v.** $P(E_2 \cup E_3)$

   **iii.** $P(E_1 \cup E_3)$     **vi.** $P(E_2 \cap E_3)$

**3.20** Let $E$ be any event in a finite outcome space $S$.

**a.** Using Definition 3.6, show that $P(E \cup \bar{E}) = 1$.

**b.** Show that $P(E \cap \bar{E}) = 0$.

**3.21** **a.** Find the probabilities of the sums 2 through 12 on the toss of two fair dice.

**b.** Use Minitab to simulate the sums on 1000 tosses of two fair dice.

**c.** Compare the relative frequencies in part b with the probabilities in part a.

**3.22** In simple Mendelian Theory, a trait is said to be determined by two genes (say A and a), one of which is inherited from each parent. The possible genetic combinations are AA, aA, Aa, and aa, where the first letter refers to the gene inherited from the first parent (say the father). The gene A is called dominant, and individuals of type AA, Aa, or aA will display the dominant trait. The gene a is called recessive, and only an individual of type aa will display the recessive trait. In hybrid crosses the four outcomes in $S = \{AA, Aa, aA, aa\}$ can be thought of as equally likely outcomes. What proportion should display the dominant trait? Simulate the outcomes of 1000 hybrid crosses using Minitab. What proportion in your simulation display the dominant trait?

**3.23** **a.** Using the information from exercise 3.19, use RANDOM to simulate the number of days required to deliver 1000 letters.

**b.** Compare the relative frequencies observed in part a with the probabilities of exercise 3.19.

**3.24** Using the probabilities of exercise 3.12, simulate the number of games played in 1000 World Series. Find the average length of these 1000 Series as in Exhibit 3.5. In Section 3.5 it will be shown that the probabilities used in this problem are reasonable for equally strong teams under an assumption to be described there (namely, the assumption of independence).

## 3.4

## Three Laws of Probability and Conditional Probability

Addition Law

We consider next three basic laws for calculating probabilities. Although these laws will be demonstrated for finite outcome spaces, they also hold for outcome spaces that are not finite.

First, suppose we want to know the probability that at least one of two events $A$ and $B$ will occur—i.e., we want to find the value of $P(A \cup B)$. This value is given by the **Addition Law**.

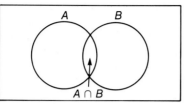

**Figure 3.5**

---

> **The Addition Law** ━━━━━━
>
> For any two events $A$ and $B$ of $S$, we have
>
> $$P(A \cup B) = P(A) + P(B) - P(A \cap B)$$
>
> In words, the probability of the union of $A$ and $B$ equals the sum of the probabilities of $A$ and of $B$ less the probability of the intersection of $A$ and $B$.
>
> Figure 3.5 makes it easy to see why the law is valid. The value of $P(A \cup B)$ is the sum of the probabilities of the outcomes in $A \cup B$. This sum is not equal to the sum of the probabilities in $A$ and in $B$ because we have counted twice the probabilities of those outcomes common to $A$ and $B$—i.e., in $A \cap B$. Hence, we have
>
> $$P(A \cup B) = P(A) + P(B) - P(A \cap B)$$

---

**Example 3.9**

---

The alumni of a particular college who graduated 20 years ago are contacted, and income data are gathered on those currently employed. The following information is obtained from 600 individuals:

| Description | Number |
|---|---|
| Male and income over $25,000 | 300 |
| Male and income $25,000 or less | 100 |
| Female and income over $25,000 | 80 |
| Female and income $25,000 or less | 120 |
| Total | 600 |

The situation is described in Figure 3.6, where $A$ = male, $B$ = income over $25,000, and the sample space is composed of 600 individuals.

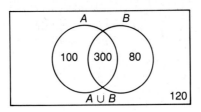

**Figure 3.6**

If we select an individual at random, assigning equal probability (i.e., a probability of 1/600) to each individual, we then have

$$P(A) = \frac{400}{600} = \frac{2}{3}$$

$$P(B) = \frac{380}{600} = \frac{19}{30}$$

$$P(A \cap B) = \frac{300}{600} = \frac{1}{2}$$

The fact that

$$P(A) + P(B) - P(A \cap B) = \frac{20}{30} + \frac{19}{30} - \frac{15}{30} = \frac{24}{30} = \frac{4}{5}$$

and

$$P(A \cup B) = (100 + 300 + 80)/600 = \frac{480}{600} = \frac{4}{5}$$

shows that the Addition Law holds, as it must. Notice that $P(A) + P(B)$ could not be the probability of any event, for its value exceeds 1, violating Definition 3.3.

In Section 3.3 we defined the complement of an event $A$, $\bar{A}$, as the set of outcomes in $S$ that are not in $A$. Therefore, we can compute $P(\bar{A})$ by the **Law of Complements.**

**Law of Complements**

---

**The Law of Complements** ▬▬▬▬▬▬▬▬▬▬▬▬▬▬▬

For any event $A$ of $S$,

$$P(\bar{A}) = 1 - P(A)$$

---

It is clear that the sum of the probabilities of the outcomes in $A$ plus the sum of the probabilities of the outcomes in $\bar{A}$ equals the sum of the probabilities of all outcomes in $S$, which is 1. Hence,

$$P(A) + P(\bar{A}) = P(S) = 1 \quad \text{or} \quad P(\bar{A}) = 1 - P(A)$$

Returning to Example 3.5 concerning the number of games in a best-of-seven-game baseball series, consider the probability of the event $E_4$ that a series will end in fewer than seven games. Clearly

$$P(E_4) = 1 - P(\bar{E}_4) = 1 - \frac{30}{79} = \frac{49}{79}$$

Now consider the special case of this law in which $A = S$. $\bar{S}$ is then a special kind of subset of $S$, namely the subset with no outcomes at all. This set, called the empty set, is denoted by $\emptyset$ and is assumed to be a subset of any set. The probability of the empty set is zero:

$$P(\bar{S}) = P(\emptyset) = 1 - P(S) = 1 - 1 = 0$$

If two events have no common outcomes, their intersection is empty. We define this situation formally as follows.

---

**Definition 3.10** ▬▬▬▬▬▬▬▬▬▬▬▬▬▬▬▬▬▬▬▬▬▬

disjoint events
mutually exclusive
events

Two events $A$ and $B$ are called **disjoint** or **mutually exclusive events** if and only if $A \cap B = \emptyset$.

---

For disjoint events $A$ and $B$,

$$\begin{aligned} P(A \cup B) &= P(A) + P(B) - P(A \cap B) \\ &= P(A) + P(B) - P(\emptyset) \\ &= P(A) + P(B) \end{aligned}$$

In Example 3.5 concerning the number of games in a best-of-seven-game series, the following events were defined:

$E_1 =$ Exactly 4 games are played.

$E_2 =$ An odd number of games are played.

Here $P(E_1) = 13/79$, $P(E_2) = 49/79$, and $(E_1 \cap E_2) = \emptyset$. Hence we have

$$P(E_1 \cup E_2) = P(E_1) + P(E_2) = \frac{13}{79} + \frac{49}{79} = \frac{62}{79}$$

It is frequently of interest to consider probabilities with respect to a subset of $S$. Such probabilities, called conditional probabilities, are calculated as if a subset of $S$, say $A$, were the outcome space. For example, with respect to the alumni in Example 3.9, we might be interested in the probability that a graduate had an income over \$25,000 *given* that the graduate was male. The formula for the calculation of a conditional probability is as follows.

### Definition 3.11

The **conditional probability** of $B$ given $A$ is defined to be

$$P(B|A) = P(A \cap B)/P(A)$$

provided $P(A) \neq 0$.

Notice that the probabilities on the right-hand side of the equal sign in this definition are unconditional probabilities.

## Example 3.10

Consider the events $A$ and $B$ described in Example 3.9. We saw that $P(B) = 19/30$ is the probability that a selected alumnus has an income exceeding $25,000. In the calculation of a conditional probability with respect to the event $A$, that a selected alumnus is male, we consider $A$ to be the "full" sample space. If we wanted to find the conditional probability that a graduate has an income exceeding $25,000 *given* that the selected graduate is a male, we would consider the event $A$ to be a sample space in its own right, as shown in the Venn diagram of Figure 3.7. As there are 400 males, 300 of whom have incomes over $25,000, we obtain

$$P(B|A) = \frac{300}{400} = \frac{3}{4}$$

Alternatively, using Definition 3.11 we get

$$P(B|A) = P(A \cap B)/P(A) = \frac{(300/600)}{(400/600)} = \frac{3}{4}$$

which agrees with the previous calculation. The probability that a graduate has an income over $25,000, given that she is a female, can be found similarly:

$$P(B|\bar{A}) = P(\bar{A} \cap B)/P(\bar{A}) = \frac{(80/600)}{(200/600)} = \frac{2}{5}$$

The conditional probability of a graduate's having an income over $25,000 given that the graduate is a female is thus less than the unconditional probability that a

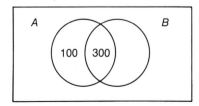

## Figure 3.7

selected graduate has an income over $25,000 and considerably less than the conditional probability for males.

Like other probabilities, conditional probabilities can be interpreted as long-run relative frequencies. $P(B|\bar{A}) = 2/5$ can be intepreted to mean that among a large number of female graduates of this college 20 years ago, about two in five have an income exceeding $25,000.

**Multiplication Law**

The **Multiplication Law** for probabilities is simply a restatement of the rule for computing conditional probabilities given in Definition 3.11. The equation of that definition is multiplied by $P(A)$ to yield the following.

---

**The Multiplication Law** ▬▬▬▬▬▬▬▬▬▬▬▬▬▬▬▬▬▬

For any events $A$ and $B$,

$$P(A \cap B) = P(A)P(B|A)$$

---

**Example 3.11**

---

Suppose a club with 40 members has only enough money to send two of its members to a conference. There are 15 men and 25 women in the club. Each member writes his or her name on a slip of paper. Two slips are selected successively from a hat to determine which two members will be sent to the meeting. We wish to know the probability that both individuals selected will be women.

Let $A$ and $B$ be defined as follows:

$A$ = the first selection is a woman.
$B$ = the second selection is a woman.

We want to know the probability that both $A$ and $B$ will occur, $P(A \cap B)$. Clearly, $P(A) = 25/40 = 5/8$. The conditional probability that a woman will be selected on the second draw given that a woman is selected on the first draw is $24/39 = 8/13$, as there are 39 members left, of whom 24 are women. Hence, using the Multiplication Law, we have

$$P(A \cap B) = P(A)P(B|A) = \left(\frac{5}{8}\right)\left(\frac{8}{13}\right) = \frac{5}{13}$$

which gives the probability that both individuals selected will be women.

Computations of probabilities using the Multiplication Law are most easily visualized by use of a tree diagram, such as the one for this example given in Figure 3.8. At each fork in such a tree all of the probabilities add up to 1. The product of the probabilities on a path gives the probabilities of interest. For example, the top path in Figure 3.8 shows the probability of the selection of two women to be $40/104 = 5/13$. To find the probability that both selected individuals

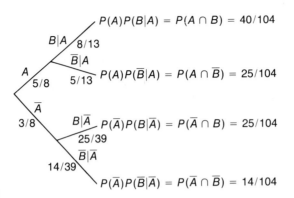

**Figure 3.8**

Tree Diagram for Selection of Two Club Members

are male, we compute

$$P(\bar{A} \cap \bar{B}) = P(\bar{A})P(\bar{B}|\bar{A}) = \left(\frac{3}{8}\right)\left(\frac{14}{39}\right) = \frac{42}{312} = \frac{7}{52}$$

as indicated by the lowest path in the tree in Figure 3.8.

The probability that one man and one woman are sent is

$$P\{(A \cap \bar{B}) \cup (\bar{A} \cap B)\} = P(A \cap \bar{B}) + P(\bar{A} \cap B)$$

(Why?) As indicated in Figure 3.8, the latter probability is equal to

$$P(A)P(\bar{B}|A) + P(\bar{A})P(B|\bar{A}) = \left(\frac{5}{8}\right)\left(\frac{5}{13}\right) + \left(\frac{3}{8}\right)\left(\frac{25}{39}\right) = \frac{25}{52}$$

Note that in this example either two women are sent, two men are sent, or one woman and one man are sent. These three events are mutually exclusive and have a union equal to $S$. The sum of the probabilities of these three events is $40/104 + 14/104 + 50/104 = 1$, as shown in Figure 3.8. The two middle paths each correspond to selection of one man and one woman. The sum of the probabilities of the ends of all the "branches" in the tree must be 1. It should be clear from Figure 3.8 that if three mutually exclusive events $E_1$, $E_2$, and $E_3$ have a union equal to $S$, then $P(E_1) + P(E_2) + P(E_3) = 1$ (see Figure 3.9).

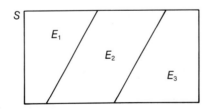

**Figure 3.9**

The Multiplication Law can be extended as follows.

---

**The Extended Multiplication Law** ━━━━━━━━

$$P(E_1 \cap E_2 \cap \cdots \cap E_k) = P(E_1)P(E_2|E_1)P(E_3|E_1 \cap E_2) \cdots$$
$$P(E_k|E_1 \cap E_2 \cdots E_{k-1})$$

for any $k \geq 1$.

---

In the case where $k = 3$, we have

$$P(E_1 \cap E_2 \cap E_3) = P(E_1)P(E_2|E_1)P(E_3|E_1 \cap E_2)$$

## Example 3.12

Suppose that the club described in Example 3.11 finds that it can send three individuals to the conference, so three slips are drawn without replacement. What is the probability that three women will be selected? Let $E_1$ be the event that the first selection is a female, $E_2$ the event that the second is a female, and $E_3$ the event that the third is a female. We have

$$P(E_1 \cap E_2 \cap E_3) = P(E_1)P(E_2|E_1)P(E_3|E_1 \cap E_2)$$
$$= \left(\frac{25}{40}\right)\left(\frac{24}{39}\right)\left(\frac{23}{38}\right) = \frac{115}{494}$$

## Example 3.13

Assume a golfer has a bag containing five clubs, only one of which is appropriate for the shot he is about to take. Assume that the probability that the golfer will make a good shot with an appropriate club is 3/4 and the probability that he will make a good shot with an inappropriate club is 1/5. He selects a club at random from his bag and takes a shot. What is the probability that it is a good shot? We make the following definitions:

$A =$ An appropriate club is selected.
$B =$ A good shot is made.

We need to compute

$$P(B) = P\{(A \cap B) \cup (\bar{A} \cap B)\} = P(A \cap B) + P(\bar{A} \cap B)$$
$$= P(A)P(B|A) + P(\bar{A})P(B|\bar{A})$$
$$= \left(\frac{1}{5}\right)\left(\frac{3}{4}\right) + \left(\frac{4}{5}\right)\left(\frac{1}{5}\right) = \frac{31}{100}$$

Thus in the long run, the probability is that the golfer will make a good shot 31 times in 100.

**3.25**  Consider the outcome space $S = \{2, 3, 4, 5, 6, 7, 8, 9, 10, 11\}$ of exercise 3.18, again assigning equal probability to each element. Using the definitions of $E_1$, $E_2$, and $E_3$ in that exercise, find $P(E_1 \cup E_2)$, $P(E_1 \cup E_3)$, and $P(E_2 \cup E_3)$ by means of the Addition Law.

**3.26**  Use the sample space $S = \{2, 3, 4, 5, 6\}$ giving the number of days it takes a letter to be sent from New York to Denver, together with the probability assignment and the definitions of $E_1$, $E_2$, and $E_3$ in exercise 3.19, to do the following:
  **a.** Verify the values of $P(E_1 \cup E_2)$, $P(E_1 \cup E_3)$, and $P(E_2 \cup E_3)$ using the Addition Law.
  **b.** Find $P(\bar{E}_1)$, $P(\bar{E}_2)$, and $P(\bar{E}_3)$ using the law for the complement.

**3.27**  The letters A, B, C can be listed in six different ways. (One such listing is BAC.) If one such listing is chosen at random, what is the probability the list will not be in alphabetical order? Use the complement rule.

**3.28**  There are 16 different forms in which a four-digit sequence of zeros and/or ones can occur. (One such form is 0101.) If each list has equal probability of selection, what is the probability of getting at least one 1 in the list? Use the complement rule.

**3.29**  A freshman college class has 400 members. Of these, 300 take English, 350 take mathematics, and 20 take neither subject. Let $A$ be the set of those taking English and $B$ be the set of those taking mathematics.
  **a.** Draw a diagram like Figure 3.6, giving the numbers of students in each of the subsets $\bar{A} \cap \bar{B}$, $A \cap \bar{B}$, $\bar{A} \cap B$, and $A \cap B$. [*Hint:* Use the fact that $N(A \cup B) = N(A) + N(B) - N(A \cap B)$, where $N(E)$ represents the number of elements in the set $E$.]
  **b.** Verify that $P(A \cup B) = P(A) + P(B) - P(A \cap B)$ for a student who is selected at random.

**3.30**  A lot of 10 items contains 3 defectives. One item is selected at random, and then a second item is selected at random from the remaining items.
  **a.** Using the Multiplication Law, find the probability that both will be defective.
  **b.** Using the Multiplication Law, find the probability that neither will be defective.
  **c.** Using the complement law, find the probability that exactly one will be defective. (Use the results of parts a and b.)

**3.31**  In a small high school there are only 40 boys eligible for sports. Two teams play in the fall—a football team and a soccer team. The football team has 25 members, and the soccer team has 15 members. Five boys play both sports. If $A$ represents playing football and $B$ represents playing soccer, find the following for a boy selected at random:
  **a.** $P(\bar{A})$      **d.** $P(B)$
  **b.** $P(\bar{A}|B)$     **e.** $P(B|A)$
  **c.** $P(\bar{A}|\bar{B})$     **f.** $P(B|\bar{A})$

**3.32**  Assuming that one student in exercise 3.29 is selected at random, find the following:
  **a.** $P(A)$
  **b.** $P(A|B)$
  **c.** $P(A|\bar{B})$

**3.33** A golfer has a bag with four clubs. Only one of these is appropriate for the shot she is about to take. The conditional probability of making a good shot given the correct club is 0.8. The conditional probability of making a good shot given the wrong club is 0.2. She chooses a club at random and takes a shot. What is the probability that she will make a good shot? *Note:* Let $C$ indicate a correct club, $\bar{C}$ indicate an incorrect club, and $G$ indicate a good shot. Then find $P\{(C \cap G) \cup (\bar{C} \cap G)\}$.

**3.34** In a year that is not evenly divisible by 4, there are seven months with 31 days, four months with 30 days, and one month with 28 days. A month is chosen at random and a date is selected at random from the selected month.
  **a.** What is the conditional probability that an odd-numbered date is chosen, *given* that a month with an odd number of days is selected?
  **b.** What is the conditional probability that an odd-numbered date is chosen, *given* that a month with an even number of days is selected?
  **c.** What is the unconditional probability that an odd-numbered date is chosen?

**3.35** The probability of a batter's getting a hit against a right-handed pitcher is 1/3, and the probability of his getting a hit against a left-handed pitcher is 2/7.
  **a.** Find the batter's long-run batting average, given that he faces equal amounts of right- and left-handed pitching.
  **b.** Find the batter's long-run batting average, given that he faces right-handed pitching twice as often as left-handed pitching.

**3.36** A basketball player has a probability of 0.8 of making her first foul shot. If she makes the first foul shot, the probability of making the second one increases to 0.9, but if she misses the first shot, the probability of making the second decreases to 0.6. She enters the game and attempts two foul shots.
  **a.** What is the probability that she will make both shots?
  **b.** What is the probability that she will miss both shots?
  **c.** What is the probability that she will make one shot and miss the other?

**3.37** Three cards are drawn from a standard deck without replacing the previous card or cards drawn. What is the probability that all three cards are hearts? What is the probability that they are of the same suit?

**3.38** There are nine books on a shelf. Of these, two have blue covers, three have red covers, and four have green covers. Two books are selected at random.
  **a.** What is the probability that both books are the same color?
  **b.** What is the probability that the two books are different colors?
  **c.** What is the probability that one book has a red cover and the other has a green cover?

**3.39** A ball is drawn at random from a box containing one red and one green ball. If the ball drawn is red, the drawing stops. If it is green, the green ball is replaced, together with another green ball, and a second ball is drawn. If it is red, the drawing stops. If it is green, it and another green ball are put in the box. This process continues until the tenth draw, when, if no red ball is found, the drawing stops. Let $S = \{1, 2, 3, \ldots, 10\}$ be the outcome set, where 1 indicates a red ball on the first draw, 2 indicates that two draws are required to get the first red, and so on. Find the following:
  **a.** $P(1)$      **c.** $P(k)$ for $2 \leqslant k \leqslant 9$
  **b.** $P(2)$      **d.** $P(10)$
  *Note:* Use the extended multiplication law in part c.

## 3.5

**Independence**  The idea of the independence of two events $A$ and $B$ is important in probability and statistics because it permits calculation of the probability of the intersection $P(A \cap B)$ using only knowledge of $P(A)$ and $P(B)$. In general, one must know $P(B|A)$ to find $P(A \cap B)$. The following definition gives the rule for calculating the probability of the intersection of two independent events.

---

**Definition 3.12** ▬▬▬▬▬▬▬▬▬▬▬▬▬▬▬▬▬▬▬▬▬▬▬▬▬▬▬▬▬▬▬▬▬▬▬▬

Two events $A$ and $B$ are said to be **independent** if and only if

$$P(A \cap B) = P(A)P(B)$$

---

This rule is closely related to the multiplication law, which states that

$$P(A \cap B) = P(A)P(B|A)$$

If $A$ and $B$ are independent events, then

$$P(A \cap B) = P(A)P(B|A) = P(A)P(B)$$

In addition, if $P(A) > 0$, we can divide the above equation by $P(A)$ to obtain

$$P(B|A) = P(B)$$

Similarly, if $P(B) > 0$, we can conclude that

$$P(A|B) = P(A)$$

Hence, if $A$ and $B$ are independent *and* have positive probability, then (1) the conditional probability of $B$ given $A$ is the same as the unconditional probability of $B$ and (2) the conditional probability of $A$ given $B$ is the same as the unconditional probability of $A$. In other words, in this case the occurrence of $B$ does not affect the *probability* of the occurrence of $A$, and the occurrence of $A$ does not affect the *probability* of the occurrence of $B$.

Note that the fact that two events are independent does not mean that they are disjoint as defined in Definition 3.10. For example, suppose we select one of the 32 chess pieces at random. If we define $A$ to be the selection of a white piece and $B$ to be the selection of a pawn, then $A \cap B$ is the selection of a white pawn. We have $P(A) = 1/2$ and $P(B) = 1/2$, as exactly one-half of the 32 pieces are white and exactly one-half are pawns. Also, $P(A \cap B) = 1/4$, because 8 of the 32 pieces are white pawns. We have $P(A)P(B) = (1/2)(1/2) = 1/4 = P(A \cap B)$, so by Definition 3.12 these events are independent. They are not disjoint, however, as it is clearly possible to obtain a white pawn on a single selection.

Often two events are *assumed* to be independent when they may not be, so that the probability that both events will occur can be considered to be equal to the product of the probabilities of the individual events. Consider the probability

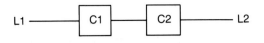

**Figure 3.10**

Two Components in Series

that two electronic components in series will work if each component has probability $p$ of working and the components act *independently*. The situation is depicted in Figure 3.10. We want to know the probability that current will flow from L1 to L2. Let $A$ be the event that component C1 works and $B$ the event that component C2 works. The desired probability is $P(A \cap B) = P(A)P(B) = p^2$ because of the assumed independence of the components. Consider the slightly more complicated situation depicted in Figure 3.11. Again, we want to calculate the probability that the current will flow from L1 to L2, given that each of the four components operates independently with probability $p$. The current can flow when both components C1 and C2 work or when both components C3 and C4 work. Letting $C_1$, $C_2$, $C_3$, and $C_4$ be the events that components C1, C2, C3, and C4 work, we can find the probability that the current will flow from L1 to L2 as follows, using the addition law:

$$P\{(C_1 \cap C_2) \cup (C_3 \cap C_4)\} = P(C_1 \cap C_2) + P(C_3 \cap C_4)$$
$$- P\{(C_1 \cap C_2) \cap (C_3 \cap C_4)\}$$

Using the independence of the components yields

$$P\{(C_1 \cap C_2) \cup (C_3 \cap C_4)\} = P(C_1)P(C_2) + P(C_3)P(C_4)$$
$$- P(C_1)P(C_2)P(C_3)P(C_4)$$
$$= p^2 + p^2 - p^4 = 2p^2 - p^4$$

The value $p^4$ is obtained from

$$P\{(C_1 \cap C_2) \cap (C_3 \cap C_4)\} = P(C_1 \cap C_2)P(C_3 \cap C_4)$$
$$= P(C_1)P(C_2)P(C_3)P(C_4)$$

using the independence of the components. The probabilities of successful operation of the systems shown in Figures 3.10 and 3.11 are given in Table 3.4. If the probability that an individual component will work is $p = 0.8$, the probability that current will flow through the first (less complicated) system is $p^2 = 0.64$

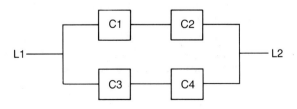

**Figure 3.11**

A More Complex System

**Table 3.4**

| $p$ | $p^2$ | $2p^2 - p^4$ |
|-----|-------|--------------|
| 0 | 0 | 0 |
| 0.2 | 0.04 | 0.0784 |
| 0.4 | 0.16 | 0.2944 |
| 0.6 | 0.36 | 0.5904 |
| 0.8 | 0.64 | 0.8704 |
| 0.9 | 0.81 | 0.9639 |
| 0.95 | 0.9025 | 0.9905 |
| 1 | 1 | 1.0000 |

and the probability that current will flow through the second system is $2p^2 - p^4 = 2(0.8)^2 - (0.8)^4 = 0.8704$.

In the system with the two components in series, the probability that the system will work, $p^2$, is always less than the probability that a component will work, $p$, because $0 < p < 1$. This is not true for the second system, as the redundancy built in by using two systems in parallel allows the *system* to operate with higher probability than a *component* for larger values of $p$. For instance, if the probability that a component will work is $p = 0.9$, then the probability that the first system will work is only 0.81, whereas the probability that the second system will work is $0.9639 > 0.9$. This example illustrates the value of redundancy in electronic systems.

The definition of independence of two events $A$ and $B$ can be extended to include three or more events.

---

**Definition 3.13** ▬▬▬▬▬▬▬▬▬▬▬▬▬▬▬▬▬▬▬▬▬▬▬▬▬▬▬▬▬▬▬

**mutually independent events**

Three events $A$, $B$, and $C$ are said to be **mutually independent** if all of the following equalities hold:
  a. $P(A \cap B) = P(A)P(B)$
  b. $P(A \cap C) = P(A)P(C)$
  c. $P(B \cap C) = P(B)P(C)$
  d. $P(A \cap B \cap C) = P(A)P(B)P(C)$

---

**Example 3.14** ▬▬▬▬▬▬▬▬

The probabilities that three students are on time for a class are 0.9, 0.95, and 0.75, respectively. Let $A$, $B$, and $C$ be the following events:

  $A$ = The first student is on time.
  $B$ = The second student is on time.
  $C$ = The third student is on time.

If $A$, $B$, and $C$ are assumed to be mutually exclusive, we can compute the probability that all of these students will be on time as follows:

$$P(A \cap B \cap C) = P(A)P(B)P(C) = (0.9)(0.95)(0.75) = 0.64125$$

It is possible for equalities a, b, and c of Definition 3.13 to hold without equality d being valid.

**Example 3.15**

Consider the following four sequences of zeros and ones.

100  010  001  111

Let each of the four sequences have an equal probability of being chosen (namely, 1/4). Define the events $A$, $B$ and $C$ as follows:

$A$ = There is a 1 in the first position of the chosen sequence.
$B$ = There is a 1 in the second position of the chosen sequence.
$C$ = There is a 1 in the third position of the chosen sequence.

We then have the following probabilities:

$$P(A) = P(B) = P(C) = \frac{1}{2}$$

$$P(A \cap B) = P(A \cap C) = P(B \cap C) = \frac{1}{4}$$

$$P(A \cap B \cap C) = \frac{1}{4}$$

Thus in this case the first three equalities of Definition 3.13 are valid, but

$$P(A \cap B \cap C) = \frac{1}{4} \neq P(A)P(B)P(C) = \frac{1}{8}$$

The events $A$, $B$, and $C$ are said to be pairwise independent but not mutually independent.

---

**Definition 3.14** ▬▬▬▬▬▬▬

Suppose that $E_1, E_2, \ldots, E_n$ are $n$ events. These events are called mutually independent if the probability of the intersection of any $j \leqslant n$ of these events equals the product of the probabilities of the $j$ events.

Frequently we assume that $n$ events are mutually independent in order to use the product rule to find the probabilities of intersections. This process will be demonstrated in connection with an important special case of independent events called binomial trials.

## Binomial Trials

In practice, situations frequently involve a sequence of independent trials, each of which can be only a success S or failure F. In many such cases the probability of success may be assumed to be a constant $p$ for each trial. Tossing a fair coin $n = 20, 50$, or $100$ times is an example of such a situation in which $p = 1/2$. Other examples come to mind quickly.

1   A football player attempts three extra points in a game. We assume that he is successful with probability $p = 3/4$ at each attempt.
2   Ten items are selected at random from the output of a production line. The probability of getting a defective item, which we call a "success," on each selection is $p = 1/20$ for a line producing five percent defectives.
3   Fifty seeds are planted. Each has a probability $p = 0.8$ of germinating successfully.

In each of these situations the outcome of greatest interest is the number of successes in the total number of trials. The extra point kicker can be successful on 0, 1, 2, or 3 attempts. A method of calculating the probability of each of these **binomial trials** events given $p$ is required. Such trials are called **binomial trials** with success probability $p$.

Let us first consider the case of two trials. The tree in Figure 3.12 indicates the possible outcomes. Each path in the tree from left to right is a possible outcome.

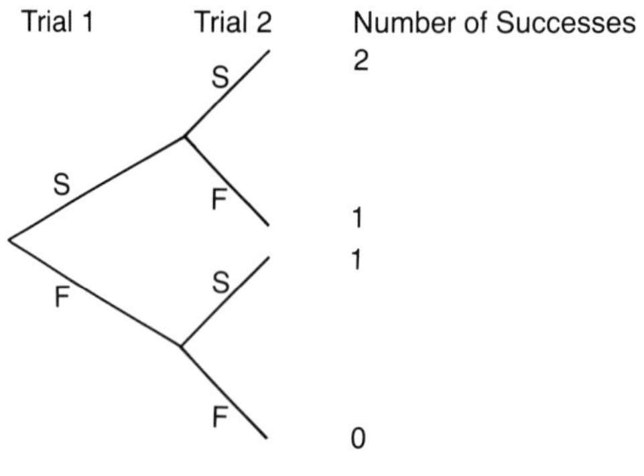

**Figure 3.12**

**Two Binomial Trials**

Because the outcomes are independent,

$$P(\text{SS}) = P(\text{S})P(\text{S}) = p^2$$
$$P(\text{SF}) = P(\text{S})P(\text{F}) = p(1 - p)$$
$$P(\text{FS}) = P(\text{F})P(\text{S}) = (1 - p)p$$
$$P(\text{FF}) = P(\text{F})P(\text{F}) = (1 - p)^2$$

Letting $q = 1 - p = P$ (failure on a single trial), we obtain the following probabilities for the number of successes $x$.

| $x$ | $P(x \text{ successes})$ |
|-----|--------------------------|
| 0 | $(1 - p)^2 = q^2$ |
| 1 | $2p(1 - p) = 2pq$ |
| 2 | $p^2$ |

Thus, for example, if a fair coin is tossed,

$$P(0 \text{ heads}) = (1 - p)^2 = \left(\frac{1}{2}\right)^2 = \frac{1}{4}$$

$$P(1 \text{ head}) = 2p(1 - p) = 2\left(\frac{1}{2}\right)\left(1 - \frac{1}{2}\right) = (1)\left(\frac{1}{2}\right) = \frac{1}{2}$$

$$P(2 \text{ heads}) = p^2 = \left(\frac{1}{2}\right)^2 = \frac{1}{4}$$

For the case of three trials, we get the tree in Figure 3.13, which has eight paths. The number of successes corresponding to each path from left to right is given at the end of the path.

It is easy to verify that we obtain the probabilities given in the table below. For example, we find three paths, SFF, FSF, and FFS, that result in exactly one success. Each such path has probability $pq^2$, as it contains one S and two F's. The total probability, $P(x = 1)$, is thus $3pq^2$.

| $x$ | $P(x \text{ successes})$ |
|-----|--------------------------|
| 0 | $q^3$ |
| 1 | $3pq^2$ |
| 2 | $3p^2q$ |
| 3 | $p^3$ |

For the case of the extra point kicker, we have $p = 3/4$ and $q = 1/4$. Hence,

$$P(0) = \left(\frac{1}{4}\right)^3 = \frac{1}{64}$$

$$P(1) = 3\left(\frac{3}{4}\right)\left(\frac{1}{4}\right)^2 = \frac{9}{64}$$

$$P(2) = 3\left(\frac{3}{4}\right)^2\left(\frac{1}{4}\right) = \frac{27}{64}$$

$$P(3) = \left(\frac{3}{4}\right)^3 = \frac{27}{64}$$

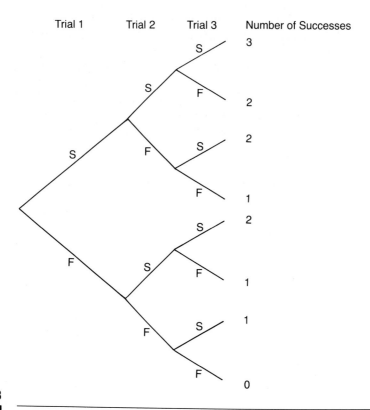

Trial 1    Trial 2    Trial 3    Number of Successes

**Figure 3.13**

It can be shown that, in general, if we make $n$ binomial trials with probability of success $p$ at each trial,

$$P(x \text{ successes}) \;=\; \left(\frac{n!}{x!(n-x)!}\right) p^x q^{n-x} \;=\; \binom{n}{x} p^x q^{n-x}$$

The notation $\binom{n}{x} = n!/x!(n-x)!$ is called a binomial coefficient and is read as "$n$ choose $x$." It represents the number of distinct subsets of size $x$ that can be chosen from a set of size $n$—for example, the number of paths in an $n$-stage tree with exactly $x$ S's and $(n-x)$ F's. Each such path has a probability of $p^x q^{n-x}$. A more detailed description of binomial coefficients is given in Appendix A.

**Example 3.16**

**BINOMIAL**
**PDF**
**CDF**

Minitab uses the above formula in the very useful subcommand **BINOMIAL** in conjunction with the commands **PDF** and **CDF** to compute probabilities for independent trials. The values of $n$ and $p$ can be chosen as desired. The output of PDF gives $P(x \text{ successes})$ and the output of CDF gives $P(x \text{ or fewer successes})$ for

$x = 0, 1, 2, 3, \ldots, n$. The probabilities for the three cases $n = 20$ and $p = 0.2$, $n = 20$ and $p = 0.5$, and $n = 20$ and $p = 0.8$, as computed by Minitab, are given in Exhibit 3.7.

The output at the upper right of the exhibit shows that when we toss a fair coin $n = 20$ times, where $p = 1/2$, the probability of getting exactly 10 heads is 0.1762. The probability of getting 12 or fewer heads is 0.8684.

As another example, assume that we are interested in knowing the probability of getting correct answers in 20 trials on a multiple-choice examination on

**Exhibit 3.7**

```
MTB > NOTE N = 20,P = 0.2,0.5, AND 0.8        MTB > PDF;
MTB > PDF;                                    SUBC> BINOMIAL N = 20 P = 0.5.
SUBC> BINOMIAL N = 20 P = 0.2.
                                                 BINOMIAL WITH N =  20  P = 0.500000
   BINOMIAL WITH N =  20  P = 0.200000            K          P( X = K)
      K          P( X = K)                        1            0.0000
      0            0.0115                          2            0.0002
      1            0.0576                          3            0.0011
      2            0.1369                          4            0.0046
      3            0.2054                          5            0.0148
      4            0.2182                          6            0.0370
      5            0.1746                          7            0.0739
      6            0.1091                          8            0.1201
      7            0.0545                          9            0.1602
      8            0.0222                         10            0.1762
      9            0.0074                         11            0.1602
     10            0.0020                         12            0.1201
     11            0.0005                         13            0.0739
     12            0.0001                         14            0.0370
     13            0.0000                         15            0.0148
MTB > CDF;                                        16            0.0046
SUBC> BINOMIAL N = 20 P = 0.2.                    17            0.0011
                                                 18            0.0002
   BINOMIAL WITH N =  20  P = 0.200000           19            0.0000
      K  P( X LESS OR = K)                  MTB > CDF;
      0            0.0115                    SUBC> BINOMIAL N = 20 P = 0.5.
      1            0.0692
      2            0.2061                          BINOMIAL WITH N =  20  P = 0.500000
      3            0.4114                             K  P( X LESS OR = K)
      4            0.6296                             1            0.0000
      5            0.8042                             2            0.0002
      6            0.9133                             3            0.0013
      7            0.9679                             4            0.0059
      8            0.9900                             5            0.0207
      9            0.9974                             6            0.0577
     10            0.9994                             7            0.1316
     11            0.9999                             8            0.2517
     12            1.0000                             9            0.4119
                                                    10            0.5881
                                                    11            0.7483
                                                    12            0.8684
                                                    13            0.9423
                                                    14            0.9793
                                                    15            0.9941
                                                    16            0.9987
                                                    17            0.9998
                                                    18            1.0000
```

**Exhibit 3.7**

(cont.)

```
MTB > PDF;
SUBC> BINOMIAL N = 20 P = 0.8.

      BINOMIAL WITH N =  20  P = 0.800000
         K          P( X = K)
         7            0.0000
         8            0.0001
         9            0.0005
        10            0.0020
        11            0.0074
        12            0.0222
        13            0.0545
        14            0.1091
        15            0.1746
        16            0.2182
        17            0.2054
        18            0.1369
        19            0.0576
        20            0.0115
MTB > CDF;
SUBC> BINOMIAL N = 20 P = 0.8.

      BINOMIAL WITH N =  20  P = 0.800000
       K   P( X LESS OR = K)
         7            0.0000
         8            0.0001
         9            0.0006
        10            0.0026
        11            0.0100
        12            0.0321
        13            0.0867
        14            0.1958
        15            0.3704
        16            0.5886
        17            0.7939
        18            0.9308
        19            0.9885
        20            1.0000
```

which we guess at each answer. Assuming that there are five possible answers, the probability of a success at each trial is $1/5 = 0.2$. In this case we see from the output on the upper left in Exhibit 3.7 that the probability of getting ten or fewer correct answers is 0.9994. One is not likely to pass by guessing! Note that when the BINOMIAL command is used, probabilities of less than 0.0001 are not printed out by CDF. In the first portion of Exhibit 3.7 no probabilities are printed by CDF for $x = 13, 14, 15, 16, 17, 18, 19,$ and 20 for this reason.

Note that if $n = 3$ and $p = 1/2$ in the independent-trials situation, the probability function for $x$ heads in three independent trials is given by

$$p(x) = \binom{3}{x} (1/2)^3 \qquad x = 0, 1, 2, 3$$

Hence, $p(0) = p(3) = 1/8$ and $p(1) = p(2) = 3/8$, verifying the statement made in Example 3.2 of Section 3.2 regarding the number of females in a three-child family when $P(\text{Female}) = P(\text{Male}) = 1/2$.

Let us return to the World Series example, and assume that the two teams are of equal ability. The outcomes AAAA (team A wins the first four games) and BBBB (team B wins the first four games) are the only ones that will result in a four-game series. As each of these outcomes has probability 1/16, we have $p(4) = 2/16$. A World Series will be won by A in five games if any one of the sequences BAAAA, ABAAA, AABAA, or AAABA occurs. Note that AAAAB cannot occur. There are four similar sequences resulting in a five-game series won by B. Hence, $p(5) = 8(1/32) = 4/16$. Verify for yourself that

$$p(x) = \binom{x-1}{x-4}(1/2)^{x-1} \qquad x = 4, 5, 6, 7$$

is the probability of an $x$-game World Series if the teams are of equal ability and the games are assumed to be independent.

## Exercises 3.5

**3.40** Suppose the probability that the 8:00 A.M. commuter train will be on time at a certain station is 0.8 on Monday and 0.9 on Tuesday. Call these events $A$ and $B$, respectively. Assuming that these two events are independent, find the following.
  **a.** The probability that the train will be on time on both Monday and Tuesday of a certain week—i.e., $P(A \cap B)$.
  **b.** The probability that the train will be on time on at least one of the two days or both—i.e., $P(A \cup B)$.
  **c.** The probability that the train will be on time on neither of the two days—i.e., $P(\bar{A} \cap \bar{B})$.

**3.41** The probabilities associated with the occurrence of various numbers of accidents in a large factory in a month are given by $p(0) = 0.7$, $p(1) = 0.2$, $p(2) = 0.08$, and $p(3) = 0.02$. If the numbers of accidents in two successive months are considered to be independent, find the following:
  **a.** The probability of having no accidents in the two months.
  **b.** The probability of having at least two accidents in both of the two months.
  **c.** The probability of having the same number of accidents in the two months.

**3.42** A single card is selected at random from a deck. The following events are defined:

$A$ = a club is selected

$B$ = a two is selected

  **a.** Are these events independent? Use Definition 3.12 to decide.
  **b.** Are these events disjoint? Use Definition 3.10 to decide.

**3.43** Consider Example 3.9 concerning the alumni of a college, with event $A$ representing being a male and event $B$ representing having an income in excess of $25,000, as before. Use the probabilities for the selection of an individual indicated in Figure 3.6 to show that $A$ and $B$ are neither independent nor disjoint.

**3.44** A sample of ten items is taken from a production line to determine whether the process is "in control." Assume that the items are classified as defective or nondefective and that the trials can be considered to be independent.

    **a.** If the proportion of defectives produced is 0.10, what is the probability that there will be two or fewer defectives in the sample?

    **b.** If the process is stopped whenever more than two defectives are obtained in the sample, what is the probability that the process will be stopped, given the proportion of defectives stated in part a?

**3.45** The probability that an archer will make a bull's-eye is $p = 2/3$. Assume that the shots are probabilistically independent.

    **a.** What is the probability of 0, 1, 2, 3 and 4 bull's-eyes in 4 shots? (Five probabilities are required.)

    **b.** Verify that the probabilities in part a add up to 1.

**3.46** An operation is successful 90 percent of the time. Assuming independence, what is the probability that, in a week in which 4 such operations are performed, 0, 1, 2, 3, and 4 will be successful? Use the formula for binomial probabilities. (Five probabilities are required.)

**3.47** Assume that $A$ and $B$ are events with $P(A) > 0$ and $P(B) > 0$.

    **a.** Show that if $A$ and $B$ are independent they cannot be disjoint. *Hint:* Consider $P(A \cap B)$.

    **b.** Show that if $A$ and $B$ are disjoint they cannot be independent.

**3.48** Suppose a fair die is tossed until the first six is obtained, and the number of tosses required is counted. Assume that the tosses are independent.

    **a.** Find the probability that one toss is required.

    **b.** Find the probability that two tosses are required; i.e., find the probability of FS, where F represents a failure on the first trial and S a success (a six) on the second trial.

    **c.** Find the probability that $x$ tosses are required to obtain a six.

**3.49** Two teams of equal ability play a best-of-five-game series. Find the probabilities that the series ends in 3, 4, and 5 games. Verify that these three probabilities add up to 1.

**3.50** The probability of success on three independent trials is not constant. The probability of success is 1/2 on the first trial, 2/3 on the second trial, and 3/4 on the third trial.

    **a.** Find the probabilities of zero, one, two, and three successes in the three trials.

    **b.** What is the probability of having more successes than failures in the three trials?

**3.51** A certain location can have three types of weather: clear, cloudy, and rainy, with probabilities of 1/6, 1/3, and 1/2, respectively. Assume that the weather on a given day is independent of the weather on other days.

    **a.** What is the probability of having three successive rainy days? clear days? cloudy days?

    **b.** What is the probability that three successive days will have three different types of weather?

    **c.** What is the probability that at least two of the three days will have the same type of weather?

**3.52** A total of $n$ binomial trials are made. The probability of success for each trial is $p = 1/n$.

    **a.** What is the probability of no successes in $n$ independent trials for $n = 3$? $n = 5$? $n = 10$?

    **b.** What appears to happen to the probability in part a as $n$ increases?

**3.53** A salesman is successful in making a sale on 50 percent of his visits. Assuming independence, what is the minimum number of visits, $n$, he should schedule in order to make sure that the probability of at least one sale is at least 0.90? *Note:* This value will be the minimum number required in order to make the probability of no sales at most 0.10.

**3.54** The first weekday flight from Omaha to Denver arrives on time with a probability of 0.9. If 20 flights are scheduled in the next four weeks, use PDF and CDF to find the following:
  **a.** The probability that at least 18 will be on time.
  **b.** The probability that 17 or less will be on time.
  **c.** The probability that exactly 18 will be on time.
  **d.** The probability that more than 16 will be on time.

**3.55** It can be shown that in the case of $n$ independent trials with probability of success $p$, the probabilities $p(x)$ first increase to a maximum, attained when $x$ is the smallest integer equal to $(n + 1)p$ or less than $(n + 1)p$ if this value is not an integer. If $(n + 1)p$ is an integer, there is a double maximum at $(n + 1)p$ and $(n + 1)p - 1$. The probabilities decrease thereafter.
  **a.** Verify that this statement is correct for the three cases with $n = 20$ and $p = 0.2$, 0.5, and 0.8 given in this section.
  **b.** Use BINOMIAL with $n = 19$ and $p = 0.5$. For which value(s) of $x$, the number of successes in the 19 trials, is the probability of $x$ successes a maximum?

**3.56 a.** Which is larger: (1) the probability of obtaining two heads in four tosses of a fair coin or (2) the probability of obtaining three heads in six tosses of a fair coin?
  **b.** Use BINOMIAL with $n = 20$, 50, and 100 and $p = 1/2$ to find the probability of 10, 25, and 50 heads, respectively. What appears to happen to the probability of obtaining $n/2$ heads in $n$ tosses of a fair coin as $n$ gets very large?

**\*3.57** In certain experiments involving expensive animals, it is important to keep the number of experimental animals used as small as possible. Suppose the person conducting such an experiment wishes to have at least eight animals survive a treatment so that they can be used in a post-treatment study. It is known that 20 percent of such animals will not survive the treatment. What is the smallest number of animals with which she should begin the study in order to have a probability of at least 0.95 that at least eight will survive? Assume independence and use Minitab.

---

**Summary**     The concepts of a theoretical random experiment, an outcome space, and a probability assignment to an outcome space provide the mathematical or axiomatic basis for the study of elementary probability. Although in many cases each outcome is given the same probability, equal probability assignment is not the only possibility for a finite outcome space.

An event is a subset of an outcome space. For a finite outcome space, the probability of an event is the sum of the probabilities that make up the event. The

---

\*An asterisk denotes a problem that is more difficult than most.

complement, intersection, and union are all new events formed from existing events.

The Addition Law, the Law of Complements, and the Multiplication Law permit the calculation of the probabilities of the union of two events, the complement of a single event, and the intersection of two events, respectively. The definition of conditional probability is just a restatement of the Multiplication Law. This definition permits the calculation of probabilities with respect to a subset $A$ of $S$.

The idea of independence permits the calculation of probabilities in more complex situations.

Minitab is an effective and easily used device for

1  illustrating the stability of long-run relative frequencies,
2  simulating the performance of random experiments with known probabilities, and
3  calculating probabilities in complex situations (e.g., the binomial trials situation).

## Key Words

| | |
|---|---|
| Addition Law | Multiplication Law |
| binomial trials | mutually exclusive events |
| complement | mutually independent events |
| conditional probability | outcome space |
| disjoint events | probability |
| event | probability assignment |
| experiment | relative frequency |
| independent events | simulation |
| intersection | union |
| Law of Complements | |

## Minitab Commands

| | | |
|---|---|---|
| BASE | INDICATOR | TALLY |
| CDF | PDF | |

# Chapter 4

# Discrete and Continuous Random Variables

## 4.1

**Introduction**

In Chapter 3 an outcome space $S$ was defined to be the set of all possible outcomes of an experiment. In this chapter we will consider rules for assigning numerical values to each outcome in $S$. A particular rule that assigns a numerical value to each of the outcomes of $S$ is called a random variable. We will study properties of random variables. As the points of an outcome space $S$ correspond to elements of a population, the properties of any random variables defined for $S$ are properties associated with a population (as opposed to a sample).

In the stock example discussed in Sections 2.1 and 2.2, the 900 stocks appearing in the 1981 year-end edition of *Business Week* are the elements of an outcome space $S$. Two random variables are defined for each element (stock) in this outcome space. The first is the annual yield in 1981, which defines a number for each of the 900 stocks. The second is the percentage change for each stock during 1981, which associates another number with each stock. Each random variable can be thought of as defining a rule that associates a number with each point of a given outcome space. There are, of course, many other random variables associated with this particular outcome space—that is, other rules that could be used to assign numbers to each stock. For example, the year-end price of the stock, the low price for the year, and the high price for the year are all random variables that could be used to assign a number to each of the 900 stocks. Each such rule that assigns a numerical value to a stock is a random variable. Hence there is no single random variable defined for an outcome space $S$, although we may be much more interested in particular random variables, (e.g., in our example, percentage price change) than in others.

In the example of two independent trials in Section 3.5, we considered the sample space

$$S = \{SS, SF, FS, FF\}$$

The random variable that was considered in that case was the number of successes associated with each outcome. As indicated in Figure 3.12, the possible values of this random variable are 0, 1, and 2. The element SS has the number 2 associated with it, as it represents two successes in a row. The elements SF and FS have the number 1 associated with them, as there is one success in each case. Finally, FF is assigned the value 0, as it represents two failures in a row.

## Example 4.1

Let $S$ be the outcome space consisting of all Canadian colleges and universities with a 1980–81 enrollment of at least 200 students. Two random variables of interest are the number of students and the number of teachers at these institutions in that year. The institutions and the values of these two random variables are listed in Table 4.1.

## Table 4.1

**Canadian Universities and Colleges**

|  | Name | Students | Teachers |
|---|---|---|---|
| 1. | Acadia Univ. | 2760 | 210 |
| 2. | Alberta, Univ. of | 18,270 | 1580 |
| 3. | Bishop's Univ. | 750 | 80 |
| 4. | Brandon | 940 | 150 |
| 5. | British Columbia, Univ. of | 19,870 | 2090 |
| 6. | Brock Univ. | 2300 | 210 |
| 7. | Calgary, Univ. of | 11,080 | 1110 |
| 8. | Canadian Bible College | 380 | 10 |
| 9. | Canadian Union College | 210 | 20 |
| 10. | Carleton Univ. | 8430 | 620 |
| 11. | Concordia Univ. | 10,780 | 700 |
| 12. | Dalhousie Univ. | 7440 | 820 |
| 13. | Guelph, Univ. of | 9390 | 770 |
| 14. | Lakeland Univ. | 2690 | 240 |
| 15. | Laurentian Univ. | 2620 | 320 |
| 16. | Laval Univeritie | 18,170 | 1470 |
| 17. | Lethbridge, Univ. of | 1490 | 170 |
| 18. | Manitoba, Univ. of | 12,860 | 1319 |
| 19. | McGill Univ. | 16,400 | 1250 |
| 20. | McMaster Univ. | 9910 | 900 |
| 21. | Mem. Univ. of N.F. | 6740 | 830 |
| 22. | Moncton, Univ. de | 2940 | 280 |
| 23. | Montreal, Univ. de | 18,000 | 1790 |
| 24. | Mount Allison Univ. | 1510 | 140 |
| 25. | Mount St. Vincent Univ. | 1440 | 110 |

**Table 4.1**

**cont.**

| | Name | Students | Teachers |
|---|---|---|---|
| 26. | New Brunswick, Univ. of | 6070 | 570 |
| 27. | Nova Scotia Coll. of Arts & Design | 430 | 40 |
| 28. | Ottawa Univ. | 11,710 | 1010 |
| 29. | Prince Edward Island, Univ. of | 1320 | 120 |
| 30. | Quebec, Univ. of | 18,850 | 1410 |
| 31. | Queen's Univ. | 11,000 | 930 |
| 32. | Regina, Univ. of | 3640 | 380 |
| 33. | Royal Military College of Canada | 680 | 150 |
| 34. | Royal Roads Military College | 250 | 40 |
| 35. | Ryerson Polytechnic Inst. | 9170 | 640 |
| 36. | St. Francis Xavier Univ. | 2740 | 790 |
| 37. | St. Mary's Univ. | 2270 | 190 |
| 38. | St. Thomas Univ. | 720 | 60 |
| 39. | Saskatchewan, Univ. of | 9760 | 1040 |
| 40. | Sherbrooke, Univ. of | 7190 | 720 |
| 41. | Simon Fraser Univ. | 5040 | 490 |
| 42. | Technical Univ. of N.S. | 790 | 70 |
| 43. | Toronto, Univ. of | 33,940 | 2840 |
| 44. | Trent Univ. | 2180 | 180 |
| 45. | Victoria, Univ. of | 5670 | 520 |
| 46. | Waterloo, Univ. of | 15,750 | 800 |
| 47. | Welfrid Laurier Univ. | 3890 | 220 |
| 48. | Western Ontario, Univ. of | 16,810 | 1420 |
| 49. | Windsor, Univ. of | 6780 | 520 |
| 50. | Winnipeg, Univ. of | 2400 | 190 |
| 51. | York Univ. | 11,820 | 1020 |

*Source:* Statistics Canada, reported in *The World Almanac and Book of Facts*, 1983, p. 200.

A particular investigator will study those random variables that are of greatest interest to him or her. Although the numbers of students and faculty were considered in Example 4.1, clearly other random variables, such as annual tuition or the proportion of faculty members with a Ph.D. degree might also be of interest.

So far in this section we have considered only finite outcome spaces. As discussed in Section 2.2, there are also populations and hence outcome spaces that are infinite.

**Example 4.2**

The length of time an individual takes to respond to a stimulus might be considered to have as an outcome space $S$ the interval $0 < t \leqslant 60$, with $t$ measured in minutes. One rule used to define a random variable on this space is given by the function $f(t) = t$. In other words, each point in $S$ is assigned to itself, the actual response time.

Suppose we were interested in singling out for remedial treatment those individuals whose response time exceeded 10 minutes but was no more than 60 minutes. Another random variable might be assigned to this sample space by the function

$$g(t) = \begin{cases} 0 & \text{if } 0 < t \leqslant 10 \\ 1 & \text{if } 10 < t \leqslant 60 \end{cases}$$

Here each value in $S$ that is less than or equal to 10 is assigned the value 0. Each value in $S$ that is greater than 10 and no more than 60 is assigned the value 1. By assigning the value 1 to all individuals with response times exceeding 10 minutes, the random variable defined by $g(t)$ would pick them out.

## 4.2
**Discrete Random Variables and the Binomial Random Variable**

The random variables defined in Section 4.1 for the sample spaces of the 900 stocks and the 51 Canadian universities and colleges have only a finite number of different values, as the outcome spaces themselves have a finite number of points. In the example in Section 3.5 of two independent trials with sample space $S = \{SS, SF, FS, FF\}$, the random variable giving the number of successes is discrete because only three values can be attained—0, 1, and 2. Random variables are generally denoted by capital letters, frequently $X$, $Y$, or $Z$. In the case of the number of successes on two independent trials, we would say the random variable $X$ takes on the values 0, 1, and 2.

discrete random variable

> **Definition 4.1** ■━━━━━━━━━━━━━━━━━━━━━━━━━━━
>
> A **discrete random variable** $X$ assigns a numerical value to each outcome of $S$. The number of values that such a random variable may attain may be either finite or countably infinite.

As an example of a situation in which a random variable has an infinite but countable number of values, consider the experiment of tossing a fair coin until the first head occurs. The outcome space $S$ for this experiment is

$$S = \{H, TH, TTH, TTTH, \ldots\}$$

If we define the random variable $Y$ by $Y(H) = 1$, $Y(TH) = 2$, $Y(TTH) = 3$, $\ldots$, and so forth, $Y$ counts the number of tosses until the first head occurs. This random variable can take on an infinite number of values—i.e., all of the positive integers, $P = \{1, 2, 3, \ldots, k, \ldots\}$.

If the values in a set can be matched with the positive integers, the set is called countably infinite. The set of *even* positive integers is countably infinite, for example, because it can be matched with the set $P$ as follows:

$$
\begin{array}{cccccc}
1 & 2 & 3 & 4 & \ldots & k & \ldots \\
\updownarrow & \updownarrow & \updownarrow & \updownarrow & & \updownarrow & \\
2 & 4 & 6 & 8 & & 2k &
\end{array}
$$

Of course, $P$ itself is countably infinite, so $Y$ is a discrete random variable.

Notice that it is the number of values the random variable can have and not the number of points of $S$ that determines whether the random variable is discrete. The random variable defined by the function $g(t)$ in Example 4.2 is discrete because it takes on only two values, 0 and 1. The random variable defined by $f(t) = t$ is not discrete because the number of points in the interval $0 < t \leqslant 60$, the possible values achieved by $f(t) = t$, is not countable. Such a random variable is called continuous. Continuous random variables will be defined and discussed in later sections of this chapter.

For the outcome space $S$ consisting of all books published in the United States in a given year, the number of pages in each such book defines a discrete random variable. The number of pages can take on only a finite number of values, with a minimum of 1 and a maximum of $N$, where $N$ is the number of pages in the longest book. Frequently, discrete random variables take on only integral values, as in this example. Such is not always the case, however. For the outcome space $S$ composed of 1000 men's hats, the size of the hats defines a discrete random variable that can have both integral and nonintegral values. The number of possible hat sizes is finite, but hat sizes such as $6\frac{3}{4}$, 7, and $7\frac{1}{4}$ are possible.

An important connection between the probabilities assigned to a sample space and a discrete random variable $X$ is made by the definition of a function called the probability function of $X$.

---

**Definition 4.2** ▬▬▬▬▬▬▬▬▬▬▬▬▬▬▬▬▬▬▬▬▬▬▬▬▬▬▬

probability function

A **probability function** $p(x)$ gives the probability that a discrete random variable $X$ will take on the value $x$. The probabilities come from the probability assignment to $S$. Such a probability function must satisfy the following conditions:

**a.** $0 \leqslant p(x) \leqslant 1$    for all $x$

**b.** $\displaystyle\sum_{\text{all } x} p(x) = 1$

---

**Example 4.3** ▬▬▬ _____

Consider the tossing of a fair die with one face numbered 1, two faces numbered 3, and three faces numbered 5. Let us define a random variable $X$ to be the number that occurs when such a die is tossed. The probability function of $X$ will give the probabilities associated with the possible outcomes. These values are inherited from the probabilities assigned to $S$. The appropriate probability function would be given by $p(x)$ defined as follows:

| $x$ | $p(x)$ |
|-----|--------|
| 1   | 1/6    |
| 3   | 2/6    |
| 5   | 3/6    |

## Example 4.4

Consider a couple with two children. The possible orderings of the sexes of the children are given by

$$S = \{FF, FM, MF, MM\}$$

Let us define the random variable $Y$ as the number of males in the family. We have $Y(FF) = 0$, $Y(FM) = 1$, $Y(MF) = 1$, and $Y(MM) = 2$. Let $p$ represent the probability of a male birth, and assume the sexes of the two children are independent. We have the probability function $p(y)$ defined as follows, where $q = 1 - p$.

| $y$ | $p(y)$ | $p(y)$ for $p = 1/2$ | $p(y)$ for $p = 0.513$ |
|-----|--------|----------------------|------------------------|
| 0   | $q^2$  | $1/4 = 0.25$         | 0.2372                 |
| 1   | $2pq$  | $1/2 = 0.50$         | 0.4997                 |
| 2   | $p^2$  | $1/4 = 0.25$         | 0.2632                 |

If we assume that the probabilities of the sexes are equal, we obtain the values 0.25, 0.50, and 0.25 for the probabilities of 0, 1, and 2 male births, respectively. If we take the proportion of male births in the United States as the value for $p$ (i.e., 0.513), we obtain slightly different values for these probabilities.

## Example 4.5

Let us now generalize to the case of three independent trials with probability of success $p$. A tennis player has probability $p = 1/3$ of beating his son at tennis. Suppose we wish to know the probability that the father will win 0, 1, 2, or 3 of the next $n = 3$ matches. We saw in Section 3.5 that there are eight possible outcomes, which may be denoted FFF, SFF, FSF, FFS, SSF, SFS, FSS, and SSS. Previously we implicitly defined a random variable by assigning to each outcome the number of successes in the three trials. The general probability function in the case of $n = 3$, where $0 \leqslant p \leqslant 1$, is given below along with the probability function for the specific case $p = 1/3$.

| $x$ | $p(x)$ | $p(x)$ for $p = 1/3$ |
|-----|--------|----------------------|
| 0 | $q^3$ | 8/27 |
| 1 | $3pq^2$ | 12/27 |
| 2 | $3p^2q$ | 6/27 |
| 3 | $p^3$ | 1/27 |

## Binomial Random Variable

**binomial random variable**

When $n$ independent trials are made, each with probability of success $p$, the number of successes $X$ is called the **binomial random variable.** We say that $X$ has distribution $B(n, p)$. We saw in Chapter 3 that the probability function in this case is given by

$$p(x) = \binom{n}{x} p^x q^{n-x} \qquad \text{for} \quad x = 0, 1, 2, \ldots, n$$

Exhibit 3.7 shows the probability function for the binomial random variable produced by Minitab for the cases of $n = 20$ and $p = 0.2, 0.5$, and $0.8$.

## Example 4.6

Consider a tireless postman who attempts each day to deliver a registered letter. Assume that the probability that the addressee will be at home is $1/2$ and that the trials are independent. Let $X$ be the random variable giving the number of the day on which the registered letter is delivered. The outcome space is

$$S = \{1, 2, 3, \ldots\} = P$$

the set of positive integers. Thus $X$ is an example of a discrete random variable with a countably infinite number of values.

Because the trials are independent, $p(1) = 1/2$, $p(2) = (1/2)^2$, $p(3) = (1/2)^3$, and, in general, $p(x) = (1/2)^x$. Does the probability function $p(x)$ satisfy the requirements of Definition 4.2? We know that, if $|r| < 1$,

$$1 + r + r^2 + r^3 + \cdots + r^x + \cdots = \frac{1}{1 - r}$$

Substituting $r = 1/2$, we find that

$$1 + (1/2) + (1/2)^2 + \cdots + (1/2)^x + \cdots = \frac{1}{1/2} = 2$$

Subtracting 1 from both sides of this equation gives

$$(1/2) + (1/2)^2 + \cdots + (1/2)^x + \cdots = \sum_{x=1}^{\infty} p(x) = 1$$

Therefore $p(x) = (1/2)^x$ for $x = 1, 2, \ldots$ satisfies the requirements of Definition 4.2.

Probabilities of various events can be found from $p(x)$. For example, the probability that three or fewer trips will be required to deliver the letter is given by $(1/2) + (1/2)^2 + (1/2)^3 = 7/8$. We shall see in the next section that this example is a particular case of the geometric random variable.

## Probability Histograms

probability histogram

The values of the probability function of a discrete random variable can be displayed by means of a **probability histogram.** The probability histogram for the number of male births when $p = 1/2$ is given in Figure 4.1. This figure is a graphical representation of the probability distribution of a binomial random variable with $n = 2$ and $p = 1/2$. In this case, where the histogram is for a probability distribution, the vertical axis represents probability rather than frequency. The probability histogram for the binomial random variable $X$ with $n = 3$ and $p = 1/3$ is given in Figure 4.2. Note that the area of the probability histogram is 1 in both of these cases. The area under a probability histogram will always be 1. Probability histograms give a visual picture of the distribution of a random variable. They are most frequently used with discrete random variables having integral values.

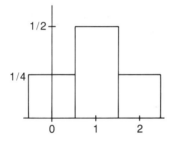

**Figure 4.1**

**Probability Histogram for Binomial Distribution $n = 2$, $p = 0.5$**

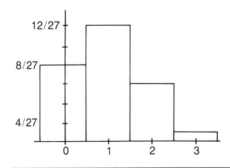

**Figure 4.2**

**Probability Histogram for Binomial Distribution $n = 3$, $p = 1/3$**

CHAPTER 4  DISCRETE AND CONTINUOUS RANDOM VARIABLES

The similarity between a histogram for a sample and a probability histogram naturally gives rise to several questions. How do we define a central or middle value of a probability distribution, which would correspond to the mean of a sample? How do we measure the degree of spread or variability of a random variable, which would correspond to the variance or standard deviation of a sample? We will turn to a consideration of these properties of a discrete random variable in the next section.

## Exercises 4.2

**4.1** Suppose a group of professional golfers play a tough par-4 golf hole. The probability of getting a birdie (a 3) is half that of getting a par, and the probability of getting a bogey (a 5) is twice that of getting a par. Twenty percent of the golfers get a par; the highest score anyone gets is a double bogey (a 6). Find the probability function $p(x)$ of $X$, the scores of the professional golfers on this hole. Construct a probability histogram for this random variable.

**4.2** Suppose a best-of-five-game series is played between two teams of equal ability. The series ends as soon as one of the teams wins three games. If the games are considered independent trials, find the probability function $p(x)$ of $X$, the number of games played in the series. Construct a probability histogram for this random variable.

**4.3** On a dangerous island in the Caribbean, there is at least one but never more than four hurricanes per year. The probability of $x$ hurricanes is inversely proportional to $x$; that is, for a constant $c$, $p(x) = c/x$ for $x = 1, 2, 3, 4$. Find the probability function for this random variable. Construct a probability histogram for this random variable.

**4.4** Find the probability function for $X$, the sum resulting from the tossing of two dice, given that the dice are fair. Construct a probability histogram for this random variable.

**4.5** Let $X$ be the random variable representing the number of males in a family of four children.
 **a.** What does the random variable $Y = 4 - X$ represent?
 **b.** What does the random variable $W = Y - X$ represent, and what values may it have?
 **c.** Considering male and female births to be independent and equally probable, find the probability functions for $X$, $Y$, and $W$.

**4.6** Define precisely several random variables associated with the population consisting of the 50 states.

**4.7** The integers $\{1, 2, 3, 4, 5, 6\}$ are assigned a probability function directly proportional to the value of each integer—that is, for a constant $c$, $p(x) = cx$ for $x = 1, 2, \ldots, 6$. Find the probability function $p(x)$.

**4.8** **a.** Find the probability function for the binomial random variable with $n = 5$ and $p = 1/2$.
 **b.** Construct a probability histogram for this distribution.

**4.9** **a.** Use the Minitab command PDF to find the probability function of the binomial random variable for the case $n = 11$ and $p = 1/2$.
 **b.** Construct a probability histogram for this random variable. With which value(s) of $x$ is the greatest probability associated?

**4.10** Assume a fair die is tossed until an even number appears. Find the probability function of $X$, the number of the trial on which an even number is first obtained.

**4.11** Minitab simulates the selection of observations of a discrete random variable by means of the RANDOM command and the DISCRETE subcommand. The values the random variable can attain are put in one column, and the corresponding values of the probability function in another column. Using RANDOM, simulate 300 tosses of a die with one face numbered 1, two numbered 3, and three numbered 5. Make a histogram of these outcomes. Is the relative frequency of these outcomes about what you expected? Why?

**4.12** Use RANDOM to simulate the outcomes of 1000 father-son tennis matches of three sets each, where the father has a probability of 1/3 of winning a set. Make a relative frequency histogram of the number of matches won by the father. Is this histogram similar in shape to the probability histogram given in Figure 4.2?

**4.13** **a.** Use RANDOM to simulate the outcomes of 1000 observations of a binomial random variable with $n = 8$ and $p = 1/4$. Do the same for the case of $n = 8$ and $p = 1/2$ and the case of $n = 8$ and $p = 3/4$. Put the observations for each case in a separate column. Use Minitab to make histograms of the observations in the three columns. What is the general appearance of each of these histograms?
**b.** Use PDF to compute the binomial probabilities for the three cases of part a. Do the relative frequencies simulated in part a match the theoretical probabilities reasonably well?

**\*4.14** The probability function of a discrete random variable defined over the positive integers $p$ is given by

$$p(k) = \frac{1}{k(k + 1)}$$

**a.** Find $p(1)$, $p(2)$, and $p(3)$.
**b.** Find an expression for $\Sigma_{k=1}^{n} p(k)$.
**c.** Show that the limiting value of the expression in part b as $n \to \infty$ is 1. In other words, show that the probabilities sum to 1.

**\*4.15** For Example 4.6 of the tireless postman, find the probability that the first successful attempt to deliver a letter will occur on an odd-numbered trial. Use the Law of Complements to find the corresponding probability for an even-numbered trial.

## 4.3

## The Expectation and Variance of a Discrete Random Variable

We next consider how to find a number that can be thought of as an "average" or representative value of a discrete random variable.

---

**Definition 4.3** ━━━━━━━━━━━━━━━━━━━━━━━━━━━━

expected value

The **expected value** $E(X)$ of a discrete random variable is given by

$$E(X) = \sum_{\text{all } x} xp(x) = \mu$$

where $p(x)$ is the probability function of $X$. As indicated, $E(X)$ is frequently denoted by the Greek symbol $\mu$.

---

The expected value of a discrete random variable is a weighted average of the values of $X$. The weight assigned to a particular value $x$ is $p(x)$, the probability that the random variable will take on the value $x$.

## Example 4.7

In Example 3.6 two fair tetrahedra were tossed. On each die, the numbers 1, 2, 3, and 4 each had a probability of 1/4 of landing facing downward. Let the random variable $T$ represent the sum of the two faces landing face downward. The probability function for $T$ given in Example 3.6 will be used here to compute the value of $E(T)$, the expected value of $T$.

$$
\begin{aligned}
E(T) &= 2\left(\frac{1}{16}\right) + 3\left(\frac{2}{16}\right) + 4\left(\frac{3}{16}\right) + 5\left(\frac{4}{16}\right) + 6\left(\frac{3}{16}\right) \\
&\quad + 7\left(\frac{2}{16}\right) + 8\left(\frac{1}{16}\right) \\
&= \frac{80}{16} = 5
\end{aligned}
$$

Thus the expected sum, the expected value of the random variable $T$, is 5.

## Example 4.8

Let us return to the seven-game series of Section 3.5 in which each team had equal probability of winning each game. Let $X$ represent the number of games played in such a series in which the probabilities of the outcomes of the games are independent. The probability function for $x$ was found to be

$$
p(x) = \binom{x-1}{x-4}\left(\frac{1}{2}\right)^{x-1} \qquad \text{for } x = 4, 5, 6, 7
$$

or

$$
p(4) = \frac{1}{8} \qquad p(5) = \frac{1}{4} \qquad p(6) = \frac{5}{16} \qquad p(7) = \frac{5}{16}
$$

Thus

$$
\begin{aligned}
E(X) &= 4\left(\frac{1}{8}\right) + 5\left(\frac{1}{4}\right) + 6\left(\frac{5}{16}\right) + 7\left(\frac{5}{16}\right) \\
&= \frac{93}{16} = 5.8125
\end{aligned}
$$

So the number of games we can expect to be played in such a series is 5.8125. Note that this number is not an integer. Just as the average number of children per family in a sample of ten families can be nonintegral, the expected value of $X$ can be a number that cannot actually be attained by the random variable.

In order to see the logic behind Definition 4.3, consider the tossing of a fair tetrahedron as described in Example 4.7. Let $n_1, n_2, n_3$, and $n_4$ represent the number of ones, twos, threes, and fours obtained in $n$ trials. We can compute the average, or mean, of the $n$ tosses as

$$\bar{x} = \frac{1n_1 + 2n_2 + 3n_3 + 4n_4}{n}$$

$$= 1\left(\frac{n_1}{n}\right) + 2\left(\frac{n_2}{n}\right) + 3\left(\frac{n_3}{n}\right) + 4\left(\frac{n_4}{n}\right)$$

$$= 1f_1 + 2f_2 + 3f_3 + 4f_4$$

Here $f_1, f_2, f_3$, and $f_4$ represent the relative frequencies of the outcomes 1, 2, 3, and 4, respectively. We have considered probabilities to be the theoretical counterpart of relative frequencies. Hence when $n$ is large, the last expression given for $\bar{x}$ above naturally leads to the definition of $E(X)$ in Definition 4.3.

## Example 4.9

Table 4.1 described a sample space $S$ that included all Canadian colleges and universities with at least 200 students. Two random variables were defined in this space: the number of students (say $X$) and the number of teachers (say $Y$). If each value in the sample space is given the same probability, namely 1/51, the expected value of $X$ from Definition 4.3 is

$$E(X) = \sum_{i=1}^{51} x_i\left(\frac{1}{51}\right) = \frac{\sum_{i=1}^{51} x_i}{51}$$

As this value is just the average of the number of students in all the 51 institutions, the AVERAGE command can be used to find the expected value of student enrollment, as shown in Exhibit 4.1.

## Exhibit 4.1

```
MTB > NOTE ENROLLMENT IN 51 CANADIAN COLLEGES AND UNIVERSITIES
MTB > SET C1
C1
   2760    18270      750      940     .    .    .

MTB > END
MTB > PRINT C1
C1
   2760    18270      750      940    19870     2300    11080      380
    210     8430    10780     7440     9390     2690     2620    18170
   1490    12860    16400     9910     6740     2940    18800     1510
   1440     6070      430    11710     1320    18850    11000     3640
    680      250     9170     2740     2270      720     9760     7190
   5040      790    33940     2180     5670    15750    16810     3890
   6780     2400    11820

MTB > AVERAGE C1
   MEAN    =       7432.2
```

CHAPTER 4  **DISCRETE AND CONTINUOUS RANDOM VARIABLES**

Note that in this case the 51 universities are considered not a sample but a population.

Consider a sequence of $n$ independent binomial trials, each with probability of success $p$. Let $X$ represent the number of successes. The expression $X \sim B(n, p)$ signifies that when $n$ independent trials are made, each with probability of success $p$, $X$ is binomially distributed. We would like to find a mathematical expression for the expectation of the binomial random variable. Consider a father who has a probability of 1/3 of beating his son at tennis. Assume that the two play a total of 30 matches which are considered probabilistically independent. The number of wins by the father is a binomial random variable $X$, where $X \sim B(30, 1/3)$. It seems that the father should, "on average," win 10 matches. The implicit assumption is that $E(X) = 30(1/3) = 10$. It can be proved that for *the binomial random variable*,

$$E(X) = np \tag{4.1}$$

the number of trials times the probability of success on an individual trial.

## Example 4.10

Suppose that the probability of a basketball player's making a foul shot is 0.7. If we consider each shot to be an independent trial, the expected number of successes in the next ten shots would be $np = 10(0.7) = 7$ using Equation 4.1. The expected number of successes in the next 15 shots would be $np = 15(0.7) = 10.5$. Again we have a situation in which the expected value is a nonintegral number that cannot be taken on by the random variable.

We now consider three properties of the expectation of a random variable, which are important and very easy to demonstrate.

---

**Property 4.1** ████████████████████████████████████████

For any random variable $X$ that is a constant $k$ on $S$,

$$E(X) = E(k) = k$$

For example, if $X$ is weight in pounds, then $16X$ is weight in ounces. Clearly $E(16X)$ should equal $16E(X)$. In words, the expected weight in ounces should be 16 times the expected weight in pounds. Similarly, if $Y$ is height in inches, then $Y/12$ is height in feet. Thus $E(Y/12)$ should equal $E(Y)/12$. In words, the expected height in feet should be 1/12th the expected height in inches.

---

**Property 4.2** ▬▬▬▬▬▬▬▬▬▬▬▬▬▬▬▬▬▬▬▬▬▬▬▬▬▬▬▬

For any random variable $X$ and constant $k$,

$$E(kX) = kE(X)$$

**Property 4.3** ▬▬▬▬▬▬▬▬▬▬▬▬▬▬▬▬▬▬▬▬▬▬▬▬▬▬▬▬

For any random variable $X$ and constant $k$,

$$E(X + k) = E(X) + k$$

In physics it is known that the relation between temperature measured in degrees Kelvin and temperature measured in degrees Celsius is given by

$$K = C + 273.15$$

Hence if $T$ is a random variable measuring temperature, $E(K)$ should equal $E(T + 273.15)$, or $E(T) + 273.15$. In words, the expected temperature in degrees Kelvin should be the expected temperature in degrees Celsius plus 273.15.

Proving Properties 4.1, 4.2, and 4.3 for discrete random variables is left to the instructor. These properties are also valid for continuous random variables.

Next we will consider how to measure the variability, or spread, of the distribution of a random variable. For example, consider two random variables $X$ and $Y$ with the following probability functions:

$$X: \ p(x) = \begin{cases} \dfrac{1}{4} \ \text{for } x = 1 \text{ and } x = -1 \\ \dfrac{1}{2} \ \text{for } x = 0 \end{cases}$$

$$Y: \ p(y) = \begin{cases} \dfrac{1}{4} \ \text{for } y = 10 \text{ and } y = -10 \\ \dfrac{1}{2} \ \text{for } y = 0 \end{cases}$$

It is easy to compute $E(X) = 0 = E(Y)$. The distribution of $Y$ clearly seems more "spread out" than that of $X$, however. The variance $\sigma^2$ of a discrete random variable is a measure of the spread of the distribution of a random variable. It is defined as follows.

**Definition 4.4** ■■■■■■■■■■■■■■■■■■■■■■■■■■■■■■■■■■■■■■■■■■■■■■■■■■

variance

The **variance** $\sigma_X^2$ of a discrete random variable is given by

$$\sum_{\text{all } x} [x - E(X)]^2 p(x) \;=\; E[(X - \mu)]^2 \;=\; \text{Var}(X)$$

For the random variables $X$ and $Y$ above,

$$\sigma_X^2 \;=\; \frac{(-1)^2 + (1)^2}{4} \;=\; \frac{1}{2}$$

and

$$\sigma_Y^2 \;=\; \frac{(-10)^2 + (10)^2}{4} \;=\; 50$$

The larger variance of $Y$ indicates that this random variable is more spread out than $X$, although $E(X) = E(Y) = 0$. The population variance $\sigma^2$ corresponds to the sample variance $s^2$. Just as $E(X)$ is not a sample mean, however, the variance $\sigma^2$ of a random variable is not equal to a sample variance $s^2$. The variance $\sigma^2$ is used as a measure of spread of the distribution of the random variable $X$.

**Example 4.11** ────────────────────────────────────────────────

Consider finding the variance of the sum $T$ of the tosses of two fair tetrahedra. Using the probability function of Example 3.6 and the value of $\mu = 5$ found in Example 4.7, we have

$$\sigma_T^2 \;=\; (2 - 5)^2 \left(\frac{1}{16}\right) + (3 - 5)^2 \left(\frac{2}{16}\right) + (4 - 5)^2 \left(\frac{3}{16}\right)$$

$$+ (5 - 5)^2 \left(\frac{4}{16}\right) + (6 - 5)^2 \left(\frac{3}{16}\right) + (7 - 5)^2 \left(\frac{2}{16}\right)$$

$$+ (8 - 5)^2 \left(\frac{1}{16}\right)$$

$$= \frac{5}{2}$$

────────────────────────────────────────────────

**Example 4.12** ────────────────────────────────────────────────

In Example 4.5, the random variable $X$ is the number of wins in three matches between a father and a son. The matches are considered independent, with the father having probability $1/3$ of winning a match. The probability function of $X$ given in Example 4.5 is

$$p(0) \;=\; \frac{8}{27} \qquad p(1) \;=\; \frac{12}{27} \qquad p(2) \;=\; \frac{6}{27} \qquad p(3) \;=\; \frac{1}{27}$$

As this is the binomial case with $n = 3$ and $p = 1/3$, $E(X) = np = 1$, and for the variance we find

$$\sigma_X^2 = (0 - 1)^2 \left(\frac{8}{27}\right) + (1 - 1)^2 \left(\frac{12}{27}\right) + (2 - 1)^2 \left(\frac{6}{27}\right) + (3 - 1)^2 \left(\frac{1}{27}\right)$$

$$= \frac{18}{27} = \frac{2}{3}$$

---

In the general case of $n$ independent trials with probability of success $p$, it may be shown that the binomial random variable $X$ giving the total number of successes in $n$ trials has a variance of $\sigma_X^2 = np(1 - p)$. We will not prove this result now, but note that in the case of father versus son in tennis,

$$np(1 - p) = 3 \left(\frac{1}{3}\right)\left(\frac{2}{3}\right) = \frac{2}{3}$$

which agrees with the value just found in Example 4.12.

Like the sample variance, the variance of a random variable is expressed in units of the original random variable squared. The variance of 2/3 computed above for the number of wins by the father is in units of $(\text{successes})^2$. In order to measure the variability (or spread) of a random variable in the original units, we must use the standard deviation.

**Definition 4.5** ▬▬▬▬▬▬▬▬▬▬▬▬▬▬▬▬▬▬▬▬▬▬▬▬▬▬▬

standard deviation of a random variable

The **standard deviation of a random variable** is the positive square root of the variance—that is, $(\sigma^2)^{1/2} = \sigma$.

Hence, for $T$ in Example 4.11,

$$\sigma_T = \left(\frac{5}{2}\right)^{1/2} = 1.581$$

For the number of wins by the father in Example 4.12,

$$\sigma_X = \left(\frac{2}{3}\right)^{1/2} = 0.816$$

We now consider three properties of the variance $\sigma_X^2$, which are analogous to Properties 4.1, 4.2, and 4.3 for the expectation.

**Property 4.4** ▬▬▬▬▬▬▬▬▬▬▬▬▬▬▬▬▬▬▬▬▬▬▬▬▬▬▬

If $X$ is a constant random variable equal to $k$,

$$\text{Var}(X) = \text{Var}(k) = 0$$

**Property 4.5** ▄▄▄▄▄▄▄▄▄▄▄▄▄▄▄▄▄▄▄▄▄▄▄▄▄▄▄▄▄▄▄▄▄▄▄▄▄▄▄▄▄▄

If $X$ is any random variable and $k$ is a constant,

$$\text{Var}(kX) = k^2 \, \text{Var}(X)$$

**Property 4.6** ▄▄▄▄▄▄▄▄▄▄▄▄▄▄▄▄▄▄▄▄▄▄▄▄▄▄▄▄▄▄▄▄▄▄▄▄▄▄▄▄▄▄

If $X$ is any random variable and $k$ is a constant,

$$\text{Var}(X + k) = \text{Var}(X)$$

Note that Property 4.5 implies that $\sigma_{kX} = |k|\sigma_X$. For example, if $k = -1$, $\sigma_{-X} = \sigma_X$; $\sigma_{-X}$ cannot be equal to $-\sigma_X$, as the standard deviation of a random variable cannot be negative. The proofs of Properties 4.4 through 4.6 are left to the instructor.

For random variables $X$ and $Y$ with probability functions given, respectively, by

$$p(x) = \begin{cases} \dfrac{1}{4} & \text{for } x = \pm 1 \\[2mm] \dfrac{1}{2} & \text{for } x = 0 \end{cases}$$

and

$$p(y) = \begin{cases} \dfrac{1}{4} & \text{for } y = \pm 10 \\[2mm] \dfrac{1}{2} & \text{for } y = 0 \end{cases}$$

we have the relationship $Y = 10X$. From Property 4.5 we should have

$$\text{Var}(Y) = 100 \, \text{Var}(X)$$

$\text{Var}(Y)$ was found to be 50 and $\text{Var}(X) = 1/2$. Thus

$$\text{Var}(Y) = 50 = 100 \left(\frac{1}{2}\right) = 100 \, \text{Var}(X)$$

so this relationship is valid in this case. Also, $\sigma_Y = 10\sigma_X$ is valid in this case, as $\sqrt{50} = 10(1/\sqrt{2})$.

**Exercises 4.3**
▄▄▄▄▄▄▄▄
_____

**4.16** Using the information given in exercise 4.1, find the expected number of shots taken on the par 4 hole by a professional golfer. Find the variance of this random variable.

**4.17** Using the probability function found in exercise 4.2, find the expected number of games played by the two teams in a best-of-five-game series. Find the variance of this random variable.

**4.18** Using the probability function found in exercise 4.3, find the expected number of hurricanes on the Caribbean island described. Find the variance of this random variable.

**4.19** Using the probability function found in exercise 4.4, find the expected sum on the toss of two fair dice.

**4.20** The number of universities and colleges in each of the fifty states in 1978–79 is given below.

| State | No. of Institutions | State | No. of Institutions |
|-------|---------------------|-------|---------------------|
| AL | 58 | MT | 13 |
| AK | 16 | NE | 31 |
| AZ | 23 | NV | 6 |
| AR | 34 | NH | 24 |
| CA | 262 | NJ | 63 |
| CO | 41 | NM | 19 |
| CT | 47 | NY | 286 |
| DE | 10 | NC | 126 |
| FL | 77 | ND | 16 |
| GA | 72 | OH | 133 |
| HI | 12 | OK | 43 |
| ID | 9 | OR | 43 |
| IL | 154 | PA | 178 |
| IN | 66 | RI | 13 |
| IA | 62 | SC | 61 |
| KS | 52 | SD | 18 |
| KY | 42 | TN | 76 |
| LA | 32 | TX | 147 |
| ME | 27 | UT | 14 |
| MD | 54 | VT | 21 |
| MA | 119 | VI | 71 |
| MI | 96 | WA | 49 |
| MN | 65 | WV | 28 |
| MS | 46 | WI | 62 |
| MO | 84 | WY | 8 |

*Source:* U.S. Department of Health, Education, and Welfare, National Center for Education Statistics, "Digest of Education Statistics, 1980," pp. 112–113.

**a.** Assume that each state is given equal probability of 1/50 of being chosen at random. Using Minitab, find the value of $E(X)$, where $X$ represents the number of institutions of higher education in the state.

**b.** Using Minitab, find the variance of this population by computing

$$\sigma_X^2 = \sum_{x=1}^{50} \frac{[x - E(X)]^2}{50}$$

**c.** Find the population standard deviation.

**4.21**  **a.** Suppose a discrete random variable $X$ has the following probability function:

| $x$ | 0 | 1 | 2 | 3 |
|---|---|---|---|---|
| $p(x)$ | 0.1 | 0.2 | 0.3 | 0.4 |

Find $E(X)$, $\sigma_X^2$, and $\sigma_X$.

**b.** Consider the random variable $Y = 10X$. Find the probability function of $Y$ and verify Properties 4.2 and 4.5.

**4.22**  A professor is on time for his class 60 percent of the time. Assuming the times of his arrivals are independent, calculate the expected number of times he will be on time over the 45 class meetings. Then determine the expected number of times he will not be on time. What is the variance of each of these two random variables?

**4.23**  The probability that first-class letters from Tampa, Florida to Des Moines, Iowa will be delivered within three days is 0.9.

**a.** If 100 such letters are sent and $X$ is defined to be the number that arrive within three days, find $E(X)$. What assumptions have you made?

**b.** What is the value of the variance $\sigma_X^2$?

**4.24**  It can be shown that for any integer $n$

$$\sum_{i=1}^{n} i = \frac{n(n + 1)}{2}$$

that is, the right-hand term is an expression for the sum of the first $n$ integers. If a number is to be chosen at random from $S = \{1, 2, \ldots, n\}$, we can assign each integer equal probability. What is the expected value of a number so chosen?

**4.25**  Find the variance of the random variable of exercise 4.7.

**4.26**  Let $-X$ be the negative of the random variable in exercise 4.21.

**a.** Find the probability function for this random variable.

**b.** Find $\text{Var}(-X)$ and show that it equals $\text{Var}(X)$.

**4.27**  The random variable $X$ has the following probability function:

| $x$ | $-2$ | $-1$ | 0 | 1 | 2 |
|---|---|---|---|---|---|
| $p(x)$ | 1/9 | 2/9 | 3/9 | 2/9 | 1/9 |

**a.** Find $E(X)$ and $\text{Var}(X)$.

**b.** Let $Y = X + 10$. Find $E(Y)$ and $\text{Var}(Y)$ by finding the probability function of $Y$.

**c.** Verify Properties 4.3 and 4.6 for $Y = X + 10$.

**4.28**  Use the command RANDOM to simulate the scores of 200 golfers on the hole described in exercise 4.1. AVERAGE these observations. Is this value close to the value for $E(X)$ found in exercise 4.16? Is it equal to it?

**4.29**  Use the command RANDOM to simulate the number of games played in 200 best-of-five-game series between two equally good teams. Use the command MEAN on these values. Is this mean close to the value for $E(X)$ found in exercise 4.17? Is it equal to it?

## 4.4

### The Geometric and Poisson Random Variables

Most of the discrete random variables discussed in the previous section were defined for finite outcome spaces. In Example 4.6, however, a discrete random variable was defined on the countably infinite outcome space $P = \{1, 2, \ldots\}$, the set of all positive integers. There we considered making independent trials, with a success or a failure on each trial, until a success was achieved. On every trial the probability of a success was taken to be 1/2. Obtaining the outcome $k$ meant that exactly $k$ trials were needed for the first success to be attained. In this section we consider two families of random variables defined on countably infinite outcome spaces: the geometric random variable and the Poisson random variable. Such outcome spaces are to some extent mathematical fictions. A real letter carrier, unlike the one in Example 4.6, would not return more than 100 times to try to deliver a letter! Nevertheless the two families of random variables to be discussed have important real-world applications.

The geometric random variable describes the number of independent trials needed for the first success to occur. The outcome space in this case is of the following form:

$$S = \{S, FS, FFS, FFFS, \ldots\}$$

The geometric random variable can have as values any of the positive integers $P = \{1, 2, 3, \ldots\}$. This random variable is used to describe such variables as the number of trips a letter carrier had to make to deliver a registered letter, the number of visits a student had to make to find a professor in his office, and the number of attempts a high jumper had to make to jump more than six feet.

The Poisson random variable can be thought of as describing the number of occurrences of an infrequent event during a fixed period of time. The Poisson random variable can take on any of the values $Q = \{0, 1, 2, \ldots\}$. Examples of this type of variable are the number of hurricanes that hit the east coast of Florida during the month of September, the number of phone calls that arrive at an exchange from 10:00 A.M. to 10:05 A.M. on a Wednesday morning, and the number of severe accidents in a large factory during a month.

In the case of the geometric random variable, the assumption is made that success occurs with probability $p$, where $0 < p < 1$. We can easily see that the probability of success on the first trial is $p$. For the first success to occur on the second trial, we must have the outcome FS, which has probability $qp$ because of the independence of the trials (where $q = 1 - p$). Similarly, the probability that the first success will occur on trial three is $P(\text{FFS}) = q^2 p$. This leads to the following definition.

---

**Definition 4.6** ▬▬▬▬▬▬▬▬▬▬▬▬▬▬▬▬▬▬▬▬▬▬▬

geometric random variable

The **geometric random variable** $X$ has the probability function

$$p(x) = q^{x-1} p \qquad \text{for } x = 1, 2, \ldots$$

---

**120**  CHAPTER 4  DISCRETE AND CONTINUOUS RANDOM VARIABLES

For this function to be a true probability function, we must have

$$\sum_{x=1}^{\infty} p(x) = \sum_{x=1}^{\infty} q^{x-1} p = 1$$

It can be shown that the sum of the infinite geometric series for $|q| < 1$ is

$$1 + q + q^2 + \cdots + q^{x-1} + q^x + \cdots = \frac{1}{1 - q} = \frac{1}{p}$$

If we multiply both sides of the above equation by $p$, it is easy to see that the sum of the geometric probabilities is equal to 1:

$$p + pq + pq^2 + \cdots + pq^{x-1} + pq^x + \cdots = p\left(\frac{1}{1 - q}\right)$$
$$= p\left(\frac{1}{p}\right) = \frac{p}{p} = 1$$

or

$$\sum_{x=1}^{\infty} q^{x-1} p = 1$$

**Example 4.13**

Suppose the probability that a high jumper will clear six feet is 1/4. Assuming that her attempts are independent, we find the following probabilities that her first success during an afternoon practice will be on trial $x$.

| $x$ | $p(x)$ |
|---|---|
| 1 | $\dfrac{1}{4}$ |
| 2 | $\dfrac{3}{4}\left(\dfrac{1}{4}\right) = \dfrac{3}{16}$ |
| 3 | $\left(\dfrac{3}{4}\right)^2 \left(\dfrac{1}{4}\right) = \dfrac{9}{64}$ |
| $\vdots$ | |
| $x$ | $\left(\dfrac{3}{4}\right)^{x-1} \left(\dfrac{1}{4}\right)$ |

Hence the probability that exactly three trials will be required to achieve success is 9/64. The probability of success in three or fewer trials is $1/4 + 3/16 + 9/64 = 37/64$. The probability that more than three attempts will be required is thus $1 - 37/64 = 27/64$.

The expected value and variance of a geometric random variable are given by

$$E(X) = \frac{1}{p} \quad \text{and} \quad \text{Var}(X) = \frac{q}{p^2} \qquad \qquad \textbf{4.2}$$

Once more, demonstrations of these results are left to the instructor.

For the high jumper of Example 4.13, $E(X) = 1/(1/4) = 4$, so the expected number of attempts required to make a successful jump is 4.

Similarly, suppose we repeatedly and independently select an integer from the set $\{0, 1, 2, \ldots, 9\}$. Let a success be defined as obtaining a zero. The number of attempts $X$ until the first zero is obtained has a geometric distribution with $p = 1/10$. Thus the expected number of selections required to obtain the first zero is $1/(1/10) = 10$.

It can be verified by direct multiplication that for any fixed positive integer $N$,

$$(1 - q^N) = (1 - q)(1 + q + q^2 + \cdots + q^{N-1})$$

The right-hand side of this identity is equal to $p \sum_{x=1}^{N} q^{x-1}$, the probability that the first success in independent trials is attained on trial $N$ or before. Thus the probability that more than $N$ trials are required to obtain the first success is given by the elementary expression

$$1 - (1 - q^N) = q^N$$

Hence the probability that the high jumper of Example 4.13 requires more than three jumps to clear the bar is $(3/4)^N = (3/4)^3 = 27/64$, which agrees with the result found in that example. Similarly, the probability that we must make more than four trials in order to select a zero from the integers $\{0, 1, 2, \ldots, 9\}$ is $(9/10)^4 = 0.6561$.

In the Poisson case we are considering situations in which the random variable is counting the number of occurrences of a relatively rare event. In order to use the Poisson random variable, we must know or assume the expected number of occurrences of the infrequent event in the fixed period of time. For example, it may be known from historical data that on the average three hurricanes hit the east coast of Florida in September. In the case of the telephone exchange, the expected number of calls arriving during the period from 10:00 A.M. to 10:05 A.M. might be assumed to be 5. Assuming that $\mu = E(X)$ denotes the expected number of such occurrences, the Poisson random variable has a probability function defined as follows.

---

**Definition 4.7** ━━━━━━━━━━━━━━━━━━━━━━━━━━━━━━

Poisson random variable

The **Poisson random variable** has the probability function

$$p(x) = e^{-\mu}\mu^x/x! \qquad \text{for } x = 0, 1, \ldots$$

---

It will be assumed (correctly) that these probabilities satisfy $\sum_{x=0}^{\infty} p(x) = 1$.

**POISSON**
**PDF**
**CDF**

This probability function would, in general, be awkward to use, but Minitab has a simple subcommand **POISSON** which, used with **PDF** and **CDF**, permits easy calculation of the individual and cumulative probabilities for a given value of $\mu = E(X)$.

**Example 4.14**

Consider the case of the number of hurricanes, $X$, hitting the east coast of Florida during September. Assume that $\mu = 3$. The commands PDF and CDF have been used with $\mu = 3$ to find the probability of exactly $k$ hurricanes in September, given by

$$p(k) = \frac{e^{-3}3^k}{k!}$$

as well as the probability of $k$ or fewer hurricanes, given by

$$p(X \leqslant k) = \sum_{x=0}^{k} \frac{e^{-3}3^x}{x!}$$

for $k = 0, 1, 2, \ldots, 12$. The Minitab output is shown in Exhibit 4.2.

**Exhibit 4.2**

```
MTB > PDF;                              MTB > CDF;
SUBC> POISSON MEAN = 3.                 SUBC> POISSON MEAN = 3.

  POISSON WITH MEAN =   3.000             POISSON WITH MEAN =   3.000
      K          P( X = K)                   K   P( X LESS OR = K)
      0            0.0498                      0           0.0498
      1            0.1494                      1           0.1991
      2            0.2240                      2           0.4232
      3            0.2240                      3           0.6472
      4            0.1680                      4           0.8153
      5            0.1008                      5           0.9161
      6            0.0504                      6           0.9665
      7            0.0216                      7           0.9881
      8            0.0081                      8           0.9962
      9            0.0027                      9           0.9989
     10            0.0008                     10           0.9997
     11            0.0002                     11           0.9999
     12            0.0001                     12           1.0000
     13            0.0000
```

Many probabilities of interest can easily be read from this output. For example, the probabilities of 0, 1, 2, 3, and 4 hurricanes are 0.0498, 0.1494, 0.2240, 0.2240, and 0.1680, respectively. The probability of six or more hurricanes in a single September is $1 - p(X \leqslant 5) = 1 - 0.9161 = 0.0839$ (about one chance in twelve).

**Example 4.15**

For the example of $X$ telephone calls arriving in a five-minute period, assume $\mu = 5$. Exhibit 4.3 shows the output obtained when the commands PDF and CDF were used with $\mu = 5$.

**Exhibit 4.3**

```
MTB > PDF;
SUBC> POISSON MEAN = 5.

     POISSON WITH MEAN =    5.000
       K           P( X = K)
       0             0.0067
       1             0.0337
       2             0.0842
       3             0.1404
       4             0.1755
       5             0.1755
       6             0.1462
       7             0.1044
       8             0.0653
       9             0.0363
      10             0.0181
      11             0.0082
      12             0.0034
      13             0.0013
      14             0.0005
      15             0.0002
      16             0.0000
MTB > CDF;
SUBC> POISSON MEAN = 5.

     POISSON WITH MEAN =    5.000
       K   P( X LESS OR = K)
       0             0.0067
       1             0.0404
       2             0.1247
       3             0.2650
       4             0.4405
       5             0.6160
       6             0.7622
       7             0.8666
       8             0.9319
       9             0.9682
      10             0.9863
      11             0.9945
      12             0.9980
      13             0.9993
      14             0.9998
      15             0.9999
      16             1.0000
```

The probabilities of $k$ phone calls are given for $k = 0, 1, \ldots, 16$, as are cumulative probabilities for $k = 0, 1, 2, \ldots, 16$. For example, the probability of ten or fewer calls is 0.9863. The probability of six or more calls in the five-minute period is $1 - p(5 \text{ or fewer calls}) = 1 - 0.6160 = 0.3840$.

The Poisson random variable is widely used to give a probabilistic model or description of the number of occurrences of a relatively rare event in a fixed period of time. It can also be used to give the probability of the number of occurrences of a rare event in space. For example, the number of houses painted orange in one square mile of a suburban town might well be described probabilistically by a Poisson random variable.

The Poisson random variable has the unusual property that $E(X) = \text{Var}(X) = \mu$. This property is not generally valid for other random variables.

Although the Poisson random variable may take on only nonnegative integers as values, it is not necessary that the expected value of $X$ be an integer. To emphasize this fact, the Minitab subcommand POISSON was used with $\mu = E(X) = 7.5$; the output is shown in Exhibit 4.4.

**Exhibit 4.4**

```
MTB > PDF;                              MTB > CDF;
SUBC> POISSON MEAN = 7.5.               SUBC> POISSON MEAN = 7.5.

  POISSON WITH MEAN =   7.500             POISSON WITH MEAN =   7.500
      K         P( X = K)                     K   P( X LESS OR = K)
      0           0.0006                       0         0.0006
      1           0.0041                       1         0.0047
      2           0.0156                       2         0.0203
      3           0.0389                       3         0.0591
      4           0.0729                       4         0.1321
      5           0.1094                       5         0.2414
      6           0.1367                       6         0.3782
      7           0.1465                       7         0.5246
      8           0.1373                       8         0.6620
      9           0.1144                       9         0.7764
     10           0.0858                      10         0.8622
     11           0.0585                      11         0.9208
     12           0.0366                      12         0.9573
     13           0.0211                      13         0.9784
     14           0.0113                      14         0.9897
     15           0.0057                      15         0.9954
     16           0.0026                      16         0.9980
     17           0.0012                      17         0.9992
     18           0.0005                      18         0.9997
     19           0.0002                      19         0.9999
     20           0.0001                      20         1.0000
     21           0.0000
```

The RANDOM command in Minitab permits the simulation of repeated observations from a Poisson distribution with a specified expected value. The RANDOM command was used similarly in Chapter 3 to simulate repeated observations from a binomial distribution with specified values of $n$ and $p$. In the output in Exhibit 4.5, the numbers of hurricanes to hit the east coast of Florida during 50 Septembers were simulated with the number expected per year ($\mu$) equal to 3. The values were stored in C1 but not printed out. In the output in Exhibit 4.6, the numbers of calls to arrive in 100 half-hour periods were simulated with the expected number to arrive per half-hour ($\mu$) equal to 5. The means ($\bar{x} = 3.02$,

**Exhibit 4.5**

```
MTB > NOTE SIMULATION OF NUMBER OF HURRICANES
MTB > BASE = 1000
MTB > RANDOM 50 OBSERVATIONS IN C1;
SUBC> POISSON MEAN = 3.
MTB > AVERAGE C1
      MEAN    =       3.0200
MTB > STDEV C1
      ST.DEV. =       1.8680
MTB > HISTOGRAM C1

Histogram of C1    N = 50

Midpoint     Count
       0         2    **
       1         8    ********
       2        12    ************
       3        10    **********
       4        11    ***********
       5         1    *
       6         5    *****
       7         0
       8         0
       9         0
      10         1    *
```

the average of the 50 observations of the number of hurricanes, and $\bar{x} = 5.20$, the average number of calls) are estimates of the population values $\mu = 3$ and $\mu = 5$. The computer-generated histograms of the observations in each of the two simulations indicate the variability that one observes when sampling from a theoretical distribution.

**Exhibit 4.6**

```
MTB > NOTE SIMULATION OF NUMBER OF CALLS
MTB > RANDOM 100 OBSERVATIONS OF CALLS IN C2;
SUBC> POISSON MEAN = 5.
MTB > AVERAGE C2
      MEAN    =       5.2000
MTB > STDEV C2
      ST.DEV. =       2.3181
MTB > HISTOGRAM C2

Histogram of C2    N = 100

Midpoint     Count
       0         1    *
       1         6    ******
       2         6    ******
       3        11    **********
       4        16    ****************
       5        11    **********
       6        17    *****************
       7        19    *******************
       8         7    *******
       9         3    ***
      10         1    *
      11         2    **
```

**4.30** **a.** The probability that an archer will hit a bull's-eye is 1/5. If she takes consecutive shots until she hits a bull's-eye, what is the probability the first bull's-eye will occur on the first attempt? The second attempt? The $k$th attempt? Assume independence.

**b.** What is the expected number of trials required to obtain the first bull's-eye?

**4.31** **a.** The probability that an electronically operated door will open is 0.99. If successive openings are considered independent trials, what is the probability function of $X$, the number of trials until the first time the door fails to open?

**b.** What is the expected number of trials until the first failure?

**c.** What is the probability the first failure will occur after the tenth trial?

**4.32** **a.** The probability that a professor will be on time for class is 1/2. If trials are assumed to be independent, what is the probability that the first class she is late for will be the first class? The second class? The $k$th class?

**b.** Using the fact that for $|x| < 1$

$$\sum_{k=0}^{\infty} x^k = 1 + x + x^2 + \cdots + \cdots = \frac{1}{1-x}$$

find the probability that the first class she is late for is (i) an odd-numbered class and (ii) an even-numbered class.

**4.33** Let $X$ have a geometric distribution with $p = 1/6$. Describe a real-world situation for which this probability model would be realistic.

**4.34** Accidents occur at a busy intersection at the rate of one per week. Find the probability function of $X$, the number of accidents per week. Use Minitab to evaluate the probability functions for $x = 0, 1, 2, 3, 4, 5, 6, 7$.

**4.35** Police call a service station to tow away cars three times a day, on average. What is the probability that the station will be called two or fewer times on a given day? more than four times? exactly three times?

**4.36** Arrivals of customers at a small bank on a Wednesday morning between 11:00 and 11:20 A.M. are random events in time. Historical data show that on average the number of such arrivals, $X$, is four.

**a.** Using Minitab, find the probability function of $X$.

**b.** The two tellers at this bank become swamped if eight or more customers arrive during this period of time. What is the probability that eight or more customers will arrive?

**4.37** The Poisson distribution can be used to approximate the binomial distribution when $n$ is large, $p$ is small, and $np = \mu$ is known. Assume that $X$ is binomially distributed with $n = 100$ and $p = 1/100$. Use PDF with the subcommand BINOMIAL to find the probability function of $X$. Compare the probabilities found with those given by the subcommand POISSON with the appropriate value of $\mu$. Do the Poisson probabilities appear to be good approximations of the corresponding binomial probabilities?

**4.38** Assume that a typist makes an error once in every 250 keystrokes, and that the paragraph about to be typed requires 1000 keystrokes. Use CDF and PDF with the subcommand POISSON to answer the following questions.

**a.** What is the expected number of errors made by the typist in typing the paragraph?

**b.** What is the probability that the typist will make two or fewer errors in typing the paragraph? three or fewer? four or fewer?

**c.** What is the most probable number or numbers of errors?

**4.39** The number of calls per day to an ambulance service can be thought of as a Poisson random variable with $\mu = 2.5$. Use Minitab to simulate the number of calls on 1000 days. Compare the relative frequencies of 0, 1, 2, . . . , 10 calls with the corresponding Poisson probabilities.

**4.40** Let $X$ have the Poisson distribution with $\mu = 5$. Using the Minitab output shown in Exhibit 4.3, construct a probability histogram for this random variable. Is this probability histogram similar to the histogram for the 100 simulated observations of this distribution given in Exhibit 4.5?

**\*4.41** Suppose $X$ has a geometric distribution (with parameter $P$).
**a.** Find $P(X > k)$ for any positive integer $k$.
**b.** Find $P(X > k + j)$ for positive integers $k$ and $j$.
**c.** Find $P(X > k + j | x > k)$ and compare this probability with $P(X > j)$. Express this relationship in words.

## 4.5
## Continuous Random Variables

A discrete random variable, as we have seen, is a function, defined on $S$, that can have a finite or countably infinite number of values. A continuous random variable, on the other hand, is a function, defined on a sample space $S$, that takes on values on an interval of the real line. Typically the sample space is considered to be an interval of the real line, and the function $X$ is taken to be the identity function $X(s) = s$ for any $s \in S$. The interval defining $S$ can be bounded or unbounded. For example, $S_1 = \{x | 0 \leqslant x \leqslant 1\}$ is a bounded interval of the real line consisting of all points on the interval from 0 to 1. On the other hand, the interval $S_2 = \{t | 0 < t < \infty\}$, the set of all positive real numbers, is unbounded. As $X(s) = s$ maps any point of $S$ to itself, the sample space for this random variable can be thought of as $S$ itself. There are many real-world situations that can be described by a continuous random variable. For example, each point of $S_1 = \{x | 0 \leqslant x \leqslant 1\}$ might be considered to represent the proportion of a water tank that is full. Similarly, each point of $S_2 = \{t | 0 < t < \infty\}$ might represent the time in seconds between a fixed time (say 5:00 P.M.) and the time a telephone call arrives. Many variables, including distances, heights, lengths, temperatures, and voltages, are naturally thought of as taking on any possible value on an interval of the real line.

A continuous random variable is formally defined as follows.

---

**Definition 4.8** ▬▬▬▬▬▬▬▬▬▬▬▬▬▬▬▬▬▬▬▬▬▬▬▬▬▬▬▬

continuous random variable

A **continuous random variable** $X$ is a function that assigns a real value to every point of a sample space $S$ in such a way that the possible values assigned make up an interval of the real line.

---

In this text the continuous function $X(s)$ will always be thought of as the identity function $X(s) = s$. Thus the sample space $S$ can be thought of as the set of possible values achieved by such a random variable. Some other examples of continuous outcome spaces are

$$S_3 = \{x \mid 28 \leqslant x \leqslant 32\}$$
$$S_4 = \{y \mid 9.5 \leqslant y \leqslant 60\}$$

$S_3$ could represent the barometric pressure at a given location at noon, measured in inches of mercury. Similarly, $S_4$ might represent the number of seconds required by a high school student to run 100 meters.

It is not possible to assign a positive probability $P_x$ to every number on an interval of the real line and still satisfy the condition $\Sigma_{\text{all } x} P_x = 1$. Thus probabilities cannot be assigned to continuous random variables in the same way as they were to discrete random variables. The idea of a probability histogram, however, does generalize. If you look at the probability histograms in Figures 4.1 and 4.2, you will note that the total area under each histogram is 1. Probabilities for a continuous random variable are assigned to an interval by means of a probability density function $f(x)$, which generalizes the idea of a probability histogram as follows.

---

**probability density function**

**Definition 4.9** ▬▬▬▬▬▬▬▬▬▬▬▬▬▬▬▬▬▬▬▬▬▬▬▬▬▬▬▬

A **probability density function** $f(x)$ for a continuous random variable is a function that satisfies the following conditions:
   **a.** $f(x) \geqslant 0$ for all $x$
   **b.** the area under $f(x)$ and above the $x$ axis is 1.

---

For a continuous random variable we assign a probability to an interval $[a, b]$ by defining $P(a \leqslant X \leqslant b)$ to be the area on the interval $[a, b]$ between the probability density function $f(x)$ and the $x$ axis.

## Example 4.16

A graph of the probability density function

$$f(x) = \begin{cases} 2x & \text{if } 0 \leqslant x \leqslant 1 \\ 0 & \text{otherwise} \end{cases}$$

defined on $S = \{x \mid 0 \leqslant x \leqslant 1\}$, is given in Figure 4.3.

The area under $f(x)$ is the area of a right triangle with base $b = 1$ and height $h = 2$. Clearly, the area of this triangle, $(1/2)bh$, is 1. Notice that $f(x)$ itself is not a probability, as it takes on values greater than 1. The probability, $P(0 \leqslant X \leqslant 1/2)$, is the area under $f(x)$ and above the $x$ axis, between $x = 0$ and

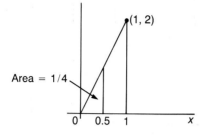

Area = 1/4

(1, 2)

0  0.5  1     x

**Figure 4.3**

$x = 1/2$. This area is that of a triangle with base $b = 1/2$ and height $h = 1$, so

$$P\left(0 \leqslant X \leqslant \frac{1}{2}\right) = \left(\frac{1}{2}\right)bh = \frac{1}{4}$$

As the total area under $f(x) = 2x$ on [0, 1] is 1,

$$P\left(\frac{1}{2} \leqslant X \leqslant 1\right) = 1 - P\left(0 \leqslant X \leqslant \frac{1}{2}\right) = 1 - \frac{1}{4} = \frac{3}{4}$$

Application of elementary principles of geometry confirms that the area of the trapezoid bounded by the $x$ axis, $x = 1/2$, $x = 1$, and $f(x) = 2x$ is 3/4.

For a continuous random variable with probability density function $f(x)$, consider the probability that $X = c$—that is, the probability that the random variable has a particular value $c$. This probability corresponds to the area of a rectangle with a base $b = 0$ and a height of $f(c)$, which is 0. Hence, the probability assigned to any fixed value $c$ by a continuous random variable is 0. A probability density function may assign positive probability to an interval, even though each point is assigned zero probability. The important idea is that for continuous random variables, probabilities are areas.

Frequently continuous distributions are symmetric about a vertical line $x = c$. In Figure 4.4 the probability density function is symmetric about $x = 0$. It is useful to know whether a function is symmetric, because the expected value, $E(X)$, of a random variable with a symmetric probability density function is equal to the value about which the probability density function is symmetric. (There are continuous random variables for which $E(X)$ does not exist, but they will not be considered here.) Hence, the random variable portrayed in Figure 4.4 has an expected value of 0. In general, the expected value of a continuous random variable cannot be defined without using calculus. Nevertheless we will frequently refer to the expected value of such a random variable, denoted by $E(X)$ or by $\mu$. For those with some calculus background, the formal definition of $E(X)$ is given here.

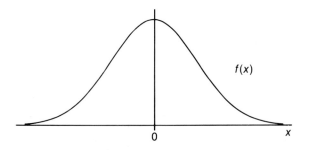

f(x)

0

x

**Figure 4.4**

**A Symmetric Probability Density Function**

**Definition 4.10** ▬▬▬

expected value

The **expected value** of a continuous random variable with probability density function $f(x)$ is

$$\mu = E(X) = \int_{-\infty}^{\infty} xf(x)\, dx$$

For Figure 4.3, the reader can check to find $E(X) = 2/3$.

**Example 4.17**

Consider the probability density function graphed in Figure 4.5. The distribution is assumed to be that of the true net weights, $W$, in ounces, of boxes of a certain brand of breakfast food. Based on the symmetry about $w = 16$, we observe that $E(W) = 16$. Probabilities for $W$ can be found by elementary geometry. For example, $P(W \leqslant 15.5)$ is given by the area of the shaded triangle. Using similar

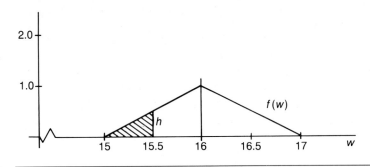

**Figure 4.5**

triangles, we have $[h/(1/2)] = 1$. Hence $h = 1/2$. Thus

$$P(W \leqslant 15.5) = \left(\frac{1}{2}\right)bh = \left(\frac{1}{2}\right)\left(\frac{1}{2}\right)\left(\frac{1}{2}\right) = \frac{1}{8}$$

By symmetry, $P(W \geqslant 16.5) = 1/8$. Using the law of complements for probabilities, we have

$$P(15.5 \leqslant W \leqslant 16.5) = 1 - P(W \leqslant 15.5) - P(W \geqslant 16.5)$$
$$= 1 - \frac{1}{8} - \frac{1}{8} = \frac{3}{4}$$

This result can be interpreted to mean that, in the long run, 75 percent of the boxes of this breakfast food have a net weight within a half-ounce of the value $E(W) = 16$.

The definition given below of the variance of a continuous random variable $X$ is exactly analogous to the definition of the variance of a discrete random variable given in Definition 4.4.

---

**Definition 4.11** ▬▬▬▬▬▬▬▬▬▬▬▬▬▬▬▬▬▬▬▬▬▬▬▬▬▬

The variance of a continuous random variable with probability density function $f(x)$ is given by

$$\sigma^2 = \text{Var}(X) = E(X - \mu)^2 = \int_{-\infty}^{\infty} (x - \mu)^2 f(x)\, dx$$

---

As for the expectation, the value of $\sigma^2$ can only be computed using calculus. The variance $\sigma^2$ [or $\text{Var}(X)$], however, may still be interpreted as the average squared distance of the values of the random variable $X$ from the center of the distribution, as defined by $\mu = E(X)$. Large values of $\sigma^2$ correspond to distributions that are spread out about $\mu$. Properties 4.1 through 4.6 of $E(X)$ and $\text{Var}(X)$ for a discrete random variable hold for a continuous random variable as well.

This section concludes with a discussion of the median $m$ of a continuous random variable.

---

**Definition 4.12** ▬▬▬▬▬▬▬▬▬▬▬▬▬▬▬▬▬▬▬▬▬▬▬▬▬▬

**median of a continuous random variable**

The **median of a continuous random variable** $X$ is a number $m$ satisfying $P(X \leqslant m) = P(X \geqslant m) = 1/2$.

---

The median divides the population in half in terms of probability. In the long run 50 percent of the observations of $X$ will exceed $m$ and 50 percent will be less than $m$. For the random variable of Example 4.16, we find that

$$P(X \leqslant a) = (1/2)a(2a) = a^2$$

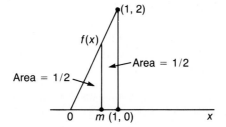

**Figure 4.6**

The Median of a Continuous Random Variable

using the expression for the area of a triangle. Hence $m$ must satisfy $P(X \leqslant m) = m^2 = 1/2$, and we have $m = \sqrt{2}/2 = 0.707$, as illustrated in Figure 4.6. If the probability density function of a continuous random variable is symmetric about a value $c$, both $E(X)$ and the median $m$ will have the value $c$. Hence, for the random variable described by the probability density function of Figure 4.4, both the expected value and the median equal 0.

**Exercises 4.5**

**4.42** Use the probability density function of $X$ graphed below to find the following probabilities.
  **a.** $P(X \leqslant 0)$
  **b.** $P(X \leqslant -1)$
  **c.** $P(X \geqslant 1)$
  **d.** $P(X \leqslant 1)$
  **e.** $P(X \geqslant -1)$
  **f.** $P(X = 0)$

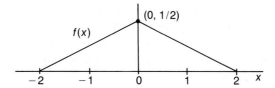

**4.43** The function

$$f(x) = \begin{cases} 1 \text{ on } [0, 1] \\ 0 \text{ elsewhere} \end{cases}$$

is the probability density function of the uniform random variable $U$ on $[0, 1]$.
  **a.** Show that the area under $f(x)$ and above the $x$ axis is 1.
  **b.** Find $P(0.1 \leqslant U \leqslant 0.3)$ and $P(0.5 \leqslant U \leqslant 0.7)$.
  **c.** In general, what can be said about the probability assigned to intervals of equal length lying entirely within $[0, 1]$?
  **d.** Determine the value of $E(U)$ and the median of $U$. *Hint*: Use the symmetry of the density function.

**4.44**  **a.** The uniform random variable on $[a, b]$ has a probability density function that is constant on $[a, b]$ and zero for values not on $[a, b]$. What is the value of this constant?

**b.** What is the expected value of this random variable? *Hint*: Draw a graph of the probability density function.

**4.45** The function $f(x)$ shown below is a probability density function.

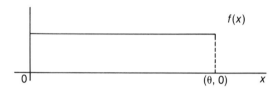

**a.** What must the height of this rectangle be as a function of $\theta$?
**b.** Find $P(0 \leqslant X \leqslant \theta/2)$.
**c.** Find $P[0 \leqslant X \leqslant (3/4)\theta]$.
**d.** Find $P(0 \leqslant X \leqslant k\theta)$ for $0 \leqslant k \leqslant 1$.

**4.46** The UNIFORM subcommand used with RANDOM permits the selection of a random sample of size $n$ from the distribution described in exercise 4.43. Select 200 such samples and AVERAGE them. What is $E(U)$? Is the average you have computed near $E(U)$? Is it equal to it?

**4.47** Consider the continuous random variable $X$ with the probability density function indicated in the figure below.

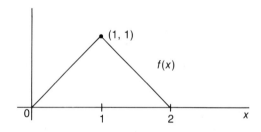

**a.** Show that the area under $f(x)$ and above the $x$ axis is 1.
**b.** Find $P(0.5 \leqslant X \leqslant 1.5)$.
**c.** Find $P(X \geqslant 1.5)$.
**d.** Find $P(X \leqslant 0.5)$.
**e.** This function is the probability density function of the sum of two independent uniform random variables on $[0, 1]$. To verify this fact, use RANDOM to select 200 observations from this distribution. Place the observations in two columns and add the corresponding elements. Then, using the COPY command with the subcommand USE and the COUNT command, find the proportion of these 200 sums on the intervals $(0.5, 1.5)$, $(1.5, 2.0)$, and $(0.0, 0.5)$. Compare these proportions with your answers to parts b, c, and d.
**f.** Find $E(X)$ and the median of $X$.

**4.48** The probability density function for a continuous random variable $X$ is presented in the figure below.

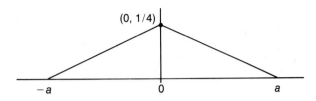

(0, 1/4)

$-a$      0      $a$

**a.** What is the value of $a$?
**b.** Find $P(3 \leqslant X \leqslant a)$ and $P(2 \leqslant X \leqslant a)$.
**c.** Find $P(-3 \leqslant X \leqslant 3)$ and $P(-2 \leqslant X \leqslant 2)$.

**4.49** The probability density function of a continuous random variable $X$ is defined by

$$f(x) = \begin{cases} 2(1 - x) & \text{if } 0 \leqslant x \leqslant 1 \\ 0 & \text{otherwise} \end{cases}$$

**a.** Graph this probability density function.
**b.** Find the median of $X$.

## 4.6

### The Normal Random Variable

**normal random variable**

**standard normal variable**

A particular continuous random variable called the Gaussian or **normal random variable** plays a crucial role in probability and statistics for many reasons. The distribution was discovered by A. DeMoivre in 1733, but it was first thoroughly investigated by the mathematicians C. F. Gauss and P. S. Laplace in the late eighteenth and early nineteenth centuries. Actually, the normal random variable is not a single random variable but rather a family of random variables. The normal family gives a different distribution corresponding to every pair of values of $\mu = E(X)$ and $\sigma^2 = \text{Var}(X)$. One reason this random variable is important is that the sums of independent random variables can be proved to have approximately a normal distribution if the number of summands is large and the contribution of any particular summand is small. Many observable random variables can be thought of as arising from such sums. For example, yields (per acre) of wheat can be thought of as the total contribution of a large number of individual stalks; weight gains in infants from birth to one year of age can be thought of as the sum of 365 daily contributions. It is not hard to think of other examples.

Fortunately, questions concerning probabilities of any normal random variable can be reduced to questions about a single normal random variable if $\mu$ and $\sigma^2$ are known. This single normal variable is called the **standard normal variable.**

The standard normal random variable, which is universally denoted by $Z$, has a probability density function given by

$$f(z) = \left(\frac{1}{\sqrt{2\pi}}\right)e^{-z^2/2}, \quad -\infty < z < \infty \qquad \textbf{4.3}$$

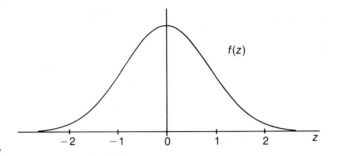

**Figure 4.7**

Probability Density Function for Standard Normal Random Variable

A graph of this probability density function appears in Figure 4.7. The area under this probability density function is 1, a fact that we will not prove but that can be demonstrated mathematically. Some characteristics of the standard normal probability density function are evident from Equation 4.3 and Figure 4.7. First, we see from the expression for $f(z)$ that the exponent of $e$ is negative unless $z = 0$. Hence, the function has its maximum at $z = 0$. Second, it is easy to check that $f(z) = f(-z)$ for all $z$, which indicates that the probability density function is symmetric about $z = 0$. Hence, $E(Z) = 0$. Third, it is clear from the symmetry that the area under $f(z)$ to the left of $-z$ is equal to the area under $f(z)$ to the right of $+z$. Hence, $P(Z \leqslant -z) = P(Z \geqslant z) = 1 - P(Z \leqslant z)$.

As an example of the latter fact, Figure 4.8 clearly shows that the area under the standard normal probability density function to the left of $-1$ is the same as the area to the right of $+1$. Table I in Appendix C gives the area under the standard normal density function to the left of $z$, $P(Z \leqslant z)$ for various values of $z$. The table indicates that $P(Z \leqslant 1) = 0.8413$. Thus $P(Z \geqslant 1) = 1 - P(Z \leqslant 1) = 1 - 0.8413 = 0.1587$. Hence the two shaded areas of Figure 4.8 represent "tail" probabilities each equal to 0.1587.

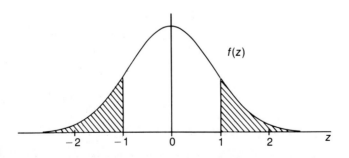

**Figure 4.8**

$P(Z \geqslant 1) = P(Z \leqslant -1)$

CHAPTER 4 DISCRETE AND CONTINUOUS RANDOM VARIABLES

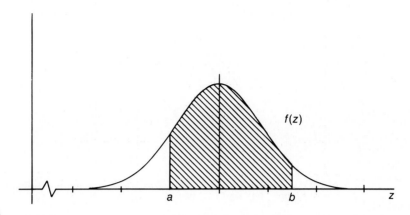

**Figure 4.9**

$P(a \leqslant Z \leqslant b)$

Suppose we want to find $P(a \leqslant Z \leqslant b)$. As Figure 4.9 shows, this area is equal to $P(Z \leqslant b) - P(Z \leqslant a)$, which can be determined from Table I. For example,

$$
\begin{aligned}
P(-1 \leqslant Z \leqslant 2) &= P(Z \leqslant 2) - P(Z \leqslant -1) \\
&= 0.9772 - 0.1587 = 0.8185
\end{aligned}
$$

In order to find $P(Z \leqslant -1)$, we use the fact that

$$
P(Z \leqslant -1) = P(Z \geqslant 1) = 1 - P(Z \leqslant 1)
$$

In general, to find $P(Z \geqslant c)$, we find

$$
P(Z \geqslant c) = 1 - P(Z \leqslant c)
$$

using the fact that $P(Z \geqslant c) + P(Z \leqslant c) = 1$. Thus

$$
P(Z \geqslant 1.5) = 1 - P(Z \leqslant 1.5) = 1 - 0.9332 = 0.0668
$$

This probability is indicated by the shaded area in Figure 4.10.

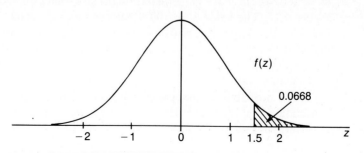

**Figure 4.10**

$P(Z \geqslant 1.5)$

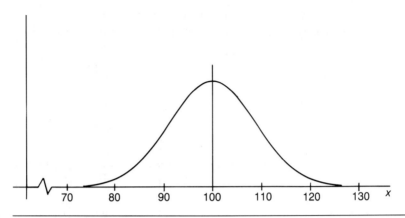

**Figure 4.11**

Probability Density Function for $\mu = 100$ and $\sigma = 10$

Next we consider the complete family of random variables. As mentioned above, corresponding to every pair of values $\mu$ and $\sigma^2$ satisfying $-\infty < \mu < \infty$ and $\sigma^2 > 0$ there is a particular continuous random variable. For example, suppose that observations over a long period of time indicate that weights of one-year-old male infants are normally distributed, with $\mu = 25$ pounds and $\sigma = 1.5$ pounds. The normal random variable with $E(X) = \mu$ and $\text{Var}(X) = \sigma^2$, where $\mu$ and $\sigma^2$ are assumed known, has a complicated probability density function given by

$$f(x; \mu, \sigma^2) = \left(\frac{1}{\sqrt{2\pi}\sigma}\right)e^{-(x-\mu)^2/2\sigma^2}, \qquad -\infty < x < \infty$$

The values $\mu$ and $\sigma^2$ are called the parameters of the distribution. The value $\mu$ is the value for which the probability density function $f(x; \mu, \sigma^2)$ is maximum, and the probability density function is symmetric about $\mu$; hence $E(X) = \mu$. This value is called the population expectation. The value of $\sigma^2$, the population variance, or $\sigma$, the population standard deviation, measures the spread of the distribution about $\mu$.

A random variable $X$ having a normal distribution with $\mu = 100$ and $\sigma^2 = 100$ would have a probability density function like the one shown in Figure 4.11. The value $\mu = 100$ is the center or expected value of this random variable. One important reason for using $\sigma$, the population standard deviation, is that it has the same units as $\mu$. If $X$ has a normal distribution with $\mu$ and $\sigma^2$ known, we write $X \sim N(\mu, \sigma^2)$. For the distribution displayed in Figure 4.11, $X \sim N(100, 100)$.

The probabilities associated with a normal random variable with known expectation and standard deviation can be calculated from Table I, because if $X \sim N(\mu, \sigma^2)$ then

$$\frac{X - \mu}{\sigma} = Z \hspace{4cm} \textbf{4.4}$$

CHAPTER 4  DISCRETE AND CONTINUOUS RANDOM VARIABLES

that is, the new random variable $(X - \mu)/\sigma$ has the standard normal distribution. Using Properties 4.1 through 4.3 of the expectation, we have

$$E\left(\frac{X - \mu}{\sigma}\right) = \frac{E(X) - \mu}{\sigma} = \frac{\mu - \mu}{\sigma} = 0$$

Also,

$$\mathrm{Var}\left(\frac{X - \mu}{\sigma}\right) = \frac{1}{\sigma^2}\mathrm{Var}(X - \mu) = \frac{\mathrm{Var}(X)}{\sigma^2} = \frac{\sigma^2}{\sigma^2} = 1$$

from Property 4.5 of the variance. Thus for the standard normal random variable $Z$, $E(Z) = 0$ and $\mathrm{Var}(Z) = 1$.

**Example 4.18**

Assume that a population of test scores is normally distributed with $\mu = 100$ and $\sigma = 10$. We write $X \sim N(100, 100)$, which is read as "$X$ is normally distributed with an expected value of 100 and a population variance of 100 or standard deviation of 10." Suppose we want to know the proportion of the population taking this test who have scores between 90 and 115. We have

$$P(90 \leqslant X \leqslant 115) = P\left[\frac{90 - 100}{10} \leqslant \frac{X - 100}{10} \leqslant \frac{115 - 100}{10}\right]$$

$$= P\left[-1 \leqslant \frac{X - \mu}{\sigma} \leqslant 1.5\right]$$

$$= P(-1 \leqslant Z \leqslant 1.5)$$

The last step makes use of fact that $(X - \mu)/\sigma$ has the standard normal distribution. Using Table I to find this area, shown graphically in Figure 4.12, we get

$$P(-1 \leqslant Z \leqslant 1.5) = P(Z \leqslant 1.5) - P(Z \leqslant -1)$$

$$= 0.9332 - 0.1587 = 0.7745$$

In other words, about 77.45% of those who take this test score between 90 and 115.

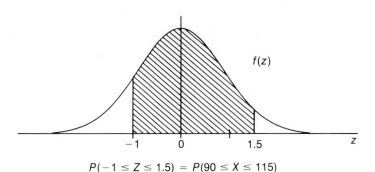

$$P(-1 \leq Z \leq 1.5) = P(90 \leq X \leq 115)$$

**Figure 4.12**

**$P(-1 \leqslant Z \leqslant 1.5)$**

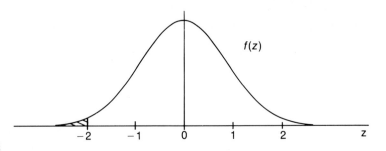

**Figure 4.13**

$P(Z < -2)$

**Example 4.19**

Let us assume that the annual increase in value of all growth mutual funds is normally distributed. Further, let us assume that the population expected value is 10 percentage points and the population standard deviation is 5 percentage points. To determine what proportion of such funds do not show a gain for the year, we want to find $P(X < 0)$. We have

$$P(X < 0) = P\left(\frac{X - 10}{5} < \frac{-10}{5}\right) = P(Z < -2)$$

From Table I we find that $P(Z < -2) = 0.0228$. Hence 2.28 percent of such funds do not show a gain. This probability calculation is illustrated graphically in Figure 4.13.

When $\mu$ and $\sigma^2$ are known, we can also find specified percentiles of a normal random variable.

**Example 4.20**

Suppose we want to find the 95th percentile of the test scores of Example 4.18. We want $P(X \leqslant c) = 0.95$, where $c$ is to be determined. $P(X \leqslant c) = 0.95$ is equivalent to

$$P\left(\frac{X - \mu}{\sigma} \leqslant \frac{c - 100}{10}\right) = 0.95$$

or

$$P\left(Z \leqslant \frac{c - 100}{10}\right) = 0.95$$

Using Table I, we see that $P(Z \leqslant 1.645) = 0.95$. As there is only one 95th

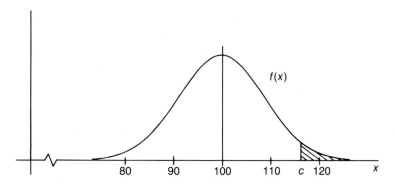

**Figure 4.14**

$P(X \leqslant c) = 0.95$

percentile for $Z$, we must have

$$\frac{c - 100}{10} = 1.645$$

and $c = 116.45$. (This calculation is illustrated in Figure 4.14.)

Hence 95 percent of individuals score at or below 116.45. A score of at least 116.45 places one in the top 5 percent of those taking the exam.

The 90th percentile of the annual yields of the growth mutual funds (see Example 4.19) can be found similarly, as follows:

$$P(X \leqslant c) = P\left(Z \leqslant \frac{c - 10}{5}\right) = 0.90$$

From Table I we have $P(Z \leqslant 1.282) = 0.90$. Thus

$$\frac{c - 10}{5} = 1.282$$

and $c = 16.41$. (This calculation is illustrated in Figure 4.15.) Hence the 90th percentile for the annual yield of these growth funds is 16.41 percent.

If $X \sim N(\mu, \sigma^2)$, then for any positive $k$ we can find $P(\mu - k\sigma \leqslant X \leqslant \mu + k\sigma)$—the probability that an observation is within $k$ standard deviations of $\mu$— from the table of the standard normal distribution:

$$
\begin{aligned}
P(\mu - k\sigma \leqslant X \leqslant \mu + k\sigma) &= P(-k\sigma \leqslant X - \mu < k\sigma) \\
&= P\left(-k \leqslant \frac{X - \mu}{\sigma} \leqslant k\right) \\
&= P(Z \leqslant k) - P(Z \leqslant -k)
\end{aligned}
$$

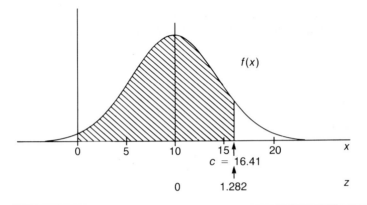

**Figure 4.15**

Ninetieth Percentile of Yields of Growth Mutual Funds

Using Table I for $k = 1, 2,$ and 3, we have

| $k$ | $P(\mu - k\sigma \leqslant X \leqslant \mu + k\sigma)$ |
|---|---|
| 1 | $0.8413 - 0.1587 = 0.6826$ |
| 2 | $0.9772 - 0.0228 = 0.9544$ |
| 3 | $0.9987 - 0.0013 = 0.9974$ |

These probabilities are helpful in describing how $\sigma$ measures spread in a normal distribution. In any normal distribution, slightly more than 68 percent of the population values are within one standard deviation of $\mu$, and slightly more than 95 percent of the observations are within two standard deviations of $\mu$. This concept is shown graphically in Figure 4.16. For any normal distribution, the probability that an observation will lie within three standard deviations of $\mu$ is

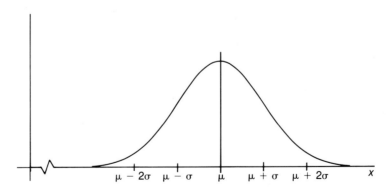

**Figure 4.16**

Probability Density Function of $N(\mu, \sigma^2)$

0.9974. Only 26 observations in 10,000 would be expected to lie more than three standard deviations away from the population expectation. Such observations are rare. For $k = 4$,

$$P(\mu - 4\sigma \leqslant X \leqslant \mu + 4\sigma) = 0.99994$$

which is essentially equal to 1.

In Minitab one can use the command RANDOM with the subcommand NORMAL to do random sampling from normal distributions. We will use this method to sample from several normal populations.

**Example 4.21**

---

Assume that two normal populations have the same expectations, $\mu_1 = \mu_2 = 70$, but different standard deviations, $\sigma_1 = 2$ and $\sigma_2 = 8$. Suppose the first population consists of male heights in inches, and the second consists of test scores (with a possible range of values from 0 to 100). In Exhibits 4.7 and 4.8, the RANDOM command in Minitab has been used to take a random sample of size 100 from the first population and a random sample of size 200 from the second population, and then the MEAN and STDEV commands have been used with each sample.

As the output shows, the histogram for the second sample is more spread out than that for the first. The means of the two samples, $\bar{x}_1 = 69.674$ and $\bar{x}_2 = 70.506$, appear to be reasonable estimates of the common expectation of 70, but notice that neither sample value equals 70. The sample standard deviations, $s_1 = 2.1987$ and $s_2 = 7.8824$, are estimates of $\sigma_1 = 2$ and $\sigma_2 = 8$. The closeness

**Exhibit 4.7**

---

```
MTB > NOTE RANDOM SAMPLE FROM N(70,4)
MTB > BASE = 1000
MTB > RANDOM 100 OBSERVATIONS IN C1;
SUBC> NORMAL MU = 70 SIGMA = 2.
MTB > MEAN C1
    MEAN     =       69.674
MTB > STDEV C1
    ST.DEV. =        2.1987
MTB > HISTOGRAM C1

Histogram of C1    N = 100

Midpoint    Count
    64        1    *
    65        3    ***
    66        4    ****
    67        6    ******
    68       13    *************
    69       24    ************************
    70       13    *************
    71       16    ****************
    72       13    *************
    73        3    ***
    74        0
    75        4    ****
```

**Exhibit 4.8**

```
MTB > NOTE RANDOM SAMPLE FROM N(70,64)
MTB > RANDOM 200 OBSERVATIONS IN C2;
SUBC> NORMAL MU = 70 SIGMA = 8.
MTB > MEAN C2
      MEAN     =        70.506
MTB > STDEV C2
      ST.DEV. =        7.8824
MTB > HISTOGRAM C2;
SUBC> INCREMENT = 2.5;
SUBC> START = 48.

Histogram of C2    N = 200

Midpoint    Count
   48.00        1  *
   50.50        2  **
   53.00        1  *
   55.50        5  *****
   58.00        7  *******
   60.50       12  ************
   63.00       12  ************
   65.50       18  ******************
   68.00       27  ***************************
   70.50       29  *****************************
   73.00       28  ****************************
   75.50       18  ******************
   78.00        9  *********
   80.50       15  ***************
   83.00       10  **********
   85.50        2  **
   88.00        3  ***
   90.50        0
   93.00        1  *
```

of these values suggests that sample calculations can be used to estimate unknown population parameters, which are assumed here to be known. In almost all real-world situations, the value of population parameters such as $\mu$ and $\sigma$ will not be known.

---

Minitab has an additional capacity that is useful for making a rough graphical check of whether a sample has come from a normal population. An artificially small value of $n = 5$ will be used to show how the graphical method, called a **normal plot**, works.

**normal plot**

In Figure 4.17, the area under the standard normal probability density function has been divided into five equal parts, each with area equal to 1/5. The points $z_{(1)}$, $z_{(2)}$, $z_{(3)}$, $z_{(4)}$, and $z_{(5)}$ are the midpoints of each of the five equal areas in terms of probability. That is,

$$P(Z \leqslant z_{(1)}) = \frac{1}{10}$$

$$P(Z \leqslant z_{(2)}) = \frac{3}{10}$$

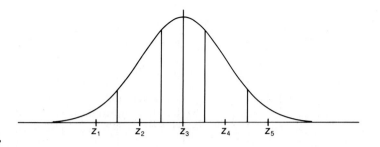

**Figure 4.17**

Normal Scores $n = 5$

$$P(Z \leqslant z_{(3)}) = \frac{5}{10}$$

$$P(Z \leqslant z_{(4)}) = \frac{7}{10}$$

$$P(Z \leqslant z_{(5)}) = \frac{9}{10}$$

If the ordered observations in a normal sample are $x_{(1)}, x_{(2)}, x_{(3)}, x_{(4)}$, and $x_{(5)}$, then, as $(X - \mu)/\sigma = Z$, we have the following approximate equalities:

$$\frac{x_{(1)} - \mu}{\sigma} \doteq z_{(1)}$$

$$\frac{x_{(2)} - \mu}{\sigma} \doteq z_{(2)}$$

$$\vdots$$

$$\frac{x_{(5)} - \mu}{\sigma} \doteq z_{(5)}$$

**NSCORES**

In general, we have $(x_{(i)} - \mu)/\sigma \doteq z_{(i)}$ for all $i$ for some constants $\mu$ and $\sigma$. This result implies that a plot of $(x_{(i)}, z_{(i)})$ will be approximately linear *if* the observations come from a normal distribution. The command **NSCORES** in Minitab produces the value of $z_{(i)}$, called the $i$th normal score. The $i$th normal score satisfies the relation

$$P(Z \leqslant z_{(i)}) = \frac{2i - 1}{2n}$$

(Minitab actually produces a slightly corrected NSCORE value. See the *Minitab Student Handbook* for details.) The graphical procedure will be illustrated with two examples of normal plots.

**Example 4.22** _____

Consider the data in exercise 2.10, which gives 25 measurements of one-pound containers of a chemical additive. In Exhibit 4.9, the Minitab command PRINT has been used to list these 25 observations, and the commands NSCORES and PLOT have been used to construct a normal plot. The ordered observations are plotted on the horizontal axis and the normal scores on the vertical axis. The plot of the ordered weights versus the corresponding normal scores appears to be reasonably linear. This linearity is a rough justification of the normality assumption for the population of weights sampled.

**Exhibit 4.9** _____

```
MTB > NOTE NORMAL PLOT OF "ONE POUND" CONTAINER DATA
MTB > SET C1
C1
   0.9473   0.9655   0.9703   0.9757     .    .    .

MTB > END
MTB > PRINT C1
C1
   0.9473   0.9655   0.9703   0.9757   0.9770   0.9775   0.9788
   0.9861   0.9887   0.9958   0.9964   0.9974   1.0002   1.0016
   1.0058   1.0077   1.0084   1.0102   1.0132   1.0173   1.0182
   1.0225   1.0248   1.0306   1.0396

MTB > NSCORES C1 IN C2
MTB > NAME C1 'WEIGHTS' C2 'NSCORES'
MTB > PLOT C2 VERSUS C1


         -
NSCORES  -                                                  *
         -
         -                                               *
    1.2+                                              *
         -                                        *  *
         -                                        *  *
         -                                     **
         -                                     **
    0.0+                                   ***
         -                                 2
         -                              **
         -                          2
         -                          **
   -1.2+                       *
         -                    *
         -
         -            *
         -
           +---------+---------+---------+---------+---------+-WEIGHTS
         0.940     0.960     0.980     1.000     1.020     1.040
```

## Example 4.23

Consider the data in exercise 2.27 giving the lengths of time in minutes spent at a grocery store checkout counter for 50 customers. A normal plot constructed for this data set is shown in Exhibit 4.10.

This plot is clearly not linear. The deviation from normality suggested by this curve is caused by the skewness of the data. There are a few large observations: 40.83, 45.95, and 69.61. On the other hand, there are a large number of short waiting times (21 of the 50 times are under six minutes). The plot reflects these facts by showing a right-hand tail that is "too far out" to be on a straight line and a

**Exhibit 4.10**

```
MTB > NOTE NORMAL PLOT OF WAITING TIMES AT CHECKOUT COUNTER
MTB > SET C1
C1
   10.41    17.79     3.99      3.94    .    .    .

MTB > END
MTB > NAME C1 'TIMES'
MTB > PRINT C1
TIMES
   10.41    17.79     3.99      3.94     5.59     2.35    18.94    21.78
    2.71    69.61    12.44     12.48     8.59     6.65    45.95    14.96
   13.98     1.33    16.94      1.09     4.59     5.85     4.36     6.97
   11.10     5.43     4.25     10.34     4.49     2.68    19.67     5.94
   18.53     1.99    37.71     13.33     2.37    21.10    13.01     6.45
   10.08    13.30     5.00      0.62     3.32     2.28     7.38    15.42
   40.83    19.86


MTB > NSCORES C1 IN C2
MTB > NAME C2 'NSCORES'
MTB > PLOT C2 VS C1


          -
NSCORES   -
          -
          -                                                   *
          -                                         *
     1.5+                              *  *
          -                  ***
          -                22
          -               22*
          -               222
     0.0+         *2*2
          -       *5
          -       5
          -       3*
          -       3
    -1.5+   2
          -   *
          -  *

          -
          +---------+---------+---------+---------+---------+-TIMES
          0        15        30        45        60        75
```

**Exhibit 4.11**

```
MTB > STEM-AND-LEAF C1

Stem-and-leaf of TIMES     N = 50
Leaf Unit = 1.0

   16      0  0111222223334444
  (10)     0  5555566678
   24      1  00012233334
   13      1  5678899
    6      2  11
    4      2
    4      3
    4      3  7
    3      4  0
    2      4  5
    1      5
    1      5
    1      6
    1      6  9
```

left-hand tail that is "too far in" to be on a straight line. Minitab has been used to create a stem-and-leaf display of these 50 times (Exhibit 4.11), which is useful in showing the skewed nature of this data set.

## Exercises 4.6

**4.50** Find the following probabilities for the standard normal random variable $Z$.
  **a.** $P(-1 \leq Z \leq 1.5)$     **d.** $P(0.4 \leq Z \leq 1)$
  **b.** $P(Z \leq -0.8)$     **e.** $P(-0.2 \leq Z \leq 0.8)$
  **c.** $P(Z \geq 1.4)$     **f.** $P(Z \geq 1.96)$

**4.51** Find the values of $c$ that satisfy the following.
  **a.** $P(Z \leq c) = 0.8159$     **d.** $P(c \leq Z) = 0.025$
  **b.** $P(Z \leq -c) = 0.0668$     **e.** $P(c \leq Z) = 0.05$ (interpolate)
  **c.** $P(Z \leq c) = 0.975$     **f.** $P(-c \leq Z \leq c) = 0.8064$

**4.52** Assume that scores $X$ on a standardized history examination are $N(71, 100)$. Find the following probabilities.
  **a.** $P(X \leq 85)$     **c.** $P(65 \leq X \leq 80)$
  **b.** $P(X \geq 60)$     **d.** $P(61 \leq X \leq 81)$

**4.53** **a.** Find the 95th percentile of the examination scores in exercise 4.52.
  **b.** Find the 5th percentile of these examination scores.

**4.54** **a.** Find $P(-2.5 \leq Z \leq 2.5)$.
  **b.** Find $P(\mu - 2.5\sigma \leq X \leq \mu + 2.5\sigma)$ for $X \sim N(\mu, \sigma^2)$, and interpret this probability statement in words.

**4.55** Weights of newborn male infants at a hospital are assumed to have distribution $X \sim N(7.75, 0.25)$ with the measurements in pounds. Find the following.
  **a.** $P(7.5 \leq X \leq 8.5)$     **c.** $P(X \geq 8)$     **e.** $P(X = 8)$
  **b.** $P(X \leq 7.0)$     **d.** $P(X \leq 8)$

**4.56**  The heights $Y$ in inches of 18-year-old females are assumed to be $N(67, 16)$. The height of the entrance to a building is only $6'2''$. What percentage of 18-year-old females will have to duck to get through the entrance?

**4.57**  The stated net weight of packages produced by a certain factory is 16 ounces. The net weights have a standard deviation of $\sigma = 0.1$ ounce, regardless of the fill level at which the packaging machine is set. If the machine is set at a level of 16.2 ounces, what percent of production will be under the stated net weight? Assume normality.

**4.58**  If three females are selected at random from the population described in exercise 4.56, what is the probability that at least two of the three will be over 67 inches tall? *Note:* Use the binomial distribution.

**4.59**  Use RANDOM to sample 200 observations from the population of examination scores in exercise 4.52.
   **a.** Calculate $\bar{x}$ and $s$. Do these appear to be reasonable approximations of the known population parameters $\mu$ and $\sigma$?
   **b.** Use HISTOGRAM with this data set. Does the histogram have a bell-shaped appearance?

**4.60**  **a.** Use RANDOM to sample the weights of 1000 male infants from the population described in exercise 4.55.
   **b.** Find the proportion of these observations in the intervals $[\mu - \sigma, \mu + \sigma]$ and $[\mu - 2\sigma, \mu + 2\sigma]$, using the COPY command with the subcommand SET and the COUNT command.
   **c.** Compare the proportions in part b with the corresponding probabilities given on page 142 for the normal distribution.

**4.61**  Use RANDOM to sample 50 observations from $X \sim N(100, 15^2)$. Make a normal plot of these observations. Do these normal data produce a plot that is close to a straight line?

**4.62**  Use RANDOM to sample 25 observations from the uniform distribution on $[0, 1]$. Make a normal plot of these observations. Do these data yield a normal plot that is close to a straight line? How does it deviate from a straight line?

**4.63**  Construct a normal plot of the yield data for the 50 stocks of Table 2.1. Does the plot suggest any deviation from normality?

**4.64**  Construct a normal plot of the weight data for the 50 women in exercise 2.7. Does the normality assumption appear to be justified for these data?

**4.65**  Construct a normal plot of the data on length of life of 58 mice given in exercise 2.41. Make a stem-and-leaf diagram for these data. What deviations from normality are suggested by these two graphical displays?

## 4.7
## Several Random Variables

In this section we consider several random variables defined at a point in an outcome space $S$, rather than a single random variable. For simplicity we focus on the case of two random variables $X$ and $Y$. In human populations it is easy to think of two measurements' being assigned to an individual: height and weight, mathematical and verbal scores on an aptitude examination, years of education and annual salary, and so forth. The discovery and quantification of relationships between two random variables is exceedingly important; one measure of association called the covariance will be considered at the end of this section. Like events, random variables are (roughly) independent if the value attained by one does not affect the probability distribution of the other. We will frequently assume that random variables are independent.

The definitions of a bivariate discrete random variable and a bivariate probability function are similar to those for the univariate case.

---

**Definition 4.13** ▬▬▬▬▬▬▬▬▬▬▬▬▬▬▬▬▬▬▬▬▬▬▬▬▬▬▬▬▬▬▬▬▬

bivariate discrete
random variable

A **bivariate discrete random variable** $(X, Y)$ assigns two numerical values to each outcome of an outcome space $S$. The number of pairs of values such a random variable may have is finite or countable.

---

**Definition 4.14** ▬▬▬▬▬▬▬▬▬▬▬▬▬▬▬▬▬▬▬▬▬▬▬▬▬▬▬▬▬▬▬▬▬

bivariate probability
function

A **bivariate probability function** for a random variable $(X, Y)$ gives the probability that $X = x$ and $Y = y$ for all pairs $(x, y)$ for which this probability is positive. This probability is denoted by $p(x, y)$.

---

**Example 4.24** ▬▬▬▬▬▬▬▬▬▬▬▬▬▬▬▬▬▬▬▬▬▬▬▬▬▬▬▬▬▬▬▬▬▬▬▬▬▬▬▬▬▬▬▬▬▬

Assume that two fair tetrahedra, one red and one green, both numbered 1, 2, 3, and 4, are tossed. Let $X$ represent the outcome of tossing the red tetrahedron, and let $Z$ represent the maximum value on the two tetrahedra. The sample space for these two random variables was given in Figure 3.4. Table 4.2 gives the bivariate probability function of $X$ and $Z$.

Consider how these probabilities are computed. The probability that $X = 3$ and $Z = 2$, for example, is clearly 0, for if a 3 is face down on the red tetrahedron, the maximum of the two tetrahedra must be at least 3. We arrive at the value $f(3, 3) = 3/16$ by observing that for $(3, 1)$, $(3, 2)$, and $(3, 3)$, a 3 is face down on

---

**Table 4.2** ▬▬▬▬▬▬▬▬▬▬▬▬▬▬▬▬▬▬▬▬▬▬▬▬▬▬▬▬▬▬▬▬▬▬▬▬▬▬▬▬▬▬▬▬▬▬▬▬▬▬▬▬▬▬▬▬

$p(x, z)$

| $z$ \ $x$ | 1 | 2 | 3 | 4 | |
|---|---|---|---|---|---|
| 1 | 1/16 | 0 | 0 | 0 | 1/16 |
| 2 | 1/16 | 2/16 | 0 | 0 | 3/16 |
| 3 | 1/16 | 1/16 | 3/16 | 0 | 5/16 |
| 4 | 1/16 | 1/16 | 1/16 | 4/16 | 7/16 |
| | 1/4 | 1/4 | 1/4 | 1/4 | |

the red tetrahedron and the maximum is 3. The other probabilities for this bivariate distribution should be verified by the reader.

## Example 4.25

Once again considering the tetrahedra described in Example 4.24, let $Y$ represent the outcome of tossing the green tetrahedron, and let $X$ represent the outcome of tossing the red tetrahedron. The bivariate probability function for $X$ and $Y$ is given in Table 4.3. The table illustrates the fact that all sixteen possible outcomes $(x, y)$, $x = 1, 2, 3, 4$ and $y = 1, 2, 3, 4$, have equal probability.

## Table 4.3

$p(x, y)$

| $y$ \ $x$ | 1 | 2 | 3 | 4 | |
|---|---|---|---|---|---|
| 1 | 1/16 | 1/16 | 1/16 | 1/16 | 1/4 |
| 2 | 1/16 | 1/16 | 1/16 | 1/16 | 1/4 |
| 3 | 1/16 | 1/16 | 1/16 | 1/16 | 1/4 |
| 4 | 1/16 | 1/16 | 1/16 | 1/16 | 1/4 |
| | 1/4 | 1/4 | 1/4 | 1/4 | |

By summing the probabilities in each row of Table 4.2, we obtain the probability that $Z$, the maximum, is 1, 2, 3, or 4. The resulting equations are called the marginal probability function of $Z$. For Table 4.2, we have

$$P(Z = 1) = \frac{1}{16}$$

$$P(Z = 2) = \frac{3}{16}$$

$$P(Z = 3) = \frac{5}{16}$$

$$P(Z = 4) = \frac{7}{16}$$

Similarly, we can find the marginal probability function of $X$ in Table 4.2 by summing the probabilities in the columns to obtain $P(X = x) = 1/4$ for $x = 1$, 2, 3, 4. The formal definition of the marginal probability function is as follows.

**Definition 4.15**

For a bivariate discrete random variable $(X, Y)$ with probability function $p(x, y)$, the **marginal probability function** of $X$ is given by

$$P(X = x) = \sum_{\text{all } y} p(x, y)$$

and the marginal probability function of $Y$ is given by

$$P(Y = y) = \sum_{\text{all } x} p(x, y)$$

The marginal probability functions of $X$ and $Y$ found by summing the rows and columns of Table 4.3 confirm what we already know—namely, that the values 1, 2, 3, and 4 each have an equal probability of $1/4$ of appearing on either the red or the green tetrahedron.

We can now make precise the idea of independence of two random variables. It is fairly clear that the random variables $X$ and $Z$ of Example 4.24 are not independent, for the value of $X$ affects the distribution of $Z$. For example, whereas the conditional probability that the maximum is 2, *given* that the red tetrahedron is 3, is 0, the unconditional probability $P(Z = 2)$ is $3/16$. Using the information from Example 4.25, however, we find that

$$P(X = x \mid Y = y) = \frac{P(X = x \text{ and } Y = y)}{P(Y = y)} = \frac{(1/16)}{(1/4)}$$

$$= \frac{1}{4} = P(X = x)$$

for any combination of values $(x, y)$ where $x = 1, 2, 3, 4$ and $y = 1, 2, 3, 4$. Thus the value of the random variable $Y$ does not affect the probability distribution of $X$.

**Definition 4.16**

Two variables are called **independent random variables** if

$$P(X = x, Y = y) = P(X = x)P(Y = y)$$

for all pairs of values $(x, y)$.

Note that if $P(Y = y) > 0$ and if $X$ and $Y$ are independent, then

$$P(X = x \mid Y = y) = \frac{P(X = x \text{ and } Y = y)}{P(Y = y)}$$

$$= \frac{P(X = x)P(Y = y)}{P(Y = y)} = P(X = x)$$

Thus for independent random variables the conditional distribution of $X$ given $Y = y$ is the same as the unconditional distribution of $X$. The same is true if $X$ and $Y$ are interchanged, as long as $P(X = x) > 0$.

The expectation of a real-valued function, $f(x, y)$, of two variables $x$ and $y$ is defined as follows.

---

**Definition 4.17** ▬▬▬▬▬▬▬▬▬▬▬▬▬▬▬▬▬▬▬▬▬▬▬▬▬▬▬▬▬▬

If $f(x, y)$ is a real-valued function of $(x, y)$ and $(X, Y)$ has the bivariate probability function $p(x, y)$,

$$E[f(X, Y)] = \sum_{\text{all } x} \sum_{\text{all } y} f(x, y)p(x, y)$$

---

The following property holds for any two random variables, whether or not they are independent.

---

**Property 4.7** ▬▬▬▬▬▬▬▬▬▬▬▬▬▬▬▬▬▬▬▬▬▬▬▬▬▬▬▬▬▬▬▬▬▬▬

For any two random variables $X$ and $Y$,

$$E(X + Y) = E(X) + E(Y)$$

---

The proof for discrete random variables is as follows:

$$E(X + Y) = \sum_x \sum_y (x + y)p(x, y) = \sum_x \sum_y xp(x, y) + \sum_y \sum_x yp(x, y)$$
$$= \sum_x xp(X = x) + \sum_y yp(Y = y) = E(X) + E(Y)$$

This property extends to the sum of any $k$ random variables.

---

**Property 4.8** ▬▬▬▬▬▬▬▬▬▬▬▬▬▬▬▬▬▬▬▬▬▬▬▬▬▬▬▬▬▬▬▬▬▬▬

For any $k$ random variables $X_1, X_2, \ldots, X_k$,

$$E\left(\sum_{i=1}^{k} X_i\right) = \sum_{i=1}^{k} E(X_i)$$

---

Consider again tosses of the red and green tetrahedra. Let $X$ represent the outcome of tossing the red tetrahedron and $Y$ the outcome of tossing the green one. We have seen that

$$E(X) = 1\left(\frac{1}{4}\right) + 2\left(\frac{1}{4}\right) + 3\left(\frac{1}{4}\right) + 4\left(\frac{1}{4}\right) = \frac{5}{2}$$

which is also the value of $E(Y)$. Using Property 4.7, we have, for $T = X + Y$,

$$E(T) = E(X + Y) = E(X) + E(Y) = \frac{5}{2} + \frac{5}{2} = 5$$

which agrees with the result in Section 4.3.

For Example 4.5, in which the probability of the father's winning a tennis match is $1/3$, let $I_1 = 1$ if the father wins the first match and $I_1 = 0$ if he loses. Similarly, let $I_2 = 1$ if the father wins the second match and $I_2 = 0$ if he loses, and so on. The number of games won by the father may then be written as $X = I_1 + I_2 + I_3$.

$$E(I_1) = 0\left(\frac{2}{3}\right) + 1\left(\frac{1}{3}\right) = \frac{1}{3}$$

and clearly $I_2$ and $I_3$ have the same expected value. Hence

$$E(X) = E(I_1) + E(I_2) + E(I_3) = 1$$

which again agrees with a previous result.

## The Expectation of a Binomial Random Variable

Using the same approach as above, it is now easy to show that $E(X) = np$ when $X$ has the binomial distribution. Let $I_k = 1$ if success occurs on trial $k$ and $I_k = 0$ if failure occurs. (Random variables that can take on only the values 0 and 1 are called indicator random variables, as they are 1 if the "indicated event" occurs and 0 if it does not.) The expected value of $I_k$ is easily computed to be

$$E(I_k) = 0(1 - p) + 1p = p$$

for each $k$. As $X = \Sigma_{i=1}^{k} I_k$, the expected number of successes in $n$ binomial trials is

$$E(X) = E\left(\sum_{k=1}^{n} I_k\right) = \sum_{k=1}^{n} E(I_k) = \sum_{k=1}^{n} p = np \qquad \textbf{4.5}$$

This result again agrees with the one in Section 4.3.

Another consequence of Property 4.8 together with Properties 4.1 and 4.2 is that the variance of a discrete random variable $X$ may be written as $E(X^2) - [E(X)]^2$.

$$
\begin{aligned}
\sigma_X^2 &= E(X - \mu_X)^2 = E(X^2 - 2X\mu_X + \mu_X^2) \\
&= E(X^2) + E(-2X\mu_X) + E(\mu_X^2) \quad \text{(Using Property 4.8)} \\
&= E(X^2) - 2\mu_X E(X) + \mu_X^2 \quad \text{(Using Properties 4.1 and 4.2)} \\
&= E(X^2) - 2\mu_X^2 + \mu_X^2 \\
&= E(X^2) - \mu_X^2 = E(X^2) - [E(X)]^2 \qquad \textbf{4.6}
\end{aligned}
$$

It is sometimes easier to use this expression for $\sigma_X^2$ rather than the expression given in Section 4.3. Consider the case of $X \sim B(3, 1/3)$.

$$E(X^2) = 0^2 \left(\frac{8}{27}\right) + 1^2 \left(\frac{12}{27}\right) + 2^2 \left(\frac{6}{27}\right) + 3^2 \left(\frac{1}{27}\right) = \frac{45}{27}$$

and

$$E(X) = 1$$

Hence

$$\sigma_X^2 = E(X^2) - [E(X)]^2 = \frac{5}{3} - 1 = \frac{2}{3}$$

This value agrees with the value of $\sigma_X^2$ found in Section 4.3.

We next consider certain properties of independent random variables $X$ and $Y$, which will be stated without proof.

---

**Property 4.9**

If $X$ and $Y$ are independent random variables, for any functions $f(X)$ and $g(Y)$,

$$E[f(X)g(Y)] = E[f(X)] \, E[g(Y)]$$

---

**Property 4.10**

If $X$ and $Y$ are independent random variables,

$$\mathrm{Var}(X + Y) = \mathrm{Var}(X) + \mathrm{Var}(Y)$$

---

*Note*: This property does not have to hold if the variables are not independent. This property can be generalized as follows.

---

**Property 4.11**

If $X_1, X_2, \ldots, X_k$ are pairwise independent random variables,

$$\mathrm{Var}\left(\sum_{i=1}^{k} X_i\right) = \sum_{i=1}^{k} \mathrm{Var}(X_i)$$

---

An example of the use of Property 4.11 is given next.

## Example 4.26

Consider the variance of the sum of the red and green tetrahedra of Example 4.25. We know that

$$\text{Var}(X) = \frac{(1^2 + 2^2 + 3^2 + 4^2)}{4} - \left(\frac{5}{2}\right)^2 = \frac{5}{4}$$

As $Y$ has the same probability function as $X$, $\text{Var}(Y) = 5/4$ also. We have seen that $X$ and $Y$ are independent. Let $T = X + Y$. Then,

$$\text{Var}(T) = \text{Var}(X + Y) = \text{Var}(X) + \text{Var}(Y) = \frac{5}{4} + \frac{5}{4} = \frac{5}{2}$$

This value agrees with the variance computed in Example 4.11.

---

Property 4.11 is used to prove the expression for the variance in the binomial case given in Section 4.3, $\text{Var}(X) = np(1 - p)$.

### The Variance of a Binomial Random Variable

Using independent indicator random variables $I_k$ as before, we have

$$\text{Var}(X) = \text{Var}\left(\sum_{i=1}^{k} I_k\right) = \sum_{i=1}^{k} \text{Var}(I_k)$$

However,

$$\begin{aligned} \text{Var}(I_k) &= E(I_k^2) - [E(I_k)]^2 \\ &= E(I_k) - [E(I_k)]^2 \\ &= p - p^2 = p(1 - p) \end{aligned}$$

Hence

$$\text{Var}(X) = \sum_{k=1}^{n} p(1 - p) = np(1 - p)$$

verifying the expression for the binomial variance. Note that $E(I_k) = E(I_k^2)$, because the indicator random variables $I_k$ and $I_k^2$ have the same distribution. That is, $I_k^2 = 1$ when $I_k = 1$, and $I_k^2 = 0$ when $I_k = 0$.

We next consider a measure of the association between two bivariate random variables—the covariance of $X$ and $Y$.

---

**Definition 4.18** ▬▬▬

covariance

The **covariance** of $X$ and $Y$ is a measure of association between two random variables.

$$\text{cov}(X, Y) = E[(X - \mu_X)(Y - \mu_Y)]$$

---

Positive values of cov($X$, $Y$) mean that $X$ tends to exceed $\mu_X$ when $Y$ exceeds $\mu_Y$ and $X$ tends to be less than $\mu_X$ when $Y$ is less than $\mu_Y$. It can be shown that

$$\text{cov}(X, Y) = E(XY) - \mu_X\mu_Y \qquad \textbf{4.7}$$

the proof of which is left to the instructor.

## Example 4.27

For the random variables ($X$, $Z$) with the probability function given in Table 4.2, using Definition 4.14 we find that

$$E(XZ) = \frac{1\cdot1}{16} + \frac{1\cdot2}{16} + (2\cdot2)\left(\frac{2}{16}\right) + (1\cdot3)\left(\frac{1}{16}\right)$$
$$+ \frac{2\cdot3}{16} + (3\cdot3)\left(\frac{3}{16}\right) + \frac{1\cdot4}{16} + (2\cdot4)\left(\frac{1}{16}\right)$$
$$+ \frac{3\cdot4}{16} + (4\cdot4)\left(\frac{4}{16}\right) = \frac{135}{16}$$

We have seen that $\mu_X = 5/2$, and it is easily checked that $\mu_Z = 25/8$. Thus

$$\text{cov}(X, Z) = E(XZ) - \mu_X\mu_Z = \frac{135}{16} - \left(\frac{5}{2}\right)\left(\frac{25}{8}\right) = \frac{10}{16}$$

and $X$ and $Z$ have positive covariance. This positive covariance can be interpreted to mean that the value on the green tetrahedron and the maximum on the two tetrahedra tend to be large or small (with respect to their expected values) at the same time.

Definitions analogous to Definitions 4.13 through 4.18 can be made for continuous bivariate random variables. Such definitions will not be given here, as the mathematics is too advanced for the level of this text. Nevertheless, it is easy to think of observable bivariate random variables that we know intuitively are continuous random variables. The heights ($X$) and weights ($Y$) of individuals mentioned at the beginning of this section are examples of continuous random variables. Properties 4.1 through 4.11 hold for continuous random variables as well as for discrete random variables.

Also, we can understand intuitively that certain continuous bivariate random variables will have positive covariance. Examples include the heights of two brothers, the noon temperature in Dallas and daily demand for electricity in that city, and the speed of an aircraft and the force of lift exerted on its wings. Other pairs of random variables are intuitively understood to have a negative covariance. One example is the latitude of a location in the northern hemisphere and the mean noon temperature in January; another is the depth below sea level of a cubic foot of water and a measure of the ambient temperature of the water.

## Exercises 4.7

**4.66** The following are bivariate probability functions for two pairs of random variables $(X, Y)$ and $(U, V)$.

| y \ x | 0 | 1 |
|---|---|---|
| 0 | 1/4 | 1/4 |
| 1 | 1/4 | 1/4 |

| v \ u | 0 | 1 |
|---|---|---|
| 0 | 1/8 | 3/8 |
| 1 | 3/8 | 1/8 |

a. Find the marginal distributions of $X$ and $Y$ and of $U$ and $V$.
b. What is the relationship between these marginal distributions?
c. Knowing the marginal distributions of two random variables does not allow us to find their bivariate probability function. We can find the bivariate distribution from the marginals only if the random variables have a certain property. What property is that?

**4.67** Consider tossing the red and green tetrahedra labeled 1, 2, 3, and 4. Let $X$ represent the outcome of tossing the red one and $W$ represent the minimum of the two tetrahedra.
a. Find the bivariate probability function of $X$ and $W$.
b. Find the marginal probability functions of $X$ and $W$.

**4.68** Let $X = 1$ represent a male and $X = 2$ represent a female. Let $Y = 1$ represent favoring the Equal Rights Amendment and $Y = 2$ represent opposing it. Suppose $P(X = 1) = P(X = 2) = 0.5$, $P(Y = 1) = 0.6$, and $P(Y = 2) = 0.4$. If $X$ and $Y$ are independent, find the bivariate probability function of $X$ and $Y$.

**4.69** A fair die is tossed twice. Let $X$ be the outcome of the first toss and $Y$ the outcome of the second.
a. Find $E(X)$ and $E(Y)$.
b. Find the expected value of the sum of the two tosses.
c. Find the expected sum of ten tosses of the die.

**4.70** In a certain IRS district, the husband's income $X$ as reported on joint income tax returns has an expected value of \$20,000 and the wife's income $Y$ has an expected value of \$12,000.
a. Find $E(X + Y)$.
b. Find $E(X - Y)$.
c. Define in words the random variables $X + Y$ and $X - Y$.

**4.71** a. Find the variance $\sigma^2$ of the outcome of a toss of a fair die, $X$, using $\sigma^2 = E(X^2) - [E(X)]^2$.
b. Find the variance of $X + Y$, the sum of the outcomes of two such dice assumed to be independent.

**4.72** Let $X$ and $Y$ be independent random variables with variances $\sigma_X^2$ and $\sigma_Y^2$.
a. Find $\text{Var}(X + Y)$ in terms of $\sigma_X^2$ and $\sigma_Y^2$.
b. Find $\text{Var}(X - Y) = \text{Var}[X + (-Y)]$ in terms of $\sigma_X^2$ and $\sigma_Y^2$.

**4.73** An integer is selected at random from the set $S = \{1, 2, 3, \ldots, n\}$. Given that

$$\sum_{i=1}^{n} i^2 = \frac{n(n + 1)(2n + 1)}{6}$$

and using the result of exercise 4.24, find $\sigma_X^2$, where $X$ represents the outcome of the selection. *Note:* Use $\sigma_X^2 = E(X^2) - [E(X)]^2$.

**4.74** Given $X \sim B(100, 1/2)$, find the values of $E(X)$ and $Var(X)$.

**4.75** Suppose two individuals are selected independently from a normal population and their weights are denoted by $X_1$ and $X_2$. Assume the normal population has variance $\sigma^2$.

 **a.** Find the variance of twice the weight of the first individual selected.
 **b.** Find the variance of the sum of the weights of the two individuals.
 *Note*: The answers should be in terms of $\sigma^2$.

**4.76** Assume that $X \sim N(72, 4)$ and $Y \sim N(69, 4)$ are distributions of the heights in inches of male and female students at a large university.

 **a.** Find $E(X - Y)$.
 **b.** Find $Var(X - Y)$, assuming that $X$ and $Y$ are independent.

**4.77** The random variables $X$ and $Y$ have the following joint probability function:

| x<br>y | 0 | 1 | 2 | 3 |
|---|---|---|---|---|
| 0 | 1/216 | 9/216 | 27/216 | 27/216 |
| 1 | 6/216 | 36/216 | 54/216 | 0 |
| 2 | 12/216 | 36/216 | 0 | 0 |
| 3 | 8/216 | 0 | 0 | 0 |

 **a.** Find the marginal probability function for $X$. Show that $X \sim B(3, 1/2)$, and find $E(X)$.
 **b.** Find the marginal probability function for $Y$. Show that $Y \sim B(3, 1/3)$, and find $E(Y)$.
 **c.** Find cov$(X, Y)$ using Equation 4.7.

**4.78** Let $X$ and $Y$ be continuous random variables, with $E(X) = 50$, $Var(X) = 100$, $E(Y) = 40$, and $Var(Y) = 25$.

 **a.** Given cov$(X, Y) = 30$, find $E(XY)$.
 **b.** In general it can be proved that for any two random variables,

$$Var(X + Y) = Var(X) + Var(Y) + 2 \text{ cov}(X, Y)$$

 Find $Var(X + Y)$ for this exercise.

**4.79** Use RANDOM to simulate the selection of two columns of 50 uniformly distributed observations on $[0, 1]$. Call the columns C1 and C2. Construct twice C2 in C3 and C1 + C2 in C4.

 **a.** PLOT C3 versus C1.
 **b.** PLOT C4 versus C1.
 **c.** How would you describe the difference between the general scatter of points of the two plots? What is causing this difference?

**4.80** Find cov$(X, Y)$ and cov$(U, V)$ for the random variables in exercise 4.66.

**4.81** Prove that cov$(X, Y) = E(XY) - E(X)E(Y)$. Use

$$cov(X, Y) = E[(X - \mu_X)(Y - \mu_Y)]$$

 and multiply out the expression in brackets before taking the expectation.

**Summary**  Random variables define rules for assigning a numerical value or values to each point of an outcome space. A discrete random variable can take on only a finite or countable number of values. A continuous random variable can take on any numerical value on an interval of the real numbers. The probability function for a discrete random variable gives a rule for assigning probabilities to the values a random variable can attain. A probability histogram gives a graphical representation of the probability function for a discrete random variable. Random variables are generally denoted by capital letters such as $X$, $Y$, $Z$, $U$, and $V$.

For a discrete random variable $X$ we define a numerical value called the expected value of $X$, written as $E(X)$. This value gives information about the location, or "center," of the distribution of $X$. It is analogous to but not the same as the mean of a sample of numerical observations. The variance of a discrete random variable $X$, written as $\sigma_X^2$ or $\mathrm{Var}(X)$, is another numerical value associated with a random variable. It gives a measure of the "spread" of the distribution of $X$. This variance is analogous to but not the same as the variance of a sample. The square root of the variance, $\sigma_X$, is called the standard deviation of $X$. It is a measure of "spread" that has the same units as the original units of $X$.

Important discrete random variables include the binomial, geometric, and Poisson random variables, each of which gives a good probabilistic description of certain real-life situations. Minitab may be used to simulate sampling from both binomial and Poisson distributions.

The probability density function gives the probability for a continuous random variable over a given interval. This probability is calculated as the area under the probability density function and above the horizontal axis for the interval in question. Although calculus is needed for a formal definition of $E(X)$ and $\mathrm{Var}(X)$ for continuous random variables, the ideas are analogous to those concerning discrete random variables. Properties of the expected value and variance are exactly the same for continuous random variables as for discrete random variables.

An important special case is the normal distribution. Probabilities for the standard normal distribution are calculated by finding appropriate areas under the probability density function for that random variable. The relationship of the general normal variable, $X \sim N(\mu, \sigma^2)$, to the standard normal variable permits calculation of probabilities associated with any normal random variable given only the probabilities associated with the standard normal variable.

The expected value of a sum of random variables is equal to the sum of the expected values. A similar property holds for the variance of a sum of independent random variables—if $k$ random variables are pairwise independent, the variance of their sum equals the sum of their individual variances. The covariance of two random variables is a measure of association between two random variables in the bivariate case.

binomial random variable
bivariate discrete random variable
bivariate probability function
continuous random variable
covariance
discrete random variable
expected value
geometric random variable
independent random variables
marginal probability function
median of a continuous random
   variable

normal random variable
normal plot
Poisson random variable
probability density function
probability function
probability histogram
standard deviation of a random
   variable
standard normal variable
variance

| CDF | PDF | POISSON |
|-----|-----|---------|
| NSCORES | | |

# Chapter 5

# Large-Sample Estimation

## 5.1

### Introduction

*parameter*

*population expectation*

*population median*

*population variance*

*population proportion*

The aim of sampling is to obtain accurate information about a population or, more exactly, the characteristics of one or more random variables defined for a population. Typically the data available are the numerical values of a random variable for those elements in a random sample. The characteristics of a random variable of interest are called population **parameters**. Examples of such parameters are the **population expectation** $\mu$, the **population median** $m$, the **population variance** $\sigma^2$, and the **population proportion** $p$. The values of such population parameters cannot be determined exactly on the basis of the sample elements alone. The sample data, however, contain information that permits estimation of population quantities. Statistics—that is, computations based on observations of a sample—are used as estimators of population parameters. The idea of estimation of population parameters will be introduced via two examples.

### Example 5.1

The lengths of time $T$ that customers must wait at a checkout counter have a continuous distribution. The waiting times of 100 customers, simulated using Minitab, are presented in Exhibit 5.1.

The sample average, median, and standard deviation have all been computed using Minitab. The average waiting time is $\bar{x} = 15.388$. This value is an estimate of $\mu_T$, the true expected waiting time. A different sample of 100 observations would yield a different average value, however, so 15.388 is not equal to $\mu_T$. Later in this chapter we will consider the question "In what sense

Exhibit 5.1

```
MTB > NOTE RANDOM SAMPLE OF 100 TIMES FROM DISTRIBUTION WITH MU = 15
MTB > BASE = 1000
MTB > RANDOM 100 OBSERVATIONS IN C1;
SUBC> UNIFORM A = 0 B = 1.
MTB > LOGE OF C1 IN C2
MTB > MULT C2 BY -15 IN C3
MTB > PRINT C3
C3
   18.533    26..752     9.109    42.079    12.225    21.270     7.402
   30.707     2.979    15.860     4.996    21.816     1.714    18.466
    8.130     2.902    28.232    25.216     9.845     0.125    10.764
   10.789    15.964    20.832    28.469    34.433    17.365     3.899
   10.472     7.293    14.601    39.751    55.551     1.709    12.639
   11.155    12.095    14.155    21.451     0.766    40.321     1.880
   10.865     7.320     3.636     3.841     7.709    15.011    27.119
   22.500     4.992     3.215    14.025   122.519     8.659    31.074
    1.549     7.717     0.335    18.888    15.895    23.875     8.444
   13.929     9.565     7.773    30.567    14.142     4.310    84.826
   17.396     2.675     6.125     0.406    17.968     0.065    46.943
   39.390     0.166     6.530    18.174    11.926     4.262     1.615
   10.987    15.528    25.926    10.241     7.352     3.105    14.494
   14.614     6.512    17.714     0.456     6.546     1.275     7.642
    2.596     1.181

MTB > AVERAGE C3
   MEAN    =      15.388
MTB > STDEV C3
   ST.DEV. =      17.295
MTB > MEDIAN C3
   MEDIAN =      10.926
```

can $\bar{x}$ be considered a good estimate of $\mu$?" In this case the actual value of $\mu_T$ is 15, but in most cases the true value of $\mu$ will not be known.

Other parameters of the distribution of waiting times of Example 5.1 are the true median waiting time, $m_T$, and the population standard deviation of the waiting times, $\sigma_T$. The sample median $\hat{m} = 10.926$ and the sample standard deviation $s = 17.295$ can be used as estimates of these quantities. In this case the true values of the population parameters are known to be $m_T = 10.397$ and $\sigma_T = 15$. Usually, however, these parameters are unknown, and thus it is important to know how well a sample estimate approximates a population parameter.

**Example 5.2**

A candidate for the U.S. House of Representatives wants to know what proportion $p$ of registered voters plan to vote for him in November. He has been able to get a list of registered voters and has selected a random sample of 1600 voters from the list of over 100,000 voters. The sampled voters are asked, "Do you plan to vote for candidate A in the November election for the House of Representatives?" Because the sample size is small in relation to the population size, it is assumed that any single reply to this question will not affect the probabilities of the replies of the other samples voters. Thus the number of "Yes" replies among the 1600 sampled responses can be assumed to have a binomial distribution. Of the 1600 voters, 840 indicate an intention to vote for candidate A. The proportion of positive responses $\hat{p} = 840/1600 = 0.525$ is a natural estimate of $p$, but how good an estimate it is depends on how closely $\hat{p}$, the sample fraction of "successes," approximates $p$.

These two examples lead to the following definition of an estimator. Let $\theta$ represent a general population parameter, of which $\mu$, $m$, $\sigma^2$, and $p$ are examples.

---

**Definition 5.1** ▆▆▆▆▆▆▆▆▆▆▆▆▆▆▆▆▆▆▆▆▆▆▆▆▆▆▆▆

estimator

An **estimator** of $\theta$ is a statistic $\hat{\theta}_n$ that is a function of the observations in a random sample used to estimate $\theta$. The subscript $n$ emphasizes that the statistic is calculated on the basis of a sample of size $n$.

---

In Example 5.1, the statistic $\bar{X}$, the mean of the sample of 100 observations, is used as the estimator of $\mu_T$, the true expected waiting time. It is crucial to understand that the estimator (in this case the sample mean $\bar{X}$) is itself a random variable. From the continuous distribution of waiting times, an infinite number of random samples of size $n = 100$ can be drawn. Each such sample will produce a different value for the estimator $\bar{X}$. These values of $\bar{X}$ themselves have a distribution. It is by conceptualizing the distribution of the random variable $\bar{X}$ that one can attack the problem of determining the probable error in the estimation of $\mu$ made by using $\bar{X}$. (Note that an estimator is represented by a capital letter; a lowercase letter identifies a single value of an estimator. Hence, although we speak of the sample mean in general as $\bar{X}$, for the data of Example 5.1 we say that the value of the sample mean is $\bar{x} = 15.388$.)

In this chapter we will consider methods of estimating population parameters,

large-sample estimation

focusing on cases of **large-sample estimation.**

## 5.2

## The Distribution of the Sample Mean $\bar{X}$ in Large Samples

A basic problem in statistical estimation is the estimation of location for a population or, more precisely, a random variable defined for a population. As we have seen, there are various measures of location for a random variable. The population expectation $\mu = E(X)$ and the population median $m$ are two such measures. In this section and the next one, we will concentrate on the estimation of $\mu$. (For symmetric continuous random variables $m = \mu$, so for symmetric distributions the estimation of $\mu$ is equivalent to the estimation of $m$.)

The expectation $\mu$ can be estimated by the estimator $\bar{X}$, the average of $n$ independent observations of the random variable $X$. But first we must clarify what is meant by a random sample of size $n$ from a statistical distribution defined by the random variable $X$.

**random sample**

**parent distribution**

### Definition 5.2 ▬▬▬▬▬▬▬▬▬▬▬▬▬▬▬▬▬▬▬▬▬▬▬▬▬

A set of $n$ random variables $(X_1, X_2, \ldots, X_n)$ is called a **random sample** from $X$ if the distribution of each observation $X_i$ is the same as the distribution of $X$ (called the **parent distribution**) and the $X_i$s are statistically independent.

For continuous random variables it is reasonable to assume that the sampling of a finite number of observations from a population will not alter the original distribution. Hence, each selection will have the original (parent) distribution, and the observations can be considered to have been independently selected. In sampling from a finite population, one generally takes a random sample without replacement—the selection of a particular observation precludes its selection later. For instance, in the survey in Example 5.2, once a voter had been asked the candidate's question, that voter would not be selected again. This practice alters the population being sampled, leading to dependence among the observations $X_i$. As long as the sample size is small in comparison to the finite population size, however, the dependence may be assumed to be slight and Definition 5.2 may be considered to hold. Technically, in order to satisfy the requirements of the definition, one would have to replace each population element selected before selecting again. In the voting example this would involve allowing the same voter to appear twice (or even more often) in the sample.

The natural way to estimate $\mu$, the expectation of $X$, is to average the observations from a random sample. It is important to differentiate between $\mu$, the theoretical population expectation, and $\bar{X}$, its estimator. The former is a population quantity and cannot be observed. The estimator $\bar{X}$ is a random variable, which can take on many values. For different random samples of size $n$, different values of $\bar{X}$ will be observed. In practice we take only one sample and observe a single value of the random variable $\bar{X}$, which we denote by $\bar{x}$. In Example 5.1, observation of a single sample of size $n = 100$ yielded a value of $\bar{x} = 15.388$. This value is our estimate of $\mu$ in this case. In order to get information about the error of this estimate of $\mu$, we must consider the possible values the estimator $\bar{X}$ may have. In other words, the **distribution of $\bar{X}$** must be investigated.

**distribution of $\bar{X}$**

Consider the random variable

$$\bar{X} = \sum_{i=1}^{n} X_i/n$$

where $X_i$ are the observations from a random sample as defined in Definition 5.2. The parent population $X$ is assumed to have expectation $\mu$ and variance $\sigma^2$. To confirm that $\bar{X}$ has a probability distribution, consider the very simple example of the outcomes of tossing a fair die with two faces labeled 1, two faces labeled 2, and two faces labeled 3. The parent population $X$ has the probability function $p(1) = p(2) = p(3) = 1/3$. By tossing two such dice, one can obtain the sums of two observations taken independently. The sample space is shown in Figure 5.1. Each of the nine points has an equal probability of $1/9$.

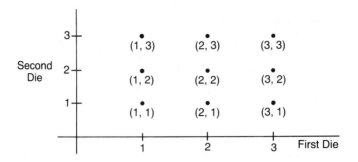

**Figure 5.1**

Outcome Space for Tosses of Two Dice Labeled Double 1, 2, and 3

Table 5.1 gives the probability function for the sum of two independent tosses. Dividing each sum by 2 yields the distribution of $\bar{X}$, the average of two independent tosses. Note that whereas the parent population assigns equal probability to each point, the same is not true of the distribution of averages. The probability function of $\bar{X}$ for three observations of $X$ appears in Table 5.2.

Tables 5.1 and 5.2 give useful general information about the distribution of a sample mean $\bar{X}$. The original population $X$ has expectation

$$E(X) = 1\left(\frac{1}{3}\right) + 2\left(\frac{1}{3}\right) + 3\left(\frac{1}{3}\right) = 2$$

From Table 5.1 we see that in the case of a sample of size $n = 2$,

$$E(\bar{X}) = 1\left(\frac{1}{9}\right) + 1.5\left(\frac{2}{9}\right) + 2\left(\frac{3}{9}\right) + 2.5\left(\frac{2}{9}\right) + 3\left(\frac{1}{9}\right) = \frac{18}{9} = 2$$

Table 5.2 shows that in the case of $n = 3$,

$$E(\bar{X}) = 1\left(\frac{1}{27}\right) + \left(\frac{4}{3}\right)\left(\frac{3}{27}\right) + \left(\frac{5}{3}\right)\left(\frac{6}{27}\right) + 2\left(\frac{7}{27}\right) + \left(\frac{7}{3}\right)\left(\frac{6}{27}\right)$$

$$+ \left(\frac{8}{3}\right)\left(\frac{3}{27}\right) + 3\left(\frac{1}{27}\right)$$

$$= \frac{54}{27} = 2$$

**Table 5.1**

Probability Function for $\bar{X}$ ($n = 2$)

| Sum | 2 | 3 | 4 | 5 | 6 |
|---|---|---|---|---|---|
| Average, $\bar{x}$ | 1 | 3/2 | 2 | 5/2 | 3 |
| Probability, $P(\bar{X} = x)$ | 1/9 | 2/9 | 3/9 | 2/9 | 1/9 |

**Table 5.2**

| Probability Function for $\bar{X}(n = 3)$ | | | | | | | |
|---|---|---|---|---|---|---|---|
| $\bar{x}$ | 1 | 4/3 | 5/3 | 2 | 7/3 | 8/3 | 3 |
| $P(\bar{X} = \bar{x})$ | 1/27 | 3/27 | 6/27 | 7/27 | 6/27 | 3/27 | 1/27 |

In each case $E(\bar{X}) = E(X) = \mu$. We will see later that in general the statistic $\bar{X}$ will have the same expectation as the original sampled random variable $X$; that is, for any sample size,

$$E(\bar{X}) = E(X) = \mu \qquad\qquad \textbf{5.1}$$

Tables 5.1 and 5.2 also show that the distribution of $\bar{X}$ is not the same as the original distribution of $X$. In fact, in these two cases the probability that $\bar{X}$ will have a value near $\mu = 2$ increases as $n$ increases. We will prove shortly that

$$\text{Var}(\bar{X}) = \frac{\text{Var}(X)}{n} = \frac{\sigma^2}{n} \qquad\qquad \textbf{5.2}$$

Hence for any value of $n > 1$, $\text{Var}(\bar{X}) = \sigma^2/n < \sigma^2$; that is, the "variation" about $\mu$ is less for $\bar{X}$ than for the $X$ original population.

## Minitab Probability Histograms for $\bar{X}$

Minitab can be used to generate histograms, which may be interpreted as probability histograms, for the sum and mean (average) of $n = 2$ and $n = 3$ independent observations of the discrete random variable $X$, which assigns equal probability to each of the integers 1, 2, . . . , $k$. We will consider the case where $k = 5$. The histogram for $n = 2$, in Exhibit 5.2, was obtained by putting the blocks of integers 11111, 22222, . . . , 55555 in C1 and the block of integers 12345 repeated five times in C2 and adding these columns in C3. The histogram for $n = 3$, in Exhibit 5.3, was obtained similarly.

It should be clear that the distribution of the sample means causes the probability to be concentrated close to the expectation, $E(X) = 3$, of the parent population. Also, the probability distribution for the averages of three such independently selected integers displays a decidedly bell-shaped appearance. In fact, the distribution of such averages approaches a normal distribution as $n$ increases.

Let us now make more precise these observations concerning the distribution of $\bar{X}$ for a random sample of size $n$. As $\bar{X}$ is a random variable, it has an expectation. To find the expectation of $\bar{X}$, we use the fact that the "expectation of the sum" is the "sum of the expectations" and the fact that $E(X_i) = \mu$ for all $i$ (because each

## Exhibit 5.2

```
MTB > NOTE HISTOGRAM OF SUMS OF PAIRS OF FIRST 5 INTEGERS
MTB > SET C1
C1
   1   1   1   1   .   .   .

MTB > END
MTB > SET C2
C2
   1   2   3   4   .   .   .

MTB > END
MTB > ADD C1 TO C2 IN C3
MTB > HISTOGRAM C3

Histogram of C3    N = 25

Midpoint    Count
      2        1    *
      3        2    **
      4        3    ***
      5        4    ****
      6        5    *****
      7        4    ****
      8        3    ***
      9        2    **
     10        1    *

MTB > NOTE HISTOGRAM OF AVERAGES OF PAIRS OF FIRST 5 INTEGERS
MTB > DIVIDE C3 BY 2 IN C3
MTB > HISTOGRAM C3

Histogram of C3    N = 25

Midpoint    Count
    1.0        1    *
    1.5        2    **
    2.0        3    ***
    2.5        4    ****
    3.0        5    *****
    3.5        4    ****
    4.0        3    ***
    4.5        2    **
    5.0        1    *
```

$X_i$ has the parent distribution):

$$E(\bar{X}) = E\left(\sum_{i=1}^{n} \frac{X_i}{n}\right) = \left(\frac{1}{n}\right) E\left(\sum_{i=1}^{n} X_i\right) = \left(\frac{1}{n}\right) \sum_{i=1}^{n} E(X_i)$$

$$= \left(\frac{1}{n}\right) \sum_{i=1}^{n} \mu = \left(\frac{1}{n}\right) n\mu = \mu$$

5.3

The expected value of the population of the averages of $n$ independent observations from the parent population is $\mu$, the expectation of the parent population. This relationship is valid for both discrete and continuous parent populations. As the probability histograms created with Minitab show, however, the distribution of $\bar{X}$ is not the same as that of the parent population.

**Exhibit 5.3**

```
MTB > NOTE HISTOGRAM OF SUMS OF TRIPLES OF FIRST 5 INTEGERS
MTB > SET C1
C1
    1    1    1    1    .    .    .

MTB > END
MTB > SET C2
C2
    1    2    3    4    .    .    .

MTB > END
MTB > SET C3
C3
    1    1    1    1    .    .    .

MTB > END
MTB > ADD C1 TO C2 IN C4
MTB > ADD C3 TO C4 IN C4
MTB > HISTOGRAM C4

Histogram of C4    N = 125

Midpoint   Count
      3      1   *
      4      3   ***
      5      6   ******
      6     10   **********
      7     15   ***************
      8     18   ******************
      9     19   *******************
     10     18   ******************
     11     15   ***************
     12     10   **********
     13      6   ******
     14      3   ***
     15      1   *


MTB > NOTE HISTOGRAM OF AVERAGES OF TRIPLES OF FIRST 5 INTEGERS
MTB > DIVIDE C4 BY 3 IN C4
MTB > HISTOGRAM C4 FIRST MIDPOINT = 1 INTERVAL = .33333

Histogram of C4    N = 125

Midpoint   Count
   1.000     1   *
   1.333     3   ***
   1.667     6   ******
   2.000    10   **********
   2.333    15   ***************
   2.667    18   ******************
   3.000    19   *******************
   3.333    18   ******************
   3.667    15   ***************
   4.000    10   **********
   4.333     6   ******
   4.667     3   ***
   5.000     1   *
```

To find the variance of the random variable $\bar{X}$, we use the fact that $\text{Var}(kX) = k^2\,\text{Var}(X)$ for any random variable $X$; the fact that for independent random variables, the variance of a sum of random variables is the sum of the variances; and the fact that $\text{Var}(X_i) = \sigma^2$ for all $i$ (because each $X_i$ has the parent population distribution):

$$\text{Var}(\bar{X}) = \text{Var}\left(\sum_{i=1}^{n}\frac{X_i}{n}\right) = \frac{1}{n^2}\sum_{i=1}^{n}\text{Var}(X_i)$$

$$= \frac{1}{n^2}\sum_{i=1}^{n}\sigma^2 = \frac{1}{n^2}n\sigma^2 = \frac{\sigma^2}{n}$$

**5.4**

For the distribution given by $P(1) = P(2) = P(3) = 1/3$, we saw that $E(X) = 2$. Hence

$$\text{Var}(X) = (1-2)^2\left(\frac{1}{3}\right) + (2-2)^2\left(\frac{1}{3}\right) + (3-2)^2\left(\frac{1}{3}\right) = \frac{2}{3}$$

From Table 5.1 we find that

$$\text{Var}(\bar{X}) = (1-2)^2\left(\frac{1}{9}\right) + (1.5-2)^2\left(\frac{2}{9}\right) + (2-2)^2\left(\frac{3}{9}\right)$$

$$+ (2.5-2)^2\left(\frac{2}{9}\right) + (3-2)^2\left(\frac{1}{9}\right) = \frac{3}{9} = \frac{1}{3}$$

Thus in this case

$$\text{Var}\,(\bar{X}) = \frac{\text{Var}(X)}{n} = \frac{2/3}{2} = \frac{1}{3}$$

as required by Equation 5.4.

Because $\text{Var}(\bar{X}) = \sigma^2/n$, $\text{Var}(\bar{X})$ must become small as $n$ becomes large. Because $E(\bar{X}) = \mu$, the probability that $\bar{X}$ will be close to $\mu$ must become close to 1 as $n$ becomes large. The relationship between the distributions of $X$ and $\bar{X}$ in the continuous case is depicted by the probability density functions in Figure 5.2. The

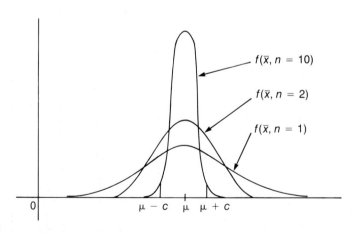

**Figure 5.2**

**Probability Densities of $\bar{X}$, $n = 1$, 2, and 10**

CHAPTER 5   LARGE-SAMPLE ESTIMATION

distributions shown have the same expectation, $\mu$, for all values of $n$. As $\sigma^2/n$ becomes smaller with increases in $n$, more and more of the area under the density functions for $\bar{X}$ falls within a fixed interval $(\mu - c, \mu + c)$. Figure 5.2 is a graphical illustration of what was established earlier—that the probability that $\bar{X}$ will attain a value near $\mu$ becomes high as $n$ becomes large. This property is, of course, a desirable one for an estimator, as the point of using $\bar{X}$ is to estimate $\mu$.

Finally, we can make the surprising observation that, as long as the parent population $X$ has a finite expectation $\mu$ and a finite variance $\sigma^2$, the distribution of sample means, $\bar{X}$, behaves like a normal random variable, with $E(\bar{X}) = \mu$ and $\text{Var}(\bar{X}) = \sigma^2/n$ for large $n$. More precisely, for large $n$ the standardized random variable

$$\frac{\bar{X} - E(\bar{X})}{\sigma_{\bar{X}}} = \frac{\bar{X} - \mu}{\sigma/\sqrt{n}}$$

can be treated as a standard normal variable $Z$. We can write

$$\frac{\bar{X} - \mu}{\sigma/\sqrt{n}} \sim Z$$

**Central Limit Theorem**

What is surprising here is that the form of the underlying parent population does not matter—the large-sample standardized distribution of $\bar{X}$ is approximately the same as that of $Z$. This result, called the **Central Limit Theorem**, is one of the most important theorems in statistics. It accounts in large part for the great importance of the normal distribution in statistics.

## Minitab Illustration of the Central Limit Theorem

In order to demonstrate the Central Limit Theorem, the Minitab command RANDOM was used to obtain 200 observations of means of samples of size $n = 12$ from the uniform distribution on $(0, 1)$. (See Exhibit 5.4.) This parent population has the probability density function

$$f(x) = \begin{cases} 1 & \text{if } 0 \leqslant x \leqslant 1 \\ 0 & \text{elsewhere} \end{cases}$$

As the graph of the density function in Figure 5.3 illustrates, distribution is decidedly nonnormal, assigning equal probabilities to intervals of $(0, 1)$ of equal length. The observations from the uniform distribution $U(0, 1)$ were stored by Minitab in the columns C1–C12. These twelve columns were then summed and divided by 12, yielding 200 sample averages from the $U(0, 1)$ distribution in C14. Two histograms were printed out. The first is the histogram of the 200 observations in C1; the second is the histogram of the 200 sample means in C14. Together they provide a **simulation of the distribution of** $\bar{X}$. In addition, AVERAGE and STDEV commands were used with columns C1 and C14.

**simulation of the distribution of** $\bar{X}$

In the first histogram the interval $[0, 1]$ is divided into ten intervals of length 0.1. The number of the 200 observations in C1 falling into each of these ten classes

**Exhibit 5.4**

```
MTB > NOTE SIMULATION OF THE AVERAGES OF 12 U(0,1) OBSERVATIONS
MTB > BASE = 1000
MTB > RANDOM 200 OBSERVATIONS IN C1-C12;
SUBC> UNIFORM A = 0 B = 1.
MTB > ADD C1-C12 IN C14
MTB > DIVIDE C14 BY 12 IN C14
MTB > AVERAGE C1
    MEAN     =      0.50826
MTB > STDEV C1
    ST.DEV. =      0.29598
MTB > HISTOGRAM C1 FIRST MIDPOINT = 0.05 INTERVAL = .1


Histogram of C1    N = 200

Midpoint    Count
   0.050      21    *********************
   0.150      19    *******************
   0.250      18    ******************
   0.350      25    *************************
   0.450      18    ******************
   0.550      20    ********************
   0.650      15    ***************
   0.750      19    *******************
   0.850      21    *********************
   0.950      24    ************************


MTB > AVERAGE C14
    MEAN     =      0.49626
MTB > STDEV C14
    ST.DEV. =      0.087496
MTB > HISTOGRAM C14


Histogram of C14    N = 200

Midpoint    Count
   0.25       1    *
   0.30       2    **
   0.35      14    **************
   0.40      28    ****************************
   0.45      43    *******************************************
   0.50      34    **********************************
   0.55      42    ******************************************
   0.60      19    *******************
   0.65      12    ************
   0.70       5    *****
```

is shown. As each interval has probability 1/10 of containing an individual observation, the expected number of observations in each interval is $200(1/10) = 20$. The observed frequencies are about the same except for sampling variation. The second histogram of the 200 sample means shows the bell-shaped form characteristic of the normal distribution, even though the original distribution from which the observations were sampled was uniform on (0, 1).

Additional information about the original distribution and the distribution of the means can be procured through use of the AVERAGE and STDEV commands. The standard deviation of the random variable $U(0, 1)$ [that is, the uniform random variable on (0, 1)], is $\sigma_U = 1/\sqrt{12} = 0.289$ with $E(U) = 0.5$. For

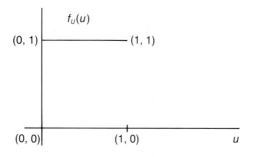

**Figure 5.3**

**Density of Uniform (0, 1) Distribution**

the 200 observations in C1, these values are reasonably approximated by $s = 0.29598$ and $\bar{x} = 0.50826$. For the means of samples of size 12, the expectation $E(\bar{U}) = E(U) = 0.5$ and the theoretical standard deviation $\sigma_{\bar{U}} = \sigma_U/\sqrt{n} = (1/\sqrt{12})/\sqrt{12} = 1/12 = 0.0833$. For the 200 sample means in C14, the corresponding average is 0.49626 and standard deviation is 0.0875, both of which approximate the theoretical values quite well.

The Central Limit Theorem can be used to approximate certain probabilities concerning the distribution of $\bar{X}$. To do so we make use of the fact that, when the sample size is reasonably large,

$$\frac{\bar{X} - \mu_X}{\sigma_X/\sqrt{n}} \sim Z \qquad \qquad \textbf{5.5}$$

The size of $n$ required in order for Equation 5.5 to be valid depends on the distribution of the parent population $X$. For $n \geqslant 30$, the normal approximation is usually quite good. For symmetric parent populations, smaller values of $n$ are adequate, as the preceding simulation of means of $n = 12$ observations illustrates.

**Example 5.3**

A machine fills packages in such a way that the standard deviation of the net weights of the packages is $\sigma = 0.25$ oz, regardless of the true expected net weight of the package, $\mu$. Suppose $n = 36$ packages are packed in each carton, and assume $\mu = 32.1$. We want to find the probability that the average net weight of a package in a carton is less than 32 oz. This probability will not depend on the distribution of the original weights. Using Table I in Appendix C, we have

$$P(\bar{X} < 32) = P\left(\frac{\bar{X} - \mu}{\sigma/\sqrt{n}} < \frac{32 - 32.1}{0.25/6}\right)$$
$$= P(Z < -2.4) = 0.0082$$

(See Figure 5.4.) This probability is quite small. Thus if $\mu = 32.1$ oz, very few cartons of 36 packages will average less than 32 oz per package.

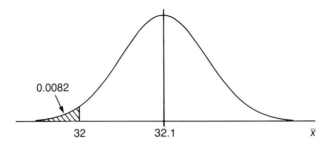

0.0082

32          32.1          $\bar{X}$

**Figure 5.4**

$P(\bar{X} < 32)$

For comparison let us compute the probability that an individual package will be less than 32 oz in net weight, *assuming the normality* of the original observations.

$$P(X < 32) = P\left(\frac{X - \mu}{\sigma} < \frac{32 - 32.1}{0.25}\right)$$

$$= P(Z < -0.40) = 0.3446$$

In this situation more than 34 percent of the original packages will have a net weight of less than 32 oz. The explanation of the difference between the two probabilities is that the values of the averages of the net weights of 36 packages will be close to $E(\bar{X}) = \mu = 32.1$ because $\sigma_{\bar{x}} = \sigma/\sqrt{n} = 0.25/6 = 0.04167$. Few cartons will have an average package weight of less than 32 oz, as this value is $2.4\sigma_{\bar{x}}$ below $E(\bar{X})$ because $2.4\sigma_{\bar{x}} = 2.4(\sigma/\sqrt{n}) = 2.4(0.25)/6 = 0.1$.

**Example 5.4**

Test scores on a standardized examination have averaged $\mu = 70$ with $\sigma = 5$ over a long period of time. The scores of the current class of 36 students average 72.5. What was the probability of this class's attaining an average of 72.5 or better?

$$P(\bar{X} \geqslant 72.5) = P\left[\frac{\bar{X} - \mu}{\sigma/\sqrt{n}} \geqslant \left(\frac{72.5 - 70}{5/6}\right)\right]$$

$$= P(Z \geqslant 3) = 0.0013$$

The probability of a sample mean of at least 72.5 is quite small. If $\sigma = 5$ is correct and a value of $\bar{X} \geqslant 72.5$ is observed, either an unusually rare event has occurred or this class of students is performing better on average than those in the past did. In practical situations we would probably decide in favor of the latter.

## Example 5.5

Waiting times at a checkout counter have a distribution with $\mu = 10$ and $\sigma = 10$. Waiting times typically are not normally distributed. We want to find the probability that the average of 64 waiting times in a randomly selected sample will exceed 11.5.

$$P(\bar{X} > 11.5) = P\left[Z > \left(\frac{11.5 - 10}{10/8}\right)\right]$$
$$= P(Z > 1.2) = 0.1151$$

With $\mu = 10$ and $\sigma = 10$, the probability that a sample mean based on a sample of size $n = 64$ will exceed 11.5 is 0.1151. Although this probability is somewhat small, it is not unusually small. An average of over 11.5 would be observed about once in every nine samples of size 64.

---

In this section we have considered the distribution of averages of samples of size $n$ from a parent population $X$. Such averages $\bar{X}$ are random variables with $E(\bar{X}) = E(X)$ and $\text{Var}(\bar{X}) = \text{Var}(X)/n$. For large samples, the standardized random variable $(\bar{X} - \mu_X)/(\sigma_X/\sqrt{n})$ has approximately a standard normal distribution. A rule of thumb is that $n \geq 30$ is adequate for the normal approximation. Although this rule is not completely valid, it is reliable for most practical purposes and can be used for the exercises of this chapter.

## Exercises 5.2

**5.1** Consider a continuous distribution with $\mu_X = 25$ and $\sigma_X^2 = 25$. Assume that a random sample of $n = 36$ observations is taken from this population.
   **a.** Find $E(\bar{X})$.
   **b.** Find $\text{Var}(\bar{X})$.
   **c.** Approximate $P(\bar{X} \geq 26)$ and $P(\bar{X} \leq 23)$.
   **d.** Approximate $P(23 \leq \bar{X} \leq 26)$.

**5.2** The dollar amount in a bank's checking accounts is a random variable $X$ with $E(X) = \$373$ and $\text{Var}(X) = \$100$. Use the Central Limit Theorem to approximate the probability that the average dollar amount of 64 randomly selected accounts will exceed $375.

**5.3** Assume that the dividends of electric utility stocks as of a given date have a distribution with $\mu = 8.5$ percent and $\sigma = 2.5$ percent. Use the Central Limit Theorem to find the probability that the average dividend of 25 such stocks will exceed 10 percent. (Assume that, because of the symmetry of the underlying population, $n = 25$ is large enough for the Central Limit Theorem to apply.)

**5.4** Test scores are assumed to have $E(X) = \mu = 75$ with $\text{Var}(X) = \sigma^2 = 16$. For a random sample of size $n = 64$, find
   **a.** $P(\bar{X} \leq 75)$       **c.** $P(\bar{X} \geq 74)$
   **b.** $P(\bar{X} \leq 76)$       **d.** $P(\bar{X} \geq 78)$

**5.5** Consider the discrete random variable $X$ with probability function $P(X) = 1/6$ for $x = 1, 2, 3, 4, 5, 6$.
  **a.** Find the probability function of the average of two independent selections from this distribution.
  **b.** Find $E(X)$ and $E(\bar{X})$ from the probability functions of $X$ and $\bar{X}$.
  **c.** Find $\text{Var}(X)$ and $\text{Var}(\bar{X})$ from the probability functions, and show that $\text{Var}(\bar{X}) = \text{Var}(X)/2$.

**5.6** Consider the discrete random variable $X$, which assigns equal probability to the integers 1, 2, 3, and 4.
  **a.** Find the probability function of the average of two selections from this distribution without replacement.
  **b.** Find $E(X)$ and $E(\bar{X})$ from the probability functions of $X$ and $\bar{X}$. Is $E(X) = E(\bar{X})$?
  **c.** Find $\text{Var}(X)$ and $\text{Var}(\bar{X})$ from the probability functions. Is $\text{Var}(\bar{X}) = \text{Var}(X)/2$?

**5.7** A fair die is tossed a total of $n$ times.
  **a.** What is the value of $E(\bar{X})$ for $n = 3$? for $n = 4$? for general $n$?
  **b.** Using $\text{Var}(\bar{X}) = \text{Var}(X)/n$, calculate $\text{Var}(\bar{X})$ for $n = 3$.
  **c.** Find $\text{Var}(\bar{X})$ for general $n$.

**5.8** In an article in the *Journal of the American Statistical Association*, D. J. Davis (1952) presents the number of correct entries between each mistake for several ledger clerks. For the first clerk he presents the following data:

734  121 404 646 1072  148  312 773   43 1102 111
641  754 598  86 2138  150 1047 907  165  166   6
 94 1023 903 355  303 1378  202 343 1266

  **a.** Assume these data come from a distribution with $\mu = 576$ and $\sigma = 576$. Find the approximate probability of observing a mean as large as that observed or larger.
  **b.** Make a histogram of these observations. Do they appear to be normally distributed?
  **c.** Why does your answer to part b not invalidate the calculation in part a?

**5.9** **a.** Employing the method described in this section, use Minitab to simulate the averages of 100 means of 16 observations from the uniform distribution on (0, 1).
  **b.** Produce histograms for the first group of 100 $U(0, 1)$ observations and for the 100 means. Describe the difference between the shapes of these two histograms.
  **c.** Given $E(U) = 0.5$ and $\text{Var}(U) = 1/12$, find $E(\bar{U})$ and $\text{Var}(\bar{U})$ in this case.

**5.10** Using Minitab, SET the values 0, 5, 10, 15 in Cl and the probabilities 0.20, 0.30, 0.30, 0.20 in C2. Use RANDOM to simulate 100 means of size 16 from this distribution.
  **a.** Make a histogram of the 100 means. What is its general appearance? Why?
  **b.** Find $E(\bar{X})$ and $\sigma_{\bar{X}}$, and compare these values with the results of applying the DESCRIBE command to the column of means.

## 5.3

### Estimation of $\mu$ in Large Samples

point estimate

It has just been demonstrated that the statistic $\bar{X}$ is a good estimate of the population expectation $\mu$. We proved that $E(\bar{X}) = \mu$, and we showed that, for large sample size $n$, the probability that $\bar{X}$ will be close to $\mu$ is high (that is, close to 1). An estimator such as $\bar{X}$, which gives a single numerical value computed from a random sample of $n$ observations, is called a **point estimate**. In Exhibit 5.4,

Minitab calculated $\bar{x} = 0.50826$ as a point estimate of $E(U) = 0.5$ for the first sample of 200 observations from $U(0, 1)$. In many applications, however, it is preferable to obtain an interval of values that has a high probability of containing $\mu$. Such intervals, called confidence intervals, are widely used in the estimation of population parameters.

**confidence interval for $\mu$**

In this section the focus is on finding a **confidence interval for** $\mu$, an unknown population expectation. The object is to obtain an interval of values that is likely to contain the unknown parameter $\mu$. The aim is to obtain $L(X_1, X_2, \ldots, X_n)$ and $U(X_1, X_2, \ldots, X_n)$ such that

$$P(L < \mu < U) = 1 - \alpha \qquad \textbf{5.6}$$

**confidence coefficient**

where $L$ stands for the lower endpoint of the confidence interval, $U$ stands for the upper endpoint of the confidence interval, and $1 - \alpha$ is called the **confidence coefficient**. The dependence of $L$ and $U$ on the sample observations $X_1, X_2, \ldots, X_n$ has been suppressed in Equation 5.6, but these endpoints do depend on the sample observations. Hence both $L$ and $U$ are random variables. The value $1 - \alpha$ is the probability that the random interval $(L, U)$ includes $\mu$. This probability can be thought of as giving the long-run frequency that intervals found using the endpoints $L$ and $U$ will include the unknown population expectation $\mu$. Because we want a high probability of coverage, $\alpha$ must be small. Frequently a value of $\alpha = 0.05$ or $\alpha = 0.01$ is chosen. Because

$$(1 - 0.05)100 = 0.95(100) = 95 \text{ percent}$$

and

$$(1 - 0.01)100 = 0.99(100) = 99 \text{ percent}$$

the corresponding intervals are called 95 percent and 99 percent confidence intervals for $\mu$, respectively.

To find $L$ and $U$ in the large-sample case, we consider the following probability statement about the standard normal distribution.

$$P(-z_{\alpha/2} < Z < z_{\alpha/2}) = 1 - \alpha \qquad \textbf{5.7}$$

The meaning of Equation 5.7 is clear from Figure 5.5. Note that the point $z_{\alpha/2}$ cuts off a tail area of $\alpha/2$ to the right and the point $-z_{\alpha/2}$ cuts off a tail area of $\alpha/2$ to the left. Hence the area under the standard normal probability density function between $-z_{\alpha/2}$ and $z_{\alpha/2}$ and above the $z$ axis must be $1 - \alpha$. Table 5.3 gives values

**Table 5.3**

Selected Values of $z_{\alpha/2}$

| $\alpha$ | 0.20 | 0.10 | 0.05 | 0.02 | 0.01 |
|----------------|-------|-------|-------|-------|-------|
| $z_{\alpha/2}$ | 1.282 | 1.645 | 1.960 | 2.326 | 2.576 |

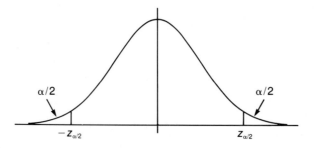

**Figure 5.5**

Tail Areas for Standard Normal Distribution

of $z_{\alpha/2}$ for a few values of $\alpha$. If $\alpha = 0.05$, for example, we find that $z_{0.025} = 1.96$, and

$$P(-1.96 < Z < 1.96) = 0.95$$

Thus 95 percent of the observations from the standard normal distribution lie between $-1.96$ and $1.96$.

In order to find a confidence interval for $\mu$, we first apply the Central Limit Theorem to Equation 5.7 and then multiply the inequality by $\sigma/\sqrt{n}$:

$$P(-z_{\alpha/2} < Z < z_{\alpha/2}) = 1 - \alpha$$

$$P\left(-z_{\alpha/2} < \frac{\bar{X} - \mu}{\sigma\sqrt{n}} < z_{\alpha/2}\right) = 1 - \alpha$$

$$P\left(-\frac{\sigma}{\sqrt{n}} z_{\alpha/2} < \bar{X} - \mu < \frac{\sigma}{\sqrt{n}} z_{\alpha/2}\right) = 1 - \alpha$$

$$P\left(\bar{X} - \frac{\sigma}{\sqrt{n}} z_{\alpha/2} < \mu < \bar{X} + \frac{\sigma}{\sqrt{n}} z_{\alpha/2}\right) = 1 - \alpha \qquad \textbf{5.8}$$

The reader should check that the final double inequality is equivalent to the preceding one. The final double inequality yields $L = \bar{X} - (\sigma/\sqrt{n})z_{\alpha/2}$ and $U = \bar{X} + (\sigma/\sqrt{n})z_{\alpha/2}$ as the required endpoints for a $(1 - \alpha)100$ percent confidence interval for $\mu$.

**Example 5.6**

Consider the $n = 200$ observations from $U(0, 1)$ in column C1 in Exhibit 5.4. Suppose we want to find the endpoints of a 95 percent confidence interval for $E(U)$, the expectation of the uniform random variable on $(0, 1)$. Using the fact that $\sigma^2 = 1/12$ for the uniform random variable and rounding to three decimals, we have

$$L = \bar{X} + \frac{\sigma}{\sqrt{n}} z_{0.025} = 0.508 - \frac{1}{\sqrt{2400}} 1.96$$

$$= 0.508 - 0.040 = 0.468$$

and

$$U = \bar{X} + \frac{\sigma}{\sqrt{n}} z_{0.025} = 0.508 + 0.040 = 0.548$$

Thus the 95 percent confidence interval is (0.468, 0.548), which certainly contains the true value of $\mu$, known in this case to be $E(U) = 0.5$.

A practical problem in carrying out computations like those in Example 5.6 is that $\sigma^2$ is generally not known. For large samples, however, one can replace $\sigma$ with the sample standard deviation and obtain an approximate $(1 - \alpha)100$ percent confidence interval using the endpoints

$$\bar{X} \pm \frac{s}{\sqrt{n}} z_{\alpha/2} \qquad\qquad \textbf{5.9}$$

## Example 5.7

Again let us consider finding a 95 percent confidence interval for the uniform distribution on (0, 1), this time using a sample of size $n = 100$ and using Equation 5.9 to find the endpoints of the confidence interval. Minitab allows quick calculation of the required endpoints. The command RANDOM is used to sample the 100 observations in C1. The standard deviation of these 100 observations is

ZINTERVAL    assigned to K1. Finally, the **ZINTERVAL** command is used to find the required endpoints. The Minitab output is shown in Exhibit 5.5; the confidence interval is given in the last line of the output.

To clarify the meaning of the confidence coefficient, Minitab was used on 19 other samples of size 100 from $U(0, 1)$. The endpoints for the intervals are given in Table 5.4. As before, $L$ stands for the lower endpoint of the confidence interval and $U$ for the upper endpoint. As Table 5.4 shows, the probability 0.95 is not associated with any particular interval. Rather, the probability 0.95 is associated with the way in which the interval was obtained. In the long run, 95 out of 100 intervals obtained using this procedure will contain $\mu$. In Table 5.4, all intervals but those with an asterisk (numbers 7 and 17) contain 0.5. Hence the proportion of these 20 intervals containing $\mu$ is 0.90. For a very large number of such calculations, one would expect this proportion to be near 0.95, the indicated confidence coefficient. The 95 percent probability is thus associated with the procedure; it is a way of expressing that we have 95 percent confidence in any particular interval arrived at with this procedure. If we happen to obtain interval number 7, we will be mistaken in assuming that it contains $\mu$. This type of error is always possible

## Exhibit 5.5

```
MTB > NOTE CONFIDENCE INTERVAL FOR EXPECTED VALUE OF UNIFORM (0,1)
MTB > BASE = 1000
MTB > RANDOM 100 OBS IN C1;
SUBC> UNIFORM A = 0 B = 1.
MTB > PRINT C1
C1
  0.290675   0.168050   0.544834   0.060491   0.442637   0.242192
  0.610525   0.129107   0.819880   0.347385   0.716742   0.233535
  0.892020   0.291974   0.581578   0.824085   0.152262   0.186173
  0.518754   0.991703   0.487927   0.487101   0.344987   0.249377
  0.149878   0.100705   0.314226   0.771125   0.497520   0.614941
  0.377796   0.070646   0.024639   0.892330   0.430579   0.475374
  0.446495   0.389205   0.239286   0.950244   0.068013   0.882213
  0.484642   0.613849   0.784735   0.774078   0.598150   0.367605
  0.163989   0.223126   0.716906   0.807070   0.392587   0.000284
  0.561427   0.125988   0.901907   0.597830   0.977930   0.283883
  0.346570   0.203587   0.569534   0.395111   0.528510   0.595584
  0.130312   0.389542   0.750269   0.003500   0.313562   0.836643
  0.664749   0.973302   0.301842   0.995667   0.043739   0.072368
  0.988979   0.647037   0.297720   0.451537   0.752641   0.897928
  0.480725   0.355160   0.177569   0.505226   0.612548   0.813013
  0.380498   0.377467   0.647810   0.306994   0.970080   0.646354
  0.918535   0.600808   0.841089   0.924262

MTB > STDEV C1 IN K1
  ST.DEV. =     0.28241
MTB > ZINTERVAL 95 PERCENT CONFIDENCE, SIGMA = K1 DATA IN C1

THE ASSUMED SIGMA =0.282

              N     MEAN    STDEV   SE MEAN    95.0 PERCENT C.I.
C1          100    0.4939   0.2824   0.0282   ( 0.4385,  0.5494)
```

## Table 5.4

**Endpoints of Twenty 95 Percent Confidence Intervals for $p = 0.5$**

| Sample No. | L | U | Sample No. | L | U |
|---|---|---|---|---|---|
| 1 | 0.4385 | 0.5494 | 11 | 0.4604 | 0.5798 |
| 2 | 0.4289 | 0.5478 | 12 | 0.4193 | 0.5443 |
| 3 | 0.4512 | 0.5608 | 13 | 0.4404 | 0.5531 |
| 4 | 0.4235 | 0.5447 | 14 | 0.4050 | 0.5106 |
| 5 | 0.4245 | 0.5377 | 15 | 0.4136 | 0.5327 |
| 6 | 0.4356 | 0.5522 | 16 | 0.4163 | 0.5256 |
| 7* | 0.3743 | 0.4925 | 17* | 0.3591 | 0.4727 |
| 8 | 0.4961 | 0.6119 | 18 | 0.4477 | 0.5647 |
| 9 | 0.4669 | 0.5776 | 19 | 0.4266 | 0.5438 |
| 10 | 0.4334 | 0.5450 | 20 | 0.4475 | 0.5606 |

with inferential procedures. However, statistical methods are constructed so that there is a known (small) probability of making such an error.

Several important observations can be made about the form of the endpoints of confidence intervals. For simplicity we will look at the case in which $\sigma$ is known and the endpoints are $\bar{x} \pm (\sigma/\sqrt{n})z_{\alpha/2}$. Ideally we would like to have a short confidence interval with a high confidence coefficient. Consider Example 5.6, in which a random sample of size 200 from $U(0, 1)$ was used with $\sigma^2 = 1/12$. If we increase the confidence coefficient from 0.95 to 0.99, the length of the confidence interval increases from $2(\sigma/\sqrt{n})z_{0.025} = 2(0.040) = 0.080$ to $2(\sigma/\sqrt{n})z_{0.005} = 2(0.0526) = 0.105$. For a given data set, increased confidence can be obtained only at the cost of having a longer interval. Similarly, $2(\sigma/\sqrt{n})z_{\alpha/2}$ decreases as $\alpha$ increases—that is, one can obtain a shorter confidence interval by increasing $\alpha$. Then, however, the confidence coefficient, $100(1 - \alpha)$, decreases. For example, if we let $\alpha = 0.10$ for the data set of Example 5.6, an interval of length $2(\sigma/\sqrt{n})z_{0.05} = 2(0.0336) = 0.067$ is obtained. The length of this interval is less than 0.080, but the confidence coefficient has now decreased to 90 percent. Only by increasing $n$ is it possible to decrease the length of the confidence interval, $2(\sigma/\sqrt{n})z_{\alpha/2}$, and simultaneously increase the confidence coefficient. Suppose in Example 5.6 that $\bar{x}$ remained the same but the sample size was increased to 400. If the confidence coefficient were increased to 99 percent, the length of the resulting interval would be $2(1/\sqrt{4800})(2.576) = 0.074$, which is less than 0.080.

One additional observation about confidence intervals is also instructive. Suppose one wanted a 100 percent confidence interval. In this case $\alpha = 0$. Then $z_{\alpha/2} = z_0 = \infty$, and the interval $\bar{x} \pm (\sigma/\sqrt{n})z_{\alpha/2}$ becomes the entire real number line. It is certainly true that, whatever the value of $\mu$, it always will fall in the interval $-\infty < \mu < \infty$, but no sampling is needed to make this not very useful conclusion. Hence one must use a value of $1 - \alpha$ that is less than but close to 1 (say 0.95 or 0.99) in order to obtain meaningful and useful confidence intervals. We will now consider several examples.

## Example 5.8

The 100 waiting times of Example 5.1 yield $\bar{x} = 15.388$ and $s = 17.295$. Let us use these sample statistics to find a 95 percent confidence interval for $\mu_T$, the expected waiting time at a checkout counter. The endpoints of the interval are given by

$$\bar{x} \pm \frac{s}{\sqrt{n}} z_{0.025}$$

or

$$15.388 \pm \left(\frac{17.295}{\sqrt{100}}\right) 1.96 = 15.388 \pm 3.390$$

The resulting confidence interval is (11.998, 18.778). This interval contains $\mu_T = 15$, the known true value of the expected waiting time.

## Example 5.9

Following are the failure times (in hours) of 49 electronic components for which $\mu$ is unknown.

| | | | | | | | | | |
|---|---|---|---|---|---|---|---|---|---|
| 1.2 | 2.2 | 4.9 | 5.0 | 6.8 | 7.0 | 12.1 | 13.7 | 15.1 | 15.2 |
| 23.9 | 24.3 | 25.1 | 35.8 | 38.9 | 47.7 | 48.4 | 49.3 | 53.2 | 55.6 |
| 62.7 | 72.4 | 73.6 | 76.8 | 83.8 | 85.1 | 97.9 | 99.6 | 102.8 | 108.5 |
| 128.7 | 133.6 | 144.1 | 147.6 | 150.6 | 151.6 | 152.6 | 164.2 | 166.8 | 178.6 |
| 185.2 | 187.1 | 203.0 | 204.3 | 229.5 | 253.1 | 304.1 | 341.7 | 354.4 | |

*Source:* Benjamin Epstein, "Tests for the Validity of the Assumption That the Underlying Distribution of Life Is Exponential: Part II," *Technometrics* 2 (1960): 168.

In the Minitab output in Exhibit 5.6, these observations have been placed in column C2, a histogram has been printed out, and the values of $\bar{x} = 104.68$, $\hat{m} = 83.8$, and $s = 90.7$ have been found. The distribution of failure times is clearly skewed to the right, with a large number (23) of failures occurring in the first 75 hours and the rest spread increasingly sparsely over the intervals 75–175, 175–275 and 275–375. The endpoints of an approximate 90 percent confidence interval for $\mu$ are given by

$$\bar{x} \pm \frac{s}{\sqrt{n}} z_{0.05} = 104.7 \pm \left(\frac{90.7}{7}\right) 1.645$$

$$= 104.7 \pm 21.31$$

## Exhibit 5.6

```
MTB > NOTE DATA FROM EPSTEIN TECHNOMETRICS 2,1960, P.168
MTB > NOTE FAILURE TIMES FOR 49 COMPONENTS
MTB > SET C2
C2
     1.2     2.2     4.9     5.0    .   .   .

MTB > END
MTB > AVERAGE C2·
   MEAN     =      104.68
MTB > STDEV C2
   ST.DEV. =      90.664
MTB > MEDIAN C2
   MEDIAN =       83.800
MTB > HISTOGRAM C2

Histogram of C2   N = 49

Midpoint   Count
      0      12    ************
     50      11    ***********
    100       7    *******
    150       9    *********
    200       5    *****
    250       2    **
    300       1    *
    350       2    **
```

The 90 percent confidence interval is thus (83.39, 126.01). The reader should find the endpoints of a 95 percent confidence interval for $\mu$.

Example 5.10

Following are the survival times in days for 52 patients who received heart transplants.

| | | | | | | | | | | | | | |
|---|---|---|---|---|---|---|---|---|---|---|---|---|---|
| 15 | 3 | 624 | 46 | 127 | 61 | 1350 | 312 | 24 | 10 | 1024 | 39 | 730 |
| 136 | 1379 | 1 | 836 | 60 | 1140 | 1153 | 54 | 47 | 0 | 43 | 971 | 868 |
| 44 | 780 | 51 | 710 | 663 | 253 | 147 | 51 | 479 | 322 | 442 | 419 | 65 |
| 362 | 64 | 228 | 65 | 264 | 25 | 193 | 196 | 63 | 12 | 103 | 60 | 43 |

*Source:* B. Turnbull, B. Brown, and M. Hu, "Survivorship Analyses of Heart Transplant Data," *Journal of the American Statistical Association* 69 (1974): 75.

Exhibit 5.7 shows the output generated when Minitab was used as in the previous example. The distribution is again very skewed, as the histogram indicates. The average survival period for these 52 patients was $\bar{x} = 330$ days with $s = 394$. A 95 percent confidence interval has endpoints

$$330 \pm \frac{394}{\sqrt{52}} 1.96 = 330 \pm 107$$

rounded to the nearest integer. Hence the interval (223, 437) is a 95 percent confidence interval for the true average survival period after a heart transplant. The interval is quite wide, because there is substantial variation in the survival periods for different patients.

**Exhibit 5.7**

```
MTB > NOTE SURVIVAL PERIOD IN DAYS FOR 52 HEART TRANSPLANT PATIENTS
MTB > HISTOGRAM C1

Histogram of C1    N = 52

Midpoint    Count
       0       24   ************************
     200        9   *********
     400        6   ******
     600        2   **
     800        5   *****
    1000        2   **
    1200        2   **
    1400        2   **

MTB > AVERAGE C1
   MEAN     =      329.94
MTB > MEDIAN C1
   MEDIAN =      131.50
MTB > STDEV C1
   ST.DEV. =      394.07
```

**5.11** Suppose we want to estimate the average time it takes a commuter to drive down Chestnut Street from 63rd to 36th Street during the morning rush hour (6:00–9:00 A.M.) in Philadelphia. A random sample of $n = 80$ such times has $\bar{x} = 12.5$ and $s = 2.2$. Find an approximate 95 percent confidence interval for $\mu$, the true unknown average time in minutes.

**5.12** In an article by W. S. Youden entitled "Systematic Errors in Physical Constants," which appeared in *Technometrics* 4 (1962), the average of 32 experimental measurements of the gravity constant $g$ (in cm/sec/sec) was given as $\bar{x} = 980.6124$ with $s = 0.60$. Find a 95 percent confidence interval for the true value of $g$.

**5.13** The table below gives the names and dates of birth of the 43 people elected to the House of Representatives from California in 1980.

| District | Representative | Date of Birth | |
|---|---|---|---|
| 1 | Eugene A. Chappie | 3-28-20 | |
| 2 | Don H. Claussen | 4-27-23 | |
| 3 | Robert T. Matsui | 9-17-41 | |
| 4 | Vic Fazio | 10-11-42 | |
| 5 | John L. Burton | 12-15-32 | |
| 6 | Phillip Burton | 6-1-26 | |
| 7 | George Miller | 5-17-45 | |
| 8 | Ronald V. Dellums | 11-24-35 | |
| 9 | Fortney H. Stark | 11-11-31 | |
| 10 | Don Edwards | 1-6-15 | |
| 11 | Tom Lantos | 2-1-28 | |
| 12 | Paul N. McCloskey, Jr. | 9-29-27 | |
| 13 | Norman Y. Mineta | 11-12-31 | |
| 14 | Norman D. Shumway | 7-28-34 | |
| 15 | Tony Coelho | 6-15-42 | |
| 16 | Leon E. Panetta | 6-28-38 | |
| 17 | Charles Pashayan, Jr. | 3-27-41 | |
| 18 | William M. Thomas | 12-6-41 | |
| 19 | Robert J. Lagomarsino | 9-4-26 | |
| 20 | Barry M. Goldwater, Jr. | 4-29-39 | |
| 21 | Bobbi Fieldler | 4-22-37 | |
| 22 | Carlos J. Moorhead | 5-6-22 | |
| 23 | Anthony C. Beilenson | 10-26-32 | |
| 24 | Henry A. Waxman | 9-12-39 | |
| 25 | Edward R. Roybal | 2-10-16 | |
| 26 | John H. Rousselot | 11-1-27 | |
| 27 | Robert K. Dornan | 4-3-33 | |
| 28 | Julian C. Dixon | 8-8-34 | |
| 29 | Augustus F. Hawkins | 8-31-07 | |
| 30 | George E. Danielson | 2-20-15 | |
| 31 | Mervyn M. Dymally | 5-12-26 | |
| 32 | Glenn M. Anderson | 2-21-13 | |
| 33 | Wayne Grisham | 1-10-23 | (cont.) |

| District | Representative | Date of Birth |
|----------|----------------|---------------|
| 34 | Daniel E. Lungren | 9-22-46 |
| 35 | David Dreier | 7-5-52 |
| 36 | George E. Brown, Jr. | 3-6-20 |
| 37 | Jerry Lewis | 10-21-34 |
| 38 | Jerry M. Patterson | 10-25-34 |
| 39 | William E. Dawnemeyer | 9-22-29 |
| 40 | Robert E. Badham | 6-9-29 |
| 41 | Bill Lowrey | 5-2-47 |
| 42 | Duncan L. Hunter | 5-31-48 |
| 43 | Clair W. Burgener | 12-5-21 |

*Source: The Almanac of American Politics* (Washington, D.C.: Barone and Co., 1982).

**a.** Find the ages of these individuals on January 1, 1981.
**b.** Find a 95 percent confidence interval for $\mu$, the average age of California representatives on January 1, 1981. The population from which we are sampling might be considered to be that of California politicians.

**5.14** The *Philadelphia Inquirer* of September 26, 1982 printed the following temperature ranges for 31 U.S. cities on the preceding day:

| City | High | Low | City | High | Low |
|------|------|-----|------|------|-----|
| Albany | 76 | 46 | Jacksonville | 82 | 63 |
| Atlanta | 70 | 58 | Los Angeles | 78 | 74 |
| Baltimore | 72 | 54 | Memphis | 74 | 59 |
| Bismark | 71 | 35 | Miami | 85 | 76 |
| Boston | 70 | 55 | Minneapolis | 61 | 42 |
| Buffalo | 68 | 53 | New Orleans | 80 | 60 |
| Charleston | 77 | 62 | New York | 71 | 57 |
| Chicago | 50 | 47 | Oklahoma City | 77 | 52 |
| Cincinnati | 63 | 58 | Phoenix | 104 | 82 |
| Cleveland | 66 | 56 | Portland | 67 | 45 |
| Dallas | 82 | 59 | St. Louis | 62 | 56 |
| Denver | 70 | 51 | San Francisco | 65 | 58 |
| Detroit | 67 | 57 | Seattle | 62 | 57 |
| Honolulu | 89 | 76 | Tampa | 85 | 72 |
| Houston | 87 | 68 | Washington | 75 | 58 |
| Indianapolis | 62 | 53 | | | |

Find a 95 percent confidence interval for the true average difference between high and low temperatures for U.S. cities on this date.

**5.15** In an article by Bryan Wilkinson, entitled "World Series Pools," in the *American Statistician* 4 (1968): 35, the following distribution was given for the difference between the numbers of runs scored by the winning and losing teams in 300 games.

| Winning Difference | Frequency |
|:---:|:---:|
| 0 | 15 |
| 1 | 27 |
| 2 | 23 |
| 3 | 49 |
| 4 | 31 |
| 5 | 41 |
| 6 | 27 |
| 7 | 38 |
| 8 | 23 |
| 9 | 26 |

**a.** Given that $\bar{x} = 4.65$ and $s = 2.59$, find a 95 percent confidence interval for $\mu$, the true mean difference between the numbers of runs scored by World Series winners and losers.
**b.** Find a 90 percent confidence interval for $\mu$ as defined in part a.
**c.** Which of these intervals should be longer—the one with the larger confidence coefficient or the one with the smaller confidence coefficient? Which one did your calculations show to be longer?

**5.16** Following are the numbers of home runs made by the National League champions from 1919 to 1981:

12 15 23 42 41 27 39 21 30 31 43 56 31
38 28 35 34 33 31 36 28 43 34 30 29 33
28 23 51 40 54 47 42 37 47 49 51 43 44
47 46 41 46 49 44 47 52 44 39 36 45 45
48 40 44 36 38 38 52 40 48 48 31

*Source:* The *Information Please Almanac*
(New York: Simon and Schuster, 1982), p. 907.

**a.** Using these data, find a 90 percent confidence interval for the population expectation.
**b.** Which assumptions made in the derivation of this confidence interval for $\mu$ may be violated in this case?

**5.17** Following are the ages of 80 randomly selected captains in the U.S. Navy. Find an approximate 90 percent confidence interval for the average age of such captains.

61 50 43 57 60 56 39 57 45 46 53 44 47 40

44 60 55 36 45 71 59 56 50 36 31 54 41 60

54 53 33 47 48 57 43 57 46 52 61 48 41 54

44 58 56 45 49 56 46 48 45 50 61 47 49 52

57 50 50 60 40 47 51 50 61 54 55 56 54 42

44 56 48 37 40 56 55 45 38 46

**5.18** Following are the true net weights in ounces of 64 two-pound packages of cheese:

32.69 31.64 32.44 32.84 32.46 32.23 32.11 32.00

32.04 32.78 31.79 31.15 32.57 32.01 32.37 32.69

32.22 32.35 33.34 31.79 32.64 32.43 32.23 32.00

31.96 32.37 33.24 32.49 32.36 33.07 32.36 31.96

32.59 32.78 32.37 32.97 32.78 32.15 33.04 32.93

32.03 32.36 32.54 32.92 33.02 32.14 31.93 32.85

33.58 31.91 33.09 33.81 33.42 32.33 33.69 32.28

33.33 31.98 32.61 32.73 32.40 32.01 32.64 32.03

**a.** Find a 95 percent confidence interval for $\mu$, the true average net weight of such packages.
**b.** Use the HISTOGRAM and BOXPLOT commands with these data.
**c.** Does the mean or the median seem to be the better measure of centrality? Why?

**5.19** Given below are the values of the coins in the pockets of 39 students, as presented by Ernest Rubin in an article entitled "Statistical Experimentation in the Classroom," published in *American Statistician* 17 (1963).

0.03 0.32 0.98 0.41 1.19 0.12 0.38 0.40 1.13 0.38

0.50 0.23 1.20 1.03 0.14 0.25 1.09 0.00 0.88 1.16

0.50 0.28 0.73 0.62 0.26 1.07 0.27 0.82 0.93 0.00

0.60 0.25 0.19 0.52 1.16 0.07 1.35 0.06 0.47

**a.** Use the DESCRIBE command to find $\bar{x}$ and $s^2$ for these data.
**b.** Calculate the endpoints of a 95 percent confidence interval for $\mu$, the true average value of the coins in the pockets of a population of similar students.
**c.** Use the HISTOGRAM and BOXPLOT commands with these data. Do the data appear to be normally distributed? Would a nonnormal distribution substantially alter the 95 percent confidence coefficient figure used in part b? Why or why not?

**5.20** A random sample of the amounts of 50 checks was taken from a list of checks issued by the Ames, Iowa Community School District. These amounts, to the nearest dollar, were as follows:

| | | | | | | | | | |
|---|---|---|---|---|---|---|---|---|---|
| 176 | 1443 | 11 | 65 | 115 | 148 | 55 | 8024 | 211 | 61 |
| 6 | 3303 | 5 | 1600 | 18 | 150 | 21 | 92 | 23 | 347 |
| 122 | 112 | 18 | 30 | 37 | 24 | 50 | 256 | 246 | 295 |
| 20 | 17639 | 115 | 50 | 70 | 556 | 78 | 237 | 51 | 77 |
| 88 | 48 | 91 | 130 | 24 | 300 | 19 | 133 | 38 | 79 |

a. Use Minitab to create a histogram, boxplot, and stem-and-leaf diagram for this data set.

b. Use Minitab to find the values of $\bar{x}$ and $s$.

c. Find a 95 percent confidence interval for $\mu$, the expected value of a check issued by this school district.

d. Why might the expectation, $\mu$, not be the best measure of location for this population?

**5.21** James A. Ohlsen and Stephen H. Penman reported on stock splits in their article "Volatility Increases Subsequent to Stock Splits, An Empirical Aberration," in the *Journal of Financial Economics* 14 (1985): 251–266. For the $n = 1257$ stock splits they studied, Ohlsen and Penman calculated the average number of days between the announcement of the split and the actual splitting of the stock to be $\bar{x} = 52.06$ days with a sample standard deviation of $s = 30.51$ days.

a. Find a 90 percent confidence interval for the value of $\mu$.

b. Find a 99 percent confidence interval for the value of $\mu$.

**5.22** The discrete uniform distribution on the outcome space $S = \{1, 2, \ldots, n\}$ assigns equal probability, $1/n$, to each of the integers in $S$. We have already seen that for this random variable, $\mu = (n + 1)/2$. It also can be shown that $\sigma^2 = (n^2 - 1)/12$. Consider this distribution for $n = 7$.

a. Find $\mu$ and $\sigma^2$.

b. Using RANDOM in Minitab, simulate the selection of 100 sample means of size 16 from this distribution. Do not print out the individual values.

c. Using the HISTOGRAM command, make a histogram of one column of 100 observations from this discrete uniform distribution. Make a histogram of the 100 means of sample size 16. Describe and compare the shapes of these two histograms. Why is there a difference in their shapes?

d. Using the simulated means and the known value of $\sigma$, use Minitab to find 100 confidence intervals for $\mu$ with confidence coefficient 90 percent.

e. What proportion of these intervals contain $\mu$? Is this proportion near the nominal 90 percent figure?

## 5.4

**Large-Sample Estimation of a Population Proportion**

confidence interval for *p*

In the previous section we saw how to estimate the expected value $\mu$ of a random variable $X$ when the sample size can be considered large. In this section we estimate an unknown population proportion $p$. As we did for $\mu$, we will find both a point estimator and a **confidence interval for p**. The values of the estimates of numerous population percentages or proportions have important ramifications. On September 4, 1982, for example, *The Washington Post* featured a point estimator in a headline on the front page:

---

### Jobless Rate in August Remained at Postwar High of 9.8 Pct

---

Another well-known source of estimates of population percentages is the *Gallup Report*, a monthly digest of the results of sampling U.S. public opinion.

Every month interviewers ask the following question of between 1500 and 3000 adults: "Do you approve of the way (the current incumbent) is handling his job as President?" The following results of the previous month's poll concerning President Reagan were published in the May 1982 issue of the *Gallup Report*:

**Approve: 46 Percent; Disapprove: 45 Percent; No Opinion: 9 Percent**

Another area in which the estimation of population proportions is important is the manufacturing of a product, such as a tire. A manufacturer would like to produce only tires without defects, but unfortunately a complicated production process will always yield some defective items. It is of considerable importance for a manufacturer to estimate accurately the proportion of those tires produced that will be defective, with the eventual aim of reducing this proportion.

Let us first consider finding a point estimator of an unknown population proportion $p$. Assume that we are sampling independent observations from a population of elements. For each observation, either the element has a certain property or it does not. An unknown proportion $p$ of the total population has the property, and it is this parameter we wish to estimate. In *The Washington Post* example, the property of interest is being unemployed. In the Gallup poll example, the property of interest is approval of the way in which the President is handling his job. In the manufacturing example, the property of interest is defectiveness. In each case the true population proportion $p$ is unknown. Just as $\bar{X}$ is used as a point estimator of $\mu$, $\hat{p}$, the proportion of elements in the sample having the property, is usually used as the point estimator of $p$. The value of $\hat{p}$ for the unemployment rate in August of 1982 is 0.098. The value of $\hat{p}$ for the presidential approval rating is 0.46.

As we did with $\bar{X}$, we now consider properties of the random variable $\hat{p}$. Each element in the sample is assumed to have probability $p$ (unknown) of having the property and probability $1 - p$ of not having it. As independence is assumed, the *number* of elements *in the sample* having the relevant property can be considered to be a random variable $X$ with a binomial distribution, $B(n, p)$. The *proportion in the sample* having the property is thus

$$\hat{p} = \frac{X}{n} \tag{5.10}$$

Recall that we can write $X$ as a sum of independent indicator random variables that have the same distribution. The common distribution is given by

$$P(I_k = 0) = 1 - p \quad \text{and} \quad P(I_k = 1) = p, \quad k = 1, 2, \dots, n$$

Thus

$$\hat{p} = \frac{X}{n} = \sum_{k=1}^{n} \frac{I_k}{n}$$

is an average of $n$ independent random variables having the same parent distribution. Using the expectation and variance of the binomial variable $X$, we find that

$$E(\hat{p}) = E\left(\frac{X}{n}\right) = \frac{E(X)}{n} = \frac{np}{n} = p \qquad \textbf{5.11}$$

and

$$\text{Var}\left(\frac{X}{n}\right) = \frac{\text{Var}(X)}{n^2} = \frac{np(1-p)}{n^2} = \frac{p(1-p)}{n} \qquad \textbf{5.12}$$

Further, as $\hat{p}$ is an average, we know from the preceding section that the probability that $\hat{p}$ is close to $p$ is near 1 for large $n$. The Central Limit Theorem applies to $X$. Thus we know that for large $n$,

$$\frac{X - np}{\sqrt{np(1-p)}} = \frac{\hat{p} - p}{\sqrt{p(1-p)/n}}$$

or

$$\frac{X - np}{\sqrt{np(1-p)}} = \frac{\hat{p} - p}{\sigma(\hat{p})} \qquad \textbf{5.13}$$

where we define $\sigma(\hat{p}) = \sqrt{p(1-p)/n}$, has approximately a standard normal distribution.

This fact can be used to find an approximate $(1 - \alpha)100$ percent confidence interval for $p$. From the Central Limit Theorem we know that the following probability statement is approximately valid:

$$P\left(-z_{\alpha/2} \leqslant \frac{\hat{p} - p}{\sigma(\hat{p})} \leqslant z_{\alpha/2}\right) = 1 - \alpha$$

We can invert this double inequality to "trap" $p$, exactly as we did $\mu$ in Equation 5.8. The expression

$$\hat{p} \pm \left(\sqrt{\frac{p(1-p)}{n}}\right) z_{\alpha/2}$$

gives the endpoints of an approximate $(1 - \alpha)100$ percent confidence interval for the unknown $p$. Unfortunately $\sigma(\hat{p})$ is a function of the unknown $p$, but for large $n$ it is justifiable to replace $p$ by $\hat{p}$ in the expression for $\sigma(\hat{p})$ to obtain

$$\hat{p} \pm \left(\sqrt{\frac{\hat{p}(1-\hat{p})}{n}}\right) z_{\alpha/2} \qquad \textbf{5.14}$$

Equation 5.14 gives the desired endpoints of a confidence interval for the unknown population proportion $p$. The confidence coefficient is approximately $(1 - \alpha)100$ percent.

We next consider some examples.

## Example 5.11

During the period from January 14 through February 10, 1985, the Gallup organization conducted a survey of 1036 women and 520 men for the American

College of Obstetricians and Gynecologists. Respondents were asked whether they agreed with the statement "There are substantial risks with using the birth control pill." The proportion that agreed with this statement was $\hat{p} = 0.78$. A confidence interval for $p$, the corresponding population proportion that agrees with this statement, with a 95 percent confidence coefficient would have endpoints

$$0.78 \pm \left( \sqrt{\frac{(0.78)(0.22)}{1656}} \right) 1.96 = 0.78 \pm 0.02$$

Hence the corresponding confidence interval would be given by (0.76, 0.80).

---

**Example 5.12**

---

In "A Study of Poisson's Models for Jury Verdicts in Criminal and Civil Trials," by A. E. Gelfand and H. Solomon, in the *Journal of the American Statistical Association* (1973), some data are reported concerning convictions in criminal trials in the Seine Department in France between 1825 and 1830. A brief summary of the data appears in Table 5.5. In 1825, 567 of 802 criminals accused of crimes in the Seine Department were convicted. The value of $\hat{p} = 567/802 = 0.707$ is an estimate of the conviction rate in Paris courts during 1825. A 90 percent confidence interval for $p$ would be given by

$$0.707 \pm \left( \sqrt{\frac{(0.707)(0.293)}{802}} \right) 1.645 = 0.707 \pm 0.026$$

The endpoints of the corresponding confidence interval are (0.681, 0.733). The conviction rate decreased following 1825, and none of the conviction rates for 1826 through 1830 lie in this interval. Hence the confidence interval just established may be considered appropriate only for 1825. This example illustrates that the parameter $p$ may not be constant over time.

---

**Table 5.5**

---

Number of Accused and Jury Decisions in the Years 1825–1830 in the Seine Department in France

|  | 1825 | 1826 | 1827 | 1828 | 1829 | 1830 |
|---|---|---|---|---|---|---|
| Number of Accused | 802 | 824 | 675 | 868 | 908 | 804 |
| Number of Convictions | 567 | 527 | 436 | 559 | 604 | 484 |
| Proportion of Convictions | 0.707 | 0.640 | 0.646 | 0.644 | 0.665 | 0.602 |

## Minitab Simulation of Confidence Intervals for $p = 1/2$

**simulation of $\hat{p}$**

Once more Minitab will be used to emphasize the meaning of a confidence coefficient. In Exhibit 5.8, the computer package was used to produce a **simulation of $\hat{p}$** values. The printout also gives 25 confidence intervals using confidence coefficient $1 - \alpha = 0.95$. The true value of $p = 1/2$ and the RANDOM command were used to obtain $X \sim B(100, 0.5)$ 25 times, and the values of $\hat{p} = x/100$ and the interval endpoints $\hat{p} - (\sqrt{\hat{p}(1 - \hat{p})/100})1.96$ and $\hat{p} + (\sqrt{\hat{p}(1 - \hat{p})/100})1.96$ were calculated. The values of $X$ and the endpoints of the confidence interval were printed out.

Of the 25 confidence intervals, exactly five do not contain the true value of $p$ (namely 1/2). The proportion of intervals containing $p$ is $20/25 = 0.80$, which is not very close to the true confidence coefficient of 0.95. Once again, note that the 0.95 probability refers to the procedure, which enables us to have 95 percent confidence in the single interval typically computed.

It should be emphasized that the confidence interval endpoints given in Equation 5.14 depend on the sample size $n$ and not on the size of the population sampled, as long as the latter is very large. This important idea seems at first counterintuitive. It goes to the heart of the reliability and effectiveness of statistical methods, however. If the opposite were the case—if substantially larger sample sizes were required for larger populations than for smaller ones in order to achieve the same confidence coefficient—much of the practical importance of statistical estimation would be lost.

## Exercises 5.4

**5.23** Four hundred undergraduate students at a large university are polled with regard to whether they approve a change in the grading system from A, B, C, D, E to A, A−, B+, B, B−, C+, C, C−, D+, D, D−, F. Of the random sample, 272 are opposed to the change.
   **a.** Find a 90 percent confidence interval for the proportion of all students opposed to the change.
   **b.** Find a 95 percent confidence interval for this proportion. What happens to the length of this interval as the confidence coefficient increases?

**5.24** In a survey for *Newsweek* magazine made public on October 9, 1982, the Gallup organization stated that 51 percent of 1018 adults interviewed by telephone between September 27 and September 30 disapproved of President Reagan's performance.
   **a.** Find a 95 percent confidence interval for the proportion of adults in the United States who disapproved of the President's performance at that time.
   **b.** Can it be said that the poll shows that a majority disapprove?

**5.25** In 1980 the City Planning Commission conducted a survey of 7800 individuals in Philadelphia. Interviewers asked those Philadelphia residents selected to respond "bad or not good," "neutral," or "good" to 13 qualities or locations. The locations receiving the most favorable responses were the Benjamin Franklin Parkway (74.7% good) and the International Airport (64.3% good). Find 95 percent confidence intervals for the corresponding population parameters.

**Exhibit 5.8**

```
MTB > NOTE SIMULATION OF 25 CONFIDENCE INTERVALS FOR P
MTB > NOTE HERE N = 100 AND P = 0.5
MTB > BASE = 1002
MTB > RANDOM 25 OBSERVATIONS IN C1;
SUBC> BINOMIAL N = 100 P = 0.5.
MTB > TALLY C1

      C1   COUNT
      39     1
      42     1
      43     2
      44     2
      45     2
      46     1
      47     2
      53     3
      54     1
      55     1
      56     1
      57     2
      58     2
      60     1
      61     3
      N=    25

MTB > DIVIDE C1 BY 100 IN C1
MTB > SUBTRACT C1 FROM 1 IN C2
MTB > MULTIPLY C1 BY C2 IN C2
MTB > DIVIDE C2 BY 100 IN C2
MTB > SQRT C2 IN C2
MTB > MULT C2 BY 1.96 IN C2
MTB > ADD C2 TO C1 IN C4
MTB > SUBTRACT C2 FROM C1 IN C3
MTB > NAME C3 'LOWER' C4 'UPPER'
MTB > PRINT C3-C4
      ROW       LOWER        UPPER

        1     0.442314     0.637686
        2     0.432177     0.627823
        3     0.372177     0.567823
        4     0.332965     0.527035
        5     0.352491     0.547509
        6     0.462708     0.657292
        7*    0.514401     0.705599
        8     0.472965     0.667035
        9*    0.294401     0.485599
       10*    0.514401     0.705599
       11     0.332965     0.527035
       12     0.472965     0.667035
       13*    0.514401     0.705599
       14*    0.503980     0.696020
       15     0.342708     0.537292
       16     0.323263     0.516737
       17     0.342708     0.537292
       18     0.372177     0.567823
       19     0.432177     0.627823
       20     0.362314     0.557686
       21     0.483263     0.676737
       22     0.483263     0.676737
       23     0.432177     0.627823
       24     0.452491     0.647509
       25     0.352491     0.547509


    * DOES NOT CONTAIN 0.5
```

**5.26** In an article entitled "On the Incidence of Swept Double-Headers," in the *American Statistician* 23 (1969), M. Goodman reported that in 1964, 113 of the 194 double-headers in the major leagues were swept.

  **a.** Using these data, find a 90 percent confidence interval for the incidence of swept double-headers.

  **b.** Find a 90 percent confidence interval for the incidence of split double-headers.

  **c.** What is the relationship between the lengths of the intervals in parts a and b?

**5.27 a.** The Gallup organization uses samples of at least 1500. If its estimate of a population proportion is $\hat{p} = 0.40$, find a confidence interval for the true proportion $p$, assuming $n = 1500$ and $\alpha = 0.05$.

  **b.** If $n$ were larger than 1500, would a confidence interval computed with $\hat{p} = 0.40$ and the same confidence coefficient be longer or shorter than the one in part a?

**5.28** Of 230 adults, 160 are able to identify both of their state senators. Find an 80 percent confidence interval for the corresponding population proportion.

**5.29** The *Public Opinion Quarterly* of March 1986 recorded the responses of 1488 individuals to a question by the Louis Harris polling company regarding risk. Eighty percent of the 1488 individuals sampled agreed that "People are subject to more risk today than twenty years ago." Find a 95 percent confidence interval for the corresponding population proportion.

**5.30** The same issue of the *Public Opinion Quarterly* recorded the results of a Roper organization poll conducted after the Challenger disaster. A question asked of 1003 respondents was "Does this week's space accident shake your faith in science and technology, or is your degree of confidence in science and technology the same now as it was before the accident?" Eighty-three percent of the respondents said that their degree of confidence in science and technology was unchanged by the accident. Find a 90 percent confidence interval for the corresponding population parameter.

**5.31** In a survey conducted by CBS/*New York Times*, voters leaving polling places in New York State were asked, "Should Jack Kemp run for president in 1988?" Of 1438 such voters, 61 percent replied negatively. Find a 99 percent confidence interval for the corresponding population value $p$.

**5.32** Using Minitab, simulate 100 confidence intervals for a proportion $p$, known to be equal to 0.25. Use $\alpha = 0.10$ and $n = 100$ for each such interval. Print out the endpoints of these confidence intervals.

  **a.** What proportion of these intervals contains 0.25?

  **b.** In the long run what proportion should contain 0.25?

# 5.5

## Large-Sample Estimation of a Population Median

For symmetric random variables the preferred parameter for measuring location is generally the expectation $\mu$. For skewed distributions, however, we have seen that the population median $m$ is the preferred measure of location. The histogram in Exhibit 5.7, for example, shows that the distribution of survival periods for the population of heart transplant patients is skewed to the right. In such cases we are interested in estimation of $m$, the population median, when the sample size can be considered to be large.

A point estimator for $m$ is the sample median $\hat{m}$, which was defined in Definition 2.12. Consider, for example, the data in Example 5.9. Because the sample size ($n = 49$) is an odd number, the sample median is the $(n + 1)/2 = 25$th largest observation, which is 83.8. The histogram in Example 5.9 strongly suggests positive skewness for the distribution of these failure times. Hence, this point estimate of $m$ would probably be preferred to the sample mean 104.7, which is a point estimate of $\mu$. The parameter $m$ represents a compelling measure of location because it divides the population of failure times in half in terms of probability. One-half of such times exceed $m$, and one-half of the such times are less than $m$.

confidence interval for $m$

The method of obtaining a **confidence interval for $m$** is somewhat different from that used in the cases of $\mu$ and $p$. The resulting computation is quite simple, however, and depends on the Central Limit Theorem, as do those for $\mu$ and $p$. We need to define the $k$th-order statistic first. Assume we have a random sample of size $n$ from a parent population $X$. We order the observations by magnitude: $X_{(1)} \leqslant X_{(2)} \leqslant \ldots \leqslant X_{(n)}$. Thus $X_{(1)}$ is the minimum observation in a random sample of size $n$. This random variable is not the same as $X_1$, the first observation in the random sample, as, of course, $X_1$ need not be the minimum in the sample. If many samples of size $n$ are taken from the population defined by $X$ and ordered by magnitude, many different values will be obtained for $X_{(1)}$, the smallest observation. Hence $X_{(1)}$ is a random variable in its own right. This random variable is the *first-order* statistic.

---

**Definition 5.3** ━━━━━━━━━━━━━━━━━━━━━━━━━━━━━━━━━━━━━━━━

$k$th-order statistic

The **$k$th-order statistic** $X_{(k)}$ is the $k$th observation by magnitude in a random sample from the parent population $X$.

---

A confidence interval for $m$ will depend on the values of two order statistics obtained in a random sample.

To understand the general reasoning, consider the random interval $[X_{(1)}, X_{(n)}]$ in the case where $X$ is continuous. This interval contains all numbers from (and including) the minimum to (and including) the maximum of a random sample from $X$. The interval is a random interval, as different random samples will yield different intervals. What is the probability that such an interval covers $m$? We have

$$P(X_{(1)} \leqslant m \leqslant X_{(n)}) \;=\; 1 - P(X_{(1)} > m) - P(X_{(n)} < m)$$

The probability that the smallest of $n$ observations is greater than the population median $m$, however, equals the probability that all observations in the random sample exceed $m$. The smallest observation exceeds $m$ only in the case in which all the sampled observations exceed $m$. Thus,

$$P(X_{(1)} > m) \;=\; P(X_i > m, \text{ for all } i) \;=\; \left(\frac{1}{2}\right)^n$$

The last equality follows from the fact that the probability that each observation exceeds $m$ is 1/2 and the fact that the observations are independent. Similarly,

$$P(X_{(n)} < m) = P(X_i < m, \text{ for all } i) = \left(\frac{1}{2}\right)^n$$

Thus,

$$P(X_{(1)} \leqslant m \leqslant X_{(n)}) = 1 - 2\left(\frac{1}{2}\right)^n$$

The interval $[X_{(1)}, X_{(n)}]$, with endpoints given by the minimum and maximum values of the random sample, is a confidence interval for $m$ with confidence coefficient $1 - 2(1/2)^n$. In the case of $n = 10$, the confidence coefficient would be

$$1 - 2\left(\frac{1}{2}\right)^{10} = 0.998$$

Although the confidence coefficient in this case is high, it is clear that $[X_{(1)}, X_{(n)}]$ will become an unacceptably long interval as $n$ becomes large, because the length of the interval $R$, the sample range, increases with $n$, as pointed out in Section 2.5.

In practice, the intervals used are of the form $[X_{(k)}, X_{(n-k+1)}]$; that is, they extend from the $k$th smallest to the $k$th largest observation. For $n = 20$ and $k = 1$, we obtain $[X_{(1)}, X_{(20)}]$; for $n = 20$ and $k = 2$, we obtain $[X_{(2)}, X_{(19)}]$; and so forth. Using reasoning similar to that above, it can be shown that

$$P(X_{(k)} \leqslant m \leqslant X_{(n-k+1)}) = 1 - 2P(Y < k)$$

where $Y \sim B(n, 1/2)$. This probability equals $1 - \alpha$ if $P(Y < k) = \alpha/2$. For large $n$, the Central Limit Theorem can be used to find $k$ for a given value of the confidence coefficient $1 - \alpha$, as follows.

$$\frac{\alpha}{2} = P(Y < k) = P\left(\frac{Y - n/2}{\sqrt{n}/2} < \frac{k - n/2}{\sqrt{n}/2}\right)$$

But for large $n$, the binomial random variable $Y$, when standardized, is approximately distributed as $Z$; that is,

$$\left(Y - \frac{n}{2}\right)\Big/\left(\frac{\sqrt{n}}{2}\right) \sim Z$$

Hence

$$\left(k - \frac{n}{2}\right)\Big/\left(\frac{\sqrt{n}}{2}\right) = -z_{\alpha/2}$$

and solving for $k$ gives

$$k = \frac{n}{2} - \left(\frac{\sqrt{n}}{2}\right)z_{\alpha/2} \qquad\qquad \textbf{5.15}$$

In general, the result of Equation 5.15 will not be an integer, so the largest integer smaller than or equal to the value given by Equation 5.15 should be used. The interval $[X_{(k)}, X_{(n-k+1)}]$ is a confidence interval for $m$ with confidence coefficient approximately equal to $1 - \alpha$.

## Example 5.13

**SORT**

Consider the data given in exercise 5.8 on the number of correct entries between errors for a clerk. This data set was entered in column C1 of the Minitab worksheet in Exhibit 5.9. The data were sorted using the **SORT** command and printed out by Minitab. The resulting histogram strongly suggests right skewness.

To find a 95 percent confidence interval for $m$, we use the smallest integer not greater than

$$k = \frac{31}{2} - \left(\frac{\sqrt{31}}{2}\right) 1.96 = 10.04$$

## Exhibit 5.9

```
MTB > NOTE DATA FOR CLERK 1;NUMBER OF CORRECT VALUES BETWEEN ERRORS
MTB > SET C1
C1
    734      121      404      646      .    .    .

MTB > END
MTB > SORT C1 IN C1
MTB > PRINT C1
C1
      6       43       86       94      111      121      148      150      165      166
    202      303      312      343      355      404      598      641      646      734
    754      773      903      907     1023     1047     1072     1102     1266     1378
   2138

MTB > HISTOGRAM C1

Histogram of C1    N = 31

Midpoint    Count
      0        4    ****
    200        7    *******
    400        5    *****
    600        3    ***
    800        3    ***
   1000        5    *****
   1200        2    **
   1400        1    *
   1600        0
   1800        0
   2000        0
   2200        1    *

MTB > SINTERVAL CONFIDENCE = 0.95 DATA IN C1

SIGN CONFIDENCE INTERVAL FOR MEDIAN

                              ACHIEVED
                 N    MEDIAN   CONFIDENCE    CONFIDENCE INTERVAL    POSITION
    CLERK        31    404.0    0.9292      (   202.0,    754.0)        11
                                0.9706      (   166.0,    773.0)        10
```

Hence an approximate 95 percent confidence interval for $m$ is $[X_{(10)}, X_{(22)}]$, or [166, 773].

SINTERVAL    Minitab has a simple command **SINTERVAL** which uses the binomial distribution to find the exact confidence coefficient for intervals having a confidence coefficient near a prescribed value. In this case the interval $[X_{(10)}, X_{(22)}] = [166, 773]$ of Exhibit 5.9 is shown to have an achieved confidence coefficient of 0.9706. The prescribed confidence coefficient in the SINTERVAL command is 0.95, but the actual achieved coefficient is slightly greater.

---

The properties of confidence intervals for $m$ are similar to those of confidence intervals for $\mu$ and $p$. Recall that $k = n/2 - (\sqrt{n}/2)z_{\alpha/2}$. When $\alpha$ is decreased, the confidence coefficient $1 - \alpha$ becomes larger. At the same time, however, $z_{\alpha/2}$ increases and $k$ becomes smaller, yielding a longer confidence interval for $m$. Conversely, when $\alpha$ is increased, the confidence coefficient decreases but $k$ increases, yielding a shorter confidence interval. Again, the confidence coefficient $(1 - \alpha)100$ percent is associated with the procedure generating the interval, and not with a particular interval observed.

## Example 5.14

---

Consider again the data on the survival period for 52 heart transplant patients in Example 5.10. The histogram very conclusively demonstrates the skewness of these data. The population median $m$ is therefore preferred to the population expectation $\mu$ as a measure of location. Calculating the value of $k$ required for a

## Exhibit 5.10

```
MTB > NOTE CONFIDENCE INTERVAL FOR MEDIAN WITH CONF COEFFICIENT = 0.90
MTB > NOTE DATA IS SURVIVAL PERIOD IN DAYS FOR HEART TRANSPLANT PATIEN
MTB > TS
MTB > NAME C1 'DAYS'
MTB > SORT C1 IN C1
MTB > PRINT C1
DAYS
     0      1      3     10     12     15     24     25     39     43
    43     44     46     47     51     51     54     60     60     61
    63     64     65     65    103    127    136    147    193    196
   228    253    264    312    322    362    419    442    479    624
   663    710    730    780    836    868    971   1024   1140   1153
  1350   1379

MTB > SINTERVAL WITH CONF COEFFICIENT = 0.90 DATA IN C1

SIGN CONFIDENCE INTERVAL FOR MEDIAN
```

| | N | MEDIAN | ACHIEVED CONFIDENCE | CONFIDENCE INTERVAL | | POSITION |
|---|---|---|---|---|---|---|
| DAYS | 52 | 131.5 | 0.8728 | ( 63.00, | 253.0) | 21 |
| | | | 0.9286 | ( 61.00, | 264.0) | 20 |

90 percent confidence interval for $m$, we have

$$k = \frac{52}{2} - \left(\frac{\sqrt{52}}{2}\right) 1.645 = 20.07$$

so a 90 percent confidence interval is given by $[X_{(20)}, X_{(33)}]$. Minitab was used to sort and print the data (Exhibit 5.10) so that the required order statistics could be found more easily. The required interval is [61, 264]. As indicated in the output of the SINTERVAL command, the achieved confidence coefficient is 0.9286.

Note that in Example 5.10 the values of point estimators of $\mu$ and $m$ are, respectively, $\bar{x} = 330$ and $\hat{m} = 131.5$. The sample median is less than one-half the sample mean, because $m < \mu$ for random variables whose distributions are very skewed to the right. Also, although the confidence interval found in Example 5.14 is about the same length as the one found in Example 5.10, it is shifted dramatically to the left. As the median $m$ is the true survival time that is exceeded by 50 percent of the population, it is almost certainly a more meaningful measure of location than the expectation $\mu$. Hence the point estimate given by $\hat{m}$ and the confidence interval of this section are appropriately used for these data.

## Exercises 5.5

**5.33** For the data in exercise 5.13 on the ages of the 43 representatives from California elected in 1980, find a confidence interval for $m$ using the method of this section. Use a confidence coefficient of 0.95. Compare this interval with that computed for $\mu$ in exercise 5.13.

**5.34** For the data on high and low temperatures given in exercise 5.14, find a 95 percent confidence interval for $m$, the median of the temperature differences, and compare it with the interval computed in exercise 5.14.

**5.35** **a.** For the data in exercise 5.16 on the number of home runs by the National League Champions (1919–1981), find a 90 percent confidence interval for $m$. Compare this interval with that found in exercise 5.16 for $\mu$.
**b.** Construct a histogram for these data, and use it to decide whether $m$ or $\mu$ seems to be the more appropriate measure of location.

**5.36** **a.** Using the ages of the 80 captains in the U.S. Navy given in exercise 5.17, find a 90 percent confidence interval for the median age of U.S. Navy captains.
**b.** Compare this interval with that found in exercise 5.17.
**c.** Decide whether $\mu$ or $m$ seems to be the better measure of location. Explain your reasoning.

**5.37** **a.** Example 5.9 gives the time (in hours) until failure of 49 electronic components. The Minitab histogram shows clearly that these data are right skewed; thus $m$ is preferred to $\mu$ as a population measure of location. Find the endpoints of a 90 percent confidence interval for $m$.
**b.** Would you expect this interval to be shifted to the right or to the left of a 90 percent confidence interval for $\mu$? Why? Is the interval found in part a shifted as expected?

**5.38 a.** For the data in exercise 5.18 on the 64 two-pound packages, find the endpoints of a 95 percent confidence interval for $m$.

    **b.** Because these data are normally distributed, $\mu = m$. Compare the interval computed in this problem with that computed in exercise 5.18. Which is shorter? Which would you prefer? Why?

**5.39 a.** For the data in exercise 5.20 on the dollar values of 50 checks, find the endpoints of a 95 percent confidence interval for $m$.

    **b.** Compare the length of the interval in part a with that found in part c of exercise 5.20.

    **c.** Which interval would you prefer and why?

## 5.6

**Consideration of Sample Size in Estimation of $E(X)$ and $p$**

**minimum sample sizes**

In the last three sections we have seen how to estimate the population parameters $\mu, p$, and $m$ in the large-sample case. In this section we will consider what **minimum sample sizes** are required to estimate $\mu$, a population expectation, and $p$, a population proportion. The issue of how large a sample size $n$ is required to estimate a population parameter is one of practical importance. In general, of course, a larger random sample will yield better estimates than a smaller one. In practice, however, sample sizes are restricted by the cost of gathering data, the time available to gather data, and, in some cases, ethical considerations. The latter might be a factor, for example, in medical trials, in which the issue is a comparison of the effectiveness of two different surgical treatments of a serious illness. Often such effectiveness is measured by a comparison of the true average length of life after treatment (for individuals of the same age) with each of the surgical procedures. It is clearly important to decide with as few observations as possible which of the two treatments yields the longer average survival period.

First we will consider the estimation of $\mu = E(X)$. The issue is how large a random sample to take from the parent population $X$ so that $\bar{X}$ differs from $\mu$ by no more than a small fixed amount $c$ with a known high probability. That is, for $c > 0$, we need to find a sample size $n$ such that

$$P(|\bar{X} - \mu| \leqslant c) \geqslant 1 - \alpha \qquad \textbf{5.16}$$

where $1 - \alpha$ is a known high probability. Standardizing $\bar{X}$, we can rewrite this probability statement as

$$P\left(\frac{|\bar{X} - \mu|}{\sigma/\sqrt{n}} \leqslant \frac{c}{\sigma/\sqrt{n}}\right) \geqslant 1 - \alpha$$

or, using the Central Limit Theorem,

$$P\left(|Z| \leqslant \frac{c\sqrt{n}}{\sigma}\right) \geqslant 1 - \alpha \qquad \textbf{5.17}$$

Again it is assumed that $n$ is large enough that the Central Limit Theorem applies. Thus no assumptions are made about the parent population $X$ except that $\mu$ and $\sigma$ exist. If $c\sqrt{n}/\sigma = z_{\alpha/2}$, Expression 5.17 holds as an equality. Solving this equation for $n$, we find the required sample size $n^*$ to be

$$n^* = \frac{(\sigma z_{\alpha/2})^2}{c^2} \qquad\qquad 5.18$$

Of course, Equation 5.18 will not in general yield an integer, so the smallest integer at least equal to $n^*$ is used. For any value of $n > n^*$ we have $c\sqrt{n}/\sigma > z_{\alpha/2}$, so

$$P\left(|Z| \leqslant \frac{c\sqrt{n}}{\sigma}\right) > 1 - \alpha$$

and hence

$$P(|\bar{X} - \mu| \leqslant c) > 1 - \alpha$$

Thus the smallest integer at least equal to $n^*$ given by Equation 5.18 is the *smallest* sample size for which the requirement expressed in Equation 5.16 will be met.

**Example 5.15**

---

A quality control specialist wishes to estimate the average amount of time a worker will take to complete a given task using a new assembly technique. Suppose the standard deviation $\sigma$ can be taken to be two minutes, and the specialist wants a probability of at least 0.90 that $\bar{X}$ will differ from $\mu$ by no more than one-half minute. How many such assembly operations should the quality control specialist observe? Using $\alpha = 0.10$, $z_{0.05} = 1.645$, $c = 0.5$, and $\sigma = 2$, we have

$$n^* = \frac{[2(1.645)]^2}{(0.5)^2} = 43.3$$

Thus at least 44 observations should be made.

---

Generally, of course, it is unrealistic to assume that $\sigma$ is known. It may be possible, however, to state a maximum value for $\sigma$. Assuming $\sigma \leqslant \sigma^*$, we can insert $\sigma^*$ into Equation 5.18 to get

$$n^* = \frac{(\sigma^* z_{\alpha/2})^2}{c^2} \qquad\qquad 5.19$$

Suppose that the quality control specialist in Example 5.15 did not know $\sigma$ but could assert that $\sigma \leqslant 4$. The value of $n^*$ given by Equation 5.19 is $[4(1.645)]^2/(0.5)^2 = 173.2$, indicating that at least 174 assembly operations should be observed in order to attain the precision desired. Alternatively, an initial sample could be taken and $\sigma$ could be estimated by using the sample standard deviation $s$ in the calculation of $n^*$. If this initial sample were not large, however, the estimate of $\sigma$ might not be very good, causing the value of $n^*$ to be inappropriately large or small. Neither of these outcomes is desirable. The former can lead to a waste of sampling resources and the latter to an inaccurate estimate of $\mu$.

Two other properties of the required sample size $n^*$ given by Equation 5.18 should be emphasized. If we improve the precision of the estimate by replacing $c$

by $c/2$, the required sample size $n^*$ will be multiplied by 4, as substitution into Equation 5.18 would show. Similarly, if $c$ is replaced by $c/3$, $n^*$ will be multiplied by 9. In general, if $c$ is replaced by $c/k$ for any positive number $k$, $n^*$ is multiplied by $k^2$. In mathematical terms, $n^*$ is inversely proportional to the square of $c$. Similarly, $n^*$ is directly proportional to the square of $\sigma$. If $\sigma$ is replaced by $k\sigma$ for any positive number $k$, $n^*$ is multiplied by $k^2$. This fact was illustrated in the example above, where $\sigma = 2$ was replaced by $\sigma^* = 4$. In that case the computed value of $n^*$ increased from 43.3 to 173.2, which is four times 43.3. Because sample sizes must be integers, the second sample size, 174, is not exactly four times 44, the sample size found in Example 5.15.

## Minitab Simulation of Error in Estimation of $\mu$

The simulation capability of Minitab can be used to illustrate further the idea of the error in estimation of $\mu$. Assume that in sampling from a *normal* distribution, we want to estimate $\mu$ with a maximum error of 1 unit, with a probability of at least 0.9544. The normal assumption has been made in this case, as $(\bar{X} - \mu)/(\sigma/\sqrt{n})$ has exactly a standard normal distribution for any fixed value of $n$. The probability 0.9544 has been used because then $\alpha = 0.0456$, $\alpha/2 = 0.0228$, and $z_{\alpha/2} = 2$, from Table I of Appendix C. Taking $\sigma = 2$, we have $n^* = (\sigma z_{\alpha/2})^2/c^2 = 16$, a convenient integer. The output in Exhibit 5.11 is the result of using Minitab to simulate the observations of 100 means of samples of size 16 from a normal population with known population expectation $\mu = 70$ and standard deviation $\sigma = 2$. The 100 means are in C17, and the values of $\bar{X} - 70$ are in C18. The

OMIT  Minitab **OMIT** command was used to place those errors whose absolute value exceeds 1 in C19. These four errors were then printed out. The ordered values of $\bar{X} - 70$ were also printed out, clearly showing that 96 of the 100 errors have a magnitude of less than 1. This result compares quite well with the theoretical probability of 0.9544.

To determine the minimum sample size needed for the estimation of $p$, a population proportion, we use reasoning similar to that used in the estimation of $\mu$. The aim is to achieve a high probability that $\hat{p}$, the sample fraction, differs from $p$ by no more than a fixed amount $d$—that is, with a maximum error of $d$. The sample size $n$ must be large enough so that

$$P(|\hat{p} - p| \leqslant d) \geqslant 1 - \alpha \qquad \textbf{5.20}$$

Standardizing as for $\mu$, we get

$$P\left(\frac{|\hat{p} - p|}{\sigma(\hat{p})} \leqslant \frac{d}{\sigma(\hat{p})}\right) \geqslant 1 - \alpha$$

or, again using the Central Limit Theorem,

$$P\left(|Z| \leqslant \frac{d}{\sigma(\hat{p})}\right) \geqslant 1 - \alpha \qquad \textbf{5.21}$$

**Exhibit 5.11**

```
MTB > NOTE SIMULATION OF 100 AVERAGES OF 16 OBS FROM N(70,4)
MTB > BASE = 1010
MTB > RANDOM 100 OBS IN C1-C16;
SUBC> NORMAL MU = 70 SIGMA = 2.
MTB > ADD C1-C16 IN C17
MTB > DIVIDE C17 BY 16 IN C17
MTB > SUBTRACT 70 FROM C17 IN C18
MTB > OMIT ROWS WITH VALUES FROM -1 TO 1 IN C18 PUT IN C19
MTB > PRINT C19
C19
  -1.14079  -1.02049   1.11797   1.21918

MTB > SORT C18 IN C18
MTB > PRINT C18
C18
  -1.14079  -1.02049  -0.89935  -0.88332  -0.87770  -0.85684  -0.77293
  -0.76283  -0.71489  -0.69304  -0.68600  -0.66096  -0.65337  -0.63109
  -0.62900  -0.59302  -0.55045  -0.54337  -0.51924  -0.50754  -0.48816
  -0.47963  -0.47603  -0.47340  -0.46785  -0.45311  -0.44777  -0.41682
  -0.38420  -0.37773  -0.34332  -0.30278  -0.30196  -0.22331  -0.22235
  -0.21169  -0.20264  -0.19363  -0.19151  -0.18922  -0.16628  -0.15733
  -0.14049  -0.12462  -0.12254  -0.12086  -0.12061  -0.11906  -0.11906
  -0.09871  -0.07619  -0.05194  -0.04810  -0.04544  -0.04472  -0.04088
  -0.03983  -0.02602  -0.02267  -0.02260  -0.01476   0.04066   0.04793
   0.08580   0.11217   0.12405   0.15199   0.16815   0.20564   0.23328
   0.23531   0.24063   0.24388   0.24837   0.25362   0.29674   0.31706
   0.31934   0.33089   0.40898   0.41312   0.43314   0.44545   0.45644
   0.45702   0.48105   0.49014   0.49185   0.52341   0.54175   0.56398
   0.56732   0.61990   0.72066   0.77019   0.89543   0.91243   0.92865
   1.11797   1.21918
```

If we choose

$$\frac{d}{\sigma(\hat{p})} = \frac{d}{\sqrt{p(1-p)/n}} = z_{\alpha/2}$$

we see that Expression 5.21 holds. Solving for $n$, we obtain

$$n^* = \frac{p(1-p)(z_{\alpha/2})^2}{d^2} \qquad \qquad \textbf{5.22}$$

Again, the smallest integer not less than the value of $n^*$ determined from Expression 5.21 is the minimum sample size required to achieve the maximum precision in estimation of $p$ required in Expression 5.20.

In this case the value of $p(1-p)$ is unknown (corresponding to the unknown $\sigma$ in the case of estimating $\mu$). From the graph of the function $p(1-p)$ in Figure 5.6 it is clear that for $0 < p < 1$ the function $p(1-p)$ has a maximum value of $1/4$ at $p = 1/2$. Hence, whatever the value of $p$, if we use the smallest integer greater than or equal to

$$n^* = \frac{(z_{\alpha/2})^2}{4d^2} \qquad \qquad \textbf{5.23}$$

the sample size will be adequate for Expression 5.20 to hold.

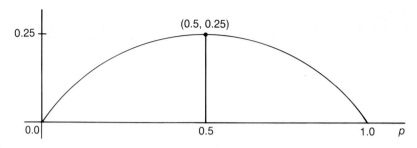

**Figure 5.6**

The Function $f(p) = p(1 - p)$

## Example 5.16

A candidate wishes to estimate the proportion $p$ of registered voters who say they will vote for her in the next election with an error of no more than 2 percentage points ($d = 0.02$), with a probability of at least 0.95. As $\alpha = 0.05$ and $d = 0.02$, using Equation 5.23 we find

$$n^* = \frac{(z_{0.025})^2}{4d^2} = \frac{(1.96)^2}{[4(0.02)^2]} = 2401$$

Sometimes it is possible to use Equation 5.22 to find $n^*$ even though $p$ is not known. If, for example, we know that $p \leqslant 0.20$, then

$$p(1 - p) \leqslant (0.2)(0.8) = 0.16$$

as $p(1 - p)$ increases on $(0, 1/2)$, as shown in Figure 5.6. Similarly, if $p \geqslant 0.7$, then

$$p(1 - p) \leqslant (0.7)(0.3) = 0.21$$

as $p(1 - p)$ decreases on $(1/2, 1)$. Use of Equation 5.22 instead of Equation 5.23 can result in significantly smaller required sample sizes, as the following example illustrates.

## Example 5.17

It is known that the percentage of homes in a given area with cable TV is less than 20 percent. Suppose we need to estimate the proportion of homes with cable TV, allowing an error of no more than 0.02, with a probability of at least 0.95. Using Equation 5.22, we have

$$n^* = \frac{(0.2)(0.8)(1.96)^2}{(0.02)^2} = 1536.64$$

**204**

**Table 5.6**

| | |
|---|---|
| **Values of $n^*$ for a Maximum Error of $d$ with Probability 0.95 in Estimation of $p$** | |

| $d$ | $n^* = 1/d^2$ |
|---|---|
| 0.05 | 400 |
| 0.025 | 1600 |
| 0.02 | 2500 |
| 0.01 | 10,000 |

A sample of 1537 homes is thus required. Example 5.16 gives a value of $n = 2401$ for the case in which nothing is known about $p$. In this example, knowledge of the maximum value possible for $p$ has significantly reduced the required sample size.

Expressions 5.22 and 5.23 show that $n^*$ is inversely proportional to the square of $d$. If we decrease the error of the estimate by replacing $d$ by $d/2$, the minimum sample size is increased by a factor of 4. If we set $1 - \alpha = 0.9544$ in Equation 5.22, $z_{\alpha/2} = 2$. For this confidence coefficient, Equation 5.22 yields the simple expression $n^* = 1/d^2$. Table 5.6 gives values of $n^*$ for certain values of the maximum error $d$. Table 5.6 indicates why sample sizes of the national polling organizations are frequently in the range of 1600 to 2500. Notice that $n^*$ does not depend on the size of the population from which sampling is done, as long as that population size can be considered very large.

**Exercises 5.6**

**5.40** The authors of the *Gallup Report* state that population percentage estimates are based on samples of 1500 or more. They also state that the estimates are in error by no more than 3 percentage points, with a probability of 0.95. Is this statement justified?

**5.41** **a.** Assume that the dividend yields of stocks of U.S. utility companies can have a true standard deviation $\sigma$ of no more than 4 percentage points. How large a random sample of such stocks is required to estimate the true average yield of all such stocks with an error of no more than 1 percentage point, with a probability of at least 0.95?

**b.** Answer part a for a probability of at least 0.99.

**5.42** Using the information given in exercise 5.11, determine the minimum sample size required to estimate the true average time required to complete the commuter trip with an error of no more than 0.5 minute, with a probability at least 0.95. Assume $\sigma \leqslant 2.5$.

**5.43** Using the information given in exercise 5.12, determine the minimum sample size required to estimate the true value of the gravitational constant $g$ with an error of no more than 0.1, with a probability of at least 0.95. Assume $\sigma^2 \leqslant 1$.

**5.44** If an error of 0.05 could be tolerated in the preceding problem, what minimum sample size would be required, using the same probability of allowable error?

**5.45** In order to estimate the proportion of defective items produced on an assembly line, a random sample is to be taken. It is quite certain that the proportion of defectives is less than 0.10. Find the sample size required to estimate the true proportion of defectives with an error of no more than 0.01, with a probability of at least 0.90.

**5.46** Many polls taken to estimate population proportions have a relatively small sample size. If $n = 100$, what type of maximum error of the estimate is possible using $1 - \alpha = 0.9544$?

**5.47** Suppose it is known that $p \geqslant 0.8$. Find the minimum sample size needed to estimate $p$ with a maximum error of 0.025, with a probability of at least 0.95.

**5.48** For a value of $d = 0.03$, what sample size is required to estimate a population proportion with a probability of error of no more than 0.0456?

**Summary**

In this chapter we considered the subject of estimating population parameters—specifically, a population expectation $\mu$, a population median $m$, and population proportion $p$, when the sample size can be considered to be large. For a random sample of size $n$ from a parent population $X$, $E(\bar{X}) = \mu$ and $\mathrm{Var}(\bar{X}) = \sigma^2/n$. The important Central Limit Theorem states that for any parent population $X$ for which $\mu$ and $\sigma$ exist, a sample mean $\bar{X}$ for large $n$ has (when standardized) approximately a standard normal distribution. This fact, expressed mathematically as $(\bar{X} - \mu)/(\sigma/\sqrt{n}) \sim Z$, permits us to find probabilities concerning sample means, even when the populations from which the means were selected are not normally distributed.

The point estimators of $\mu$, $p$, and $m$ are, respectively, the sample mean $\bar{X}$, the sample proportion $\hat{p}$, and the sample median $\hat{m}$. These point estimators are not as useful as interval estimates. Using the Central Limit Theorem, it is possible to derive confidence intervals for a population expectation, median, and proportion. These confidence intervals are calculated by procedures that yield intervals containing the unknown parameter with a given (high) probability. The confidence coefficient is associated with the procedure generating the interval and not with the particular observed interval. With a given sample, a higher required confidence coefficient results in a longer interval, and a shorter required interval results in a lower confidence coefficient. Increasing the sample size is the only way to obtain shorter intervals with higher confidence coefficients.

For estimation of $\mu$, the required sample size is inversely proportional to the square of the allowable error $c$ and directly proportional to the square of the standard deviation $\sigma$ of the parent population. For $p$, the required sample size is inversely proportional to the square of the maximum error $d$. In the estimation of $p$, the required sample size depends only on the confidence coefficient $1 - \alpha$ and $d$. The required sample size does not depend on the size of the population, as long as the latter can be considered very large. Knowledge of the possible values of $p$ can considerably reduce the required sample size.

Central Limit Theorem
confidence coefficient
confidence interval for $m$
confidence interval for $\mu$
confidence interval for $p$
distribution of $\bar{X}$
estimator
$k$th-order statistic
large-sample estimation
minimum sample sizes

parameter
parent distribution
point estimate
population expectation
population median
population proportion
population variance
random sample
simulation of the distribution of $\bar{X}$
simulation of $\hat{p}$

## Minitab Commands

| OMIT | SORT | ZINTERVAL |
| SINTERVAL | | |

# Chapter 6

# Hypothesis Testing in Large Samples

## 6.1

**Introduction**

In a scientific study an investigator is trying to obtain new insights and knowledge in his or her field. Statistics provides methods for making decisions in such investigations. The general method of inquiry is called the scientific method. In this type of inquiry an investigator begins with a hypothesis or several hypotheses about a question or a problem. The hypotheses lead to predictions about some aspect of physical or social behavior. The investigator then collects data (typically in numerical form) to use in deciding whether these predictions—and hence the hypotheses that led to them—are justified. This process is followed by a synthesis of valid new hypotheses and existing theory. New conjectures are made, beginning the cycle again. Although in practice the scientific process may deviate in one way or another from this well-ordered sequence, the accumulation of statistical evidence in support of scientific hypotheses plays a very important role in the development of knowledge in a complex technological society.

Examples of hypotheses abound. Here are a few:

1 Large doses of vitamin C will reduce the incidence of the common cold.
2 Requiring students to take four years of high school mathematics will increase mathematics scores on the Scholastic Aptitude Test (SAT).
3 Curfews for 16- to 18-year-old drivers will substantially reduce automobile accident rates for this group.

In order to find evidence to deny or verify such hypotheses, numerical observations are made. In the first example, the incidence of colds among a sample of individuals taking a large dose of vitamin C might be observed and then compared with the incidence of colds in the general population. In the second example, the average score on the mathematics portion of the SAT for a sample of students with four years of mathematics would be compared with a known expected score for the general population. In the last example, the automobile accident rate for 16- to 18-year-old drivers in a state with a driving curfew would be compared with the rate for teenage drivers in similar states without such a curfew. The task of the investigator is to decide, using statistical methods, in favor of or against the hypothesis being considered.

Statistical methods used to make such decisions should have certain properties. First, objective criteria should be used to make the decision. Second, the probability of making an incorrect decision should be controlled and known. Third, the results should be reported in a form understandable to other investigators in the same scientific area. In order to achieve these aims, it is necessary to understand several concepts in hypothesis testing, which are formalized in the definitions that follow.

---

**Definition 6.1** ▬▬▬▬▬▬▬▬▬▬▬▬▬▬▬▬▬▬▬▬▬▬▬▬▬▬▬

statistical hypothesis

A **statistical hypothesis** is a statement about the value or values of a population parameter.

---

Suppose $p$ represents the probability of an individual's getting a cold during the period from October 1 through March 31. It is known that the incidence of the common cold during the period mentioned among individuals who do not receive large doses of vitamin C is about 40 percent. The statement

H: $p = 0.4$

null hypothesis

is a statistical hypothesis. A hypothesis such as H is referred to as a **null hypothesis** and is denoted by $H_0$. A null hypothesis generally declares that no change from the current situation exists. For the vitamin C example, the null hypothesis would be that large doses of vitamin C *do not* reduce the incidence of the common cold. For the second example, the null hypothesis would be that a requirement of four years of high school mathematics *does not* increase mathematics scores on the SAT examinations. For the third example, the null hypothesis would be that a curfew for 16- to 18-year-old drivers *does not* affect the automobile accident rate of such drivers.

In contrast to a null hypothesis is a research hypothesis, defined as follows.

---

**Definition 6.2** ▬▬▬▬▬▬▬▬▬▬▬▬▬▬▬▬▬▬▬▬▬▬▬▬▬▬▬

research hypothesis

A **research hypothesis** is a statistical hypothesis indicating that a conjecture or new idea of an investigator is true.

---

Like a null hypothesis, a research hypothesis must be stated in terms of the value or values of a population parameter. For instance, the research hypothesis concerning the effectiveness of vitamin C in reducing the incidence of the common cold would be stated as

$$H_1: p < 0.4$$

In words, the research hypothesis is that use of vitamin C reduces the incidence of the common cold.

In connection with the second example, suppose that mathematics scores for all students taking the SAT had averaged 470 over the twenty years preceding a state's introduction of four-year mathematics requirement in high school. The statistical hypothesis

$$H_1: \mu > 470$$

states that the true average SAT math score for students taking four years of high school mathematics is above the previous long-term average. We say that $\mu$ exceeds its "null value" of 470. The research hypothesis is also referred to as the **alternative hypothesis**, because it is an alternative to the null hypothesis.

**alternative hypothesis**

The statistical task is to decide, on the basis of sample data, between the null and alternative hypotheses. In the vitamin C example, the statistical problem is to decide between

$$H_0: p = 0.4 \qquad \text{(vitamin C does not affect the incidence of colds)} \qquad \textbf{6.1}$$

and

$$H_1: p < 0.4 \qquad \text{(vitamin C reduces the incidence of colds)} \qquad \textbf{6.2}$$

A typical procedure for testing these hypotheses would be for the experimenter to select a group of $n$ individuals at random. The members of the group would agree to adhere to a prescribed dosage of vitamin C over the period from October 1 to March 31. (This group is referred to as the treatment group.) The proportion of individuals in this group who got a cold during this six-month period would be calculated. Based on the value of the sample statistic $\hat{p}$, the fraction of the treatment group that got a cold, a choice could be made between the null hypothesis and the research hypothesis.

---

**Definition 6.3** ━━━━━━━━━━━━━━━━━━━━━━━━━━━━━━

**test statistic**

A **test statistic** is a calculation from the sampled data, the value of which will be used to decide whether to accept or reject the null hypothesis.

---

The null and alternative hypotheses about the effect of math programs on SAT scores are as follows.

$$H_0: \mu = 470 \qquad \text{(SAT mathematics scores have not increased)} \qquad \textbf{6.3}$$
$$H_1: \mu > 470 \qquad \text{(SAT mathematics scores have increased)} \qquad \textbf{6.4}$$

To test these hypotheses, an investigator would select $n$ students completing a four-year mathematics requirement in high school. These students' average mathematics score on the SAT, $\bar{X}$, would be the test statistic.

In the vitamin C case, one would reject the null hypothesis in favor of the research hypothesis for small values of $\hat{p}$. The region of values leading to rejection of the null hypothesis would be of the form

$$\hat{p} \leqslant \text{constant} \qquad \qquad \textbf{6.5}$$

This inequality makes sense, as small values of $\hat{p}$ mean that a small fraction of the individuals taking the vitamin C got colds, which implies that vitamin C is effective in reducing the incidence of the common cold.

---

**Definition 6.4** ▬▬▬▬▬▬▬▬▬▬▬▬▬▬▬▬▬▬▬▬

critical region

The **critical region** for a test statistic is the set of values of the test statistic that lead to the rejection of the null hypothesis $H_0$. The critical region is also known as the rejection region.

---

The critical region for deciding between the null and research hypotheses in the SAT score example would be based on the average SAT mathematics score of those selected by the investigator to take the examination. An appropriate critical region would be of the form

$$\bar{X} \geqslant \text{constant} \qquad \qquad \textbf{6.6}$$

Again this critical region makes sense, as large values of $\bar{X}$ correspond to improved average performance on the examination.

It is crucial that the constants indicated in Equations 6.5 and 6.6 be chosen carefully. Such constants should be selected so that the hypothesis-testing procedure is objective and the probability of error is controlled and known.

## 6.2
### Type I and Type II Errors

In order to determine appropriate critical regions for a decision between a null hypothesis $H_0$ and an alternative $H_1$, we must first define the two types of errors that can be made. We will refer throughout this section to the vitamin C example and the associated hypotheses:

$$H_0: p = 0.4 \quad \text{and} \quad H_1: p < 0.4 \qquad \qquad \textbf{6.7}$$

One error that can be made is to reject $H_0$ when it is true. That is, we might decide that vitamin C is effective in reducing the incidence of the common cold when actually it is not. Such an error—rejecting a null hypothesis when it is true —is referred to as a Type I error. As Table 6.1 shows, in the vitamin C example this type of error would occur if the research hypothesis $H_1: p < 0.4$ were chosen

## Table 6.1

**Type I and Type II Errors in Vitamin C Example**

| Decision in Favor of Hypothesis | True Situation | |
|---|---|---|
| | $p = 0.4$ | $p < 0.4$ |
| $H_0$ | No Error | Type II Error |
| $H_1$ | Type I Error | No Error |

when the true situation was that $p = 0.4$. A Type I error in this case might lead to widespread use of a nostrum or ineffective cure for the common cold, which would help those selling vitamin C, but perhaps no one else.

---

**Definition 6.5**

**Type I error**

A **Type I error** is made if the null hypothesis is rejected when it is true.

---

### Minitab Simulation of Type I Error

Minitab's simulation capacity can be used to illustrate the relative frequency of occurrence of a Type I error in the vitamin C example. The decision rule is as follows: If 30 or fewer of the 100 individuals in the treatment group get colds during the six-month period, a decision is made that vitamin C is effective in reducing the incidence of the common cold. Thus the critical region can be written as $\hat{p} \leqslant 0.30$. Let us assume that the null hypothesis is in fact true—that is, the probability of an individual's getting a cold is actually 0.4. Exhibit 6.1 shows the output generated when RANDOM was used to simulate 1000 examples of treatment groups of size 100.

As the computer output shows, in 26 of the 1000 cases, 30 or fewer of the 100 individuals in the simulated treatment group got colds. In each of these 26 cases, therefore, a decision would be made in favor of $H_1 : p < 0.4$ (effective treatment) even though $H_0 : p = 0.4$ (ineffective treatment) is true. The simulated Type I error rate is thus 0.026.

The normal approximation to the binomial distribution can be used to obtain a theoretical value of the probability of a Type I error. For the vitamin C example, if the true probability of getting a cold is $p = 0.4$, a Type I error will be made if 30 or fewer individuals get colds in 100 independent trials. Let $X$ be the number of

**Exhibit 6.1**

```
MTB > NOTE SIMULATION OF 1000 TREATMENT GROUPS IN VITAMIN EXAMPLE
MTB > NOTE FOR REDUCING INCIDENCE OF THE COMMON COLD
MTB > BASE = 4000
MTB > RANDOM 1000 OBSERVATIONS IN C1;
SUBC> BINOMIAL N = 100 P = 0.4.
MTB > TALLY C1

      C1   COUNT
      23     1
      26     3
      27     1
      28     6
      29     5
      30    10
      31    15
      32    16
      33    31
      34    32
      35    45
      36    66
      37    75
      38    65
      39    76
      40    81
      41    83
      42    81
      43    66
      44    78
      45    49
      46    34
      47    23
      48    20
      49    13
      50     8
      51     6
      52     4
      53     3
      54     1
      55     2
      56     1
      N=  1000
```

trials out of 100 on which a cold occurs. Then $X \sim B(100, 0.4)$. Thus

$$P(X \leqslant 30) = P\left(\frac{X - 40}{\sqrt{100(0.6)(0.4)}} \leqslant \frac{30.5 - 40}{\sqrt{24}}\right)$$

$$\doteq P(Z \leqslant -1.94) = 0.0262$$

which is in remarkably good agreement with the simulated value.

$\alpha$     The probability of a Type I error is universally denoted by $\alpha$. The estimate of $\alpha$ calculated from the Minitab simulation is 0.026. The normal approximation to the binomial distribution yields $\alpha = 0.0262$.

In the computation of the approximation of the binomial probability $P(X \leqslant 30)$, 30 was replaced by 30.5. Because a continuous distribution is being

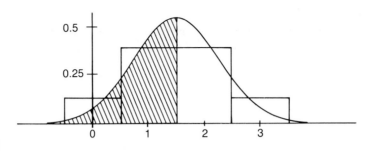

**Figure 6.1**

Normal Approximation to $B(3, 0.5)$

used to approximate the area under a discrete probability histogram, this substitution improves the accuracy of the normal approximation to the binomial distribution. See Figure 6.1 for an illustration of this principle for the simple case $B(3, 0.5)$. Clearly, we get a better approximation of the probability $P(X \leqslant 1)$ if we use the shaded area to the left of 1.5 rather than that to the left of 1. If we use 1, the approximation yields

$$P\left(Z \leqslant \frac{1 - 1.5}{\sqrt{3/4}}\right) = P(Z \leqslant -0.58) = 0.2810$$

If we use 1.5, we obtain

$$P(Z \leqslant 0) = 0.5$$

which is the actual probability. Hence, to approximate $P(X \leqslant k_1)$ for $X \sim B(n, p)$, replace $k_1$ by $(k_1 + 1/2)$ before standardization. Similarly, to approximate $P(X \geqslant k_2)$, replace $k_2$ by $(k_2 - 1/2)$ before standardization. This procedure is called using the normal approximation to the binomial distribution with a **continuity correction**  **continuity correction**.

The second type of error that can be made in choosing between the hypotheses is to retain $H_0$ when in fact $H_1$ is true. This kind of error is called a Type II error. In the vitamin C example, a Type II error would mean deciding that vitamin C is ineffective when in fact its use reduces the incidence of the common cold below its "null value" of $p = 0.4$.

---

**Definition 6.6** ▬▬▬▬▬▬▬▬▬▬▬▬▬▬▬▬▬▬▬▬▬▬▬▬▬▬▬▬▬▬▬▬▬▬▬▬▬▬

**Type II error**  A **Type II error** is made if the null hypothesis is accepted when the research (or alternative) hypothesis is true.

---

$\beta$    The probability of a Type II error is universally denoted by $\beta$. In the vitamin C example, we can see from the statement of $H_1$: $p < 0.4$ that there are many possible values of $p$ that satisfy $H_1$. The probability of a Type II error will depend on the actual value of $p$. Hence $\beta$ is a function of $p$, $\beta(p)$. If $p = 0.2$, the probability

**Table 6.2**

| Type II Error Values for Vitamin C Example | | | | |
|---|---|---|---|---|
| $p$ | 0.2 | 0.25 | 0.30 | 0.35 | 0.4 |
| $\beta(p)$ | 0.0043 | 0.1020 | 0.4562 | 0.8264 | 0.9738 |

of a Type II error can be calculated as

$$\begin{aligned}
\beta(0.2) &= P(\text{deciding for } H_0 | n = 100, p = 0.2) \\
&= 1 - P(\text{rejecting } H_0 | n = 100, p = 0.2) \\
&= 1 - P(X \leqslant 30 | n = 100, p = 0.2)
\end{aligned}$$

for $X \sim B(100, 0.2)$. This probability can then be approximated by the normal distribution, yielding

$$\begin{aligned}
\beta(0.2) &= 1 - P\left(\frac{X - np}{\sqrt{np(1-p)}} \leqslant \frac{30.5 - 20}{\sqrt{100(0.2)(0.8)}}\right) \\
&= 1 - P(Z \leqslant 2.63) = 1 - 0.9957 = 0.0043
\end{aligned}$$

A similar calculation would be required to find the probability of a Type II error, $\beta(p)$, for every other value of $p < 0.4$. A few of these probabilities are given in Table 6.2. The probabilities in the table were calculated just as for $p = 0.2$, using the normal approximation with the continuity correction. It is clear that the consequences of a Type II error are different from those of a Type I error. If a Type II error is made, it is because the research hypothesis is true but the experiment did not produce the evidence necessary to reach that conclusion; therefore the null hypothesis is accepted as valid instead. In the case of the vitamin C example, a treatment that reduced the incidence of the common cold would be ignored. As almost everyone can survive having a cold, a Type II error might not be too critical in this example. To miss an effective treatment for a serious disease, however, would be a very bad error indeed.

As you can see from Table 6.2, the more $p$ is less than 0.4, the smaller the value of $\beta(p)$. The test is most effective in distinguishing between hypotheses when the value of $p$ in the alternative hypothesis is not close to the null value of $p = 0.40$. On the other hand, the value of $\beta(p)$ is large when $p$ is near 0.4. A plot of $\beta(p)$ as a function of $p$ appears in Figure 6.2. This curve is called the operating characteristic (OC) curve for the test. It clearly shows that $\beta(p)$ increases as $p$ increases on $(0, 0.4)$. For $p = 0.4$, $\beta(0.4) = 0.9738$. Note that this value is equal to $1 - \alpha = 1 - 0.0262 = 0.9738$, the probability of accepting $H_0$ given that $H_0$ is true.

## Minitab Simulation of Type II Error

The simulation capacity of Minitab can be used to illustrate the relative frequency of occurrence of a Type II error. Once again the decision rule is to reject

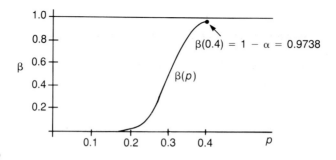

**Figure 6.2**

Type II Error Curve

$H_0: p = 0.4$ if 30 or fewer of the 100 individuals in the treatment group get colds during the observation period. If the number who get colds exceeds 30, the null hypothesis is retained. Let us assume that the treated group has only probability $p = 0.25$ of getting a cold. Exhibit 6.2 presents the output generated when RANDOM was used with $p = 0.25$ and $n = 100$ to simulate 1000 observations of $X \sim B(100, 0.25)$.

The output indicates that 94 of the 1000 observations exceed 30, so the observed Type II error rate is 0.094 in this simulation. In Table 6.2, the theoretical value of $\beta(0.25)$, given by $P(X > 30 | p = 0.25)$, was found to be 0.102. Again the simulated error rate, in this case for a Type II error, is in fairly good agreement with the theoretical value.

In the vitamin C example, the test statistic used was $X$, the number of persons in the treatment group who got colds. The critical region was arbitrarily chosen to be $X \leqslant 30$. The probability of a Type I error $\alpha$ was then computed to be approximately 0.0262. Similarly, the probabilities of Type II errors, $\beta(p)$, were computed for different values of $p$. Usually the critical or rejection region is chosen in such a way that $\alpha$ is controlled so as to be some small value, often in the range from 0.01 to 0.05. In order to illustrate the process, an artificially small sample size $n = 10$ will be used to decide between the two vitamin C hypotheses.

The test statistic will again be $X$, defined this time as the number out of the ten individuals taking vitamin C who do not get a cold during the period from October 1 to March 31. As before, appropriate critical regions are of the form

$$X \leqslant k \qquad \qquad \textbf{6.8}$$

for some constant $k$. We can use Minitab to find the value of $P(X \leqslant k | n = 10, p = 0.4)$ for various values of $k$.

The output in Exhibit 6.3 shows that for $k = 0$ the value of $\alpha$ is 0.0060; for $k = 1$ the value of $\alpha$ is 0.0464; and for $k = 2$ the value of $\alpha$ is 0.1673. The critical region for achieving a value of $\alpha$ in the desired range is $X \leqslant 1$. In other words, if one or fewer of the ten treated individuals gets a cold, we decide that vitamin C is effective. If two or more get colds, we have to say that there is not sufficient

**Exhibit 6.2**

```
MTB > OUTPUT WIDTH = 70
MTB > NOTE SIMULATION OF 1000 TREATMENT GROUPS IN VITAMIN EXAMPLE
MTB > NOTE FOR REDUCING INCIDENCE OF THE COMMON COLD
MTB > BASE = 5000
MTB > RANDOM 1000 OBSERVATIONS IN C1;
SUBC> BINOMIAL N = 100 P = 0.25.
MTB > TALLY C1

         C1  COUNT
         13    3
         14    2
         15    8
         16   12
         17   26
         18   25
         19   42
         20   45
         21   73
         22   78
         23   87
         24   78
         25   90
         26   94
         27   74
         28   74
         29   56
         30   39
         31   30
         32   22
         33   18
         34    9
         35    6
         36    6
         37    2
         40    1
         N= 1000
```

evidence to decide that vitamin C is effective in treating the common cold. The value of $\alpha = 0.0464$ is referred to as the significance level of the test.

---

**Definition 6.7** ▪▪▪▪▪▪▪▪▪▪▪▪▪▪▪▪▪▪▪▪▪▪▪▪▪▪▪▪▪▪▪▪▪▪▪▪▪▪▪▪▪▪▪▪▪▪

**significance level**

The **significance level** of a test is the probability that the test statistic will fall within the critical region if $H_0$ is true; that is, it is equal to $\alpha$, the probability of a Type I error for the test.

---

It should be emphasized that a decision to retain the null hypothesis does not mean that the hypothesis is correct. For example, suppose the incidence of getting a common cold were reduced from 0.4 to 0.30 by use of vitamin C. We would use the Minitab command CDF to find

$$P(X > 1 | n = 10, p = 0.30)$$

Exhibit 6.3

```
MTB > NOTE BINOMIAL PROBABILITIES FOR N = 10 AND P = 0.4
MTB > PDF;
SUBC> BINOMIAL PROBABILITIES N = 10 P = 0.4.

      BINOMIAL WITH N =  10  P = 0.400000
           K         P( X = K)
           0            0.0060
           1            0.0403
           2            0.1209
           3            0.2150
           4            0.2508
           5            0.2007
           6            0.1115
           7            0.0425
           8            0.0106
           9            0.0016
          10            0.0001
MTB > CDF;
SUBC> BINOMIAL CUMULATIVE PROB N = 10 P = 0.4.

      BINOMIAL WITH N =  10  P = 0.400000
        K  P( X LESS OR = K)
        0            0.0060
        1            0.0464
        2            0.1673
        3            0.3823
        4            0.6331
        5            0.8338
        6            0.9452
        7            0.9877
        8            0.9983
        9            0.9999
       10            1.0000
```

The output is shown below.

```
MTB > CDF;
SUBC> BINOMIAL N = 10 P = 0.30.

      BINOMIAL WITH N =  10  P = 0.300000
        K  P( X LESS OR = K)
        0            0.0282
        1            0.1493
        2            0.3828
        3            0.6496
        4            0.8497
        5            0.9527
        6            0.9894
        7            0.9984
        8            0.9999
        9            1.0000
```

The output shows that $P(X > 1) = 1 - 0.1493 = 0.8507$. In other words, even though $p = 0.3 < 0.4$, use of the critical region $X \leqslant 1$ would result in a decision that $p = 0.4$ about 85 percent of the time. Hence a decision to retain $H_0$

means only that the data are not inconsistent with $H_0$. The fact that $H_0$ is not unreasonable in view of the data does not necessarily mean that it is true.

The steps used in deciding between two statistical hypotheses can be summarized as follows:

1 Establish $H_0$, the null hypothesis, and $H_1$, the research hypothesis.
2 Decide on $\alpha$, the probability of a Type I error (frequently in the range 0.01 to 0.05).
3 Choose an appropriate test statistic.
4 On the basis of $H_0$, $H_1$, $n$, and $\alpha$, find a critical region for the test statistic.
5 Compute the value of the test statistic from a random sample. Choose $H_1$ if this value lies in the critical region, or $H_0$ if it does not.

Subsequent sections show how the critical region can be selected so as to make the value $\alpha$ equal to a chosen small probability. It should be emphasized that by controlling $\alpha$ we are controlling the probability of stating that the research hypothesis is true when in fact it is not. The burden is on the research hypothesis, as it should be. We want to control $\alpha$ so that an erroneous decision in favor of the research hypothesis will be made only $100\alpha$ percent of the time.

## Exercises 6.2

**6.1** A box contains six balls, of which an unknown number $\theta$ are green and the rest are red. Two balls are drawn from the box randomly without replacement. We wish to decide between

$H_0: \theta = 2$     and     $H_1: \theta = 4$

We are to reject $H_0$ in favor of $H_1$ if both balls are green.
**a.** Find the probability of a Type I error—that is, the probability of obtaining two green balls from the box on two successive selections when there are two green and four red balls in the box.
**b.** Find the probability of a Type II error—that is, the probability of obtaining fewer than two green balls from the box in the two selections when four of the six balls in the box are green.

**6.2** **a.** A coin is tossed five times. It is declared to be fair ($H_0$) if the number of heads is neither 0 nor 5. Find the probability of a Type I error.
**b.** Find the probability of a Type II error if the probability of heads is actually 2/3. *Note:* This probability is most easily found using the rule for the probability of a complement.

**6.3** A production process is said to be "in control" if the proportion of defectives produced is 0.05. A random sample of 20 items is taken from the output. We wish to decide between

$H_0: p = 0.05$     and     $H_1: p > 0.05$

If $H_1$ is true, the process is out of control and should be stopped and adjusted. We decide to stop the process if 3 or more of the 20 items sampled are defective.
**a.** State in words the meaning of a Type I error.
**b.** State in words the meaning of a Type II error.
**c.** Use Minitab to find the probability of a Type I error.

**d.** Use Minitab to find the probability of a Type II error if $p = 0.10, 0.15, 0.20, 0.25, 0.30, 0.40,$ and $0.50$.

**e.** Sketch a graph of the OC curve for this test, analogous to the one in Figure 6.2.

**f.** Does the curve in part e decrease as a function of $p$ for $p > 0.05$? Why is this trend to be expected?

**6.4** A university is said to have an equal number of male and female undergraduates. A student doubts this statement; he believes that the proportion of females is less than 0.5. A random sample of 16 students is taken from a student phone directory. The student wishes to test the hypotheses

$$H_0: p = 0.5 \quad \text{and} \quad H_1: p < 0.5$$

**a.** Use Minitab to find an appropriate critical region with significance level $\alpha = 0.0384$.

**b.** Use Minitab and the critical region from part a to calculate the probability of a Type II error for $p = 0.45, 0.4, 0.35, 0.3, 0.2,$ and $0.1$.

**c.** Sketch a graph of the OC curve for the critical region of part a.

**6.5** **a.** General Motors is reputed to have more than 50 percent of the automobile market in a certain state. Suppose that $n = 100$ cars are observed and that $X$, the number of these cars manufactured by GM, is established. Assuming the trials are independent, use $X$ to test $H_0: p = 1/2$ versus $H_1: p > 1/2$, where $p$ is the proportion of GM cars in the state. Assume that $X \geq 58$ is the critical region. Calculate the probability of a Type I error, using the normal approximation with the continuity correction.

**b.** Assuming $p = 0.6$, calculate the probability of a Type II error, using the normal approximation with the continuity correction.

**c.** Find $\beta(0.55)$, $\beta(0.65)$, and $\beta(0.75)$, and sketch the OC curve for this test.

**6.6** **a.** Use the RANDOM command in Minitab to carry out the test in the preceding problem 1000 times, as in the example of this section. Use $p = 0.5$ and $n = 100$. What is the simulated Type I error rate? How does this rate compare with your answer to part a of exercise 6.5?

**b.** Use RANDOM to approximate the value of $\beta(0.60)$ by making 1000 observations of $X$, given $p = 0.6$. How does the simulated value compare with the calculation in part b of exercise 6.5?

**6.7** Television network A claims that one of its programs has more than 40 percent of the network television audience at 7:00 P.M. Another network doubts this claim and hires a television rating service to test $H_0: p = 0.4$ versus $H_1: p > 0.4$, where $p$ is the proportion of viewers watching network A's program. A total of 400 viewers are surveyed. A decision will be made to reject $H_0$ in favor of $H_1$ if 180 or more of these viewers are, in fact, watching network A's show.

**a.** Find the probability of a Type I error $\alpha$, using the normal approximation with the continuity correction.

**b.** Find the probability of a Type II error for $p = 0.5$ and $p = 0.8$, using the normal approximation with the continuity correction. Is the relationship between these probabilities what you would expect? Explain.

**6.8** Test the hypothesis that one-half of the applicants to a medical school are male versus the alternative that more males than females apply, by counting the number of males, $X$, in only ten admissions. A decision in favor of the hypothesis that there are more males than females is to be made if eight or more of the ten applicants are male.

**a.** Using the subcommand BINOMIAL with CDF, determine the probability of a Type I error by finding $P(X \geqslant 8 | n = 10, p = 0.5)$ for $X \sim B(10, 0.5)$.

**b.** Use $B(10, p)$ for $p = 0.6, 0.7, 0.8, 0.9$, and 1 to find $\beta(p)$. Graph $\beta(p)$ versus $p$ for these values and for $p = 0.5$. Does this curve appear to decrease as $p$ increases? Is this trend to be expected? Why?

**6.9**  **a.** The advertising manager of a brewery wishes to test the hypothesis $H_0: p = 0.6$ versus $H_1: p > 0.6$, where $p$ is the proportion of beer drinkers in a certain adult population. A sample of $n = 600$ adults is to be taken, and a decision will be made in favor of $H_1$ if the number of beer drinkers in the sample is 390 or more. Find $\alpha$ as in exercise 6.5.

**b.** If the critical region were changed to $X \geqslant 400$, would you expect $\alpha$ to increase or decrease?

**c.** Calculate $\alpha$ for $X \geqslant 400$. Is the result consistent with your answer to part b?

**6.10**  Using RANDOM, simulate 1000 samplings of 20 items from a production line with 5 percent defective items. Use the TALLY command with the column in which the output of RANDOM is stored.

**a.** In what proportion of these 1000 observations are 3 or more defectives found? Compare this proportion with the binomial probability found in part c of exercise 6.3.

**b.** Carry out the simulation described above with 20 percent defective items. What proportion of the observations now have 3 or more defective items? Compare this proportion with the theoretical probability $1 - \beta(0.2)$ found in part d of exercise 6.3.

## 6.3

## Hypothesis Testing for $\mu$ in Large Samples

Section 6.2 introduced several ideas about tests of hypotheses concerning a population proportion $p$. In this section we consider tests for $\mu = E(X)$, the expectation of a random variable $X$. The null hypothesis is stated as

$$H_0: \mu = \mu_0 \qquad\qquad \text{6.9}$$

where $\mu_0$ is a particular fixed number. The standard alternatives to this null hypothesis are the following:

$$H_1: \mu > \mu_0 \qquad H_1: \mu < \mu_0 \qquad H_1: \mu \neq \mu_0 \qquad \text{6.10}$$

The first step in deciding between Equation 6.9 and one of the alternatives in 6.10 is to select $\alpha$, the probability of a Type I error. In order to guard against deciding in favor of the research hypothesis when the data do not support it, the value of $\alpha$ must be set at some small value (typically $\alpha = 0.10, 0.05$, or $0.01$).

Once $H_0$ and $H_1$ have been stated and a value of $\alpha$ has been selected, the next step in the decision procedure outlined in Section 6.2 is to select a test statistic. As the hypotheses in Equations 6.9 and 6.10 involve $\mu$, it should not be surprising that the test statistic will depend on $\bar{X}$, the sample average. Assuming that the sample size is large, we have seen that the random variable $\bar{X}$, when standardized, satisfies

$$\frac{\bar{X} - \mu}{\sigma/\sqrt{n}} \sim Z$$

that is, when standardized $\bar{X}$ has approximately the standard normal distribution. Suppose we want to test the null hypothesis in 6.9 against the first alternative in 6.10,

$$H_1: \mu > \mu_0 \tag{6.11}$$

**Z-value** We use the **Z-value**, or observed value, of the test statistic:

$$Z = \frac{\bar{X} - \mu_0}{\sigma/\sqrt{n}} \tag{6.12}$$

The next step is to find the critical region for the test. *If $H_0$ is valid, $\mu$ will be equal to $\mu_0$* and $Z$ in Equation 6.12 will, in fact, have a standard normal distribution. If, however, the alternative in 6.11 is true, the observed value of $Z$ in Equation 6.12 will tend to be positive because $E(\bar{X}) = \mu > \mu_0$. Further, the more positive $Z$ is, the more convinced we ought to be that $H_1$ is true. Thus the critical region will be of the form

$$\frac{\bar{X} - \mu_0}{\sigma/\sqrt{n}} \geqslant c_\alpha \qquad \text{or} \qquad Z \geqslant c_\alpha$$

where the constant $c_\alpha$ is chosen so as to make the probability of a Type I error equal to $\alpha$. We require

$$P\left(\frac{\bar{X} - \mu_0}{\sigma/\sqrt{n}} \geqslant c_\alpha | H_0\right) = \alpha \tag{6.13}$$

But under $H_0$, $(\bar{X} - \mu_0)/(\sigma/\sqrt{n})$ has the standard normal distribution. Thus $c_\alpha$ must be chosen so that

$$P(Z \geqslant c_\alpha) = \alpha \qquad \text{or} \qquad c_\alpha = z_\alpha$$

The rejection region in Equation 6.13 may be rewritten in terms of $\bar{X}$ as

$$\bar{X} \geqslant \mu_0 + \frac{\sigma}{\sqrt{n}} z_\alpha \tag{6.14}$$

As is reasonable, the null hypothesis should be rejected in favor of the alternative in 6.11 for large values of the sample mean. Notice that the critical region depends on knowledge of $H_0$, $H_1$, the sample size $n$, and the significance level for the test. Also, as Equation 6.12 shows, the value of $\sigma$ must be known or assumed in order to calculate the required test statistic $Z$. A graphical representation of the critical region is given in Figure 6.3. The region is all values of $Z$ greater than or equal to $z_\alpha$.

    In general, in carrying out a test of $H_0: \mu = \mu_0$ against the alternatives mentioned above, we obtain the critical regions indicated in Table 6.3. (Refer to Table 5.3 for several useful values of $z_{\alpha/2}$.) In Minitab these alternatives are coded as $+1$, $-1$, and 0. The one-sided critical region $Z \geqslant z_\alpha$ is also appropriate for testing

$$H_0: \mu \leqslant \mu_0 \qquad \text{versus} \qquad H_1: \mu > \mu_0$$

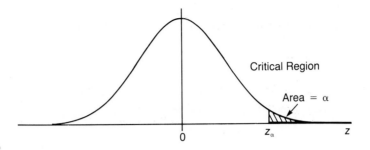

**Figure 6.3**

Rejection Region for $H_1: \mu > \mu_0$

**Table 6.3**

Critical Regions for $H_0: \mu = \mu_0$

| Alternative | Critical Region | Minitab Alternative |
|---|---|---|
| $\mu > \mu_0$ | $Z \geqslant z_\alpha$ | $+1$ |
| $\mu < \mu_0$ | $Z \leqslant -z_\alpha$ | $-1$ |
| $\mu \neq \mu_0$ | $|Z| \geqslant z_{\alpha/2}$ | $0$ |

Similarly, $Z \leqslant -z_\alpha$ is appropriate for testing

$$H_0: \mu \geqslant \mu_0 \qquad \text{versus} \qquad H_1: \mu < \mu_0$$

(Although analogous remarks are true for subsequent tests, they will not be explicitly stated in each case.) The critical region in the case of the third alternative in Table 6.3 consists of two separate parts, as $|Z| \geqslant z_{\alpha/2}$ includes $Z \leqslant -z_{\alpha/2}$ and $Z \geqslant z_{\alpha/2}$. Such a critical region, which is called two-sided or two-tailed, is shown in Figure 6.4.

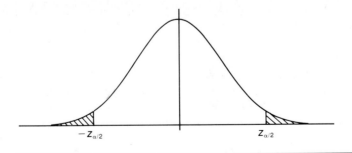

**Figure 6.4**

Critical Region for $H_1: \mu \neq \mu_0$

For large samples, the value of $Z$ is often computed by replacing $\sigma$ with the sample standard deviation:

$$Z = \frac{\bar{X} - \mu_0}{s/\sqrt{n}}$$

6.15

This approach is generally satisfactory for large samples, unless there is good reason to believe that $\sigma$ will not be well estimated by $s$.

## Example 6.1

Consider the data on stocks in Section 2.1. Suppose past experience indicates that the true average dividend yield of highly capitalized companies is about 5 percent. An economist doubts that the yield is this high. It would be appropriate to test the following hypotheses:

$$H_0: \mu = 5 \text{ (percent)} \quad \text{versus} \quad H_1: \mu < 5$$

Notice that the alternative is chosen to correspond to the economist's research hypothesis.

For the above hypotheses, the critical region for a test at significance level 0.05 is of the form

$$Z \leqslant -z_{0.05} \quad \text{or} \quad Z \leqslant -1.645$$

The sample mean and standard deviation for the 50 stocks are $\bar{x} = 4.784$ and $s = 2.982$. We calculate

$$Z = \frac{4.784 - 5}{2.982/\sqrt{50}} = -0.512$$

This value does not fall into the critical region, so we retain the null hypothesis $H_0: \mu = 5$; that is, we decide that it is reasonable to assume that the true average yield for the stocks is 5 percent.

Consider the percentage price change for the 50 stocks, also given in Section 2.1. Suppose that we test the following hypotheses:

$$H_0: \mu = 0 \quad \text{versus} \quad H_1: \mu \neq 0$$

Using $\alpha = 0.05$, from Table 6.3 we obtain the critical region

$$|Z| \geqslant z_{0.025} \quad \text{or} \quad |Z| \geqslant 1.96$$

For the 50 observed percentage price changes in 1981, we found that $\bar{x} = -8.14$ and $s = 28.571$. Hence,

$$Z = \frac{-8.14}{28.571/\sqrt{50}} = -2.01$$

This value of $Z$ *is* in the critical region, as $|-2.01| = 2.01 \geqslant 1.96$. The data strongly suggest a negative percentage change for stocks in 1981.

## Minitab Example of Test for $\mu$

Section 2.4 gave the number of runs scored during one year by major league batters hitting at least 0.300. Suppose that for a theoretical population of major league batters hitting over 0.300 for a season we wish to test, using $\alpha = 0.05$, the hypotheses

$$H_0: \mu = 80 \quad \text{versus} \quad H_1: \mu \neq 80$$

where $\mu = E(X)$, the expected number of runs scored by such batters per season. The number of runs scored by each of the 44 batters sampled has been SET into column C1 of the Minitab worksheet in Exhibit 6.4. The value of the sample standard deviation has been computed using the command STDEV and has been stored as K1. Note that the two-sided alternative $H_1$ is coded using the number zero, as shown in Table 6.3.

**ZTEST**      The command **ZTEST** has been used to compute the observed value of $Z = -0.96$. The fact that this value is not in the critical region $|Z| \geq z_{0.025} = 1.96$ means that the null hypothesis (of an expected value of 80 runs) cannot be rejected. Hence we retain the null hypothesis as a reasonable possibility.

The output in Exhibit 6.4 includes a *p*-value of 0.34, which is defined as follows.

**Exhibit 6.4**

```
MTB > NOTE TEST OF AVERAGE RUNS = 80 FOR BASEBALL DATA OF CH 2
MTB > SET C1
C1
     69     66     45     69     .    .    .

MTB > END
MTB > PRINT C1
C1
     69     66     45     69     47    111     83     40     68     70
     96     31     78     58     84     94     73     79     91     87
     96     87     96     74     76    134     61    117     96     42
     62     57     81     94     86    111     84     67    100     67
     54     62     42     94

MTB > STDEV C1 PUT IN K1
    ST.DEV. =      22.147
MTB > ZTEST OF MU = 80 ALTERNATIVE = 0, SIGMA = K1, FOR C1

TEST OF MU = 80.00 VS MU N.E. 80.00
THE ASSUMED SIGMA = 22.1

                N       MEAN    STDEV    SE MEAN       Z    P VALUE
C1             44      76.80    22.15       3.34    -0.96       0.34
```

**Definition 6.8** ━━━━━━━━━━

A **p-value** for a test is the minimum value, $\alpha^*$, of the significance level for which the null hypothesis being tested can be rejected. Taken into account in its computation are the alternative hypothesis and the observed value of Z. The p-value is also known as the attained significance level for the test.

For the Minitab output of Exhibit 6.4 on runs scored by major league batters, the rejection region is of the form $|Z| \geqslant z_{\alpha/2}$. The computed value of $z$ is $-0.96$. The null hypothesis can be rejected if $|Z| \geqslant 0.96$ is chosen to be the critical region. From Table I of Appendix C we find that

$$P(|Z| \geqslant 0.96) = 2(1 - 0.8315) = 0.3370 = \alpha^*$$

This value agrees with the Minitab p-value to two significant decimal places. If the significance level $\alpha$ is any *smaller* than 0.34 (for instance, $\alpha = 0.05$), we cannot reject $H_0$ in favor of $H_1$. Only if the significance level is at least 0.34 can we reject $H_0$ on the basis of these data. As significance levels are chosen to be small probabilities (generally no more than 0.20), there is no reasonable significance level at which the null hypothesis should be rejected on the basis of these data.

The p-value gives a probability which in a sense measures the agreement of the data with the null hypothesis. If the p-value is high, the agreement with the null hypothesis is good. If the p-value is low, the agreement is not very good. Small p-values lead to the rejection of $H_0$. In Example 6.1 the observed value of Z was $-2.01$. The relevant p-value is

$$P(|Z| \geqslant 2.01) = 2(1 - 0.9778) = 0.0444$$

for a two-sided alternative. Only for values of $\alpha \geqslant \alpha^* = 0.0444$ should the null hypothesis of no percentage price change for the population of stocks be rejected. Hence for $\alpha = 0.05$ the null hypothesis would be rejected, but for $\alpha = 0.01$ it would be retained. We can thus use the p-value $\alpha^*$ to test a null hypothesis, as follows: Given a formal significance level of $\alpha$, we retain $H_0$ when $\alpha^* > \alpha$ and reject $H_0$ when $\alpha^* \leqslant \alpha$.

There is an important connection between confidence intervals for $\mu$ and a test of $H_0: \mu = \mu_0$ versus $H_1: \mu \neq \mu_0$. For large $n$, $(1 - \alpha)100$ percent confidence interval for $\mu$ is given by

$$\bar{X} - \frac{\sigma}{\sqrt{n}} z_{\alpha/2} < \mu < \bar{X} + \frac{\sigma}{\sqrt{n}} z_{\alpha/2}$$

We have seen that this expression is equivalent to

$$-z_{\alpha/2} < \frac{(\bar{X} - \mu)}{\sigma/\sqrt{n}} < z_{\alpha/2} \qquad \text{or} \qquad -z_{\alpha/2} < Z < z_{\alpha/2}$$

(See Section 5.3.) As the critical region for a test of $H_0: \mu = \mu_0$ versus $H_1: \mu \neq \mu_0$ is given by $|Z| \geqslant z_{\alpha/2}$, however, the confidence interval contains exactly those values of $\mu_0$ that would result in *retaining* $H_0$: $\mu = \mu_0$ at significance level $\alpha$ for a two-sided alternative. Hence, if we know the confidence interval and $\mu_0$ is in that interval, $H_0$: $\mu = \mu_0$ can be retained. If not, $H_0$ should be rejected.

Again it should be emphasized that a decision to retain $H_0$ is a "weak" decision. The fact that the calculated statistic does not lie in the critical region means that no evidence has been found to declare the null hypothesis incorrect. The data are thus consistent with the null hypothesis, but they do not prove that $H_0$ is correct. A decision is considered "strong" when the statistic computed lies in the critical region leading to rejection of $H_0$—in this case, the probability that $H_0$ is in fact true is only $\alpha$. Hence the probability of rejection of $H_0$ when it is true is controlled to have a preselected (small) probability $\alpha$.

## Example 6.2

A sample of the heights (in inches) of 64 females yielded an average height of $\bar{x} = 68.5$. The population of heights has an assumed variance of $\sigma^2 = 4$. A 95 percent confidence interval for $\mu$ has endpoints

$$68.5 \pm (2/8)z_{0.025} \qquad \text{or} \qquad 68.5 \pm 0.49$$

Thus any value of $\mu_0$ in the interval (68.01, 68.99) would be retained in testing

$$H_0: \mu = \mu_0 \qquad \text{versus} \qquad H_1: \mu \neq \mu_0$$

All other values would be rejected at significance level $\alpha = 0.05$.

---

Let us now turn to the calculation of $\beta$, the probability of a Type II error. Consider the hypotheses of Example 6.1 regarding stock yields,

$$H_0: \mu = 5 \qquad \text{and} \qquad H_1: \mu < 5$$

A Type II error is made if $H_0$ is accepted when $H_1$ is correct. Whether a Type II error occurs will be a function of $\mu$. The required probability is

$$\beta(\mu) = P\left(\frac{\bar{X} - \mu_0}{\sigma/\sqrt{n}} > -1.645 | \mu \text{ is the true expectation}\right)$$

$$= P\left(\bar{X} - \mu_0 > -\frac{\sigma}{\sqrt{n}} 1.645 | \mu \text{ is the true expectation}\right)$$

$$= P\left(\frac{\bar{X} - \mu}{\sigma/\sqrt{n}} > \frac{\mu_0 - \mu}{\sigma/\sqrt{n}} - 1.645 | \mu\right)$$

$$= P\left(Z > \frac{5 - \mu}{2.982/\sqrt{50}} - 1.645\right)$$

Once again, the substitution of $Z$ is justified by the Central Limit Theorem. For

**Table 6.4**

**The Probabilities of Type II Errors for Example 6.1**

| $\mu$ | 3 | 3.5 | 4 | 4.5 | 5 |
|---|---|---|---|---|---|
| $\beta(\mu)$ | 0.0010 | 0.0281 | 0.2327 | 0.6772 | 0.95 |

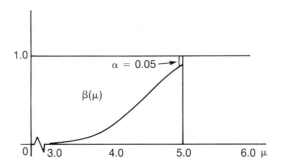

**Figure 6.5**

**Graph of Type II Error as a Function of $\mu$**

example, if $\mu = 4$, we have

$$\beta(4.5) = P\left(Z > \frac{5-4}{2.982/\sqrt{50}} - 1.645\right)$$
$$= P(Z > 0.73) = 0.2327$$

where the probability has been found from the table of the standard normal distribution. The values of $\beta(\mu)$ for various values of $\mu$ are given in Table 6.4.

A graph of the Type II error curve has been plotted in Figure 6.5, using the values of $\beta(\mu)$ in Table 6.4. It can readily be seen that for values of $\mu$ close to but less than $\mu_0 = 5$ the probability of a Type II error is high, whereas for values substantially less than $\mu = \mu_0$ (for example, $\mu = 3$) the probability of this type of error is small. As before, the test is most effective in distinguishing between hypotheses when the values of $\mu$ are far apart.

**Exercises 6.3**

**6.11** In exercise 5.11, calculation of summary statistics for 80 commuting times over a specified route yielded $\bar{x} = 12.5$ and $s = 2.2$. Test the null hypothesis that it takes an average of 12 minutes to travel this route. Use the alternative $H_1: \mu > 12$.
  **a.** Find the critical region in terms of $Z$ for a test using $\alpha = 0.05$.
  **b.** Compute the observed value of $Z$ and decide between $H_0: \mu = 12$ and $H_1: \mu > 12$.
  **c.** Find the probability of a Type II error for $\mu = 12.5$ and $\mu = 13$.
  **d.** Answer parts a and b for a test using $\alpha = 0.01$.

**6.12** Use the 32 measurements of the gravity constant $g$ given in exercise 5.12 to test $H_0$: $\mu = 980.665$ versus a two-sided alternative. ($\mu = 980.665$ is the value given in the

*Standard Mathematical Tables* published by The Chemical Rubber Company, Cleveland, Ohio.) Use $\alpha = 0.01$.

**6.13** Determine the ages on January 1, 1981 of the 43 California representatives listed in exercise 5.13. Use the ZTEST command to decide between $H_0: \mu = 45$ and $H_1: \mu \neq 45$, using significance level $\alpha = 0.05$. Clearly state the critical region for this test.

**6.14** Use the confidence interval for the difference between high and low temperatures on September 26, 1982 obtained in exercise 5.14 to test the hypothesis that the true average difference between high and low temperatures on that date was 20 degrees against a two-sided alternative, using $\alpha = 0.05$. Use Minitab as needed.

**6.15** Exercise 5.15 gives data on the difference in the number of runs scored by World Series teams in 300 games. The average difference is $\bar{x} = 4.64$, and the standard deviation of the differences is $s = 2.59$. If each of the values $0, 1, 2, \ldots, 9$ were assigned an equal probability of $1/10$, we would have $\mu = 4.5$ for the population. Test $H_0: \mu = 4.5$ versus $H_1: \mu \neq 4.5$, using these data.

**6.16** Consider the data on home runs by National League champions given in exercise 5.16. Test the hypothesis $H_0: \mu = 40$ (that is, the average number of home runs required to win the championship is 40) versus $H_1: \mu \neq 40$, using $\alpha = 0.05$. Clearly state the rejection region. Use Minitab as needed. (The assumption implied here —that the game has not changed with regard to home runs over the years—is, of course, rather shaky.)

**6.17** Use the data of exercise 5.17 and the confidence interval for the average age of the U.S. Navy captains to test $H_0: \mu = 50$ versus $H_1: \mu \neq 50$, using $\alpha = 0.05$.

**6.18** Using Minitab, store the integers from 1 to 100 in C1, and put 0.01 in all 100 rows of C2. Use RANDOM to simulate the means of 200 samples of size 16 from this population, for which $\mu = 50.5$ and $\sigma = 28.866$.
   **a.** Compute a column of 200 observed $Z$ values, using the true values of $\mu$ and $\sigma$.
   **b.** Using the COPY command and the OMIT subcommand, find the proportion of these values that are at least 1.282 and the proportion that are at least 1.645. Compare these results with the theoretical values of 0.10 and 0.05.
   **c.** Have the computer generate a histogram of the observed $Z$ values. Inspect the histogram to determine whether the $Z$ values appear to be normally distributed. Note that the parent population has the discrete uniform distribution on $1, 2, \ldots, 100$.
   **d.** Generate a normal plot of the observed $Z$ values and make another visual test for normality.

**6.19** Consider the data on the net weights of 64 two-pound packages of cheese, given in exercise 5.18.
   **a.** Use the ZTEST command to test $H_0: \mu = 32$ versus $H_1: \mu \neq 32$. Use $\alpha = 0.05$.
   **b.** Use the output from ZTEST to find a $p$-value for this test.

**6.20** In cases where one actually is sampling from a normal distribution, $Z = (\bar{X} - \mu_0)/(\sigma/\sqrt{n})$ has an exact standard normal distribution.
   **a.** Restate the critical region for testing $H_0: \mu = \mu_0$ versus $H_1: \mu < \mu_0$ in terms of $\bar{X}$. That is, find the value $c$ such that $P(\bar{X} \leq c | H_0) = \alpha$. The value $c$ will be a function of $\alpha$, $n$, and $\sigma$.
   **b.** Find the critical region for the stock yields of Example 6.1 in terms of $\bar{X}$, assuming $\sigma = 3$. Does the observed value $\bar{x} = 4.784$ fall in this region?

**Hypothesis Testing for _p_ in Large Samples**

Section 6.3 described large-sample tests concerning the expectation $E(X)$ of a random variable. In this section we will consider tests concerning an unknown population proportion $p$. The null hypothesis, which is analogous to the one in Equation 6.9 for $\mu$, is stated as

$$H_0: p = p_0 \qquad\qquad\qquad \textbf{6.16}$$

where $p_0$ is a fixed number on the interval [0, 1]. Standard alternatives to this null hypothesis are

$$H_1: p > p_0 \qquad H_1: p < p_0 \qquad H_1: p \neq p_0 \qquad\qquad \textbf{6.17}$$

The same critical region used in the tests for $\mu$ to test

$$H_0: p = p_0 \qquad \text{versus} \qquad H_1: p > p_0$$

will be used in testing

$$H_0: p \leqslant p_0 \qquad \text{versus} \qquad H_1: p > p_0$$

Similarly, the same critical region used to test

$$H_0: p = p_0 \qquad \text{versus} \qquad H_1: p < p_0$$

will be used in testing

$$H_0: p \geqslant p_0 \qquad \text{versus} \qquad H_1: p < p_0$$

In order to decide between the null hypothesis and one of the alternatives in Equation 6.17, we must find a critical region of values of a test statistic. Suppose that the alternative is of the first type in Equation 6.17. We require a test with significance level $\alpha$. As the null and alternative hypotheses both involve a population proportion $p$, it is reasonable that the test statistic should depend on the sample fraction $\hat{p}$. For a large sample, we have seen that the random variable $\hat{p}$, when standardized, satisfies

$$\frac{\hat{p} - p}{\sqrt{p(1-p)/n}} \sim Z$$

That is, the random variable has approximately the standard normal distribution, where $p$ is the true population proportion. As we did for the test statistic of Section 6.3, we compute

$$Z = \frac{\hat{p} - p_0}{\sqrt{p_0(1-p_0)/n}} \qquad\qquad\qquad \textbf{6.18}$$

as the observed value of $Z$. If $H_0$ is true, $Z$ in Equation 6.18 will have approximately a standard normal distribution for large $n$. As $E(\hat{p}) = p$, $\hat{p}$ is on the average equal to the unknown proportion $p$. If $H_1: p > p_0$ is true, the test statistic $Z$ will tend to be positive, as $\hat{p}$ estimates $p$ (not $p_0$). The more positive $Z$ is, the more evidence

## Table 6.5

**Critical Regions for Tests of $H_0: p = p_0$**

| Alternative | Critical Region |
|---|---|
| $p > p_0$ | $Z \geqslant z_\alpha$ |
| $p < p_0$ | $z \leqslant -z_\alpha$ |
| $p \neq p_0$ | $|Z| \geqslant z_{\alpha/2}$ |

there is in favor of $H_1$. Hence the critical region will be chosen to be

$$\frac{\hat{p} - p_0}{\sqrt{p_0(1 - p_0)/n}} \geqslant z_\alpha \qquad \qquad \textbf{6.19}$$

This critical region, which corresponds to the critical regions of the preceding section, provides an approximate $\alpha$-level test for the null hypothesis versus $H_1: p > p_0$ when $n$ is large. The test is approximate because the normality of $Z$ in 6.18 under $H_0$ depends on the Central Limit Theorem. In this section we assume a sample large enough that the Central Limit Theorem provides a good approximation to normality.

Critical regions for the other alternative hypotheses are listed in Table 6.5. They were arrived at through the same type of reasoning as was used to derive $Z \geqslant z_\alpha$.

## Example 6.3

Prior to an election, a poll of 1600 registered voters is taken by a candidate who wishes to decide between

$$H_0: p \leqslant 1/2 \qquad \text{and} \qquad H_1: p > 1/2$$

Here $p$ is the proportion of voters in the voting population who say that they will vote for this candidate in the coming election. Notice that the alternative hypothesis states that more than 50 percent of the voting population say that they will vote for the candidate. This is the research hypothesis for which the candidate would presumably be pleased to find evidence.

Of the 1600 registered voters polled, 840 state that they will vote for the candidate in the forthcoming election. For $\alpha = 0.05$, the critical region for the test is

$$Z \geqslant z_{0.05} = 1.645$$

The computed value of the test statistic is

$$Z = \frac{\hat{p} - p_0}{\sqrt{p_0(1 - p_0)/n}}$$

$$= \frac{0.525 - 0.5}{\sqrt{(0.5)(0.5)/1600}} = 2.00$$

As this value lies in the critical region, the appropriate conclusion is in favor of $H_1: p > 1/2$. There is evidence that, at the time at which the poll was taken, the proportion of registered voters favoring the candidate exceeded 0.5.

The $p$-value for this testing situation is $P(Z \geqslant 2.00) = 0.0228$. This $p$-value is computed as a one-tailed value because the alternative is one-sided. At any significance level $\alpha \geqslant 0.0228$, $H_0$ should be rejected in favor of $H_1$; for $\alpha < 0.0228$, $H_0$ should be retained. For example, if $\alpha = 0.01$ were chosen as the significance level, $H_0$ would be retained. We say that the value of $Z = 2.00$ is significant at the 0.05 level of significance, but not at the 0.01 level.

## Example 6.4

In 1982, 11 higher education associations sponsored a survey concerning the attitudes of the U.S. adult population toward higher education. The survey, conducted by Group Attitudes Corporation of New York, was released to the press in October 1982 by J. W. Peltason, President of the American Council on Education. Of the 1200 respondents, 55 percent stated that they had major concerns about their ability to pay for a child's college education. Suppose we wish to decide whether the proportion of the U.S. adult population with such concerns exceeds 1/2. The appropriate hypotheses are

$$H_0: p \leqslant 0.5 \qquad \text{and} \qquad H_1: p > 0.5$$

The computed value of $Z$ is found to be

$$Z = \frac{0.55 - 0.5}{\sqrt{(0.5)(0.5)/1200}} = 3.46$$

For $\alpha = 0.01$, the rejection region is

$$Z \geqslant 2.326$$

The value 3.46 is clearly in the critical region. The appropriate decision is to accept $H_1$; that is, that more than half of the adult U.S. population is concerned about its ability to pay for the college education of a child. The $p$-value for this test, $P(Z \geqslant 3.46) = 0.0003$, is strong evidence in favor of $H_1$.

## Example 6.5

Consider the data on the survival of heart transplant patients given in Example 5.10. One null hypothesis of interest is

$$H_0: p = 1/2$$

where $p$ is the probability of surviving for at lease one year (365 days) following a heart transplant. An appropriate alternative would be

$$H_1: p < 1/2$$

which indicates that the true probability of surviving for a year is less than 1/2. The critical region for a test using $\alpha = 0.05$ is

$$Z \leqslant -z_{0.05} \quad \text{or} \quad Z \leqslant -1.645$$

Of the 52 heart transplant patients, 16 survived 365 or more days. We calculate

$$Z = \frac{(16/52) - 1/2}{\sqrt{(1/2)(1/2)/52}} = -2.77$$

This value is in the critical region. The appropriate conclusion is that the probability of patients' surviving for at least one year after this medical procedure is less than 1/2. The $p$-value of $P(Z \leqslant -2.77) = 0.0028$ is strong evidence against the null hypothesis and in favor of $H_1$.

---

The critical or rejection region for $H_0: p = p_0$ versus $H_1: p > p_0$ can be written as in Equation 6.19. It can also be expressed in terms of $\hat{p}$ as

$$\hat{p} \geqslant p_0 + \sqrt{\frac{p_0(1 - p_0)}{n}} z_\alpha \qquad \textbf{6.20}$$

For Example 6.3, in which $\alpha = 0.05$, the critical region would be written as

$$\hat{p} \geqslant 0.5 + \sqrt{\frac{1}{6400}} \, 1.645 = 0.5206$$

For the data of Example 6.3, $\hat{p} = 0.525$, which would be in the critical region as before.

The value of $\beta(p)$, the probability of a Type II error, can be found from the critical region given by Equation 6.20. The probability of accepting $H_0$ given that $p$ is the true population proportion is

$$\begin{aligned}
\beta(p) &= P(\hat{p} < 0.5206 | p \text{ is the true population value}) \\
&= P\left(\frac{\hat{p} - p}{\sqrt{p(1 - p)/n}} < \frac{0.5206 - p}{\sqrt{p(1 - p)/n}}\right) \\
&= P\left(Z < \frac{0.5206 - p}{\sqrt{p(1 - p)/n}}\right)
\end{aligned}$$

Once again the Central Limit Theorem has been used. For $p = 0.55$ in Example 6.3, we calculate

$$\begin{aligned}
\beta(0.55) &= P\left(Z < \frac{0.5206 - 0.55}{\sqrt{(0.55)(0.45)/1600}}\right) \\
&= P(Z < -2.36) = 0.0094
\end{aligned}$$

Values of $\beta(p)$ calculated for several values of $p$ in Example 6.3 are given in Table 6.6.

In Figure 6.6, a graph of the Type II error curve has been plotted using values of $\beta(p)$.

## Table 6.6

**Probabilities of Type II Errors for Example 6.3**

| $p$ | 0.5 | 0.51 | 0.52 | 0.53 | 0.54 | 0.55 |
|-----|-----|------|------|------|------|------|
| $\beta(p)$ | 0.9503 | 0.8023 | 0.5199 | 0.2266 | 0.0594 | 0.0094 |

Again, some interesting properties of the test procedure are illustrated by the values of $\beta(p)$ in Table 6.6 and the graph of $\beta(p)$ in Figure 6.6. For $p = p_0$, the value of $\beta(p_0) = 1 - \alpha$. The probability of rejecting $H_0$ given $p = p_0$ is chosen to be $\alpha$; hence the probability of accepting $H_0$ given $p = p_0$ must be $1 - \alpha$. For values of $p$ in the alternative hypothesis that are only slightly greater than $1/2$, the probability of Type II errors is large [for example, $\beta(0.51) = 0.8023$]. The test procedure is least effective in distinguishing between values of $p$ that differ by a small amount. On the other hand, if $p = 0.55$, the probability of a Type II error is only 0.0094. Thus, in Example 6.3, if 55 percent of the registered voters polled are in favor of the candidate, the test will result in an incorrect decision for $H_0: p = 1/2$ only about 0.94 percent of the time.

It is important to understand that it is *always possible* for a statistical test to lead to an erroneous decision, no matter which decision is made. In Example 6.3 a significance level of $\alpha = 0.05$ was used. There is thus a 5 percent chance that it will be concluded that $p > 1/2$ (more than one-half of the registered voters intend to vote for the candidate) when in fact $p = 1/2$. The candidate must accept the fact that this inferential procedure will result in such an error about 5 times in 100 decisions. On the other hand, if the actual value of $p$ is 0.53, Table 6.6 indicates that an incorrect decision for $H_0: p \leqslant 1/2$ will be made about 22.7 percent of the time.

Students sometimes ask, "Why not choose $\alpha = 0$?" This could be done, but it would be unwise. As $\alpha$ is the probability of rejection of the null hypothesis when it is true, if we choose the empty set as the critical region, the probability of a Type I error will be zero and the null hypothesis will never be rejected. In the context of Example 6.3, even if all of the 1600 sampled voters expressed the intention to vote

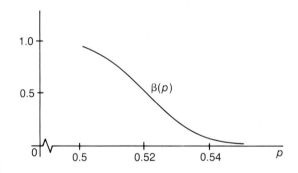

**Figure 6.6**

**Type II Error Curve for Example 6.3**

CHAPTER 6   HYPOTHESIS TESTING IN LARGE SAMPLES

for the candidate, we would not decide for $H_1: p > 1/2$. In fact, for any $p > 1/2$, $\beta(p) = 1$, as the null hypothesis would always be retained. When the critical region is chosen to be the empty set, the test is no longer sensitive to the data. Hence for statistical tests the value of $\alpha$ is chosen to be small, but not zero, as in the examples of this section.

## Exercises 6.4

**6.21** At one point in a production process, 100 items of a certain type were selected for inspection. Of these, eight were found to be defective. Is this sufficient reason to reject $H_0: p = 0.05$ in favor of $H_1: p > 0.05$, where $p$ represents the true proportion of defectives? Use $\alpha = 0.05$.

**6.22** Exercise 5.24 described the Gallup organization's poll of October 1982 showing that 51 percent of 1018 adults disapproved of the performance of President Reagan. If $p$ is the true proportion of the adult population disapproving of the President's performance, test

$$H_0: p \leqslant 0.48 \qquad \text{versus} \qquad H_1: p > 0.48$$

Determine the $p$-value for these data, using the above hypotheses.

**6.23** Test $H_0: p = 1/6$ versus $H_1: p \neq 1/6$, where $p$ is the probability that a die will land with a one showing, given that in 500 tosses of the die there were 75 ones. Assume $\alpha = 0.10$. Find the $p$-value for the hypotheses.

**6.24** Mendelian theory predicts that in hybrid crosses, traits that are determined by a single genetic locus are inherited according to a simple probabilistic model. The offspring of hybrid crosses display the dominant trait three-fourths of the time. Suppose that of 1000 such offspring, 725 display the dominant trait. Test $H_0: p = 3/4$ versus $H_1: p \neq 3/4$. Use $\alpha = 0.05$. Does Mendelian Theory seem to apply?

**6.25** In 1,000,000 selections of an integer from $\{1, 2, \ldots, 10\}$, a total of 501,000 even integers are obtained.
  **a.** State in statistical form the null hypothesis that even and odd integers are equally likely.
  **b.** Test the hypothesis in part a against a two-sided alternative. Use $\alpha = 0.05$.
  **c.** Find the $p$-value for this test.

**6.26** The article mentioned in exercise 5.26 reported that 113 of 194 major-league double headers were swept (rather than split). Defining $p$ to be the probability that a double header is swept, test

$$H_0: p = 2/3 \qquad \text{versus} \qquad H_1: p < 2/3$$

using $\alpha = 0.05$. Find the $p$-value for this test.

**6.27** An aging baseball player has a lifetime batting average of 0.300. This year he hit 0.272 in 400 at bats. We wish to know if his current performance is statistically below his previous performance.
  **a.** State appropriate null and alternative hypotheses.
  **b.** Carry out a test of the hypotheses in part a using $\alpha = 0.05$.
  **c.** Calculate the $p$-value for this test.
  **d.** Find $\beta(0.280)$ and state the meaning of this probability in words.

**6.28** Over a period of time, 36 percent of the freshmen at a large university have received grade point averages of 3.00 or more. In the current year, 400 freshmen in a class of 1000 have GPAs of 3.00 or higher.

   **a.** State the null hypothesis that the percentage of the current freshman class with a GPA of 3.00 or better is no different from the percentage of past classes.

   **b.** State the alternative—that this class is better than those in the past.

   **c.** Test the hypotheses in parts a and b, using $\alpha = 0.05$.

   **d.** Find $\beta(0.4)$.

**6.29** Exercise 5.29 reported the results of a survey of a sample of $n = 1488$ people, 80 percent of whom agreed with the statement "People are subject to more risk today than twenty years ago." Let $p$ represent the true population proportion agreeing with this statement.

   **a.** Test $H_0: p = 0.75$ versus $H_1: p > 0.75$, using $\alpha = 0.05$.

   **b.** Carry out the test in part a at significance levels of $\alpha = 0.01$ and $\alpha = 0.001$.

**6.30** In Exercise 5.31 it was reported that of a sample of $n = 1438$ voters leaving the polls in New York State, 61 percent stated that Jack Kemp should not run for the Presidency in 1988. Let $p$ be the corresponding population proportion.

   **a.** Test $H_0: p = 0.5$ versus $H_1: p > 0.5$, using $\alpha = 0.01$.

   **b.** How strong is the evidence that the population of voters represented by the sample is opposed to Kemp's presidential candidacy?

**6.31** Use RANDOM to simulate 1000 observations from $B(100, 0.8)$. Standardize these values using $Z = (\hat{p} - 0.8)/0.04$, where $\hat{p}$ is the observed proportion of successes in the 1000 cases.

   **a.** Find the proportion of $Z$ values that are less than or equal to $-1.282$, and compare it with the appropriate probability from the standard normal distribution.

   **b.** Have the computer print out a histogram of the observed $Z$ values. Does this histogram have the expected bell-shaped form?

   **c.** Assume that we test $H_0: p \geqslant 0.9$ versus $H_1: p < 0.9$. Using the same $\hat{p}$ values, compute the observed values of $Z$ under $H_0$. Show that the correct standardization is $(\hat{p} - 0.9)/0.03$. What proportion of $Z$ values are now less than or equal to $-1.282$?

   **d.** Using $\alpha = 0.10$, find the estimated Type II error rate in part c for $p = 0.8$; that is, estimate $\beta(0.8)$ using the results of part c.

   **e.** Use

$$P(Z > -1.282 | p = 0.8)$$

$$= P\left(\frac{\hat{p} - 0.9}{0.03} > -1.282 | p = 0.8\right)$$

$$= P(\hat{p} > 0.86154 | p = 0.8)$$

to calculate $\beta(0.8)$ using the normal approximation to the binomial distribution. Compare this probability with the result of part d.

## 6.5

**Hypothesis Testing for *m* in Large Samples**

In this section we will consider tests of hypotheses concerning the population median *m*. A parent random variable $X$ is assumed to have a population median *m*. The statement of the null hypothesis, which corresponds to that for $\mu$, is given by

$$\text{H}_0: m = m_0 \qquad\qquad 6.21$$

We wish to test the hypothesis that the population median *m* is equal to a hypothesized value $m_0$. The usual alternatives correspond to those for tests concerning $\mu$ given earlier:

$$\text{H}_1: m > m_0 \qquad \text{H}_1: m < m_0 \qquad \text{H}_1: m \neq m_0 \qquad 6.22$$

We again assume that the sample size is large.

The test statistic used to define appropriate critical regions for the alternatives in 6.22 is not as obvious as those discussed in Sections 6.3 and 6.4. A test statistic for *m* is based on the signs of the deviations between the sample observations and the hypothesized median—that is,

$$X_1 - m_0, X_2 - m_0, \ldots, X_n - m_0 \qquad 6.23$$

This test statistic, called the sign test statistic, is defined as follows.

---

**Definition 6.9** ▄▄▄▄▄▄▄▄▄▄▄▄▄▄▄▄▄▄▄▄▄▄▄▄▄▄▄▄▄▄▄▄▄▄▄▄▄▄▄▄▄▄

*sign test statistic*

The **sign test statistic** $S$ is the number of positive signs among the differences $X_1 - m_0, X_2 - m_0, \ldots, X_n - m_0$.

---

If *m* is the true population median, the number of positive signs $S$ among $X_1 - m, X_2 - m, \ldots, X_n - m$ is exactly the number of successes in $n$ independent trials with probability of success $p = 1/2$. This statement is true because each of the $n$ independent differences $X_i - m$ is positive with probability $1/2$ and negative with probability $1/2$. (Technically it is true only if $X$ is a continuous random variable, but it can be assumed to be approximately valid for discrete random variables taking on a large number of values.) Thus, if Equation 6.21 is true, $S$ has the binomial distribution with parameters $n$ and $1/2$; that is, $S \sim B(n, 1/2)$.

When $\text{H}_0$ is true, the test statistic $S$ has the binomial distribution regardless of the form of the parent distribution (assuming $X$ is continuous). Because, *under $\text{H}_0$*, the distribution of $S$ does not depend on the distribution of $X$, $S$ is called distribution-free or nonparametric. We will see additional examples of distribution-free statistics in more complicated estimation and testing situations in later chapters.

We now seek critical regions for $\alpha$-level tests of the null hypothesis in Equation 6.21 versus the alternatives in 6.22. Suppose $\text{H}_1: m < m_0$ is the appropriate

**Table 6.7**

**Critical Regions for Large–Sample Tests for m**

| Alternative | Critical Region | Minitab Alternative |
|---|---|---|
| $m > m_0$ | $Z \geqslant z_\alpha$ | 1 |
| $m < m_0$ | $Z \leqslant -z_\alpha$ | $-1$ |
| $m \neq m_0$ | $\lvert Z \rvert \geqslant z_{\alpha/2}$ | none |

alternative. Because $S \sim B(n, 1/2)$, if $H_0$ is true $E(S) = n/2$. That is, the expected number of positive signs is $n/2$ if $H_0$ is true. If $m < m_0$ is true, the number of positive signs $S$ will tend to be smaller than $n/2$, the number expected under $H_0$. Hence small values of $S$ lead to rejection of $H_0$ for this alternative. In the extreme case, if all signs $X_i - m_0$ were negative, there would certainly be reason to believe that $m$ was less than $m_0$. The large-sample test is based on the computed statistic

$$Z = \frac{S - n/2}{\sqrt{n}/2} \qquad\qquad \textbf{6.24}$$

As observed in Chapter 5, this standardized binomial random variable is approximately distributed as the standard normal random variable for large $n$. The appropriate critical region for $H_0$ versus $H_1$: $m < m_0$, using significance level $\alpha$, is

$$Z = \frac{S - n/2}{\sqrt{n}/2} \leqslant -z_\alpha \qquad\qquad \textbf{6.25}$$

Critical regions for $\alpha$-level tests of $H_0$: $m = m_0$ versus the alternatives in 6.22 are given in Table 6.7.

**Example 6.6**

Refer again to the survival data for heart transplant patients given in Example 5.10. The histogram for these data suggests right skewness. As mentioned previously, the population median $m$ is the preferred population location parameter. Assume that a critic of heart transplants asserts that the median survival period is less than 200 days. The appropriate null and alternative hypotheses for testing this assertion are

$$H_0\colon m \geqslant 200 \qquad \text{and} \qquad H_1\colon m < 200$$

Note that we wish to keep $\alpha$ small so that the burden of proof is on the critic's alternative.

In looking at the heart transplant data, we find that of the 52 patients involved in the study, 22 lived longer than 200 days after a heart transplant. Hence

$$Z = \frac{22 - (52/2)}{\sqrt{13}} = -1.11$$

For an $\alpha = 0.05$ level test, the critical region is

$$Z < -z_{0.05} = -1.645$$

The computed value of $Z$ is not in the critical region, so the hypothesis that the median survival period is at least 200 days cannot be rejected.

---

**Example 6.7**

---

For the stock yields of Example 6.1, consider testing

$$\text{H}_0\colon m = 5 \qquad \text{versus} \qquad \text{H}_1\colon m \neq 5$$

where the observations are the annual yields of the stocks given in Table 2.1. Exactly 27 of the 50 values of $X_i - 5$ are positive. The calculated value of the test statistic is

$$Z = \frac{27 - 25}{\sqrt{50}/2} = 0.566$$

For $\alpha = 0.05$, the rejection region is

$$|Z| \geqslant z_{0.025} = 1.96$$

so $m_0 = 5$ would be retained.

Suppose that the hypotheses to be tested were changed to

$$\text{H}_0\colon m = 3 \qquad \text{and} \qquad \text{H}_1\colon m > 3$$

For the same data, we have $S = 35$ and $Z = 2.828$. Using $\alpha = 0.05$, the critical region is

$$Z \geqslant 1.645$$

so we would certainly reject $\text{H}_0$ in favor of $\text{H}_1\colon m > 3$. The statistical evidence suggests that the true yield of these stocks exceeds 3 percent.

---

The calculations required to determine the sign test statistic and the corresponding value of $Z$ are straightforward; a computer is not required to carry them out. If there are many such tests to be made, however, it can be helpful to use the computer.

## Minitab Sign Test Procedure

Exhibit 6.5 shows the output generated when Minitab was used to test the null hypotheses $\text{H}_0\colon m = 5$ and $\text{H}_0\colon m = 3$ of Example 6.7 for the stock yield data.

STEST    The **STEST** command calculates the number of observations exceeding the hypothesized value of the median $m$. There are 27 observations for $m = 5$ and 35 for $m = 3$, as previously found in Example 6.7. Calculation of $p$-values for the

**Exhibit 6.5**

```
MTB > NOTE TEST OF MEDIAN = 5 FOR STOCK YIELD DATA
MTB > PRINT C1
YIELD
     0.00     0.00     0.00     0.32     0.58     0.74     0.80     0.93
     1.07     1.91     2.18     2.42     2.58     2.61     2.71     3.02
     3.15     3.49     3.81     3.88     4.09     4.57     4.62     5.05
     5.15     5.18     5.23     5.31     5.41     5.45     5.63     5.74
     5.97     6.17     6.32     6.51     6.61     6.89     6.96     7.09
     7.11     7.61     7.74     8.00     8.16     8.42     9.09     9.80
    10.53    12.58

MTB > STEST MEDIAN = 5 DATA IN C1

SIGN TEST OF MEDIAN = 5.000 VERSUS  N.E.   5.000

                 N  BELOW  EQUAL  ABOVE   P-VALUE     MEDIAN
YIELD           50     23      0     27    0.6718      5.165

MTB > NOTE TEST OF MEDIAN = 3 FOR STOCK YIELD DATA
MTB > STEST MEDIAN = 3 DATA IN C1;
SUBC> ALTERNATIVE = 1.

SIGN TEST OF MEDIAN = 3.000 VERSUS  G.T.   3.000

                 N  BELOW  EQUAL  ABOVE   P-VALUE     MEDIAN
YIELD           50     15      0     35    0.0033      5.165
```

appropriate Minitab alternatives given in Table 6.7 yields *p*-values of 0.6718 and 0.0033. These results lead to the same decisions made in Example 6.7—namely, to retain the first hypothesis and to reject the second.

The test described in this section is referred to as the sign test. It is easy to see that

$$\frac{S - n/2}{\sqrt{n}/2} = \frac{\hat{p} - 1/2}{\sqrt{(1/2)(1/2)(1/n)}}$$

is just the statistic used to test the null hypothesis $H_0$: $p = 1/2$ in Section 6.4. We are simply testing whether the proportion of positive signs among the $X_i - m_0$ is equal to 1/2, which will be the case if, in fact, $m = m_0$.

## Exercises 6.5

**6.32** Automotive engineers are interested in knowing whether the mileage of a given make of car has improved as the result of an engineering change in this model year. Previously such cars averaged 18 miles per gallon when driven at an average speed of 40 miles per hour on a ten-mile route. The average mileage for a total of 50 new cars was calculated to be $\bar{x} = 19.5$ miles per gallon with a standard deviation $s = 3$. Thirty-five cars exceeded the 18-miles-per-gallon mark.

**a.** State the null hypothesis of no improvement and the appropriate alternative hypothesis in terms of $\mu$, assuming a symmetric population distribution.

**b.** State the hypotheses of part a in terms of $m$.

**c.** Employing the method of Section 6.3, test the hypotheses in part a using $\alpha = 0.05$ and the parameter $\mu$.

**d.** Test the hypotheses in part b, using $\alpha = 0.05$ and the parameter $m$.

**e.** Do the tests in parts c and d lead to the same decision?

**6.33** Using the data given in exercise 5.13, carry out the sign test for $m$, the population median of the ages of the California legislators on January 1, 1981. If a legislator's age is exactly 45, delete it from the data set in the computation of $S$. The random variable of interest here is discrete, but the sign test is approximately valid nonetheless.

**6.34** As the histogram for hits in Chapter 2 indicates, the baseball data in Exhibits 2.7 and 2.8 are skewed to the left, and hence the population median is the preferred location measure. Test $H_0: m = 160$ versus $H_1: m \neq 160$ for the population of major leaguers who bat 0.300 or better.

**6.35** Using the data on home runs by National League champions given in exercise 5.16, test $H_0: m = 40$ versus $H_1: m \neq 40$, using $\alpha = 0.05$. Does your conclusion agree with what you found out about $\mu$ in exercise 6.16?

**6.36** The data in Example 5.9 for failure times of electronic components are quite skewed to the right, and hence the median is the preferred location measure. Test $H_0: m = 75$ versus $H_1: m \neq 75$, using $\alpha = 0.10$.

**6.37** The number of correct entries between errors for a clerk is given in exercise 5.8. Test $H_0: m = 300$ versus $H_1: m \neq 300$, using $\alpha = 0.05$.

**6.38** The lengths of 64 bluegill sunfish given in exercise 2.40 come from a nonnormal population.

**a.** Use the sign test statistic $S$ and the large-sample test statistic $Z$ to decide between

$$H_0: m = 125 \quad \text{and} \quad H_1: m > 125$$

using $\alpha = 0.05$.

**b.** Carry out the same test procedure for the hypotheses

$$H_0: m = 151 \quad \text{and} \quad H_1: m \neq 151$$

**6.39** The data on the annual rainfall in 34 cities of El Salvador given in exercise 2.15 appear not to be normally distributed.

**a.** Test the hypotheses

$$H_0: m = 1980 \quad \text{and} \quad H_1: m \neq 1980$$

with $\alpha = 0.10$, using the method described in this section.

**b.** Test the hypotheses

$$H_0: \mu = 1980 \quad \text{and} \quad H_1: \mu \neq 1980$$

with $\alpha = 0.10$, using the method described in Section 6.3.

**c.** Do your answers to parts a and b agree?

**6.40** The confidence intervals described in Section 5.5 can be used to carry out a test of $H_0: m = m_0$ versus a two-sided alternative. Suppose that we find a confidence interval with a confidence coefficient of $(1 - \alpha)100$ percent. If this interval contains the hypothesized median value $m_0$, we retain $H_0$ at significance level $\alpha$; otherwise $H_0$ is rejected. Use the confidence interval for $m$ found in Section 5.5 to carry out the test of exercise 6.37.

**6.41** Use the confidence interval of exercise 5.39 to carry out a test of

$$H_0: m = 100 \quad \text{versus} \quad H_1: m \neq 100$$

using a significance level of $\alpha = 0.05$.

**Summary**     There are two basic types of errors in hypothesis tests. A Type I error is an incorrect rejection of the null hypothesis; a Type II error is an incorrect acceptance of the null hypothesis. The meaning and importance of $\alpha$, the probability of a Type I error, was stressed. The value $\alpha$ is also called the significance level of the test. The probability of a Type II error, denoted by $\beta$, depends on which value a parameter in the research alternative assumes. Type II errors can be calculated using a normal approximation and simulated using Minitab.

Hypotheses to be tested may concern the expectation of a random variable $\mu$, a population proportion $p$, and a population median $m$. If sample sizes can be assumed to be large enough that the Central Limit Theorem can be applied, the *standardized* values of $\bar{X}$, $\hat{p}$, and the sign test statistic $S$ can all be assumed to have approximate standard normal distributions under the null hypothesis. Using the appropriate percentile points of the standard normal distribution, it is relatively straightforward to determine appropriate critical regions for tests involving these population parameters.

In testing situations, the probability of a Type I error, $\alpha$, is set at some small value (often 0.05 or 0.01). There is a close connection between statistical tests and confidence intervals. Suppose a $(1 - \alpha)100$ percent confidence interval is found for a parameter $\theta$. An $\alpha$-level test of $H_0$: $\theta = \theta_0$ will result in retaining $H_0$ if $\theta_0$ is in the interval and rejecting $H_0$ otherwise. A probability called a *p*-value may be used in conducting statistical tests. The *p*-value is the smallest level of significance at which the null hypothesis can be rejected for the data observed. This probability gives an indication of the agreement of the data with the null hypothesis. For a given significance level $\alpha$, $H_0$ is retained if $\alpha$ is smaller than the computed *p*-value and rejected otherwise. Small *p*-values suggest little agreement between the data and the null hypothesis and indicate support of the alternative hypothesis.

## Key Words

| | |
|---|---|
| $\alpha$ | significance level |
| alternative hypothesis | statistical hypothesis |
| $\beta$ | test statistic |
| continuity correction | tests for $m$ |
| critical (rejection) region | tests for $p$ |
| null hypothesis | tests for $\mu$ |
| *p*-value | Type I error |
| research hypothesis | Type II error |
| sign test statistic | Z-value (observed value) |

## Minitab Commands

STEST                    ZTEST

# Chapter 7

# Small-Sample Inference

**Introduction**

In Chapters 5 and 6 we considered methods of inference to use when sample sizes can be assumed to be large. Both estimation and hypothesis testing were discussed under the assumption that sample sizes were large enough that the Central Limit Theorem applied. This assumption yielded confidence intervals and tests based on the standard normal distribution. Frequently, however, because of sampling costs, the time involved, or other considerations, investigators must use samples that cannot be considered large. In this chapter we will consider both estimation and hypothesis testing for the expectation $\mu$ in the case **small sample size** of a **small sample size**. We will begin by defining two properties of small (and large) sample estimates.

---

**Definition 7.1**

**unbiased estimator**

A statistic $\hat{\theta}_n$ based on a random sample of size $n$ from $X$ is an **unbiased estimator** of the parameter $\theta$ if $E(\hat{\theta}_n) = \theta$.

---

Definition 7.1 states that $E(\hat{\theta}_n)$ must be equal to $\theta$ regardless of the value of $n$. The following equalities have been demonstrated or accepted as valid.

$$E(\bar{X}) = \mu \qquad \textbf{7.1a}$$

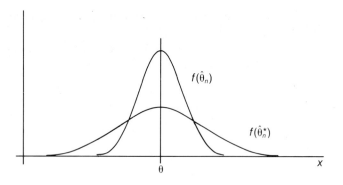

**Figure 7.1**

Density Functions of Two Unbiased Estimators of $\theta$

$$E(\hat{p}) = p$$  7.1b
$$E(S^2) = \sigma^2$$  7.1c

Thus, according to Definition 7.1, the sample mean is an unbiased estimate of a population expectation, the sample fraction is an unbiased estimate of a population proportion, and the sample variance is an unbiased estimator of the population variance. (The sample median $\hat{m}$, on the other hand, is not, in general, an unbiased estimator of $m$.) Loosely, unbiasedness means that "on the average" the statistic $\hat{\theta}_n$ will equal the unknown parameter $\theta$.

Intuitively we can see that unbiasedness is a reasonable property for an estimator to have. Nevertheless, such an estimator may not be a very good estimator of $\theta$ if its variance is large. In Figure 7.1, both $\hat{\theta}_n$ and $\hat{\theta}_n^*$ have density functions that are symmetric about $\theta$. Hence, assuming the expectations of each of these statistics exist, both are unbiased estimators of $\theta$. Nonetheless, $\hat{\theta}_n^*$ would not be a very good estimator of $\theta$, because, although "on the average" it is equal to $\theta$, single observations of this statistic would frequently be far away from $\theta$.

The best unbiased estimator of $\theta$ is the one with the smallest possible variance. Such an estimator, if it exists, is called a minimum variance unbiased estimator.

---

**Definition 7.2** ▬▬▬▬▬▬▬▬▬▬▬▬▬▬▬▬▬▬▬▬▬▬

MVUE (minimum variance unbiased estimator)

An unbiased estimator of $\theta$ based on a sample of size $n$ is a **minimum variance unbiased estimator** (**MVUE**) of $\theta$ if it has the smallest possible variance of all such unbiased estimators.

---

It can be shown that $\bar{X}$ is an MVUE for $\mu$ if $\sigma^2$ exists, and that $\hat{p}$ is an MVUE for $p$. If the parent random variable $X$ is normally distributed, $S^2$ is an MVUE for $\sigma^2$. The fact that these variables are MVUEs justifies their use as estimators for the corresponding parameters. The endpoints of confidence intervals and the test statistics of Sections 7.2, 7.4, and 7.5 will be functions of $\bar{X}$, $\hat{p}$, and $S^2$, respectively.

For the population median $m$ in Section 7.3, various estimators will be used, but none can claim to be an MVUE.

The following three data sets will be used in this chapter to illustrate estimation of population parameters such as $\mu$, $m$, and $\sigma^2$.

Data Set 1: Weights of One-Pound Containers of a Chemical Additive

| | | | | |
|---|---|---|---|---|
| 0.9473 | 0.9655 | 0.9703 | 0.9757 | 0.9770 |
| 0.9775 | 0.9788 | 0.9861 | 0.9887 | 0.9958 |
| 0.9964 | 0.9974 | 1.0002 | 1.0016 | 1.0058 |
| 1.0077 | 1.0084 | 1.0102 | 1.0132 | 1.0173 |
| 1.0182 | 1.0225 | 1.0248 | 1.0306 | 1.0396 |

*Source:* G. J. Hahn and S. S. Shapiro, *Statistical Models in Engineering* (New York: John Wiley and Sons, 1967), p. 258.

**Exhibit 7.1**

```
MTB > NOTE WEIGHTS OF ONE-POUND CONTAINERS OF A CHEMICAL ADDITIVE
MTB > SET C1
C1
   0.9473    0.9655    0.9703    0.9757    .   .   .

MTB > END
MTB > DESCRIBE C1

                N      MEAN    MEDIAN    TRMEAN     STDEV    SEMEAN
C1             25   0.99826   1.00020   0.99868   0.02228   0.00446

              MIN       MAX        Q1        Q3
C1        0.94730   1.03960   0.97815   1.01525

MTB > MEDIAN C1
   MEDIAN =       1.0002
MTB > HISTOGRAM C1

Histogram of C1    N = 25

Midpoint   Count
    0.95      1   *
    0.96      0
    0.97      2   **
    0.98      4   ****
    0.99      2   **
    1.00      5   *****
    1.01      5   *****
    1.02      4   ****
    1.03      1   *
    1.04      1   *

MTB > BOXPLOT C1


                              -------------------
             --------------I        +        I-------------
                              -------------------
        +---------+---------+---------+---------+---------+-C1
      0.940     0.960     0.980     1.000     1.020     1.040
```

**Exhibit 7.2**

```
MTB > NOTE "NO CAR" DATA (PER 1000) FOR 21 WARDS IN HULL, ENGLAND
MTB > SET C2
C2
     506    511    549    553    .    .    .

MTB > END
MTB > DESCRIBE C2

                 N      MEAN    MEDIAN    TRMEAN    STDEV    SEMEAN
C2              21     663.3     673.0     662.5    102.2      22.3

               MIN       MAX        Q1        Q3
C2           506.0     836.0     572.0     744.0

MTB > MEDIAN C2
   MEDIAN =       673.00
MTB > HISTOGRAM C2

Histogram of C2    N = 21

Midpoint    Count
    500       2    **
    550       3    ***
    600       3    ***
    650       3    ***
    700       4    ****
    750       2    **
    800       3    ***
    850       1    *

MTB > BOXPLOT C2


                        ---------------------
            -----------I           +          I---------------
                        ---------------------
          +---------+---------+---------+---------+---------+-C2
         490       560       630       700       770       840
```

Elementary summary statistics, a histogram, and a boxplot are given for this data set in the Minitab output in Exhibit 7.1. The histogram shows a generally symmetric appearance. The normal plot for these data given in Section 4.6 indicated good agreement with the normality assumption. Values of the sample mean, median, and standard deviation computed by DESCRIBE are $\bar{x} = 0.99826$, $\hat{m} = 1.0002$, and $s = 0.02228$, respectively. The minimum and maximum values are 0.9473 and 1.0396, and the first and third quartiles are Q1 = 0.97815 and Q3 = 1.01525, respectively. The remaining two statistics computed by DESCRIBE are referred to as TRMEAN and SEMEAN. The first of these is the trimmed mean, which will be discussed in Section 7.3. SEMEAN, which represents the "standard error of the mean," is simply defined as SEMEAN $= s/\sqrt{n}$. In this case, $s/\sqrt{n} = 0.02228/\sqrt{25} = 0.00446$. The standard error of the mean is useful in the calculation of endpoints of confidence intervals. It is part of the large-sample expression

**Exhibit 7.3**

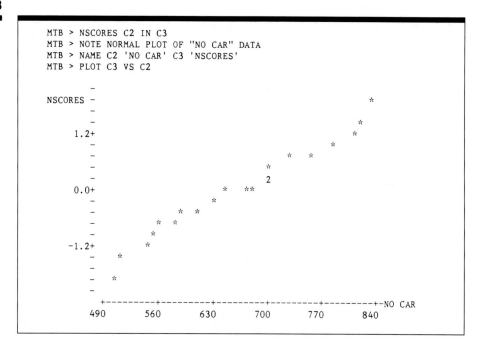

```
MTB > NSCORES C2 IN C3
MTB > NOTE NORMAL PLOT OF "NO CAR" DATA
MTB > NAME C2 'NO CAR' C3 'NSCORES'
MTB > PLOT C3 VS C2
```

for the endpoints of a $(1 - \alpha)100$ percent confidence interval for $\mu$, namely

$$\bar{x} \pm \frac{s}{\sqrt{n}} z_{\alpha/2}$$

Data Set 2: Rates (per thousand) of Individuals Owning No Car (1971) in 21 Wards of Hull, England

| | | | | | | |
|---|---|---|---|---|---|---|
| 506 | 511 | 549 | 553 | 560 | 584 | 591 |
| 612 | 627 | 644 | 673 | 678 | 699 | 699 |
| 703 | 729 | 759 | 783 | 812 | 822 | 836 |

*Source:* M. Goldstein, "Preliminary Inspection of Multivariate Data," *The American Statistician* 36, No. 4 (1982): 358.

Minitab output, including summary statistics, a histogram, and a boxplot, for this data set is shown in Exhibit 7.2. The histogram for this data set is almost rectangular, indicating that the observations form a distribution more like a uniform distribution than a normal distribution. A normal plot of the "no car" data appears in Exhibit 7.3. This normal plot suggests that both left and right tails are "too far in" for the data to be from a normal distribution.

**Exhibit 7.4**

```
MTB > NOTE ESTIMATES OF WHEN 60 SECONDS HAVE PASSED BY 20 PERSONS
MTB > SET C3
C3
     25    30    35    35    .    .    .

MTB > END
MTB > DESCRIBE C3

                    N      MEAN    MEDIAN    TRMEAN    STDEV    SEMEAN
C3                 20     52.95     52.00     52.44    16.99      3.80

                   MIN      MAX       Q1        Q3
C3               25.00    90.00     40.50     67.75

MTB > MEDIAN C3
   MEDIAN =        52.000
MTB > HISTOGRAM C3

Histogram of C3    N = 20

Midpoint   Count
      30      2    **
      40      5    *****
      50      5    *****
      60      1    *
      70      5    *****
      80      1    *
      90      1    *

MTB > BOXPLOT C3

                         -------------------
            ----------I        +        I---------------
                         -------------------
         --------+---------+---------+---------+---------+---C3
               30        45        60        75        90
```

Data Set 3: Estimates by 20 Persons of When 60 Seconds Have Passed
(second trial, given first trial result)

25  30  35  35  40
42  42  45  45  51
53  53  60  65  67
68  68  70  75  90

*Source:* T. M. Smith and B. Iglewicz, "An Effective Classroom
Technique for Comparison of Robust Estimators,"
*The American Statistician* 36, No. 3 (1982): 167.

Minitab output for these data appears in Exhibit 7.4. A normal plot is shown in Exhibit 7.5. The histogram for this data set does not suggest any very smooth shape. It appears that the largest observation is quite large—more than two sample standard deviations larger than $\bar{x}$. Observations that are unusually distant from others in a data set are called **outliers**. The value 90 would be considered a moderate **outliers** outlier for this data set. The boxplot for these data, in which outliers are approximately based on what is to be expected if the population is normally distributed, indicates that it is not an extreme outlier.

**Exhibit 7.5**

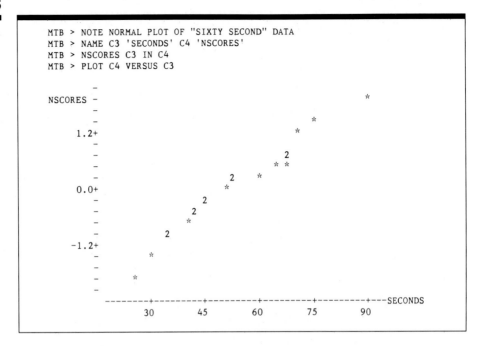

```
MTB > NOTE NORMAL PLOT OF "SIXTY SECOND" DATA
MTB > NAME C3 'SECONDS' C4 'NSCORES'
MTB > NSCORES C3 IN C4
MTB > PLOT C4 VERSUS C3
```

Outliers or disparate observations may affect inference in the small-sample situation by substantially affecting the values of $\bar{x}$ and $s$. For Data Set 3, $\bar{x}$ may be "too large" an estimate of $\mu$. Also, $s$ may be "too large" an estimate of $\sigma$ if the outlier actually comes from a different population than the other observations. This would result in confidence intervals for $\mu$ that were inappropriately centered and overly long. This issue will be addressed in Section 7.3, where several methods of inference for a location parameter of a distribution are discussed.

**Exercises 7.1**

**7.1** The final standings in the National Hockey League in 1974 are presented below, along with some other statistics. Points were computed by adding twice the number of wins and the number of ties.

| Team | Wins | Losses | Ties | GF | GA | Points |
|------|------|--------|------|-----|-----|--------|
| *East Division* | | | | | | |
| Boston | 52 | 17 | 9 | 349 | 221 | 113 |
| Montreal | 45 | 24 | 9 | 293 | 240 | 99 |
| N.Y. Rangers | 40 | 24 | 14 | 300 | 251 | 94 |
| Toronto | 35 | 27 | 16 | 274 | 230 | 86 |
| Buffalo | 32 | 34 | 12 | 242 | 250 | 76 |
| Detroit | 29 | 39 | 10 | 255 | 319 | 68 |
| Vancouver | 24 | 43 | 11 | 224 | 296 | 59 |
| N.Y. Islanders | 19 | 41 | 18 | 182 | 247 | 56 |

| Team | Wins | Losses | Ties | GF | GA | Points |
|------|------|--------|------|-----|-----|--------|
| *West Division* | | | | | | |
| Philadelphia | 50 | 16 | 12 | 273 | 164 | 112 |
| Chicago | 41 | 14 | 23 | 272 | 164 | 105 |
| Los Angeles | 33 | 33 | 12 | 233 | 231 | 78 |
| Atlanta | 30 | 34 | 14 | 214 | 238 | 74 |
| Pittsburgh | 28 | 41 | 9 | 242 | 273 | 65 |
| St. Louis | 26 | 40 | 12 | 206 | 248 | 64 |
| Minnesota | 23 | 38 | 17 | 235 | 275 | 63 |
| California | 13 | 55 | 10 | 195 | 342 | 36 |

*Source:* Stan and Shirley Fischler, *The Hockey Encyclopedia* (New York: Macmillan, 1983), p. 561.

**a.** Construct a boxplot, histogram, and normal plot for the 16 values of GF (Goals For). Does the normality assumption appear to be justified?

**b.** Construct a boxplot, histogram, and normal plot for the 16 values of GA (Goals Against). Does the normality assumption appear to be justified?

**7.2** The data below give the total number of articles and pages in 18 statistical journals from 1968 to 1971.

| Journal | Articles | Pages |
|---------|----------|-------|
| *American Statistician* | 194 | 1008 |
| *Annals of Math. Stat.* | 903 | 8834 |
| *Annals of Inst. Math. Stat.* | 200 | 2164 |
| *Applied Statistics* | 163 | 1239 |
| *Australian Journal of Stat.* | 69 | 684 |
| *Biometrics* | 310 | 3879 |
| *Biometrika* | 331 | 2689 |
| *Calcutta Stat. Assn.* | 44 | 535 |
| *Journal American Stat. Assn.* | 518 | 5945 |
| *Journal Combinatorial Theory* | 396 | 3712 |
| *Journal Indian Soc. Agri. Stat.* | 74 | 1044 |
| *Journal of Royal Stat. Soc. B* | 169 | 2044 |
| *Proc. Conf. Design Expt. Army* | 123 | 2451 |
| *Reports Stat. Appl. Res.* | 60 | 661 |
| *Rev. Int. Stat. Inst.* | 92 | 1569 |
| *Sankhya A* | 177 | 1942 |
| *Sankhya B* | 101 | 2038 |
| *Technometrics* | 304 | 3623 |

*Source:* W. T. and A. J. Federer, "A Study of Statistical Design Publications from 1968 through 1971," *American Statistician* 27, No. 4 (1973): 163.

**a.** Construct boxplots, histograms, and normal plots for these two variables.

**b.** Is the normality assumption justified for articles? for pages? If not, what type of deviation from normality is observed in each of these cases?

**7.3** In a study of relative hyperinsulinemia, standard glucose tolerance level tests were administered to 20 obese individuals. The level of plasma inorganic phosphate in the blood was measured at the time of the glucose challenge and at fixed time intervals thereafter. The data below give these levels 0, 1, and 2 hours after the glucose challenge, in mg/dl.

| Patient | Hours after Glucose Challenge | | | Patient | Hours after Glucose Challenge | | |
|---------|-----|-----|-----|---------|-----|-----|-----|
|         | 0   | 1   | 2   |         | 0   | 1   | 2   |
| 1  | 4.3 | 3.0 | 2.2 | 11 | 4.8 | 4.7 | 4.7 |
| 2  | 5.0 | 4.1 | 3.7 | 12 | 4.4 | 4.2 | 3.5 |
| 3  | 4.6 | 3.9 | 3.7 | 13 | 4.9 | 4.0 | 3.3 |
| 4  | 4.3 | 3.1 | 3.1 | 14 | 5.1 | 4.6 | 3.4 |
| 5  | 3.1 | 3.3 | 2.6 | 15 | 4.8 | 4.6 | 4.1 |
| 6  | 4.8 | 2.9 | 2.2 | 16 | 4.2 | 3.8 | 3.3 |
| 7  | 3.7 | 3.3 | 2.9 | 17 | 6.6 | 5.2 | 4.3 |
| 8  | 5.4 | 3.9 | 2.8 | 18 | 3.6 | 3.1 | 2.1 |
| 9  | 3.0 | 2.3 | 2.1 | 19 | 4.5 | 3.7 | 2.4 |
| 10 | 4.9 | 4.1 | 3.7 | 20 | 4.6 | 3.8 | 3.8 |

*Source:* G. O. Zerbe, "Randomized Analysis of the Completely Randomized Design Extended to Growth and Response Curves," *Journal of the American Statistical Association* 74, No. 365 (1979): 219.

**a.** Construct a boxplot, histogram, and normal plot for these three variables.
**b.** Does the normality assumption appear justified for these data sets?
**c.** What is the value of a possible outlier for the observations at time zero?
**d.** Define a fourth variable to represent the difference of the inorganic phosphate levels at times $t = 0$ and $t = 1$. Construct a histogram and normal plot for these differences. Does the normality assumption appear to be justified for these differences?

**7.4** Construct a boxplot, histogram, and normal plot for the 25 batting averages of American League batters given in Exhibit 2.10. These data are clearly skewed to the right, as the histogram shows. How is the skewness indicated by the boxplot and the normal plot?

**7.5** Consider the 32 scores on a statistics exam shown below.

69 57 83 82 99 75 58 78

66 61 71 70 68 70 65 86

65 64 47 68 93 66 51 80

61 80 62 61 63 62 89 84

Do you think it is reasonable to hypothesize that the underlying distribution is normal? What evidence do you have for your decision?

## 7.2

**Small-Sample Inference for $\mu$ in Normal Populations**

Chapters 5 and 6 discussed inference for the expectation $\mu$ of a random variable $X$ when the sample size $n$ is large. Tests and confidence intervals were based on the approximate normality of

$$Z = \frac{\bar{X} - \mu}{\sigma/\sqrt{n}} \quad \text{or} \quad Z = \frac{\bar{X} - \mu}{S/\sqrt{n}} \qquad \text{7.2}$$

for large $n$. The confidence intervals and critical regions found in those chapters are not justified for small $n$. Even in sampling from a normal population, the use of the sample standard deviation $S$ in place of $\sigma$, as in the second expression of Equation 7.2, does not produce a standard normal random variable for small $n$. In this chapter we will assume that the observations $X_1, X_2, \ldots, X_n$ are independent with parent population distribution $X \sim N(\mu, \sigma^2)$, with both $\mu$ and $\sigma^2$ unknown.

The inferential methods considered in this chapter are based on the random variable defined by

$$t = \frac{\bar{X} - \mu}{S/\sqrt{n}} \qquad \text{7.3}$$

As you can see from the above expression, this $t$ statistic has the same form as the second $Z$ statistic of Equation 7.2. Here, however, we assume $X_i \sim N(\mu, \sigma^2)$ for $i = 1, 2, \ldots, n$. The distribution of $t$ in Equation 7.3 is not standard normal, even with normal observations. The correct distribution was discovered by W. S. Gosset (1908), writing under the pseudonym Student. The random variable in Equation 7.3 is said to have **Student's $t$ distribution**. Student's $t$ distribution is a class of

**Student's $t$ distribution**

**degrees of freedom**

distributions defined by a single parameter $v$, depending not on $\mu$ or $\sigma$, but on the sample size $n$. The parameter $v$ is called the **degrees of freedom** of the $t$ distribution. For the random variable of Equation 7.3, $v = n - 1$ and we say that $t$ has Student's $t$ distribution with $n - 1$ degrees of freedom.

In Figure 7.2 the probability density function for the $t$ distribution with $v = 4$ degrees of freedom and that for the standard normal distribution, $Z$, are graphed. The density function for the $t$ statistic is symmetric about zero, as is the

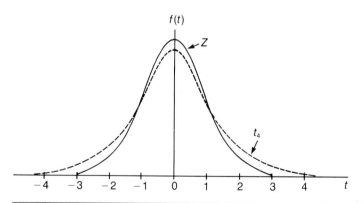

**Figure 7.2**

**Student's $t$ Distribution ($v = 4$)**

**Table 7.1**

| Ninety-ninth Percentile Points of $t$ Distributions | | | | | | | |
|---|---|---|---|---|---|---|---|
| $v$ | 1 | 2 | 5 | 10 | 20 | 30 | $\infty$ |
| $t_{0.01,v}$ | 31.821 | 6.965 | 3.365 | 2.764 | 2.528 | 2.457 | 2.326 |

*Source:* E. S. Pearson and H. O. Hartley, eds., *Biometrika Tables for Statisticians*, 3rd ed., Vol. 1 (Cambridge: Cambridge University Press, 1966). Adapted from Table 12 with the permission of the *Biometrika* Trustees.

density function for $Z$; but the $t$ distribution is more "spread out" than the standard normal distribution. Hence there is more probability in the "tails" of a $t$ distribution than in those of the standard normal distribution. As $v \to \infty$ (the number of degrees of freedom becomes arbitrarily large), the $t_v$ distribution approaches the standard normal distribution. We write $t_\infty = Z$; that is, the $t$ distribution with infinite degrees of freedom is a standard normal random variable.

An examination of Table II of Appendix C will clarify the relationship between the $Z$ and $t$ percentiles. For the $t$ distribution with $v$ degrees of freedom, the value exceeded with probability $\alpha$ is defined to be $t_{\alpha,v}$; that is, $P(t_v \geq t_{\alpha,v}) = \alpha$. Table 7.1 is an abbreviated table of $t_{\alpha,v}$ for $\alpha = 0.01$. It is clear that the 99th percentile of the $t$ distribution approaches the same percentile of the standard normal distribution as the number of degrees of freedom increases. The value of $t_{0.01,\infty} = 2.326 = Z_{0.01}$ is the 99th percentile of the standard normal distribution.

Let us now consider small-sample estimation of $\mu$, based on a confidence interval with confidence coefficient $(1 - \alpha)$ and assuming $X \sim N(\mu, \sigma^2)$, with $\sigma^2$ unknown. We know from the preceding remarks about Equation 7.3 that the following probability statement is valid:

$$P\left(-t_{\alpha/2,n-1} < \frac{\bar{X} - \mu}{S/\sqrt{n}} < t_{\alpha/2,n-1}\right) = 1 - \alpha \qquad \textbf{7.4}$$

This equation corresponds to the probability statements in Equation 5.8, except that $S$ has replaced $\sigma$ and $t_{\alpha/2,n-1}$ has replaced $z_{\alpha/2}$. Using the argument of Section 5.3 with these substitutions yields the endpoints

$$\bar{X} \pm \frac{S}{\sqrt{n}} t_{\alpha/2,n-1} \qquad \textbf{7.5}$$

for a $(1 - \alpha)100$ percent confidence interval for $\mu$.

**Example 7.1**

Using the data in Data Set 1 on weights of nominal one-pound containers, we can calculate the endpoints of a 95 percent confidence interval for $\mu$ as follows:

$$\bar{x} \pm \frac{s}{\sqrt{n}} t_{0.025,24} = 0.99826 \pm \frac{0.0223}{\sqrt{25}} 2.064$$

$$= 0.99826 \pm 0.00921$$

**Table 7.2**

**Critical Regions for $t$ Tests for $\mu$**

| Alternative | Critical Region | Minitab Alternative |
|---|---|---|
| $\mu > \mu_0$ | $t \geq t_{\alpha,n-1}$ | $+1$ |
| $\mu < \mu_0$ | $t \leq -t_{\alpha,n-1}$ | $-1$ |
| $\mu \neq \mu_0$ | $|t| \geq t_{\alpha/2,n-1}$ | $0$ |

Note that the number of degrees of freedom is 24, as $n = 25$. Hence (0.989, 1.007) is the required confidence interval. This interval contains 1, so a test of

$$H_0: \mu = 1 \quad \text{versus} \quad H_1: \mu \neq 1$$

at significance level $\alpha = 0.05$ would result in retaining $H_0$. In other words, the data suggest that the hypothesis of a true average weight of one pound should not be rejected.

In carrying out tests of $H_0: \mu = \mu_0$ for small $n$, where we assume that $X \sim N(\mu, \sigma^2)$ and $\sigma^2$ is unknown, the statistic

$$\frac{\bar{X} - \mu_0}{S/\sqrt{n}} \tag{7.6}$$

is used in place of $Z = (\bar{X} - \mu_0)/(\sigma/\sqrt{n})$. Table 7.2 gives the critical regions to be used in testing the null hypothesis against the three standard alternatives. The critical regions are for $\alpha$-level tests against the indicated alternatives. For example, if $H_0$ is in fact true (that is, $\mu = \mu_0$), testing against the first alternative yields

$$P\left(\frac{\bar{X} - \mu_0}{S/\sqrt{n}} \geq t_{\alpha,n-1}\right) = P(t_{n-1} \geq t_{\alpha,n-1}) = \alpha$$

In other words, the probability of rejecting $H_0: \mu = \mu_0$ when $H_0$ is true equals $\alpha$, the required significance level.

**Example 7.2**

The measurements in Data Set 3 reflect the amount of time that had actually passed when individuals without watches estimated that 60 seconds had passed. Assuming we accept the somewhat shaky assumption of normality, reasonable null and alternative hypotheses would be

$$H_0: \mu = 60 \quad \text{versus} \quad H_1: \mu \neq 60$$

Using $\alpha = 0.05$, we find the critical region to be

$$|t| \geq t_{0.025,19} \quad \text{or} \quad |t| \geq 2.093$$

The calculated value of the test statistic is

$$t = \frac{52.95 - 60}{16.99/\sqrt{20}} = -1.856$$

Thus, at the 5 percent level of significance, $H_0$ is retained. If instead we use $\alpha = 0.10$, the critical region becomes

$$|t| \geq t_{0.05,19} \quad \text{or} \quad |t| \geq 1.729$$

and $H_0$ is rejected.

Next are illustrated two Minitab commands that are very useful for finding confidence intervals for $\mu$ and carrying out tests of $H_0$: $\mu = \mu_0$. The observations are assumed to be from a normal distribution, with small $n$ and unknown $\sigma^2$.

## Minitab Analyses of Data Set 1

Minitab was used with the 25 observations of one-pound containers in Data Set 1 to produce the output shown in Exhibit 7.6. The observations were SET in C1. Then 90, 95, and 99 percent confidence intervals were found for $\mu$, using the

**Exhibit 7.6**

```
MTB > NOTE INFERENCE FOR "ONE-POUND" CONTAINER DATA
MTB > SET C1
C1
   0.9473   0.9655   0.9703   0.9757   .  .  .

MTB > END
MTB > TINTERVAL WITH 90 PERCENT CONFIDENCE FOR DATA IN C1

              N      MEAN     STDEV    SE MEAN    90.0 PERCENT C.I.
C1           25   0.99826   0.02227   0.00445   ( 0.99064, 1.00589)

MTB > TINTERVAL WITH 95 PERCENT CONFIDENCE FOR DATA IN C1

              N      MEAN     STDEV    SE MEAN    95.0 PERCENT C.I.
C1           25   0.99826   0.02227   0.00445   ( 0.98907, 1.00746)

MTB > TINTERVAL WITH 99 PERCENT CONFIDENCE FOR DATA IN C1

              N      MEAN     STDEV    SE MEAN    99.0 PERCENT C.I.
C1           25   0.99826   0.02227   0.00445   ( 0.98580, 1.01073)

MTB > TTEST OF MU = 1 ALTERNATIVE = 0 FOR DATA IN C1

TEST OF MU = 1.00000 VS MU N.E.  1.00000

              N      MEAN     STDEV    SE MEAN         T    P VALUE
C1           25   0.99826   0.02227   0.00445      -0.39      0.70
```

**TINTERVAL** command. Finally, the **TTEST** command was used to test the null hypothesis $H_0$: $\mu = 1$ versus a two-sided alternative. Each of the confidence intervals given contains the value 1, indicating that $H_0$: $\mu = 1$ cannot be rejected against a two-sided alternative for $\alpha = 0.10, 0.05$, or $0.01$. The test of $H_0$: $\mu = 1$ versus $H_1$: $\mu \neq 1$ yielded a computed $t$ value of $-0.390$, which is consistent with the null hypothesis. The $p$-value of $0.70$ clearly indicates that the data are consistent with $H_0$ for any value of $\alpha < 0.70$ (that is, for any reasonable significance level).

### Minitab Analyses of Data Set 3

Minitab was used with the 60-second data of Data Set 3 to produce the output shown in Exhibit 7.7. The data set is in C3. TINTERVAL was used to obtain confidence intervals with 90 and 95 percent confidence, and then TTEST was used to test $H_0$: $\mu = 60$ versus $H_1$: $\mu \neq 60$. The first of the two confidence intervals does not contain 60; the second does. Hence, in testing $H_0$: $\mu = 60$ versus $H_1$: $\mu \neq 60$, we would reject $H_0$ for $\alpha = 0.10$ but not for $\alpha = 0.05$. The $p$-value for this test was given by TTEST to be $0.079$. Hence the smallest significance level for which the null hypothesis would be rejected in favor of a two-sided alternative is $0.079$. Note that as $\bar{x} = 52.95$ and $t = -1.86 < 0$, the data suggest that individuals tend to underestimate the length of a 60-second interval. In fact, against the alternative $H_1$: $\mu < 60$, the critical region is $t \leqslant -1.729$ for a 5 percent level test, and thus $H_0$ would be rejected.

**Exhibit 7.7**

```
MTB > NOTE INFERENCE FOR "SIXTY SECOND" DATA
MTB > SET C2
C2
      25    30    35    35     .   .   .

MTB > END
MTB > TINTERVAL WITH 90 PERCENT CONFIDENCE FOR DATA IN C2

              N       MEAN     STDEV   SE MEAN    90.0 PERCENT C.I.
C2           20      52.95     16.99    3.80    (   46.38,    59.52)

MTB > TINTERVAL WITH 95 PERCENT CONFIDENCE FOR DATA IN C2

              N       MEAN     STDEV   SE MEAN    95.0 PERCENT C.I.
C2           20      52.95     16.99    3.80    (   45.00,    60.90)

MTB > TTEST OF MU = 60 ALTERNATIVE = 0 FOR DATA IN C2

TEST OF MU = 60.00 VS MU N.E. 60.00

              N       MEAN     STDEV   SE MEAN        T     P VALUE
C2           20      52.95     16.99    3.80       -1.86     0.079
```

**7.6** Find $t_{0.05,2}$, $t_{0.05,5}$, $t_{0.05,10}$, $t_{0.05,20}$, and $z_{0.05}$.

**7.7** Find the following probabilities:
  **a.** $P(t_5 \geqslant 3.365)$    **d.** $P(t_{10} \geqslant 2.764)$
  **b.** $P(|t_5| \geqslant 2.015)$    **e.** $P(t_{20} \geqslant 2.528)$
  **c.** $P(-1.943 < t_6 < 1.943)$    **f.** $P(t_\infty \geqslant 1.645)$

**7.8** Use the data given in exercise 7.1 on GF (Goals For) for the 16 hockey teams in the NHL in 1973–1974.
  **a.** Assuming normality, find a 95 percent confidence interval for $\mu_{GF}$, the true average number of goals scored during a playing season by a team in the NHL.
  **b.** Answer part a using a 99 percent confidence coefficient.

**7.9** The annualized returns on ten stocks during December 1980 are given below. Consider this list a random sample of yields from a larger population of stocks.

| Company | Return | Company | Return |
|---|---|---|---|
| Abbot Labs | 0.056 | Apache Corp. | −0.071 |
| Aetna | 0.068 | Armstrong Corp. | −0.034 |
| Alcoa | −0.079 | Atlantic Richfield | −0.122 |
| American Brands | 0.013 | Bank of N.Y. | 0.030 |
| Amsted Industries | −0.055 | Bell and Howell | −0.045 |

*Source:* Center for Research and Security Prices, University of Chicago, as reported in J. D. Jobson, "Testing for Zero Intercept in Multivariate Normal Regression Using the Univariate Multiple-Regression F Test," *The American Statistician* 36 (1982): 371.

  **a.** Assuming normality, find a 95 percent confidence interval for the average yield $\mu$ of the population of stocks during December 1980.
  **b.** Test the hypothesis $H_0$: $\mu = 0$ versus a two-sided alternative, using $\alpha = 0.05$. Find the $p$-value for this test.

**7.10** The following data (ordered by magnitude) give the daily income in dollars from the game of 21 at a small Las Vegas casino during February 1976.

  416  594 1192 1269 1453 1555 2065 2070 2438 2497

  2595 2845 2967 2999 3130 3162 3251 3283 3414 3467

  3516 3729 3963 4006 4388 5395 5520 5885 7059

*Source:* W. M. Visscher and Aaron S. Goldman, "Optimization of Earnings in Stochastic Industries, with Applications to Casinos," *Journal of the American Statistical Association* 73, No. 363 (1978): 502.

  Use Minitab to do the following.
  **a.** Make a normal plot of these data to determine whether the assumption of normality is justified.
  **b.** Find a 90 percent confidence interval for $\mu$, the daily average take for this casino from the game of 21, assuming normality.

**7.11** Using the data on glucose tolerance levels from exercise 7.3, find the values of the variable defined in part d of that exercise to represent the difference of the inorganic phosphate levels at times $t = 0$ and $t = 1$. Use Minitab to do the following.
  **a.** Assuming normality, find a 95 percent confidence interval for $\mu_D$, the true average differences in inorganic levels of plasma for the 20 patients between times $t = 0$ and $t = 1$.

**b.** Assuming normality, test the null hypothesis $H_0: \mu_D = 0$ versus $H_1: \mu_D > 0$, using $\alpha = 0.05$.

**7.12** Would it be appropriate to use the $t$ statistic to find a confidence interval for the average number of pages in a statistics journal over the years 1968–1971, using the data for the 20 journals in exercise 7.2? Explain why or why not.

**7.13** The following is another set of 20 estimates of a 60-second period by individuals without watches. In this case no trial run was allowed.

20 23 35 42 44 45 45 46 47 49

51 54 62 65 70 70 70 80 89 138

*Source:* T. M. Smith and B. Iglewicz, "An Effective Classroom Technique for Comparison of Robust Estimators," *The American Statistician* 36, No. 3 (1982): 167.

Use Minitab as needed to do the following.
**a.** Make a normal plot of these observations. Which observation is a good candidate for an outlier?
**b.** Find a 95 percent confidence interval for $\mu$, using these observations and assuming normality.
**c.** Delete the outlier and make a normal plot of the remaining observations. Does the normality assumption seem more reasonable now?
**d.** Find a 95 percent confidence interval for $\mu$, using these 19 observations. What comparisons can you make between this interval and the one in part b?

**7.14** The following are the times in minutes taken by 25 students to complete a quiz.

29.6 31.6 32.0 29.5 31.6 31.8 30.9 31.2

31.1 29.4 31.3 32.8 31.2 35.0 30.1 33.1

31.9 29.0 34.7 35.1 30.3 31.9 30.3 37.4

26.8

Use Minitab as needed to do the following.
**a.** Construct a histogram and normal plot of these observations. Is the normality assumption justified?
**b.** Test $H_0: \mu = 30$ versus $H_1: \mu > 30$, using $\alpha = 0.05$. What is the $p$-value for this test?

**7.15** The following are the times in minutes taken by another group of 25 students to complete a quiz.

40.0 34.1 29.4 27.9 42.4 28.5 35.0 28.6

39.5 41.3 32.8 36.1 42.9 35.4 29.1 34.0

36.7 31.5 29.7 31.1 26.9 40.7 29.2 37.4

35.7

Use Minitab as needed to do the following.
**a.** Construct a histogram and normal plot of these observations. Is the normality assumption justified?
**b.** Regardless of your answer to part a, test $H_0: \mu = 30$ versus $H_1: \mu > 30$, using a $t$ test. Use $\alpha = 0.05$.

**7.16** Suppose a sample of size 20 is obtained from a normal distribution and a 95 percent confidence interval is found to have endpoints 20.1 and 24.9.
**a.** What is the value of $\bar{x}$?

**b.** What decision would be made if $H_0: \mu = 25$ were tested against $H_1: \mu \neq 25$, using $\alpha = 0.05$?

**7.17** Use the test score data of exercise 7.5 and the value of $t_{0.025,31} = 2.040$ to do the following.

**a.** Test $H_0: \mu = 70$ versus $H_1: \mu > 70$. (Seventy percent has been the average score of students on this test over a period of years.) Use $\alpha = 0.025$.

**b.** Find a 95 percent confidence interval for $\mu$, using the $t$ statistic.

## 7.3

**Robust Inference for Location in Small Samples**

In Section 7.2 we looked at small-sample inference for $\mu$ in cases where normality of the population sampled could be assumed. In many cases, however, the shape of a histogram or the lack of linearity of a normal plot of the data indicates that the normality assumption is not justified. The rectangular shape of the histogram of the "no car" data in Data Set 2, for example, rules out the normality assumption. For nonsymmetric distributions, the median $m$ is frequently the best measure of population location. Two point estimates of the median $m$ will be considered in this section. One is the sample median $\hat{m}$, and the other is the Hodges-Lehmann estimator. In addition, there are various robust statistics that are used to measure

**robust estimator**     location. The term **robust estimator** means that these sample estimators are not greatly affected by deviations of the parent population from normality. In particular, these estimates are not strongly affected by the presence of one or two outliers. A robust estimator called the trimmed mean will be introduced in this section. Confidence intervals for $m$ in the small-sample case will also be discussed.

Consider the case of estimating $m$, the population median. In Chapter 5 the sample median $\hat{m}$ was suggested as a point estimate of $m$. A second point estimate

**Walsh averages**     of $m$ is based on what are called Walsh averages. **Walsh averages** are averages of the form

$$U_{ij} = \frac{X_i + X_j}{2} \qquad \text{7.7}$$

namely, the pairwise average of the $i$th and $j$th observations in the sample (including the case for which $i = j$). Using these $U_{ij}$, we can define the Hodges-Lehmann estimator of $m$.

---

**Definition 7.3** ▰▰▰▰▰▰▰▰▰▰▰▰▰▰

**Hodges-Lehmann estimator**

The **Hodges-Lehmann estimator** is defined by

$$mw = \underset{i \leqslant j}{\text{median }} U_{ij}$$

where the median is taken over all $n(n + 1)/2$ such averages.

---

For certain symmetric nonnormal distributions, this statistic can be shown to be a better estimate of the population median $m$ than is the sample median $\hat{m}$.

Another type of point estimator for location that is insensitive to moderate deviations from normality is the trimmed mean.

**Definition 7.4** ▬▬▬▬▬▬▬▬▬▬▬▬▬▬▬▬▬▬▬▬▬▬▬▬

*trimmed mean*

The **trimmed mean** with $k$th-level trimming is

$$T_n(k) = \sum_{i=k+1}^{n-k} \frac{X_{(i)}}{n - 2k}$$

For first-level trimming, we omit the largest and smallest observations in the sample and average the rest. For $k$th-level trimming, we omit the $k$ smallest and $k$ largest observations and average the rest. This procedure has the advantage of reducing the effect of extreme observations in the estimation of location. The trimmed mean is said to be robust against outliers.

## Example 7.3
▬▬▬▬▬▬▬▬

Suppose the following five ordered observations are obtained in a random sample:

$$X_{(1)} = 1, \quad X_{(2)} = 3, \quad X_{(3)} = 5, \quad X_{(4)} = 8, \quad X_{(5)} = 15$$

For this sample, $\hat{m} = 5$ and $\bar{x} = 6.4$. The 15 Walsh averages are

$$1 \quad 2 \quad 3 \quad 3 \quad 4 \quad 4.5 \quad 5 \quad 5.5 \quad 6.5 \quad 8 \quad 8 \quad 9 \quad 10 \quad 11.5 \quad 15$$

The Hodges-Lehmann estimator is the median of these 15 numbers:

$$\text{mw} = 5.5$$

The trimmed mean for first-level trimming is given by

$$t_5(1) = \frac{3 + 5 + 8}{3} = 5.333$$

It is clear that the influence of the largest observation is reduced in both the sample median $\hat{m} = 5$ and the trimmed mean $t_5(1) = 5.333$. The sample mean $\bar{x} = 6.4$ is most affected by the largest observation. In this case, the advantage of the Hodges-Lehmann estimate, $\text{mw} = 5.5$, is that it is a compromise between the trimmed mean and the sample mean.

## Example 7.4
▬▬▬▬▬▬▬▬

Again let us consider Data Set 2, which gives the number of people per thousand individuals in 21 wards of Hull, England, who owned no car in 1971. Exhibit 7.8 shows the output generated when Minitab was used to compute $\bar{x}$, $\hat{m}$, mw, and

*WALSH*  the first-level trimmed mean. The **WALSH** command was used to compute the

Exhibit 7.8

```
MTB > NOTE ESTIMATES OF LOCATION FOR "NO CAR" DATA
MTB > SET C1
C1
    506     511     549     553     .   .   .

MTB > END
MTB > PRINT C1
C1
    506     511     549     553     560     584     591     612     627     644
    673     678     699     699     703     729     759     783     812     822
    836

MTB > AVERAGE C1
    MEAN    =       663.33
MTB > MEDIAN C1
    MEDIAN =        673.00
MTB > WALSH OF C1 IN C2 INDICES IN C3,C4
MTB > MEDIAN C2
    MEDIAN =        663.00
MTB > PICK ROWS 2 TO 20 OF C1 IN C5
MTB > AVERAGE C5
    MEAN    =       662.53
```

**PICK** averages required for the estimator based on the Walsh averages. The **PICK** command was used to trim the unwanted values for the trimmed mean.

The DESCRIBE command in Minitab can also be used to calculate and print a trimmed mean. In this calculation of the trimmed mean, called TRMEAN, the smallest 5 percent and the largest 5 percent of the observations are first deleted. The average of the remaining observations is then calculated. In Exhibit 7.2, the DESCRIBE command was used with the car data from Data Set 2. As $n = 21$, 5 percent of the sample size is $(0.05)21 = 1.05$. This result was rounded to 1 by Minitab, and the extreme observations 506 and 836 were deleted. The average of the remaining 19 observations was calculated as 662.5. This value is equal, except for rounding, to the first-level trimmed mean of 662.53 calculated using the PICK command in Exhibit 7.8.

To summarize, we have

$$\bar{x} = 663.33 \qquad \hat{m} = 673 \qquad mw = 663 \qquad t_{21}(1) = 662.53$$

For this data set, use of the Hodges-Lehmann estimator rather than the sample median substantially alters the estimate of the population median. As the values of $\bar{x}$, mw, and $t_{21}(1)$ are not very different, perhaps $mw = 663$ is a sensible compromise estimate of $m$.

## Example 7.5

Exhibit 7.9 shows the output generated when Minitab was used as in the previous example to find $\bar{x}$, $\hat{m}$, mw, and $t_{20}(1)$ for the twenty estimates of 60 seconds in Data Set 3.

Exhibit 7.9

```
MTB > NOTE ESTIMATES OF LOCATION FOR "SIXTY SECOND" DATA
MTB > SET C1
C1
    25    30    35    35    .    .    .

MTB > END
MTB > PRINT C1
C1
    25    30    35    35    40    42    42    45    45    51    53
    53    60    65    67    68    68    70    75    90

MTB > AVERAGE C1
    MEAN    =       52.950
MTB > MEDIAN C1
    MEDIAN =       52.000
MTB > WALSH OF C1 IN C2 INDICES IN C3,C4
MTB > MEDIAN C2
    MEDIAN =       52.500
MTB > SORT C1 IN C1
MTB > PICK ROWS 2 TO 19 OF C1 IN C5
MTB > AVERAGE C5
    MEAN    =       52.444
```

Here we have

$$\bar{x} = 52.95 \qquad \hat{m} = 52 \qquad mw = 52.5 \qquad t_{20}(1) = 52.444$$

In this case, the values of the Hodges-Lehmann estimator and the trimmed mean are close to each other. Either of these appears to be a reasonable point estimate for location.

---

In Chapter 5 it was noted that for asymmetric populations the population median $m$ is usually preferred over the expectation $\mu$ as a measure of location. For a continuous random variable $X$, $m$ satisfies $P(X \leqslant m) = P(X \geqslant m) = 0.5$. If $X_{(1)}, X_{(2)}, \ldots, X_{(n)}$ are the order statistics from a random sample,

$$P[X_{(k)} < m < X_{(n-k+1)}] = 1 - 2 \sum_{i=0}^{k-1} \binom{n}{i} \left(\frac{1}{2}\right)^n$$

The last expression is the probability that in a binomial distribution, $B(n, 1/2)$, between $i = k$ and $i = n - k + 1$ successes will be obtained—that is, $P[k \leqslant B \leqslant (n - k + 1)]$. Thus for small sample sizes, we can find a confidence interval for $m$ with confidence coefficient $(1 - \alpha)$, where

$$\alpha = 2 \sum_{i=0}^{k-1} \binom{n}{i} \left(\frac{1}{2}\right)^n = 2P[(X \leqslant (k - 1)] \qquad \text{for } X \sim B(n, 1/2)$$

by using the interval $(X_{(k)}, X_{(n-k+1)})$. The value of $\alpha$ can be found easily using the Minitab command BINOMIAL.

**Example 7.6**

Consider again the car data in Data Set 2. Exhibit 7.10 shows the output generated when Minitab was used with the 21 observations ordered by magnitude in C1. The BINOMIAL command was used to print out the binomial distribution for $n = 21$ and $p = 1/2$, required in order to find a confidence interval for $m$.

**Exhibit 7.10**

```
MTB > NOTE CONFIDENCE INTERVAL FOR "NO CAR" DATA ASSUMING NORMALITY
MTB > SET C1
C1
    506    511    549    553    .   .   .

MTB > END
MTB > PRINT C1
C1
    506    511    549    553    560    584    591    612    627    644
    673    678    699    699    703    729    759    783    812    822
    836

MTB > CDF;
SUBC> BINOMIAL N = 21 P = 0.5.

     BINOMIAL WITH N =  21   P = 0.500000
       K   P( X LESS OR = K)
       1        0.0000
       2        0.0001
       3        0.0007
       4        0.0036
       5        0.0133
       6        0.0392
       7        0.0946
       8        0.1917
       9        0.3318
      10        0.5000
      11        0.6682
      12        0.8083
      13        0.9054
      14        0.9608
      15        0.9867
      16        0.9964
      17        0.9993
      18        0.9999
      19        1.0000
```

For $k = 6$, we have

$$1 - \alpha = 1 - 2P[B(21, 0.5) \leqslant 5] = 1 - 2(0.0133) = 0.9734$$

Hence $(X_{(6)}, X_{(16)})$, or $(584, 729)$, is a confidence interval for $m$ with confidence coefficient 0.9734. Similarly, $(X_{(7)}, X_{(15)}) = (591, 703)$ is a 92.16 percent confidence interval for $m$.

It is interesting to compare a normal-theory confidence interval for $\mu$ with the corresponding interval for $m$. Following is the output generated for this data set when the TINTERVAL command was used with confidence coefficient 0.9216.

```
MTB > TINTERVAL WITH 92.16 PERCENT CONFIDENCE FOR DATA IN C1

            N      MEAN    STDEV   SE MEAN    92.2 PERCENT C.I.
    C1     21     663.3    102.2     22.3   (  621.9,    704.7)
```

Thus, using the shaky normality assumption, we find a 92.2 percent confidence interval for $\mu$ to be (621.9, 704.7). The intervals for $\mu$ and $m$ are not too different. Whereas the confidence coefficient for the interval based on the order statistics is exact, however, the confidence coefficient for the interval based on the $t$ statistic is only an approximation, because the data are not normally distributed. For this reason, the former interval would be preferred.

---

For symmetric populations, the Walsh averages $U_{ij}$ can be used to find a confidence interval for $m$. The interested reader is referred to G. Noether, *Introduction to Statistics—A Fresh Approach* (Boston: Houghton Mifflin, 1971), pp. 110–112, for the details. Tests of the hypothesis $H_0: m = m_0$ versus standard

**sign test**  alternatives can easily be constructed using the **sign test** statistic

$$S = \sum \text{sgn}(X_i - m_0) \qquad X_i > m_0$$

with the binomial distribution used to find critical regions. The development of such tests is left to the next section, as they are equivalent to tests concerning the value of a population proportion $p$.

## Exercises 7.3

**7.18**  Use the data given in exercise 7.1 on GF and GA for the NHL.
   **a.** Calculate $\bar{x}$, $m$, mw, and $t_{16}(1)$ for both "goals for" data and "goals against" data.
   **b.** Which statistical estimate of location in part a would you choose for GF and GA? Why?

**7.19**  Use the data given in exercise 7.13 on 20 individual estimates of a 60-second period.
   **a.** Find $\bar{x}$, $m$, mw, and $t_{20}(1)$. Which of these statistics would you prefer as a measure of location? Why?
   **b.** Find a confidence interval for the population median $m$ with confidence coefficient 0.9586.

**7.20**  Use the differences in the levels of inorganic phosphate found in exercise 7.3(d) for the 20 patients.
   **a.** Calculate $\bar{x}$, $m$, mw, and $t_{20}(1)$ for these data.
   **b.** Which statistical estimate of location would you prefer? Why?

**7.21** The following are the initial weights of 20 animals in an agricultural experiment.

61 59 76 50 61 54 57 45 41 40

74 75 64 48 62 42 52 43 50 40

*Source:* G. W. Snedecor and W. G. Cochran, *Statistical Methods*, 6th Ed. (Ames, Iowa: Iowa State University Press, 1967), p. 440.

**a.** Make a normal plot of these data. How does it deviate from normality?

**b.** If the underlying distribution of weights is symmetric, $m = \mu$. Find a confidence interval for $m$ with confidence coefficient 0.9586, using the method of this section. Use TINTERVAL with the same confidence coefficient to find a confidence interval for $\mu$.

**c.** Which of the two intervals in part b would you prefer to present to a group of animal scientists?

**7.22** **a.** If the interval $(X_{(3)}, X_{(22)})$? is used for a sample of size 24 as a confidence interval for $m$, what is the corresponding confidence coefficient?

**b.** What is the corresponding confidence coefficient if the interval used is $(X_{(4)}, X_{(21)})$?

**c.** Which of the two confidence intervals is shorter? Which has the smaller confidence coefficient?

**7.23** A random sample of 18 money market funds revealed the following 30-day average yields for the funds as of December 1, 1982.

| Fund | Yield (%) |
|---|---|
| American General | 9.6 |
| Capital Preservation | 6.8 |
| Cash Equivalent Govt. Only | 8.4 |
| Current Interest | 8.8 |
| Delaware Cash Reserve | 9.2 |
| ED Jones Daily Passport | 8.9 |
| Fahnestock Daily Income | 8.4 |
| First Investors Cash Management | 8.8 |
| Fund/Gov't Investors | 8.1 |
| Hutton Cash Reserve Management | 8.8 |
| Kemper Gov't Money Market | 8.2 |
| Lexington Money Market | 8.9 |
| McDonald Money Market | 8.5 |
| Morgan Keegan Daily Cash | 8.9 |
| Putnam Daily Div. Trust | 9.5 |
| Seligman Cash Mgt. Fund | 8.8 |
| Sutro Money Market Fund | 8.9 |
| United Cash Management | 8.9 |

*Source: The Wall Street Journal*, December 1, 1982.

**a.** Make a normal plot of these observations. What statements can be made about this data set from examination of this normal plot? Is the assumption of normality justified?

**b.** Calculate $\bar{x}$, $m$, mw, and $t_{18}(1)$. What statistical estimate of location do you prefer?

**c.** Find a confidence interval for $m$ with confidence coefficient 0.9692.

**7.24** The ages at inauguration of the first twenty presidents are given below.

| President | Age | President | Age |
|---|---|---|---|
| Washington | 57 | Polk | 49 |
| J. Adams | 61 | Taylor | 64 |
| Jefferson | 57 | Fillmore | 50 |
| Madison | 57 | Pierce | 48 |
| Monroe | 58 | Buchanan | 65 |
| J. Q. Adams | 57 | Lincoln | 52 |
| Jackson | 61 | A. Johnson | 56 |
| Van Buren | 54 | Grant | 46 |
| W. H. Harrison | 68 | Hayes | 54 |
| Tyler | 51 | Garfield | 49 |

*Source: Information Please Almanac* (Boston: Houghton Mifflin, 1986), p. 594.

**a.** Find $\bar{x}$, $m$, mw, and $t_{20}(1)$.
**b.** Find a 0.8846 percent confidence interval for $m$.

**7.25** The ages at inauguration of the second twenty presidents are given below.

| President | Age | President | Age |
|---|---|---|---|
| Arthur | 50 | Hoover | 54 |
| Cleveland | 47 | F. D. Roosevelt | 51 |
| B. Harrison | 55 | Truman | 60 |
| Cleveland | 55 | Eisenhower | 62 |
| McKinley | 54 | Kennedy | 43 |
| T. Roosevelt | 42 | L. B. Johnson | 55 |
| Taft | 51 | Nixon | 56 |
| Wilson | 56 | Ford | 61 |
| Harding | 55 | Carter | 52 |
| Coolidge | 51 | Reagan | 69 |

*Source: Information Please Almanac* (Boston: Houghton Mifflin, 1986), p. 594.

**a.** Answer the questions of exercise 7.24 for these data.
**b.** It is sometimes argued that presidents are getting younger. Do the confidence intervals here and in exercise 7.24 tend to support or refute this claim?

**7.26** Simulate 20 observations from $N[100, (15)^2]$. For this distribution, $\mu = m = 100$. Use Minitab to do the following.
**a.** Find a 0.8846 confidence interval for $m$, using the method of this section.
**b.** Find a 0.8846 confidence interval for $\mu$, using the $t$ distribution.
**c.** Repeat parts a and b 25 times. How many of each type of confidence interval cover $\mu$?
**d.** Find the average length of the 25 intervals of each type found in part c. Which procedure appears to yield the shorter average confidence interval?

**7.27** For the survival time data for the 52 heart transplant patients in Example 5.10, estimate $m$ using $\hat{m}$ and mw.

**7.28** Use the data of exercise 2.40 on the lengths of 64 bluegill sunfish.
   **a.** Estimate $m$ using $\hat{m}$ and mw.
   **b.** Use DESCRIBE to calculate a trimmed mean for this data set.

**7.29** Use the data of exercise 2.41 on the times in days until death of 58 mice in a radiation experiment.
   **a.** Estimate $\mu$ using $\bar{x}$, $t_n(1)$, and the trimmed mean from Minitab.
   **b.** Estimate $m$ using $\hat{m}$ and mw.
   **c.** Which estimate of $\mu$ in part a do you prefer? Which estimate of $m$ in part b do you prefer?

## 7.4

## Small-Sample Inference for $p$

In Sections 5.4 and 6.4, the discussion of estimation and hypothesis testing for an unknown population proportion $p$ focused on the large-sample case. Calculations of confidence intervals and critical regions for hypothesis tests were based on the normal approximation to the distribution of $\hat{p}$, the sample fraction of successes. In this section we will discuss the case where $n$ cannot be considered large. In estimation, a refinement of the technique employed to find the large-sample confidence interval will be used to improve the accuracy of the method for small and intermediate-sized $n$. In hypothesis testing, the binomial distribution will be used instead of the normal approximation to find exact values for the probabilities of Type I and Type II errors. The small-sample test of the null hypothesis $H_0$: $p = 0.5$ provides a test of the null hypothesis $H_0$: $m = m_0$, where $m$ is the median of a continuous random variable.

Let us first consider estimation of $p$, a population proportion, when the sample size cannot be assumed to be large. Assume, as before, that $n$ independent observations are taken, and let $X$ be the number of observations in the sample that have the property of interest. Then $X$ has the binomial distribution $B(n, p)$, with $p$ unknown. To derive an improved confidence interval, we again begin with the normal approximation. This approximation will be quite good for rather small $n$ as long as $p$ is not too close to either 0 or 1. We have

$$P\left(\frac{|\hat{p} - p|}{\sqrt{p(1 - p)/n}} < z_{\alpha/2}\right) = 1 - \alpha \qquad 7.8$$

If we replace $z_{\alpha/2}$ by $z$, the inequality statement above becomes

$$|\hat{p} - p| < \sqrt{\frac{p(1 - p)}{n}}\, z$$

Squaring this expression yields

$$(\hat{p} - p)^2 < p(1 - p)\left(\frac{z^2}{n}\right) \qquad 7.9$$

Equation 7.9 can be further simplified to

$$p^2\left(1 + \frac{z^2}{n}\right) - p\left(2\hat{p} + \frac{z^2}{n}\right) + (\hat{p})^2 < 0 \qquad 7.10$$

## Table 7.3

**Endpoints of Confidence Intervals**

| $n$ | Confidence Coefficient | Small-Sample Interval (Equation 7.11) | | Large-Sample Interval (Equation 7.12) | |
|---|---|---|---|---|---|
| | | Lower | Upper | Lower | Upper |
| 40 | 90 | 0.432 | 0.676 | 0.499 | 0.751 |
| 40 | 95 | 0.383 | 0.670 | 0.475 | 0.775 |
| 80 | 90 | 0.501 | 0.675 | 0.536 | 0.714 |
| 80 | 95 | 0.470 | 0.677 | 0.519 | 0.731 |
| 800 | 90 | 0.593 | 0.649 | 0.597 | 0.653 |
| 800 | 95 | 0.586 | 0.653 | 0.591 | 0.659 |

The quadratic expression in $p$ on the left side of Equation 7.10 can be negative only for values of $p$ between its roots, which are therefore the endpoints of the desired confidence interval. The roots of the polynomial are

$$\left( \hat{p} - \frac{z^2}{2n} \pm \frac{z}{\sqrt{n}} \sqrt{\hat{p}(1 - \hat{p}) + \frac{z^2}{4n}} \right) \bigg/ \left( 1 + \frac{z^2}{n} \right) \qquad \textbf{7.11}$$

Note that when the terms of size $1/n$ are set equal to 0, we obtain

$$\hat{p} \pm z \sqrt{\frac{\hat{p}(1 - \hat{p})}{n}} \qquad \textbf{7.12}$$

The endpoints in Equation 7.12 agree with those found in Section 5.4.

To see the effect of using the corrected endpoints given by Equation 7.11, consider estimation of $p$ for $n = 40$, 80, and 800. Suppose $\hat{p} = 5/8$ is observed in each case—that is, $X = 25$, 50, and 500, respectively. Endpoints of 90 and 95 percent confidence intervals obtained by using Equations 7.11 and 7.12 are given in Table 7.3. For $n = 40$ and $n = 80$, the small-sample and large-sample intervals have approximately the same length but are centered quite differently. For these cases, the small-sample interval is more appropriate. When $n = 800$, it is clear that there is little difference between the small-sample and large-sample confidence intervals. The large-sample interval with endpoints given by Equation 7.12 may therefore be used in that case.

We again consider testing the null hypothesis

$$H_0: p = p_0 \qquad \textbf{7.13}$$

just as we did in Section 6.4. The standard alternatives are those given in Table 7.4. The critical regions are stated in terms of $X$, the number of "successes" observed in $n$ independent selections from a population with a proportion $p$ of elements having the property defining a success. For the first alternative in Table 7.4, $H_1: p > p_0$, a large number of "successes" corresponds to the null hypothesis's being false and the alternative's being true. Thus the critical region is of the form

## Table 7.4

**Critical Regions for Testing $H_0: p = p_0$**

| Alternative | Critical Region |
|---|---|
| $p > p_0$ | $X \geqslant c_1$ |
| $p < p_0$ | $X \leqslant c_2$ |
| $p \neq p_0$ | $X \leqslant c_2^*$ or $X \geqslant c_1^*$ |

$X \geqslant c_1$. The value of $\alpha = P(X \geqslant c_1 | p = p_0)$ can be calculated from the binomial distribution. As in Chapter 6, the constant $c_1$ must be chosen so that $\alpha$ is small but not zero. The value of the Type II error $\beta(p) = P(X < c_1 | p)$ can also be calculated from the binomial distribution, with $n$ equal to the number of observations taken and $p$ a value of the population proportion under $H_1$. Example 7.7 illustrates these ideas by means of a familiar example.

## Example 7.7

To study the question of whether large doses of vitamin C are effective in preventing the common cold, we decide to make a pilot study using only 40 individuals. As in Chapter 6, we will assume that, in the absence of treatment, about 40 percent of individuals get colds during the period from October 1 to March 31. The 40 individuals are given the vitamin C dosage, and the number of the forty who get colds $(X)$ is observed. $X$ has the binomial distribution with $n = 40$. The task is to decide between

$$H_0: p = 0.4 \quad \text{and} \quad H_1: p < 0.4$$

The alternative hypothesis states that the treatment has reduced the frequency of colds. If we use the command BINOMIAL with $n = 40$ and $p = 0.4$, it is very easy to find a rejection region for a suitable $\alpha$ value and to find $p$-values for a test. The Minitab output that will allow us to obtain an appropriate critical region is given in Exhibit 7.11.

The choice of the critical region $\{X \leqslant 10\}$ yields a significance level in the right-hand column of $\alpha = P(X \leqslant 10 | p = 0.4) = 0.0352$. Typically a critical region with a significance level near 0.05 or 0.01 is selected. If $X = 7$ were observed, the corresponding $p$-value would be 0.0021. A smaller value of $p$ is much more likely, however, as a value such as $X = 7$ is not likely to arise from a population with a true probability of 0.4 of getting a cold.

It is also easy to find the probability of Type II errors using the BINOMIAL command. For example, using the $B(40, 0.2)$ output in Exhibit 7.12 with rejection region $X \leqslant 10$, we find that

$$\begin{aligned}
\beta(0.20) &= P(\text{accepting } H_0 | p = 0.2) = 1 - P(\text{rejecting } H_0 | p = 0.2) \\
&= 1 - P(X \leqslant 10 | p = 0.2) = 1 - 0.8392 = 0.1608
\end{aligned}$$

**Exhibit 7.11**

```
MTB > CDF;
SUBC> BINOMIAL N = 40 P = 0.4.

    BINOMIAL WITH N =   40  P = 0.400000
      K  P( X LESS OR = K)
      4          0.0000
      5          0.0001
      6          0.0006
      7          0.0021
      8          0.0061
      9          0.0156
     10          0.0352
     11          0.0709
     12          0.1285
     13          0.2112
     14          0.3174
     15          0.4402
     16          0.5681
     17          0.6885
     18          0.7911
     19          0.8702
     20          0.9256
     21          0.9608
     22          0.9811
     23          0.9917
     24          0.9966
     25          0.9988
     26          0.9996
     27          0.9999
     28          1.0000
```

**Exhibit 7.12**

```
MTB > CDF;
SUBC> BINOMIAL N = 40 P = 0.2.

    BINOMIAL WITH N =   40  P = 0.200000
      K  P( X LESS OR = K)
      0          0.0001
      1          0.0015
      2          0.0079
      3          0.0285
      4          0.0759
      5          0.1613
      6          0.2859
      7          0.4371
      8          0.5931
      9          0.7318
     10          0.8392
     11          0.9125
     12          0.9568
     13          0.9806
     14          0.9921
     15          0.9971
     16          0.9990
     17          0.9997
     18          0.9999
     19          1.0000
```

## Table 7.5

| | | | | | | | |
|---|---|---|---|---|---|---|---|
| **Type II Error Probabilities in Vitamin C Case ($n = 40$)** | | | | | | | |
| $p$ | 0.10 | 0.15 | 0.20 | 0.25 | 0.30 | 0.35 | 0.40 |
| $\beta(p)$ | 0.0015 | 0.0299 | 0.1608 | 0.2849 | 0.6913 | 0.8785 | 0.9648 |

## Table 7.6

**Critical Regions in Terms of $S$**

| Alternative | Alternative Expressed in Terms of $p$ | Critical Region |
|---|---|---|
| $m > m_0$ | $p > 1/2$ | $S \geqslant c_1$ |
| $m < m_0$ | $p < 1/2$ | $S \leqslant c_2$ |
| $m \neq m_0$ | $p = 1/2$ | $S \leqslant c_2^*$ or $S \geqslant c_1^*$ |

Other values of $\beta(p)$ found similarly are given in Table 7.5. Again, the fact that the test distinguishes least clearly between $p = 0.4$ and values of $p$ close to but less than 0.4 is illustrated by the high probability of Type II errors for such values of $p$. In practice, however, it may only be important to determine when the frequency of colds has been substantially reduced, so $\beta(0.2) = 0.1608$ may be acceptable for an initial study with a small sample.

In testing the null hypothesis $H_0$: $m = m_0$, we have used the signs of the differences $X_1 - m_0, \ldots, X_n - m_0$. When $H_0$ is true, we have $X \sim B(n, 1/2)$. The critical regions used against the three standard alternatives have the forms given in Table 7.6, where $S$ denotes the number of these $n$ differences with positive signs, as before.

The sign test is just a test of $H_0$: $p = 1/2$ versus the appropriate alternative. For small samples the test can be carried out using CDF with the subcommand BINOMIAL, as explained in Example 7.7.

## Example 7.8

Consider the 30-day average yields of the 18 money market funds of exercise 7.23. Assume that we wish to test

$$H_0: m \leqslant 8.6 \qquad \text{versus} \qquad H_1: m > 8.6$$

Exhibit 7.13 shows the output generated when Minitab was used to find the cumulative probabilities for $X \sim B(18, 1/2)$.

**Exhibit 7.13**

```
MTB > CDF;
SUBC> BINOMIAL N = 18 P = 0.5.

      BINOMIAL WITH N =  18  P = 0.500000
         K  P( X LESS OR = K)
         0        0.0000
         1        0.0001
         2        0.0007
         3        0.0038
         4        0.0154
         5        0.0481
         6        0.1189
         7        0.2403
         8        0.4073
         9        0.5927
        10        0.7597
        11        0.8811
        12        0.9519
        13        0.9846
        14        0.9962
        15        0.9993
        16        0.9999
        17        1.0000


MTB > NOTE TEST OF MEDIAN = 8.6 VERSUS MEDIAN > 8.6
MTB > NOTE DATA IS 30 DAY AVERAGE YIELDS FROM PROBLEM 7.23
MTB > SET C1
C1
    9.6     6.8     8.4     8.8    .    .    .

MTB > NAME C1 '30DAYLD'
MTB > PRINT C1
30DAYLD
    9.6     6.8     8.4     8.8     9.2     8.9     8.4     8.8     8.1     8.8     8.2
    8.9     8.5     8.9     9.5     8.8     8.9     8.9

MTB > STEST MEDIAN = 8.6 DATA IN C1;
SUBC> ALTERNATIVE = 1.

SIGN TEST OF MEDIAN = 8.600 VERSUS   G.T.   8.600

                 N   BELOW  EQUAL  ABOVE   P-VALUE    MEDIAN
30DAYLD         18      6      0     12    0.1189     8.800
```

We see that if we use the critical region $S \geqslant 13$, we obtain a significance level of $\alpha = 1 - P(S \leqslant 12 | p = 0.5) = 0.0481$. As $S = 12$ in this case, we would retain $H_0$. The $p$-value for the test is

$$P(S \geqslant 12 | H_0) \ = \ 1 - P(S \leqslant 11 | H_0) \ = \ 1 - 0.8811 \ = \ 0.1189$$

In light of the fact that the evidence is not conclusive, it might be reasonable to test these hypotheses again with a larger sample of money market funds. The Minitab command STEST was also used to test these two hypotheses.

**7.30** In an article published on November 28, 1982, the *Philadelphia Inquirer* reported on research conducted by San Francisco child psychologist Dr. Lenore Terr. Dr. Terr had examined 25 "normal" children and compared them with 26 children who had been traumatized by the kidnapping of the school bus on which they were riding. Among the 25 "normal" children, she found 10 extremely frightened and 5 traumatized children.

    **a.** Find a 90 percent confidence interval for the proportion $p$ of traumatized children among the "normal" children, using the method described in this section.

    **b.** Answer part a using the large-sample method of Section 5.4.

    **c.** Compare the lengths and locations of these two intervals.

**7.31** At a recent meeting of the American Statistical Association, 3 of the 30 members elected to be Fellows of the American Statistical Association were female.

    **a.** Find a 90 percent confidence interval for the proportion of female Fellows of ASA, using the method of this section.

    **b.** Why is this interval not necessarily a good one to use to estimate the proportion of female Fellows of ASA?

**7.32** Of the 52 heart transplant patients considered in Example 5.10, 16 survived longer than 365 days.

    **a.** Find a 90 percent confidence interval for $p$, the true proportion of such heart transplant patients surviving for at least 365 days, using Equations 7.11 and 7.12.

    **b.** Is there much difference in the lengths of these two intervals? in their midpoints? Which would you use and why?

**7.33** Use the data of exercise 5.26 to find a 95 percent confidence interval for $p$, the proportion of major league double headers that are swept.

    **a.** Use the method of this section.

    **b.** Use the large-sample method of Chapter 5.

    **c.** Compare these two intervals as in exercise 7.32.

**7.34** Use the method of this section together with the data given in exercise 7.13 to test $H_0$: $m = 60$ versus $H_1$: $m \neq 60$ for the 20 estimates of 60 seconds. Use as a significance level the closest possible value less than 0.05. Each tail of the critical region should have probability $\alpha/2$. Use the Minitab command CDF with the BINOMIAL subcommand.

**7.35** In a small-sample test of the Mendelian hypothesis regarding the incidence of the recessive trait controlled by a single pair of genes, 40 observations were made. According to the Mendelian theory, the proportion of observations displaying the recessive trait should be 1/4. Of the 40 observations, 15 displayed the recessive trait. Test $H_0$: $p = 1/4$ versus $H_1$: $p > 1/4$, using the Minitab command CDF. Choose as $\alpha$ the closest possible value less than 0.05.

    **a.** What is the rejection region for the test?

    **b.** What is the $p$-value for the 15 observations of the recessive trait?

    **c.** What is $\beta(p)$ for $p = 0.30, 0.35$, and $0.40$?

**7.36** For a sample of size $n = 20$, use the CDF command to test $H_0$: $p = 1/2$ versus $H_1$: $p \neq 1/2$, using a rejection region of $X \leqslant 5$ and $X \geqslant 15$.

    **a.** What is the value of $\alpha$?

    **b.** For $p = 0.4$, find the value of $\beta$, the probability of a Type II error.

**7.37**  For the data on rates of return in exercise 7.9, use the Minitab command CDF with the BINOMIAL subcommand to test $H_0: m = 0$ versus $H_1: m \neq 0$, choosing as $\alpha$ the closest possible value less than 0.05.

**7.38**  For the initial-weight data of exercise 7.21, use Minitab to test $H_0: m = 49$ versus $H_1: m > 49$, selecting $\alpha$ as in exercise 7.37.

**7.39**  For the data in exercise 7.3 on 20 observations of plasma inorganic phosphate at time zero, use Minitab to test $H_0: m = 4$ versus $H_1: m > 4$, choosing as $\alpha$ the closest possible value less than 0.10.

## 7.5

### Small-Sample Inference for $\sigma^2$

**Bernoulli random variable**

We have focused on inference for the parameters $\mu$, $m$, and $p$, all of which can be considered to be measures of location. We can consider $p$ to be the expectation of the **Bernoulli random variable** $X$, which is simply the binomial random variable with $n = 1$, having probability function

$$P(x) = p^x(1 - p)^{1-x} \qquad \text{for} \qquad x = 0, 1$$

We find that $E(X) = 0(1 - p) + 1 \cdot p = p$.

As our last illustration of small-sample inference, we shift attention to the population variance $\sigma^2$, a population parameter measuring variability. In production processes one frequently wants to control the variability of some characteristic of the items being produced—for example, the density, length, or weight of the items. Many times products will not even perform their intended function if stated specifications are not met. In such cases it is particularly important to ensure that few items exceed tolerances. In this section observations are assumed to come from normal distributions with expectation $\mu$ and variance $\sigma^2$.

A new distribution related to the normal distribution is required in order to make inference with regard to $\sigma^2$: the chi-square distribution with parameter $v$. As in the case of the $t$ distribution, $v$ is called the degrees of freedom.

---

**Definition 7.5** ▬▬▬▬▬▬▬▬▬▬▬▬▬▬▬▬▬▬▬▬▬▬▬▬▬▬▬▬▬▬▬▬▬▬▬▬▬

**chi-square distribution**

The **chi-square distribution** with $v$ degrees of freedom, denoted by $\chi_v^2$, is the distribution of $\sum_{i=1}^{v}(Z_i)^2$, the sum of the squares of $v$ independent standard normal random variables.

---

A $\chi^2$ random variable can have only positive values, as it is a sum of squares. The general form of the probability density function for the chi-square distribution is shown in Figure 7.3. The fact that the chi-square random variables have only positive values is reflected by the fact that the probability density functions are zero for $\chi^2 < 0$ and positive for $\chi^2 > 0$, as shown in the figure. It can be shown that the expectation of a chi-square random variable is equal to its degrees of freedom,

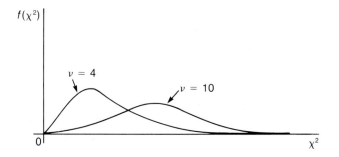

**Figure 7.3**

**Chi-Square Distribution**

$$E(\chi_v^2) = v \qquad\qquad 7.14$$

and also that

$$\mathrm{Var}\ (\chi_v^2) = 2v \qquad\qquad 7.15$$

Thus both the expectation and the variance of $\chi_v^2$ increase with $v$. These trends are reflected in the probability density functions of Figure 7.3.

Percentile points for the chi-square random variables are required for estimation and hypothesis testing regarding $\sigma^2$. Table III in Appendix C gives percentile points frequently used in practice. The percentile point $\chi_{\alpha,v}^2$ satisfies

$$P(\chi^2 > \chi_{\alpha,v}^2) = \alpha \qquad\qquad 7.16$$

This point is exceeded with probability $\alpha$ by the chi-square random variable with $v$ degrees of freedom. For example,

$$P(\chi_4^2 > \chi_{0.05,4}^2) = P(\chi_4^2 > 9.4808) = 0.05$$

Similarly,

$$P(\chi_{10}^2 > \chi_{0.05,10}^2) = P(\chi_{10}^2 > 18.307) = 0.05$$

It is clear from Table III of Appendix C that the 95th percentile point $\chi_{0.05,v}^2$ increases as $v$ increases. This trend is also reflected in Figure 7.3.

The importance of the chi-square distribution for inference with regard to $\sigma^2$ in the normal case arises from the following theorem, which is stated without proof.

---

**Theorem 7.1** ▪▪▪▪▪▪▪▪▪▪▪▪▪▪▪▪▪▪▪▪▪▪▪▪▪▪▪▪▪▪▪▪

The random variable

$$\frac{(n-1)S^2}{\sigma^2} = \sum_{i=1}^{n} \frac{(X_i - \bar{X})^2}{\sigma^2}$$

where the $X_i$ are a random sample from $X \sim N(\mu, \sigma^2)$, has the chi-square distribution with $(n-1)$ degrees of freedom.

---

The sample variance $S^2$ is used as a point estimator for $\sigma^2$. Assuming the sample is a random sample from $X \sim N(\mu, \sigma^2)$, we see from Equation 7.14 and Theorem 7.1 that

$$E\left(\frac{(n-1)S^2}{\sigma^2}\right) = n - 1$$

so

$$\frac{n-1}{\sigma^2} E(S^2) = n - 1$$

Multiplying both sides of this equation by $\sigma^2/(n-1)$ yields

$$E(S^2) = \sigma^2 \qquad\qquad\qquad \textbf{7.17}$$

Equation 7.17 shows that in sampling from a normal distribution the sample variance $S^2$ is an unbiased estimator of the population variance (see Definition 7.1). The sample variance is also a minimum variance unbiased estimator (MVUE) of the population variance $\sigma^2$ in this case. As such, $S^2$ is almost always the appropriate point estimator of $\sigma^2$ in sampling from a normal distribution.

The result stated in Theorem 7.1 will now be used to find confidence intervals for $\sigma^2$ in the small-sample case for $X \sim N(\mu, \sigma^2)$. In sampling from a normal distribution, the following three probability statements are equivalent:

$$P(\chi^2_{1-\alpha/2} < \chi^2 < \chi^2_\alpha) = 1 - \alpha$$

$$P\left(\chi^2_{1-\alpha/2} < \frac{(n-1)S^2}{\sigma^2} < \chi^2_{\alpha/2}\right) = 1 - \alpha$$

$$P\left(\frac{(n-1)S^2}{\chi^2_{\alpha/2}} < \sigma^2 < \frac{(n-1)S^2}{\chi^2_{1-\alpha/2}}\right) = 1 - \alpha \qquad \textbf{7.18}$$

(The appropriate number of degrees of freedom, $n - 1$, has been omitted from the subscripts.) The second statement in Equation 7.18 follows from Theorem 7.1. The reader should check that the double inequality in the third line of Equation 7.18 is equivalent to the one in the second line. Hence,

$$\frac{(n-1)S^2}{\chi^2_{\alpha/2}} \qquad \text{and} \qquad \frac{(n-1)S^2}{\chi^2_{1-\alpha/2}} \qquad\qquad \textbf{7.19}$$

are the endpoints of a $(1 - \alpha)100$ percent confidence interval for $\sigma^2$. It is clear from Equation 7.19 that the square root of these numbers yields a $(1 - \alpha)100$ percent confidence interval for $\sigma$.

## Example 7.9

For Data Set 1, on the 25 one-pound containers of a chemical additive, the normality assumption appears to be justified. The value of the standard deviation is $s = 0.0223$, so Equation 7.19 gives

$$L = \frac{(24)(0.0223)^2}{39.36} \qquad \text{and} \qquad U = \frac{(24)(0.0223)^2}{12.40}$$

the endpoints of a 95 percent confidence interval for $\sigma^2$. The confidence interval is thus (0.00030323, 0.00096242). Taking the square root of these endpoints yields (0.0174, 0.310) as a 95 percent confidence interval for $\sigma$.

## Example 7.10

For Data Set 3 (the 60-second estimations) we found that $s = 17.0$ and $n = 20$. Hence the endpoints of a 95 percent confidence interval for $\sigma^2$, assuming normality, are given by

$$L = \frac{(19)(17)^2}{32.582} \quad \text{and} \quad U = \frac{(19)(17)^2}{8.907}$$

Thus the confidence interval is (168.53, 616.48). Taking square roots, we find the confidence interval for $\sigma$ to be (12.98, 24.83). It is important to remember that the units of the latter interval are those of $s$ and are in seconds, the original unit of measurement. This interval indicates that the approximations of the length of a 60-second period by individuals without watches vary quite a lot.

In order to test $H_0: \sigma^2 = \sigma_0^2$ against standard alternatives, we use the calculated statistic

$$\chi^2 = \frac{(n-1)S^2}{\sigma_0^2}$$

7.20

Table 7.7 provides critical regions for the standard alternatives at significance level $\alpha$.

The reasoning leading to these critical regions is similar to that used previously for other parameters. The statistic $S^2$ is an unbiased estimate of $\sigma^2$. For example, if in fact $\sigma^2 > \sigma_0^2$, the calculated chi-square test statistic given by Equation 7.20 will tend to be larger than if $\sigma^2 = \sigma_0^2$. Hence large values of the calculated statistic $\chi^2$ indicate that $H_0: \sigma^2 = \sigma_0^2$ should be rejected in favor of $H_1: \sigma^2 > \sigma_0^2$.

## Table 7.7

**Critical Regions for Tests of $\sigma^2$ in the Normal Case**

| Alternative | Critical Region |
|---|---|
| $\sigma^2 > \sigma_0^2$ | $\chi^2 \geq \chi^2_{\alpha,n-1}$ |
| $\sigma^2 < \sigma_0^2$ | $\chi^2 \leq \chi^2_{1-\alpha,n-1}$ |
| $\sigma^2 \neq \sigma_0^2$ | $\chi^2 \geq \chi^2_{\alpha/2,n-1}$ or $\chi^2 \leq \chi^2_{1-\alpha/2,n-1}$ |

## Example 7.11

Again using the data on the 25 one-pound containers in Data Set 1, let us test

$$H_0: \sigma^2 \leqslant 0.0016 \qquad \text{versus} \qquad H_1: \sigma^2 > 0.0016$$

or the equivalent statements,

$$H_0: \sigma \leqslant 0.04 \qquad \text{and} \qquad H_1: \sigma > 0.04$$

The value of chi-square is found using Equation 7.20:

$$\chi^2 = \frac{(24)(0.0223)^2}{0.0016} = 7.459$$

From Table 7.7 we see that the critical region for an $\alpha = 0.05$ level test is

$$\chi^2 \geqslant \chi^2_{0.05,24} = 36.415$$

There is insufficient evidence to reject $H_0$ at significance level $\alpha = 0.05$. If $\sigma = 0.04$ is the largest tolerable value of $\sigma$, the data suggest weakly (why?) that the true standard deviation is within tolerance.

## Exercises 7.5

**7.40** Find the values of the following:
   **a.** $\chi^2_{0.05,5}$     **c.** $\chi^2_{0.01,9}$
   **b.** $\chi^2_{0.05,20}$     **d.** $\chi^2_{0.01,20}$

**7.41** Use Definition 7.5 and the fact that $\text{Var}(Z) = E(Z^2) = 1$ to show that $E(\chi^2_v) = v$.

**7.42** Using the data in Exhibit 2.10 on runs by 25 American League batters in 1980, test $H_0: \sigma \leqslant 20$ versus $H_1: \sigma > 20$. Assume that the normality assumption is justified.

**7.43** **a.** Use the data in exercise 2.34 on male life expectancy in 22 European countries to test $H_0: \sigma \leqslant 1.5$ versus $H_1: \sigma > 1.5$. Again assume the normality assumption is justified.
   **b.** Find a 90 percent confidence interval for $\sigma$.

**7.44** Use the test-score data of exercise 7.5 to find a 95 percent confidence interval for $\sigma$, assuming normality. *Note:* $\chi^2_{0.975,31} = 17.539$ and $\chi^2_{0.025,31} = 48.232$.

**7.45** **a.** Use the data in exercise 7.9 on the yields of ten stocks to test $H_0: \sigma^2 = 0.002$ versus $H_1: \sigma^2 \neq 0.002$. Assume normality.
   **b.** Find 95 percent confidence intervals for $\sigma^2$ and $\sigma$.

**7.46** **a.** Using the data of exercise 7.10 on the income from the game of 21, find a 95 percent confidence interval for $\sigma$, assuming normality.
   **b.** Test $H_0: \sigma \leqslant 1000$ versus $H_1: \sigma > 1000$, using a significance level of $\alpha = 0.05$.

**7.47** Assuming that the normality assumption is justified, use the data given in exercise 7.14 on the times taken by 25 students to complete a quiz.
   **a.** Find a 99 percent confidence interval for $\sigma$.
   **b.** Test $H_0: \sigma \leqslant 1.5$ versus $H_1: \sigma > 1.5$, using $\alpha = 0.05$.

**\*7.48**  It can be shown that the random variable

$$\frac{\chi_v^2 - v}{\sqrt{2v}}$$

has approximately a standard normal distribution for large values of $v$. Why does this statement follow from Definition 7.5, Equations 7.14 and 7.15, and the Central Limit Theorem?

**\*7.49**  **a.** Use the preceding exercise to show that for large $v$,

$$\chi_{\alpha,v}^2 \doteq \sqrt{2v}\, z_\alpha + v$$

**b.** It can also be shown that

$$(2\chi_v^2)^{1/2} - (2v - 1)^{1/2}$$

is approximately distributed as a standard normal variable for large $v$. Show that this fact implies that

$$\chi_{\alpha,v}^2 \doteq \frac{[z_\alpha + (2v - 1)^{1/2}]^2}{2}$$

**c.** Using $\alpha = 0.05$ and parts a and b, estimate $\chi_{0.05,100}^2$. Compare these values with that given in Table III of Appendix C.

---

**Summary**

In this chapter we considered inference for a population expectation, median, proportion, and variance in cases where the sample size is small. For symmetric distributions, $n < 30$ is normally considered "small," although there is no standard definition for all populations. Unbiasedness is a property of estimators shared by the sample mean, proportion, and variance as estimators of $\mu$, $p$, and $\sigma^2$, respectively. Unbiasedness means that "on the average" the sample estimator is equal to the parameter being estimated. The best unbiased estimators are minimum variance unbiased estimators (MVUEs). The sample mean and proportion are MVUEs for $\mu$ and $p$, respectively, and the sample variance is an MVUE for $\sigma^2$ in the normal case. These characteristics of $\bar{X}$, $\hat{p}$, and $S^2$ make them appropriate estimators of the corresponding population parameters for small $n$.

In small-sample estimation it is frequently assumed that the populations being sampled are normally distributed. If a population being sampled is not symmetric, the population median $m$ is an appropriate location measure and is preferred over the population expectation $\mu$. A population may be symmetric but not normally distributed. Departures from normality can often be determined by using graphical methods such as a boxplots, histograms, or normal plots. The statistics used for nonnormal symmetric populations must be insensitive to deviations from normality in the parent population. Such statistics are called robust.

Two statistics used as robust estimates of location are the median of the Walsh averages, called the Hodges-Lehmann estimator, and the trimmed mean. For symmetric distributions, the former is frequently a more efficient estimate of the population median than is the sample median. Both of these estimators are less sensitive to outliers than is the sample mean. The Minitab command DESCRIBE computes a trimmed mean with a specific proportion of trimming. The binomial distribution can also be used to find a confidence interval for $m$. The command CDF with the subcommand BINOMIAL is helpful in obtaining the order statistics required to calculate an appropriate confidence interval for $m$.

For small-sample tests for $p$, the binomial distribution may be used to find probabilities of Type I and Type II errors. There is a correspondence between the sign test for the median and the test of the null hypothesis $H_0: p = 1/2$. Tests of the null hypothesis $H_0: m = m_0$ are based on this correspondence. In sampling from a normal distribution, tests and confidence intervals for $\sigma^2$, the population variance, depend on the chi-square random variable.

## Key Words

| | |
|---|---|
| Bernoulli random variable | small sample size |
| chi-square distribution | Student's $t$ distribution |
| degrees of freedom | test for $m$ |
| Hodges-Lehmann estimator | test for $p$ |
| MVUE (minimum variance unbiased estimator) | test for $\sigma$ |
| | test for $\mu$ |
| outliers | unbiased estimator |
| robust estimator | trimmed mean |
| sign test | Walsh average |

## Minitab Commands

| | | |
|---|---|---|
| PICK | TTEST | WALSH |
| TINTERVAL | | |

# Chapter 8

# Two-Sample Comparisons

## 8.1

**Introduction**

**two-sample procedures**

The preceding three chapters introduced methods of statistical inference aimed at allowing conclusions to be drawn about a single parameter. The methods were based on a single random sample from a population. It is often important to compare corresponding parameters of two populations. This chapter discusses the comparison of the expectations, proportions, and variances of two populations. The general methods used are referred to as **two-sample procedures.**

For example, it may be important to decide whether a new method of accomplishing a task is an improvement over an old method. Is teaching algebra made more effective by replacing the lecture format by a new method of computer-assisted instruction (CAI)? This question can be addressed by comparing the true mean examination scores of students taught by the traditional method with the scores earned on the same exam by students taught by a new method. Similarly, it may be informative to compare two groups (say males and females) with regard to corresponding population proportions. For example, is the proportion of women of voting age who favor the ERA amendment higher than that of men? If indeed it is greater, an estimate of the difference of these two proportions would be useful. To state the goal in statistical terminology, we want to compare the effects of two treatments (the types of instruction) or to compare two groups (voting-age women and men). Two-sample comparisons in many diverse fields can be made with a relatively small number of statistical methods.

A few basic ideas of experimental design will be introduced here to provide some orientation before we consider particular two-sample statistical procedures. In some situations, an investigator may be in a position to determine in advance which individual elements (called experimental units) are to receive treatment 1 and which are to receive treatment 2. For example, in medical experiments in which animals are to receive two different types of drug, say A and B, the experimenter is free to assign the animals to the two treatments (drugs) as he or she chooses. This assignment is often done by randomly assigning $n_1$, a predetermined number of the $n$ available animals, to drug A and the remainder to drug B. Random selection is used in order to eliminate, as nearly as possible, the effects of other characteristics of the animals that might affect their response to the drugs. For example, if the $n_1$ oldest animals were assigned to drug A, it would not be possible to separate the effect of the drug from that of age. Random selection makes the assignment of all the older animals to one treatment very improbable. An experiment in which the treatments are assigned randomly to the experimental units is an example of a **designed experiment.** In general, the experimenter attempts to use an allocation method that will reflect **treatment differences**, if any exist.

In other situations, an investigator is not free to make an assignment of the treatments to the experimental units. For example, suppose an experimenter wanted to compare males and females with regard to their performance in introductory college chemistry. The only information available might well be the common final examination scores of those females and males who happened to be enrolled in an introductory chemistry course. When the investigator is not able to assign individual units to treatments, the data are said to arise from an **observational study**. An observer of an observational study must be very careful in making decisions about treatment differences. As a fictitious example, consider a chemistry course taught in two lecture sections for which a common final examination is given. If female students were drawn to a handsome but incompetent chemistry instructor, a higher average score by males on the final might appear to indicate superior male performance, when actually it only reflected differences in the abilities of the instructors.

To clarify the difference between a designed experiment and an observational study, consider two possible ways of carrying out an experiment comparing the effectiveness of computer-assisted instruction with that of the standard lecture format in teaching algebra. Suppose 100 students are to take algebra in two sections, in which the two different methods are to be used. One way to set up the experiment would be to randomly assign 50 students to the first section and the remainder to the second. We might then reasonably attribute an observed difference in final examination scores to the method of instruction. On the other hand, those students wishing to try the CAI class could be allowed to make this choice, with the remainder going to the section employing the standard lecture format. Differences in exam scores in that case might be due to the students' choice of treatment and not to the two teaching methods. On average, for example, the students with higher mathematical skills might choose the standard lecture format. Such differences are said to be due to **self-selection bias**.

*Margin notes:*
designed experiment
treatment differences

observational study

self-selection bias

**Table 8.1**

---

Masters Tournament Winners 1934–1981

| Year | Name | Score | Year | Name | Score |
|------|------|-------|------|------|-------|
| 1934 | Smith | 284 | 1960 | Palmer | 282 |
| 1935 | Sarazen | 282 | 1961 | Player | 280 |
| 1936 | Smith | 285 | 1962 | Palmer | 280 |
| 1937 | Nelson | 283 | 1963 | Nicklaus | 286 |
| 1938 | Picard | 285 | 1964 | Palmer | 276 |
| 1939 | Guldahl | 279 | 1965 | Nicklaus | 271 |
| 1940 | Demaret | 280 | 1966 | Nicklaus | 288 |
| 1941 | Wood | 280 | 1967 | Brewer | 280 |
| 1942 | Nelson | 280 | 1968 | Goalby | 277 |
| 1946 | Keiser | 282 | 1969 | Archer | 281 |
| 1947 | Demaret | 281 | 1970 | Casper | 279 |
| 1948 | Harman | 279 | 1971 | Coody | 279 |
| 1949 | Snead | 282 | 1972 | Nicklaus | 286 |
| 1950 | Demaret | 283 | 1973 | Aaron | 283 |
| 1951 | Hogan | 280 | 1974 | Player | 278 |
| 1952 | Snead | 286 | 1975 | Nicklaus | 276 |
| 1953 | Hogan | 274 | 1976 | Floyd | 271 |
| 1954 | Snead | 289 | 1977 | Watson | 276 |
| 1955 | Middlecoff | 279 | 1978 | Player | 277 |
| 1956 | Burke | 289 | 1979 | Zoeller | 280 |
| 1957 | Ford | 283 | 1980 | Ballesteros | 275 |
| 1958 | Palmer | 284 | 1981 | Watson | 280 |
| 1959 | Wall | 284 | | | |

*Source: The Information Please Almanac* (Boston: Houghton Mifflin, 1982), p. 896.

In spite of difficulties that arise in the random assignment of experimental units to treatments, the comparison of two methods of carrying out an action or the comparison of a characteristic exhibited by two populations is an important statistical problem.

One area in which two-sample comparisons are common is sports analysis. Table 8.1 presents the scores of the winners of the Masters Tournament between 1934 and 1981. There is widespread belief that improvements in both golfing equipment and players' skills have led to improved scores over this period. This view is summed up in the often-quoted remark, attributed to Bobby Jones, about the game of Jack Nicklaus: "He plays a game with which I am not familiar." If it is true that scores have improved over the course of the 45 tournaments between 1934 and 1981, the average winning score should be lower for the last 22 tournaments than for the first 23. This chapter will outline statistical procedures that can be used to provide a justification (or refutation) of the belief that winning scores are declining.

## Comparison of Location of Two Populations for Large Samples

In Section 8.1, the comparison of two methods of teaching algebra was presented as an example of a two-sample problem. Two populations were described—those taught algebra through the standard lecture format and those taught by a new CAI method. The random variables of interest are the scores on a common final examination of those taught in the conventional way (say $X$) and those taught by the CAI method (say $Y$). One way to compare these populations is to compare $E(X) = \mu_x$ and $E(Y) = \mu_y$, the expectations of these two random variables. We can conceptualize the two populations as shown in Figure 8.1. There the difference $\mu_x - \mu_y$ appears to be negative, suggesting superiority of the new teaching method. One approach is to test the null hypothesis $H_0: \mu_x = \mu_y$ versus an appropriate alternative. In this case, a sensible alternative is $H_1: \mu_x < \mu_y$—that is, the true average examination score is higher for those taught using the CAI method. It is

**difference of two expectations**

also important to find a confidence interval for $\mu_y - \mu_x$, the **difference of two expectations**. In practice, a confidence interval is frequently more important than a statistical test, as the size of a difference due to treatments (teaching methods) is often of more interest than the simple determination that there is such a difference.

In the two-sample situation considered here, it will be assumed that random samples of sizes $n_x$ and $n_y$, respectively, are available from each of the two populations. These observations will be denoted by

$$X_i, i = 1, 2, \ldots, n_x \quad \text{and} \quad Y_j, j = 1, 2, \ldots, n_y \qquad \textbf{8.1}$$

It will also be assumed that the observations from the first population in Equation 8.1 are independent of those from the second population, and that the first population has variance $\sigma_x^2$ and the second has variance $\sigma_y^2$. Thus we have

$$E(X_i) = \mu_x, \text{ all } i \quad \text{and} \quad E(Y_j) = \mu_y, \text{ all } j$$

and

$$\text{Var}(X_i) = \sigma_x^2, \text{ all } i \quad \text{and} \quad \text{Var}(Y_j) = \sigma_y^2, \text{ all } j$$

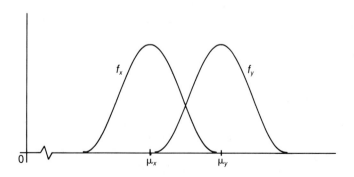

**Figure 8.1**

Two Symmetric Populations with Different Expected Values

**Table 8.2**

| Large-Sample Critical Regions for Tests of Two Population Means | | |
|---|---|---|
| Alternative | Critical Region | Minitab Alternative |
| $\mu_x > \mu_y$ | $Z \geqslant z_\alpha$ | $+1$ |
| $\mu_x < \mu_y$ | $Z \leqslant -z_\alpha$ | $-1$ |
| $\mu_x \neq \mu_y$ | $|Z| \geqslant z_{\alpha/2}$ | |

as the observations are random samples from the respective parent populations $X$ and $Y$. As a parameter of major interest is the difference $\mu_x - \mu_y$, it should not be surprising that the fundamental statistic for inference here is $\bar{X} - \bar{Y}$, the difference of the two sample means. These means are given by

$$\bar{X} = \sum_{i=1}^{n_x} \frac{x_j}{n_x} \quad \text{and} \quad \bar{Y} = \sum_{j=1}^{n_y} \frac{Y_j}{n_y}$$

We can easily find

$$E(\bar{X} - \bar{Y}) = E(\bar{X}) - E(\bar{Y}) = \mu_x - \mu_y \qquad \text{8.2}$$

and

$$\text{Var}(\bar{X} - \bar{Y}) = \text{Var}(\bar{X}) + \text{Var}(\bar{Y}) = \frac{\sigma_x^2}{n_x} + \frac{\sigma_y^2}{n_y} \qquad \text{8.3}$$

using the independence of $\bar{X}$ and $\bar{Y}$ and standard properties of the expectation and variance. Equation 8.2 states that the difference of the sample means unbiasedly estimates $\mu_x - \mu_y$, the difference of the population means. Equation 8.3 shows that, as $n_x$ and $n_y$ both become large, the variance of $\bar{X} - \bar{Y}$ becomes small. Hence, we see intuitively that, for large $n_x$ and $n_y$, $\bar{X} - \bar{Y}$ should be a good estimator of $\mu_x - \mu_y$.

Assuming that $n_x$ and $n_y$ can both be considered to be large, we consider first the hypothesis-testing situation. A standard null hypothesis is $H_0: \mu_x = \mu_y$ (or, equivalently, $H_0: \mu_x - \mu_y = 0$). The null hypothesis says that there is no difference in location as measured by $\mu_x$ and $\mu_y$ for the two populations. Standard alternatives are given in Table 8.2.

In the large-sample case, the test statistic used is

$$Z = \frac{\bar{X} - \bar{Y}}{\sqrt{S_x^2/n_x + S_y^2/n_y}} \qquad \text{8.4}$$

If the true variances $\sigma_x^2$ and $\sigma_y^2$ were known, these would be used, but as this is almost never the case, the two sample variances are used as estimates of $\sigma_x^2$ and $\sigma_y^2$ in the denominator of Equation 8.4. For large $n_x$ and $n_y$, an extension of the Central Limit Theorem guarantees that the statistic in Equation 8.4 has approximately a standard normal distribution *if $H_0$ is true*. The choice of the critical regions in Table 8.2 can be justified as before. For example, if $\mu_x > \mu_y$ is correct, $\bar{X}$ will generally be larger than $\bar{Y}$. The $Z$ statistic of Equation 8.4 will thus be positive, and hence the rejection region $Z \geqslant z_\alpha$ is appropriate for the first case in Table 8.2.

As noted above, $\bar{X} - \bar{Y}$ is an unbiased estimator of $\mu_x - \mu_y$. The standardized random variable given by

$$\frac{\bar{X} - \bar{Y} - (\mu_x - \mu_y)}{\sqrt{S_x^2/n_x + S_y^2/n_y}} \qquad \textbf{8.5}$$

will have approximately a standard normal distribution for large $n_x$ and $n_y$. This fact may be used to find the endpoints of an approximate $(1 - \alpha)100$ percent confidence interval for $\mu_x - \mu_y$. The endpoints, which are analogous to those found for a large-sample confidence interval for $\mu$ in Equation 5.9, are

$$\bar{X} - \bar{Y} \pm \sqrt{\frac{S_x^2}{n_x} + \frac{S_y^2}{n_y}} \; z_{\alpha/2} \qquad \textbf{8.6}$$

As in Equation 8.4, the theoretical variances have been replaced by the sample variances.

## Example 8.1

Consider the following data concerning the number of children born in Sri Lanka to uneducated women (the $X$ population) in comparison to those born to women with 10 or more years of education (the $Y$ population). Both samples include women married for 15 to 19 years.

| Sample | Sample Size | Mean | Standard Deviation |
|--------|-------------|------|--------------------|
| $X$    | 239         | 5.13 | 2.35               |
| $Y$    | 95          | 4.13 | 2.10               |

*Source:* Sri Lanka Fertility Study (1975), as reported in Roderick J. A. Little, "Direct Standardization: A Tool for Teaching Linear Models for Unbalanced Data," *The American Statistician* 36 (1982): 39.

As an alternative to $H_0$: $\mu_x = \mu_y$ we take $H_1$: $\mu_x > \mu_y$—that uneducated women will have more children on the average than will educated women. The value of $Z$ computed from Equation 8.4 is

$$Z = \frac{5.13 - 4.13}{\sqrt{(2.35)^2/239 + (2.10)^2/95}}$$

$$= \frac{1}{0.26368} = 3.79$$

This value of $Z$ exceeds $z_\alpha$ for any reasonable value of $\alpha$ such as $\alpha = 0.005$, as $Z_{0.005} = 2.576$. The evidence for the alternative hypothesis is compelling.

A confidence interval for $\mu_x - \mu_y$, the difference between the true average number of children for those in the $X$ population and the true average number of children for those in the $Y$ population, has endpoints given by Equation 8.6. A 95 percent confidence interval has the endpoints

$$5.13 - 4.13 \pm (0.26368)(1.96) = 1 \pm 0.517$$

The interval is thus given by (0.483, 1.517). The point estimate of $\mu_x - \mu_y$ is, of course, $\bar{x} - \bar{y} = 1$; that is, Sri Lankan women in the first population have one more child on average than do those in the second population.

## Example 8.2

Assume that we have obtained the following summary data for 100 students taught by method A and 100 students taught by method B. The observations are scores on a common final examination.

| Method | Sample Size | Mean | Standard Deviation |
|--------|-------------|------|--------------------|
| A      | 100         | 83   | 5.6                |
| B      | 100         | 77   | 8.2                |

There is some reason to believe that teaching method A may be superior. We test

$$H_0\colon \mu_A = \mu_B \qquad \text{versus} \qquad H_1\colon \mu_A > \mu_B$$

The calculated value of the $Z$ statistic is

$$Z = \frac{83 - 77}{\sqrt{(5.6)^2/100 + (8.2)^2/100}} = 6.04$$

As in Example 8.1, it is clear that $H_0$ should be rejected. A 95 percent confidence interval for $\mu_A - \mu_B$ is given by

$$(83 - 77) \pm (0.99298)(1.96) = 6 \pm 1.946$$

The confidence interval is thus (4.054, 7.946). The evidence for superior performance on the common final examination by those taught by method A is clear.

## Exercises 8.2

**8.1** The 1975 Sri Lanka Fertility Study mentioned in this section gave the following data, by educational group, for the number of children born to Sri Lankan women married for 10–14 years.

| Group | Sample Size | Average Number of Children | Standard Deviation |
|-------|-------------|----------------------------|--------------------|
| 1–5 years of school | 482 | 3.91 | 1.72 |
| 10+ years of school | 145 | 3.14 | 1.47 |

**a.** Use the large-sample $Z$ statistic to test $H_0\colon \mu_x = \mu_y$ versus an appropriate alternative, with $\alpha = 0.10$.

**b.** Find a 90 percent confidence interval for $\mu_x - \mu_y$, using the large-sample procedure.

**8.2** A random sample of 50 males and 50 females was selected from an introductory statistics course. The following average scores on an examination were obtained.

| Group | $n$ | Mean | Standard Deviation |
|---|---|---|---|
| Female | 50 | 76.1 | 12.3 |
| Male | 50 | 77.2 | 10.8 |

**a.** Test

$$H_0: \mu_x = \mu_y \quad \text{versus} \quad H_1: \mu_x \neq \mu_y$$

using $\alpha = 0.10$. Let $x$ refer to the male population and $y$ to the female population.

**b.** Find an approximate 90 percent confidence interval for $\mu_x - \mu_y$. What important value does this interval contain, and why is it important?

**8.3** In the Spring 1986 edition of the *Journal of Experimental Education*, an article on the effectiveness of CAI (computer-assisted instruction) reported pretest and posttest scores on two 50-item tests administered to 100 U.S. Navy yeoman "A" students.

| | Pretest | | | Posttest | | |
|---|---|---|---|---|---|---|
| | $n$ | $\bar{x}$ | $s$ | $n$ | $\bar{x}$ | $s$ |
| CAI Group | 50 | 18.0 | 3.56 | 50 | 45.78 | 4.46 |
| Traditional Group | 50 | 18.92 | 3.6 | 50 | 44.34 | 3.70 |

J. R. Enochs, H. M. Handley, and J. P. Wollenberg, "Relating Learning Style, Reading Vocabulary, Reading Comprehension and Aptitude for Learning to Achievement in Self-Paced and CAI Modes," *Journal of Experimental Education*, Spring (1986): 135–139.

**a.** Do the two groups differ on average performance on the pretests? Use $\alpha = 0.05$.

**b.** Do the two groups differ on average performance on the posttests? Use $\alpha = 0.05$.

**8.4** In the Summer 1986 edition of the *Journal of Experimental Education*, S. L. Stallings and S. J. Derry reported on a comparison of student performance in reading comprehension with and without organizers. (An "organizer" is an introduction that orients students to the nature of the reading material on a test.) The test consisted of 32 items. Each answer was given a score of 2, 1, or 0, so the maximum score that could be obtained was 64. The following data were reported:

| | No Organizer | | | Organizer | | |
|---|---|---|---|---|---|---|
| $n$ | $\bar{x}$ | $s_x$ | $n$ | $\bar{y}$ | $s_y$ |
| 100 | 32.82 | 9.95 | 100 | 32.96 | 9.24 |

S. L. Stallings and S. J. Derry, "Can an Advance Organizer Technique Compensate for Poor Reading Conditions?" *Journal of Experimental Education*, Summer (1986): 217–222.

**a.** Does there appear to be a significant difference in the two groups' performance on this test? Use $\alpha = 0.05$.

**b.** Find a 95 percent confidence interval for $\mu_x - \mu_y$.

**8.5** Turnpike officials obtained two random samples of 50 cars traveling between two exits on the Indiana Turnpike. In the first sample the cars were traveling east to west, and in the second sample the cars were traveling west to east. The following observations were made for the two groups of time spent traveling (in minutes).

| | East to West | | | West to East | |
|---|---|---|---|---|---|
| $n_x$ | $\bar{x}$ | $s_x$ | $n_y$ | $\bar{y}$ | $s_y$ |
| 50 | 40 | 15 | 50 | 34.5 | 10 |

**a.** Test

$$H_0: \mu_x = \mu_y \qquad \text{versus} \qquad H_1: \mu_x > \mu_y$$

using $\alpha = 0.05$. State the meaning of $H_1$ in words.

**b.** Find a 90 percent confidence interval for $\mu_x - \mu_y$.

## 8.3

## Comparison of Location of Two Populations for Small Samples

Sometimes inference about $\mu_x - \mu_y$ is required when the sample sizes $n_x$ and $n_y$ are not large. In such cases, additional distributional assumptions must be made about the populations sampled in order to make inferences. The following additional assumptions about the $X$ and $Y$ populations are frequently made.

$$X \sim N(\mu_x, \sigma^2) \qquad Y \sim N(\mu_y, \sigma^2) \qquad\qquad \textbf{8.7}$$

In other words, both populations are considered to be normally distributed with possibly different expectations $\mu_x$ and $\mu_y$ but *common* variance $\sigma^2$, which is assumed to be unknown. Under the assumptions of Equation 8.6, the statistic $\bar{X} - \bar{Y}$ can be shown to have a normal distribution with expectation $\mu_x - \mu_y$ and variance $\sigma^2[(1/n_x) + (1/n_y)]$. Hence the random variable

$$\frac{\bar{X} - \bar{Y} - (\mu_x - \mu_y)}{\sigma\sqrt{(1/n_x) + (1/n_y)}} = Z \qquad\qquad \textbf{8.8}$$

has a standard normal distribution. This result is not an approximation; it follows exactly from the normality assumptions of Equation 8.7.

Calculation of the random variable $Z$ in Equation 8.8 under the null hypothesis $H_0: \mu_x = \mu_y$ is not possible, because the variance $\sigma^2$ is not known. The estimator of $\sigma^2$ used in such situations is called the pooled estimate of the common variance.

---

**Definition 8.1** ▬▬▬

**pooled estimate of variance**

The **pooled estimate of** the common **variance** $\sigma^2$ is

$$S_p^2 = \frac{(n_x - 1)S_x^2 + (n_y - 1)S_y^2}{n_x + n_y - 2}$$

---

[Note that $(n_x - 1)S_x^2$ is the same as $\sum_{i=1}^{n_x} (x_i - \bar{x})^2$, the sum of the squares of the deviations from $\bar{x}$ of the $x_i$; similarly, $(n_y - 1)S_y^2$ is the same as $\sum_{i=1}^{n_y} (y_i - \bar{y})^2$. See

**Table 8.3**

**Critical Regions for Small-Sample Tests of the Equality of Two Population Expectations (Equal Variances)**

| Alternative | Critical Region | Minitab Alternative |
|---|---|---|
| $\mu_x > \mu_y$ | $t \geqslant t_{\alpha, n_x + n_y - 2}$ | $+1$ |
| $\mu_x < \mu_y$ | $t \leqslant -t_{\alpha, n_x + n_y - 2}$ | $-1$ |
| $\mu_x = \mu_y$ | $\lvert t \rvert \geqslant t_{\alpha/2, n_x + n_y - 2}$ | |

exercise 8.7.] As $S_x^2$ and $S_y^2$ are both unbiased estimates of $\sigma^2$, we have

$$
\begin{aligned}
E(S_p^2) &= \frac{(n_x - 1)E(S_x^2) + (n_y - 1)E(S_y^2)}{n_x + n_y - 2} \\
&= \frac{(n_x - 1)\sigma^2 + (n_y - 1)\sigma^2}{n_x + n_y - 2} = \sigma^2
\end{aligned}
$$

Hence the pooled estimate is an unbiased estimator of the assumed common variance $\sigma^2$. If we replace $\sigma$ by $S_p$ in Equation 8.8, the resulting random variable

$$
\frac{\bar{X} - \bar{Y} - (\mu_x - \mu_y)}{S_p \sqrt{1/n_x + 1/n_y}} \tag{8.9}
$$

can be shown to have Student's $t$ distribution with $n_x + n_y - 2$ degrees of freedom.

In order to test the null hypothesis $H_0$: $\mu_x = \mu_y$, we compute Equation 8.9 for this hypothesis, obtaining as the test statistic

$$
t = \frac{\bar{X} - \bar{Y}}{S_p \sqrt{1/n_x + 1/n_y}} = \frac{\bar{X} - \bar{Y}}{S_d} \tag{8.10}
$$

which replaces $Z$ in Equation 8.4. Critical regions for $\alpha$-level tests versus standard alternatives are given in Table 8.3.

Using familiar reasoning, the endpoints of a $(1 - \alpha)100$ percent confidence interval for $\mu_x - \mu_y$ can be found to be

$$
\bar{X} - \bar{Y} \pm S_d t_{\alpha/2, n_x + n_y - 2} \tag{8.11}
$$

**Example 8.3**

Wire cable is being manufactured by two processes. We wish to determine whether the process used affects the mean breaking strength of the cable. Laboratory tests are performed by putting samples under tension and recording the load required to break the cable. Assume that the observations are random samples taken independently from two normal populations with the same variance. The following sample data are obtained.

| Sample | Sample Size | Mean Load (Pounds) | Variance |
|--------|-------------|--------------------|----------|
| $X$ | 6 | 8.2 | 2.0 |
| $Y$ | 7 | 11.2 | 4.0 |

We test the following hypotheses, using $\alpha = 0.05$:

$$H_0: \mu_x = \mu_y \quad \text{versus} \quad H_1: \mu_x \neq \mu_y$$

The pooled estimate of variance is

$$S_p^2 = \frac{5(2) + 6(4)}{11} = \frac{34}{11}$$

and the calculated $t$ statistic is found to be

$$t = \frac{8.2 - 11.2}{\sqrt{34/11(1/6 + 1/7)}} = -3.067$$

The appropriate critical region is

$$|t| \geq t_{0.025,11} = 2.201$$

The observed $t$ is in the critical region, so $H_0$ is rejected. The data suggest that the true mean breaking strengths of wires produced by the two processes are not equal and that $\mu_y > \mu_x$.

## Example 8.4

**TWOSAMPLE POOLED**   Exhibit 8.1 shows the output generated when the Minitab command **TWOSAMPLE** was used with the subcommand **POOLED** to carry out the calculations required under the normality assumptions of Equation 8.7 on the Masters Tournament scores of Table 8.1. The first 23 winning Masters scores are stored in C1 and the next 22 winning scores in C2. Normal plots of the two groups indicate tolerably good agreement with the normality assumption.

To test the null hypothesis $H_0: \mu_x = \mu_y$ against the alternative $H_1: \mu_x > \mu_y$ (that the winning scores are declining) the Minitab command TWOSAMPLE was used with Minitab alternative $+1$ specified in a subcommand. The following statistics were obtained:

$$\bar{x} = 282.30 \qquad \bar{y} = 279.14 \qquad t = 2.74$$

The appropriate number of degrees of freedom for the test is

$$n_x + n_y - 2 = 43$$

Minitab gives a $p$-value of 0.0044, which implies a significant difference between $\mu_x$ and $\mu_y$ at any significance level $\alpha \geq 0.0044$. A 95 percent confidence interval for $\mu_x - \mu_y$ has been calculated from Equation 8.11 to be (0.84, 5.50). The point estimate of $\mu_x - \mu_y$ is $\bar{x} - \bar{y} = 282.30 - 279.14 = 3.16$. It appears reasonable to assume that the variances are equal, as $s_x = 3.39$ and $s_y = 4.32$, although a test of $H_0$: $\sigma_x = \sigma_y$ has not yet been presented. (This will be done in Section 8.6.) There appears to be statistical evidence that the winning Masters scores have been declining.

---

If a common variance $\sigma^2$ cannot be assumed, it may be necessary to carry out inference for the difference of population expectations for small samples. In that case,

$$X \sim N(\mu_x, \sigma_x^2) \qquad \text{and} \qquad Y \sim N(\mu_y, \sigma_y^2) \qquad\qquad \textbf{8.12}$$

**Exhibit 8.1**

```
MTB > NOTE COMPARISON OF OLD AND RECENT MASTERS WINNERS
MTB > SET C1
C1
      284     282     285     283     .    .    .

MTB > END
MTB > SET C2
C2
      282     280     280     286     .    .    .

MTB > END
MTB > PRINT C1-C2
 ROW      C1      C2

   1     284     282
   2     282     280
   3     285     280
   4     283     286
   5     285     276
   6     279     271
   7     280     288
   8     280     280
   9     280     277
  10     282     281
  11     281     279
  12     279     279
  13     282     286
  14     283     283
  15     280     278
  16     286     276
  17     274     271
  18     289     276
  19     279     277
  20     289     280
  21     283     275
  22     284     280
  23     284
```

```
MTB > NOTE NORMAL PLOT FOR FIRST 23 YEARS MASTERS DATA
MTB > NSCORES C1 IN C3
MTB > NAME C1 'OLDSCOR' C3 'NSCORE'
MTB > PLOT C3 C1
```

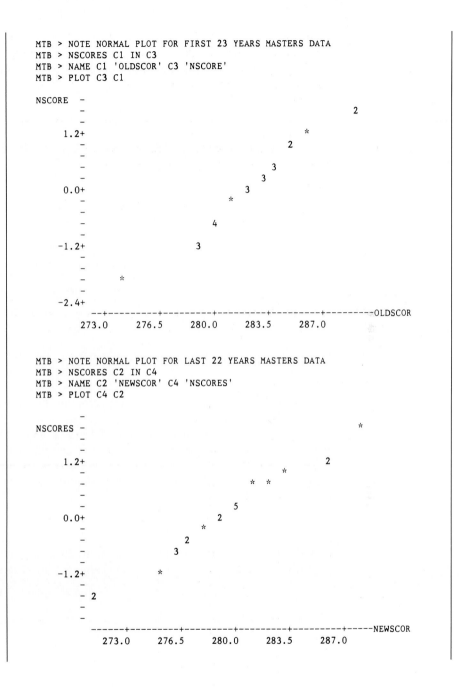

```
MTB > NOTE NORMAL PLOT FOR LAST 22 YEARS MASTERS DATA
MTB > NSCORES C2 IN C4
MTB > NAME C2 'NEWSCOR' C4 'NSCORES'
MTB > PLOT C4 C2
```

Exhibit 8.1
(cont.)

```
MTB > TWOSAMPLE T DATA IN C1 C2;
SUBC> POOLED;
SUBC> ALTERNATIVE +1.

TWOSAMPLE T FOR C1 VS C2
       N      MEAN    STDEV   SE MEAN
C1    23    282.30     3.39      0.71
C2    22    279.14     4.32      0.92

95 PCT CI FOR MU C1 - MU C2: (0.84, 5.50)
TTEST MU C1 = MU C2 (VS GT): T=2.74 P=0.0044 DF=43.0
```

## Table 8.4

**Critical Regions for Small-Sample Tests of Two Population Means (Unequal Variances)**

| Alternative | Critical Region | Minitab Alternative |
|---|---|---|
| $\mu_x > \mu_y$ | $t' \geqslant t_{\alpha,\nu}$ | $+1$ |
| $\mu_x < \mu_y$ | $t' \leqslant -t_{\alpha,\nu}$ | $-1$ |
| $\mu_x \neq \mu_y$ | $|t'| \geqslant t_{\alpha/2,\nu}$ | |

**approximate degrees of freedom**

Under these normality assumptions we compute the statistic given by Equation 8.4, labeling it $t'$ instead of $Z$. Under $H_0$: $\mu_x = \mu_y$, $t'$ has an approximate $t$ distribution with **approximate degrees of freedom** equal to $\nu$. The value of $\nu$ is calculated from the data using a somewhat complicated formula. The critical regions for $\alpha$-level tests are given in Table 8.4. The endpoints of the confidence interval for $\mu_x - \mu_y$ with a confidence coefficient of $(1 - \alpha)100$ percent are like those in Equation 8.6, with $t_{\alpha/2,\nu}$ replacing $z_{\alpha/2}$.

## Example 8.5

Exhibit 8.2 shows the output generated when the Minitab command TWO-SAMPLE was used with the data in Table 8.1 to compute the $t'$ statistic, a

## Exhibit 8.2

```
MTB > TWOSAMPLE T DATA IN C1 C2;
SUBC> ALTERNATIVE +1.

TWOSAMPLE T FOR C1 VS C2
       N      MEAN    STDEV   SE MEAN
C1    23    282.30     3.39      0.71
C2    22    279.14     4.32      0.92

95 PCT CI FOR MU C1 - MU C2: (0.82, 5.52)
TTEST MU C1 = MU C2 (VS GT): T=2.73 P=0.0048 DF=39.8
```

$p$-value, and a confidence interval for $\mu_x - \mu_y$, under the assumption of unequal variances.

We obtain $t' = 2.73$ with approximately $v = 39.8$ degrees of freedom. The $p$-value of 0.0048, which is very close to the value of 0.0044 that was found by assuming equal variances, would lead to rejection of $H_0$ in favor of $H_1$: $\mu_x > \mu_y$ for any $\alpha \geqslant 0.0048$. The 95 percent confidence interval for $\mu_x - \mu_y$ is (0.82, 5.52), which also agrees well with that computed under the equal variance assumption.

Finally, it should be noted that the two samples are not really independent, as several players participated in the Masters both before and after the cutoff year —in fact, Arnold Palmer won in 1958, 1960, 1962, and 1964. Nevertheless, the evidence for a decline in winning scores is quite strong.

---

In many cases, normality of the $X$ and $Y$ observations cannot be assumed. In such cases differences in location between the two populations are often measured by the difference between the population medians, $m_x - m_y$. Figure 8.2 indicates how two such populations may be conceptualized. The inferential tasks in such a situation are to test the null hypothesis $H_0$: $m_x = m_y$ versus standard alternatives and to find a confidence interval for $m_x - m_y$. Standard alternatives are given in Table 8.5. A test of the null hypothesis that both samples come from the same (but unspecified) distribution can be carried out by pooling the random samples from **ranks** the two populations and replacing the observations by their **ranks** by magnitude in the combined sample. The smallest observation in the combined sample is replaced by 1, the next smallest by 2, and so forth, with the largest observation being replaced by $n_x + n_y$. The ranks of the observations that originally came from the first $(X)$ sample are then summed. The sum of these ranks is denoted by

$$W = \sum_{i=1}^{n_x} R_i \qquad \text{where } R_i \text{ is the rank of } X_i$$

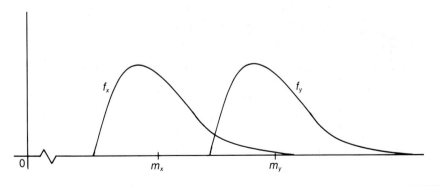

**Figure 8.2**

Two Skewed Populations

## Table 8.5

**Critical Regions for Test of Population Medians**

| Alternative | Critical Region |
|---|---|
| $m_x > m_y$ | $Z \geqslant z_\alpha$ |
| $m_x < m_y$ | $Z \leqslant -z_\alpha$ |
| $m_x \neq m_y$ | $|Z| \geqslant z_{\alpha/2}$ |

**Wilcoxon rank sum test**

If $W$ is either much smaller or much larger than $E(W)$ under $H_0$, the hypothesis that the medians of the two distributions are equal is rejected. This test is referred to as the **Wilcoxon rank sum test**. Under the null hypothesis, the test statistic $W$ has a distribution that does not depend on that of the $X$ and $Y$ populations, *as long as* these populations have the *same* continuous distribution. Thus the Wilcoxon rank sum test is a distribution-free or nonparametric test, as was the sign test.

The details of testing the null hypothesis $H_0$: $m_x = m_y$ will be considered next. *Under $H_0$* it can be shown that for the $W$ statistic we have

$$E(W) = \frac{n_x(n_x + n_y + 1)}{2} \qquad \textbf{8.13}$$

and

$$\text{Var}(W) = \frac{n_x n_y(n_x + n_y + 1)}{12} \qquad \textbf{8.14}$$

Under the null hypothesis, the standardized Wilcoxon statistic,

$$Z = \frac{W - n_x(n_x + n_y + 1)/2}{\sqrt{n_x n_y(n_x + n_y + 1)/12}} \qquad \textbf{8.15}$$

is approximately distributed as the standard normal variable for $n_x \geqslant 8$ and $n_y \geqslant 8$.

The Wilcoxon rank sum test statistic is equivalent to a test statistic called the **Mann-Whitney statistic**.

**Mann-Whitney statistic**

## Example 8.6

Table 8.6 gives per capita state and local taxes in 8 northern ($X$) and 15 sunbelt ($Y$) states in 1980, stated in terms of taxes per \$1000 of personal income. The numbers in parentheses are the ranks of the states by level of state and local taxes in the combined sample. Note that when two values are equal, the averge of the ranks is assigned to each. Similarly, if three values were equal, each would receive the average of the three ranks to be assigned.

As it is frequently assumed that taxes are higher in northern states, the following null and alternative hypotheses seem reasonable:

$$H_0: m_x = m_y \qquad \text{and} \qquad H_1: m_x > m_y$$

**Table 8.6**

| Per Capita State and Local Taxes per $1000 of Personal Income | | | | | |
|---|---|---|---|---|---|
| Northern State | Tax | | Sunbelt State | Tax | |
| Illinois | 112 | (14) | Alabama | 96 | (4) |
| Indiana | 88 | (1) | Arizona | 133 | (21) |
| Massachusetts | 139 | (22) | Arkansas | 99 | (7) |
| Michigan | 115 | (15) | California | 122 | (19.5) |
| New Jersey | 117 | (18) | Florida | 97 | (5) |
| New York | 163 | (23) | Georgia | 108 | (12) |
| Ohio | 94 | (2.5) | Louisiana | 116 | (16.5) |
| Pennsylvania | 116 | (16.5) | Mississippi | 109 | (13) |
| | | | New Mexico | 122 | (19.5) |
| | | | North Carolina | 106 | (10) |
| | | | Oklahoma | 102 | (8.5) |
| | | | South Carolina | 107 | (11) |
| | | | Tennessee | 94 | (2.5) |
| | | | Texas | 98 | (6) |
| | | | Virginia | 102 | (8.5) |

*Source: Florida Statistical Abstract 1982, p. 612.*

Finding that $W = 112$, we calculate

$$Z = \frac{112 - 8(12)}{\sqrt{8 \cdot 15 \cdot 24/12}} = 1.03$$

The associated $p$-value is $P(Z \geq 1.03) = 0.1515$. The case for higher local and state taxes in northern states is not conclusively demonstrated. For example, for $\alpha = 0.10$ and $0.05$ the null hypothesis of equal medians would be retained. Only for significance levels $\alpha \geq 0.1515$ would $H_0$ be rejected in favor of $H_1$.

**MANN-WHITNEY**   The Minitab system uses the command **MANN-WHITNEY** to carry out the computations of the Wilcoxon statistic $W$ and related inferential procedures. Use of this command produces a $p$-value for testing $H_0$: $m_x = m_y$ (the population medians are equal) versus $H_1$: $m_x \neq m_y$.

**Example 8.7**

Exhibit 8.3 shows the output generated when the Minitab command MANN-WHITNEY was used with the data of Table 8.1 on the Masters Tournament winners. The first 23 winning scores were stored in C1 and the last 22 winning scores in C2.

Note that $m_x$ is referred to as ETA1 and $m_y$ as ETA2. The command produces a $p$-value for testing $H_0$: $m_x = m_y$ versus $H_1$: $m_x \neq m_y$, a point estimate of

Exhibit 8.3

```
MTB > NOTE MANN-WHITNEY TEST FOR MASTERS DATA
MTB > MANN-WHITNEY DATA IN C1 C2

Mann-Whitney Confidence Interval and Test

C1          N =  23      MEDIAN =        282.00
C2          N =  22      MEDIAN =        279.50
POINT ESTIMATE FOR ETA1-ETA2 IS          2.9995
95.0  PCT C.I. FOR ETA1-ETA2 IS (       1.0,       5.0)
W =    645.5
TEST OF ETA1 = ETA2  VS.  ETA1 N.E. ETA2 IS SIGNIFICANT AT   0.0084
```

**difference of two medians** $m_x - m_y$, the **difference of two medians**, and a confidence interval for $m_x - m_y$ with a confidence coefficient of 95 percent. The point estimate of $m_x - m_y$ is 2.9995 (or 3), and a 95 percent confidence interval for $m_x - m_y$ has endpoints (1.0, 5.0). In other words, the point estimate of the decrease of the winning score is 3.0 strokes. In order to obtain a $p$-value for a test of $H_0$: $m_x = m_y$ versus $H_1$: $m_x > m_y$, a one-sided alternative, the Minitab $p$-value is divided by 2, giving a $p$-value of 0.0042. The reader should note that these results are in excellent agreement with those of Example 8.4, in which normal theory was used. The corresponding $p$-value found in Example 8.4 was 0.0044, the point estimate of $\mu_x - \mu_y$ was 3.16, and the 95 percent confidence interval for $\mu_x - \mu_y$ was (0.84, 5.5). In this case the distribution-free method confirms the normal theory results.

In some cases the Wilcoxon procedure is more appropriate than the normal theory methods because of a lack of normality of the original populations.

## Example 8.8

The data of Example 8.6 on state taxes have been used to illustrate how the Wilcoxon test is carried out by Minitab. The northern state data have been stored in C1 and the sunbelt state data in C2. The normal plots produced for each column are given in Exhibit 8.4, together with the output from the MANN-WHITNEY command.

The point estimate of $m_x - m_y$ is calculated to be 9.5. A 90 percent confidence interval for $m_x - m_y$ is given by $(-6.0, 19.0)$, suggesting no statistical difference in the population medians. The value of the statistic, $W = 112$, agrees with the computation of Example 8.6. The $p$-value is $0.3171/2 = 0.1586$. The slight difference from the value of 0.1515 found for the one-sided alternative considered in Example 8.6 is due to the use of the normal approximation in Equation 8.15. As in Example 8.6, a decision for higher state and local taxes in the northern states is not found to be statistically significant for $\alpha = 0.05$ or $\alpha = 0.10$.

**Exhibit 8.4**

```
MTB > NOTE COMPARISON OF TAX DATA FOR NORTHERN AND SUNBELT STATES
MTB > SET C1
C1
    112      88     139     115    .   .   .

MTB > END
MTB > SET C2
C2
     96     133      99     122    .   .   .

MTB > END
MTB > NAME C1 'NORTH' C2 'SUNBELT'
MTB > PRINT C1,C2
 ROW   NORTH  SUNBELT

   1     112       96
   2      88      133
   3     139       99
   4     115      122
   5     117       97
   6     163      108
   7      94      116
   8     116      109
   9              122
  10              106
  11              102
  12              107
  13               94
  14               98
  15              102




MTB > NOTE NORMAL PLOT FOR NORTHERN STATES
MTB > NSCORES C1 C3
MTB > NAME C3 'NSCORE'
MTB > PLOT C3 C1


         -                                              *

NSCORE   -
         -
         -
   0.80+                              *
         -
         -                 *
         -
         -              *
   0.00+
         -              *
         -
         -           *
         -
  -0.80+        *
         -
         -
         -
         -    *
       --------+---------+---------+---------+---------+---NORTH
             96        112       128       144       160
```

Exhibit 8.4
(cont.)

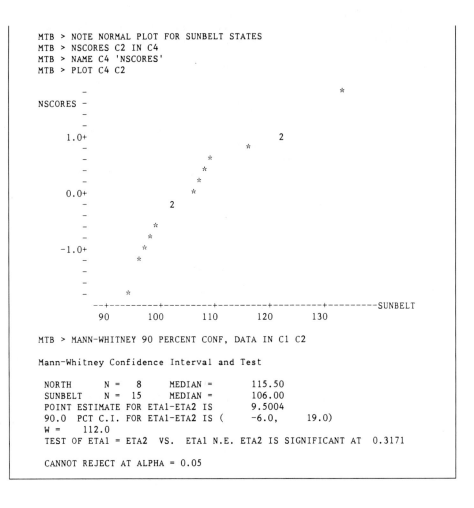

```
MTB > NOTE NORMAL PLOT FOR SUNBELT STATES
MTB > NSCORES C2 IN C4
MTB > NAME C4 'NSCORES'
MTB > PLOT C4 C2


          -                                             *
NSCORES -
          -
          -
    1.0+                                    2
          -                            *
          -                  *
          -                 *
          -                *
    0.0+               *
          -        2
          -
          -         *
          -          *
   -1.0+          *
          -        *
          -
          -
          -    *
       --+---------+---------+---------+---------+---------+---------SUNBELT
         90       100       110       120       130

MTB > MANN-WHITNEY 90 PERCENT CONF, DATA IN C1 C2

Mann-Whitney Confidence Interval and Test

   NORTH      N =   8     MEDIAN =       115.50
   SUNBELT    N =  15     MEDIAN =       106.00
   POINT ESTIMATE FOR ETA1-ETA2 IS       9.5004
   90.0  PCT C.I. FOR ETA1-ETA2 IS (    -6.0,      19.0)
   W =    112.0
   TEST OF ETA1 = ETA2  VS.  ETA1 N.E. ETA2 IS SIGNIFICANT AT  0.3171

   CANNOT REJECT AT ALPHA = 0.05
```

## Exercises 8.3

**8.6** Two groups of employees are trained to assemble a complex item by two different methods. Ten employees trained by each method are timed as they assemble the item. The following are summary data on the times required to complete the task.

| Method | Sample Size | Mean Time (minutes) | Standard Deviation |
|--------|-------------|---------------------|--------------------|
| X | 10 | 32.5 | 5.8 |
| Y | 10 | 37.6 | 6.4 |

**a.** Assuming normality and equal population variances, test

$$H_0: \mu_x = \mu_y \quad \text{versus} \quad H_1: \mu_x < \mu_y$$

using $\alpha = 0.05$.

**b.** Find a 95 percent confidence interval for $\mu_x - \mu_y$.

**c.** Does the confidence interval in part b contain zero? Does this result contradict your decision in part a?

**8.7** The typing speeds of 9 boys and 16 girls are sampled; the data are summarized below. Let $X$ represent the population of boys and $Y$ represent the population of girls. Assume that the data can be considered independent samples from two normal populations with the same variance.

| Sample | Number | Mean (w.p.m.) | Sum of Squares |
|--------|--------|---------------|----------------|
| Boys ($X$) | 9 | 36 | 24 |
| Girls ($Y$) | 16 | 38.5 | 68 |

*Note:* The values in the last column are $\sum_{i=1}^{9}(x_i - \bar{x})^2$ and $\sum_{j=1}^{16}(y_j - \bar{y})^2$.

**a.** Find the pooled estimate of the variance.

**b.** Test $H_0: \mu_x = \mu_y$ versus $H_1: \mu_y > \mu_x$, using $\alpha = 0.05$. State clearly the rejection region.

**c.** Find a 95 percent confidence interval for $\mu_y - \mu_x$.

**8.8** Independent random samples from normal populations with the same variance yielded the following data. The $X$ sample gives the scores of 12 freshmen on an English examination, and the $Y$ sample gives the scores of 18 sophomores on the same test.

| Sample | Number | Mean Score | Sum of Squares |
|--------|--------|------------|----------------|
| $X$ | 12 | 86 | 264 |
| $Y$ | 18 | 90 | 636 |

**a.** Find the estimate of the common variance.

**b.** Test $H_0: \mu_x = \mu_y$ versus $H_1: \mu_y > \mu_x$, using $\alpha = 0.05$. State clearly the rejection region.

**c.** Find a 90 percent confidence interval for $\mu_y - \mu_x$, the true mean difference between the scores of sophomores and freshmen in this experiment.

**8.9** Consider the two sets of estimates of a 60-second interval given in Chapter 7. After the first set was obtained, the individuals were told the results of their first trial (that is, the actual length of time of their first guess). The data are reprinted below.

Set 1:   25 30 35 35 40 42 42 45 45 51 53 53 60 65 67 68 68 70 75   90

Set 2:   20 23 35 42 44 45 45 46 47 49 51 54 62 65 70 70 70 80 89 138

Use Minitab to carry out the following.

**a.** Test $H_0: \mu_x = \mu_y$ versus $H_1: \mu_x \neq \mu_y$, using $\alpha = 0.05$. Use both the pooled $t$ test and the alternative two-sample test based on normal theory.

**b.** Use the Mann-Whitney test statistic to test $H_0: m_x = m_y$ versus $H_1: m_x \neq m_y$, using $\alpha = 0.05$.

**c.** Find 95 percent confidence intervals for $\mu_x - \mu_y$ and $m_x - m_y$.

**8.10** The following data give per capita personal income in 1978 in 15 sunbelt $(X)$ and 8 northern $(Y)$ states in dollars.

| Sunbelt State | Personal Income | Northern State | Personal Income |
|---|---|---|---|
| Alabama | 6291 | Illinois | 8903 |
| Arizona | 7372 | Indiana | 7706 |
| Arkansas | 5969 | Massachusetts | 7924 |
| California | 8927 | Michigan | 8483 |
| Florida | 7573 | New Jersey | 8773 |
| Georgia | 6705 | New York | 8224 |
| Louisiana | 6716 | Ohio | 7855 |
| Mississippi | 5529 | Pennsylvania | 7740 |
| New Mexico | 6574 | | |
| North Carolina | 6515 | | |
| Oklahoma | 7137 | | |
| South Carolina | 6288 | | |
| Tennessee | 6547 | | |
| Texas | 7730 | | |
| Virginia | 7671 | | |

*Source:* Bureau of Economic Analysis, U.S. Department of Commerce, as reported in *The Information Please Almanac* (Boston: Houghton Mifflin, 1980), p. 41.

Use Minitab to carry out the following.

**a.** Assuming equal population variances, use a normal theory test to test $H_0: \mu_x = \mu_y$ versus $H_1: \mu_x < \mu_y$, with $\alpha = 0.05$. Find a 95 percent confidence interval for the difference $\mu_y - \mu_x$.

**b.** Use the Mann-Whitney test statistic to test $H_0: m_x = m_y$ versus $H_1: m_x < m_y$, using $\alpha = 0.05$. Find a 95 percent confidence interval for $m_y - m_x$.

**8.11** The per capita debt (1978) for eight midwestern and eight eastern states is given below.

| Midwestern State | Per Capita Debt ($) | Eastern State | Per Capita Debt ($) |
|---|---|---|---|
| Illinois | 509.21 | Connecticut | 1152.79 |
| Indiana | 107.49 | Maine | 634.05 |
| Iowa | 128.45 | Massachusetts | 938.55 |
| Kansas | 193.81 | New York | 1302.29 |
| Michigan | 272.13 | New Jersey | 734.11 |
| Missouri | 146.21 | Pennsylvania | 549.66 |
| Nebraska | 33.46 | Rhode Island | 1267.92 |
| Ohio | 349.01 | Vermont | 1035.74 |

*Source:* Bureau of the Census and U.S. Commerce and Treasury Departments, as reported in *The World Almanac and Book of Facts*, 1981, p. 165.

Use Minitab to carry out the following.

**a.** There is little doubt that there is a difference in the per capita debt of these two areas. Find a 95 percent confidence interval for the average difference, using an appropriate normal theory statistic and assuming equal variances.

**b.** Find a 95 percent confidence interval for the difference in median per capita debt between eastern and midwestern states in 1978.

**8.12** Using the data on American League and National League batters given in Exhibits 2.10 and 2.11, carry out comparisons of these two groups of batters, using tests with $\alpha = 0.05$ and 95 percent confidence intervals for the variables hits, runs, and runs batted in. Justify your choice of statistical procedures for each variable. Use Minitab as needed.

**8.13** Compare the per capita personal income in the plains states $(X)$ and in the southeastern states $(Y)$, using the following information for 1980.

| Plains States | Per Capita Income ($) | Southeastern States | Per Capita Income ($) |
|---|---|---|---|
| Iowa | 9358 | Arkansas | 7268 |
| Kansas | 9983 | Florida | 8996 |
| Minnesota | 9724 | Georgia | 8073 |
| Missouri | 8982 | Kentucky | 7613 |
| Nebraska | 9365 | Louisiana | 8458 |
| North Dakota | 8747 | Mississippi | 6580 |
| South Dakota | 7806 | N. Carolina | 7819 |
| | | S. Carolina | 7266 |
| | | Tennessee | 7720 |
| | | Virginia | 9392 |
| | | West Virginia | 7800 |

*Source:* Bureau of Economic Analysis, U.S. Commerce Department, as reported in *The World Almanac and Book of Facts*, 1983, p. 126.

Use Minitab to carry out the following.

**a.** Use both a normal theory test statistic (assuming equal variances) and a distribution-free test statistic to test $H_0$: $\mu_x = \mu_y$ versus $H_1$: $\mu_x \neq \mu_y$, with $\alpha = 0.10$.

**b.** Use both types of statistics to find 95 percent confidence intervals for $\mu_x - \mu_y$ and $m_x - m_y$.

**8.14** Use Minitab to sample 50 observations from $X \sim N(50, 9)$ and 50 observations from $Y \sim N(55, 16)$. *Note:* $\sigma_x = 3$ and $\sigma_y = 4$.

**a.** Use the command TWOSAMPLE without the subcommand POOLED to test $H_0$: $\mu_x = \mu_y$ versus $H_1$: $\mu_x \neq \mu_y$ for these data, with $\alpha = 0.10$.

**b.** Use the subcommand POOLED to test the hypotheses in part a.

**c.** Find 90 percent confidence intervals for $\mu_y - \mu_x$ using both procedures. Do the intervals contain the true difference of $\mu_y - \mu_x = 5$?

**8.15** Use the Minitab command RANDOM to sample 12 observations from $X \sim N(100, 25)$ and 15 observations from $Y \sim N(100, 16)$.

**a.** Carry out tests of $H_0$: $\mu_x = \mu_y$ versus $H_1$: $\mu_x \neq \mu_y$ using both normal theory methods discussed in this section, with $\alpha = 0.10$.

**b.** Find 90 percent confidence intervals using both methods. Is the value zero in these intervals? Why is this relevant?

## Paired Comparisons

In the last section we compared the expectations of two populations under the assumption that *independent* random samples from the two populations were available. There are cases in which a comparison of population expectations is required, but the two random samples are not independent. In fact, often experiments are intentionally designed so that dependence is a result of the method by which the observations are selected. For example, suppose a company was interested in comparing the effectiveness of two different types of suntan lotion (say A and B) in preventing sunburn. It is known that individuals differ greatly in their susceptibility to sunburn. Thus a reasonable plan would be to select a number of individuals who are at present untanned and apply lotion A to one arm chosen at random and lotion B to the other arm. After a given period of time in the sun, measurements of the degree of sunburn on each arm would be made for each individual. These observations would not be independent because the arms would belong to the same person. The *difference* in the degrees of sunburn on the two arms of each individual would be the observation used to make conclusions about the effectiveness of the two lotions.

Thus we have $n$ paired observations, denoted by $(X_i, Y_i)$, $i = 1, 2, \ldots, n$. The first observation in each pair is a measurement of a particular individual's response to application of treatment 1 (lotion A), and the second observation is a measure of his or her response to treatment 2 (lotion B). The basic observations used for inference are the differences, $D_i = X_i - Y_i$, $i = 1, 2, \ldots, n$. For each $i$, we have

$$E(D_i) = E(X_i - Y_i) = E(X_i) - E(Y_i) = \mu_x - \mu_y = \mu_d$$

As before, the basic inferential task is to test the null hyothesis,

$$H_0: \mu_x - \mu_y = \mu_d = 0 \qquad \text{8.16}$$

and to find a confidence interval for $\mu_x - \mu_y = \mu_d$. We treat the $n$ differences as if they were $n$ observations from a single population. Hence, the tests and confidence intervals employed will be the one-sample tests and confidence intervals described in Chapters 6 and 7. Such a comparison of differences is referred to as a **paired** **comparison** or a comparison of matched pairs. If the number of differences is small, normality of the differences must be assumed. Tests and confidence intervals will be based on the $t$ distribution. If the number of differences is large ($n \geqslant 30$), the Central Limit Theorem permits use of the standard normal distribution $Z$ for such inference.

**paired comparison**

## Example 8.9

A hypothetical administrator from the University of Pennsylvania wished to determine whether there was a statistically significant difference between classroom use on Mondays and Wednesdays. He knew that use of the 138 rooms available varied greatly depending on the hour of the day. Table 8.7 presents information on the use of the available rooms for fall 1981.

**Table 8.7**

**Number of Rooms in Use by Time and Day for Fall 1981**

| Time | Monday | Wednesday | Difference |
|------|--------|-----------|------------|
| 9:00 | 89 | 95 | 6 |
| 10:00 | 129 | 133 | 4 |
| 11:00 | 121 | 128 | 7 |
| 12:00 | 105 | 107 | 2 |
| 1:00 | 94 | 95 | 1 |
| 2:00 | 103 | 112 | 9 |
| 3:00 | 78 | 86 | 8 |
| 4:00 | 59 | 80 | 21 |
| 5:00 | 35 | 46 | 11 |

*Source: University of Pennsylvania Almanac,* Vol. 29 (3), 1982.

Exhibit 8.5 shows the output generated when Minitab was used to carry out two analyses of these data. The numbers of rooms in use on Mondays during the hours 9:00–5:00 were set in Cl, and the corresponding numbers of rooms in use on Wednesday were set in C2. The differences (Wednesday − Monday) were set in C3. The matched-pairs analysis was carried out by means of the TTEST and TINTERVAL commands, using the differences in room use from C3. The second analysis, using the independent two-sample method of the previous section, was carried out by means of the TWOSAMPLE command, using the data in Cl and C2.

We first test

$$H_0: \mu_d = 0 \qquad \text{versus} \qquad H_1: \mu_d \neq 0$$

In the matched-pairs analysis of the data, the differences in room usage for each of the nine hours in C3 are considered to be a single sample. The test of the hypotheses above is carried out using the output from the TTEST command. The point estimate of $\mu_d$ is $\bar{d} = 7.67$ classrooms. The calculated value of the test statistic is $t = 3.86$ with 8 degrees of freedom. A 95 percent confidence interval for $\mu_d$ is (3.09, 12.25). The $p$-value of 0.0048 requires that $H_0: \mu_d = 0$ be *rejected* for any significance level $\alpha \geq 0.0048$, and hence for $\alpha = 0.05$ or $\alpha = 0.01$. The clear conclusion is that classroom usage is higher on Wednesdays than on Mondays.

The TWOSAMPLE command was also used with these data, in order to demonstrate that use of an inappropriate statistical analysis can lead to errors. The $t$ test of the hypotheses of the previous paragraph is based on a $v$-value of approximately 15.8 degrees of freedom. The calculated $t$ value is $-0.58$. The corresponding $p$-value of 0.57 suggests that the null hypothesis of no difference in average room usage should be retained. Also, the 95 percent confidence interval $(-35.9, 20.6)$ contains 0, indicating that $H_0: \mu_d = 0$ should not be rejected. The conclusion of the two-sample analysis is just the opposite of that of the matched-pairs analysis.

**Exhibit 8.5**

```
MTB > NOTE ROOM ASSIGNMENT DATA
MTB > SET C1
C1
    89     129     121     105     .    .    .

MTB > SET C2
C2
    95     133     128     107     .    .    .

MTB > LET C3 = C2 - C1
MTB > NAME C1 'MON' C2 'WED' C3 'DIFF'
MTB > PRINT C1-C3
 RQW    MON     WED     DIFF

   1     89      95       6
   2    129     133       4
   3    121     128       7
   4    105     107       2
   5     94      95       1
   6    103     112       9
   7     78      86       8
   8     59      80      21
   9     35      46      11


MTB > TTEST MU = 0 DATA IN C3

TEST OF MU = 0.00 VS MU N.E. 0.00

               N      MEAN    STDEV    SE MEAN       T    P VALUE
DIFF           9      7.67     5.96       1.99    3.86     0.0048

MTB > TINTERVAL WITH 95 PERCENT CONF DATA IN C3

               N      MEAN    STDEV   SE MEAN    95.0 PERCENT C.I.
DIFF           9      7.67     5.96      1.99  (    3.09,    12.25)

MTB > TWOSAMPLE T C1 C2

TWOSAMPLE T FOR MON VS WED
        N      MEAN    STDEV    SE MEAN
MON  9      90.3      29.6       9.9
WED  9      98.0      26.4       8.8

95 PCT CI FOR MU MON - MU WED: (-35.9, 20.6)
TTEST MU MON = MU WED (VS NE): T=-0.58 P=0.57 DF=15.8
```

One reason the two-sample analysis is inappropriate is that the estimated variance of the difference $\bar{X} - \bar{Y}$, $s_x^2/n_x + s_y^2/n_y$, is inflated because of varying classroom usage at different times during the day. The use of differences at each hour substantially reduces the effects of this variability. The variability itself is not of interest because the administrator already knows that classroom usage varies greatly at different hours of the day, and the reduction in the effects of this variability increases the precision of the estimate of $\mu_d$.

**Example 8.10**

The following data reflect enrollment in eight summer courses offered by an academic department in 1985 and 1986.

| Course | 1985 | 1986 |
|--------|------|------|
| 1 | 35 | 33 |
| 2 | 67 | 59 |
| 3 | 25 | 22 |
| 4 | 38 | 28 |
| 5 | 32 | 24 |
| 6 | 38 | 43 |
| 7 | 39 | 26 |
| 8 | 7 | 6 |

The faculty in the department is interested in knowing whether there was a significant change in course enrollment over these two years. The null hypothesis is that there was no difference—that is, $\mu_1 - \mu_2 = \mu_d = 0$. The Minitab output for the two types of analyses is shown in Exhibit 8.6, with the 1985 and 1986 enrollments for each of eight courses set in C1 and C2, respectively, and the eight differences (1985 − 1986) set in C3.

Using the inappropriate two-sample test, we get a $p$-value of 0.62 for testing $H_0: \mu_d = 0$ versus $H_1: \mu_d \neq 0$. The corresponding $t$ value is 0.62. This analysis strongly suggests retention of $H_0$. The implied conclusion is that there was no difference in enrollment between 1985 and 1986.

Using the differences between the two years and the single-sample procedure, we get $t = 2.44$. The $p$-value versus a two-sided alternative is 0.045. This value is much smaller than 0.62, suggesting that the null hypothesis is not strongly supported by the data. In fact, against the alternative $H_1: \mu_x > \mu_y$ we have a critical region of $t > t_{0.05,7} = 1.895$. The calculated $t = 2.44$ implies rejection of $H_0$ in favor of the one-sided alternative at the $\alpha = 0.05$ level of significance. This result also follows from calculation of the one-sided $p$-value of $0.045/2 = 0.0225$. The explanation of the differing conclusions arising from the two-sample and single-sample analyses is as in Example 8.9. The varying sizes of the classes produce a large unexplained estimated variance in the two-sample analysis.

---

Several important ideas are highlighted by the matched-pairs method of analysis. First, the investigator can play an important role in the design of a statistical study before data are gathered. By matching experimental units in pairs whose elements are as similar as possible, an investigator can increase the likelihood that an observed difference in responses is actually due to the different treatments. Second, uninformed use of an inappropriate statistical method can cause an investigator to go badly wrong in making inferences. Third, in reading reports containing statistical analyses of data, one must be on the alert for badly designed experimental studies and the use of inappropriate statistical techniques.

**Exhibit 8.6**

```
MTB > NOTE COURSE ENROLLMENT EXAMPLE
MTB > READ INTO C1-C3
      8 ROWS READ
 ROW   C1    C2    C3

   1    1    35    33
   2    2    67    59
   3    3    25    22
   4    4    38    28
   .    .    .

MTB > NAME C1 'COURSE' C2 '1985' C3 '1986'
MTB > LET C4 = C2 - C3
MTB > NAME C4 'DIFF'
MTB > PRINT C1-C4
 ROW   COURSE   1985   1986   DIFF

   1      1      35     33      2
   2      2      67     59      8
   3      3      25     22      3
   4      4      38     28     10
   5      5      32     24      8
   6      6      38     43     -5
   7      7      39     26     13
   8      8       7      6      1

MTB > TWOSAMPLE C2 C3

TWOSAMPLE T FOR 1985 VS 1986
        N      MEAN    STDEV   SE MEAN
1985    8      35.1    16.7      5.9
1986    8      30.1    15.7      5.5

95 PCT CI FOR MU 1985 - MU 1986: (-12.5, 22.5)
TTEST MU 1985 = MU 1986 (VS NE): T=0.62 P=0.55 DF=13.9

MTB > TTEST MU = 0 DATA IN C4

TEST OF MU = 0.00 VS MU N.E. 0.00

              N      MEAN    STDEV   SE MEAN       T    P VALUE
DIFF          8      5.00    5.81     2.05       2.44    0.045

MTB > TINT 95 PERCENT CONF DATA IN C4

              N      MEAN    STDEV   SE MEAN   95.0 PERCENT C.I.
DIFF          8      5.00    5.81     2.05    (  0.14,   9.86)
```

**8.16** The numbers of rooms being used each hour on Fridays at the University of Pennsylvania are given below.

| Time | 9:00 | 10:00 | 11:00 | 12:00 | 1:00 | 2:00 | 3:00 | 4:00 | 5:00 |
|------|------|-------|-------|-------|------|------|------|------|------|
| Rooms in Use | 83 | 133 | 131 | 107 | 83 | 63 | 21 | 15 | 3 |

*Source: University of Pennsylvania Almanac* 29, No. 3 (1982).

   **a.** Use this information, together with the information on room usage for Wednesdays given in Table 8.7, to find a point estimate for $\mu_x - \mu_y$. Let $X$ represent Wednesday and $Y$ represent Friday.

   **b.** Use both two-sample and Minitab single-sample methods to carry out a test of $H_0: \mu_x = \mu_y$ versus $H_1: \mu_x \neq \mu_y$ at level $\alpha = 0.10$. Which analysis is appropriate?

**8.17** The Associate Dean of Student Life at Iowa State University summarized the number of student misconduct cases at the university for 1981–1982 and 1982–1983 as follows:

| Class Standing | Year | |
|---|---|---|
| | 1981–1982 ($X$) | 1982–1983 ($Y$) |
| Freshman | 67 | 66 |
| Sophomore | 27 | 44 |
| Junior | 39 | 42 |
| Senior | 42 | 40 |
| Graduate Student | 10 | 11 |
| Totals | 185 | 203 |

*Source: Annual Report of Student Conduct Violations,* 1982–83, Office of Student Life, Iowa State University, 1983.

   **a.** Use the independent two-sample test to decide between $H_0: \mu_d = 0$ and $H_1: \mu_y - \mu_x = \mu_d > 0$, using $\alpha = 0.10$.

   **b.** Use the matched-pairs test to decide between the hypotheses in part a.

   **c.** Do the methods in parts a and b lead to the same decision?

**8.18** The data below give the gold reserves (in millions of ounces) in the banks of ten industrialized countries during 1979 and 1980.

| Country | 1979 | 1980 |
|---------|------|------|
| Belgium | 34.21 | 34.18 |
| Canada | 22.18 | 20.98 |
| France | 81.92 | 81.85 |
| Italy | 66.71 | 66.67 |
| Japan | 24.23 | 24.23 |
| Netherlands | 43.97 | 43.94 |
| Switzerland | 83.28 | 83.28 |
| U.K. | 18.25 | 18.84 |
| U.S. | 260.60 | 264.32 |
| W. Germany | 95.25 | 95.18 |

*Source: IMF, International Financial Statistics, as reported in The World Almanac and Book of Facts,* 1983, p. 122.

   Test the hypothesis that gold reserves in the central banks remained the same in these two years against the hypothesis that they decreased. Use $\alpha = 0.05$.

**8.19** The following data give the average life expectancy in 15 sunbelt states by gender for the years 1969–1971.

| State | Male | Female |
|---|---|---|
| Alabama | 64.90 | 73.41 |
| Arizona | 66.57 | 75.04 |
| Arkansas | 66.68 | 74.97 |
| California | 68.19 | 75.37 |
| Florida | 66.61 | 74.96 |
| Georgia | 64.27 | 73.01 |
| Louisiana | 64.85 | 72.88 |
| Mississippi | 64.06 | 72.40 |
| New Mexico | 66.51 | 74.51 |
| North Carolina | 64.94 | 73.78 |
| Oklahoma | 67.40 | 75.70 |
| South Carolina | 63.85 | 72.29 |
| Tennessee | 66.15 | 74.26 |
| Texas | 67.05 | 74.99 |
| Virginia | 66.26 | 74.17 |

*Source:* U.S. Department of Commerce, Bureau of the Census, *Statistical Abstract of the United States*, 1981.

**a.** Using TWOSAMPLE, find a 95 percent confidence interval for the difference $\mu_y - \mu_x$, where $\mu_y$ represents average life expectancy for women and $\mu_x$ the average life expectancy for men.

**b.** Find a 95 percent confidence interval for $\mu_y - \mu_x$, using TINTERVAL.

**c.** Which interval is shorter? Why?

**8.20** The following table gives the average salaries for male ($X$) and female ($Y$) civilians employed full-time in federal white-collar positions in 1981.

| Occupation | Men | Women | |
|---|---|---|---|
| Accountant | 31,261 | 24,593 | |
| Architect | 32,775 | 28,588 | |
| Attorney | 40,092 | 34,578 | |
| Chaplain | 31,948 | 16,789 | |
| Chemist | 33,684 | 27,310 | |
| Clerk/Typist | 11,703 | 11,593 | |
| Dental assistant | 13,653 | 13,560 | |
| Editor/Writer | 29,000 | 23,418 | |
| Editor, technical | 28,278 | 24,038 | |
| Engineer, civil | 33,197 | 24,417 | |
| Engineer, electrical | 33,084 | 26,482 | |
| Engineer, mechanical | 33,121 | 25,082 | |
| Law clerk | 23,164 | 23,187 | |
| Librarian | 30,728 | 27,473 | |
| Messenger | 10,277 | 10,906 | |
| Nurse | 21,498 | 22,840 | |
| Paralegal | 30,042 | 23,501 | (cont.) |

| Occupation | Men | Women |
|---|---|---|
| Personnel management | 33,306 | 26,868 |
| Pharmacist | 27,286 | 24,906 |
| Public relations | 33,531 | 26,654 |
| Purchasing | 17,022 | 15,723 |
| Secretary | 14,823 | 15,836 |
| Social work | 28,675 | 27,164 |
| Statistician | 33,817 | 28,770 |
| Technician | 17,011 | 15,819 |
| Therapist, occupational | 23,274 | 21,943 |
| Therapist, physical | 23,842 | 21,748 |

*Source:* Office of Personnel Management, October 31, 1981, as reported in *The World Almanac and Book of Facts*, 1983, p. 129.

**a.** Find a 95 percent confidence interval for $\mu_x - \mu_y$, using TWOSAMPLE.
**b.** Find a 95 percent confidence interval for $\mu_x - \mu_y$, using TINTERVAL.
**c.** Which confidence interval do you prefer? Why?

## 8.5

## Comparison of Population Proportions

*difference of two proportions*

It is often of interest to consider whether the proportion of individuals having a characteristic is the same in one population as in another. In Chapter 1 we considered the *New York Times*/CBS election poll regarding voter preference for the two major parties. In Table 1.1, the sample responses were broken down on the basis of sex, race, and other variables. Whereas 41 percent of prospective white voters favored the Republican Party, only 6 percent of the prospective black voters favored the Republicans. This difference would probably be large enough to convince most readers that there was a significant difference between races, even though the number of respondents in each group was not given. The statistics on gender differences were much less definitive, however: 41 percent of the men and 35 percent of the women favored the Republican Party. It is not clear whether this difference reflects a true difference between male and female preferences in the voting population. This section presents the statistical methods used to test $H_0: p_1 = p_2$, the null hypothesis that two population proportions are equal, against standard alternatives. We will also consider estimation of $p_1 - p_2$, the **difference of two proportions**, both with a point estimate and with a confidence interval.

First, however, we must define the statistics that will be used. Let us assume that there are two populations, in each of which there are some members with a given characteristic and some without it. We randomly sample $n_1$ observations from the first population and $n_2$ observations from the second. The random variables $X_1$ and $X_2$ are the numbers of observations in the samples from the first and second populations, respectively, having the given characteristic. The statistics

$$\hat{p}_1 = X_1/n_1 \quad \text{and} \quad \hat{p}_2 = X_2/n_2 \qquad \textbf{8.17}$$

are defined to be the sample proportions possessing the characteristic. Given that

$$X_1 \sim B(n_1, p_1) \quad \text{and} \quad X_2 \sim B(n_2, p_2)$$

that is, that both have the binomial distribution with the corresponding sample sizes and population proportions as the relevant parameters, we have

$$E(\hat{p}_1 - \hat{p}_2) = E(\hat{p}_1) - E(\hat{p}_2) = p_1 - p_2 \qquad \textbf{8.18}$$

Hence, the expectation of the difference between the sample proportions is an unbiased estimator of the difference between the true population proportions. We assume that $X_1$ and $X_2$ are independent, as in the two-sample situation of Section 8.2. For the estimated variance of the difference of the sample proportions we have

$$\begin{aligned}
\text{Var}(\hat{p}_1 - \hat{p}_2) &= \text{Var}(\hat{p}_1) + \text{Var}(\hat{p}_2) \\
&= \frac{p_1(1 - p_1)}{n_1} + \frac{p_2(1 - p_2)}{n_2}
\end{aligned} \qquad \textbf{8.19}$$

Consider the estimation of $p_1 - p_2$. It is clear that $\hat{p}_1 - \hat{p}_2$ is a natural point estimate. For sufficiently large $n_1$ and $n_2$, the standardized statistic

$$\frac{(\hat{p}_1 - \hat{p}_2) - (p_1 - p_2)}{\sqrt{p_1(1 - p_1)/n_1 + p_2(1 - p_2)/n_2}} \qquad \textbf{8.20}$$

has approximately a standard normal distribution, by extension of the Central Limit Theorem. The $(1 - \alpha)100$ percent confidence interval, obtained in the standard way, would have endpoints given by

$$\hat{p}_1 - \hat{p}_2 \pm \sqrt{\frac{p_1(1 - p_1)}{n_1} + \frac{p_2(1 - p_2)}{n_2}}\, z_{\alpha/2} \qquad \textbf{8.21}$$

As $p_1$ and $p_2$ are unknown, we obtain an approximate $(1 - \alpha)100$ percent confidence interval for $p_1 - p_2$ by using the endpoints

$$\hat{p}_1 - \hat{p}_2 \pm \sqrt{\frac{\hat{p}_1(1 - \hat{p}_1)}{n_1} + \frac{\hat{p}_2(1 - \hat{p}_2)}{n_2}}\, z_{\alpha/2} \qquad \textbf{8.22}$$

The procedure is analogous to the one-sample procedure of Section 5.4. As before in the estimation of variance, unknown population parameters are replaced by sample estimates. The question of how large $n_1$ and $n_2$ must be for the interval to be appropriate depends on the values of $p_1$ and $p_2$. If $0.1 \leqslant p_i \leqslant 0.9$, $i = 1, 2$, an interval for which $n_1 \geqslant 30$ and $n_2 \geqslant 30$ usually has approximately the correct confidence coefficient. For comparison of $p_1$ and $p_2$ when both are close to 0 or to 1, larger samples are required.

**Example 8.11**

_____

Let us compare the accuracy of two field goal kickers, using their 1983 season records as the available data. In that year Nick Lowrey scored field goals on 24 out of 30 attempts. Mark Mosely made field goals on 33 out of 47 attempts. (This information appeared in an article by Donald A. and Timothy D. Berry entitled

"The Probability of a Field Goal: Rating Kickers" which appeared in *The American Statistician* 39, No. 2 (1985): 154.) We will assume that $p_1$ and $p_2$ represent the long-run percentages of field goals made by Lowrey and Moseley. The fractions of successes observed are thus

$$\hat{p}_1 = \frac{24}{30} = 0.8 \quad \text{and} \quad \hat{p}_2 = \frac{33}{47} = 0.702$$

A point estimate for $p_1 - p_2$ is given by $\hat{p}_1 - \hat{p}_2 = 0.800 - 0.702 = 0.098$. Using Equation 8.22, we obtain the endpoints of a 95 percent confidence interval for $p_1 - p_2$:

$$0.800 - 0.702 \pm \sqrt{\frac{(0.8)(0.2)}{30} + \frac{(0.702)(0.298)}{47}} \, (1.96)$$

$$= 0.098 \pm 0.194$$

The confidence interval is thus $(-0.096, 0.292)$. As this interval contains the value zero, we conclude that there is no statistically evident difference in the field-goal-kicking proficiency of these two players.

## Example 8.12

The Alfred B. Nobel Prize has been awarded since 1901 for contributions in the fields of chemistry, literature, peace, physics, and physiology (or medicine). Of a total of 98 recipients or co-recipients of the Nobel Prize for chemistry, 25 have been from the United States. Of 80 awards in literature, 9 have been to individuals from the United States. Letting $p_1$ represent the long-run proportion of recipients of Nobel Prizes in chemistry who come from the United States and $p_2$ represent the corresponding proportion of recipients of prizes in literature, we find that

$$\hat{p}_1 - \hat{p}_2 = 0.255 - 0.112 = 0.143$$

A 95 percent confidence interval for $p_1 - p_2$ has endpoints given by $0.143 \pm 0.111$. The interval is $(0.032, 0.254)$, which suggests that a greater proportion of chemistry prize winners than literature prize winners come from the United States.

In the testing situation,

$$H_0: p_1 = p_2 = p \quad (p \text{ unknown}) \tag{8.23}$$

is tested against standard alternatives, which are listed in Table 8.8 along with appropriate critical regions for $\alpha$-level tests. The test statistic is derived from

$$Z = \frac{\hat{p}_1 - \hat{p}_2}{\sqrt{p(1-p)/n_1 + p(1-p)/n_2}}$$

which has approximately a standard normal distribution for large $n_1$ and $n_2$. The

**Table 8.8**

---

**Critical Regions for Tests of the Equality of Two Proportions**

| Alternative | Critical Region |
|---|---|
| $p_1 > p_2$ | $Z \geqslant z_\alpha$ |
| $p_1 < p_2$ | $Z \leqslant -z_\alpha$ |
| $p_1 \neq p_2$ | $|Z| \geqslant z_{\alpha/2}$ |

---

unknown common value of $p$ is estimated by

$$\hat{p} = \frac{X_1 + X_2}{n_1 + n_2}$$

the fraction of successes in the combined sample. This type of pooled estimate of $p$ is appropriate *under* $H_0$, which assumes that $p_1$ and $p_2$ are equal. Hence the calculated value is

$$Z = \frac{\hat{p}_1 - \hat{p}_2}{\sqrt{\hat{p}(1 - \hat{p})(1/n_1 + 1/n_2)}} \qquad\qquad \textbf{8.24}$$

**Example 8.13**

---

In 1981 two former Notre Dame players, Joe Montana and Joe Theisman, were playing quarterback in the National Football League. Montana completed 311 of 488 passes and Theisman 293 of 496. Let us test the hypothesis that completion percentages are the same for the two athletes.

$$\hat{p}_1 = 0.637 \qquad \hat{p}_2 = 0.591$$

$$\hat{p} = \frac{311 + 293}{488 + 496} = \frac{604}{984} = 0.614$$

$$Z = \frac{0.637 - 0.591}{\sqrt{(0.614)(0.386)(1/488 + 1/496)}}$$

$$= 1.482$$

Against a two-sided alternative, the $p$-value is $2P(Z \geqslant 1.482) = 0.138$. Hence at levels $\alpha = 0.05$ and $0.10$ we would retain $H_0$: $p_1 = p_2$. There is insufficient statistical evidence to conclude that a true difference in completion rates exists between these two passers.

---

**Example 8.14**

Members of the Department of Statistics at Iowa State University collected the following data on grades in an introductory business statistics course and an introductory engineering statistics course.

| Course | Number of Students | Number of A Grades |
|---|---|---|
| Business Statistics | 571 | 82 |
| Engineering Statistics | 156 | 25 |

The null hypothesis that the proportion of A grades in the two courses is equal can be tested by calculating

$$\hat{p}_1 = \frac{82}{571} = 0.1436 \qquad \hat{p}_2 = \frac{25}{156} = 0.1603$$

$$\hat{p} = \frac{82 + 25}{571 + 156} = 0.1472$$

$$Z = \frac{0.1436 - 0.1603}{\sqrt{(0.1472)(0.8528)(1/571 + 1/156)}}$$

$$= -0.52$$

Against a two-sided alternative, the p-value is $2P(Z \leqslant -0.52) = 0.6030$. The null hypothesis, $H_0: p_1 = p_2$, would not be rejected at any reasonable level of significance. It appears that the proportion of A's does not differ significantly in the two courses.

**Exercises 8.5**

**8.21** Al Oliver won the National League batting championship in 1982 with 204 hits in 617 at bats. The runner-up was Bill Madlock, with 181 hits in 568 at bats. (*Source: World Almanac*, 1983, p. 904.)
  **a.** Find a 95 percent confidence interval for $p_1 - p_2$, where $p_1$ and $p_2$ are the theoretical averages for these two hitters.
  **b.** Test $H_0: p_1 = p_2$ versus $H_1: p_1 \neq p_2$ at level $\alpha = 0.05$.

**8.22** In 1982 in the National Basketball Association, Artis Gilmore made 546 of 837 field goal attempts and Kareem Abdul Jabbar made 753 of 1301 attempts. (*Source: World Almanac*, 1983, pp. 842–43.) Let $p_1$ and $p_2$ be the percentages of field goals made by the two players. Answer the questions in exercise 8.21 for these data.

**8.23** The information in the table on page 316 was presented in an article on an animal husbandry experiment.
  **a.** Find a 95 percent confidence interval for $p_1 - p_2$.
  **b.** Find a 95 percent confidence interval for $p_3 - p_2$.
  **c.** Using $\alpha = 0.05$, test $H_0: p_2 = p_3$ versus $H_1: p_3 > p_2$.

| | Number of Conceptions | Number of Services |
|---|---|---|
| Bull 1 | $x_1 = 42$ | $n_1 = 101$ |
| Bull 2 | $x_2 = 36$ | $n_2 = 69$ |
| Bull 3 | $x_3 = 77$ | $n_3 = 135$ |

*Source:* Joel C. Kelinman, "Proportions with Extraneous Variance: Single and Independent Samples," *Journal of the American Statistical Association* 68 (1973): 52.

**8.24** Suppose that two difficult problems appear on a college entrance examination. On one administration of the examination, 12 percent of 500 students answer the first difficult problem correctly. On another administration of the examination, 18 percent of 400 students answer the second difficult problem correctly. Let $p_1$ and $p_2$ be the theoretical proportions of students who answer the corresponding questions correctly.
**a.** Using $\alpha = 0.05$, test $H_0: p_1 = p_2$ versus $H_1: p_1 \neq p_2$.
**b.** Find a 90 percent confidence interval for $p_2 - p_1$.

**8.25** The following data give the numbers of individuals in the United States who are of Mexican and Cuban origin.

| Origin | Number | Percent Male |
|---|---|---|
| Mexican | 10,269,000 | 51.1 |
| Cuban | 1,036,000 | 48.7 |

*Source: Current Population Survey, 1983,* U.S. Department of Commerce, Bureau of Census.

**a.** Let $p_1$ represent the proportion of males of Mexican origin and $p_2$ the proportion of males of Cuban origin. Test $H_0: p_1 = p_2$ versus $H_1: p_1 \neq p_2$ at a level of significance of $\alpha = 0.01$.
**b.** Find a 95 percent confidence interval for $p_1 - p_2$.

**8.26** An ethnographic analysis revealed the following information about students enrolled in 1971 and 1984 in Field High School, near San Francisco.

| Year | Total Number of Students | Number of Students with Spanish Surnames |
|---|---|---|
| 1971 | 2507 | 847 |
| 1984 | 2377 | 1357 |

*Source:* Maria E. Matute-Bianchi, "Ethnic Identities and Patterns of School Success and Failure among Mexican-Descent and Japanese-American Students in a California High School: An Ethnographic Analysis," *American Journal of Education,* November (1986), 233–255.

**a.** Let $p_1$ be the proportion of students with Spanish surnames in 1971 and $p_2$ the proportion of such students in 1984. Test $H_0: p_1 = p_2$ versus $H_1: p_1 < p_2$, using $\alpha = 0.05$.
**b.** Find a 95 percent confidence interval for $p_1 - p_2$. What appears to be happening over time to the proportion of students at Field High School with Spanish surnames?

**8.27** In 1975, 488 of 3922 permits for new construction in Iowa were issued in the university towns of Ames and Iowa City. In 1979, the number was 294 of 3338. (*Source: Statistical Profile of Iowa, 1981*, Iowa Development Commission, Des Moines, 1981, p. 80.)

**a.** Test the hypothesis that the proportion of new construction in Iowa in the two university cities was the same in 1979 as it had been in 1975 against the alternative that this proportion decreased. Use $\alpha = 0.05$.

**b.** Find a 95 percent confidence interval for the change in the proportion (1975 less 1979).

**8.28** The total number of male births and the total number of births in Australia during 1975 and 1979 are given below.

| Year | Births | Male Births |
|------|--------|-------------|
| 1975 | 233,012 | 119,850 |
| 1979 | 223,132 | 114,616 |

*Source: Year Book 1981, Australia, Australia Bureau of Statistics, Canberra, 1981, p. 94.*

Test $H_0: p_1 = p_2$ versus $H_1: p_1 \neq p_2$, where $p_1$ is the proportion of male births in 1975 and $p_2$ the proportion of male births in 1979. Use $\alpha = 0.05$.

**8.29** Of 40 persons suffering from a disease, 20 are cured within two weeks with the conventional treatment. With a new treatment, 40 of 49 persons with the disease are cured within two weeks. Find a 95 percent confidence interval for the increase in the proportion cured within two weeks with the new treatment.

**8.30** Suppose 10 of 100 workers on a day shift have accidents during a year and 18 of 120 workers on a night shift have accidents during the same time period. Is there statistical evidence ($\alpha = 0.05$) that more accidents occur on the night shift than on the day shift? Carry out the test versus a one-sided alternative.

## 8.6

**Comparison of Population Variances**

In Sections 8.2, 8.3, and 8.4, the locations of two random variables were compared. It is also frequently important to test whether two populations differ in terms of variability. Figure 8.3 presents the density functions of two random variables with the same expectation ($\mu_x = \mu_y$). The fact that its density function is more "spread out" about the common expectation indicates that the random variable $Y$ is more variable than $X$. A practical situation in which the variance is crucial is the filling of containers in a manufacturing process. It is important that the variation of the fill be kept as small as possible, so that the fraction of under-filled containers produced is not substantial. The manufacturer would much prefer that the distribution of the fillings look like that of the random variable $X$ in Figure 8.3 rather than that of $Y$. Another situation in which it is important to compare the variance of two random variables is the testing of $\mu_x = \mu_y$ in the normal case. Table 8.3 gave

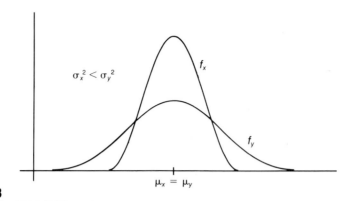

**Figure 8.3**

Densities of X and Y with $\mu_x = \mu_y$ but $\sigma_x^2 < \sigma_y^2$

the appropriate critical regions for $\sigma_x^2 = \sigma_y^2$, and Table 8.4 gave the appropriate critical regions for $\sigma_x^2 \neq \sigma_y^2$. It is thus natural to want to test the null hypothesis $H_0: \sigma_x^2 = \sigma_y^2$ versus $H_1: \sigma_x^2 \neq \sigma_y^2$ in the normal case before carrying out a test for equality of expectations.

Before we consider the question of tests of hypotheses about the variances of two normal populations and the estimation of $\sigma_x^2/\sigma_y^2$, however, it is necessary to introduce one further distribution related to the chi-square random variable: the

*F distribution*     **F distribution**. The $F$ distribution was named after Sir Ronald Fisher (1890–1962), one of the most distinguished statistical thinkers of this century.

---

**Definition 8.2** ▌━━━━━━━━━━━━━━━━━━━━━━━━━━━━━━━━━━━━━━

The random variable that is equal to the ratio of two independent chi-square random variables each divided by its degrees of freedom,

$$\frac{\chi_m^2/m}{\chi_n^2/n} \;=\; F(m, n)$$

*F random variable*     is called the **F random variable** with $m$ and $n$ degrees of freedom.

---

The $F$ distribution is extremely important in statistics. It is a two-parameter family of distributions, with one random variable defined for each pair of parameters. The parameters are called the numerator and denominator degrees of freedom (indicated as $m$ and $n$ in Definition 8.2). Probability density functions for the $F$ distribution are similar to that of the chi-square random variable. Like the chi-square random variable, the $F$ random variable can take on only positive values, as it is a ratio of two chi squares divided by positive integers. Two probability density functions for $F$ random variables are given in Figure 8.4. The expectation

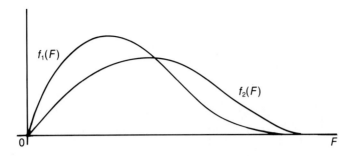

**Figure 8.4**

**Typical F Densities**

and variance of an $F$ random variable are given by

$$E[F(m, n)] = \frac{n}{n - 2} \qquad \textbf{8.25}$$

and

$$\text{Var}[F(m, n)] = \frac{2n^2[1 + (n - 2)/m]}{(n - 2)^2(n - 4)} \qquad \textbf{8.26}$$

It is not necessary to memorize these formulas. Note, however, that as $n$ becomes large, the expectation of $F$ approaches 1. This trend can be verified intuitively—the denominator of $F(m, n)$, $\chi_n^2/n$, approaches 1 for large $n$, and thus $F(m, n)$ behaves like the numerator, $\chi_m^2/m$, which has an expectation equal to 1.

Table IV of Appendix C gives values of the $F(m, n)$ random variable that are exceeded with probabilities 0.05 and 0.01 for various combinations of values of $m$ and $n$. For example, we find from Table IV of Appendix C that

$$P[F(3, 5) \geqslant F_{0.05}(3, 5)] = P[F(3, 5) \geqslant 5.41] = 0.05$$

Also,

$$P[F(5, 3) \geqslant F_{0.05}(5, 3)] = P[F(5, 3) \geqslant 9.01] = 0.05$$

It is clear that the order of the parameters $m$ and $n$ makes a difference. The 95th percentile for the $F(3, 5)$ distribution is 5.41, whereas for the $F(5, 3)$ distribution it is 9.01. This should not be too surprising, as Equation 8.25 gives

$$E[F(3, 5)] = \frac{5}{5 - 2} = \frac{5}{3}$$

and

$$E[F(5, 3)] = \frac{3}{3 - 2} = 3$$

Given that the expectation of the latter distribution is more than one unit to the right of that of the former, it is consistent to find that the right-tail percentile points of the $F(5, 3)$ distribution lie to the right of the corresponding points of the $F(3, 5)$ distribution.

It is also possible to use Table IV of Appendix C to obtain values of the $F(m, n)$ random variable exceeded with probabilities 0.95 and 0.99, because the reciprocal of an $F(m, n)$ variable is clearly an $F(n, m)$ random variable (note the reversed degrees of freedom). This result, which is an immediate consequence of Definition 8.2, is expressed in the following sequence of equivalent probability statements.

$$P\left(F(m, n) \geqslant \frac{1}{F_{0.05}(n, m)}\right) = P\left(\frac{1}{F(n, m)} \geqslant \frac{1}{F_{0.05}(n, m)}\right)$$
$$= P[F(n, m) \leqslant F_{0.05}(n, m)] \qquad \textbf{8.27}$$
$$= 0.95$$

Hence $1/F_{0.05}(n, m)$, the *reciprocal* of the upper 5th percentile of the $F$ distribution *with n and m degrees of freedom*, is exceeded with probability 0.95 by the $F(m, n)$ random variable. Thus,

$$F_{0.95}(m, n) = \frac{1}{F_{0.05}(n, m)} \qquad \textbf{8.28}$$

and similarly,

$$F_{0.99}(m, n) = \frac{1}{F_{0.01}(n, m)} \qquad \textbf{8.29}$$

For example,

$$F_{0.95}(3, 5) = \frac{1}{F_{0.05}(5, 3)} = \frac{1}{9.01} = 0.111$$

and similarly,

$$F_{0.95}(5, 3) = \frac{1}{F_{0.05}(3, 5)} = \frac{1}{5.41} = 0.185$$

Now let us consider testing the null hypothesis $H_0: \sigma_x^2 = \sigma_y^2$ in the case of random samples from $X \sim N(\mu_x, \sigma_x^2)$ and $Y \sim N(\mu_y, \sigma_y^2)$. The samples will be assumed to be independent and to have sizes $n_x$ and $n_y$, respectively. From Theorem 7.1 it is known that

$$\frac{(n_x - 1)S_x^2}{\sigma_x^2} \sim \chi^2 \text{ with } n_x - 1 \text{ degrees of freedom}$$

and

$$\frac{(n_y - 1)S_y^2}{\sigma_y^2} \sim \chi^2 \text{ with } n_y - 1 \text{ degrees of freedom}$$

Dividing each of the these independent chi squares by its degrees of freedom,

## Table 8.9

**Critical Regions for a Test of Equality of Two Variances**

| Alternative | Critical Region |
|---|---|
| $\sigma_x > \sigma_y$ | $F \geqslant F_\alpha(n_x - 1, n_y - 1)$ |
| $\sigma_x < \sigma_y$ | $F \leqslant F_{1-\alpha}(n_x - 1, n_y - 1)$ |
| $\sigma_x \neq \sigma_y$ | $F \leqslant F_{1-\alpha/2}(n_x - 1, n_y - 1)$ or |
| | $F \geqslant F_{\alpha/2}(n_x - 1, n_y - 1)$ |

$(n_x - 1)$ and $(n_y - 1)$, respectively, yields

$$\left(\frac{S_x^2}{\sigma_x^2}\right) \bigg/ \left(\frac{S_y^2}{\sigma_y^2}\right) \sim F(n_x - 1, n_y - 1) \qquad\qquad 8.30$$

In other words, this ratio has an $F$ distribution with $(n_x - 1)$ and $(n_y - 1)$ degrees of freedom. Under $H_0$: $\sigma_x = \sigma_y$, but not otherwise, this ratio reduces to

$$\frac{S_x^2}{S_y^2} \sim F(n_x - 1, n_y - 1) \qquad\qquad 8.31$$

that is, the ratio of the sample variances. Under $H_0$, $S_x^2/S_y^2$ has an $F$ distribution with the degrees of freedom indicated in Equation 8.31. The critical regions given in Table 8.9 are appropriate for the indicated alternatives for $\alpha$-level tests of the null hypothesis,

$$H_0: \sigma_x^2 = \sigma_y^2 \qquad \text{or, equivalently,} \qquad H_0: \sigma_x = \sigma_y \qquad\qquad 8.32$$

## Example 8.15

Using the data of Example 8.4 on the Masters Tournament, consider testing

$$H_0: \sigma_x^2 = \sigma_y^2 \qquad \text{versus} \qquad H_1: \sigma_x^2 \neq \sigma_y^2$$

prior to a $t$ test for the comparison of the expectations of these two populations, assuming normality. For these two samples the following values were observed:

$$n_x = 23 \qquad S_x^2 = (3.39)^2 = 11.492$$
$$n_y = 22 \qquad S_y^2 = (4.32)^2 = 18.662$$

The appropriate critical region for an $\alpha = 0.02$ level test (using interpolation in the $F$ table) is

$$F \leqslant F_{0.99}(22, 21) = \frac{1}{F_{0.01}}(21, 22) = \frac{1}{2.81} = 0.356$$

or

$$F \geqslant F_{0.01}(22, 21) = 2.84$$

The computed value of $F$ is $11.492/18.662 = 0.616$, which satisfies neither of these inequalities. Hence we retain $H_0$: $\sigma_x^2 = \sigma_y^2$, which suggests that the pooled $t$ test is reasonable for these data.

## Example 8.16

Consider the data on National and American League batters hitting 0.300 or more in 1980, shown in Exhibits 2.10 and 2.11. The data on runs appear to be symmetrically distributed, so we test

$$H_0: \sigma_x^2 = \sigma_y^2 \quad \text{versus} \quad H_1: \sigma_x^2 \neq \sigma_y^2$$

assuming normality. For the American League batters, $n_x = 25$ and $s_x = 22.7$. For the National League batters, $n_y = 19$ and $s_y = 20.6$. If the *larger* sample variance is placed in the *numerator* of the calculated $F$ statistic, we need only compare this value with the right-tailed value from the $F$ distribution. In that case,

$$F = \frac{(22.7)^2}{(20.6)^2} = 1.21$$

and from Table IV we find that the right-tailed value that defines the critical region is

$$F \geq F_{0.05}(24, 18) = 2.15$$

As $F$ does not exceed 2.15, we retain $H_0: \sigma_x^2 = \sigma_y^2$. The significance level for the test, however, is $2(0.05) = 0.10$, as this test is carried out against a two-sided alternative.

---

It is a straightforward matter to find a confidence interval for $\sigma_x^2/\sigma_y^2$ for samples from two independent normal populations. The endpoints for a $(1 - \alpha)100$ percent confidence interval are given by

$$\frac{[F_{1-\alpha/2}(n_y - 1, n_x - 1)]S_x^2}{S_y^2} \quad \text{and} \quad \frac{[F_{\alpha/2}(n_y - 1, n_x - 1)]S_x^2}{S_y^2} \qquad \textbf{8.33}$$

You will be asked to justify these endpoints in exercise 8.33. Because of the limited nature of the tables available in this book, the confidence coefficient should be chosen to be 0.90 or 0.98 or, equivalently, $\alpha = 0.10$ or $\alpha = 0.02$.

## Example 8.17

A 90 percent confidence interval for $\sigma_x^2/\sigma_y^2$ for the Masters Tournament data has endpoints

$$\frac{[F_{0.95}(21, 22)]s_x^2}{s_y^2} \quad \text{and} \quad \frac{[F_{0.05}(21, 22)]s_x^2}{s_y^2}$$

or

$$(0.482)(0.616) = 0.297 \quad \text{and} \quad (2.06)(0.616) = 1.269$$

---

CHAPTER 8  **TWO-SAMPLE COMPARISONS**

**Example 8.18**

In Example 8.16, $\sigma_x^2$ represented the true variance of runs scored for American League batters and $\sigma_y^2$ represented the true variance for National League batters. From Equation 8.33 we see that a 90 percent confidence interval for $\sigma_x^2/\sigma_y^2$ is given by the endpoints

$$\frac{[F_{0.95}(24,\ 18)]s_x^2}{s_y^2} \quad \text{and} \quad \frac{[F_{0.05}(24,\ 18)]s_x^2}{s_y^2}$$

or

$$\frac{(1/2.15)(22.7)^2}{(20.6)^2} \quad \text{and} \quad \frac{(2.06)(22.7)^2}{(20.6)^2}$$

The interval is thus given by

$$(0.565,\ 2.502)$$

A word of caution is in order about using $F$ tests to compare variances before doing $t$ tests. It is known that the $F$ test is highly affected by nonnormality, whereas the $t$ test is much less affected. When sample sizes are small, it is not easy to check on the normality assumption, which must hold if the $F$ test is to be reliable. Thus it may be better not to use $t$ if gross nonnormality is suspected or if nothing is known about the distribution that generated the data. If you are reasonably certain about the normality, use $t$ in whichever form (pooled or unpooled variances) is appropriate, as indicated by an $F$ test.

**Exercises 8.6**

**8.31** Find the values of the following:
  **a.** $F_{0.05}(3,\ 7)$  **b.** $F_{0.05}(7,\ 3)$
  **c.** $F_{0.01}(2,\ 6)$  **d.** $F_{0.01}(6,\ 2)$

**8.32** Find the values indicated:
  **a.** $F_{0.95}(3,\ 7)$  **b.** $F_{0.95}(7,\ 3)$
  **c.** $F_{0.99}(2,\ 6)$  **d.** $F_{0.99}(6,\ 6)$

**8.33** Show that the endpoints for a $(1 - \alpha)100$ percent confidence interval for $\sigma_x^2/\sigma_y^2$ are given by Expression 8.33.

**8.34** Use the data from Example 8.3 on the mean breaking strength of two different types of cable.
  **a.** Test $H_0: \sigma_x^2 = \sigma_y^2$ versus $H_1: \sigma_x^2 \neq \sigma_y^2$, using $\alpha = 0.10$.
  **b.** Does the use of the pooled $t$ test appear to be reasonable in testing $H_0: \mu_x = \mu_y$ versus $H_1: \mu_x \neq \mu_y$? Why?

**8.35** Use the data in exercise 8.6 on the assembly times of ten employees taught by two methods.
  **a.** Test $H_0: \sigma_x^2 = \sigma_y^2$ versus $H_1: \sigma_x^2 \neq \sigma_y^2$. Use $\alpha = 0.02$.
  **b.** Find a 98 percent confidence interval for $\sigma_x^2/\sigma_y^2$.

**8.36** **a.** Using the data on boys' and girls' typing speeds from exercise 8.7, test $H_0: \sigma_x^2 = \sigma_y^2$ versus $H_1: \sigma_x^2 \neq \sigma_y^2$, using $\alpha = 0.10$ and assuming normality.
**b.** Find a 90 percent confidence interval for $\sigma_x^2/\sigma_y^2$.

**8.37** **a.** Use the data of exercise 8.8 to test $H_0: \sigma_x^2 = \sigma_y^2$ versus $H_1: \sigma_x^2 \neq \sigma_y^2$, using $\alpha = 0.02$. Here $\sigma_x^2$ is the variance of freshman scores and $\sigma_y^2$ the corresponding variance for sophomores.
**b.** Find a 98 percent confidence interval for $\sigma_x^2/\sigma_y^2$.

**8.38** Use the per capita income data from exercise 8.10 to test $H_0: \sigma_x^2 = \sigma_y^2$ versus $H_1: \sigma_x^2 \neq \sigma_y^2$, with $\alpha = 0.10$.

**8.39** Show that the square roots of the endpoints given by Equation 8.33 provide the endpoints of a $(1 - \alpha)100$ percent confidence interval for $\sigma_x/\sigma_y$.

**8.40** Find confidence intervals for $\sigma_x/\sigma_y$ in the following cases.
**a.** For the data of exercise 8.36 with a 90 percent confidence coefficient.
**b.** For the data of exercise 8.37 with a 98 percent confidence coefficient.

## Summary

The comparison of corresponding parameters of two populations is based on random samples from the two populations. In statistics such comparisons are referred to as two-sample problems.

Two-sample problems can involve the comparison of the locations of two populations. There are several methods appropriate for testing $H_0: \mu_x = \mu_y$ (or $m_x = m_y$) and finding confidence intervals for $\mu_x - \mu_y$ (or $m_x - m_y$). The size and normality or nonnormality of a sample will determine which testing method is appropriate. In the large-sample case, the normality of the statistic $\bar{X} - \bar{Y}$, guaranteed by the Central Limit Theorem, provides tests and confidence intervals analogous to the one-sample cases of Chapters 5 and 6. In the small-sample case where normality can be assumed, Student's $t$ distribution is the basis for tests and confidence intervals analogous to those of Chapter 7. When normality cannot be assumed, nonparametric procedures based on the Wilcoxon rank sum statistic permit inference to be carried out for location in the two-sample case. In the latter case comparisons are made between population medians.

In one type of designed experiment, the experimental units are grouped in pairs, and the experimental units within the pairs are made as similar as possible with respect to extraneous characteristics that might influence the response to the two treatments. An experimenter then observes the difference in the responses of the paired units to the two treatments. Single-sample procedures can be used with the observed differences, in this case to test $H_0: \mu_d = \mu_x - \mu_y = 0$ and to find a confidence interval for $\mu_d$.

There are methods for comparing two population proportions $p_1$ and $p_2$. For cases in which $n_1 \geqslant 30$ and $n_2 \geqslant 30$, there are procedures for finding critical regions for tests of $H_0: p_1 = p_2$ against standard alternatives and confidence intervals for $p_1 - p_2$. These procedures are quite naturally based on the corresponding sample proportions $\hat{p}_1$ and $\hat{p}_2$. The Central Limit Theorem justifies the use of the standard normal distribution for these inferential methods.

The $F$ distribution is used to test the equality of the variances $\sigma_x^2$ and $\sigma_y^2$ of two normal populations. The ratio of the sample variances, $S_x^2/S_y^2$, is the appropriate statistic for carrying out such tests. The $F$ distribution can be used to find a confidence interval for $\sigma_x^2/\sigma_y^2$. The $F$ distribution is very important in statistics; its fundamental use is in the comparison of the theoretical variances of two normal populations.

## Key Words

| | |
|---|---|
| approximate degrees of freedom | observational study |
| designed experiment | paired comparison |
| difference of two expectations | pooled estimate of variance |
| difference of two medians | ranks |
| difference of two proportions | self-selection bias |
| $F$ distribution | treatment differences |
| $F$ random variable | two-sample procedures |
| Mann-Whitney statistic | Wilcoxon rank sum test |

## Minitab Commands

MANN-WHITNEY          TWOSAMPLE

# Chapter 9

# Categorical Data

## 9.1

**Introduction**

*categorical data*
*count data*
*enumerative data*

In many situations the data obtained are in the form of a number of observations, which fall into certain categories. Such data are referred to variously as **categorical data**, **count data**, and **enumerative data**. A simple example of categorical data is provided by the binomial distribution. The binomial random variable yields a count of the number of successes, $X$, in $n$ independent trials. In this case there are only two categories, success and failure. The numbers falling into the two categories are given by

Successes: $X$ and Failures: $n - X$

In other cases there may be more than two categories. For example, observations of a production process might be divided by quality into three groups: nondefectives, seconds, and defectives. The production of a certain item on a given shift will yield $n_1$ nondefectives, $n_2$ seconds, and $n_3$ defectives, where $n_1 + n_2 + n_3 = n$, the total number of items produced on the shift.

Measurement scales may be classified by level of precision. At the lower levels of precision the observations are naturally recorded as counts. The four types of measurement scales, by level of precision, are the nominal, ordinal, interval, and ratio scales.

---

**Definition 9.1** ▰▰▰▰

*nominal scale*

If observations in a sample are measured with respect to a quality, the measurement scale is called a **nominal scale**.

---

Classification of items into "successes" and "failures" is an example of the use of a nominal scale. Classification of individuals by eye color (blue, brown, and green) is another example of the use of a nominal scale. No ordering is implied by these categories.

Measurements are often made on the basis of a scale that allows the observations to be ordered according to a particular quality. Such a scale is said to be ordinal.

---

**Definition 9.2** ▬▬▬▬▬▬▬▬▬▬▬▬▬▬▬▬▬▬▬▬▬▬▬▬▬

ordinal scale | If observations in a sample are measured using a scale that allows all pairs of items to be compared with respect to a certain quality, the measurement scale is called an **ordinal scale.**

---

Advanced placement examinations given to high school students are graded on a scale of 1 to 5, with 5 being the highest score. This is an example of an ordinal scale. Frequently the integers $1, 2, 3, \ldots, k$ are used to represent an ordinal scale, with $k$ representing either the highest or the lowest score. For example, the eight horses in a horse race might be ranked in the order in which they finished the race, $1, 2, \ldots, 8$. Although the rankings are meaningful in an ordinal scale, the differences between the numbers are not. For example, the fact that the difference between the ranks of the third and first horses is the same as the difference between the eighth and sixth horses (2) does not imply a meaningful relationship. There is no implication that the third horse differs from the first in the same way as the eighth does from the sixth. The integers $2, 4, 6, \ldots, 16$ could just as well be used to order the finishers. Further, the second horse is not one-half as good as the first horse, so ratios have no meaning on an ordinal scale. Such a scale permits only the ordering of any two elements with regard to the quality or characteristic of interest.

Two other measurement scales that provide greater precision of measurement than nominal and ordinal scales are the interval and ratio scales.

---

**Definition 9.3** ▬▬▬▬▬▬▬▬▬▬▬▬▬▬▬▬▬▬▬▬▬▬▬▬▬

interval scale | If observations in a sample are measured using a scale in which the differences between elements are meaningful, the measurement scale is called an **interval scale**.

---

**Definition 9.4** ▬▬▬▬▬▬▬▬▬▬▬▬▬▬▬▬▬▬▬▬▬▬▬▬▬

ratio scale | If observations in a sample are measured using an interval scale that has a natural origin or zero point, the scale is called a **ratio scale**.

---

A frequently used interval scale is the Fahrenheit scale for temperature. The difference of 5°F between 45°F and 50°F is meaningful and is thought of as equivalent to the difference of 5°F between 55°F and 60°F. There is no natural zero for this scale, however, as temperatures can range below 0°F.

The U.S. scale for the measurement of lengths uses inches and feet. This scale has a natural zero value, as nothing can have a length of less than zero. Also, a board that is two feet long is twice as long as a board that is one foot long, so ratios have meaning. Thus this scale is a ratio scale.

Observations on a nominal or an ordinal scale are often categorized into groups, and the number of observations in each category is observed. Observations on an interval or ratio scale are not so obviously categorized, but frequently the scale is divided into nonoverlapping intervals to form groups. For example, grouping was done in the case of the stock yield data presented in Table 2.1.

## Example 9.1

Consider the data given in Table 9.1 concerning the number of intellectually gifted students who withdrew from Penn State University. The subjects were 80 students who scored at or above the 90th percentile in tests of intelligence and changed their majors following enrollment at Penn State. These students were categorized by whether they withdrew after changing their major and by whether the change in major was "positive" (in a direction indicated as desirable by the Strong Vocational Interest Test). Ten of the students who withdrew made a "positive" change, and eleven made a "negative" change. Forty-six of the students who remained for four years made a "positive" change, and thirteen made a "negative" change. The measurement scale in this case is a nominal one, resulting in the four categories of Table 9.1. One question of interest is whether there is a relationship between students' remaining enrolled and the direction of curriculum change. For example, do the data suggest that students who make a "positive" change have a greater likelihood of staying in college?

## Table 9.1

**Curriculum Change and Withdrawal from College by Bright Students**

| Status | Direction of Curriculum Change | |
| --- | --- | --- |
| | Positive | Negative |
| Withdrew | 10 | 11 |
| Remained | 46 | 13 |

*Source:* Lois Adams, unpublished master's thesis, 1955, as reported in Sidney Siegel, *Nonparametric Statistics for the Behavioral Sciences* (New York: McGraw-Hill, 1956).

## Example 9.2

Another example of categorical data is the number of observations of a continuous random variable falling into adjacent nonoverlapping classes in a frequency table. Such data are often used to carry out a statistical test of whether the original data came from a specified distribution. In Table 9.2 the 49 failure times of Example 5.9 are classified into six nonoverlapping classes. Can we conclude from these counts that the assumption that the parent population is normal should be rejected?

This chapter will present methods that can be used to address the types of questions asked in the preceding examples.

## Table 9.2

**Failure Times**

| Failure Time | $0 < t \leqslant 50$ | $50 < t \leqslant 100$ | $100 < t \leqslant 150$ |
|---|---|---|---|
| Observations | 18 | 10 | 6 |
| Failure Time | $150 < t \leqslant 200$ | $200 < t \leqslant 250$ | $t > 250$ |
| Observations | 8 | 3 | 4 |

## Exercises 9.1

**9.1** Identify the measurement scale implied by each of the following:
   **a.** The classification of books into groups by the Library of Congress.
   **b.** The assignment of grades A, B, C, D, and F to student performances.
   **c.** The measurement of the heights of males in inches.
   **d.** The ordering of wines on the basis of dryness.
   **e.** The measurement of atmospheric pressure in inches of mercury.
   **f.** The measurement of the volume of water in a tank in cubic feet.
   **g.** The categorizing of individuals by sex.
   **h.** The categorizing of naval officers by rank.

**9.2** Give four examples of measurements made on an ordinal scale.

**9.3** Give four examples of measurements made on a nominal scale.

**9.4** Give five examples of measurements made on a ratio scale.

## 9.2

**The Multinomial Distribution and Elementary Tests for Categorical Data**

It is useful to have a probability model for the number of observations falling into each of $k$ mutually exclusive classes. Such a model is given by the **multinomial random variable**, for which it is assumed that

1   A total of $n$ **independent trials** are made.
2   At each trial an observation will fall into exactly one of $k$ mutually exclusive classes.
3   The probabilities of falling into the $k$ classes are $p_1, p_2, \ldots, p_k$, where $p_i$ is the probability of falling into class $i$, $i = 1, 2, \ldots, k$. These probabilities are constant for all trials, with $\Sigma_{i=1}^{k} p_i = 1$.

**multinomial random variable**

**independent trials**

If $k = 2$, we have the binomial situation. Let us define $X_1$ to be the number of type 1 outcomes in the $n$ trials, $X_2$ to be the number of type 2 outcomes, $\ldots$, and $X_k$ to be the number of type $k$ outcomes. As there are $n$ trials,

$$\sum_{i=1}^{k} X_i = n \qquad \qquad 9.1$$

The joint probability function for these random variables can be shown to be

$$P(X_1 = x_1, X_2 = x_2, \ldots, X_k = x_k) = \left( \frac{n!}{x_1! x_2! \cdots x_k!} \right) p_1^{x_1} p_2^{x_2} \cdots p_k^{x_k}$$

$$9.2$$

where again $\Sigma_{i=1}^{k} x_i = n$. We shall not need Equation 9.2 very often. Note, however, that for $k = 2$ the probability function reduces to

$$P(X_1 = x_1, X_2 = n - x_1) = \binom{n}{x_1} p_1^{x_1} (1 - p_1)^{n - x_1} \qquad 9.3$$

which is the binomial probability of $x_1$ successes in $n$ trials, each with probability of success $p_1$. Notice also that if there are $x_1$ successes in the case where $k = 2$, the number of outcomes of type 2 is $n - x_1$ (that is, the number of failures in the $n$ trials). Thus, in general, when the values of the first $(k - 1)$ $X_i$ random variables are known, the last is determined.

## Example 9.3

A simple example of multinomial trials is the tossing of a die $n$ times. At each trial the outcome is one of the values 1, 2, 3, 4, 5, or 6. Here $k = 6$. If $n = 10$, the probability of 2 ones, 2 twos, 2 threes, no fours, 2 fives, and 2 sixes is

$$\frac{10!}{2! 2! 2! 0! 2! 2!} \left( \frac{1}{6} \right)^2 \left( \frac{1}{6} \right)^2 \left( \frac{1}{6} \right)^2 \left( \frac{1}{6} \right)^0 \left( \frac{1}{6} \right)^2 \left( \frac{1}{6} \right)^2 = 0.001875$$

Generally, attention will be directed not to the individual probabilities that can be found using Equation 9.2, but instead to testing hypotheses concerning the $p_i$. For example, the null hypothesis for this example,

$$H_0: p_1 = p_2 = \cdots = p_6 = \frac{1}{6}$$

states that the die is fair. We would like to find a procedure for testing such a hypothesis against the alternative,

$$H_1: H_0 \text{ is false}$$

which, of course, means that the die is not fair.

---

From the assumptions concerning the multinomial random variable given earlier in this section, we can conclude that the *individual* random variables $X_i$ are binomially distributed with parameters $n$ and $p_i$. This is because at each trial there occurs an event that has a probability of $p_i$ of being of type $i$ and a probability of $1 - p_i$ of being of another type. The trials are independent, and $X_i$ counts the number of type $i$ occurrences in the $n$ trials. In the case of a fair die, each of the $X_i$ has distribution $B(n, 1/6)$. Because of the general form of the expectation of a binomial random variable, $E(X_i) = np_i$, $i = 1, 2, \ldots, k$. Another important distributional fact is that under the assumptions given earlier,

$$\sum_{i=1}^{k} \frac{(X_i - np_i)^2}{np_i} \; \dot\sim \; \chi^2_{k-1} \qquad\qquad \textbf{9.4}$$

that is, this random variable has approximately a chi-square distribution with $k - 1$ degrees of freedom. The left-hand side of Equation 9.4 can be thought of as the sum of the terms

$$\sum_{i=1}^{k} \frac{(\text{observed number} - \text{expected number})^2}{\text{expected number}}$$

where the observed number is the number of observations in a class and the expected number is the number expected for the same class, with the sum taken over the $k$ classes. This distributional fact will not be proved but will be used in testing

$$H_0: p_1 = p_1^*, \ldots, p_k = p_k^* \qquad \text{versus} \qquad H_1: H_0 \text{ is false} \qquad \textbf{9.5}$$

where the $p_i^*$ are hypothesized values of the $p_i$. An example will help clarify the nature of tests of this type.

## Example 9.4

Suppose there is doubt that the Minitab command RANDOM is in fact producing the integers 0, 1, 2, . . . , 9 with equal probability. This hypothesis can be tested easily using the output from the RANDOM command. The following is a summary of 1000 integers obtained from RANDOM.

**Exhibit 9.1**

```
MTB > NOTE RANDOM SAMPLE OF 1000 INTEGERS FROM 0,1,2,...,9
MTB > BASE = 6000
MTB > RANDOM 1000 OBSERVATIONS IN C1;
SUBC> UNIFORM A = 0 B = 1.
MTB > HISTOGRAM C1;
SUBC> START WITH 0.05;
SUBC> INCREMENT = 0.1.

Histogram of C1   N = 1000
Each * represents 5 obs.

Midpoint   Count
   0.050     105   *********************
   0.150      97   *******************
   0.250     102   *********************
   0.350      89   ******************
   0.450     107   **********************
   0.550     111   ***********************
   0.650      85   *****************
   0.750     115   ***********************
   0.850      96   *******************
   0.950      93   *******************
```

| Integer | 0 | 1 | 2 | 3 | 4 | 5 | 6 | 7 | 8 | 9 |
|---|---|---|---|---|---|---|---|---|---|---|
| Observed | 105 | 97 | 102 | 89 | 107 | 111 | 85 | 115 | 96 | 93 |
| Expected | 100 | 100 | 100 | 100 | 100 | 100 | 100 | 100 | 100 | 100 |

The Minitab output, including a histogram of these values, appears in Exhibit 9.1.

We want to test

$$H_0: p_i = \frac{1}{10}, i = 0, 1, 2, \ldots, 9 \qquad \text{versus} \qquad H_1: H_0 \text{ is false}$$

The null hypothesis states that each of the integers $0, 1, 2, \ldots, 9$ is equally likely, a property one would wish for from a random number generator. We compute the statistic

$$\chi^2 = \sum_{i=0}^{9} \frac{(x_i - np_i^*)^2}{np_i^*} = 8.44$$

using $n = 1000$ and $p_i^* = 1/10$, $i = 0, 1, 2, \ldots, 9$. If $H_0$ is true, this value will be a single observation from the chi-square distribution with $k - 1 = 10 - 1 = 9$ degrees of freedom. If $H_0$ is false, the true $p_i$ will not all be equal to $1/10$ and the computed **chi-square statistic** will tend to be large (positive) because the observed numbers in the classes will not be close to the common expected value of

chi-square statistic

$$np_i^* = 1000 \left(\frac{1}{10}\right) = 100$$

From Table III of Appendix C, an appropriate critical region for an $\alpha = 0.05$ level test is

$$\chi^2 \geqslant \chi^2_{\alpha,k-1} = \chi^2_{0.05,9} = 16.919$$

Because the computed value of 8.44 is less than 16.919, at significance level $\alpha = 0.05$ the decision is to retain the null hypothesis, $H_0$, which implies that RANDOM has been producing the integers 0, 1, 2, . . . , 9 with equal probability.

Example 9.4 shows that the following equation defines a critical region for testing the null hypothesis and alternative stated in Equation 9.5:

$$\chi^2 \geqslant \chi^2_{\alpha,k-1} \tag{9.6}$$

## Example 9.5

Consider testing the validity of the hypothetical probabilities of a four-, five-, six-, and seven-game World Series suggested in Section 3.5—namely, $P(4) = 1/8$, $P(5) = 1/4$, and $P(6) = P(7) = 5/16$. These probabilities are based on the assumptions that the outcomes of the individual games are independent and that the teams are of equal ability. The observed lengths of 79 series (1903–1986) are given in Table 9.3, along with the expected numbers of four-, five-, six-, and seven-game series.

## Table 9.3

**World Series Lengths (1903–1986)**

|  | Number of Games | | | | |
|---|---|---|---|---|---|
|  | 4 | 5 | 6 | 7 | Total |
| Observed | 13 | 19 | 17 | 30 | 79 |
| Expected | 9.875 | 19.75 | 24.6875 | 24.6875 | 79 |

*Source:* Adapted from *The Information Please Almanac* (Boston: Houghton Mifflin, 1986), pp. 930–932.

The computed value of chi-square is

$$\chi^2 = \frac{(13 - 9.875)^2}{9.875} + \frac{(19 - 19.75)^2}{19.75} + \frac{(17 - 24.6875)^2}{24.6875}$$

$$+ \frac{(30 - 24.6875)^2}{24.6875}$$

$$= 4.55$$

As $\chi^2 < \chi^2_{0.05,3} = 7.815$, this test suggests that there is no reason to reject these hypothetical probabilities. In other words, we could retain the probabilities given in Section 3.5 and use them as a tentative model for the length of World Series.

**test of $H_0: p = p^*$**   In the special case of $k = 2$, there are only two possible outcomes at each trial, which can be called success and failure. A **test of $H_0: p = p^*$** is a test of the same null hypothesis ($H_0: p = p_0$) that was considered in Chapter 6. The following are observed and expected values for this situation:

|          | Success | Failure     | Total |
|----------|---------|-------------|-------|
| Expected | $np^*$  | $n(1 - p^*)$ | $n$   |
| Observed | $X$     | $n - X$     | $n$   |

(Note that the subscript 1 has been dropped from $X_1$, as it is not needed.) The computed value of chi-square is

$$\chi^2 = \frac{(X - np^*)^2}{np^*} + \frac{[(n - X) - n(1 - p^*)]^2}{n(1 - p^*)}$$

$$= \left(\frac{(X - np^*)^2}{n}\right)\left(\frac{1}{p^*} + \frac{1}{1 - p^*}\right)$$

$$= \frac{(X - np^*)^2}{np^*(1 - p^*)}$$

$$= \frac{(\hat{p} - p^*)^2}{p^*(1 - p^*)/n} \tag{9.7}$$

which is the square of the $Z$ statistic of Section 6.4. For an $\alpha$-level test, a rejection region for testing $H_0: p = p^*$ versus $H_1: p \neq p^*$ is given by

$$\chi^2 \geqslant \chi^2_{\alpha,1}$$

## Example 9.6

Consider testing the null hypothesis that in the United States male and female births occur with equal probability. In 1975 there were 3,144,198 births in the United States, of which 1,613,135 were male births. Calculation shows that $n/2 = 1,572,099$ and $n(1/2)(1/2) = 786,049.5$. Use of the next-to-last line of Equation 9.7 yields

$$\chi^2 = \frac{(1,613,135 - 1,572,099)^2}{786,049.5} = 2142.3$$

This extremely large value of $\chi^2$ leads to the conclusion that the assumption that $p = 1/2$ for male births is not correct. As observed in Chapter 3, the proportion of male births in the United States exceeds that of female births. To three significant figures, the actual proportion of male births for the period 1950–1980 is 0.513.

In the case of $k = 2$, we can denote the computed value of a test statistic by the subscript c. From Equation 9.7 we see that

$$\chi^2_c = Z^2_c \tag{9.8}$$

where $Z_c$ is the computed value of the test statistic of Section 6.4. (Note that the hypothesized value of $p$ under $H_0$ is written here as $p^*$ and in Section 6.4 as $p_0$.) One might ask whether these two tests can lead to different conclusions in testing

$$H_0: p = p^* \quad \text{versus} \quad H_1: p \neq p^* \qquad\qquad 9.9$$

From Definition 7.5 we know that $Z^2$ has a chi-square distribution with *one* degree of freedom. Hence

$$\alpha = P(|Z| \geqslant z_{\alpha/2}) = P(Z^2 \geqslant z_{\alpha/2}^2) = P(\chi^2 \geqslant z_{\alpha/2}^2)$$

where $\chi^2$ has one degree of freedom. By definition, however,

$$P(\chi^2 \geqslant \chi_{\alpha,1}^2) = \alpha$$

As the chi-square distribution with one degree of freedom has only one upper $\alpha$th percentile point, we have

$$\chi_{\alpha,1}^2 = z_{\alpha/2}^2 \qquad\qquad 9.10$$

Using $Z_c^2 = \chi_c^2$, we see that

$$|Z_c| \geqslant z_{\alpha/2} \quad \text{if and only if} \quad \chi_c^2 \geqslant z_{\alpha/2}^2 = \chi_{\alpha,1}^2 \qquad\qquad 9.11$$

The equivalence in Equation 9.11 means that an $\alpha$-level test of the hypotheses in Equation 9.9 will always yield the same conclusion, whether the chi-square test of this section or the $Z$ test of Section 6.4 is used.

In chi-square tests of the type considered in this chapter, the expected number of observations in a class should be made large enough to ensure that the chi-square approximation in Equation 9.4 is reasonably good. A typical rule of thumb is to combine adjacent classes until the expected number in each class is at least five. There is evidence that this rule is rather conservative, but it will be used in this chapter.

**Exercises 9.2**

---

**9.5** A die is tossed 120 times with the following outcomes:

| Face | 1 | 2 | 3 | 4 | 5 | 6 |
|---|---|---|---|---|---|---|
| Observed | 19 | 16 | 24 | 26 | 17 | 18 |

Test the hypothesis that the die is fair, using $\alpha = 0.05$.

**9.6** As noted before, Mendelian theory predicts that for simple traits the offspring of hybrid crosses will display the dominant trait three-fourths of the time and the recessive trait one-fourth of the time. For a certain flower, the color green is dominant and the color white is recessive. Among 1000 hybrid offspring, there are 725 with green flowers and 275 with white flowers. Are these data sufficient to cast doubt on the applicability of this genetic theory for this trait? Use $\alpha = 0.05$.

**9.7** An employer believes that absences from work are twice as likely on Mondays and Fridays as on other days. The distribution of 200 days missed by employees is given below:

| Day | M | T | W | Th | F |
|---|---|---|---|---|---|
| Observed Absences | 50 | 30 | 35 | 30 | 55 |

**a.** Test the null hypothesis that there is equal probability that an absence will occur on each day of the week. Use $\alpha = 0.05$.
**b.** Test the employer's hypothesis, using $\alpha = 0.05$.

**9.8** Of the 40 individuals who were president of the United States before January 1, 1984, 27 were born in the period from October to March and 13 were born in the months from April to September. Test the null hypothesis that presidents were equally likely to be born in each of these periods. Use $\alpha = 0.05$.

**9.9** Many horse racing enthusiasts are of the opinion that the post position of a horse has an effect on whether the horse wins a race. In order to investigate this question, information was gathered on 160 races, in each of which there were eight starting horses. The number of winners from each of the post positions is shown below.

| Post Position | 1 | 2 | 3 | 4 | 5 | 6 | 7 | 8 |
|---|---|---|---|---|---|---|---|---|
| Number of Winners | 25 | 27 | 18 | 16 | 12 | 21 | 22 | 19 |

**a.** Find the expected number of winners from each of the post positions if each is considered equally likely to produce a winner.
**b.** Test the null hypothesis that post position does not determine the winner of a horse race. Use $\alpha = 0.05$.

**9.10** The total number of Ph.D.s in statistics granted in the United States over the years 1972–1981 is as follows.

| Year | 1972 | 1973 | 1974 | 1975 | 1976 | 1977 | 1978 | 1979 | 1980 | 1981 |
|---|---|---|---|---|---|---|---|---|---|---|
| Number of Ph.D.s | 213 | 252 | 221 | 234 | 246 | 247 | 289 | 232 | 227 | 250 |

*Source:* Donald S. Moore and Ingram Olkin, "Academic Statistics: Growth, Change and Federal Support," *The American Statistician* 38, No. 1 (1984): 2.

Test the null hypothesis that the rate of graduation of Ph.D. statisticians has been the same over this ten-year period. Use $\alpha = 0.01$.

**9.11** Use the World Series data of this section to test the null hypothesis that series of four, five, six, and seven games are equally probable. That is, test $p_4 = p_5 = p_6 = p_7 = 1/4$, using $\alpha = 0.10$.

**9.12** A total of 73 major railroad wrecks that occurred between 1876 and 1977 have been classified by the quarter of the year in which they occurred.

| Quarter | Jan.–Mar. | April–June | July–Sept. | Oct.–Dec. |
|---|---|---|---|---|
| Number of Wrecks | 19 | 6 | 30 | 18 |

*Source:* Adapted from reports of the Office of Safety, Federal Railroad Administration, as reported in *The World Almanac and Book of Facts*, 1983, p. 749.

Does a chi-square test suggest that there is a "quarterly effect" for these wrecks?

**Table 9.4**

| Opinion on ERA | | | | |
|---|---|---|---|---|
| Sex | Favors | Opposes | Neutral (No Opinion) | Totals |
| Female | $X_{11}$ | $X_{12}$ | $X_{13}$ | $R_1$ |
| Male | $X_{21}$ | $X_{22}$ | $X_{23}$ | $R_2$ |
| Totals | $C_1$ | $C_2$ | $C_3$ | $n$ |

## 9.3
## Contingency Tables

contingency table

In many cases data can be classified into categories on the basis of two criteria. In Table 9.1, 80 Penn State students were classified by direction of curriculum change and whether they withdrew or remained enrolled. Similarly, respondents to a survey on a political issue such as the ERA amendment might be classified on the basis of sex and opinion on the ERA amendment: in favor, opposed, or neutral (no opinion). After the number of individuals in each of the six classifications had been counted, the data could be displayed in a **contingency table** of two rows and three columns, such as Table 9.4. The number of females in the sample who favor the ERA amendment is represented by the random variable $X_{11}$ (row class 1, column class 1). The number of males in the sample who are neutral on the ERA amendment is denoted by $X_{23}$ (row class 2, column class 3). The values $R_i$, $i = 1, 2$, and $C_j$, $j = 1, 2, 3$, are the two row sums and the three column sums, respectively. Hence, $R_1$ is the total number of females in the sample and $C_2$ is the number of those in the sample who oppose the ERA amendment.

row criteria
column criteria

In a contingency table the statistical question is whether the **row criteria** and **column criteria** are independent. The null and alternative hypotheses are

$H_0$: The row and column criteria are independent.

$H_1$: The row and column criteria are associated.

association

In this example it is natural to suspect that there is an **association** between opinion on the ERA amendment and sex. Although it may not be the case, one would assume that the proportion of females favoring the ERA amendment would exceed the corresponding proportion of males. If so, sex and opinion on the ERA are associated and not independent.

## Example 9.7

In Table 9.5 the 50 states are classified in columns according to geographical region (North and Central, South, and West). The states are also classified according to growth in population during the decade from 1970 to 1980. The first row class contains those states that had either a percentage loss in population or a gain of less than 15 percent during the decade. The second row class contains those states that experienced a population growth of 15 percent or more during the decade. Most of us would assume that Table 9.5 would reflect the geographical shift of

## Table 9.5

**States by Region and Population Change**

| Population Change 1970–1980 | Region | | | Totals |
|---|---|---|---|---|
| | North & Central | South | West | |
| Less than 15% gain | 18 | 7 | 1 | 26 |
| Gain of 15% or more | 3 | 9 | 12 | 24 |
| Totals | 21 | 16 | 13 | 50 |

*Source:* Department of Commerce, Bureau of the Census, as reported in *The Information Please Almanac* (Boston: Houghton Mifflin, 1982), p. 755.

cross classifications

population that occurred during the 1970–1980 decade, and that this shift would be indicated by an association between the row and column criteria. Such **cross classifications** and their analysis will be considered next.

Consider a contingency table with $r$ rows and $c$ columns. The number of elements in the sample that are observed to fall into row class $i$ and column class $j$ is denoted by $X_{ij}$. The row sum for the $i$th row is $R_i = \Sigma_{j=1}^{c} X_{ij}$, and the column sum for the $j$th column is $C_j = \Sigma_{i=1}^{r} X_{ij}$. The total number of observations in the entire table is $n = \Sigma_{i=1}^{r} R_i = \Sigma_{j=1}^{c} C_j$. The contingency table for the general case is given in Table 9.6. There are several probabilities of importance associated with the table. The probability of an element's being in row class $i$ and column class $j$ in the population is denoted by $p_{ij}$. The probability of being in row class $i$ is denoted by $p_{i.}$, and the probability of being in column class $j$ is denoted by $p_{.j}$. Null and alternative hypotheses regarding the **independence** of these probabilities would be

## Table 9.6

**The General $r \times c$ Contingency Table**

$$
\begin{array}{ccccccc|c}
X_{11} & X_{12} & \cdots & X_{1j} & \cdots & X_{1c} & & R_1 \\
X_{21} & X_{22} & \cdots & X_{2j} & \cdots & X_{2c} & & R_2 \\
\cdot & \cdot & & \cdot & & \cdot & & \cdot \\
\cdot & \cdot & \cdots & \cdot & \cdots & \cdot & & \cdot \\
\cdot & \cdot & & \cdot & & \cdot & & \cdot \\
X_{i1} & X_{i2} & \cdots & X_{ij} & \cdots & X_{ic} & & R_3 \\
\cdot & \cdot & & \cdot & & \cdot & & \cdot \\
\cdot & \cdot & \cdots & \cdot & \cdots & \cdot & & \cdot \\
\cdot & \cdot & & \cdot & & \cdot & & \cdot \\
X_{r1} & X_{r2} & \cdots & X_{rj} & \cdots & X_{rc} & & R_r \\
\hline
C_1 & C_2 & \cdots & C_j & \cdots & C_c & & n
\end{array}
$$

stated as follows:

$$H_0: p_{ij} = p_{i.}p_{.j} \quad \text{for all pairs } (i, j)$$
$$H_1: H_0 \text{ is false} \tag{9.12}$$

That $H_0$ is a correct statement of independence follows from Definition 3.12 for the independence of two events. $H_1$ means that there is some form of association between the row and column criteria of classification.

As $p_{ij}$, $p_{i.}$, and $p_{.j}$ are all unknown, it is necessary to estimate these probabilities. The parameters $p_{i.}$ and $p_{.j}$ are estimated using the "natural" estimates

$$\hat{p}_{i.} = \frac{R_i}{n}, i = 1, 2, \ldots, r \quad \text{and} \quad \hat{p}_{.j} = \frac{C_j}{n}, j = 1, 2, \ldots, c \tag{9.13}$$

Under the hypothesis of independence, $p_{ij} = (p_{i.})(p_{.j})$, so $p_{ij}$ would be estimated by

$$\hat{p}_{ij} = \hat{p}_{i.}\hat{p}_{.j} = \left(\frac{R_i}{n}\right)\left(\frac{C_j}{n}\right) \tag{9.14}$$

**expected number of observations in cell $(i, j)$** The **expected number of observations in cell $(i, j)$** is $E_{ij} = np_{ij}$. *Under the null hypothesis*, $H_0$, the estimate of $E_{ij}$ is

$$\hat{E}_{ij} = n\hat{p}_{i.}\hat{p}_{.j} = \frac{R_i C_j}{n} \tag{9.15}$$

In order to test the hypothesis of Equation 9.12, the chi-square statistic is computed as

$$\chi^2 = \sum_{i=1}^{r} \sum_{j=1}^{c} \frac{(X_{ij} - \hat{E}_{ij})^2}{\hat{E}_{ij}} \tag{9.16}$$

As before, we can conclude that $H_0$ is false if the computed value of $\chi^2$ is too large, because the $\hat{E}_{ij}$ have been estimated assuming independence. If the assumption of independence is not justified, some of the $X_{ij}$ should be far from the corresponding $\hat{E}_{ij}$ values. The actual critical region is given by

$$\chi^2 \geq \chi^2_{\alpha,(r-1)(c-1)} \tag{9.17}$$

**degrees of freedom** The critical region is determined by the upper $\alpha$th percentile of the chi-square random variable with $v = (r-1)(c-1)$ **degrees of freedom.** A reason for this will be given at the end of this section.

## Example 9.8

Using the data in Table 9.5, the $\hat{E}_{ij}$ may be calculated for $i = 1, 2$ and $j = 1, 2, 3$. For example, $\hat{E}_{11} = (21)(26)/50 = 10.92$. Table 9.7 gives the required $\hat{E}_{ij}$ values. The calculated value of the chi-square statistic is

$$\frac{(18 - 10.92)^2}{10.92} + \frac{(7 - 8.32)^2}{8.32} + \frac{(1 - 6.76)^2}{6.76} + \frac{(3 - 10.08)^2}{10.08} + \frac{(9 - 7.68)^2}{7.68}$$
$$+ \frac{(12 - 6.24)^2}{6.24} = 20.22$$

**Table 9.7**

$\hat{E}_{ij}$ **Values for the Data of Table 9.5**

|        | $j = 1$ | $j = 2$ | $j = 3$ | Totals |
|--------|---------|---------|---------|--------|
| $i = 1$ | 10.92   | 8.32    | 6.76    | 26     |
| $i = 2$ | 10.08   | 7.68    | 6.24    | 24     |
| Totals | 21      | 16      | 13      | 50     |

For an $\alpha = 0.01$ level test, the critical region would be

$$\chi^2 \geq \chi^2_{0.01,2} = 9.21$$

The value 20.22 is clearly in the critical region, giving strong statistical evidence for a relationship between region and population change in the United States during the decade 1970–1980.

---

Notice that the row sums and column sums for the table of $\hat{E}_{ij}$ values are the same in Table 9.5 and Table 9.7. This will always be the case for tables of the $X_{ij}$ and $\hat{E}_{ij}$. Proof of this fact is left as an optional exercise.

## Minitab Analysis of a Contingency Table

CHISQUARE

Exhibit 9.2 shows the output generated when the Minitab command **CHISQUARE** was used to analyze the data in Table 9.5. The data of this table were read into the first two rows of C1, C2, and C3.

The value of the chi-square statistic and the correct degrees of freedom were printed out by Minitab. The output also gives the individual components of the chi-square computations. This information is useful because those cells that make a large contribution to the computed chi-square statistic provide information about the nature of the association between the variables. In the case of the data on population change, cells (1, 1), (1, 3), (2, 1), and (2, 3) make substantial contributions to the chi-square statistic. This is because a much larger number of North and Central states had below-average population gains than would be predicted by the independence assumption. Correspondingly, a much larger number of states in the West had above-average population gains than independence would suggest.

**Example 9.9**

---

A study comparing the automobile safety records of urban and rural drivers was based on a random sample of 613 drivers in Wisconsin, who were classified by residence (rural/urban); the categories are shown in Table 9.8. The urban drivers lived in cities with populations of at least 150,000. The drivers in the sample were

**Exhibit 9.2**

```
MTB > NOTE ANALYSIS OF REGIONAL DATA FOR POPULATION MOVEMENT 1970-80
MTB > READ TABLE INTO C1-C3
      2 ROWS READ
 ROW    C1    C2    C3

   1    18     7     1
   2     3     9    12

MTB > CHISQUARE ANALYSIS FOR DATA IN C1-C3

Expected counts are printed below observed counts

              C1        C2        C3     Total
    1         18         7         1        26
            10.9       8.3       6.8

    2          3         9        12        24
            10.1       7.7       6.2

 Total        21        16        13        50

ChiSq =    4.59 +    0.21 +    4.91 +
           4.97 +    0.23 +    5.32 = 20.22
df = 2
```

**Table 9.8**

|  | Place of Residence | | |
| Accidents | Urban | Rural | |
| --- | --- | --- | --- |
| 0 | 29 | 32 | 61 |
| 1+ | 247 | 305 | 552 |
| Totals | 276 | 337 | 613 |

*Source:* Camil Fuchs, "Possible Biased Inferences in Tests for Average Partial Association," *American Statistician* 33, No. 3 (1979): 121.

also categorized by safety records into two categories: (1) zero accidents or (2) one or more accidents. In the case of a 2 × 2 contingency table, there is a relatively simple formula for computing the value of $\chi^2$:

$$\chi^2 = \frac{n(X_{11}X_{22} - X_{12}X_{21})^2}{R_1 R_2 C_1 C_2}$$

**9.18**

Using Equation 9.18 we find that $\chi^2 = 0.173$. This very small value of $\chi^2$ is certainly not significant at any reasonable level of significance (for example, $\chi^2_{0.05,1} = 3.841$). The data suggest no association between frequency of automobile accidents and place of residence.

## Minitab Analysis of Table 9.8

The Minitab output for the command CHISQUARE using the data of Table 9.8 is shown in Exhibit 9.3. The output agrees with the calculations in Example 9.9.

**Exhibit 9.3**

```
MTB > NOTE ANALYSIS OF AUTOMOBILE ACCIDENT DATA BY RESIDENCE
MTB > READ TABLE INTO C1-C2
      2 ROWS READ
  ROW     C1     C2

    1      29     32
    2     247    305

MTB > CHISQUARE ANALYSIS FOR DATA IN C1-C2

Expected counts are printed below observed counts

            C1       C2     Total
    1       29       32        61
          27.5     33.5

    2      247      305       552
         248.5    303.5

Total      276      337       613

ChiSq =   0.09 +   0.07 +
          0.01 +   0.01 = 0.17
  df = 1
```

The reason why $v = (r - 1)(c - 1)$ provides the appropriate number of degrees of freedom for contingency table analysis is as follows. The general rule for establishing the appropriate number of degrees of freedom for categorical data is

$$\text{Degrees of freedom} = \begin{pmatrix} \text{Number of} \\ \text{classes} \end{pmatrix} - 1 - \begin{pmatrix} \text{Number of parameters} \\ \text{estimated from the data} \end{pmatrix} \qquad \textbf{9.19}$$

In the case of the general contingency table, $(r - 1)$ row probabilities are estimated, as the last probability is obtained from the relation $\Sigma \hat{p}_{i.} = 1$. Similarly, $(c - 1)$ column probabilities are estimated. Use of Equation 9.19 yields

$$\begin{aligned} v &= rc - 1 - (r - 1) - (c - 1) \\ &= rc - r - c + 1 = (r - 1)(c - 1) \end{aligned} \qquad \textbf{9.20}$$

as the appropriate number of degrees of freedom for an $r \times c$ contingency table. (This explanation is only a partial one because Equation 9.19 involves justification requiring mathematics beyond the level of this text.)

**9.13** Members of a sample of 1000 persons were asked their opinion on the Equal Rights Amendment, and the following responses, classified as in Table 9.4, were recorded.

Opinion on the ERA

| Sex | Favors | Opposes | Neutral |
|-----|--------|---------|---------|
| Female | 280 | 40 | 80 |
| Male | 300 | 150 | 150 |

**a.** Find the value of the chi-square statistic for these data and compare it with $\chi^2_{0.05,2}$.
**b.** Do the data suggest an association between sex and opinion on the ERA? What type of association is suggested?

**9.14** In an article in *The Professional Geographer*, the following data were presented on chemical companies in Brazil.

Number of Enterprises by Ownership Category

| Sector | Public | Multinational | Brazil (Group ownership) | Brazil (Single ownership) | Totals |
|--------|--------|---------------|--------------------------|---------------------------|--------|
| Chemical | 21 | 56 | 41 | 101 | 219 |
| Plastics | 0 | 15 | 20 | 56 | 91 |
| Pharmaceutical | 3 | 20 | 2 | 26 | 51 |
| Totals | 24 | 91 | 63 | 183 | 361 |

*Source:* Susan M. Cunningham, "Multinational Enterprises in Brazil, Locational Patterns and Implications for Regional Development," *The Professional Geographer* 33, No. 1 (1981): 48–62.

From these data, would you conclude that there is a relationship between the sector a company is in and the type of ownership? Use $\alpha = 0.05$. If your answer is yes, give a description of the relationship.

**9.15** In a particular statistics course there were 30 liberal arts students and 90 business school students. The scores on an exam were classified as follows:

| | Median or Below | Above Median | Totals |
|-----|-----------------|--------------|--------|
| Liberal Arts | 13 | 17 | 30 |
| Business | 47 | 43 | 90 |
| Totals | 60 | 60 | 120 |

**a.** Calculate the table of $\hat{E}_{ij}$ values.
**b.** Does there appear to be a relationship between performance on the exam and college of registration? Use $\alpha = 0.05$.

**9.16** In their book *The People's Choice*, P. F. Lazarsfeld, B. Berelson, and H. Gaudet presented data on 1655 potential voters who described themselves as having moderate interest in politics. Two variables of classification are intention to vote and level of education. A two-way table is shown below.

|                        | Intention to Vote |      |       |
|------------------------|-------------------|------|-------|
| Educational Level      | Yes               | No   | Total |
| At least some high school | 917            | 69   | 986   |
| No high school         | 602               | 67   | 669   |
| Total                  | 1519              | 136  | 1655  |

*Source:* P. F. Lazarsfeld, B. Berelson, and H. Gaudet, *The People's Choice*, 3rd edition (New York: Columbia University Press, 1968), p. 47. Reprinted with permission of the Columbia University Press.

**a.** Test the null hypothesis that there is no association between level of education and stated intention to vote. Use Equation 9.18 to compute the chi-square statistic with $\alpha = 0.05$.

**b.** How would you describe any indicated associations?

**9.17** The table below gives information on 3242 male employees of Royal Ordinance factories in the United Kingdom during 1943–1946. One variable of classification is a measure of visual acuity in the right eye, and the other is a similar measure for the left eye.

|           | Left Eye |        |       |        |        |
|-----------|----------|--------|-------|--------|--------|
| Right Eye | Highest Grade | Second Grade | Third Grade | Lowest Grade | Totals |
| Highest grade | 821  | 112    | 85    | 35     | 1053   |
| Second grade  | 116  | 494    | 145   | 27     | 782    |
| Third grade   | 72   | 151    | 583   | 87     | 893    |
| Lowest grade  | 43   | 34     | 106   | 331    | 514    |
| Totals        | 1052 | 791    | 919   | 480    | 3242   |

*Source:* A. Stuart, "The Estimation and Comparison of Strengths of Association on Contingency Tables," *Biometrika* 40 (1953): 109.

Test the null hypothesis that there is no association between left and right eye acuity for this group. Use $\alpha = 0.01$.

**9.18** The data below were obtained in a pilot study of the relationship between homework performance and conditions under which the work was done.

| Teachers' Ratings | Homework Conditions |      |        |
|-------------------|---------------------|------|--------|
|                   | Good                | Poor | Totals |
| High              | 208                 | 118  | 326    |
| Low               | 50                  | 44   | 94     |
| Totals            | 258                 | 162  | 420    |

*Source:* F. Yates, "The Analysis of Contingency Tables with Grouping Based on Quantitative Characters," *Biometrika* 35 (1948): 177.

**a.** Does there appear to be a significant association between the two variables of classification? Use $\alpha = 0.05$.

**b.** State in words how you would interpret these data.

**9.19** **a.** Show that $\Sigma_{j=1}^c \hat{E}_{ij} = R_i$ for $i = 1, 2, \ldots, r$.
   **b.** Show that $\Sigma_{i=1}^r \hat{E}_{ij} = C_j$ for $j = 1, 2, \ldots, c$.

## 9.4
## Goodness-of-Fit Methods

When statistical methods are being used, it is important to test whether the data actually come from the distribution assumed in the analysis. We already considered a test of this type for discrete variables in Section 9.2. In Example 9.4 it was assumed that the integers $0, 1, \ldots, 9$ came from a distribution with probability function $p(x) = 1/10$, $x = 0, 1, \ldots, 9$. In a random sample of 1000 observations, we would expect 100 of each integer on the average if the random number generator were functioning correctly. Using RANDOM to generate the 1000 observations, we conducted a chi-square test of

$$H_0: p_i = \frac{1}{10}, \, i = 0, 1, \ldots, 9 \quad \text{versus} \quad H_1: p_i \neq \frac{1}{10} \text{ for some } i$$

**goodness-of-fit**

and found no reason to reject this hypothesis. Tests of whether observations come from a particular distribution are called **goodness-of-fit** tests. We will first consider another example of a discrete case.

## Example 9.10

Consider a test of

$$H_0: X \sim B(10, 0.5) \quad \text{versus} \quad H_1: H_0 \text{ is false}$$

that is, observations are from a binomial distribution with parameters $n = 10$ and $p = 1/2$. The Minitab command RANDOM with the subcommand BINOMIAL has been used to generate 1000 observations from each of the binomial distributions with $n = 10$ and $p = 0.5$, $p = 0.6$, and $p = 0.7$. The Minitab output is shown in Exhibit 9.4.

For the first simulation ($p = 1/2$), the numbers of observations in each of the classes have been listed in Table 9.9. Using the computer, hand computation, or binomial tables, one can find the expected numbers of observations in the indicated classes under $H_0$. For example,

$$P(X = 5 | n = 10, p = 0.5) = \binom{10}{5}\left(\frac{1}{2}\right)^{10} = \frac{252}{1024} = 0.2461$$

## Table 9.9

**Observed and Expected Values ($n = 10$, $p = 0.5$)**

| Class | 0–1 | 2 | 3 | 4 | 5 | 6 | 7 | 8 | 9–10 |
|---|---|---|---|---|---|---|---|---|---|
| Observed | 8 | 45 | 108 | 199 | 239 | 222 | 124 | 49 | 6 |
| Expected | 10.8 | 43.9 | 117.2 | 205.1 | 246.1 | 205.1 | 117.2 | 43.9 | 10.8 |

**Exhibit 9.4**

```
MTB > NOTE BINOMIAL TRIALS WITH N = 10, P =  0.5,0.6,0.7
MTB > BASE = 10000
MTB > RANDOM 1000 OBS IN C1;
SUBC> BINOMIAL N = 10 P = 0.5.
MTB > TALLY C1

       C1  COUNT
        0    1
        1    7
        2   45
        3  108
        4  199
        5  239
        6  222
        7  124
        8   49
        9    6
       N= 1000

MTB > RANDOM 1000 OBS IN C2;
SUBC> BINOMIAL N = 10 P = 0.6.
MTB > TALLY C2

       C2  COUNT
        1    1
        2    8
        3   46
        4  118
        5  183
        6  237
        7  237
        8  117
        9   44
       10    9
       N= 1000

MTB > RANDOM 1000 OBS IN C3;
SUBC> BINOMIAL N = 10 P = 0.7.
MTB > TALLY C3

       C3  COUNT
        2    3
        3   10
        4   50
        5   93
        6  199
        7  256
        8  234
        9  120
       10   35
       N= 1000
```

so the expected number of observations in the fifth class is $1000(0.2461) = 246.1$. These expected numbers are also given in Table 9.9. Note that each of the two end classes has been combined. If they had not been combined, for the class corresponding to $X = 0$ we would have an expectation of $1000(1/1024) = 0.9766$, which is less than 5. Using both $X = 0$ and $X = 1$, we have as the expectation

**Table 9.10**

| Class | 0–1 | 2 | 3 | 4 | 5 | 6 | 7 | 8 | 9–10 |
|---|---|---|---|---|---|---|---|---|---|
| Observed ($p = 0.6$) | 1 | 8 | 46 | 118 | 183 | 237 | 237 | 117 | 53 |
| Observed ($p = 0.7$) | 0 | 3 | 10 | 50 | 93 | 199 | 256 | 234 | 155 |

$1000(1/1024 + 10/1024) = 10.8$. The value of chi-square is

$$\chi^2 = \frac{(8 - 10.8)^2}{10.8} + \cdots + \frac{(6 - 10.8)^2}{10.8} = 6.375$$

The appropriate number of degrees of freedom is one less than the number of classes, $9 - 1 = 8$, and a critical region for the test using $\alpha = 0.05$ is

$$\chi^2 \geqslant \chi^2_{0.05,8} = 15.507$$

The indicated decision is to retain the null hypothesis, which is in fact true in this case.

The two other simulations ($p = 0.6$ and $p = 0.7$) yielded the numbers given in Table 9.10. Using the observed values for $X \sim B(10, 0.6)$ and the expected values for $X \sim B(10, 0.5)$, we can calculate the value of $\chi^2 = 548.7$. Using the critical region

$$\chi^2 \geqslant \chi^2_{0.05,8} = 15.507$$

the decision would be to reject $H_0$. This test clearly indicates that $B(10, 0.5)$, the distribution hypothesized under $H_0$, is not correct. The observed values for $X \sim B(10, 0.7)$ would produce an even larger value of $\chi^2$ when calculated with the expected values assuming $X \sim B(10, 0.5)$. Again this would lead to the correct decision to reject $H_0$. Verification is left to the reader.

The chi-square statistic can also be used to test goodness-of-fit hypotheses for continuous distributions. This section will describe a test to determine whether the **normality assumption** is justified. The validity of other continuous distributions can be tested as well. The basic idea is to separate the observations into disjoint classes as in a frequency table, recording the number in each class. The hypothesized distribution is used to find the expected numbers falling into these classes. A statistic of the form

$$\chi^2 = \sum_{\text{all classes}} \frac{(\text{observed} - \text{expected})^2}{\text{expected}}$$

is used to test $H_0$: The observations come from a normal distribution, versus $H_1$: $H_0$ is false, with the rejection region for an $\alpha$-level test again of the form

$$\chi^2 \geqslant \chi^2_{\alpha,d}$$

The symbol $d$ denotes the appropriate number of degrees of freedom. An example will illustrate these ideas.

## Example 9.11

To determine whether the hypothesis $H_0$: $X \sim N(70, 4)$ is justified, let us test the data of Example 4.21 giving a simulated sample of size 100 from $X \sim N(70, 4)$. The data are summarized in Table 9.11.

## Table 9.11

**Standardized Values for Simulation of Example 4.21**

| $X$ Values | $Z$ Interval | Observed | Expected |
|---|---|---|---|
| $x \leqslant 65.5$ | $z \leqslant -2.25$ | 1 | 1.22 |
| $65.5 < x \leqslant 67.5$ | $-2.25 < z \leqslant -1.25$ | 10 | 9.34 |
| $67.5 < x \leqslant 69.5$ | $-1.25 < z \leqslant -0.25$ | 23 | 29.57 |
| $69.5 < x \leqslant 71.5$ | $-0.25 < z \leqslant 0.75$ | 46 | 37.21 |
| $71.5 < x \leqslant 73.5$ | $0.75 < z \leqslant 1.75$ | 14 | 18.65 |
| $73.5 < x$ | $1.75 < z$ | 6 | 4.01 |
| | | 100 | 100.00 |

The $Z$ intervals shown in Table 9.11 are found by using the transformation $Z = (X - \mu)/\sigma = (X - 70)/2$ for both the lower and upper endpoints for each interval of Example 4.21. For example, the interval $69.5 < x \leqslant 71.5$ corresponds to $(69.5 - 70)/2 < z \leqslant (71.5 - 70)/2$, or $-0.25 < z \leqslant 0.75$. The probabilities associated with each $Z$ interval can then be found from the table of the normal distribution in Appendix C. The numbers expected under the normality assumption are found by multiplying these probabilities by 100 (the number of observations). For example, for the interval just discussed, the table gives

$$P[-0.25 < Z \leqslant 0.75] = 0.3721$$

Hence the expected number of observations in the corresponding interval is $100(0.3721) = 37.21$. Combining the first two classes and the last two classes, we compute

$$\frac{\Sigma(\text{observed} - \text{expected})^2}{\text{expected}} = \frac{(11 - 10.56)^2}{10.56} + \cdots + \frac{(20 - 22.66)^2}{22.66}$$
$$= 3.867$$

as the value of the chi-square statistic. Using three degrees of freedom, a rejection region of the form $\chi^2 \geqslant \chi^2_{0.05,3} = 7.815$ would be appropriate. Three degrees of freedom is appropriate, as there are four classes and no parameters are estimated. Hence there is no reason to reject the hypothesis that $X \sim N(70, 4)$.

A similar test of goodness-of-fit to the normal distribution will now be carried out for data that actually come from a uniform distribution.

## Example 9.12

Suppose that we wish to test a null hypothesis similar to the one in Example 9.11, namely $H_0$: $X \sim N(70, 4)$, but the data actually come from a uniform distribution with $\mu = 70$ and $\sigma^2 = 12$. Minitab was used to obtain a sample of 1000 observations from this uniform distribution. Exhibit 9.5 shows the output generated when the HISTOGRAM command was used to find the number of observations in the indicated intervals.

The observed and expected numbers of observations in each of six classes are presented in Table 9.12. The computed value of $\chi^2$ is 2068.9 in this case, clearly leading to rejection of the normality assumption. Technically, the rejection region is $\chi^2 > \chi^2_{0.05,5} = 11.07$. With 1000 observations, the chi-square test should be able to discriminate easily between a uniform and a normal random variable.

## Exhibit 9.5

```
MTB > NOTE RANDOM SAMPLE FROM UNIFORM DISTRIBUTION WITH
MTB > NOTE EXPECTATION = 70 AND VARIANCE = 2
MTB > BASE = 2000
MTB > RANDOM 1000 OBSERVATIONS IN C1;
SUBC> UNIFORM A = 0 B = 1.
MTB > SUBTRACT 0.5 FROM C1 IN C1
MTB > MULTIPLY C1 BY 12 IN C1
MTB > ADD 70 TO C1 IN C1
MTB > HISTOGRAM C1;
SUBC> START = 65;
SUBC> INCREMENT = 2.

Histogram of C1    N = 1000
Each * represents 5 obs.

Midpoint   Count
   65.00     182   ****************************************
   67.00     140   ****************************
   69.00     187   *****************************************
   71.00     159   ********************************
   73.00     176   ************************************
   75.00     156   *******************************
```

## Table 9.12

**One Thousand Observations from a Uniform Distribution**

| $X$ Values | $Z$ Interval | Observed | Expected |
|---|---|---|---|
| $64 < x \leqslant 66$ | $z \leqslant -2$ | 182 | 22.8 |
| $66 < x \leqslant 68$ | $-2 < z \leqslant -1$ | 140 | 135.9 |
| $68 < x \leqslant 70$ | $-1 < z \leqslant 0$ | 187 | 341.3 |
| $70 < x \leqslant 72$ | $0 < z \leqslant 1$ | 159 | 341.3 |
| $72 < x \leqslant 74$ | $1 < z \leqslant 2$ | 176 | 135.9 |
| $74 < x \leqslant 76$ | $2 < z$ | 156 | 22.8 |

## Example 9.13

As a last example of a goodness-of-fit test, consider the data on the survival periods of 52 patients following heart transplants, shown in Example 5.10. A frequency table for these data is given in Table 9.13. The value of $\bar{x}$ is 329.75 and that of $s$ is 394.21. These values have been used as estimates of $\mu$ and $\sigma$, respectively, to find $z$ values corresponding to the endpoints of intervals. For example, the $z$ value corresponding to 100 is $z = (100 - 329.75)/394.21 = -0.58$.

## Exhibit 9.6

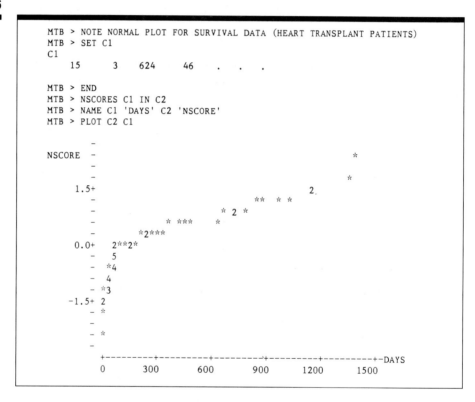

```
MTB > NOTE NORMAL PLOT FOR SURVIVAL DATA (HEART TRANSPLANT PATIENTS)
MTB > SET C1
C1
        15      3    624     46    .    .    .

MTB > END
MTB > NSCORES C1 IN C2
MTB > NAME C1 'DAYS' C2 'NSCORE'
MTB > PLOT C2 C1
```

The computed value of the chi-square statistic is $\chi^2 = 13.1$ One degree of freedom is subtracted for each parameter estimated to get the appropriate degrees of freedom, $v = k - 1 - (2) = 5 - 3 = 2$. The critical region ($\alpha = 0.05$) is $\chi^2 \geqslant \chi^2_{0.05,2} = 5.991$, so we would reject the hypothesis of the normality of these data. Exhibit 9.6 shows the Minitab normal plot of the data. As this plot and the histogram of Section 5.3 indicate, these data are far too skewed to the right to be considered a sample from a normal distribution.

**Table 9.13**

**Survival Data for Heart Transplant Patients**

| X Values | Z Interval | Observed | Expected |
|---|---|---|---|
| $x \leqslant 100$ | $z \leqslant -0.58$ | 24 | 14.61 |
| $100 < x \leqslant 300$ | $-0.58 < z \leqslant -0.08$ | 9 | 9.73 |
| $300 < x \leqslant 500$ | $-0.08 < z \leqslant 0.43$ | 6 | 10.31 |
| $500 < x \leqslant 700$ | $0.43 < z \leqslant 0.94$ | 2 | 8.32 |
| $700 < x <$ | $0.94 < z <$ | 11 | 9.03 |

*Source:* B. Turnbull, B. Brown, and M. Hu, "Survivorship Analyses of Heart Transplant Data," *Journal of the American Statistical Association* 69 (1974): 75.

A final observation should be made about chi-square goodness-of-fit tests: for these tests the null hypothesis specifies the distribution we believe to be correct. In general the research hypothesis should be stated as the alternative hypothesis, in order to minimize the probability of incorrectly deciding for the research hypothesis. In goodness-of-fit tests, however, the hypothesized distribution is stated as the null hypothesis because a strong statistical statement can be made only if the null hypothesis is rejected. Hence goodness-of-fit tests should really be called **badness-of-fit** tests. A strong statistical statement can only be made in cases such as Example 9.12, where normality ($H_0$) is *rejected*. If the null hypothesis is retained, one can only state that no serious inconsistency exists between the data observed and the hypothesized distribution under $H_0$.

**badness-of-fit**

# Exercises 9.4

**9.20** The number of hurricanes to hit the coast of a certain state in the last 100 years is given below.

| Number of Hurricanes ($x$) | Number of Years |
|---|---|
| 0 | 10 |
| 1 | 30 |
| 2 | 28 |
| 3 | 17 |
| 4 | 10 |
| 5 | 5 |

**a.** Find the expected number of years in which $x$ hurricanes would occur if $X$ were a Poisson random variable with $\mu = 2$. Use $P(X \geqslant 5)$ for the last class.

**b.** Carry out a goodness-of-fit test to the Poisson distribution with $\mu = 2$. Use $\alpha = 0.05$.

**c.** Carry out a goodness-of-fit test to the Poisson distribution, using $\bar{x}$ as an estimate of $\mu$.

Combine extreme classes, if necessary, so that the expected value in each class is at least 5.

**9.21** In a classical example from Prussian army data, Bortkiewicz compiled the number of soldiers in ten cavalry corps who died within a period of twenty years from being kicked by horses. The total number of corp years observed was 200. Let $X$ represent the number of such deaths observed in a corps year. The data are summarized below.

| Number of Deaths ($x$) | 0 | 1 | 2 | 3 | 4 |
|---|---|---|---|---|---|
| Number of Corps Years | 109 | 65 | 22 | 3 | 1 |

Use a goodness-of-fit test to decide whether the Poisson distribution can be used as a model for the random variable $X$. Use $\alpha = 0.05$ and combine classes as necessary. *Note:* Estimate $\mu$ by $\bar{x}$.

**9.22** In 1910, E. Rutherford and H. Geiger collected some now-classical data on the number of scintillations in one-eighth-minute intervals caused by radioactive decay of polonium. There were 2608 such intervals. The data are shown in the table below, in which $x$ represents the number of scintillations in such an interval.

| $x$ | Number of Intervals |
|---|---|
| 0 | 57 |
| 1 | 203 |
| 2 | 383 |
| 3 | 525 |
| 4 | 532 |
| 5 | 408 |
| 6 | 273 |
| 7 | 139 |
| 8 | 45 |
| 9 | 27 |
| 10 | 10 |
| 11 or more | 6 |

*Source:* Data quoted in David C. Hoaglin, "A Poissonness Plot," *The American Statistician* 34 (1980): 147.

Carry out a goodness-of-fit test to the Poisson distribution as in exercise 9.21, but use $\alpha = 0.01$.

**9.23** Using RANDOM, simulate 400 observations from a binomial distribution with $n = 10$ and $p = 0.4$. Use the output from the subcommand BINOMIAL with $n = 10$ and $p = 0.4$ to find the expected number of observations in each class under $H_0: X \sim B(10, 0.4)$. Combine beginning and ending classes until the expected number in each class is at least 5. Compute the value of $\chi^2$ to decide whether $H_0$ should be retained or rejected. State the rejection region for $\alpha = 0.05$.

**9.24** Use the data from exercise 9.23 to test $H_0: X \sim B(10, 0.5)$. State the rejection region for $\alpha = 0.05$. Calculate $\chi^2$ and make a decision as to whether to retain $H_0: X \sim B(10, 0.5)$.

**9.25** The following are the short interest positions as of August 15, 1984 of 67 stocks listed on the New York Stock Exchange (in thousands of shares). Short interest refers to all the securities sold short as of a given date. Selling short involves agreeing to sell at some specified time in the future a stock that one does not currently own. If the price of the stock declines in the meantime, the seller will make a profit, because the cost to the seller of buying the stock will be less than the amount received from the buyer.

| Stock | Short Interest | Stock | Short Interest |
|---|---|---|---|
| Alexanders | 1 | Lilco | 117 |
| Amer Broadcasting | 327 | Louisiana Pacific | 55 |
| Amer Home Prod | 330 | Manville | 145 |
| ATT | 1973 | Mattel | 924 |
| Apache | 76 | McLean Ind | 775 |
| AVCO | 272 | Middle South Util | 595 |
| Bank of NY | 50 | Motorola | 836 |
| Bell Canada Emt | 373 | Nat Semiconductor | 753 |
| Boston Edison | 12 | Niagara Share | 43 |
| Burroughs | 524 | Norton | 327 |
| Caterpillar | 335 | Orange Co | 185 |
| Chemical NY | 32 | Pan Amer World Air | 5483 |
| Circle K | 52 | Pennzoil | 217 |
| Community Psy | 38 | Philip Morris | 346 |
| Cont Telcom | 287 | P & G | 183 |
| Cullinet | 166 | Ralston Purina | 214 |
| Deluxe Check | 18 | Reynolds (RJ) | 281 |
| Donnelley (RR) | 42 | Sabine | 212 |
| DuPont | 715 | Seagrams | 235 |
| Elec Data Sys | 222 | Signal Cos | 360 |
| Fed Nat Mtge | 91 | Southmark | 31 |
| First Penn | 566 | Stop & Shop | 1304 |
| GCA | 117 | Tambrands | 1310 |
| Gen Motors | 1881 | Teradyne | 63 |
| Gillette | 60 | Thrifty Corp | 53 |
| Great Western Fin | 284 | Transamerica | 237 |
| Halliburton | 186 | UAL | 312 |
| Holiday Inns | 207 | United Brands | 59 |
| Houston Nat Gas | 199 | Unocal | 229 |
| Ill Power | 345 | Viacom Int | 53 |
| Inland Steel | 67 | Walgreen | 62 |
| Intl Paper | 258 | Western Air | 1531 |
| Kansas P & L | 53 | Wis P & L | 4 |
| Kyocera | 25 | | |

*Source: The Wall Street Journal*, August 22, 1984.

Use Minitab to test the data above for normality. Use $\bar{x}$ and $s$ to find appropriate $z$ intervals. Use $\alpha = 0.05$.

**9.26** **a.** Test the data of exercise 5.16 on the number of home runs by National League home run champions for normality as in exercise 9.25. Use $\alpha = 0.05$.

**b.** Make a normal plot of these observations as a rough visual check of normality. Does your conclusion agree with your answer to part a?

**9.27** Use the 100 waiting times of Section 5.1 to test $H_0$: $X \sim N(15, 225)$. Carry out the test using $\alpha = 0.10$.

**9.28** Record the final digits of the telephone numbers of a randomly selected page of a telephone directory. Carry out a test of goodness-of-fit to the discrete uniform distribution described in the first paragraph of this section.

**Summary**

In this chapter we considered categorical or count data. This type of data consists of counts of the number of observations falling into specific categories. The multinomial distribution, a generalization of the binomial distribution, gives a theoretical description of the number of observations falling into each of $k$ mutually exclusive classes in $n$ independent trials. At each trial the probabilities of an outcome in classes $1, 2, \ldots, k$ are considered to be given by $p_1, p_2, \ldots, p_k$, where $\sum_{i=1}^{k} p_i = 1$. The emphasis here is not on this distribution, but on the statistic

$$\chi^2 = \sum_{i=1}^{k} \frac{(X_i - np_i)^2}{np_i}$$

where $X_i$ is the number of observations in class $i$. For large $n$, the statistic has approximately a chi-square distribution with $k - 1$ degrees of freedom, if the $p_i$ are the correct probabilities. This distributional fact leads to a test of

$$H_0: p_i = p_i^*, \quad i = 1, 2, \ldots, k \quad \text{versus} \quad H_1: H_0 \text{ false}$$

where the $p_i^*$ are hypothesized probabilities.

Contingency tables provide a way of classifying observations by two criteria in a table with $r$ rows and $c$ columns. The question of interest is whether the two criteria are independent (in the probabilistic sense) or associated. A chi-square statistic with $(r - 1)(c - 1)$ degrees of freedom is used to carry out a test of independence. The Minitab program can quickly calculate expected values under the independence assumption, as well as the required test statistic. It also gives some information about how the variables are associated if an association exists.

A chi-square test can also be used to test whether data can reasonably be assumed to come from a hypothesized distribution. Such a test may be carried out for either discrete or continuous distributions.

## Key Words

| | |
|---|---|
| association | goodness-of-fit |
| badness-of-fit | independence |
| categorical data | independent trials |
| chi-square statistic | interval scale |
| column criteria | multinomial random variable |
| contingency table | nominal scale |
| count data | normality assumption |
| cross classifications | ordinal scale |
| degrees of freedom | ratio scale |
| enumerative data | row criteria |
| expected number of observations in cell $(i, j)$ | test of $H_0: p = p^*$ |

## Minitab Command

CHISQUARE

# Chapter 10

# Simple Linear Regression

## 10.1

**Introduction**

Two of the main objectives of the scientific method are discovering the relationships between variables and finding a mathematical description of such relationships. Many of the mathematical models considered in the physical sciences are of a deterministic type. For example, the mass of a radioactive substance remaining after a period of time $t$ can be expressed as

$$A(t) = M_0 e^{-\lambda t}$$

**deterministic relationship**

Here $M_0$ is the mass at time zero, $e = 2.71828$ is the base of the natural logarithms, and $\lambda$ is a positive constant determined by the half-life of the substance. This is called a **deterministic relationship** because for any value of $t$ we get precisely one value of $A(t)$—that is, the value of $t$ determines the value of $A(t)$. For example, if $t^* = \ln(2)/\lambda$, then $A(t^*) = M_0/2$, so $t^*$ is the actual half-life of the substance (that is, at $t = t^*$, exactly one-half of the original mass remains). In other situations, although it is known that a variable depends on a real variable, the relationship is not deterministic. For example, it is known that, on the average, a student scoring 1400 out of 1600 on the Scholastic Aptitude Test (SAT) examination will tend to have a high GPA at the end of the freshman year. Not all students scoring 1400 will have the *same* GPA at the end of the first year, however, so the GPA cannot be computed as a function of the SAT score. Similarly, it is known that the average weight of male infants will be related to the number of months since birth. Clearly, however, the actual

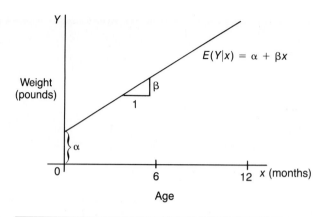

**Figure 10.1**

The Theoretical Regression Line

weight of a male infant cannot be determined exactly as a function of age. These two examples illustrate a **stochastic relationship**.

**stochastic relationship**

This chapter presents a mathematical model that is often used to explain the relationship between a random variable $Y$, thought of as a dependent random variable, and a real variable $x$, considered to be an independent variable. The model is called the simple linear regression model. The assumption of this model is that the *expectation of Y* depends linearly on $x$, so

$$E(Y|x) \;=\; \alpha + \beta x \qquad\qquad \textbf{10.1}$$

Figure 10.1 shows a graph of this expectation as a function of $x$ in the case where $\alpha > 0$ and $\beta > 0$. The value $\boldsymbol{\alpha}$ is the **intercept** of this **theoretical regression line**, and $\boldsymbol{\beta}$ is the **slope** of this line. The line in Figure 10.1 could be interpreted as giving the relationship between the age ($x$) of male infants and their true average (expected) weight ($Y$) during the first twelve months after birth. The value of $\alpha = E(Y|x=0)$ would then represent the true average weight of a male infant at birth. The value of $\beta$ is the slope of the theoretical regression line and thus represents the change in true average weight per unit increase in age (a month in this case). The values of the intercept $\alpha$ and slope $\beta$ of the theoretical regression line are unknown and must be estimated from data.

**α (intercept)**

**theoretical regression line**

**β (slope)**

As Figure 10.1 suggests, in cases where $\beta$ is assumed to be positive, the average value of $Y$ increases by $\beta$ units when $x$ increases by a single unit. As shown in Figure 10.2, if $\beta > 0$, then $E(Y|x_1) = \alpha + \beta x_1$, the average value of $Y$ at $x = x_1$, will be less than $E(Y|x_2) = \alpha + \beta x_2$, the average value of $Y$ at $x = x_2$. In the linear regression model it is assumed that $\text{Var}(Y|x) = \sigma^2$. Thus the variance of $Y$ does not depend on $x$. This feature is suggested in Figure 10.2 by the identical symmetric density functions centered about $E(Y|x_1)$ and $E(Y|x_2)$. The simple linear regression model is more precisely described by the equation

$$Y_i \;=\; \alpha + \beta x_i + \varepsilon_i, \qquad i = 1, 2, \ldots, n \qquad\qquad \textbf{10.2}$$

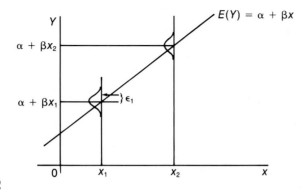

**Figure 10.2**

Distributions of Y at $x = x_1$ and $x = x_2$

where we assume that

$$E(\varepsilon_i) = 0 \qquad \text{Var}(\varepsilon_i) = \sigma^2 \tag{10.3}$$

and that the $\varepsilon_i$ are independently distributed for $i = 1, 2, \ldots, n$. At $x = x_i$ we have

$$E(Y_i) = E(\alpha + \beta x_i + \varepsilon_i) = \alpha + \beta x_i + E(\varepsilon_i) = \alpha + \beta x_i \tag{10.4}$$

Thus an observation of $Y_i$ at $x = x_i$ is composed of the real unknown expectation plus an observation of a random error term, $\varepsilon_i$, which has an expectation of zero. These components are shown for $i = 1$ in Figure 10.2. As the constant $\alpha + \beta x_i$ is independent of $\varepsilon_i$, we have

$$\text{Var}(Y_i) = \text{Var}(\alpha + \beta x_i + \varepsilon_i) = \text{Var}(\alpha + \beta x_i) + \text{Var}(\varepsilon_i) = 0 + \sigma^2 = \sigma^2 \tag{10.5}$$

This equation shows that the variance associated with any observation of $Y$, regardless of the value of $x$, is the same constant—namely, $\sigma^2$. The constant $\sigma^2$ is an unknown parameter, as are $\alpha$ and $\beta$, which must also be estimated from data.

**Example 10.1**

Let us consider once again the data of Exhibit 2.7 concerning the top 25 batters in the American League in 1980. The numbers of hits ($x$) and runs ($y$) for each of the 25 batters who hit 0.300 or better in that year were SET in C1 and C2 of the Minitab output shown in Exhibit 10.1, and the PRINT, MEAN, and STDEV commands were used with these two columns. Exhibit 10.2 shows a plot of the 25 data points constructed by Minitab. The least squares line and its equation have been added to the exhibit; these will be discussed subsequently.

It has been assumed that for every fixed value of $x$, the number of hits, there is a distribution of $Y$, the number of runs scored by the batter. It seems clear from Exhibit 10.2 that there is a relationship between the number of runs scored by a

**Exhibit 10.1**

```
MTB > NOTE REGRESSION OF RUNS ON HITS
MTB > SET C1
C1
    175    219    180    210    .   .   .

MTB > END
MTB > SET C2
C2
     87     96     87     96    .   .   .

MTB > END
MTB > NAME C1 'HITS' C2 'RUNS'
MTB > PRINT C1,C2
  ROW   HITS    RUNS

     1    175      87
     2    219      96
     3    180      87
     4    210      96
     5    179      74
     6    161      76
     7    230     134
     8    144      61
     9    205     117
    10    209      96
    11    124      42
    12    144      62
    13    138      57
    14    137      81
    15    180      94
    16    179      86
    17    179     111
    18    175      84
    19    165      67
    20    187     100
    21    125      67
    22    112      54
    23    156      62
    24    102      42
    25    154      94

MTB > MEAN C1
   MEAN     =        166.76
MTB > STDEV C1
   ST.DEV. =        33.553
MTB > MEAN C2
   MEAN     =        81.080
MTB > STDEV C2
   ST.DEV. =        22.748
```

batter and the number of hits made by a batter. When the number of hits tends to be high, so does the number of runs. This makes good baseball sense, because a hitter with a large number of hits will be on base more frequently and thus will have more opportunities to score a run. As is abundantly clear from the plot, there is no line that will pass through all of these points. We will use the data to construct a line that is as close as possible to all of the 25 points. The line that provides a "best

**Exhibit 10.2**

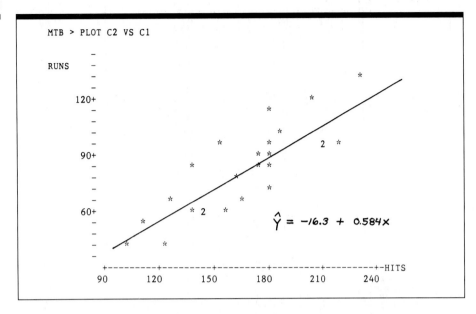

```
MTB > PLOT C2 VS C1

RUNS    -
        -
        -
  120+                                                       *
        -
        -                                     *
        -                                  *
        -                         *              *
        -                      *            *      2   *
   90+                                      * *
        -                   *              * *
        -                                  * *
        -                                     *
   60+
        -               * 2     *              Ŷ = -16.3 + 0.584x
        -        *
        -   *            *
        -
        +---------+---------+---------+---------+---------+-HITS
        90       120       150       180       210       240
```

least squares line     fit" to all of the points is called the **least squares line**. In this case, the equation of
the line produced by the least squares technique is

$$\hat{y} = -16.3 + 0.584x$$

This chapter will discuss how the equation of the least squares line is determined. This line is an "estimate" of the theoretical regression line,

$$E(Y|x) = \alpha + \beta x$$

The estimates of the intercept and the slope ($-16.3$ and $0.584$ in Example 10.1) are
estimates of the unknown parameters $\alpha$ and $\beta$, just as previously $\bar{x}$ estimated $\mu$ and
$\hat{p}$ estimated $p$. Although properties of these estimators of $\alpha$ and $\beta$ will be discussed
in this chapter, it is important to remember that these parameters will never be
known exactly.

## Exercises 10.1

**10.1**  Graph $E(Y|x) = \alpha + \beta x$ for a case in which $\alpha > 0$ and $\beta < 0$. Label the points of
intersection of this theoretical line with the $x$ and $y$ axes in terms of $\alpha$ and $\beta$.

**10.2**  Suppose that $E(Y) = \gamma x$, where $x$ is an independent real variable, $Y$ is a random
variable with the expectation given, and $\gamma$ is a real but unknown parameter.
   **a.** Make a graph similar to that of Figure 10.1 for the case in which $\gamma > 0$. Indicate
the expected values of $Y$ for $x = x_1$ and $x = x_2 > x_1$, as in Figure 10.2.
   **b.** Suggest an example for which this graph might be an appropriate model. Note that
$E(Y) = 0$ when $x = 0$.

**10.3** Suggest possible random variables $Y$, with expectations dependent on the following independent real variables.

    **a.** Assume $x$ is the age of the wife in a family in which both husband and wife are living.

    **b.** Assume $x$ represents the high temperature in Miami, Florida on a given day.

    **c.** Assume $x$ represents the average score of a student on the two examinations in a course.

**10.4** Why is the variance of $\alpha + \beta x_i$, $i = 1, 2, \ldots, n$ in Equation 10.5 equal to 0?

**10.5** Use Minitab with the data in Exhibit 2.7 for home runs $(x)$ and RBIs $(y)$ to plot the 25 points $(x_i, y_i)$, $i = 1, 2, \ldots, 25$. Does there seem to be a relation between these two variables? What kind of relationship?

**10.6** Let $Y$ represent the total cost of publishing a text with $x$ pages. Assume that $E(Y|x) = \alpha + \beta x$ is a reasonable description of how $Y$ depends on $x$.

    **a.** How would $\alpha$ be defined in economic terms? What sign would $\alpha$ have?

    **b.** How would $\beta$ be defined in economic terms? What sign would $\beta$ have?

## 10.2

## The Least Squares Line

As mentioned in Section 10.1, it is important to find a line that provides the best fit to a set of points in the plane. The points $(x_i, y_i)$, $i = 1, 2, \ldots, n$ represent the basic data set available in a simple linear regression model.

### Example 10.2

Consider a small data set in which $x$ represents the number of years of college completed by an individual and $Y$ represents that person's current salary (in thousands of dollars). A sample of size $n = 5$ is taken from a certain population of high school graduates who have gone on to further education. The observed

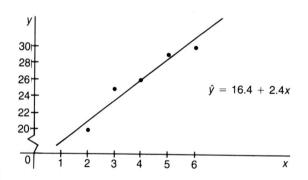

**Figure 10.3**

Plot of Data from Example 10.2

values $(x_i, y_i)$, $i = 1, 2, 3, 4, 5$ are

| $x$ | 2 | 3 | 4 | 5 | 6 |
|---|---|---|---|---|---|
| $y$ | 20 | 25 | 26 | 29 | 30 |

The data are plotted in Figure 10.3. Certainly these points do not lie on a line. To choose a best-fitting line, it is necessary to have a criterion sensitive to the requirement that the line should fit all the points well.

To obtain the best-fitting line, we begin by considering all possible lines. These lines are denoted by $y = a + bx$, where $a$ and $b$ can take on all possible real values. The value of $y$ at $x = x_i$ for such an arbitrary line is denoted by $\hat{y}_i = a + bx_i$. The vertical distance between the observed value at $x = x_i$ and $y_i$ is then given by

$$y_i - \hat{y}_i = y_i - (a + bx_i) \qquad \textbf{10.6}$$

A typical vertical distance of this kind is shown in Figure 10.4. We would like to make all deviations of the type described by Equation 10.6 as small as possible simultaneously. The deviations cannot all be made equal to zero unless the observed points lie exactly on a line. We can, however, achieve a reasonable solution by considering the expression

$$\sum (y_i - \hat{y}_i)^2 = \sum [y_i - (a + bx_i)]^2 \qquad \textbf{10.7}$$

namely, the sum of the squares of the vertical deviations. (As all sums discussed in this chapter are from $i = 1$ to $i = n$, the indices will be omitted on the summation signs.) The second expression in Equation 10.7 is a function of the values $a$ and $b$ only, as the values of the observations $(x_i, y_i)$ are known. The line providing the best fit to the data points is the one that minimizes the expression in Equation 10.7.

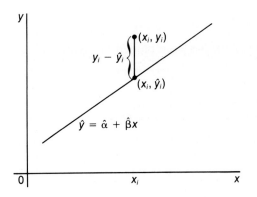

**Figure 10.4**

**A Typical Deviation from the Least Squares Line**

It can be shown that there is only one such line, $\hat{y} = \hat{\alpha} + \hat{\beta}x$, called the least squares line. $\hat{\beta}$ (the **slope**) and $\hat{\alpha}$ (the **intercept**) for the least squares line are given respectively by

$$\hat{\beta} = \frac{\Sigma(x_i - \bar{x})(y_i - \bar{y})}{\Sigma(x_i - \bar{x})^2} \quad \text{and} \quad \hat{\alpha} = \bar{y} - \hat{\beta}\bar{x} \qquad \qquad \textbf{10.8}$$

Given that

$$\hat{y} = \hat{\alpha} + \hat{\beta}x = \bar{y} - \hat{\beta}\bar{x} + \hat{\beta}x = \bar{y} + \hat{\beta}(x - \bar{x}) \qquad \qquad \textbf{10.9}$$

if $x = \bar{x}$, then $\hat{y} = \bar{y}$. Thus the least squares line always passes through the point $(\bar{x}, \bar{y})$. The reader should verify that the point $(\bar{x}, \bar{y}) = (4, 26)$ in Example 10.2 lies on $\hat{y} = 16.4 + 2.4x$.

## Example 10.3

Let us now compute the values of $\hat{\alpha}$ and $\hat{\beta}$ for the data of Example 10.2. Using $\bar{x} = 4$ and $\bar{y} = 26$, the following values can be calculated.

| $i$ | $x_i$ | $y_i$ | $x_i - \bar{x}$ | $y_i - \bar{y}$ | $(x_i - \bar{x})^2$ | $(x_i - \bar{x})(y_i - \bar{y})$ | $(y_i - \bar{y})^2$ |
|-----|-------|-------|-----------------|-----------------|---------------------|----------------------------------|---------------------|
| 1 | 2 | 20 | $-2$ | $-6$ | 4 | 12 | 36 |
| 2 | 3 | 25 | $-1$ | $-1$ | 1 | 1 | 1 |
| 3 | 4 | 26 | 0 | 0 | 0 | 0 | 0 |
| 4 | 5 | 29 | 1 | 3 | 1 | 3 | 9 |
| 5 | 6 | 30 | 2 | 4 | 4 | 8 | 16 |
| Totals | | | 0 | 0 | 10 | 24 | 62 |

(Note that the sums of the deviations of $x$ and $y$ about their means must always be zero. You can use this fact to check your calculations.) Using the values above, we have

$$\hat{\beta} = \frac{\Sigma(x_i - \bar{x})(y_i - \bar{y})}{\Sigma(x_i - \bar{x})^2} = \frac{24}{10} = 2.4$$

and

$$\hat{\alpha} = \bar{y} - \hat{\beta}\bar{x} = 26 - (2.4)4 = 16.4$$

The least squares line has been plotted in Figure 10.3.

## Use of Minitab to Determine and Plot the Least Squares Line

The data of Example 10.2 will be used to show how Minitab can be employed to find the equation of the least squares line. The values of $(x_i, y_i)$ were SET in C1 and C2. The command **REGRESS** is the crucial one; it is shown in the Minitab output in Exhibit 10.3. The REGRESS command caused the intercept and the slope of the least squares line to be printed out under the title Coef. The command also produced some other statistical data which will be explained shortly. The

**Exhibit 10.3**

```
MTB > NOTE LEAST SQUARES LINE FOR SALARY (Y) VS YEARS OF COLLEGE (X)
MTB > BRIEF 1
MTB > REGRESS Y IN C2 VS 1 X IN C1 RESIDS IN C3 PRED IN C4

The regression equation is
C2 = 16.4 + 2.40 C1

Predictor        Coef        Stdev      t-ratio
Constant        16.400       1.625       10.09
C1               2.4000      0.3830       6.27

s = 1.211       R-sq = 92.9%     R-sq(adj) = 90.5%
```

**standardized residuals**
**predicted values**

**MPLOT**

values of the **standardized residuals**, $(y_i - \hat{y}_i)/s_{(y_i - \hat{y}_i)}$, were put in the first five rows of C3, and the **predicted values**, $\hat{y}_i = \hat{\alpha} + \hat{\beta}x_i = 16.4 + 2.4x_i$, were put in the first five rows of C4.

Additionally, the **MPLOT** command was used to make plots of both $(x_i, y_i)$ and $(x_i, \hat{y}_i)$ for $i = 1, 2, 3, 4, 5$ on the same axes. These plots appear in Exhibit 10.4. The original observations are denoted by A's. The values of the $\hat{y}_i$ (the predicted values of income at each $x_i$) are denoted by B's. If an A and a B coincide, the MPLOT command prints a 2, indicating that two observations fall in the same place. The least squares line appears to provide a good fit to the original data. Later in this chapter a statistical method will be introduced for judging the goodness-of-fit of the least squares line.

**Exhibit 10.4**

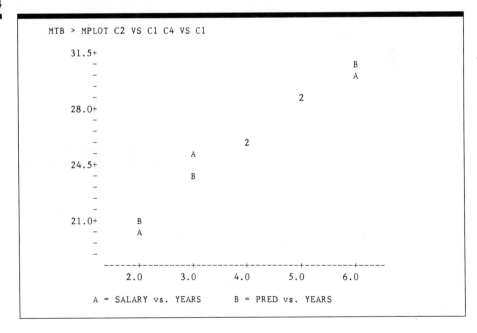

```
MTB > MPLOT C2 VS C1 C4 VS C1

    31.5+
        -                                                    B
        -                                                    A
        -
        -                                            2
    28.0+
        -
        -
        -                                    2
        -                    A
    24.5+
        -                    B
        -
        -
        -
    21.0+        B
        -        A
        -
        -
        ------+---------+---------+---------+---------+-----
             2.0       3.0       4.0       5.0       6.0

    A = SALARY vs. YEARS      B = PRED vs. YEARS
```

**10.7** The following are observations of a dependent random variable $Y$ and the seven corresponding observations of an independent real variable $x$:

| $x$ | 2 | 4 | 6 | 8 | 10 | 12 | 14 |
|---|---|---|---|---|---|---|---|
| $y$ | 17 | 21 | 30 | 33 | 37 | 43 | 50 |

**a.** Find the equation of the least squares line for these data.
**b.** Find $\bar{x}$ and $\bar{y}$ and show that the point $(\bar{x}, \bar{y})$ lies on the least squares line.

**10.8** The following observations show the number of days, $x$, on which each of five salespeople travel away from home in a month and the monthly sales, $y$, of each, in thousands of dollars.

| Salesperson | Days $(x)$ | Sales $(y)$ |
|---|---|---|
| 1 | 2 | 4 |
| 2 | 4 | 6 |
| 3 | 6 | 7 |
| 4 | 8 | 9 |
| 5 | 10 | 14 |

**a.** Find the equation of the least squares line.
**b.** Estimate the increase in sales (in thousands of dollars) for each additional day spent traveling, using your answer to part a.

**10.9** In a study relating expenditures $(Y)$ to income $(x)$, the following summary data were calculated for 27 families. The units are dollars per month for each variable.

$$\sum (x_i - \bar{x})^2 = 400{,}000 \qquad \bar{x} = 2000$$
$$\sum (y_i - \bar{y})^2 = 200{,}000 \qquad \bar{y} = 1600$$
$$\sum (x_i - \bar{x})(y_i - \bar{y}) = 280{,}000$$

**a.** Find the equation of the least squares line.
**b.** Show that $(\bar{x}, \bar{y})$ lies on this line.

**10.10** A sample of 27 income tax returns was used for a study of the relationship between the number of dependents $(x)$ a person has and the amount of income tax due $(Y)$ measured in thousands of dollars. The sample yielded the following summary data:

$$\sum (x_i - \bar{x})^2 = 2000 \qquad \bar{x} = 2$$
$$\sum (y_i - \bar{y})^2 = 900 \qquad \bar{y} = 1$$
$$\sum (x_i - \bar{x})(y_i - \bar{y}) = -1000$$

**a.** What is the value of the estimate of $\beta$ in the expression $E(Y) = \alpha + \beta x$?
**b.** What is the value of the estimate of $\alpha$?
**c.** Explain in words the meaning of the estimate in part a.

**10.11** Let $x$ represent the amount of time an individual works and $Y$ the number of pieces of work completed in this time. The following observations were made for seven different workers.

| Hours $(x)$ | Pieces $(y)$ |
|---|---|
| 1 | 1 |
| 2 | 2 |
| 3 | 3 |
| 4 | 5 |
| 5 | 8 |
| 6 | 11 |
| 7 | 12 |

**a.** Find the least squares line, using Minitab.
**b.** Interpret the meaning of $\alpha$ and $\beta$.
**c.** What are the estimates of $\alpha$ and $\beta$?

**10.12** The following table shows the results of measurements of the electrical resistance in (ohms/cm) $\times 10^{-6}$ of platinum at several temperatures in degrees Kelvin.

| Temperature $(x)$ | 100 | 200 | 300 | 400 | 500 |
|---|---|---|---|---|---|
| Resistance $(y)$ | 2 | 9 | 12 | 16 | 21 |

Find the least squares line using Minitab, and show that $(\bar{x}, \bar{y})$ is on this line.

**\*10.13** Consider the model $E(Y|x) = \gamma x$, where $Y$ is a random variable, $x$ is a real variable, and $\gamma$ is an unknown parameter. *Hint:* The quadratic expression $ax^2 + bx + c$, with $a > 0$, can be written as $a(x + b/2a)^2 + c - b^2/4a$. Hence the value of the quadratic is a minimum for $x = -b/2a$.
   **a.** Consider the problem of minimizing $\sum_{i=1}^{n}(y_i - \gamma x_i)^2$ as a function of $\gamma$. Rewrite this expression as a quadratic expression in $\gamma$, and use the result noted above to find an expression for $\hat{\gamma}$, the minimizing value, in terms of $x_i$ and $y_i$.
   **b.** On one graph, plot functions $\gamma x$ for several values of $\gamma$.
   **c.** Suggest several examples for which this model could be appropriate.

**10.14** Use Minitab to check your calculations of $\hat{\alpha}$ and $\hat{\beta}$ in exercise 10.8.

**10.15** The table on page 366 gives data on voter registration and turnout in 24 cities in the 1960 presidential election (expressed as percentages of the voting-age population).

| City | Registration ($x$) | Turnout ($y$) |
|---|---|---|
| Atlanta, GA | 33.8 | 25.6 |
| Baltimore, MD | 68.1 | 54.0 |
| Birmingham, AL | 39.1 | 13.8 |
| Boston, MA | 74.0 | 63.3 |
| Charlotte, NC | 69.9 | 54.5 |
| Dallas, TX | 65.0 | 57.3 |
| Detroit, MI | 92.0 | 70.0 |
| Honolulu, HI | 60.0 | 54.7 |
| Los Angeles, CA | 77.0 | 64.2 |
| Miami, FL | 59.2 | 43.7 |
| Minneapolis, MN | 92.5 | 58.5 |
| New Orleans, LA | 55.6 | 45.9 |
| New York, NY | 65.7 | 58.8 |
| Newark, NJ | 61.4 | 50.4 |
| Oklahoma City, OK | 80.4 | 62.7 |
| Philadelphia, PA | 77.6 | 69.8 |
| Pittsburgh, PA | 81.2 | 68.3 |
| Richmond, VA | 46.5 | 31.2 |
| Salt Lake City, UT | 87.0 | 76.6 |
| San Antonio, TX | 42.6 | 31.4 |
| San Francisco, CA | 68.0 | 64.4 |
| Seattle, WA | 92.0 | 70.8 |
| Tampa, FL | 68.8 | 63.6 |
| Topeka, KA | 81.9 | 69.3 |

*Source:* Edward R. Tufte, "Registration and Voting" in *Statistics: A Guide to the Unknown*, ed. J. Tanur (New York: Holden Day, 1972), pp. 153–161.

It has been suggested that the relatively low voter turnout was related to the difficulty of registering to vote. Using Minitab, carry out the following.
**a.** Find the least squares line $\hat{y} = \hat{\alpha} + \hat{\beta}x$, using voter turnout as the dependent variable and registration as the independent variable.
**b.** Construct a multiple plot of the observed $y_i$ values and the predicted $\hat{y}_i$ values versus $x_i$.
**c.** Estimate the increase in voter turnout (in percentage points) for an increase of 1 percent in voter registration.

**10.16** The data on page 367 give the weight (in thousands of pounds) and the average mileage per gallon for 32 automobiles. Use Minitab to carry out the following.
**a.** Find the least squares line $\hat{y} = \hat{\alpha} + \hat{\beta}x$, using mpg as the dependent variable.
**b.** Construct a multiple plot of $y_i$ and $\hat{y}_i$ versus $x_i$.
**c.** Estimate the change in mpg for an increase of 1000 pounds in vehicle weight and for an increase of 100 pounds in vehicle weight.

| Automobile | Weight | mpg | Automobile | Weight | mpg |
|---|---|---|---|---|---|
| Mazda RX-4 | 2.620 | 21.0 | Chrysler Imperial | 5.345 | 14.7 |
| Mazda RX-4 Wagon | 2.875 | 21.0 | Fiat 128 | 2.200 | 32.4 |
| Datsun 710 | 2.320 | 22.8 | Honda Civic | 1.615 | 30.4 |
| Hornet 4 Drive | 3.215 | 21.4 | Toyota Corolla | 1.835 | 33.9 |
| Hornet Sportabout | 3.440 | 18.7 | Toyota Corona | 2.465 | 21.5 |
| Valiant | 3.460 | 18.1 | Dodge Challenger | 3.520 | 15.5 |
| Duster 360 | 3.570 | 14.3 | AMC Javelin | 3.435 | 15.2 |
| Mercedes 240D | 3.190 | 24.4 | Camaro Z-28 | 3.840 | 13.3 |
| Mercedes 230 | 3.150 | 22.8 | Pontiac Firebird | 3.845 | 19.2 |
| Mercedes 280 | 3.440 | 19.2 | Fiat X1-9 | 1.935 | 27.3 |
| Mercedes 280C | 3.440 | 17.8 | Porsche 914-2 | 2.140 | 26.0 |
| Mercedes 450SE | 4.070 | 16.4 | Lotus Europa | 1.513 | 30.4 |
| Mercedes 450SL | 3.730 | 17.3 | Ford Pantera L | 3.170 | 15.8 |
| Mercedes 450SLC | 3.780 | 15.2 | Ferrari Dino 1973 | 2.770 | 19.7 |
| Cadillac Fleetwood | 5.250 | 10.4 | Maserati Bora | 3.570 | 15.0 |
| Lincoln Continental | 5.424 | 10.4 | Volvo 142E | 2.780 | 21.4 |

*Source:* H. V. Henderson and P. F. Vellman, "Building Multiple Regression Models Interactively," *Biometrics* 37 (1981): 396.

## 10.3

## The ANOVA Table and the Coefficient of Determination

ANOVA

Estimators of the unknown parameters $\alpha$ and $\beta$ of the simple linear regression model were given in Equation 10.8 of Section 10.2. Section 10.1 stated that the assumed common variance $\sigma^2$ of the $\varepsilon_i$ (and thus of the $Y_i$) must be estimated from the $(x_i, y_i)$ values. This section presents a method for doing so, using the **ANOVA** table for the simple linear regression model. The abbreviation ANOVA stands for ANalysis Of VAriance. In an ANOVA table the variability in $Y$ is partitioned into two nonnegative parts: a part explained by $x$ and a residual or unexplained part. The residual part provides an estimate of $\sigma^2$. A statistical measure of the goodness-of-fit of the data to the linear model is provided by the ratio of the portion of the variability in $Y$ explained by $x$ to the total variability in $Y$. This ratio, called the coefficient of determination, gives a statistical measure of the goodness-of-fit of the data to a line. The basic decomposition is stated precisely as follows:

$$y_i - \bar{y} = y_i - \hat{y}_i + (\hat{y}_i - \bar{y})$$

Squaring both sides and summing yields

$$\sum (y_i - \bar{y})^2 = \sum (y_i - \hat{y}_i)^2 + \sum (\hat{y}_i - \bar{y})^2 \qquad \textbf{10.10}$$

or

$$SST = SSE + SSR$$

total sum of squares (SST)

as the sum of the cross products is zero. The left-hand term in Equation 10.10 represents the total variability in $Y$. This nonnegative quantity is called the **total sum of squares (SST)**. The first term to the right of the equal sign in Equation 10.10

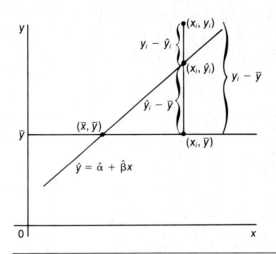

**Figure 10.5**

Decomposition of $y_i - \bar{y}$

is the sum of the squares of the residuals. This term is referred to as either the
**sum of squares for error (SSE)** residual sum of squares or the **sum of squares for error (SSE)**.

---

**Definition 10.1** ▄▄▄▄▄▄▄▄▄▄▄▄▄▄▄▄▄▄▄▄▄▄▄▄▄▄▄▄▄▄▄▄▄

In the simple linear regression model for which $\hat{y}_i = \hat{\alpha} + \hat{\beta}x_i$ (that is, $\hat{y}_i$ is the least squares prediction at $x = x_i$), the difference $y_i - \hat{y}_i$ is called the $i$th **residual**.

---

**sum of squares for regression (SSR)** The second term to the right of the equal sign represents the variability explained by the model. Another nonnegative quantity, it is referred to as the **sum of squares for regression (SSR)**. This term is the same as the term to the left of the equal sign except that the predicted values $\hat{y}_i = \hat{\alpha} + \hat{\beta}x_i$ have replaced the $y_i$ values.

The graph of the least squares line in Figure 10.5 indicates how the distance $y_i - \bar{y} = (y_i - \hat{y}_i) + (\hat{y}_i - \bar{y})$ is partitioned into two parts. The first part, $y_i - \hat{y}_i$, is considered to be unexplained by the regression line; it is thought of as a deviation from the regression line. The second part, $\hat{y}_i - \bar{y}$, is thought of as explained by the regression line.

The basic decomposition of Equation 10.10 is displayed in the analysis of variance (ANOVA) table given in Table 10.1. The heading "Source" refers to the source of the variability. The heading "d.f." refers to the degrees of freedom of the individual sums of squares. At this point the reader is asked to accept without explanation that the degrees of freedom for regression and error are correct. The "Mean Squares" are the sum of squares divided by the corresponding degrees of

## Table 10.1

**Analysis of Variance Table for Simple Linear Regression**

| Source | d.f. | Sum of Squares | Mean Square | Expected Mean Square |
|--------|------|----------------|-------------|----------------------|
| Regression | 1 | $SSR = \Sigma(\hat{y}_i - \bar{y})^2$ | $MSR = SSR/1$ | $\sigma^2 + \beta^2 \Sigma(x_i - \bar{x})^2$ |
| Error | $n - 2$ | $SSE = \Sigma(y_i - \hat{y}_i)^2$ | $MSE = SSE/(n - 2)$ | $\sigma^2$ |
| Total | $n - 1$ | $SST = \Sigma(y_i - \bar{y})^2$ | | |

**mean square for regression (MSR)**

**mean square for error (MSE)**

freedom. The table provides a **mean square for regression (MSR)** and a **mean square for error (MSE)**. It can be shown that

$$E(\text{MSE}) = E\left(\sum \frac{(y_i - \hat{y}_i)^2}{n - 2}\right) = \sigma^2 \qquad \textbf{10.11}$$

Equation 10.11 states that the mean square for error is an unbiased estimator of the unknown variance $\sigma^2$. It is not equal to $\sigma^2$, just as the sample variance is not equal to the population variance. Observations of a different set of five individuals with the same number of years of college education as those in Example 10.2 would produce different $y_i$ (income) values—for example, $(2, y_1)$, $(3, y_2)$, $(4, y_3)$, $(5, y_4)$, and $(6, y_5)$. Hence, the least squares line would have different values of $\hat{\alpha}$ and $\hat{\beta}$, and the MSE would be different as well. Similarly, it can be shown that

$$E(\text{MSR}) = \sigma^2 + \beta^2 \sum (x_i - \bar{x})^2 \qquad \textbf{10.12}$$

The last column of the ANOVA table (Table 10.1) gives the expected values of MSR and MSE. Notice that, as $\sigma^2$ and $\beta^2$ are unknown, these expected values cannot be computed from a given set of data.

When making calculations by hand, first find SST and SSR. Then the sum of squares for error can be computed from SSE = SST − SSR. An alternative expression for SSR which is frequently used for such calculations is

$$SSR = \sum (\hat{y}_i - \bar{y})^2 = \sum [\bar{y} + \hat{\beta}(x_i - \bar{x}) - \bar{y}]^2 = \hat{\beta}^2 \sum (x_i - \bar{x})^2 \qquad \textbf{10.13}$$

The term $\hat{y}_i = \bar{y} + \hat{\beta}(x_i - \bar{x})$ has been substituted from Equation 10.9.

## Example 10.4

We can compute the mean squares and construct an ANOVA table for the data of Example 10.2. Given that SSR = $(2.4)^2(10) = 57.6$ and SST = 62,

$$SSE = SST - SSR = 62 - 57.6 = 4.4$$

The ANOVA table for these data is shown in Table 10.2.

Table 10.2

**ANOVA Table for Data of Example 10.2**

| Source | d.f. | SS | MS | EMS |
|--------|------|------|-------|-------------------|
| Regression | 1 | 57.6 | 57.6 | $\sigma^2 + 10\beta^2$ |
| Error | 3 | 4.4 | 1.467 | $\sigma^2$ |
| Total | 4 | 62.0 | | |

The value of the mean square for error is MSE $= 1.467$; this is the estimate of $\sigma^2$. The expressions for the expected mean squares are given in terms of $\sigma^2$ and $\beta$ and cannot be further reduced, as $\sigma^2$ and $\beta$ are unknown parameters.

## Minitab Display of the ANOVA Table

The data for the top 25 batters in the American League in 1980 will be used to illustrate the way an ANOVA table is presented by Minitab. The number of hits and runs for each batter were stored in C1 and C2, respectively, and then the REGRESS command was used to yield the output in Exhibit 10.5. The output includes the equation of the least squares line and the analysis of variance table, as well as some other statistics which will be explained later. The equation of the least squares line (also called the regression equation) for these data is given by

$$\hat{y} = -16.3 + 0.584x$$

The value of the MSE is 139.6. (Note that Minitab denotes the MSE by $s^2$ and

**Exhibit 10.5**

```
MTB > REGRESS Y IN C2 ON 1 X IN C1 RESIDS IN C3 PRED C4

The regression equation is
RUNS = - 16.3 + 0.584 HITS

Predictor      Coef        Stdev     t-ratio
Constant      -16.27       12.22      -1.33
HITS          0.58380     0.07189      8.12

s = 11.82      R-sq = 74.1%     R-sq(adj) = 73.0%

Analysis of Variance

SOURCE       DF        SS          MS
Regression    1      9208.6      9208.6
Error        23      3211.3       139.6
Total        24     12419.8
```

calculates $s = 11.82$. In this text the MSE will be denoted by $\hat{\sigma}^2$, however, because $s^2$ has been used to denote the sample variance.)

One additional statistic of importance in the simple linear regression model will now be considered—the coefficient of determination.

---

**Definition 10.2** ▪▪▪▪▪▪▪▪▪▪▪▪▪▪▪▪▪▪▪▪▪▪▪▪▪▪▪▪▪▪▪▪▪▪▪▪▪▪▪▪▪▪

coefficient of determination

The **coefficient of determination** is given by $r^2 = \text{SSR}/\text{SST}$.

---

The coefficient of determination represents the proportion of total variability in $Y$ explained by the model. Minitab converts the ratio SSR/SST to a percentage, which is labeled R-sq. For Example 10.4, the Minitab output shows that 74.1 percent of the variation in the number of runs scored by a batter is explained by the number of his hits.

Several properties of the coefficient of determination are important. We know from Equation 10.10 that SST = SSE + SSR. As all the sums of squares are nonnegative,

$$0 \leqslant \text{SSR} \leqslant \text{SST}$$

Thus

$$0 \leqslant \frac{\text{SSR}}{\text{SST}} = r^2 \leqslant 1 \qquad \qquad \textbf{10.14}$$

The extreme values of $r^2$, namely 0 and 1, are informative. If $r^2 = 0$,

$$\text{SSR} = \sum (\hat{y}_i - \bar{y})^2 = \hat{\beta}^2 \sum (x_i - \bar{x})^2 = 0$$

Assuming that the values of the $x_i$ are not all equal, $\Sigma(x_i - \bar{x})^2 \neq 0$, so $\hat{\beta} = 0$. Hence, $r^2 = 0$ implies $\hat{\beta} = 0$. The least squares line is in this case given by

$$\hat{y} = \hat{\alpha} + 0 \cdot x = \bar{y}, \qquad i = 1, 2, \ldots, n \qquad \qquad \textbf{10.15}$$

The least squares line for $r = 0$ is horizontal, and the estimator of $E(Y|x)$, namely $\hat{y} = \bar{y}$, does not depend on $x$ at all. In words, $r^2 = 0$ means that $Y$ does not depend linearly on $x$.

The other extreme case, $r^2 = 1$, implies that SST = SSR, or

$$\text{SSE} = \sum (y_i - \hat{y}_i)^2 = 0$$

For a sum of squares to equal zero, each term must be zero. Hence $r^2 = 1$ implies that $y_i = \hat{y}_i$, $i = 1, 2, \ldots, n$. As the $(x_i, \hat{y}_i)$ values lie on a line, however, $r^2 = 1$ implies that the original observations $(x_i, y_i)$ also must have been on a line. In this case the fit of the least squares line to the data is perfect. This will hardly ever occur with real data. We can conclude, however, that values of the coefficient of determination that are close to but less than 1 suggest strong linear dependence of $E(Y)$ on the independent variable $x$. An example of close correspondence is given by the data of Example 10.4, for which $r^2 = \text{SSR}/\text{SST} = 57.6/62 = 0.929$.

**10.17 a.** Construct an analysis of variance table for the data of exercise 10.7.
  **b.** Find an unbiased estimate of $\sigma^2$ under the assumptions of the simple linear regression model.
  **c.** Find the coefficient of determination for this data set.

**10.18** Answer the questions in parts a–c of exercise 10.17 for the data of exercise 10.8.

**10.19 a.** Construct an analysis of variance table for the data of exercise 10.9.
  **b.** What proportion of the variability in expenditures of these families is explained by their incomes?
  **c.** Estimate $\sigma^2$ using an unbiased estimate, assuming that $Y_i = \alpha + \beta x_i + \varepsilon_i$, where the $\varepsilon_i$ are independent, $E(\varepsilon_i) = 0$, and $\text{Var}(\varepsilon_i) = \sigma^2$.

**10.20 a.** Answer the questions in parts a and c of exercise 10.19 for the data of exercise 10.10.
  **b.** What proportion of the variability in taxes due from each taxpayer is explained by the number of dependents the taxpayer has?

**10.21** Using Minitab, construct an ANOVA table and find the coefficient of determination for the data of exercise 10.11.

**10.22** Using Minitab, construct an ANOVA table and find the coefficient of determination for the data of exercise 10.12. Interpret in words the meaning of $r^2$.

**10.23** The amounts of thermal energy and total energy (in trillions of kilowatt hours) produced in 1979 by the ten countries producing the most energy are given below.

| Country | Thermal Energy | Total Energy |
|---|---|---|
| U.S. | 1,783.028 | 2,323.806 |
| U.S.S.R. | 1,015.000 | 1,240.000 |
| Japan | 435.504 | 581.441 |
| West Germany | 313.078 | 373.618 |
| Canada | 75.988 | 352.304 |
| U.K. | 258.582 | 299.960 |
| China | 208.950 | 281.950 |
| France | 134.266 | 241.124 |
| Italy | 127.194 | 180.522 |
| Poland | 115.000 | 117.460 |

*Source: United Nations 1979 Yearbook of World Energy Statistics,*
Statistical Papers, Series J23 (New York: Statistical Office of the
United Nations).

  Use Minitab to carry out the following.
  **a.** Find the regression equation $\hat{y} = \hat{\alpha} + \hat{\beta}x$ for thermal energy ($Y$) on total energy ($x$).
  **b.** Construct an ANOVA table for these data.
  **c.** Calculate an unbiased estimate of $\sigma^2$.
  **d.** Find $r^2$.

**10.24** Use Minitab to answer the questions in parts b, c, and d of exercise 10.23 for the voter registration and turnout data of exercise 10.15.

**10.25** Use Minitab to answer the questions in parts b, c, and d of exercise 10.23 for the data on automobile weight and mpg in exercise 10.16.

## 10.4

**Inference for**
**α and β**

In Chapter 7 it was shown how inference for the unknown parameter $\mu$ in the normal case led to confidence intervals and tests. In this section we will apply similar methods of inference for the parameters of the simple linear regression model. In order to carry out tests of hypotheses and find confidence intervals for the unknown values of $\alpha$ and $\beta$, three assumptions must be made.

**1** $Y_i = \alpha + \beta x_i + \varepsilon_i$, $i = 1, 2, \ldots, n$, where $\alpha$ and $\beta$ are unknown constants and the $x_i$ are known real numbers.

**normality of $\varepsilon_i$** **2** $\varepsilon_i \sim N(0, \sigma^2)$ for all $i$ **(normality of $\varepsilon_i$).** That is, each $\varepsilon_i$ is normally distributed with expectation 0 and variance $\sigma^2$.

**3** The $\varepsilon_i$ are independently distributed.

In this text the emphasis will be on inference for $\beta$. This unknown constant is important, as it represents the true average change in $Y$ per unit increase in $x$. Thus, in Example 10.2 concerning salary ($Y$) and years of college ($x$), $\beta$ represents the average change in annual salary (in thousands of dollars) associated with each additional year of college.

The expression for the statistic $\hat{\beta}$ may be written as

$$\hat{\beta} = \frac{\Sigma(x_i - \bar{x})(Y_i - \bar{Y})}{\Sigma(x_i - \bar{x})^2}$$
$$= \frac{\Sigma(x_i - \bar{x})Y_i}{\Sigma(x_i - \bar{x})^2} \qquad \textbf{10.16}$$

The $\bar{Y}$ term may be dropped, as $\Sigma(x_i - \bar{x}) = 0$. Then it is a straightforward matter to show that

$$E(\hat{\beta}) = \beta \qquad \textbf{10.17}$$

Equation 10.17 states that $\hat{\beta}$ is an unbiased estimate of $\beta$. Similarly, it can be shown that

$$\text{Var}(\hat{\beta}) = \frac{\sigma^2}{\Sigma(x_i - \bar{x})^2} = \sigma_{\hat{\beta}}^2 \qquad \textbf{10.18}$$

It is known that any linear combination of mutually independent normal variables $Y_i$—that is, any expression of the form $\Sigma_{i=1}^n a_i Y_i$ for constants $a_i$—is normally distributed. As the $x_i$ are fixed real numbers, Equation 10.16 shows that $\hat{\beta}$ has a normal distribution. Hence the standardized random variable $(\hat{\beta} - \beta)/\sigma_{\hat{\beta}}$ has (exactly) a standard normal distribution. Because $\sigma$ is unknown, this parameter is replaced by its estimate $\hat{\sigma} = \sqrt{\text{MSE}}$. Given that $s_{\hat{\beta}}^2 = \hat{\sigma}^2/\Sigma(x_i - \bar{x})^2$, it can be shown that

$$\frac{\hat{\beta} - \beta}{s_{\hat{\beta}}} \sim t_{n-2} \qquad \textbf{10.19}$$

that is, this new expression has Student's $t$ distribution with $n - 2$ degrees of freedom under assumptions 1–3 above. This discussion is entirely analogous to

**Table 10.3**

| Critical Regions for Tests of $H_0$: $\beta = \beta_0$ | |
|---|---|
| Alternative | Critical Region |
| $\beta > \beta_0$ | $t \geqslant t_{\alpha, n-2}$ |
| $\beta < \beta_0$ | $t \geqslant -t_{\alpha, n-2}$ |
| $\beta \neq \beta_0$ | $|t| \geqslant t_{\alpha/2, n-2}$ |

that of Chapter 7, in which it was argued that $(\bar{X} - \mu)/(S/\sqrt{n})$ had a $t$ distribution with $n - 1$ degrees of freedom.

**confidence intervals for $\beta$**   We can now use familiar methods to find **confidence intervals for $\beta$**, the unknown parameter, and carry out tests of hypotheses about $\beta$. A $(1 - \alpha)100$ percent confidence interval for $\beta$ has endpoints given by

$$\hat{\beta} \pm s_{\hat{\beta}}(t_{\alpha/2, n-2}) \tag{10.20}$$

Tests concerning the value of $\beta$ are analogous to small-sample tests of $\mu$. To test the null hypothesis $H_0$: $\beta = \beta_0$, we use the calculated value of

$$t = \frac{\hat{\beta} - \beta_0}{s_{\hat{\beta}}} \tag{10.21}$$

The rejection regions for standard alternatives are presented in Table 10.3.

**Example 10.5**

For the data of Example 10.2 relating salary $(Y)$ to years of college $(x)$, we have

$$s_{\hat{\beta}} = \sqrt{\frac{\text{MSE}}{\Sigma(x_i - \bar{x})^2}} = \sqrt{\frac{1.467}{10}} = 0.383$$

Endpoints for a 95 percent confidence interval for $\beta$ can be calculated using Equation 10.20:

$$2.4 \pm (0.383)t_{0.025, 3} = 2.4 \pm (0.383)(3.182) = 2.4 \pm 1.22$$

The required confidence interval is (1.18, 3.62). Thus for each additional year of college the estimated increase in salary is $\hat{\beta} = 2.4$ thousand dollars annually.

## Use of Minitab to Calculate Confidence Interval

The Minitab output in Exhibit 10.5 gave $\hat{\beta} = 0.584$ and $s_{\hat{\beta}} = 0.07189$ for the data on hits and runs by American League players. The value of $s_{\hat{\beta}}$ is given as the "Stdev" associated with the variable $x$ (HITS). The endpoints of a 95 percent confidence interval are given by

$$0.584 \pm (0.07189)t_{0.025,23} = 0.584 \pm (0.07189)(2.069)$$
$$= 0.584 \pm 0.149$$

The interval is (0.435, 0.733). Thus for each additional hit he makes, the number of runs a 0.300-plus hitter scores is increased by a true average amount $\beta$. This amount is estimated by the point estimate $\hat{\beta} = 0.584$ and the confidence interval just calculated. The point estimate $\hat{\beta}$ implies an estimated average increase of $100\hat{\beta} = 58.4$ runs for 100 additional hits, which makes good baseball sense. The corresponding 95 percent confidence interval for 100 additional hits is (43.5, 73.3).

## Example 10.6

Suppose a friend has asserted that an additional year of college increases an individual's salary by more than $2000 annually. To evaluate this assertion, we test

$$H_0: \beta \leqslant 2 \qquad \text{versus} \qquad H_1: \beta > 2$$

The rejection region for an $\alpha = 0.05$ level test is

$$t \geqslant t_{0.05,3} = 2.353$$

For the data of Example 10.2, where $n = 5$, the correct number of degrees of freedom is $n - 2 = 3$. Using these data we calculate

$$t = \frac{2.4 - 2.0}{0.07189} = 5.56$$

The calculated value of the test statistic lies in the critical region, so there is statistical evidence to support the friend's assertion.

Often it is important to test

$$H_0: \beta = 0 \qquad \text{versus} \qquad H_1: \beta \neq 0 \qquad \qquad \textbf{10.22}$$

The model assumption is $E(Y|x) = \alpha + \beta x$, so the null hypothesis means that $E(Y|x) = \alpha$. In other words, the null hypothesis states that the value of $x$ does not influence the average value of $Y$. The calculated test statistic is

$$t = \frac{\hat{\beta}}{s_{\hat{\beta}}} \qquad \qquad \textbf{10.23}$$

## Use of Minitab to Test $H_0: \beta = 0$

The value of $t$ in Equation 10.23 is identified by Minitab as the $t$ ratio. For the data of Example 10.1, the null hypothesis $H_0: \beta = 0$ means that the number of hits by a 0.300-plus hitter does not affect (on average) the number of runs scored.

Intuitively, this null hypothesis seems absurd. The $t$ value computed by the REGRESS command in Exhibit 10.5 is $t = 8.12$; this value will lie in the rejection region for $H_0$ at any reasonable level of $\alpha$. For example, for $\alpha = 0.01$ the critical region is

$$|t| \geqslant t_{0.005,23} = 2.807$$

so the correct decision is to reject $H_0$ in favor of $H_1: \beta \neq 0$.

Note that the ANOVA table given in Table 10.1 states that both $E(\text{MSR})$ and $E(\text{MSE})$ equal $\sigma^2$ under the null hypothesis $H_0: \beta = 0$. Thus we can also test the hypotheses in Equation 10.22 using the statistic

$$F = \frac{\text{MSR}}{\text{MSE}} \qquad\qquad \textbf{10.24}$$

Recall that the $F$ statistic originally was introduced to test the equality of variances of two independent normal distributions. It can be shown that MSR and MSE are independent under $H_0$ and that $\text{MSR} \sim \chi_1^2$ and $\text{MSE} \sim (\chi_{n-2}^2)/(n-2)$; that is, the numerator and denominator of the $F$ statistic have degrees of freedom equal to 1 and $n - 2$, respectively. From Table 10.1 we see that under $H_1: \beta \neq 0$, $E(\text{MSR}) > \sigma^2$, so an appropriate critical region for the hypotheses of Equation 10.22 is

$$F \geqslant F_\alpha(1, n - 2) \qquad\qquad \textbf{10.25}$$

Using the values shown in the Minitab output in Exhibit 10.5, we find that

$$F = \frac{9208.6}{139.6} = 65.96$$

For $\alpha = 0.01$, $F_{0.01}(1, 23) = 7.88$, so $H_0: \beta = 0$ clearly should be rejected in favor of $H_1: \beta \neq 0$ (as before). It can be shown that in testing of the null and alternative hypotheses of Equation 10.22, an $\alpha$-level $t$ test and an $\alpha$-level $F$ test will always yield the same conclusion.

Inference for the unknown intercept $\alpha = E(Y|x = 0)$ proceeds along lines similar to those described for $\beta$. Most of the details will be omitted, as they are analogous to those just presented. It can be shown that $\hat{\alpha}$ is an unbiased estimator for $\alpha$—that is,

$$E(\hat{\alpha}) = \alpha \qquad\qquad \textbf{10.26}$$

Also,

$$\text{Var}(\hat{\alpha}) = \sigma^2 \left( \frac{1}{n} + \frac{\bar{x}^2}{\Sigma(x_i - \bar{x})^2} \right) \qquad\qquad \textbf{10.27}$$

Replacing $\sigma^2$ by $\hat{\sigma}^2$, we have

$$s_{\hat{\alpha}}^2 = \hat{\sigma}^2 \left( \frac{1}{n} + \frac{\bar{x}^2}{\Sigma(x_i - \bar{x})^2} \right) \qquad\qquad \textbf{10.28}$$

Just as $(\hat{\beta} - \beta)/s_{\hat{\beta}} \sim t_{n-2}$,

$$\frac{\hat{\alpha} - \alpha}{s_{\hat{\alpha}}} \sim t_{n-2}$$

The endpoints of a $(1 - \alpha)100$ percent confidence interval for $\alpha$ are given by

$$\hat{\alpha} \pm (s_{\hat{\alpha}})t_{\alpha/2,\,n-2} \qquad\qquad \textbf{10.29}$$

Tests for $\alpha$ are based on the statistic

$$t = \frac{\hat{\alpha} - \alpha_0}{s_{\hat{\alpha}}}$$

The critical regions for appropriate alternatives are exactly the same as those of Table 10.3.

## Exercises 10.4

**10.26 a.** Find a 95 percent confidence interval for $\beta$ using the data of exercise 10.7. Use the ANOVA table created in exercise 10.17.
  **b.** Test $H_0$: $\beta = 0$ versus $H_1$: $\beta \neq 0$, using the $t$ statistic. Assume that $\alpha = 0.05$. Do not use a computer for this problem.

**10.27 a.** Find a 90 percent confidence interval for the increase in sales for each additional day a salesperson travels, using the data of exercise 10.8 and the ANOVA table constructed in exercise 10.18.
  **b.** Test $H_0$: $\beta = 0$ versus $H_1$: $\beta \neq 0$, using both the $t$ test and the $F$ test. Use $\alpha = 0.05$. Do not use a computer for this problem.

**10.28 a.** Use the data of exercise 10.9 to find a 95 percent confidence interval for $\beta$, the increase in average family expenditure per additional dollar of income. Use the ANOVA table constructed in exercise 10.19.
  **b.** Test $H_0$: $\beta = 0.7$ versus $H_1$: $\beta \neq 0.7$, using $\alpha = 0.05$.

**10.29 a.** Use the data of exercise 10.10 to find a 90 percent confidence interval for $\beta$, the decrease in income tax due in thousands of dollars for each additional dependent. Use the ANOVA table constructed in exercise 10.20.
  **b.** Test $H_0$: $\beta = -0.8$ versus $H_1$: $\beta < -0.8$, using $\alpha = 0.10$.

**10.30 a.** Use the data of exercise 10.11 and the Minitab output from exercise 10.21 to find a 95 percent confidence interval for $\beta$, the average increase in pieces produced for an additional hour of work.
  **b.** Test $H_0$: $\beta = 0$ versus $H_1$: $\beta \neq 0$, using $\alpha = 0.05$. Use both the $t$ test and the $F$ test.

**10.31** Use the data of exercise 10.12 and the Minitab output from exercise 10.22 to estimate the average increase in electrical resistance [in (ohms/cm) $\times$ $10^{-6}$] per unit increase in degrees Kelvin, by finding a 99 percent confidence interval for $\beta$.

**10.32** Using the data of exercise 10.15 and the Minitab output from exercise 10.24, find a 95 percent confidence interval for the percentage increase in voter turnout for each additional 1 percent of the population registered.

**10.33** Use the data of exercise 10.16 and the Minitab output from exercise 10.25 to estimate the decrease in mpg for each additional thousand pounds of weight of an automobile by finding a 95 percent confidence interval for $\beta$.

**10.34** Use the Minitab output from exercise 10.23 to find a 95 percent confidence interval for the 1979 average increase in thermal energy production per unit increase in total energy production (in trillions of kilowatt hours).

## 10.5

**Estimation and Prediction**

The simple linear regression model is often used to estimate an average value of $Y$, the dependent random variable, at a particular value of $x$, say $x = x_0$. For instance, for Example 10.1, it would be interesting to predict the average number of runs scored by a batter getting 200 hits. The estimate is found by evaluating the expression $\hat{Y} = \hat{\alpha} + \hat{\beta}x$ at $x = x_0 = 200$. In this case the expression yields

$$-16.3 + (0.5838)200 = 100.49 \text{ (runs)}$$

The estimate of the average value of $Y$ at $x = x_0$ is denoted by

$$\hat{\mu}_{Y|x_0} = \hat{\alpha} + \hat{\beta}x_0 \qquad \textbf{10.30}$$

**confidence intervals for** $\mu_{Y|x_0}$

As usual, **confidence intervals for** $\mu_{Y|x_0}$ are generally more useful than point estimates. This fact leads to consideration of the statistical properties of $\hat{\mu}_{Y|x_0}$.

First, the expectation of this estimated average value is given by

$$E(\hat{\mu}_{Y|x_0}) = E(\hat{\alpha} + \hat{\beta}x_0) = \alpha + \beta x_0 \qquad \textbf{10.31}$$

which is the true average value of $Y$ at $x = x_0$. Given the model assumptions presented in the previous section, the estimate is unbiased. The variance of $\hat{\mu}_{Y|x_0}$ can be found to be given by

$$\text{Var}(\hat{\alpha} + \hat{\beta}x_0) = \sigma^2 \left( \frac{1}{n} + \frac{(x_0 - \bar{x})^2}{\Sigma(x_i - \bar{x})^2} \right) \qquad \textbf{10.32}$$

If $\hat{\sigma}$ is substituted for $\sigma$ in the above expression for the variance of $\hat{\mu}_{Y|x_0}$, the expression becomes

$$\widehat{\text{Var}}(\hat{\mu}_{Y|x_0}) = \hat{\sigma}^2 \left( \frac{1}{n} + \frac{(x_0 - \bar{x})^2}{\Sigma(x_i - \bar{x})^2} \right) \qquad \textbf{10.33}$$

It can be shown that

$$\frac{\hat{\mu}_{Y|x_0} - (\alpha + \beta x_0)}{\sqrt{\widehat{\text{Var}}(\hat{\mu}_{Y|x_0})}} \sim t_{n-2} \qquad \textbf{10.34}$$

that is, the expression on the left-hand side of Equation 10.34 has a $t$ distribution with $n - 2$ degrees of freedom. Thus the endpoints of a $(1 - \alpha)100$ percent confidence interval for $\mu_{Y|x_0}$ are given by

$$\hat{\mu}_{Y|x_0} \pm \hat{\sigma} \sqrt{\frac{1}{n} + \frac{(x_0 - \bar{x})^2}{\Sigma(x_i - \bar{x})^2}} \, t_{\alpha/2, n-2} \qquad \textbf{10.35}$$

## Use of Minitab to Find Confidence Intervals for $\mu_{Y|x=x_0}$

Using Equation 10.35 with the baseball data of Example 10.1, we find that the average number of runs scored by a 0.300-plus batter with 200 hits has endpoints given by

$$100.49 \pm 11.82 \sqrt{\frac{1}{25} + \frac{1104.90}{27019.29}} \; t_{0.025,23} = 100.49 \pm 6.96$$

The confidence interval is (93.53, 107.45). We know from the Minitab output of Exhibit 10.1 that $x_0 = 200$ and $\bar{x} = 166.76$. The value of $\Sigma(x_i - \bar{x})^2$ can be obtained from the value of the standard deviation of the $x_i$ values given in the same output. The value of $\hat{\sigma} = 11.82$ is obtained from the REGRESS command, as shown in Exhibit 10.5.

**PREDICT**   Minitab can be used to find a 95 percent confidence interval for the average value of $Y$ at $x = x_0$. The subcommand **PREDICT** used with the Minitab command REGRESS produces such a confidence interval and the predicted value given by Equation 10.30. Exhibit 10.6 shows the outcome generated when Minitab was used to perform these calculations for the data of Example 10.1. Note that the 95 percent confidence interval produced by Minitab agrees with that computed using Expression 10.35 (except for roundoff error).

It is clear from Expression 10.35 that, for a given set of $(x_i, y_i)$ values ($i = 1, 2, \ldots, n$) and confidence coefficient $(1 - \alpha)$, the confidence interval for $\mu_{Y|x_0}$ is

## Exhibit 10.6

```
MTB > REGRESS Y IN C2 ON 1 X IN C1 RESIDS IN C3 PRED C4;
SUBC> PREDICT 200.

The regression equation is
RUNS = - 16.3 + 0.584 HITS

Predictor        Coef        Stdev      t-ratio
Constant       -16.27        12.22        -1.33
HITS          0.58380      0.07189         8.12

s = 11.82       R-sq = 74.1%     R-sq(adj) = 73.0%

Analysis of Variance

SOURCE        DF          SS           MS
Regression     1       9208.6       9208.6
Error         23       3211.3        139.6
Total         24      12419.8


      Fit   Stdev.Fit        95% C.I.          95% P.I.
   100.49        3.36   ( 93.53, 107.44)  ( 75.07, 125.90)
```

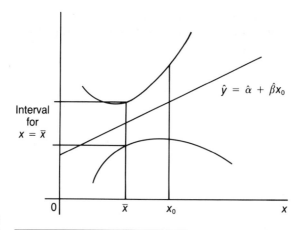

**Figure 10.6**

Endpoints of Confidence Intervals for $\mu_{Y|x_0}$

shortest when $x = \bar{x}$. Estimation of $\mu_{Y|x = x_0}$ for values of $x_0$ that are not close to $\bar{x}$ will produce a very wide confidence interval. The relationship is graphically displayed in Figure 10.6. Also, the relationship of $Y$ and $x$ may be roughly linear over a range of values of $x$ near $\bar{x}$, but not linear outside of this range. For example, in Example 10.2, where $Y$ was salary and $x$ the number of years of college, an individual's salary was estimated to increase 2.4 thousand dollars for each year of college. Clearly the model is not designed to apply to values of $x$ such as 30 (that is, 30 years of college). The predicted salary of $16.4 \pm 2.4(30) = 88.4$ thousand dollars would be a gross overestimate. Frequently the linearity assumption is valid only over a relatively small range of $x$ values. For this reason, estimation should be restricted to values of $x$ not far from the values of $x$ at which $Y$ has actually been observed.

It is possible to predict an individual future value of $Y$ at $x = x_0$, $Y_0$, rather than an average value of $Y$ at $x = x_0$. The predicted value for $\hat{Y}_0$ is the same as that for $\mu_{Y|x = x_0}$, namely

$$\hat{Y}_0 = \hat{\alpha} + \hat{\beta}x_0 \qquad \textbf{10.36}$$

The variance of the prediction is different from that of $\mu_{Y|x_0}$, however, because we are predicting $\mu_{Y|x_0} + \varepsilon_0$, the true average plus an individual value of the error term. Thus

$$\begin{aligned} \mathrm{Var}(\hat{Y}_0) &= \mathrm{Var}(\hat{\mu}_{Y|x_0}) + \mathrm{Var}(\varepsilon_0) \\ &= \sigma^2 \left( \frac{1}{n} + \frac{(x_0 - \bar{x})^2}{\Sigma(x_i - \bar{x})^2} + 1 \right) \qquad \textbf{10.37} \end{aligned}$$

**prediction interval for $Y_0$**  A **prediction interval for $Y_0$** with confidence coefficient $1 - \alpha$ has endpoints given by

$$\hat{\alpha} + \hat{\beta}x_0 \pm \hat{\sigma} \left[ \sqrt{\frac{1}{n} + \frac{(x_0 - \bar{x})^2}{\Sigma(x_i - \bar{x})^2} + 1} \, \right] t_{\alpha/2, n-2} \qquad \textbf{10.38}$$

The point predictor of the number of runs scored by a 0.300-plus batter who achieves $x_0 = 200$ hits is, like the predicted average value, 100.5. A 95 percent prediction interval is

$$100.5 \pm 11.82 \left[ \sqrt{\frac{1}{25} + 0.04089 + 1} \right] 2.069 = 100.5 \pm 25.43$$

The prediction interval becomes (75.07, 125.93). Again, except for roundoff error, this result agrees with the Minitab output in Exhibit 10.6. That this prediction interval is wider than that for the average number of runs scored by a hitter with 200 hits follows from a comparison of Expressions 10.35 and 10.38. It makes sense that an average value of $Y$ at $x_0$ can be predicted with more precision than can an individual observation of $Y$ at $x_0$.

## Exercises 10.5

**10.35 a.** Using the data and results of exercise 10.7 and the ANOVA table of exercise 10.17, estimate the average value of $Y$ at $x = 15$.
   **b.** Predict an individual value of $Y$ at $x = 15$.
   **c.** For what value of $x$ will a confidence interval for the average value of $Y$ (for fixed $\alpha$) be shortest?

**10.36 a.** Using the data and results of exercise 10.8 and the ANOVA table of exercise 10.18, estimate the average monthly sales (in thousands of dollars) of a salesperson who travels away from home seven days in a month.
   **b.** Find a 90 percent confidence interval for your estimate in part a.

**10.37 a.** Use the data and results of exercise 10.9 and the ANOVA table of exercise 10.19 to find a 95 percent confidence interval for the average expenditures of a family with an income of $2500 per month.
   **b.** For what value of $x_0$ will a 95 percent confidence interval for $\mu_{Y|x_0}$ be shortest?

**10.38 a.** Use the data and results of exercise 10.10 and the ANOVA table of exercise 10.20 to find a 95 percent confidence interval for the average income tax due from an individual with four dependents.
   **b.** For what value of $x_0$ will a 95 percent confidence interval be shortest?

**10.39** Use Minitab with the data of exercise 10.11 to find a 90 percent confidence interval for the average number of pieces completed by a worker working for four hours.

**10.40 a.** Use Minitab with the data of exercise 10.23 to predict the amount of thermal energy produced in a country with a total energy production of 500 trillion kilowatt hours.
   **b.** Find a 95 percent prediction interval for the value estimated in part a.

**10.41** Use Minitab with the data of exercise 10.15 to find the following:
   **a.** The estimated average percentage of voter turnout in a city with 70 percent of voting-age adults registered.
   **b.** The estimated percentage of voter turnout in a particular city with the same level of voter registration.
   **c.** Appropriate 95 percent intervals associated with the estimates in parts a and b.

**10.42** The following data give the 1980 sales and assets of the 25 largest U.S. corporations in millions of dollars.

| Corporation | Sales ($Y$) | Assets ($x$) |
|---|---|---|
| Exxon | 103,143 | 56,577 |
| Mobil | 59,510 | 32,705 |
| GM | 57,729 | 34,581 |
| Texaco | 51,196 | 26,430 |
| Standard Oil (Cal.) | 40,479 | 22,162 |
| Ford | 37,086 | 24,348 |
| Gulf | 26,483 | 18,638 |
| IBM | 26,213 | 26,703 |
| Standard Oil (Ind.) | 26,133 | 20,167 |
| GE | 24,959 | 18,511 |
| Atlantic Richfield | 23,744 | 16,605 |
| Shell | 19,830 | 17,615 |
| ITT | 18,530 | 15,417 |
| DuPont | 13,652 | 9,560 |
| Phillips Petroleum | 13,377 | 9,844 |
| Tenneco | 13,226 | 13,853 |
| Sun | 12,945 | 10,955 |
| U.S. Steel | 12,492 | 11,748 |
| Occidental Petroleum | 12,476 | 6,630 |
| United Technologies | 12,324 | 7,326 |
| Western Electric | 12,032 | 8,048 |
| Standard Oil (Ohio) | 11,023 | 12,080 |
| Procter and Gamble | 10,772 | 6,553 |
| Dow | 10,626 | 11,538 |
| Getty Oil | 10,150 | 8,267 |

*Source: Fortune* magazine, as reported in *The Information Please Almanac* (Boston: Houghton Mifflin, 1982), p. 44.

Use Minitab as needed to do the following.
**a.** Find the regression equation.
**b.** Find $r^2$.
**c.** Find a 95 percent confidence interval for the average sales of a large corporation with assets of $20,000,000,000.
**d.** Given that the assets of corporation A are $20,000,000,000, find a 95 percent confidence interval for the sales of this particular corporation.

**10.43** The following data give the average weekly gross earnings of employees in 12 nonmanufacturing industries in the United States in 1980 and the average number of hours worked weekly in these industries.

| Industry | Weekly Earnings ($) | Hours/Week |
|---|---|---|
| Bituminous Coal & Lignite Mining | 435.89 | 40.5 |
| Metal Mining | 415.53 | 40.5 |
| Nonmetallic Minerals | 327.87 | 43.6 |
| Telephone Communications | 350.54 | 40.2 |

(cont.)

| Industry | Weekly Earnings ($) | Hours/Week |
|---|---|---|
| Radio and TV Broadcasting | 286.46 | 38.1 |
| Electric, Gas, and Sanitary Services | 371.13 | 41.7 |
| Local and Suburban Transport | 275.01 | 39.4 |
| Wholesale Trade | 268.35 | 38.5 |
| Retail Trade | 146.89 | 30.1 |
| Hotels, Motels | 134.81 | 30.5 |
| Laundries & Dry Cleaning | 151.42 | 33.8 |
| General Building & Contracting | 333.04 | 36.2 |

*Source:* Department of Labor, Bureau of Statistics, as reported in *The Information Please Almanac* (Boston: Houghton Mifflin, 1982), p. 53.

**a.** Using earnings per week as the dependent variable, $Y$, and hours per week as the independent random variable, $x$, find the regression equation of $Y$ on $x$.

**b.** What are the values of $\hat{\sigma}^2$, $r^2$, and $s_\beta$?

**c.** Estimate the average weekly earnings in a nonmanufacturing industry in which the number of hours worked per week is 40.

**d.** Find a 95 percent confidence interval for the estimate in part c.

## 10.6
## Residual Plots

When the simple linear regression model is used to describe the relationship between a dependent variable $Y$ and an independent real variable $x$, it is important to get some indication of the validity of the model assumptions. There are three assumptions for which Minitab can provide useful graphical checks.

1    $E(Y|x) = \alpha + \beta x$ (the linearity assumption)
2    $\varepsilon_i \sim N(0, \sigma^2)$, $i = 1, 2, \ldots, n$ (the normality assumption)
3    $\text{Var}(Y|x) = \sigma^2$ (the constant variance assumption)

The invalidation of one or more of these assumptions casts doubt on the validity of inference based on the simple linear regression model. More positively, plotting may suggest ways in which the model or data set may be altered to improve inference. Because Minitab (and other statistical packages) can be used in an interactive fashion, comparisons of several statistical analyses of a data set can be made efficiently. Examples 10.7 and 10.8 illustrate the way Minitab provides visual checks of the above assumptions.

## Example 10.7

In the Minitab output in Exhibit 10.7, C1 gives the abbreviation for the state and C2 gives per capita income in 1980 for that state in thousands of dollars [*Source: Survey of Current Business*, U.S. Department of Commerce, as reported in *The Information Please Almanac* (Boston: Houghton Mifflin, 1982), p. 37]. In C3 the average annual salary ($Y$) in thousands of dollars for elementary

**Exhibit 10.7**

```
MTB > NAME C1 'STATE' C2 'INC' C3 'SALARY'
MTB > FPRINT C1-C3
 MTB > (1X,A3,2F10.1)
AL        7.5      14.6
AK       12.8      28.9
AZ        8.8      17.0
AR        7.3      12.9
CA       10.9      19.4
CO       10.0      16.9
CT       11.7      17.3
DE       10.3      17.0
FL        9.0      15.8
GA        8.1      15.2
HI       10.1      22.0
ID        8.1      14.8
IL       10.5      18.7
IN        8.9      17.6
IA        9.4      15.5
KS       10.0      15.0
KY        7.6      15.1
LA        8.5      14.7
ME        7.9      13.2
MD       10.5      19.1
MA       10.1      18.5
MI        9.9      21.0
MN        9.7      17.4
MS        6.6      12.7
MO        9.0      14.9
MT        8.5      14.8
NE        9.4      14.2
NV       10.7      17.0
NH        9.1      12.5
NJ       10.9      18.0
NM        7.8      15.5
NY       10.3      20.3
NC        7.8      15.7
ND        8.7      13.7
OH        9.5      15.7
OK        9.1      14.4
OR        9.3      17.2
PA        9.4      17.4
RI        9.4      19.3
SC        7.3      13.6
SD        7.8      13.5
TN        7.7      14.9
TX        9.5      14.8
UT        7.6      16.1
VT        7.8      12.6
VA        9.4      14.2
WA       10.3      20.3
WV        7.8      14.3
WI        9.3      16.3
WY       10.9      18.1
```

school teachers is listed (*Source:* National Educational Association Research: *Estimates of School Statistics*, 1980–81). We will assume that the average salary paid to elementary school teachers in a state depends linearly on per capita income in the state. The Minitab output giving the regression equation, the

**Exhibit 10.8**

```
MTB > BRIEF = 3
MTB > NOTE REGRESSION OF TEACHERS SALARIES ON STATE PER CAPITA INCOME
MTB > REGRESS Y IN C3 ON 1 X IN C2 RESIDS C4 PRED C5

The regression equation is
SALARY = 0.66 + 1.71 INC

Predictor        Coef        Stdev        t-ratio
Constant         0.660       1.992         0.33
INC              1.7142      0.2150        7.97

s = 1.938        R-sq = 57.0%      R-sq(adj) = 56.1%

Analysis of Variance

SOURCE         DF          SS           MS
Regression      1        238.88       238.88
Error          48        180.30         3.76
Total          49        419.18
```

analysis of variance table, and associated statistics such as $r^2$ and $\hat{\sigma}$ is shown in Exhibit 10.8.

**BRIEF**      Exhibit 10.9 shows tabular output generated by using the **BRIEF** = 3 command before the REGRESS command. The headings of this six-column table are INC, SALARY, Fit, Stdev.Fit, Residual, and St.Resid. In the notation of this chapter, these values are

$$x_i \qquad y_i \qquad \hat{y}_i = \hat{\alpha} + \hat{\beta}x_i \qquad s_{\hat{y}_i} \qquad y_i - \hat{y}_i \qquad \frac{y_i - \hat{y}_i}{s_{y_i - \hat{y}_i}} \qquad \textbf{10.39}$$

There are $n$ rows in this table—one row for each data point. Here $n = 50$. The values $s_{\hat{y}_i}$ in column 4 represent the estimated standard deviations of the predicted values $\hat{y}_i$. The residuals are in column 5. The quotients in column 6 are the residuals divided by their estimated standard deviations. If the model assumptions are correct, these standardized residuals can be taken to be $n$ (approximately independent) observations from a standard normal distribution.

Values of the standardized residuals will generally have a magnitude of 2 or less. Larger values are indicated in Exhibit 10.9 by an "R" following the standardized residual. A large value suggests an original observation that is very **outlier**   different from the others. Such an observation is called an **outlier**. In this case the second observation has a standardized residual of 3.6 and the eleventh observation has a standardized residual of 2.11. All the others are less than 2 in magnitude. The second observation is for Alaska, which is distinct in that its annual per capita income is by far the highest of all the states' at 12.8 thousand dollars. Also, the average salary of elementary school teachers in Alaska, $28,900, is by far the highest observed. The eleventh observation is for Hawaii. That state's annual per capita income is only thirteenth highest, but the average salary of teachers, $22,000,

**Exhibit 10.9**

| Obs. | INC | SALARY | Fit | Stdev.Fit | Residual | St.Resid |
|---|---|---|---|---|---|---|
| 1 | 7.5 | 14.600 | 13.496 | 0.455 | 1.104 | 0.59 |
| 2 | 12.8 | 28.900 | 22.584 | 0.823 | 6.316 | 3.60RX |
| 3 | 8.8 | 17.000 | 15.729 | 0.286 | 1.271 | 0.66 |
| 4 | 7.3 | 12.900 | 13.118 | 0.494 | -0.218 | -0.12 |
| 5 | 10.9 | 19.400 | 19.410 | 0.467 | -0.010 | -0.01 |
| 6 | 10.0 | 16.900 | 17.844 | 0.329 | -0.944 | -0.49 |
| 7 | 11.7 | 17.300 | 20.750 | 0.611 | -3.450 | -1.88 |
| 8 | 10.3 | 17.000 | 18.383 | 0.371 | -1.383 | -0.73 |
| 9 | 9.0 | 15.800 | 16.081 | 0.277 | -0.281 | -0.15 |
| 10 | 8.1 | 15.200 | 14.498 | 0.363 | 0.702 | 0.37 |
| 11 | 10.1 | 22.000 | 17.975 | 0.338 | 4.025 | 2.11R |
| 12 | 8.1 | 14.800 | 14.469 | 0.365 | 0.331 | 0.17 |
| 13 | 10.5 | 18.700 | 18.695 | 0.398 | 0.005 | 0.00 |
| 14 | 8.9 | 17.600 | 15.978 | 0.279 | 1.622 | 0.85 |
| 15 | 9.4 | 15.500 | 16.701 | 0.277 | -1.201 | -0.63 |
| 16 | 10.0 | 15.000 | 17.772 | 0.324 | -2.772 | -1.45 |
| 17 | 7.6 | 15.100 | 13.710 | 0.434 | 1.390 | 0.74 |
| 18 | 8.5 | 14.700 | 15.158 | 0.315 | -0.458 | -0.24 |
| 19 | 7.9 | 13.200 | 14.245 | 0.384 | -1.045 | -0.55 |
| 20 | 10.5 | 19.100 | 18.590 | 0.389 | 0.510 | 0.27 |
| 21 | 10.1 | 18.500 | 18.016 | 0.341 | 0.484 | 0.25 |
| 22 | 9.9 | 21.000 | 17.716 | 0.320 | 3.284 | 1.72 |
| 23 | 9.7 | 17.400 | 17.329 | 0.298 | 0.071 | 0.04 |
| 24 | 6.6 | 12.700 | 11.939 | 0.622 | 0.761 | 0.41 |
| 25 | 9.0 | 14.900 | 16.057 | 0.277 | -1.157 | -0.60 |
| 26 | 8.5 | 14.800 | 15.292 | 0.307 | -0.492 | -0.26 |
| 27 | 9.4 | 14.200 | 16.713 | 0.277 | -2.513 | -1.31 |
| 28 | 10.7 | 17.000 | 19.048 | 0.431 | -2.048 | -1.08 |
| 29 | 9.1 | 12.500 | 16.312 | 0.274 | -3.812 | -1.99 |
| 30 | 10.9 | 18.000 | 19.386 | 0.465 | -1.386 | -0.74 |
| 31 | 7.8 | 15.500 | 14.101 | 0.397 | 1.399 | 0.74 |
| 32 | 10.3 | 20.300 | 18.247 | 0.360 | 2.053 | 1.08 |
| 33 | 7.8 | 15.700 | 14.063 | 0.401 | 1.637 | 0.86 |
| 34 | 8.7 | 13.700 | 15.654 | 0.289 | -1.954 | -1.02 |
| 35 | 9.5 | 15.700 | 16.879 | 0.281 | -1.179 | -0.62 |
| 36 | 9.1 | 14.400 | 16.286 | 0.274 | -1.886 | -0.98 |
| 37 | 9.3 | 17.200 | 16.631 | 0.276 | 0.569 | 0.30 |
| 38 | 9.4 | 17.400 | 16.831 | 0.280 | 0.569 | 0.30 |
| 39 | 9.4 | 19.300 | 16.849 | 0.280 | 2.451 | 1.28 |
| 40 | 7.3 | 13.600 | 13.115 | 0.494 | 0.485 | 0.26 |
| 41 | 7.8 | 13.500 | 14.041 | 0.403 | -0.541 | -0.29 |
| 42 | 7.7 | 14.900 | 13.893 | 0.416 | 1.007 | 0.53 |
| 43 | 9.5 | 14.800 | 17.022 | 0.285 | -2.222 | -1.16 |
| 44 | 7.6 | 16.100 | 13.772 | 0.428 | 2.328 | 1.23 |
| 45 | 7.8 | 12.600 | 14.077 | 0.399 | -1.477 | -0.78 |
| 46 | 9.4 | 14.200 | 16.759 | 0.278 | -2.559 | -1.33 |
| 47 | 10.3 | 20.300 | 18.331 | 0.366 | 1.969 | 1.03 |
| 48 | 7.8 | 14.300 | 14.030 | 0.404 | 0.270 | 0.14 |
| 49 | 9.3 | 16.300 | 16.684 | 0.277 | -0.384 | -0.20 |
| 50 | 10.9 | 18.100 | 19.341 | 0.460 | -1.241 | -0.66 |

R denotes an obs. with a large st. resid.
X denotes an obs. whose X value gives it large influence.

is second highest. The notation "X" following a standardized residual means that the corresponding observation has a strong influence on the slope of the least squares line. An explanation of the reason for this influence is beyond the scope of this text, but this information may be helpful in a general way.

## Exhibit 10.10

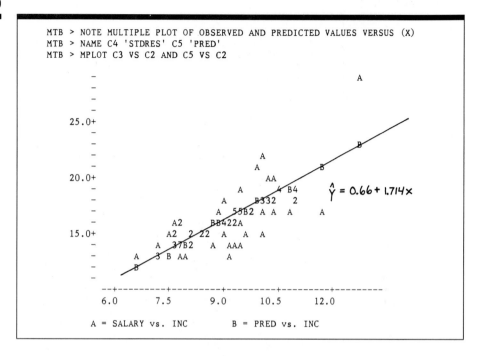

```
MTB > NOTE MULTIPLE PLOT OF OBSERVED AND PREDICTED VALUES VERSUS (X)
MTB > NAME C4 'STDRES' C5 'PRED'
MTB > MPLOT C3 VS C2 AND C5 VS C2
```

$$\hat{Y} = 0.66 + 1.714x$$

A = SALARY vs. INC          B = PRED vs. INC

Several plots have been generated to give an indication of the validity of the assumptions mentioned above. Exhibit 10.10 is a plot of $y_i$ and $\hat{y}_i$ versus per capita income, $x_i$. The original observations are denoted by the letter A; the predicted values are denoted by the letter B. The least squares line passing through the B values has been roughly sketched on this graph. There is a tendency for salaries of teachers to increase with per capita income, but the linearity assumption is only roughly justified. This fact is indicated both by this plot and by the $r^2$ value of 0.57, which can be interpreted to mean that 57 percent of the variability in the salaries of teachers is explained by the per capita income of the state in which they work. The $t$ value of 7.97 means that in testing of $H_0: \beta = 0$ versus $H_1: \beta \neq 0$, at any reasonable level of significance $H_0$ should be rejected. Hence per capita income is one variable explaining teacher income, but perhaps there are others.

**normal plot of the standardized residuals**     Exhibit 10.11 is a **normal plot of the standardized residuals**. It was obtained by plotting the normal scores of the standardized residuals created in C7 versus the standardized residuals themselves in C4. The plot is not too unsatisfactory (that is, it is reasonably linear), except for the extreme outlier, which also can be observed in the first plot. This plot suggests relatively good agreement of the data with the normality assumption. The largest standardized residual represents Alaska, where per capita income is $12,800 and elementary school teachers' salaries average

**Exhibit 10.11**

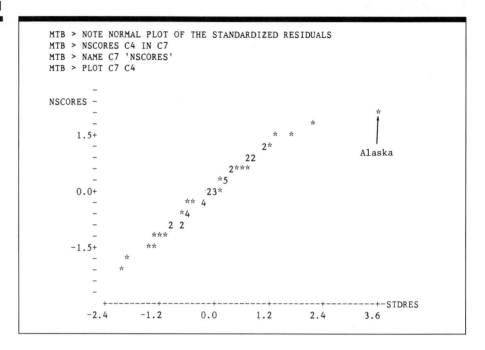

```
MTB > NOTE NORMAL PLOT OF THE STANDARDIZED RESIDUALS
MTB > NSCORES C4 IN C7
MTB > NAME C7 'NSCORES'
MTB > PLOT C7 C4
```

$28,900. As these values are far above comparable observations for other states, the normal plot also suggests that the observation for Alaska is not consonant with the other observations.

One additional plot is used to check the assumption of constant variance $\sigma^2$ (and the general goodness-of-fit of the model): a plot of the standardized residuals in C4 versus the predicted values in C5 (Exhibit 10.12). A random scatter of points indicates that the model is satisfactory. The plot for this model shows some tendency for the "spread" of the residuals to increase as the predicted values (and hence the $x_i$ values) increase. This tendency, highlighted by the dashed lines added to the plot, suggests that the assumption of constant variance $\sigma^2$ for all $x$ values is somewhat questionable for this data set.

Given plots like Exhibits 10.10–10.12, it is sometimes recommended that the extreme outlier be deleted and the regression analysis be performed again without this data point. This approach was used to generate the output shown in Exhibits 10.13 through 10.17. The new analysis differs from the old one in several ways. First, $r^2$ has decreased from 0.570 to 0.493, indicating that the outlier Alaska contributed to the linearity of the data. Second, the estimate $\hat{\beta}$ of the amount of increase in the average salary of a teacher for a $1000 increase in per capita income has declined from 1.71 to 1.37. Deleting the observation for Alaska has reduced $s_{\hat{\beta}}$ from the 0.215 to 0.203, yielding a more precise estimate of $\beta$. Also, the positive bias introduced in the estimation of $\beta$ by inclusion of Alaska in the first regression

## Exhibit 10.12

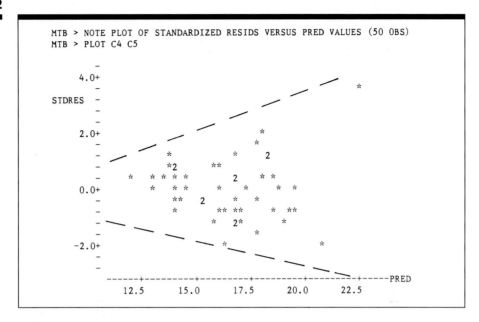

```
MTB > NOTE PLOT OF STANDARDIZED RESIDS VERSUS PRED VALUES (50 OBS)
MTB > PLOT C4 C5

           -
    4.0+
           -                                                              *
STDRES     -
           -
           -
    2.0+                                           *
           -                                       *
           -                       *           *         2
           -                       *2          **
           -        *    * * * *            2      *   *
    0.0+             *     *  *       *       *        *   *
           -              **     2        *    *
           -              *            ** **       *   **
           -                    *    2*              *
           -                        *         *
   -2.0+                              *             *
           -
           -
         ------+---------+---------+---------+---------+-----PRED
            12.5      15.0      17.5      20.0      22.5
```

## Exhibit 10.13

```
MTB > NOTE REGRESSION OF SALARIES ON PER CAPITA INCOME OMITTING ALASKA
MTB > BRIEF = 3
MTB > REGRESS Y IN C3 ON 1 X IN C2 RESIDS C4 PRED C5

The regression equation is
SALARY = 3.65 + 1.37 INC

Predictor      Coef        Stdev      t-ratio
Constant       3.649       1.863        1.96
INC            1.3717      0.2030       6.76

s = 1.673      R-sq = 49.3%     R-sq(adj) = 48.2%

Analysis of Variance

SOURCE       DF          SS          MS
Regression    1       127.91      127.91
Error        47       131.62        2.80
Total        48       259.53
```

**Exhibit 10.14**

| Obs. | INC | SALARY | Fit | Stdev.Fit | Residual | St.Resid |
|---|---|---|---|---|---|---|
| 1 | 7.5 | 14.600 | 13.920 | 0.406 | 0.680 | 0.42 |
| 2 | 8.8 | 17.000 | 15.707 | 0.247 | 1.293 | 0.78 |
| 3 | 7.3 | 12.900 | 13.618 | 0.443 | -0.718 | -0.45 |
| 4 | 10.9 | 19.400 | 18.653 | 0.442 | 0.747 | 0.46 |
| 5 | 10.0 | 16.900 | 17.400 | 0.303 | -0.500 | -0.30 |
| 6 | 11.7 | 17.300 | 19.725 | 0.582 | -2.425 | -1.55 |
| 7 | 10.3 | 17.000 | 17.831 | 0.346 | -0.831 | -0.51 |
| 8 | 9.0 | 15.800 | 15.989 | 0.240 | -0.189 | -0.11 |
| 9 | 8.1 | 15.200 | 14.723 | 0.318 | 0.477 | 0.29 |
| 10 | 10.1 | 22.000 | 17.504 | 0.313 | 4.496 | 2.73R |
| 11 | 8.1 | 14.800 | 14.699 | 0.320 | 0.101 | 0.06 |
| 12 | 10.5 | 18.700 | 18.081 | 0.374 | 0.619 | 0.38 |
| 13 | 8.9 | 17.600 | 15.906 | 0.241 | 1.694 | 1.02 |
| 14 | 9.4 | 15.500 | 16.485 | 0.245 | -0.985 | -0.60 |
| 15 | 10.0 | 15.000 | 17.343 | 0.298 | -2.343 | -1.42 |
| 16 | 7.6 | 15.100 | 14.092 | 0.386 | 1.008 | 0.62 |
| 17 | 8.5 | 14.700 | 15.251 | 0.273 | -0.551 | -0.33 |
| 18 | 7.9 | 13.200 | 14.520 | 0.338 | -1.320 | -0.81 |
| 19 | 10.5 | 19.100 | 17.997 | 0.365 | 1.103 | 0.68 |
| 20 | 10.1 | 18.500 | 17.537 | 0.316 | 0.963 | 0.59 |
| 21 | 9.9 | 21.000 | 17.297 | 0.294 | 3.703 | 2.25R |
| 22 | 9.7 | 17.400 | 16.987 | 0.270 | 0.413 | 0.25 |
| 23 | 6.6 | 12.700 | 12.675 | 0.565 | 0.025 | 0.02 |
| 24 | 9.0 | 14.900 | 15.969 | 0.240 | -1.069 | -0.65 |
| 25 | 8.5 | 14.800 | 15.358 | 0.265 | -0.558 | -0.34 |
| 26 | 9.4 | 14.200 | 16.495 | 0.245 | -2.295 | -1.39 |
| 27 | 10.7 | 17.000 | 18.363 | 0.407 | -1.363 | -0.84 |
| 28 | 9.1 | 12.500 | 16.174 | 0.239 | -3.674 | -2.22R |
| 29 | 10.9 | 18.000 | 18.633 | 0.440 | -0.633 | -0.39 |
| 30 | 7.8 | 15.500 | 14.404 | 0.351 | 1.096 | 0.67 |
| 31 | 10.3 | 20.300 | 17.723 | 0.335 | 2.577 | 1.57 |
| 32 | 7.8 | 15.700 | 14.374 | 0.354 | 1.326 | 0.81 |
| 33 | 8.7 | 13.700 | 15.647 | 0.250 | -1.947 | -1.18 |
| 34 | 9.5 | 15.700 | 16.628 | 0.250 | -0.928 | -0.56 |
| 35 | 9.1 | 14.400 | 16.153 | 0.239 | -1.753 | -1.06 |
| 36 | 9.3 | 17.200 | 16.429 | 0.243 | 0.771 | 0.47 |
| 37 | 9.4 | 17.400 | 16.589 | 0.248 | 0.811 | 0.49 |
| 38 | 9.4 | 19.300 | 16.603 | 0.249 | 2.697 | 1.63 |
| 39 | 7.3 | 13.600 | 13.616 | 0.443 | -0.016 | -0.01 |
| 40 | 7.8 | 13.500 | 14.356 | 0.356 | -0.856 | -0.52 |
| 41 | 7.7 | 14.900 | 14.238 | 0.369 | 0.662 | 0.41 |
| 42 | 9.5 | 14.800 | 16.742 | 0.255 | -1.942 | -1.17 |
| 43 | 7.6 | 16.100 | 14.141 | 0.380 | 1.959 | 1.20 |
| 44 | 7.8 | 12.600 | 14.385 | 0.353 | -1.785 | -1.09 |
| 45 | 9.4 | 14.200 | 16.532 | 0.246 | -2.332 | -1.41 |
| 46 | 10.3 | 20.300 | 17.790 | 0.342 | 2.510 | 1.53 |
| 47 | 7.8 | 14.300 | 14.348 | 0.357 | -0.048 | -0.03 |
| 48 | 9.3 | 16.300 | 16.472 | 0.244 | -0.172 | -0.10 |
| 49 | 10.9 | 18.100 | 18.598 | 0.436 | -0.498 | -0.31 |

R denotes an obs. with a large st. resid.

## Exhibit 10.15

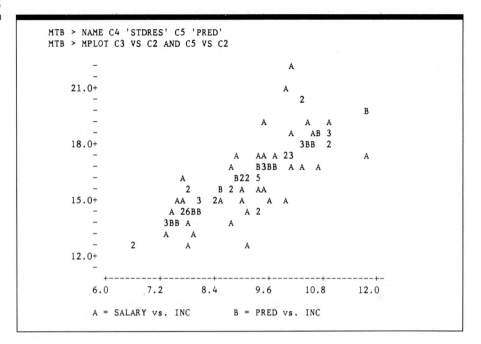

```
MTB > NAME C4 'STDRES' C5 'PRED'
MTB > MPLOT C3 VS C2 AND C5 VS C2

       -                                        A
       -
 21.0+                                          A
       -                                         2
       -                                                        B
       -                              A       A   A
       -                                  A  AB  3
 18.0+                                     3BB    2
       -                     A    AA A 23              A
       -                      A   B3BB  A  A
       -           A        B22  5
       -           2      B 2 A  AA
 15.0+          AA   3   2A   A    A   A
       -        A  26BB        A  2
       -        3BB  A      A
       -         A    A
       -      2        A         A
 12.0+
       -
         +---------+---------+---------+---------+---------+-
         6.0      7.2       8.4       9.6      10.8      12.0

         A = SALARY vs. INC        B = PRED vs. INC
```

## Exhibit 10.16

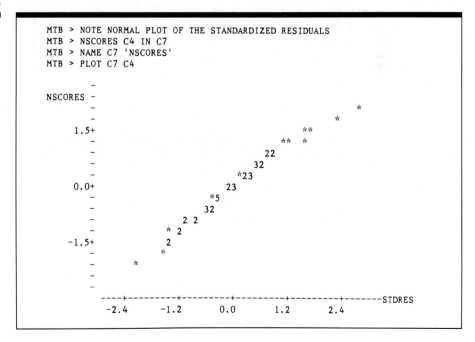

```
MTB > NOTE NORMAL PLOT OF THE STANDARDIZED RESIDUALS
MTB > NSCORES C4 IN C7
MTB > NAME C7 'NSCORES'
MTB > PLOT C7 C4

         -
NSCORES  -
         -                                          *
         -                                    *
 1.5+                               **
         -                        ** *
         -                    22
         -                  32
         -               *23
 0.0+                  23
         -           *5
         -          32
         -       2 2
         -    * 2
-1.5+       2
         -    *
         -  *
         -
         -
     ----+---------+---------+---------+---------+---------+------STDRES
        -2.4      -1.2       0.0       1.2       2.4
```

**Exhibit 10.17**

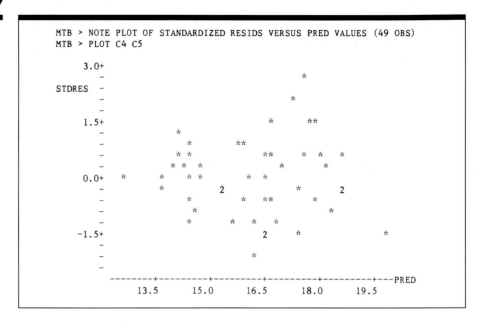

```
MTB > NOTE PLOT OF STANDARDIZED RESIDS VERSUS PRED VALUES (49 OBS)
MTB > PLOT C4 C5

     3.0+
        -                                              *
 STDRES -                                         *
        -
        -
     1.5+                                    *       **
        -          *
        -            *              **
        -          * *         *  *      *  *   *
        -        * * *          *
     0.0+    *       *    * *      *  *
        -          *         2      *         *         2
        -            *          *   **      *
        -          *                          *
        -          *       *   *   *
    -1.5+                   2      *              *
        -
        -                      *
        -
         --------+---------+---------+---------+---------+---PRED
             13.5      15.0      16.5      18.0      19.5
```

has been reduced. Third, the value of $\hat{\sigma}$, which indicates the variability of the observations about the least squares line, has been reduced from 1.938 to 1.673. Fourth, the normal plot of the standardized residuals appears more linear, suggesting better agreement with the normality assumption. Finally, instead of two observations with large standardized residuals (greater than 2 in magnitude), there are now three.

---

The situation described in the preceding example is typical of the good news/bad news conflict that applied statisticians confront daily. The first regression seems preferable on the basis of a larger $r^2$ and a smaller number of outliers. The second seems better from the point of view of a better estimate of $\beta$, a smaller value of $\hat{\sigma}$, and a more linear normal plot of the residuals. Both models indicate some deviation from the constant variance assumption. In any case the maximum percentage of variability explained by per capita income is only 57 percent. This figure clearly suggests that other variables affecting teachers' salaries should be included in the model.

**Example 10.8**

---

Let us consider a final example in which the dependent random variable $Y$ is the total number of farms in the United States. The independent variable $x$ is time measured in years. Table 10.4 gives data on the number of farms in the United States. The year 1880 is coded as zero, so, in general, we have $x = $ years $-$ 1880. The output, shown in Exhibit 10.18, is in three parts. In the first part the values of

$x_i$, $x_i^2$, and $y_i$ are printed out. (The inclusion of $x_i^2$ will be explained below.) In the second part the output from the regression command is displayed. In the last part plots of $y_i$ and $\hat{y}_i$ versus $x_i$ and of the standardized residuals versus the predicted values $\hat{y}_i$ are presented.

It is readily apparent from the regression output and the plots that the linearity assumption is invalid for these data. The proportion of variability explained is only 27.8 percent. The $t$ statistic for the variable $x$ (time) is $-2.40$,

**Exhibit 10.18**

```
MTB > NAME C1 'TIME' C2 'TIMESQ' C3 'FARMS'
MTB > PRINT C1-C3
  ROW   TIME  TIMESQ  FARMS

    1      0       0   4009
    2     10     100   4565
    3     20     400   5740
    4     30     900   6362
    5     40    1600   6454
    6     45    2025   6372
    7     50    2500   6295
    8     55    3025   6812
    9     60    3600   6102
   10     65    4225   5859
   11     70    4900   5388
   12     74    5476   4782
   13     79    6241   3711
   14     84    7056   3158
   15     89    7921   2730
   16     94    8836   2314
   17     98    9604   2479


MTB > BRIEF 2
MTB > NOTE REGRESSION OF NUMBER OF FARMS IN THE U.S. ON TIME
MTB > REGRESS Y IN C3 ON 1 X IN C1 RESIDUALS C4 PREDICTED C5

The regression equation is
FARMS = 6459 - 27.7 TIME

Predictor       Coef       Stdev      t-ratio
Constant      6458.6       731.3         8.83
TIME          -27.69       11.53        -2.40

s = 1357        R-sq = 27.8%     R-sq(adj) = 23.0%

Analysis of Variance

SOURCE        DF         SS           MS
Regression     1   10624592     10624592
Error         15   27628736      1841915
Total         16   38253328

Unusual Observations
Obs.    TIME     FARMS     Fit  Stdev.Fit  Residual  St.Resid
   1     0.0      4009    6459        731     -2450     -2.14R

R denotes an obs. with a large st. resid.
```

**Exhibit 10.18**

**(cont.)**

```
MTB > NAME C4 'RESIDS' C5 'PRED'
MTB > MPLOT C3 VS C1 C5 VS C1
```

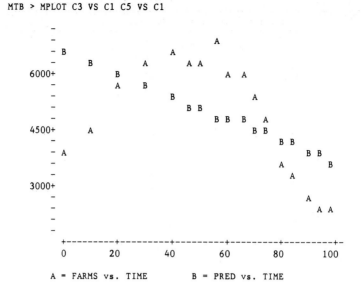

```
        A = FARMS vs. TIME      B = PRED vs. TIME
```

```
MTB > PLOT C4 C5
```

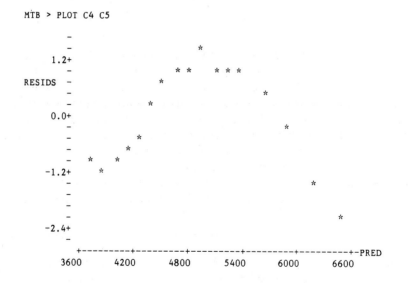

**Table 10.4**

| Farms in the United States, 1880–1978 | |
| --- | --- |
| Year | Number of Farms (in thousands) |
| 1880 | 4009 |
| 1890 | 4565 |
| 1900 | 5740 |
| 1910 | 6362 |
| 1920 | 6454 |
| 1925 | 6372 |
| 1930 | 6295 |
| 1935 | 6812 |
| 1940 | 6102 |
| 1945 | 5859 |
| 1950 | 5388 |
| 1954 | 4782 |
| 1959 | 3711 |
| 1964 | 3158 |
| 1969 | 2730 |
| 1974 | 2314 |
| 1978 | 2479 |

*Source: Agricultural Statistics 1983*, U.S. Department of Agriculture, Washington, D.C.

which would be significant in a test of $H_0$: $\beta = 0$ versus $H_1$: $\beta \neq 0$ at the $\alpha = 0.05$ level. The plot of $y_i$ and $\hat{y}_i$ versus $x_i$ gives a clear indication of what has happened since 1880. The number of farms increased from 1880 until 1920, when it reached a peak, and then began to decrease (except for an aberrant peak in the Great Depression). The rate of decrease has been particularly sharp since 1940. No straight line can fit these data well. The plot of the standardized residuals versus the predicted values would be a random scatter if the model assumptions were valid. Here there is a clear pattern over time of negative, positive, and then negative residuals. This pattern is typical of a relationship in which $E(Y)$ increases as a function of $x$ to a maximum and then decreases. The simple linear model is not appropriate for these data.

Briefly, the procedure for extending the ideas of simple linear regression to more complex models is as follows. Instead of assuming that $E(Y) = \alpha + \beta x$, we assume that

$$E(Y) = \alpha + \beta x + \gamma x^2 \qquad \qquad \textbf{10.40}$$

that is, the average value of $Y$ is a quadratic function in $x$. We then find the values of $\alpha$, $\beta$, and $\gamma$ that minimize the expression

$$\sum [y_i - (\alpha + \beta x_i + \gamma x_i^2)]^2 \qquad \qquad \textbf{10.41}$$

obtaining a best-fitting parabola for the given data, just as we found the best-fitting line by minimizing Expression 10.7. Much of the statistical analysis of simple linear regression carries over to the **quadratic model**. In particular, we still have the identity SST = SSR + SSE, where SST is defined as before and

**quadratic model**

$$\text{SSE} = \sum_{i=1}^{} [y_i - (\hat{\alpha} + \hat{\beta}x_i + \hat{\gamma}x_i^2)]^2 \qquad \textbf{10.42}$$

The values of SSE in the quadratic case can be no more than the value of SSE in the simple linear case, and it is generally less. The value of $R^2 = \text{SSR}/\text{SST}$, known as the multiple correlation coefficient, can be no smaller than the corresponding value of $r^2$. The $t$ tests for this model have $n - 3$ degrees of freedom. In general, the number of degrees of freedom for error is established by reducing the total number of degrees of freedom $(n)$ by 1 for each parameter $(\alpha, \beta, \gamma)$.

## Example 10.9

Exhibit 10.19 shows the Minitab output generated when the quadratic model was used with the data on U.S. farms in Example 10.8.

The most striking feature of the quadratic analysis is that inclusion of the second term has increased the amount of variability explained from 27.8 to 94.2

## Exhibit 10.19

```
MTB > NOTE REGRESSION OF FARMS ON TIME USING A QUADRATIC MODEL
MTB > REGRESS Y IN C3 ON 2 XS IN C1 C2 RESIDUALS C4 PREDICTED C5

The regression equation is
FARMS = 3843 + 126 TIME - 1.51 TIMESQ

Predictor       Coef         Stdev      t-ratio
Constant       3843.0        298.5        12.87
TIME           125.63        12.60         9.97
TIMESQ        -1.5083        0.1194       -12.63

s = 399.0        R-sq = 94.2%      R-sq(adj) = 93.3%

Analysis of Variance

SOURCE       DF          SS            MS
Regression    2      36024784      18012384
Error        14       2228543        159182
Total        16      38253312

SOURCE       DF       SEQ SS
TIME          1     10624592
TIMESQ        1     25400192

Unusual Observations
Obs.     TIME      FARMS      Fit  Stdev.Fit  Residual  St.Resid
  1       0.0     4009.0    3843.0     298.5     166.0      0.63 X
 17      98.0     2479.0    1669.1     236.7     809.9      2.52R

R denotes an obs. with a large st. resid.
X denotes an obs. whose X value gives it large influence.
```

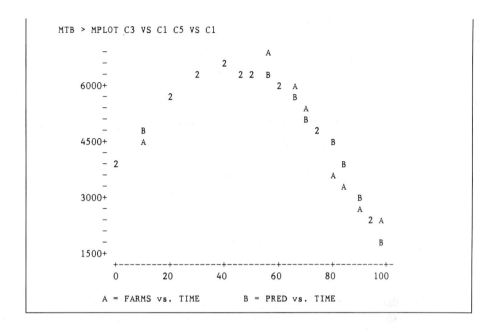

```
MTB > MPLOT C3 VS C1 C5 VS C1

         -                              A
         -                       2
         -                  2       2 2  B
      6000+                              2   A
         -             2                 B
         -                                 A
         -                                 B
         -       B                           2
      4500+      A                            B
         -
         - 2                                    B
         -                                       A
         -                                        A
      3000+                                        B
         -                                         A
         -                                          2  A
         -
         -                                            B
      1500+
          +---------+---------+---------+---------+---------+-
          0        20        40        60        80       100

          A = FARMS vs. TIME      B = PRED vs. TIME
```

percent. Additionally, the value of $\hat{\sigma}$ in the quadratic model is less than one-tenth of the corresponding value in the simple linear model. The plot of $y_i$ and $\hat{y}_i$ versus time shows quite a good approximation of the $(x_i, y_i)$ values by the $(x_i, \hat{y}_i)$ values, which lie on the best-fitting parabola.

Further details of polynomial regression will be discussed in the next chapter. This last example was introduced simply to suggest that generalization of the simple linear regression model can be valuable in interpreting data.

## Exercises 10.6

**10.44** Use Minitab with the data of exercise 10.15 on voter registration ($x$) and turnout ($y$) in 24 cities. (Use the REGRESS command with the BRIEF = 3 command.)

    **a.** Are there observations with standardized residuals exceeding 2 in magnitude? Which cities do these observations represent? In what way do these observations differ from the others?

    **b.** Make a normal plot of the standardized residuals. Does the normality assumption appear to be justified? Does the normal plot indicate any outliers?

    **c.** Plot the standardized residuals on the vertical axis versus the predicted values on the horizontal axis. Under the standard assumptions the residuals and predicted values should be independent. Is this roughly true, or is there a pattern in these residuals?

    **d.** Comment on the assumption that $\mathrm{Var}(Y|x) = \sigma^2$.

**10.45** As in exercise 10.44, use Minitab with the data of exercise 10.16 on the miles per gallon ($y$) and weights ($x$) of 32 automobiles.

    **a.** Which observations have standardized residuals exceeding 2 in magnitude? Which cars are associated with these observations? What is the sign of these residuals? What does this imply concerning these observations?

    **b.** Construct the plots required in parts b and c of exercise 10.44.

    **c.** Does the normality assumption appear to be justified?

    **d.** Is there a pattern in the plot of the standardized residuals versus the predicted values? If so, what does the pattern appear to imply?

**10.46** Use Minitab with the data of exercise 10.23 concerning total energy and total thermal energy produced in 1979.

    **a.** Which observation is an outlier? What country does this outlier represent?

    **b.** Plot $y_i$ and $\hat{y}_i$ versus $x_i$, $i = 1, 2, \ldots, 10$.

    **c.** Construct a normal plot of the standardized residuals and a plot of the standardized residuals versus the predicted values.

    **d.** What conclusions can you draw from the plots in parts b and c?

**10.47** Use the data of exercise 10.42 on the sales and assets of the 25 largest U.S. corporations in 1980.

    **a.** Which observation is an outlier? What corporation does this outlier represent?

    **b.** Plot $y_i$ and $\hat{y}_i$ versus $x_i$, $i = 1, 2, \ldots, 25$.

    **c.** Construct plots as in part c of exercise 10.46.

    **d.** Comment on the linearity and normality assumptions.

**10.48** For the data given in Example 10.8 on the number of U.S. farms ($Y$) over time ($x$), use the quadratic model to make a plot of the standardized residuals on the vertical axis versus the predicted values on the horizontal axis. Does the plot appear to reflect random scatter, or is there a pattern in this residual plot?

**10.49** The table on pages 398 and 399 gives information on the life expectancy at birth and the annual average per capita income in 19 industrialized countries.

    **a.** Using per capita income as the independent variable, find the regression equation $\hat{y} = \hat{\alpha} + \hat{\beta}x$.

    **b.** Use Minitab plotting methods to determine whether life expectancy (by country) can be explained by per capita income alone.

    **c.** What, in your opinion, is needed to obtain a better model of life expectancy (by country)?

| Country | Life Expectancy | Per Capita Income | |
|---|---|---|---|
| Australia | 71.0 | 3426 | |
| Austria | 70.4 | 3350 | |
| Belgium | 70.6 | 3346 | |
| Canada | 72.0 | 4751 | |
| Denmark | 73.3 | 5029 | |
| Finland | 69.8 | 3312 | |
| France | 72.3 | 3403 | |
| West Germany | 70.3 | 5040 | |
| Ireland | 70.7 | 2009 | |
| Italy | 70.6 | 2298 | |
| Japan | 73.2 | 3292 | |
| Netherlands | 73.8 | 4103 | (cont.) |

| Country | Life Expectancy | Per Capita Income |
|---------|-----------------|-------------------|
| New Zealand | 71.1 | 3723 |
| Norway | 73.9 | 4102 |
| Portugal | 68.1 | 956 |
| Sweden | 74.7 | 5596 |
| Switzerland | 72.1 | 2963 |
| United Kingdom | 72.0 | 2503 |
| United States | 71.3 | 5523 |

*Source:* "Vital Dialogue Is Beginning Between the Rich and Poor," *New York Times*, September 28, 1975, quoted from a report by Ann Crittendon.

## Summary

A model used to describe a relationship between a dependent random variable $Y$ and an independent real variable $x$ is called *stochastic*. The basic idea of a stochastic model is that the *expected value* of $Y$ is a function of $x$. In the simple linear regression situation, we assume that $E(Y|x) = \alpha + \beta x$ or

$$Y_i = \alpha + \beta x_i + \varepsilon_i$$

where $\alpha$ and $\beta$ are unknown parameters to be estimated from the data. The $\varepsilon_i$ are independent random variables with $E(\varepsilon_i) = 0$ and $\text{Var}(\varepsilon_i) = \sigma^2$; $\sigma^2$ is also an unknown parameter to be estimated from the data. Each observation is thus composed of an expected value $\alpha + \beta x_i$, a real-valued function of $x_i$, and a random component $\varepsilon_i$.

The least squares line $\hat{y} = \hat{\alpha} + \hat{\beta}x$ is the line that best fits the observed points $(x_i, y_i)$, $i = 1, 2, \ldots, n$. The values of the slope and the intercept of this line are, respectively,

$$\hat{\beta} = \frac{\Sigma(x_i - \bar{x})(y_i - \bar{y})}{\Sigma(x_i - \bar{x})^2} \quad \text{and} \quad \hat{\alpha} = \bar{y} - \hat{\beta}\bar{x}$$

The values $\hat{\alpha}$ and $\hat{\beta}$ are functions of the data and hence are random variables. Different observations of $Y_i$ for the same set of $x_i$, $i = 1, 2, \ldots, n$ will give different values of $\hat{\alpha}$ and $\hat{\beta}$. The least squares line $\hat{y} = \hat{\alpha} + \hat{\beta}x$ can be thought of as an estimator of the regression line $E(Y|x) = \alpha + \beta x$. The REGRESS command in Minitab permits easy calculation of the intercept and the slope of the least squares line.

The variability of the $Y$ observations is divided into two parts through the relationship

$$\text{SST} = \text{SSR} + \text{SSE}$$

The sum of squares for regression (SSR) refers to the portion of the data explained by the model; the sum of squares for error (SSE) refers to the portion of the data unexplained by the model. An unbiased estimate of $\sigma^2$ is given by the mean square for error, $\text{MSE} = (\text{SSE})/(n - 2)$. The ratio $\text{SSR}/\text{SST} = r^2$ is called the coefficient of determination; loosely speaking, it represents the proportion of the variability of the observed $y$ values explained by $x$. The coefficient $r^2$ describes the degree of linear relationship between the two variables. Values of $r^2$ near 1 suggest a strong linear relationship.

In order for inference concerning $\alpha$ and $\beta$ to be carried out, the error terms $\varepsilon_i$ must be assumed to be normally distributed. The statistics $\hat{\alpha}$ and $\hat{\beta}$ are shown to be unbiased estimates of $\alpha$ and $\beta$. Procedures for finding confidence intervals for $\alpha$ and $\beta$ and carrying out tests of hypotheses for these parameters are based on Student's $t$ distribution with $n - 2$ degrees of freedom in the simple linear regression model.

Important tasks are estimation of an average value of $Y$ at $x = x_0$, $\mu_{Y|x_0}$, and prediction of an individual value of $Y$ at $x = x_0$, $Y_0$. In both cases we evaluate the least squares line at $x = x_0$ using

$$\hat{y}(x_0) = \hat{\alpha} + \hat{\beta} x_0$$

Establishing a confidence interval for the estimate of $\mu_{Y|x_0}$ and a prediction interval for $Y_0$ is also important. For fixed $1 - \alpha$, the interval for $Y_0$ is wider than that for $\mu_{Y|x_0}$, as would be expected. Predictions of $Y$ values at $x$ values far from those at which $Y$s have been observed are quite unreliable. If such predictions must be used, the extreme variability of such estimates must be kept in mind.

Minitab plots may be used to verify the linearity assumption, the normality assumption, and the constant variance assumption or to detect deviations from these assumptions. These plots generally involve use of the standardized residuals. Of particular importance is the plot of these residuals versus the predicted values $\hat{y}_i$. If the assumptions of the simple linear regression model hold, this plot will reflect random scatter. A normal plot of the standardized residuals is used to provide a rough check of normality of the $\varepsilon_i$. It is important to remember that assuming $E(Y|x) = \alpha + \beta x$ does not make it so. The expectation may not be such a simple function of $x$. A better fit of the data than that provided by the simple linear regression model can often be found by using the multiple regression model,

$$E(Y|x) = \alpha + \beta x + \gamma x^2$$

## Key Words

| | |
|---|---|
| $\alpha$ (intercept of theoretical regression line) | deterministic relationship |
| $\hat{\alpha}$ (intercept of least squares line) | least squares line |
| ANOVA | mean square for error (MSE) |
| $\beta$ (slope of theoretical regression line) | mean square for regression (MSR) |
| $\hat{\beta}$ (slope of least squares line) | normality of $\varepsilon_i$ |
| coefficient of determination | normal plot of the standardized residuals |
| confidence intervals for $\beta$ | outlier |
| confidence intervals for $\mu_{Y|x_0}$ | prediction interval for $Y_0$ |

predicted values ($\hat{y}_i$)
quadratic model
residual
standardized residuals
stochastic relationship

sum of squares for error (SSE)
sum of squares for regression (SSR)
theoretical regression line
total sum of squares (SST)

## Minitab Commands

BRIEF
MPLOT
REGRESS

# Chapter 11

# Multiple Regression

## 11.1

**Introduction**
In Chapter 10 we considered the simple linear regression model. In that case the expectation of a dependent random variable $Y$ is assumed to be related to an independent real variable $x$ by a linear equation of the form

$$E(Y|x) = \alpha + \beta x \qquad \textbf{11.1}$$

In many real-world cases, however, the expectation of a dependent random variable will be a function not of a single real variable, but of two or more real variables. Consider the example of the selling price, $Y$ (in thousands of dollars), of a house in a city of moderate size. The average selling price $E(Y)$ will depend on such variables as

$x_1$: The size of the house (in hundreds of square feet of living space)

$x_2$: The distance from the house to the nearest elementary school (in miles)

and probably others. As another example, suppose $Y$ represents the annual sales of a large corporation by state. The expected sales, $E(Y)$, will depend on such variables as

$x_1$: The population of the state (in millions of persons)

$x_2$: The per capita income in the state (in thousands of dollars)

$x_3$: The annual advertising expenditure by the company in the state (in thousands of dollars)

In order to expand the simple linear regression model to take into account $k \geqslant 2$ explanatory real variables, we must replace the original linear equation by

$$E(Y|x_1, x_2, \ldots, x_k) = \beta_0 + \beta_1 x_1 + \beta_2 x_2 + \cdots + \beta_k x_k \qquad \textbf{11.2}$$

The unknown parameters $\beta_0, \beta_1, \ldots, \beta_k$ in Equation 11.2 replace the unknown parameters $\alpha$ and $\beta$ in Equation 11.1. Like $\alpha$ and $\beta$, these parameters must be estimated from the data. Equation 11.2 is a linear function in $x_1, x_2, \ldots, x_k$. For this reason the model described by Equation 11.2 is referred to as the multiple linear regression model, generally shortened to **multiple regression model**. The independent variables $x_1, x_2, \ldots, x_k$ are often called **regressors** or **explanatory variables**.

*multiple regression model*

*regressors*

*explanatory variables*

For ease of explanation we will concentrate initially on the case where $k = 2$—namely, that of two explanatory variables. In this case Equation 11.2 reduces to

$$E(Y|x_1, x_2) = \beta_0 + \beta_1 x_1 + \beta_2 x_2 \qquad \textbf{11.3}$$

More precisely, each $Y_i$ observation is composed of a true expected value and an error observation of the form

$$Y_i = \underbrace{\beta_0 + \beta_1 x_{i1} + \beta_2 x_{i2}} + \varepsilon_i$$

$$= E(Y|x_1 = x_{i1}, x_2 = x_{i2}) + \varepsilon_i, \qquad i = 1, 2, \ldots, n \qquad \textbf{11.4}$$

*error terms*

Here, as in the simple linear model, the **error terms** $\varepsilon_i$ are assumed to satisfy the following assumptions:

**1** $E(\varepsilon_i) = 0$
**2** $\mathrm{Var}(\varepsilon_i) = \sigma^2, i = 1, 2, \ldots, n$
**3** The $\varepsilon_i$ are independent.

The expectation of $Y$ for particular values of $x_1$ and $x_2$—namely, for $x_1 = x_{i1}$ and $x_2 = x_{i2}$—is given by Equation 11.3, just as the expectation for the simple linear regression situation is given by Equation 11.1. In fact, for $k = 1$, Equation 11.2 for the multiple regression model reduces to

$$E(Y|x_1) = \beta_0 + \beta_1 x_1 \qquad \textbf{11.5}$$

which is equivalent to the equation for the simple linear regression model given in Equation 11.1 except that $\beta_0$ has replaced $\alpha$, $\beta_1$ has replaced $\beta$, and $x_1$ has replaced $x$.

Consider the following typical data set for the selling price of a house, with regressors $x_1$ (hundreds of square feet of living space) and $x_2$ (miles to the nearest elementary school).

| House Number, $i$ | Sales Price of House, $y_i$ | Living Space, $x_{i1}$ | Distance to Elementary School, $x_{i2}$ |
|---|---|---|---|
| 1 | 76.5 | 12.1 | 2.0 |
| 2 | 84.2 | 14.0 | 1.2 |
| 3 | 100.1 | 18.5 | 1.0 |
| . | . | . | . |
| . | . | . | . |
| . | . | . | . |
| 25 | 55.2 | 8.5 | 1.8 |

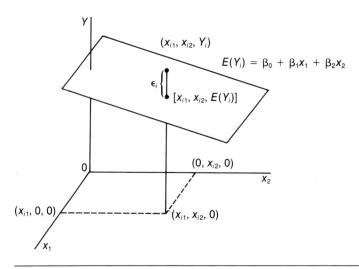

**Figure 11.1**

Theoretical Regression Plane ($k = 2$)

The first house sold for \$76,500. It had 1210 square feet of living space and was located 2.0 miles from the nearest elementary school. Given corresponding values of $y_i$, $x_{i1}$, and $x_{i2}$ for each of the $n = 25$ houses in the data set (as shown for houses 1, 2, 3, and 25), we can estimate $\beta_0$, $\beta_1$, and $\beta_2$ of Equation 11.3 and $\sigma^2$, using methods analogous to those used in the simple linear regression case.

A graphical display of the data in the case where $k = 2$ requires three dimensions. An expression of the form

$$E(Y|x_1, x_2) = \beta_0 + \beta_1 x_1 + \beta_2 x_2$$

represents a plane in three-dimensional space for every fixed set of the parameters $\beta_0$, $\beta_1$, and $\beta_2$. An individual observation of the dependent random variable $Y$ is plotted in Figure 11.1. The value of $y_i$ is indicated by the vertical height of the plotted point with coordinates $(x_{i1}, x_{i2}, Y_i)$. As indicated by Equation 11.3, the value of $Y_i$ is composed of an expected value given by the height of the plane,

$$E(Y|x_1, x_2) = \beta_0 + \beta_1 x_1 + \beta_2 x_2 \qquad \text{at } x_1 = x_{i1}, x_2 = x_{i2}$$

plus an error term $\varepsilon_i$. The theoretical regression plane of Figure 11.1 is analogous to the theoretical regression line of Chapter 10.

The goal of multiple regression analysis is to find the equation of the plane that best fits the $n$ observed points $(x_{i1}, x_{i2}, y_i)$. The method for finding this **least squares plane** is analogous to that used to determine the least squares line. We will begin with a discussion of multiple regression in the case where $k = 2$.

least squares plane

CHAPTER 11 **MULTIPLE REGRESSION**

In the case where $k = 2$, the multiple **regression equation** is assumed to be of the form

$$Y_i = \beta_0 + \beta_1 x_{i1} + \beta_2 x_{i2} + \varepsilon_i, \qquad i = 1, 2, \ldots, n \qquad \textbf{11.6}$$

The expected value of $Y$ in this model has the form

$$E(Y|x_1, x_2) = \beta_0 + \beta_1 x_1 + \beta_2 x_2 \qquad \textbf{11.7}$$

where $\beta_0$, $\beta_1$, and $\beta_2$ are fixed unknown constants. As explained in Section 11.1, a data set consists of $n$ values of $Y$ together with observed values of $x_1$ and $x_2$ for each $Y$, denoted by

$$(x_{i1}, x_{i2}, y_i), \qquad i = 1, 2, \ldots, n \qquad \textbf{11.8}$$

The $n$ triples of Equation 11.8 can be plotted in three-dimensional space as indicated in Figure 11.2. The first step is to find the plane that best fits all of these $n$ points.

To determine the coefficients $\hat{\beta}_0$, $\hat{\beta}_1$, $\hat{\beta}_2$ of the equation of the plane that best fits the $n$ points, we consider the expression

$$Q(\beta_0, \beta_1, \beta_2) = \sum [y_i - (\beta_0 + \beta_1 x_{i1} + \beta_2 x_{i2})]^2 \qquad \textbf{11.9}$$

(The sum in Equation 11.9 is taken over $i = 1, 2, \ldots, n$. As in Chapter 10, all sums without indicated limits on $i$ are from $i = 1$ to $i = n$.) The difference

$$y_i - (\beta_0 + \beta_1 x_{i1} + \beta_2 x_{i2}) \qquad \textbf{11.10}$$

is the vertical deviation between the point $(x_{i1}, x_{i2}, y_i)$ and the point on the plane

$$y = \beta_0 + \beta_1 x_1 + \beta_2 x_2 \qquad \text{at } x_1 = x_{i1} \text{ and } x_2 = x_{i2}$$

as indicated in Figure 11.2. The best-fitting plane is the one that minimizes the sum of squares of the vertical deviations in Equation 11.10. It can be shown that this plane is given by

$$\hat{y} = \hat{\beta}_0 + \hat{\beta}_1 x_1 + \hat{\beta}_2 x_2 \qquad \textbf{11.11}$$

where $\hat{\beta}_0$, $\hat{\beta}_1$, and $\hat{\beta}_2$ are the solutions to the following set of three linear equations in three unknowns:

$$n\hat{\beta}_0 + \left(\sum x_{i1}\right)\hat{\beta}_1 + \left(\sum x_{i2}\right)\hat{\beta}_2 = \sum y_i$$

$$\left(\sum x_{i1}\right)\hat{\beta}_0 + \left(\sum x_{i1}^2\right)\hat{\beta}_1 + \left(\sum x_{i1}x_{i2}\right)\hat{\beta}_2 = \sum x_{i1}y_i \qquad \textbf{11.12}$$

$$\left(\sum x_{i2}\right)\hat{\beta}_0 + \left(\sum x_{i1}x_{i2}\right)\hat{\beta}_1 + \left(\sum x_{i2}^2\right)\hat{\beta}_2 = \sum x_{i2}y_i$$

The coefficients of the unknowns are calculated directly from the data, as are the values on the right-hand sides of Equations 11.12. These equations are referred to

normal equations

as the **normal equations**.

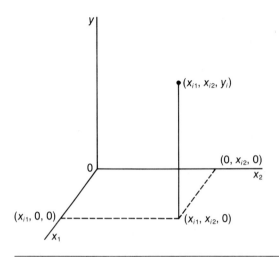

**Figure 11.2**

**A Typical Observation (k = 2)**

The Minitab statistical package is extremely useful for carrying out the computations required for multiple regression. For example, solutions to the normal equations can be obtained easily with Minitab. Almost all multiple regression calculations required in this chapter will be carried out using the computer package. Although calculating by hand is feasible for cases in which $k = 2$, it is tedious and time-consuming for cases in which $k > 2$, which are common in applications.

**Example 11.1**

Exhibit 2.7 in Chapter 2 presented data on the 25 American League batters who hit 0.300 or more in 1980. We will use this data set again to obtain a relationship between runs batted in ($Y$) and the independent variables home runs ($x_1$) and batting average ($x_2$). The multiple regression model in Equation 11.6 is assumed to be appropriate. In Exhibit 11.1 the values of the dependent variable ($Y$) have been stored in C9 and the values of the independent variables have been stored in C8 and C10. The output consists of a printout of the data, the output from use of the REGRESS command with a single explanatory variable $x_1$ (home runs) as before, and the output from use of the REGRESS command with both regressors $x_1$ and $x_2$. In the case of the simple linear regression model, the least squares line is given by the regression equation

$$\hat{y} = 42.4 + 2.17x_1$$

In the case of the multiple regression model, the relationship among the variables is estimated by the regression equation

$$\hat{y} = -76.1 + 2.22x_1 + 372x_2$$

**Exhibit 11.1**

```
MTB > PRINT C9 C8 C10
 ROW    RBI   HOMERS    AVE

   1    118     24    0.390
   2    122     25    0.352
   3     40      0    0.341
   4     60      7    0.333
   5     59      3    0.331
   6     83     17    0.329
   7     50      3    0.326
   8     45      7    0.321
   9     53      9    0.320
  10    117     19    0.319
  11     65      8    0.318
  12     68     13    0.307
  13     58      6    0.305
  14     37      9    0.304
  15    117     41    0.304
  16     85     11    0.304
  17     53      9    0.303
  18    103     24    0.302
  19     64     13    0.302
  20    115     32    0.302
  21     61     12    0.301
  22     47     15    0.300
  23     78     13    0.300
  24     55      9    0.300
  25    111     41    0.300

MTB > NOTE MULTIPLE REGRESSION EXAMPLE
MTB > READ INTO C5-C10
MTB > NOTE DEPENDENT VARIABLE (Y) IS RBIS
     25 ROWS READ
 ROW    C5      C6     C7    C8    C9     C10

   1   449      87    175    24   118   0.390
   2   622      96    219    25   122   0.352
   3   528      87    180     0    40   0.341
   4   630      96    210     7    60   0.333
   .    .    .

MTB > NOTE DEPENDENT VARIABLE (Y) IS RBIS
MTB > NOTE INDEPENDENT VARIABLES X1,X2 ARE HOMERS AND AVERAGE
MTB > NAME C8 'HOMERS'
MTB > NAME C9 'RBI'
MTB > NAME C10 'AVE'
MTB > BRIEF = 3
MTB > REGRESS C9 ON 1 X IN C8 RESIDS IN C11 PREDICTED IN C12

The regression equation is
RBI = 42.4 + 2.17 HOMERS

Predictor       Coef        Stdev     t-ratio
Constant       42.412       5.250       8.08
HOMERS          2.1722      0.2873      7.56

s = 15.40      R-sq = 71.3%    R-sq(adj) = 70.1%

Analysis of Variance

SOURCE      DF         SS          MS
Regression   1       13560       13560
Error       23        5456         237
Total       24       19016
```

Exhibit 11.1

(cont.)

```
MTB > REGRESS C9 ON 2 XS IN C8 C10 RESIDS IN C11 PREDICTED IN C12

The regression equation is
RBI = - 76.1 + 2.22 HOMERS + 372 AVE

Predictor      Coef         Stdev       t-ratio
Constant      -76.09        41.37        -1.84
HOMERS        2.2237        0.2509        8.86
AVE           371.9         129.0         2.88

s = 13.42        R-sq = 79.2%      R-sq(adj) = 77.3%

Analysis of Variance

SOURCE        DF           SS            MS
Regression    2         15056.0        7528.0
Error         22         3960.1         180.0
Total         24        19016.2

SOURCE        DF         SEQ SS
HOMERS        1        13560.4
AVE           1         1495.6
```

The computer has thus calculated

$$\hat{\beta}_0 = -76.1 \qquad \hat{\beta}_1 = 2.22 \qquad \hat{\beta}_2 = 372$$

---

As in the case of simple linear regression, the REGRESS command provides a substantial amount of information in addition to the regression equation itself. We will now consider the meaning of this output.

In Equations 11.6 and 11.7, the coefficient $\beta_1$ represents the true *average* change in $Y$ per unit change in $x_1$, *with $x_2$ held constant*. Similarly, $\beta_2$ represents the true *average* change in $Y$ per unit change in $x_2$, *with $x_1$ held constant*. In Example 11.1, $\beta_1$ represents the true average increase in RBIs for an additional home run, with batting average held constant. The point estimate of $\beta_1$ in the multiple regression model is $\hat{\beta}_1 = 2.22$; that is, we could expect an estimated average increase of 2.22 RBIs for each home run, assuming a player's batting average remained constant. The point estimate of $\beta_2$ is $\hat{\beta}_2 = 371.9$. Of course, a batting average cannot increase by a full unit. A "ten point" increase in a player's batting average, however, corresponds to an increase of 0.01 in $x_2$. Thus, a point estimate of the true average increase in RBIs for a "ten point" increase in batting average is 3.72 RBIs (with the number of home runs held constant). This result was obtained by multiplying $\hat{\beta}_2$ by 1/100, as the corresponding change in $x_2$ is 0.01 unit.

Notice that the parameter $\beta$ in the simple linear regression model of Example 11.1 represents the true average increase in RBIs as a function of home runs, ignoring the player's batting average. The first regression of Example 11.1 shows that the point estimate of $\beta$ is $\hat{\beta} = 2.17$. This value is close to the estimate of

$\hat{\beta}_1 = 2.22$ in the multiple regression model, but the two point estimates are not equal.

In the multiple regression case ($k = 2$), we are interested in finding confidence intervals and tests of hypotheses for both $\beta_1$ and $\beta_2$. Inference is possible if, in addition to making the assumptions listed on page 403 and in Equation 11.6, we can assume that the $\varepsilon_i$ are normally distributed. Then the estimators $\hat{\beta}_1$ and $\hat{\beta}_2$ are random variables satisfying

$$E(\hat{\beta}_1) = \beta_1 \qquad E(\hat{\beta}_2) = \beta_2 \qquad\qquad\qquad \textbf{11.13}$$

and we can assume that

$$\frac{\hat{\beta}_1 - \beta_1}{s_{\hat{\beta}_1}} \sim t_{n-3} \qquad \text{and} \qquad \frac{\hat{\beta}_2 - \beta_2}{s_{\hat{\beta}_2}} \sim t_{n-3} \qquad\qquad \textbf{11.14}$$

that is, each of the standardized random variables has Student's $t$ distribution with $n - 3$ degrees of freedom. The appropriate number of degrees of freedom is 1 less in the multiple regression case ($k = 2$) than in the simple linear regression case.

Confidence intervals for $\beta_1$ and $\beta_2$ with confidence coefficients of $(1 - \alpha)100$ percent are given by

$$\hat{\beta}_1 \pm (s_{\hat{\beta}_1})t_{\alpha/2,n-3} \qquad \text{and} \qquad \hat{\beta}_2 \pm (s_{\hat{\beta}_2})t_{\alpha/2,n-3} \qquad\qquad \textbf{11.15}$$

respectively. The Minitab output in Exhibit 11.1 includes the values $s_{\hat{\beta}_1} = 0.2509$ and $s_{\hat{\beta}_2} = 129.0$. A 95 percent confidence interval for $\beta_1$ has endpoints given by

$$2.224 \pm 0.2509(t_{0.025,23}) = 2.224 \pm 0.2509(2.069) = 2.224 \pm 0.519$$

Hence the interval is $(1.705, 2.743)$. This is a confidence interval for the average increase in RBIs per home run, with batting average held constant. Baseball sense says that the value must be at least 1, so this interval makes sense. A 95 percent confidence interval for $\beta_2$ has endpoints given by

$$371.9 \pm 129.0(2.069)$$

In this case it is best to move the decimal point to the left by two positions in $\hat{\beta}_2$ and $s_{\hat{\beta}_2}$, to obtain an interval with endpoints

$$3.719 \pm 1.29(2.069) = 3.719 \pm 2.669$$

Hence, the confidence interval for the true average additional number of RBIs per "ten point" increase in batting average over the season (that is, a change of 0.01 in $x_2$), with home runs held constant, is $(1.050, 6.388)$.

Typically the statistical task is to carry out tests of the null hypotheses

$$H_0: \beta_1 = 0 \qquad \text{and} \qquad H_0: \beta_2 = 0 \qquad\qquad\qquad \textbf{11.16}$$

The first null hypothesis means that $x_1$ does not contribute to the explanation of the change in $Y$. Similarly, the second null hypothesis means that $x_2$ does not contribute to the explanation of the change in $Y$. Critical regions for these tests are based on the $t$ statistics.

## Table 11.1

| Critical Regions for Testing $H_0$: $\beta_i = 0$, $i = 1, 2$ | |
| --- | --- |
| Alternative | Critical Region |
| $\beta_i > 0$ | $t \geqslant t_{\alpha,n-3}$ |
| $\beta_i < 0$ | $t \leqslant -t_{\alpha,n-3}$ |
| $\beta_i \neq 0$ | $\lvert t \rvert \geqslant t_{\alpha/2,n-3}$ |

$$t = \frac{\hat{\beta}_1}{s_{\hat{\beta}_1}} \quad \text{and} \quad t = \frac{\hat{\beta}_2}{s_{\hat{\beta}_2}} \qquad \qquad \textbf{11.17}$$

Appropriate critical regions for both of the null hypotheses in Equations 11.16 are given in Table 11.1. In Example 11.1, in a test at the 0.05 significance level against two-sided alternatives, we would reject the null hypotheses if

$$\lvert t \rvert \geqslant t_{0.025,23} = 2.069 \qquad \qquad \textbf{11.18}$$

In the Minitab output of Exhibit 11.1, the two $t$ values of Equations 11.17 are calculated; these values are 8.86 and 2.88, respectively. Both of these values lie in the critical region given in Equation 11.18. Hence $H_0$: $\beta_1 = 0$ and $H_0$: $\beta_2 = 0$ should be rejected at the $\alpha = 0.05$ level—that is, both home runs and batting average should be kept in the model, because they both contribute to the explanation of runs batted in.

ANOVA tables for multiple regression are analogous to those for simple linear regression. Table 11.2 is the ANOVA table for the case where $k = 2$. The basic decomposition corresponds to that shown in Equation 10.10 for the simple linear regression case. The total variability of the $Y$ observations is decomposed into two parts—one part explained by the regression model and the other part unexplained. The decomposition is written as

$$\text{SST} = \text{SSR} + \text{SSE} \qquad \qquad \textbf{11.19}$$

## Table 11.2

| ANOVA Table for Multiple Regression ($k = 2$) | | | |
| --- | --- | --- | --- |
| Source | d.f. | SS | MS |
| Regression | 2 | SSR | MSR = SSR/2 |
| Error (Residual) | $n - 3$ | SSE | MSE = SSE/$(n - 3)$ |
| Total | $n - 1$ | SST | |

where

$$SST = \sum (y_i - \bar{y})^2$$
$$SSE = \sum [y_i - (\hat{\beta}_0 + \hat{\beta}_1 x_{i1} + \hat{\beta}_2 x_{i2})]^2$$
$$SSR = SST - SSE$$

The total sum of squares (SST) is computed as in the simple linear model. The sum of squares for error (SSE) is the sum of the squares of the terms

$$y_i - (\hat{\beta}_0 + \hat{\beta}_1 x_{i1} + \hat{\beta}_2 x_{i2}), \quad i = 1, 2, \ldots, n \qquad \text{11.20}$$

The term in Equation 11.20 is the difference between the observed value of $Y$ at $x_1 = x_{i1}, x_2 = x_{i2}$ and that given by the least squares plane at $x_1 = x_{i1}, x_2 = x_{i2}$. This difference is generally written as

$$y_i - \hat{y}_i = y_i - (\hat{\beta}_0 + \hat{\beta}_1 x_{i1} + \hat{\beta}_2 x_{i2}), \quad i = 1, 2, \ldots, n$$

and is called the $i$th residual. The sum of squares for error is the sum of the squares of such residuals. The difference $SST - SSE = SSR$ thus represents that part of the total variability in $Y$ explained by the model.

As before, it can be shown that

$$E(MSE) = \sigma^2 \qquad \text{11.21}$$

Hence, in the second ANOVA table of Exhibit 11.1, $\hat{\sigma}^2 = MSE = 180.0$ is a point estimate of the unknown value of $\sigma^2$. The ratio

$$R^2 = \frac{SSR}{SST} \qquad \text{11.22}$$

is the **multiple regression coefficient**. As for the coefficient of determination, it is easy to see that

$$0 \leqslant R^2 \leqslant 1 \qquad \text{11.23}$$

As with $r^2$ in the simple linear regression model, the value of $R^2$ can be interpreted as the proportion of the variability in $Y$ explained by $x_1$ and $x_2$ jointly. In Example 11.1 the value of the multiple regression coefficient is

$$R^2 = \frac{15056.0}{19016.2} = 0.792$$

indicating that the two variables home runs ($x_1$) and seasonal batting average ($x_2$) explain 79.2 percent of the variability in runs batted in ($Y$). In the Minitab output this value is computed as a percentage and labeled "R-Sq."

## Example 11.2

Turning once again to the baseball data, let us consider the additional output that can be obtained from Minitab by using the **NOBRIEF** command before the REGRESS command. The tabular output shown in Exhibit 11.2 has columns headed Obs., HOMERS, RBI, Fit, Stdev.Fit, Residual, and St.Resid. There is one

**Exhibit 11.2**

| Obs. | HOMERS | RBI | Fit | Stdev.Fit | Residual | St.Resid |
|------|--------|--------|--------|-----------|----------|----------|
| 1 | 24.0 | 118.00 | 122.33 | 10.27 | -4.33 | -0.50 X |
| 2 | 25.0 | 122.00 | 110.42 | 6.03 | 11.58 | 0.97 |
| 3 | 0.0 | 40.00 | 50.74 | 5.41 | -10.74 | -0.87 |
| 4 | 7.0 | 60.00 | 63.33 | 3.87 | -3.33 | -0.26 |
| 5 | 3.0 | 59.00 | 53.69 | 4.32 | 5.31 | 0.42 |
| 6 | 17.0 | 83.00 | 84.08 | 3.19 | -1.08 | -0.08 |
| 7 | 3.0 | 50.00 | 51.83 | 4.12 | -1.83 | -0.14 |
| 8 | 7.0 | 45.00 | 58.87 | 3.35 | -13.87 | -1.07 |
| 9 | 9.0 | 53.00 | 62.94 | 3.07 | -9.94 | -0.76 |
| 10 | 19.0 | 117.00 | 84.81 | 2.91 | 32.19 | 2.46R |
| 11 | 8.0 | 65.00 | 59.97 | 3.18 | 5.03 | 0.39 |
| 12 | 13.0 | 68.00 | 67.00 | 3.00 | 1.00 | 0.08 |
| 13 | 6.0 | 58.00 | 50.69 | 3.84 | 7.31 | 0.57 |
| 14 | 9.0 | 37.00 | 56.99 | 3.50 | -19.99 | -1.54 |
| 15 | 41.0 | 117.00 | 128.15 | 7.18 | -11.15 | -0.98 |
| 16 | 11.0 | 85.00 | 61.44 | 3.31 | 23.56 | 1.81 |
| 17 | 9.0 | 53.00 | 56.62 | 3.57 | -3.62 | -0.28 |
| 18 | 24.0 | 103.00 | 89.60 | 3.93 | 13.40 | 1.04 |
| 19 | 13.0 | 64.00 | 65.14 | 3.32 | -1.14 | -0.09 |
| 20 | 32.0 | 115.00 | 107.39 | 5.31 | 7.61 | 0.62 |
| 21 | 12.0 | 61.00 | 62.55 | 3.45 | -1.55 | -0.12 |
| 22 | 15.0 | 47.00 | 68.85 | 3.43 | -21.85 | -1.68 |
| 23 | 13.0 | 78.00 | 64.40 | 3.48 | 13.60 | 1.05 |
| 24 | 9.0 | 55.00 | 55.50 | 3.79 | -0.50 | -0.04 |
| 25 | 41.0 | 111.00 | 126.66 | 7.28 | -15.66 | -1.39 |

R denotes an obs. with a large st. resid.
X denotes an obs. whose X value gives it large influence.

line of output for each observation, as in the simple linear regression case. In statistical notation, the column headings are

$$ i \qquad x_{i1} \qquad y_i \qquad \hat{y}_i \qquad s_{\hat{y}_i} \qquad y_i - \hat{y}_i \qquad \frac{(y_i - \hat{y}_i)}{s_{y_i - \hat{y}_i}} $$

Note that there is no column for the $x_{i2}$ values, although the predicted values are a function of both regressors. The standardized residuals in the last column are those stored by Minitab in C11. The graph in Exhibit 11.3 is a plot of the standardized residuals in C11 on the vertical axis versus the predicted values in C12 on the horizontal axis. The graph in Exhibit 11.4 is a plot of the normal scores for the standardized residuals in C14 on the vertical axis versus the standardized residuals in C11 on the horizontal axis.

The table in Exhibit 11.2 contains the interesting information that the tenth observation has a standardized residual of 2.46. Any standardized residual with a magnitude exceeding 2 should be examined critically. The tenth observation represents batter Al Oliver, who had 117 runs batted in, 19 home runs, and a batting average of 0.319. The regression equation gives $\hat{y}_i$(Fit) = 84.81 for the predicted number of runs batted in. The nonstandardized residual is $y_i - \hat{y}_i = 32.19$, which indicates that Oliver had (roughly) 32 more runs batted in than the model predicts. Another hitter, Buddy Bell (the sixth observation in Exhibit 11.2), had 17

**Exhibit 11.3**

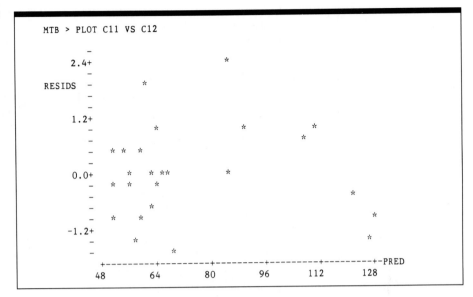

```
MTB > PLOT C11 VS C12

        _
   2.4+                                    *
        _
 RESIDS _          *
        _
        _
   1.2+
        _         *              *          *
        _                                 *
        _   * *  *
   0.0+      *   * **      *
        _   *  *    *
        _                                           *
        _          *
        _   *   *                                      *
  -1.2+
        _      *                                       *
        _           *
        +---------+---------+---------+---------+---------+-PRED
        48        64        80        96       112       128
```

**Exhibit 11.4**

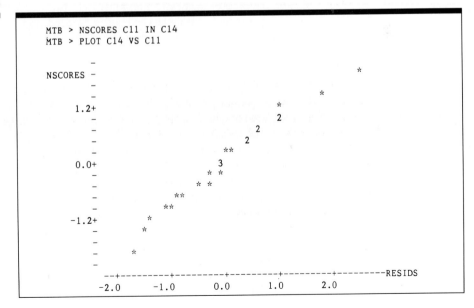

```
MTB > NSCORES C11 IN C14
MTB > PLOT C14 VS C11

        _
 NSCORES _                                       *
        _
        _
        _                                  *
   1.2+                            *
        _                          2
        _                     2
        _                  2
        _              **
   0.0+             3
        _             * *
        _          * *
        _        **
        _       **
  -1.2+      *
        _     *
        _
        _   *
        _
        --+---------+---------+---------+---------+---------RESIDS
        -2.0      -1.0       0.0       1.0       2.0
```

home runs and a batting average of 0.329, close to Oliver's record. He had 83 runs batted in, which is very close to the value of 84.08 predicted by the model. One explanation of the difference in these two batters' RBIs is that Oliver had 209 hits whereas Bell had only 161. The largest negative residual, $-21.85$, is associated with hitter number 22, Alvin Woods, who hit 15 home runs and had a batting average of 0.300. The model predicts 68.85 runs batted in, but Woods had only 47. In this case the hitter had only 112 hits for the year, the second smallest number among the 25 observations. These observations suggest that addition of the variable hits might improve the model.

The plot of the residuals versus the predicted values (Exhibit 11.3) can be used to check the overall appropriateness of the model and the constant variance assumption, with a random scatter of points suggesting that the model provides a reasonable fit. The plot for these data indicates that the residuals tend to be negative for large predicted values (greater than 120), positive for intermediate predicted values (80 to 110), and randomly distributed for predictions in the lower range (40 to 80). The plot of the normal scores of the standardized residuals versus the standardized residuals (Exhibit 11.4) should be approximately linear if the normality assumption is valid. In this case the linearity of the plot gives reasonable support to the normality assumption. The deviations from randomness in the first plot suggest that use of a model with other regressors might improve the fit—this possibility will be examined in the next section.

## Exercises 11.2

**11.1** A financial analyst is using observations of 18 companies to study the relationship between the price of a stock $(Y)$ in dollars and two regressors. The regressors are dividends per share $(x_1)$ in dollars and rate of dividend growth over the previous three years $(x_2)$ in percent. Minitab has been used to find the following regression equation and standard deviations:

$$\hat{y} = 12 + 3x_1 + 1.5x_2 \qquad s_{\beta_1} = 0.8 \qquad s_{\beta_2} = 0.75$$

Assume that the regression model of this section is valid.
**a.** Find 95 percent confidence intervals for $\beta_1$ and $\beta_2$.
**b.** Test the null hypothesis $H_0: \beta_1 = 0$ versus $H_1: \beta_1 \neq 0$. Use $\alpha = 0.05$ and state clearly the rejection region for the test.
**c.** Estimate the average price of a stock with a dividend of $x_1 = 5$ dollars and a growth rate of $x_2 = 4$ percent.

**11.2** In a regression study of teenage girls, the dependent variable is weight in pounds $(Y)$ and the independent variables are height in inches $(x_1)$ and age in years $(x_2)$. The regression equation and standard deviations for $n = 25$ individuals are

$$\hat{y} = -120 + 4.8x_1 + 0.75x_2 \qquad s_{\beta_1} = 2.4 \qquad s_{\beta_2} = 0.25$$

Assume that the regression model of this section is valid.
**a.** Find 90 percent confidence intervals for $\beta_1$ and $\beta_2$.
**b.** Test the null hypotheses $H_0: \beta_1 = 0$ and $H_0: \beta_2 = 0$ versus two-sided alternatives, using $\alpha = 0.01$. State clearly the rejection region.

**11.3** In the following data set, $Y$ represents the number of new resident students entering a university during a given year. The independent variables are the number of junior college graduates $(x_1)$ and the number of high school graduates $(x_2)$ from the region in which the university is located. All figures are in thousands of students.

| $y_i$ | $x_{i1}$ | $x_{i2}$ |
|---|---|---|
| 4.6 | 1.5 | 7.3 |
| 4.0 | 1.4 | 6.8 |
| 4.5 | 2.2 | 7.2 |
| 4.6 | 2.3 | 8.4 |
| 4.3 | 1.8 | 7.1 |
| 4.6 | 1.9 | 6.9 |
| 5.3 | 2.6 | 8.2 |
| 4.4 | 1.7 | 5.8 |
| 4.6 | 1.5 | 6.1 |
| 4.8 | 2.2 | 6.8 |
| 1.8 | 0.8 | 4.3 |
| 3.3 | 1.2 | 4.8 |
| 3.6 | 1.4 | 5.1 |
| 2.0 | 0.9 | 3.3 |
| 4.5 | 1.9 | 6.1 |
| 5.0 | 2.7 | 7.5 |
| 4.1 | 1.6 | 5.5 |
| 3.5 | 1.3 | 3.2 |
| 4.0 | 1.5 | 5.2 |

Use Minitab as needed.
**a.** Find the regression equation for these data.
**b.** In what units should $\beta_1$ and $\beta_2$ be expressed?
**c.** Test the null hypotheses $H_0$: $\beta_1 = 0$ and $H_0$: $\beta_2 = 0$ versus two-sided alternatives, using $\alpha = 0.05$.
**d.** Find 95 percent confidence intervals for $\beta_1$ and $\beta_2$.

**11.4** The following data set gives annual family expenditures $(Y)$ in thousands of dollars. The regressors $x_1$ and $x_2$ represent the husband's annual income and the wife's annual income, respectively, before taxes in thousands of dollars.

| $y_i$ | $x_{i1}$ | $x_{i2}$ |
|---|---|---|
| 60 | 42 | 37 |
| 44 | 23 | 34 |
| 41 | 33 | 22 |
| 50 | 38 | 26 |
| 34 | 18 | 21 |
| 45 | 35 | 30 |
| 46 | 38 | 32 |
| 60 | 50 | 39 |
| 61 | 42 | 43 |
| 52 | 30 | 36 |
| 28 | 9 | 26 |
| 38 | 21 | 31 |
| 31 | 10 | 23 |

(cont.)

| $y_i$ | $x_{i1}$ | $x_{i2}$ |
|-------|----------|----------|
| 61    | 43       | 39       |
| 46    | 39       | 28       |
| 53    | 33       | 42       |

Use Minitab to do the following.
a. Determine the regression equation.
b. Estimate the average increase in family expenditures for each additional dollar of husband's income, holding wife's income constant.
c. Estimate the average increase in family expenditures for each additional dollar of wife's income, holding husband's income constant.
d. Find $R^2$.
e. Find $\hat{\sigma}^2$.
f. Make a plot of the standardized residuals versus the predicted values.
g. Make a normal plot of the residuals.
h. What conclusions can you draw from the plots in part f and g?

**11.5** The following are data on motor vehicle registration, population, and per capita income for 11 states:

| State | Motor Vehicle Registration, 1984 (1000s) | Population, 1980 (1000s) | Per Capita Income ($) |
|-------|------------------------------------------|--------------------------|-----------------------|
| Alabama | 3,286 | 3,894 | 9,242 |
| Colorado | 2,896 | 2,890 | 12,770 |
| Georgia | 4,405 | 5,463 | 10,379 |
| Iowa | 2,773 | 2,913 | 10,705 |
| Maryland | 3,263 | 4,217 | 12,994 |
| Missouri | 3,551 | 4,917 | 10,969 |
| New Jersey | 5,072 | 7,365 | 14,122 |
| Ohio | 8,158 | 10,798 | 11,216 |
| South Carolina | 2,188 | 3,122 | 9,187 |
| Vermont | 409 | 511 | 9,979 |
| Wyoming | 536 | 470 | 11,911 |

*Source:* Data from the Department of Transportation, Federal Highway Administration, as presented in *The Information Please Almanac* (Boston: Houghton Mifflin, 1986), p. 70.

Use Minitab as needed for the following.
a. Find the regression equation $\hat{y} = \hat{\beta}_0 + \hat{\beta}_1 x_1 + \hat{\beta}_2 x_2$.
b. Which variable, population or per capita income, is more useful in explaining the variation in motor vehicle registrations by state? Why?
c. What proportion of the variability in $Y$ is explained by the model containing $x_1$ and $x_2$?
d. Make a plot of the standardized residuals versus the predicted values and a normal plot of the residuals. What general conclusions can you draw from these plots?

**11.6** Use the data for the 19 batters in Exhibit 2.8. Let the dependent random variable $Y$ represent runs batted in and the independent variables $x_1$ and $x_2$ be home runs and batting average, respectively.
  **a.** Find the regression equation using Minitab.
  **b.** Find point estimates of $\beta_1$ and $\beta_2$. Does the point estimate of $\beta_1$ lie in the 95 percent confidence interval for $\beta_1$ found in Example 11.1?
  **c.** Find $R^2$.
  **d.** Construct residual plots as in part d of exercise 11.5. What do you conclude from these plots?

**11.7** The following are data on the number of home runs scored by the team, the distance from home plate to the left-field foul pole in the team's home baseball park, and the club batting average for the 14 American League teams in 1985.

| Team | Home Runs | Left-Field Distance | Team Batting Average |
|------|-----------|---------------------|----------------------|
| Baltimore | 214 | 309 | 0.263 |
| Boston | 162 | 315 | 0.282 |
| California | 152 | 333 | 0.250 |
| Chicago | 146 | 341 | 0.253 |
| Cleveland | 116 | 320 | 0.265 |
| Detroit | 202 | 340 | 0.254 |
| Kansas City | 154 | 330 | 0.252 |
| Milwaukee | 101 | 315 | 0.263 |
| Minnesota | 141 | 343 | 0.263 |
| New York | 176 | 312 | 0.267 |
| Oakland | 153 | 330 | 0.264 |
| Seattle | 171 | 316 | 0.255 |
| Texas | 129 | 330 | 0.254 |
| Toronto | 158 | 330 | 0.269 |

*Source: The Information Please Almanac* (Boston: Houghton Mifflin, 1986), p. 942.

  Let $Y$ be home runs, $x_1$ the distance from home plate to left field, and $x_2$ the team batting average.
  **a.** By using the model expressed in Equation 11.7, what assumption is one making about the expected number of home runs by an American League team?
  **b.** Find the regression equation and $R^2$ for these data, using the model in Equation 11.7.
  **c.** Test $H_0: \beta_1 = 0$ and $H_0: \beta_2 = 0$ versus two-sided alternatives, using $\alpha = 0.05$.
  **d.** What conclusion can be drawn about the model hypothesized in part a?

**11.8** The following data set gives the rate of weight gain in pounds per day ($Y$), the initial age in days ($x_1$), and the initial weight in pounds ($x_2$) of 40 pigs.

| y | $x_1$ | $x_2$ | y | $x_1$ | $x_2$ |
|------|-------|-------|------|-------|-------|
| 1.40 | 78 | 61 | 1.67 | 78 | 80 |
| 1.79 | 90 | 59 | 1.41 | 83 | 61 |
| 1.72 | 94 | 76 | 1.73 | 79 | 62 |
| 1.47 | 71 | 50 | 1.23 | 70 | 47 |
| 1.26 | 99 | 61 | 1.49 | 85 | 59 |
| 1.28 | 80 | 54 | 1.22 | 83 | 42 | (cont.) |

| y | $x_1$ | $x_2$ | y | $x_1$ | $x_2$ |
|------|------|------|------|------|------|
| 1.34 | 83 | 57 | 1.39 | 71 | 47 |
| 1.55 | 75 | 45 | 1.39 | 66 | 42 |
| 1.57 | 62 | 41 | 1.56 | 67 | 40 |
| 1.26 | 67 | 40 | 1.36 | 67 | 40 |
| 1.61 | 78 | 74 | 1.40 | 77 | 62 |
| 1.31 | 99 | 75 | 1.47 | 71 | 55 |
| 1.12 | 80 | 64 | 1.37 | 78 | 62 |
| 1.35 | 75 | 48 | 1.15 | 70 | 43 |
| 1.29 | 94 | 62 | 1.22 | 95 | 57 |
| 1.24 | 91 | 42 | 1.48 | 96 | 51 |
| 1.29 | 75 | 52 | 1.31 | 71 | 41 |
| 1.43 | 63 | 43 | 1.27 | 63 | 40 |
| 1.29 | 62 | 50 | 1.22 | 62 | 45 |
| 1.26 | 67 | 40 | 1.36 | 67 | 39 |

*Source:* George W. Snedecor and William G. Cochran, *Statistical Methods*, 6th ed. (Ames, IA: Iowa State University Press, 1967), p. 440.

**a.** Find the regression equation $\hat{y} = \hat{\beta}_0 + \hat{\beta}_1 x_1 + \hat{\beta}_2 x_2$.
**b.** Does either of the variables $x_1$ or $x_2$ appear helpful in explaining the variability of $Y$? Explain.
**c.** Does the model expressed in Equation 11.6 appear to be adequate to explain a substantial proportion of the variability in weight gain?

**11.9** The following table gives the number of coins minted in the United States (in millions) for selected years from 1920 to 1960.

| Year | Total | Cents | Nickels | Dimes |
|------|--------|--------|---------|-------|
| 1920 | 630.5 | 405.7 | 82.2 | 92.0 |
| 25 | 286.8 | 188.9 | 46.3 | 36.6 |
| 30 | 265.9 | 221.8 | 28.3 | 8.6 |
| 35 | 557.2 | 331.1 | 80.7 | 85.1 |
| 40 | 1209.5 | 781.2 | 259.7 | 108.1 |
| 45 | 2060.7 | 1448.6 | 215.5 | 241.3 |
| 50 | 928.7 | 726.1 | 12.5 | 117.4 |
| 55 | 1091.4 | 938.8 | 82.7 | 45.3 |
| 60 | 2810.7 | 2169.0 | 249.7 | 272.2 |

*Source:* Ernest Rubin, "Statistical Experimentation in the Classroom," *American Statistician* 17, No. 5 (1963): 23.

**a.** Use the total number of coins minted as the dependent variable and the numbers of cents and nickels minted as the independent variables. Use the Minitab command REGRESS with the BRIEF = 3 command to find the regression equation for these data.
**b.** Test $H_0: \beta_1 = 0$ and $H_1: \beta_2 = 0$ versus two-sided alternatives, using $\alpha = 0.05$.
**c.** Find $R^2$.
**d.** Estimate the total number of coins produced in the United States in a year in which 4 billion cents are minted and 500 million nickels are minted.

**11.10** A multiple regression model of the form

$$Y_i = \beta_0 + \beta_1 x_{i1} + \beta_2 x_{i2} + \varepsilon_i, \qquad i = 1, 2, \ldots, 16$$

is used to explain household expenditures $(Y)$ as a function of income $(x_1)$ and size of family $(x_2)$. (The variables $Y$ and $x_1$ are measured in dollars and $x_2$ in number of persons.) Minitab yields the regression function

$$\hat{y} = -240 + 0.81x_1 + 420x_2$$

**a.** In what units are $\hat{\beta}_1$ and $\hat{\beta}_2$ measured?
**b.** Explain in words the meaning of $\beta_1$ and $\beta_2$.
**c.** If $s_{\hat{\beta}_1} = 0.25$ and $s_{\hat{\beta}_2} = 112.5$, find 95 percent confidence intervals for $\beta_1$ and $\beta_2$.

## 11.3

## The General Linear Regression Model

general linear regression model

The general linear regression model is a direct extension of the model defined in Equations 11.6 and 11.7 for the case of two regressors. The assumption in the **general linear regression model** is that the expected value of a dependent random variable $Y$ is a linear function of $k \geqslant 2$ real variables $x_i$, so

$$E(Y|x_1, x_2, \ldots, x_k) = \beta_0 + \beta_1 x_1 + \beta_2 x_2 + \cdots + \beta_k x_k \qquad \textbf{11.24}$$

where, as before, the $\beta_i$ are unknown parameters that must be estimated from the data. An individual observation is thus given by

$$Y_i = \underbrace{\beta_0 + \beta_1 x_{i1} + \beta_2 x_{i2} + \cdots + \beta_k x_{ik}}_{} + \varepsilon_i, \qquad i = 1, 2, \ldots, n$$

$$= E(Y_i | x_1 = x_{i1}, \ldots, x_k = x_{ik}) + \varepsilon_i \qquad \textbf{11.25}$$

As before, the observation is composed of a real expected value plus a random component, $\varepsilon_i$. Again it is assumed that $E(\varepsilon_i) = 0$ and $\text{Var}(\varepsilon_i) = \sigma^2$ for $i = 1, 2, \ldots, n$ and that the $\varepsilon_i$ are independent random variables.

The data used to estimate the $\beta_i$ and $\sigma^2$ are $n$ observations of the dependent variable $Y$, together with the corresponding values of $x_1, x_2, \ldots, x_k$. Hence a data set is of the form

$$(y_i, x_{i1}, x_{i2}, \ldots, x_{ik}), \qquad i = 1, 2, \ldots, n \qquad \textbf{11.26}$$

To estimate the $\beta_i$, we must minimize the expression

$$Q(\beta_0, \beta_1, \ldots, \beta_k) = \sum [y_i - (\beta_0 - \beta_1 x_{i1} - \beta_2 x_{i2} - \cdots - \beta_k x_{ik})]^2$$
$$\textbf{11.27}$$

The resulting regression equation is given by

$$\hat{y} = \hat{\beta}_0 + \hat{\beta}_1 x_1 + \hat{\beta}_2 x_2 + \cdots + \hat{\beta}_k x_k \qquad \textbf{11.28}$$

The values $\hat{\beta}_0, \hat{\beta}_1, \ldots, \hat{\beta}_k$ are the values that minimize Equation 11.27.

As in the case where $k = 2$, the total sum of squares can be decomposed into a sum of squares for error and a sum of squares for regression:

$$\text{SST} = \text{SSE} + \text{SSR}$$

**Table 11.3**

**ANOVA Table for General Linear Regression**

| Source | d.f. | SS | MS |
|--------|------|----|----|
| Regression | $k$ | SSR | MSR $=$ SSR/$k$ |
| Error (Residual) | $n - k - 1$ | SSE | MSE $=$ SSE/$(n - k - 1)$ |
| Total | $n - 1$ | SST | |

where

$$\text{SST} = \sum (y_i - \bar{y})^2$$
$$\text{SSE} = \sum (y_i - \hat{y}_i)^2 = \sum (y_i - \hat{\beta}_0 - \hat{\beta}_1 x_{i1} - \cdots - \hat{\beta}_k x_{ik})^2$$
$$\text{SSR} = \text{SST} - \text{SSE}$$

As before, the sum of squares for error (SSE) is the sum of the squares of the residuals of the form $y_i - \hat{y}_i$, where $y_i$ is the value of $Y$ observed at $x_1 = x_{i1}, \ldots,$ $x_k = x_{ik}$ and $\hat{y}_i$ is the value predicted by the regression equation (Equation 11.28) at the same values of $x_1, \ldots, x_k$. This information is summarized in the ANOVA table presented in Table 11.3. Under the assumptions of the first paragraph of this section, it can be shown that

$$E(\text{MSE}) = \sigma^2 \tag{11.29}$$

that is, the mean square for error is an unbiased estimator of $\sigma^2$. Thus the estimator of $\sigma^2$ used is $\hat{\sigma}^2 = \text{MSE}$. The multiple regression coefficient is the ratio $R^2 = $ SSR/SST, and $0 \leqslant R^2 \leqslant 1$. Again the value of $R^2$ can be interpreted as the proportion of the total variability in $Y$ that is explained by the model using all the regressors $x_1, x_2, \ldots, x_k$. It is always the case that adding a regressor to the model will increase $R^2$. In general, we want a *parsimonious* model—that is, a model with as small a number of regressors as possible explaining a large proportion of the variability in $Y$.

**Example 11.3**

The analysis of the residuals in Example 11.2 suggested that we might be able to explain more of the variation in runs batted in if we included in the analysis the regressor variable hits, in addition to the variables home runs and batting average. The regression output from Minitab in Exhibits 11.5 through 11.7 includes this third regressor variable.

The variables HOMERS, RBI, and AVE are in C8, C9, and C10, respectively, as before. The variable HITS is in C7. The regression was carried out with home runs ($x_1$), batting average ($x_2$), and hits ($x_3$) as regressors and runs batted in ($Y$) as the dependent variable. The regression equation is

$$\hat{y} = -67.1 + 2.16x_1 + 264x_2 + 0.157x_3$$

**Exhibit 11.5**

```
MTB > NOTE MULTIPLE REGRESSION EXAMPLE WITH K = 3
MTB > READ INTO C5-C10
MTB > NOTE DEPENDENT VARIABLE (Y) IS RBIS
      25 ROWS READ
  ROW     C5     C6     C7    C8     C9     C10

   1      449    87    175    24    118    0.390
   2      622    96    219    25    122    0.352
   3      528    87    180     0     40    0.341
   4      630    96    210     7     60    0.333
       .   .   .

MTB > NOTE DEPENDENT VARIABLE (Y) IS RBIS
MTB > NOTE INDEPENDENT VARIABLES X1,X2,X3, ARE HOMERS,BA AND HITS
MTB > NAME C7 'HITS' C8 'HOMERS' C9 'RBI' C10 'AVE'
MTB > PRINT C9 C8 C10 C7
  ROW    RBI  HOMERS      AVE    HITS

   1     118     24    0.390     175
   2     122     25    0.352     219
   3      40      0    0.341     180
   4      60      7    0.333     210
   5      59      3    0.331     179
   6      83     17    0.329     161
   7      50      3    0.326     230
   8      45      7    0.321     144
   9      53      9    0.320     205
  10     117     19    0.319     209
  11      65      8    0.318     124
  12      68     13    0.307     144
  13      58      6    0.305     138
  14      37      9    0.304     137
  15     117     41    0.304     180
  16      85     11    0.304     179
  17      53      9    0.303     179
  18     103     24    0.302     175
  19      64     13    0.302     165
  20     115     32    0.302     187
  21      61     12    0.301     125
  22      47     15    0.300     112
  23      78     13    0.300     156
  24      55      9    0.300     102
  25     111     41    0.300     154
```

The ANOVA table is shown in Table 11.4. Note that the value of SST = 19016.2 is the same as that in Example 11.1, as the $y_i$ values have not changed. The values of SSR has increased from 15056.0 for the regression with $k = 2$ to 15588.1 for $k = 3$. The value of $R^2$ has increased from 0.792 in the model with two regressors to

$$R^2 = \frac{15588.1}{19016.2} = 0.820$$

This increase is modest, but it is not the only change that must be considered. The value of the mean square for error in MSE = 163.2 for this model, whereas it was

## Exhibit 11.6

```
MTB > BRIEF = 3
MTB > REGRESS C9 ON 3 XS IN C8 C10 C7 RESIDS IN C11 PREDICTED IN C12

The regression equation is
RBI = - 67.1 + 2.16 HOMERS + 264 AVE + 0.157 HITS

Predictor       Coef        Stdev       t-ratio
Constant       -67.07       39.71        -1.69
HOMERS          2.1603       0.2415       8.95
AVE           263.7        136.7         1.93
HITS            0.15693      0.08692      1.81

s = 12.78       R-sq = 82.0%    R-sq(adj) = 79.4%

Analysis of Variance

SOURCE          DF          SS           MS
Regression       3       15588.1       5196.0
Error           21        3428.1        163.2
Total           24       19016.2

SOURCE          DF        SEQ SS
HOMERS           1       13560.4
AVE              1        1495.6
HITS             1         532.0
```

## Exhibit 11.7

```
Obs.   HOMERS      RBI        Fit  Stdev.Fit  Residual   St.Resid
  1     24.0    118.00    115.10    10.57       2.90      0.40 X
  2     25.0    122.00    114.14     6.10       7.86      0.70
  3      0.0     40.00     51.11     5.16     -11.11     -0.95
  4      7.0     60.00     68.83     4.78      -8.83     -0.75
  5      3.0     59.00     54.80     4.16       4.20      0.35
  6     17.0     83.00     81.69     3.32       1.31      0.11
  7      3.0     50.00     61.48     6.63     -11.48     -1.05
  8      7.0     45.00     55.31     3.75     -10.31     -0.84
  9      9.0     53.00     68.94     4.42     -15.94     -1.33
 10     19.0    117.00     90.91     4.37      26.09      2.17R
 11      8.0     65.00     53.54     4.68      11.46      0.96
 12     13.0     68.00     64.58     3.16       3.42      0.28
 13      6.0     58.00     47.99     3.95      10.01      0.82
 14      9.0     37.00     54.05     3.71     -17.05     -1.39
 15     41.0    117.00    129.93     6.91     -12.93     -1.20
 16     11.0     85.00     64.96     3.71      20.04      1.64
 17      9.0     53.00     60.37     3.99      -7.37     -0.61
 18     24.0    103.00     91.89     3.95      11.11      0.91
 19     13.0     64.00     66.56     3.26      -2.56     -0.21
 20     32.0    115.00    111.05     5.45       3.95      0.34
 21     12.0     61.00     57.85     4.19       3.15      0.26
 22     15.0     47.00     62.03     4.99     -15.03     -1.28
 23     13.0     78.00     64.62     3.32      13.38      1.08
 24      9.0     55.00     47.50     5.71       7.50      0.66
 25     41.0    111.00    124.79     7.01     -13.79     -1.29

R denotes an obs. with a large st. resid.
X denotes an obs. whose X value gives it large influence.
```

**Table 11.4**

**ANOVA Table**

| Source | d.f. | SS | MS |
|---|---|---|---|
| Regression | 3 | 15588.1 | 5196.0 |
| Error | 21 | 3428.1 | 163.2 |
| Total | 24 | 19016.2 | |

180.0 in Example 11.1. Thus the estimate of the unknown variance $\sigma^2$ has been reduced by $[(180 - 163.2)/180]100 = 9.3$ percent, which is not negligible.

Let us now consider inference for the general linear model, using the output from Example 11.3. First we will consider a test of the following two hypotheses:

$$H_0: \beta_1 = \beta_2 = \cdots = \beta_k = 0 \qquad \text{versus} \qquad H_1: H_0 \text{ is false} \qquad \textbf{11.30}$$

The null hypothesis in Equation 11.30 means that $E(Y|x_1, \ldots, x_k) = \beta_0$—that is, the true average value of $Y$ does not depend on any of the regressors. As before, in order to carry out inference, we must add to the assumptions in the first paragraph of this section the assumption that the $\varepsilon_i$ are normally distributed. Under $H_0$, both MSR and MSE are unbiased estimates of $\sigma^2$ and MSR/MSE has an $F$ distribution with $k$ and $n - k - 1$ degrees of freedom, as shown in the ANOVA table (Table 11.4). If at least one $\beta_i$ is not 0, $E(\text{MSR})$ will be greater than $\sigma^2$ and MSE will still be an unbiased estimate of $\sigma^2$. Hence the critical region for

*F* test    the *F* test of Equation 11.30 should be of the form

$$F \geqslant F_\alpha(k, n - k - 1)$$

For the data of Example 11.3 we have

$$F = \frac{5196.0}{163.2} = 31.84$$

for $\alpha = 0.05$, and from Table IV of Appendix C we find that

$$F_{0.05}(3, 21) = 3.07$$

Clearly the hypothesis $H_0: \beta_1 = \beta_2 = \beta_3 = 0$ should be rejected. Note that $H_0$ means that the variable runs batted in ($Y$) is not explained at all by home runs, batting average, or hits. Obviously this hypothesis is not likely to be tenable.

The interpretation of $\beta_i$ in the general linear model parallels the interpretation of $\beta_1$ and $\beta_2$ in the case where $k = 2$. The parameter $\beta_i$ represents the true average change in $Y$ per unit change in $x_i$, with all the other regressors held constant. Again,

$$E(\hat{\beta}_i) = \beta_i, \qquad i = 1, 2, \ldots, k$$

In Example 11.3, the point estimates are

$$\hat{\beta}_1 = 2.16 \qquad \hat{\beta}_2 = 264 \qquad \hat{\beta}_3 = 0.157$$

Thus, holding home runs and batting average fixed, we estimate that there will be 0.157 additional runs batted in per hit (or, multiplying the units by a factor of ten, 1.57 runs batted in for every ten additional hits).

Tests and confidence intervals for the $\beta_i$ are based on the fact that

$$\frac{\hat{\beta}_i - \beta_i}{s_{\hat{\beta}_i}} \sim t_{n-k-1}, \qquad i = 1, 2, \ldots, k \qquad\qquad \textbf{11.31}$$

that is, the properly standardized regression coefficients $\hat{\beta}_i$ have Student's $t$ distribution with $n - k - 1$ degrees of freedom. Using this fact, we find that $(1 - \alpha)100$ percent confidence intervals for $\beta_i$ have endpoints given by

$$\hat{\beta}_i \pm s_{\hat{\beta}_i} t_{\alpha/2, n-k-1}$$

The required values of the $s_{\hat{\beta}_i}$ are given in Exhibit 11.6 under the heading Stdev. For 95 percent confidence intervals, we have

$$
\begin{aligned}
\hat{\beta}_1 \pm s_{\hat{\beta}_1} t_{0.025,21} &= 2.16 \pm 0.2415(2.08) \\
&= 2.16 \pm 0.50 \\
\hat{\beta}_2 \pm s_{\hat{\beta}_2} t_{0.025,21} &= 263.7 \pm 136.7(2.08) \\
&= 263.7 \pm 284.3 \\
\hat{\beta}_3 \pm s_{\hat{\beta}_3} t_{0.025,21} &= 0.157 \pm 0.0869(2.08) \\
&= 0.157 \pm 0.181
\end{aligned}
$$

The confidence intervals for $\beta_1$, $\beta_2$, and $\beta_3$ are thus $(1.66, 2.66)$, $(-20.6, 548)$, and $(-0.024, 0.338)$, respectively.

To test the individual null hypotheses $H_0: \beta_i = 0$, the test statistics $t = \hat{\beta}_i / s_{\hat{\beta}_i}$ are used. Rejection regions versus standard alternatives are given in Table 11.5. The values of the $t$ statistics computed by Minitab are shown in Exhibit 11.6 under the heading t-ratio. For Example 11.3, the values are $t = 8.95$, $t = 1.93$, and $t = 1.81$ for $i = 1, 2, 3$, respectively. Against a two-sided alternative, the rejection region for $\alpha = 0.05$ is

$$|t| \geq t_{0.025,21} = 2.08$$

**Table 11.5**

**Critical Regions for Tests of $H_0: \beta_i = 0$**

| Alternative | Critical Region |
|---|---|
| $\beta_i > 0$ | $t > t_{\alpha, n-k-1}$ |
| $\beta_i < 0$ | $t < -t_{\alpha, n-k-1}$ |
| $\beta_i \neq 0$ | $|t| > t_{\alpha/2, n-k-1}$ |

Note that $H_0: \beta_2 = 0$ and $H_0: \beta_3 = 0$ would be retained using this rejection region. When the test statistics $t = \hat{\beta}_i/s_{\hat{\beta}_i}$ are used to test the individual null hypotheses, each test is carried out under the assumption that the other variables are all included in the model. If two variables provide very comparable information in explaining the dependent variable, it is possible that neither one will show up as significant (given that the other one is in the model already). This problem of the multicollinearity of the regressors is generally discussed in courses in regression analysis.

More reasonable alternatives than those used above would be

$$H_1: \beta_i > 0, \qquad i = 1, 2, 3$$

as one would expect runs batted in to increase with home runs, batting average, and hits. Table 11.5 indicates that against these alternatives a critical region for $\alpha = 0.05$ is

$$t > t_{0.05,21} = 1.721$$

Each of the alternative hypotheses, $H_1: \beta_1 > 0$, $H_1: \beta_2 > 0$, and $H_1: \beta_3 > 0$, would be declared valid versus the null hypotheses. In other words, given these alternative hypotheses, $x_1$, $x_2$, and $x_3$ should each be kept in the model to explain runs batted in. Each variable contributes in the expected way to the explanation of runs batted in.

Finally, let us consider the last table of the output from the REGRESS command, shown in Exhibit 11.7, and the two standard residual plots, presented in Exhibits 11.8 and 11.9. The table shows one large standardized residual—that

**Exhibit 11.8**

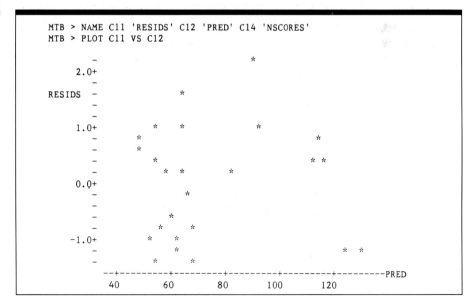

**Exhibit 11.9**

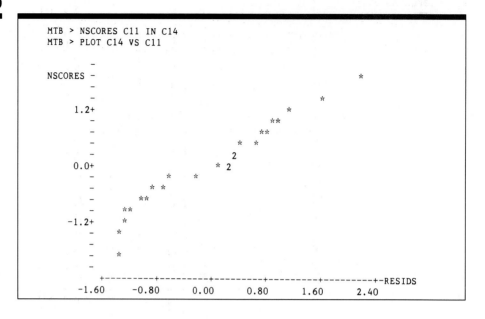

```
MTB > NSCORES C11 IN C14
MTB > PLOT C14 VS C11


          -
NSCORES   -                                                      *
          -
          -                                                *
      1.2+                                          *
          -                                    **
          -                                   **
          -                             *   *
          -                            2
      0.0+                        *  2
          -               *     *
          -            *  *
          -            **
          -         **
     -1.2+         *
          -       *
          -
          -       *

          +---------+---------+---------+---------+---------+-RESIDS
        -1.60     -0.80     0.00      0.80      1.60      2.40
```

associated with the tenth batter, Al Oliver. The standardized residual has been reduced from 2.46 in the case where $k = 2$ to 2.17. Still, the new model predicts only 90.91 runs batted in by a batter with 19 home runs, a 0.319 batting average, and 209 hits, whereas Oliver actually had batted in 117 runs in 1980. A tentative conclusion that can be drawn about Al Oliver in 1980 is that when he came to bat with runners on base, he was more likely than other good American League batters to bat them in.

The regression plot of the standardized residuals versus the predicted values (Exhibit 11.8) is similar in general form to the plot for $k = 2$. The magnitudes of the largest standardized residuals have been somewhat reduced. The largest positive residual is the one just discussed, for Al Oliver. The largest negative standardized residual went from $-1.68$ to $-1.39$. Previously the largest negative standardized residual was associated with the 22nd batter (Woods); in the current model it is associated with the 14th batter (Molitor). The normal plot of the residuals (Exhibit 11.9) is not quite as linear for $k = 3$ as it was for $k = 2$. The reduction in linearity is accounted for by the lack of large negative standardized residuals. This deviation from the model assumptions would not cause a statistician to reject the model for $k = 3$, however.

**11.11** A multiple regression model has been developed to explain $Y$, the monthly sales of a furniture store, measured in thousands of dollars. The model for the average monthly sales is given by

$$E(Y) = \beta_0 + \beta_1 x_1 + \beta_2 x_2 + \beta_3 x_3$$

where $x_1$, $x_2$, and $x_3$ represent the amount of money (in thousands of dollars) spent during a month on newspaper, radio, and television advertising, respectively. The following information has been obtained from Minitab:

| Predictor | Coefficient | $t$ ratio |
|---|---|---|
| – | 100 | 12.15 |
| $x_1$ | 20 | 3.14 |
| $x_2$ | 5 | 3.85 |
| $x_3$ | 10 | 2.15 |

Given that $\Sigma(y_i - \bar{y})^2 = 2000$, $R^2 = 0.85$, and $n = 18$, do the following.
  **a.** Construct an ANOVA table for these data.
  **b.** Test the null hypothesis $H_0: \beta_1 = \beta_2 = \beta_3 = 0$, using $\alpha = 0.05$.
  **c.** Calculate an unbiased estimate of $\sigma^2$.
  **d.** Test the individual hypotheses

$$H_0: \beta_i = 0, \qquad i = 1, 2, 3$$

versus two-sided alternatives, using $\alpha = 0.05$.
  **e.** Interpret the meaning of $\beta_1$ in words, and find a 95 percent confidence interval for $\beta_1$ using $s_{\beta_1} = 3.41$.

**11.12** A firm that sells hospital supplies is interested in estimating the relationship in sales districts among $x_1$, the amount spent for direct-mail distribution; $x_2$, the size of the sales staff; $x_3$, per capita income; and $Y$, sales. The variable $x_1$ is measured in tens of thousands of dollars, $x_2$ in individuals, $x_3$ in dollars, and $Y$ in hundreds of thousands of dollars. To estimate this relationship the firm uses the following model:

$$E(Y) = \beta_0 + \beta_1 x_1 + \beta_2 x_2 + \beta_3 x_3$$

The following information is obtained from 20 sampled sales districts.

| Predictor | Coefficient | Standard Deviation of Coefficient |
|---|---|---|
| Constant | 20.1 | 4.41 |
| $x_1$ | 4.2 | 1.52 |
| $x_2$ | −0.5 | 0.20 |
| $x_3$ | +0.025 | 0.15 |

  **a.** Test the null hypotheses

$$H_0: \beta_i = 0, \qquad i = 1, 2, 3$$

versus two-sided alternatives, using $\alpha = 0.05$.
  **b.** What are the units of $\beta_1$? What interpretation should be given to the point estimate $\hat{\beta}_1 = 4.2$?
  **c.** What are the units of $\beta_2$? What interpretation should be given to the point estimate $\hat{\beta}_2 = -0.5$?
  **d.** Find 95 percent confidence intervals for $\beta_1$, $\beta_2$, and $\beta_3$.

**11.13** The following are data on price per share of 13 U.S. airline stocks as of June 30, 1986. The information on earnings per share, cash flow per share, and revenue per share is for fiscal year 1985. All variables are measured in dollars.

| Name of Company | Price/ Share ($y$) (6-30-86) | Earnings/ Share ($x_1$) (1985) | Cash Flow/ Share ($x_2$) (1985) | Revenue/ Share ($x_3$) (1985) |
|---|---|---|---|---|
| AMR | 55 | 5.94 | 11.49 | 104.48 |
| Delta Air Lines | 43 | 6.50 | 15.23 | 117.22 |
| Eastern Air Lines | 9.25 | −0.36 | 4.20 | 79.26 |
| Northwest Airlines | 50 | 3.18 | 11.74 | 121.96 |
| Ozark Holdings | 18 | 1.08 | 2.02 | 40.80 |
| Pacific Southwest Airlines | 26 | 3.88 | 13.85 | 150.28 |
| Piedmont Aviation | 40 | 3.89 | 10.24 | 91.07 |
| Republic Airlines | 17 | 1.80 | 4.23 | 51.67 |
| Southwest Airlines | 20 | 1.54 | 3.13 | 21.07 |
| Texas Air Corp. | 35 | 1.47 | 4.99 | 84.40 |
| UAL Inc. | 55 | −4.21 | 11.17 | 181.03 |
| US Air Group | 32 | 4.05 | 7.21 | 65.61 |
| Western Airlines | 10 | 0.86 | 1.94 | 29.04 |

*Source: The Value Line Investment Survey, July 4, 1986.*

Use Minitab as needed.
**a.** Find the fitted model $\hat{y} = \hat{\beta}_0 + \hat{\beta}_1 x_1 + \hat{\beta}_2 x_2 + \hat{\beta}_3 x_3$.
**b.** What is the value of $R^2$?
**c.** Test the null hypothesis $H_0$: $\beta_1 = \beta_2 = \beta_3 = 0$, using $\alpha = 0.05$.

**11.14** The designer of a model to explain 1986 electric company dividends ($Y$) proposes using three explanatory variables:

**1** $x_1$, earnings per share (1985)
**2** $x_2$, percent of net worth earned per share (1985)
**3** $x_3$, percent of total power generated with nuclear fuel

The table gives data on dividends per share and the three explanatory variables for 21 eastern electric companies ($y$ and $x_1$ are measured in dollars and $x_2$ and $x_3$ in percentage points).

| Company | Dividend Indicated ($y$) (1986) | Earnings/ Share ($x_1$) (1985) | Percent of Net Worth Earned ($x_2$) (1985) | Percent of Power That Is Nuclear ($x_3$) |
|---|---|---|---|---|
| Allegheny Power | 2.80 | 3.59 | 12.8 | 0.0 |
| American Electric Power | 2.26 | 2.54 | 11.9 | 9.0 |
| Atlantic City Electric | 2.60 | 3.00 | 11.5 | 32.0 |
| Baltimore Gas and Electric | 1.75 | 2.80 | 13.5 | 47.0 |
| Boston Edison | 2.52 | 2.52 | 12.9 | 40.0 |
| Carolina Power | 2.68 | 3.86 | 12.6 | 33.0 |
| Consolidated Edison | 2.68 | 4.26 | 12.2 | 30.0 |
| Dominion Resources | 2.84 | 3.60 | 11.3 | 47.0 |

(cont.)

| Company | Dividend Indicated ($y$) (1986) | Earnings/ Share ($x_1$) (1985) | Percent of Net Worth Earned ($x_2$) (1985) | Percent of Power That Is Nuclear ($x_3$) |
|---|---|---|---|---|
| Duke Power | 2.60 | 3.72 | 12.1 | 54.0 |
| FPL Group | 2.02 | 3.11 | 13.5 | 35.0 |
| Florida Progress | 2.28 | 3.53 | 14.6 | 13.0 |
| New England Electric | 1.92 | 3.15 | 15.0 | 13.0 |
| N.E. Utilities | 1.68 | 2.72 | 15.0 | 48.0 |
| Pennsylvania Power & Light | 2.56 | 2.68 | 10.3 | 27.0 |
| Philadelphia Electric | 2.20 | 2.56 | 12.9 | 32.0 |
| Public Service Ent. Group | 2.93 | 3.96 | 12.4 | 24.0 |
| SCANA Corp. | 2.22 | 2.82 | 13.2 | 24.0 |
| Savannah Electric | 1.72 | 2.90 | 13.8 | 0.0 |
| Southern Company | 2.04 | 3.20 | 14.3 | 13.0 |
| TECO Energy, Inc. | 2.49 | 3.58 | 13.0 | 0.0 |
| United Illuminating | 2.32 | 5.82 | 14.7 | 8.0 |

*Source: The Value Line Investment Survey, June 27, 1986.*

Use Minitab to do the following.

**a.** Find the fitted regression equation $\hat{y} = \hat{\beta}_0 + \hat{\beta}_1 x_1 + \hat{\beta}_2 x_2 + \hat{\beta}_3 x_3$ for these data.

**b.** Find $R^2$, $\hat{\sigma}^2$, and $\hat{\sigma}$.

**c.** Test the null hypothesis $H_0: \beta_1 = \beta_2 = \beta_3 = 0$ versus $H_1: H_0$ false, using $\alpha = 0.05$. What is the meaning of your decision?

**d.** Test the individual hypotheses

$H_0: \beta_i = 0, \quad i = 1, 2, 3$

versus two-sided alternatives, using $\alpha = 0.10$.

**e.** Are the signs of the estimated regression coefficients $\hat{\beta}_1, \hat{\beta}_2$, and $\hat{\beta}_3$ those you would have predicted? If not, explain why you would have predicted different results.

**f.** Make a plot of the standardized residuals versus the predicted values for these data. What do you conclude from this plot?

**g.** Make a normal plot of the standardized residuals. Does the normality assumption appear justified?

**11.15** Use the data from Exhibit 2.8 with the addition of the regressor hits ($x_3$), as in Example 11.3. Fit the data to the model

$$E(Y|x_1, x_2, x_3) = \beta_0 + \beta_1 x_1 + \beta_2 x_2 + \beta_3 x_3$$

using Minitab.

**a.** Answer parts a–g of exercise 11.14 for this data set.

**b.** Find confidence intervals for $\beta_1, \beta_2$, and $\beta_3$ with a confidence coefficient of 95 percent.

**c.** Do the values $\hat{\beta}_1, \hat{\beta}_2$, and $\hat{\beta}_3$ fall into the confidence interval for American League batters found in this section?

### Polynomial Regression

polynomial regression

When the assumption of the linearity of $E(Y|x)$ is not justified but a higher-degree polynomial relationship is justified, a special case of the multiple regression model is frequently useful in the fitting of data. In **polynomial regression** it is assumed that

$$E(Y|x) = \beta_0 + \beta_1 x + \beta_2 x^2 + \cdots + \beta_k x^k \qquad \text{11.32}$$

In Example 10.8, in which $Y$ represented the number of farms in the United States (1880–1978), we found that no linear function of $x$ fit the number of farms well. When Equation 11.32 was used with $k = 2$ (referred to as the quadratic model), however, a fairly good fit to the data was obtained. In fact, a review of the Minitab output for Examples 10.8 and 10.9 shows that use of a quadratic model instead of a linear one increased $R^2$ from 0.278 to 0.942. In this section we will study the model in Equation 11.32 in more detail.

In polynomial regression we assume that the $i$th observation of $y$ is of the form

$$Y_i = \underbrace{\beta_0 + \beta_1 x_i + \beta_2 x_i^2 + \cdots + \beta_k x_i^k}_{} + \varepsilon_i, \qquad i = 1, 2, \ldots, n$$

$$= E(Y|x = x_i, x^2 = x_i^2, \ldots, x^k = x_i^k) + \varepsilon_i \qquad \text{11.33}$$

Comparing Equation 11.33 with Equation 11.25, we see that the following replacements have been made:

$$x_i = x_{i1}, x_i^2 = x_{i2}, \ldots, x_i^k = x_{ik} \qquad \text{11.34}$$

In other words, the variable $x_1$ is now $x$, $x_2$ is now $x^2$, $x_3$ is now $x^3$, ..., and $x_k$ is now $x^k$. In general, the $j$th regressor has become $x^j$, the $j$th power of $x$ for $j = 1, 2, \ldots, k$. The $i$th observation $Y_i$ is assumed to be composed of a $k$th-degree polynomial in $x$ evaluated at $x = x_i$ (a real value), plus a random error term $\varepsilon_i$. The assumptions with respect to the $\varepsilon_i$ made in the first paragraph of Section 11.3 are assumed to be valid here also. The values of $\beta_0, \beta_1, \ldots, \beta_k$ are estimated from the data by minimizing the equation

$$Q(\beta_0, \beta_1, \ldots, \beta_k) = \sum [y_i - (\beta_0 + \beta_1 x_i + \beta_2 x_i^2 + \cdots + \beta_k x_i^k)]^2 \quad \text{11.35}$$

which is analogous to Equation 11.27. The best-fitting $k$th-degree polynomial is given by an equation analogous to Equation 11.28:

$$\hat{y} = \hat{\beta}_0 + \hat{\beta}_1 x + \hat{\beta}_2 x^2 + \cdots + \hat{\beta}_k x^k \qquad \text{11.36}$$

where the values $\hat{\beta}_0, \hat{\beta}_1, \ldots, \hat{\beta}_k$ are those that minimize Equation 11.27. As in Section 11.3, all computations necessary to find the $\hat{\beta}_0, \hat{\beta}_1, \ldots, \hat{\beta}_k$ in Equation 11.36 will be carried out by the Minitab computer package.

Because the variable $x$ in Equation 11.32 is often chosen to be time (as in Examples 10.8 and 10.9), this section will emphasize use of the polynomial model to describe data collected on individual variables at equally spaced points in time. This type of data is extremely important in business and economics, as well as in engineering, medicine, and social policy making. Businesses frequently report sales, expenses, net income, income per share, and many other variables on a quarterly

## Table 11.6

**Work Stoppages in the United States**

| Year | Number | Year | Number |
|------|--------|------|--------|
| 1952 | 5117 | 1967 | 4595 |
| 53 | 5091 | 68 | 5045 |
| 54 | 3486 | 69 | 5700 |
| 55 | 4320 | 70 | 5716 |
| 56 | 3825 | 71 | 5138 |
| 57 | 5673 | 72 | 5010 |
| 58 | 3694 | 73 | 5353 |
| 59 | 3708 | 74 | 6074 |
| 60 | 3333 | 75 | 5031 |
| 61 | 3367 | 76 | 5648 |
| 62 | 3614 | 77 | 5506 |
| 63 | 3362 | 78 | 4230 |
| 64 | 3655 | 79 | 4827 |
| 65 | 3963 | 80 | 3885 |
| 66 | 4405 | 81 | 2568 |

*Source: Bureau of Labor Statistics*, reported in *The World Almanac and Book of Facts*, 1983, p. 134.

basis. The government reports such economic variables as the unemployment rate, the number of housing starts, and various figures related to national income on a monthly basis. Other economic variables are reported on a yearly basis. Table 11.6 gives an example of one such variable: the number of work stoppages (labor strikes) in the United States over the thirty-year period from 1952 to 1981. Such a set of observations of a single variable over equally spaced time periods is called a **time series**.

**time series**

Generally the first step in analyzing a time series is to plot time on the horizontal axis and the value of the variable of the time series at times $t = 1, 2, \ldots, n$, denoted by $y_t$, on the vertical axis. (Note that $i$ has been replaced by $t$. The coding of the dependent variable is somewhat arbitrary, but particularly for yearly data, this convention is frequently used. For the data of Table 11.6, 1952 would be coded as 1, 1953 as 2, . . . , and 1981 as 30. For many purposes, it is clearly easier to use the integers from 1 to 30 than the actual years.) It is extremely easy to obtain a plot of $(t, Y_t)$, $t = 1, 2, \ldots, n$ from Minitab. The plot of the time series in Table 11.6 is shown in Exhibit 11.10.

## Example 11.4

In order to show that a simple linear model does not describe the time series for work stoppages very well, the simple linear regression model was used with these data. The output is given in Exhibit 11.11, with $y_t$ in C2 and $t = 1, 2, \ldots, 30$ in C1.

**Exhibit 11.10**

```
MTB > NOTE TIME SERIES OF WORK STOPPAGES 1952-1981
MTB > SET C1
C1
     1    2    3    4    .    .    .

MTB > END
MTB > SET C2
C2
   5117  5091  3486  4320    .    .    .

MTB > END
MTB > NAME C1 'TIME' C2 'STRIKES'
MTB > PLOT C2 VS C1


          -
          -
    6000+                                       *
          -                          *  *           *
STRIKES   -                                         *
          -
          -        **                 *     *  *   *
    4800+                                                *
          -                        *
          -           *          *                    *
          -                      *
    3600+        *     *  **      *   *                   *
          -                   *  *  *
          -
          -
          -                                          *
    2400+
          -
          +---------+---------+---------+---------+---------+-TIME
         0.0       6.0      12.0      18.0      24.0      30.0
```

**Exhibit 11.11**

```
MTB > NOTE LINEAR REGRESSION MODEL FOR WORK STOPPAGE DATA
MTB > BRIEF 2
MTB > REGRESS Y IN C2 ON 1 X IN C1 RES C3 PRED C4

The regression equation is
STRIKES = 3934 + 32.1 TIME

Predictor      Coef       Stdev     t-ratio
Constant      3934.0      328.1      11.99
TIME           32.08      18.48       1.74

s = 876.0      R-sq = 9.7%      R-sq(adj) = 6.5%

Analysis of Variance

SOURCE        DF          SS          MS
Regression     1       2313134     2313134
Error         28      21488832      767458
Total         29      23801952

Unusual Observations
Obs.    TIME    STRIKES      Fit   Stdev.Fit   Residual   St.Resid
30      30.0      2568      4896       312       -2328      -2.84R

R denotes an obs. with a large st. resid.
```

**Exhibit 11.12**

```
MTB > NOTE CUBIC REGRESSION MODEL FOR WORK STOPPAGE DATA
MTB > MULT C1 C1 IN C3
MTB > MULT C1 C3 IN C4
MTB > NAME C3 'TSQR' NAME C4 'TCUBE'
MTB > REGRESS Y IN C2 ON 3 XS IN C1 C3 C4 RES C5 PRED C6
* NOTE *     TIME is highly correlated with other  predictor variables
* NOTE *     TSQR is highly correlated with other  predictor variables
* NOTE *     TCUBE is highly correlated with other  predictor variables

The regression equation is
STRIKES = 6068 - 782 TIME + 67.2 TSQR - 1.48 TCUBE


Predictor        Coef         Stdev        t-ratio
Constant        6068.4        332.8         18.23
TIME           -782.12        91.46         -8.55
TSQR            67.181        6.796          9.89
TCUBE          -1.4828        0.1443       -10.28


s = 400.0       R-sq = 82.5%      R-sq(adj) = 80.5%

Analysis of Variance

SOURCE          DF          SS            MS
Regression       3      19641680       6547226
Error           26       4160292        160011
Total           29      23801968


SOURCE          DF        SEQ SS
TIME             1       2313134
TSQR             1        420744
TCUBE            1      16907808


Unusual Observations
Obs.    TIME    STRIKES      Fit Stdev.Fit  Residual   St.Resid
  1      1.0     5117.0    5352.0    259.1     -235.0     -0.77 X
  3      3.0     3486.0    4286.7    160.8     -800.7     -2.19R
 30     30.0     2568.0    3031.4    259.1     -463.4     -1.52 X

R denotes an obs. with a large st. resid.
X denotes an obs. whose X value gives it large influence.
```

The value of $r^2 = 0.097$ indicates that less than 10 percent of the variability in $y$ is explained by the model—or, more accurately, that this time series is not very linear. Notice that the BRIEF = 2 command results in a printout of only those observations with unusually large standardized residuals (labeled R) and those observations that are very influential in the fit (labeled X).

It is a straightforward procedure to use a higher degree polynomial to find a better fit to these data. For $k = 3$ (a cubic polynomial), it is only necessary to construct $t^2$ and $t^3$. The best-fitting cubic polynomial can be found by using the REGRESS command with $y_t$ in C1 and regressors $t$, $t^2$, and $t^3$ in C2, C3, and C4, respectively. This procedure minimizes the expression

$$\sum_{t=1}^{30} [y_t - (\beta_0 + \beta_1 t + \beta_2 t^2 + \beta_3 t^3)]^2$$

The Minitab output is shown in Exhibit 11.12.

The best-fitting cubic equation is

$$y_t = 6068 - 782t + 67.2t^2 - 1.48t^3$$

The multiple correlation coefficient is

$$R^2 = \frac{SSR}{SST} = 0.825$$

indicating that 82.5 percent of the variation in $Y$ has been explained. This is about as well as one can expect to do using only powers of the variable time ($t$). Clearly there are other factors that affect the number of work stoppages. For example, the economic recessions of 1954, 1960–1961, 1974–1975, and 1980–1981 coincided with declines in the number of work stoppages. A good multiple regression model of the number of work stoppages would include additional variables reflecting, for example, the level of economic activity in a given year. Here we restricted ourselves to a polynomial model in $t$, so the cubic equation describes what is called the historical trend for the time series on work stoppages.

## Minitab Plots of Polynomial Regression

Exhibit 11.13 shows two plots arising from the cubic regression in Exhibit 11.12: a plot of $\hat{y}$ against $t$, which displays the general properties of a third-degree polynomial, and a multiple plot of $y_t$ and $\hat{y}_t$ versus time, which graphically indicates the goodness-of-fit. The points denoted by A are the original observations; those denoted by B are the values of $\hat{y}_t$. The plot of the standardized residuals versus the predicted values, shown in Exhibit 11.14, reveals a general scatter, consistent with the model assumptions for polynomial regression.

One must be very cautious in using a polynomial model based on historic data to forecast a future value for the number of work stoppages in a year. Substituting $t = 31$ into the equation for $\hat{y}_t$ would yield a point estimate of 2314.5 for the number of stoppages in 1982. Such an estimate would have to be treated very suspiciously, however. Whereas the cubic equation $\hat{y}_t = 6068 - 782t + 67.2t^2 - 1.48t^3$ will continue to decline very sharply for $t > 30$, in reality the number of work stoppages will not continue to decline indefinitely.

In examining the trend component of time series, we will consider only time series collected on an annual basis. The seasonal components (fall, winter, summer, and spring effects) will thus be minimized, as each observation will contain all 4 quarters, 12 months, or 52 weeks.

trend component

> **Definition 11.1** ■
>
> The **trend component** of a time series describes the long-run behavior of the series.

**Exhibit 11.13**

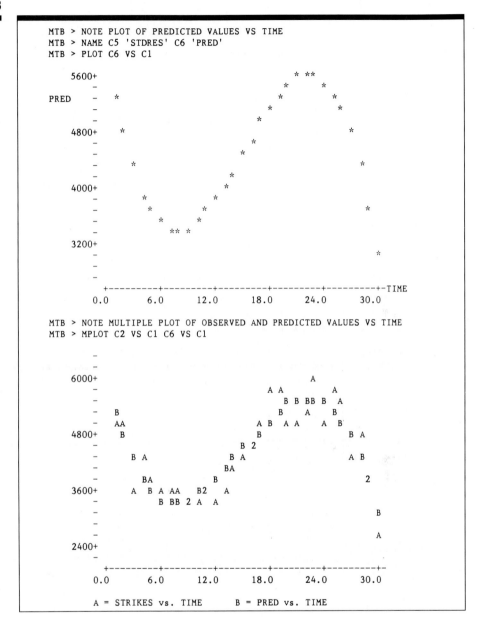

```
MTB > NOTE PLOT OF PREDICTED VALUES VS TIME
MTB > NAME C5 'STDRES' C6 'PRED'
MTB > PLOT C6 VS C1
```

```
      5600+                                        *  **
          -                                    *          *
PRED      -       *                          *
          -                                *
      4800+       *                                        *
          -                              *
          -          *                                        *
      4000+                            *
          -       *                  *
          -          *             *                          *
          -            *         *
          -              **  *
      3200+
          -                                                *
          -
          -
          +---------+---------+---------+---------+---------+-TIME
         0.0       6.0      12.0      18.0      24.0      30.0
```

```
MTB > NOTE MULTIPLE PLOT OF OBSERVED AND PREDICTED VALUES VS TIME
MTB > MPLOT C2 VS C1 C6 VS C1
```

```
          -
          -
      6000+                                    A
          -                          A A          A
          -                            B B BB B  A
          -       B                     B   A   B
          -       AA                  A B  A A     A B
      4800+       B                          B          B A
          -                                B 2
          -          B A                  B  A            A B
          -                                BA
          -            BA             B                        2
      3600+       A  B  A AA   B2    A
          -          B BB 2 A  A                             B
          -                                                  A
          -
      2400+
          -
          +---------+---------+---------+---------+---------+-
         0.0       6.0      12.0      18.0      24.0      30.0
```

```
        A = STRIKES vs. TIME      B = PRED vs. TIME
```

**Exhibit 11.14**

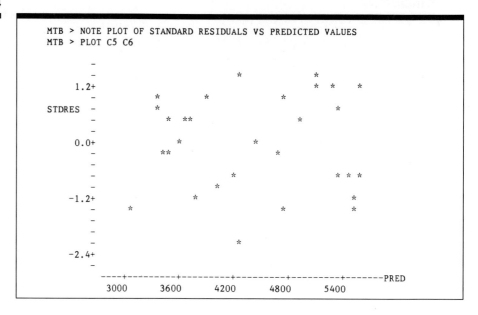

```
MTB > NOTE PLOT OF STANDARD RESIDUALS VS PREDICTED VALUES
MTB > PLOT C5 C6

         -
         -                                   *          *
   1.2+                                              *  *    *
         -              *          *            *
STDRES   -              *                                 *
         -                 *    **                  *
         -
   0.0+              *             *
         -            **                     *
         -
         -                            *             *  *  *
         -                         *
  -1.2+                    *                            *
         -        *                          *         *
         -
         -
         -
  -2.4+                          *
         -
         ----+---------+---------+---------+---------+-------PRED
           3000      3600      4200      4800      5400
```

**Exhibit 11.15**

```
MTB > NOTE POPULATION OF US (1940-1979) IN MILLIONS
MTB > SET C1
C1
      1     2     3     4    .    .    .

MTB > END
MTB > SET C2
C2
   132.6  133.9  135.4  137.3   .    .    .

MTB > END
MTB > NAME C1 'TIME' C2 'POP'
MTB > PLOT C2 VS C1

POP    -
       -                                              *
       -                                        ** **
   210+                                     ** **
       -                                   * *
       -                                 ***
       -                           ***
       -                        * *
   180+                       **
       -                    * *
       -                  **
       -                **
       -              **
   150+            *  **
       -            **
       -        *** *
       -    * *
       -
   120+
       +---------+---------+---------+---------+---------+-TIME
      0.0       8.0      16.0      24.0      32.0      40.0
```

# Table 11.7

**Population of the United States, 1940–1979 (in millions)**

| Year | Population | Year | Population |
|------|-----------|------|-----------|
| 1940 | 132.6 | 1960 | 180.7 |
| 41 | 133.9 | 61 | 183.7 |
| 42 | 135.4 | 62 | 186.6 |
| 43 | 137.3 | 63 | 189.2 |
| 44 | 138.9 | 64 | 191.9 |
| 45 | 140.5 | 65 | 194.3 |
| 46 | 141.9 | 66 | 196.6 |
| 47 | 144.7 | 67 | 198.7 |
| 48 | 147.2 | 68 | 200.7 |
| 49 | 149.8 | 69 | 202.7 |
| 1950 | 152.3 | 1970 | 204.9 |
| 51 | 154.9 | 71 | 207.1 |
| 52 | 157.6 | 72 | 208.8 |
| 53 | 160.2 | 73 | 210.4 |
| 54 | 163.0 | 74 | 211.9 |
| 55 | 165.9 | 75 | 213.6 |
| 56 | 168.9 | 76 | 215.2 |
| 57 | 172.0 | 77 | 216.9 |
| 58 | 174.9 | 78 | 218.5 |
| 59 | 177.8 | 79 | 220.6 |

*Source:* U.S. Bureau of Census, as reported in *The Statistical Abstract of the U.S. 1980*, Table 2.

## Example 11.5

Consider the data given in Table 11.7 on the resident U.S. population from 1940 to 1979. Exhibit 11.15 shows the output generated when Minitab was used to plot time on the horizontal axis (with 1940 coded as 1, 1941 as 2, . . . , 1979 as 40) and population on the vertical axis. The plot suggests a reasonably linear relationship between $y_t$ and $t$. Exhibit 11.16 shows the output generated when a polynomial of degree one (simple linear regression) was used to estimate the trend in population over time. The resulting trend estimate is

$$\hat{y}_t = \hat{\alpha} + \hat{\beta}t = 128 + 2.44t$$

The computed $t$-value of 77.94 is certainly statistically significant, and the $r^2$ value of 0.994 indicates that a first-degree polynomial is quite adequate for describing the historical trend of this time series.

Although it fits historical data well, the simple linear regression model is unlikely to be useful in forecasting future values of $Y$. The simple linear model $E(Y_t) = \alpha + \beta t$ assumes that there will be a constant *amount* of population growth per year, estimated by $\hat{\beta} = 2.44$ million persons per year. This idea of a constant amount of population growth per year does not seem realistic for the U.S. population.

**Exhibit 11.16**

```
MTB > NOTE REGRESSION OF POPULATION VERSUS TIME
MTB > BRIEF 2
MTB > REGRESS Y IN C2 ON 1 X IN C1 RESIDS C3 PREDICTED C4

The regression equation is
POP = 128 + 2.44 TIME

Predictor      Coef        Stdev      t-ratio
Constant     127.554       0.736      173.20
TIME           2.43969     0.03130     77.94

s = 2.285      R-sq = 99.4%     R-sq(adj) = 99.4%

Analysis of Variance

SOURCE        DF          SS           MS
Regression     1        31725        31725
Error         38          198            5
Total         39        31923

Unusual Observations
Obs.    TIME       POP       Fit  Stdev.Fit  Residual   St.Resid
 40     40.0    220.600   225.141    0.709     -4.541      -2.09R

R denotes an obs. with a large st. resid.
```

## Minitab Residual Plots

Residual plots are useful for determining whether the assumptions of the regression model given in the first paragraph of Section 11.3 are valid. The residual plots in Exhibits 11.17–11.19 are all for the population data of Example 11.5. The plot in Exhibit 11.17 is of the (unstandardized) residuals $y_t - \hat{y}_t$ versus the predicted values $\hat{y}_t$. The plot in Exhibit 11.18 is of the (unstandardized) residuals versus time ($t$). The plot in Exhibit 11.19 is of the standardized residuals versus the predicted values.

If the assumptions about the independence and constant variance of the error terms $\varepsilon_t$ were correct, each of these residual plots would exhibit an approximately patternless scatter of points. Such randomness certainly is not reflected in Exhibits 11.17–11.19. These residuals display a definite pattern related to the way in which the population changed over the years. This pattern is particularly clear in the plot of the residuals versus time (Exhibit 11.18). From 1940 to 1946 (1–7), the residuals declined from positive to negative values—that is, population levels went from above to below those predicted by a linear trend. From 1947 to 1966 (8–27), with the "baby boom," the residuals smoothly increased from negative values to a positive peak in the mid-1960s. From 1967 until 1979 (28–40), the residuals decreased from positive values ($y_t$ exceeding $\hat{y}_t$) to quite negative values (population levels below those predicted by a linear trend). A projection for the 1980 population that was based solely on the least squares line and did not take into account these patterns would doubtless be quite bad.

## Exhibit 11.17

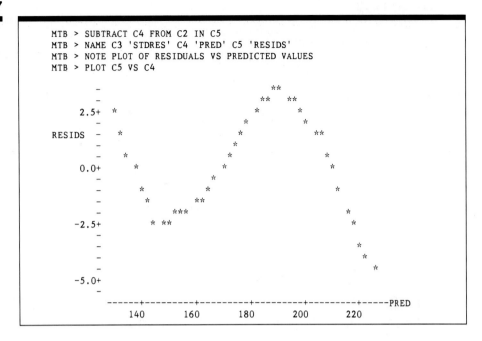

```
MTB > SUBTRACT C4 FROM C2 IN C5
MTB > NAME C3 'STDRES' C4 'PRED' C5 'RESIDS'
MTB > NOTE PLOT OF RESIDUALS VS PREDICTED VALUES
MTB > PLOT C5 VS C4


              -                              **
              -                           **    **
        2.5+   *                        *       *
              -      *                  *           *
   RESIDS -    *                      *            **
              -
              -       *              *
              -        *            *             *
        0.0+      *               *              *
              -                  *
              -       *         *
              -        *        *                    *
              -         *      **
              -          ***                        *
       -2.5+        * **                            *
              -                                      *
              -                                       *
              -                                         *
       -5.0+
              -
              ------+---------+---------+---------+---------+-----PRED
                  140       160       180       200       220
```

## Exhibit 11.18

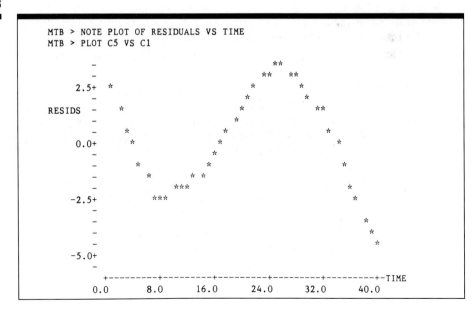

```
MTB > NOTE PLOT OF RESIDUALS VS TIME
MTB > PLOT C5 VS C1


              -                            **
              -                          **    **
        2.5+   *                        *       *
              -                        *          *
   RESIDS -       *                    *         **
              -                      *
              -      *              *
              -       *            *            *
        0.0+      *               *            *
              -
              -        *        *
              -         *      **               *
              -          ***                     *
       -2.5+        ***                          *
              -                                   *
              -                                    *
              -                                     *
       -5.0+
              -
              +---------+---------+---------+---------+---------+-TIME
             0.0       8.0      16.0      24.0      32.0      40.0
```

**Exhibit 11.19**

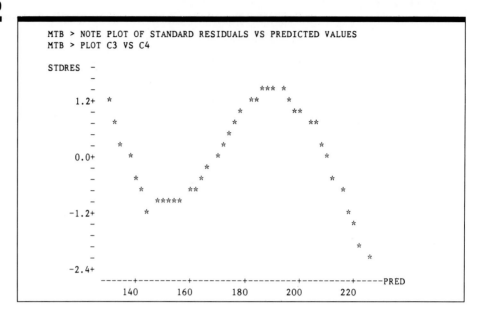

**Exercises 11.4**

**11.16** Employing Minitab as needed, use the information in exercise 10.15 concerning voter registration $(x)$ and voter turnout $(Y)$ to do the following.

    **a.** Estimate $\beta_0$, $\beta_1$, and $\beta_2$ in the model $E(Y) = \beta_0 + \beta_1 x + \beta_2 x^2$.

    **b.** Construct an ANOVA table for the quadratic model.

    **c.** Test the null hypothesis $H_0: \beta_1 = \beta_2 = 0$ versus $H_1: H_0$ false, using $\alpha = 0.05$ and the standard $F$ test.

    **d.** Test the individual null hypotheses $H_0: \beta_1 = 0$ and $H_0: \beta_2 = 0$ versus two-sided alternatives, using $\alpha = 0.05$.

    **e.** Find $R^2$. What is the increase in the explanation of $Y$ when this model is used instead of the simple linear regression model?

    **f.** Construct the standard residual plots using the quadratic model. What do you conclude from these plots?

**11.17** Employing Minitab as needed, use the information in exercise 10.16 relating the mileage per gallon $(y)$ to the weight $(x)$ of automobiles to do parts a–f of exercise 11.16.

**11.18** The data below give total U.S. crude oil reserves (in millions of barrels) from 1948 to 1975.

| Year | Oil Reserves | Year | Oil Reserves |
|------|--------------|------|--------------|
| 1948 | 23,280 | 1962 | 31,389 |
| 49 | 24,649 | 63 | 30,970 |
| 50 | 25,268 | 64 | 30,991 |
| 51 | 27,468 | 65 | 31,352 |
| 52 | 27,961 | 66 | 31,452 |
| 53 | 28,945 | 67 | 31,377 |
| 54 | 29,561 | 68 | 30,707 |
| 55 | 30,012 | 69 | 29,632 |
| 56 | 30,435 | 70 | 39,001 |
| 57 | 30,300 | 71 | 38,063 |
| 58 | 30,536 | 72 | 36,339 |
| 59 | 31,719 | 73 | 35,300 |
| 60 | 31,613 | 74 | 34,250 |
| 61 | 31,759 | 75 | 32,682 |

*Source:* American Petroleum Institute, as reported in *The World Almanac and Book of Facts*, 1983.

Use Minitab as needed to do the following.
**a.** Fit a linear model in time (coding 1948 as 1, 1949 as 2, etc.) to the oil reserve data. Find $\hat{y}_t = \hat{\alpha} + \hat{\beta}t$.
**b.** Plot $y_t$ and $\hat{y}_t$ simultaneously against time.
**c.** Find the value of $r^2$. How would you describe the goodness-of-fit of this model?
**d.** Plot the standardized residuals versus $\hat{y}_t$ and also versus time ($t$). Does there appear to be a pattern in the residuals?
**e.** Using Minitab, find $\hat{\beta}_0$, $\hat{\beta}_1$, and $\hat{\beta}_2$ for the model $E(Y_t) = \beta_0 + \beta_1 t + \beta_2 t^2$. Does using a quadratic model rather than a linear model substantially improve the goodness-of-fit? Explain.

**11.19** The data below give per capita consumption of malt beverages in the United States in gallons over the period 1950–1980.

| Year | Consumption | Year | Consumption | Year | Consumption | Year | Consumption |
|------|-------------|------|-------------|------|-------------|------|-------------|
| 1950 | 17.2 | 1965 | 16.0 | 1958 | 15.0 | 73 | 19.6 |
| 51 | 16.8 | 66 | 16.1 | 59 | 15.0 | 74 | 20.7 |
| 52 | 16.8 | 67 | 16.8 | 60 | 15.4 | 75 | 21.1 |
| 53 | 16.6 | 68 | 16.7 | 61 | 14.9 | 76 | 21.2 |
| 54 | 16.5 | 69 | 17.2 | 62 | 15.1 | 77 | 22.1 |
| 55 | 15.9 | 70 | 18.7 | 63 | 15.0 | 78 | 22.0 |
| 56 | 15.9 | 71 | 18.6 | 64 | 15.6 | 79 | 23.2 |
| 57 | 15.3 | 72 | 19.4 | | | 80 | 23.2 |

*Source:* U.S. Treasury, Bureau of Alcohol, Tobacco, and Firearms, reported in U.S. Bureau of the Census, *The Statistical History of the United States*, 1976.

**a.** Plot $y_t$ versus $t$ to obtain a general impression of the form of the long-term trend.

**b.** Fit second- and third-degree polynomials to the data, using Minitab. What is the increase in $R^2$ as the degree of the polynomial is increased from 2 to 3? Does $\hat{\sigma}$ decrease? Which of these two models do you think better describes the long-term trend in per capita malt beverage consumption?

**11.20** Total annual energy sales in the United States for the years 1967–1976 is given below (in billions of kilowatt hours).

| Year | Total Sales | Year | Total Sales |
|------|------------|------|------------|
| 1967 | 1196 | 1972 | 1735 |
| 68 | 1309 | 73 | 1850 |
| 69 | 1422 | 74 | 1845 |
| 70 | 1510 | 75 | 1889 |
| 71 | 1596 | 76 | 2003 |

*Source: Electric Power Statistics, Dec. 1978* (Washington, D.C.: Department of Energy, Energy Information Administration), p. 17.

**a.** Use Minitab with the **REGRESS** command to obtain $\hat{y}_t = \hat{\alpha} + \hat{\beta}t$. Plot $y_t$ and $\hat{y}_t$ simultaneously versus time (coding 1967 as 1, 1968 as 2, . . . , 1976 as 10). Plot the standardized residuals versus the predicted values. Is there a pattern in the residuals? What does it suggest?

**b.** What low-degree polynomial would you use to estimate trends in energy sales over this period?

**11.21** The table below gives the number of females in the U.S. labor force from 1968 to 1979 in millions.

| Year | Female Labor Force | Year | Female Labor Force |
|------|-------------------|------|-------------------|
| 1968 | 28.78 | 1974 | 35.32 |
| 69 | 29.90 | 75 | 36.50 |
| 70 | 31.23 | 76 | 37.82 |
| 71 | 31.68 | 77 | 39.37 |
| 72 | 32.94 | 78 | 40.97 |
| 73 | 33.90 | 79 | 42.97 |

*Source:* U.S. Bureau of the Census, *Statistical Abstract of the U.S., 1980*, Table No. 668, p. 402.

**a.** Fit a low-degree polynomial model to these data. Support your choice by plots and appropriate statistics.

**b.** Estimate the female labor force in 1980. Suggest why this forecast value might not be very accurate.

## 11.5

**Estimation and Prediction in Multiple Regression**

Like the simple linear regression model, the multiple regression model in Equation 11.25 can be used to estimate the average value of $Y$, the dependent variable, at particular values of the independent variables $x_1, x_2, \ldots, x_k$. Suppose the particular values of the regressors are $x_1 = x_1^*, x_2 = x_2^*, \ldots, x_k = x_k^*$. Then the estimate of $\mu_{Y|x_1=x_1^*,\ldots,x_k=x_k^*}$ is given by the regression function in Equation 11.28, evaluated at the chosen values $x_1^*, \ldots, x_k^*$. Hence the required point estimate is

$$\hat{\mu}_{Y|x_1=x_1^*,\ldots,x_k=x_k^*} = \hat{\beta}_0 + \hat{\beta}_1 x_1^* + \hat{\beta}_2 x_2^* + \cdots + \hat{\beta}_k x_k^* \qquad \textbf{11.37}$$

**estimator of $\mu_{Y|x^*}$**

This **estimator of $\mu_{Y|x^*}$** is denoted in abbreviated notation as $\hat{\mu}_{Y|x^*}$.

As in the simple linear regression case, a confidence interval for $\mu_{Y|x^*}$ is probably of more practical use than is the point estimate. To determine the expression for the endpoints of a confidence interval, we need to consider the properties of the estimate given in Equation 11.37. It can be shown that

$$E(\hat{\mu}_{Y|x_1=x_1^*,\ldots,x_k=x_k^*}) = \beta_0 + \beta_1 x_1^* + \beta_2 x_2^* + \cdots + \beta_k x_k^* \qquad \textbf{11.38}$$

is the true average value of $Y$ for the particular value of the regressors chosen (under the model assumptions). In other words, the estimator in Equation 11.37 is an unbiased estimate of the true expectation of $Y$ given on the right-hand side of Equation 11.38. The variance of the estimator is a function of $x_1^*, \ldots, x_k^*$ and the unknown variance $\sigma^2$. This variance will not be formally presented but will be denoted by

$$\text{Var}(\hat{\mu}_{Y|x_1=x_1^*,\ldots,x_k=x_k^*}) = \text{Var}(\hat{\mu}_{Y|x^*}) \qquad \textbf{11.39}$$

Substituting $\hat{\sigma}^2$ for $\sigma^2$, we estimate the value of Equation 11.39 by

$$\widehat{\text{Var}}(\hat{\mu}_{Y|x^*}) = s^2_{\hat{\mu}_{Y|x^*}} \qquad \textbf{11.40}$$

A confidence interval for the average value of $Y$ at $x_1 = x_1^*, \ldots, x_k = x_k^*$ has endpoints given by

$$\mu_{Y|x^*} \pm (s_{\hat{\mu}_{Y|x^*}})t_{\alpha/2,n-k-1} \qquad \textbf{11.41}$$

where the confidence coefficient is $(1 - \alpha)100$ percent. Equations 11.37 through 11.41 are analogous to Equations 10.30 through 10.33 and 10.35 in the simple linear regression case. These expressions are somewhat complex, but most of the required computations can be carried out by the Minitab package.

As an illustration of the estimation discussed in the two previous paragraphs, consider again Example 11.1, in which $Y$ represented runs batted in, $x_1$ represented home runs, and $x_2$ represented batting average. In that example we found the regression equation

$$\hat{y} = -76.09 + 2.2237x_1 + 371.9x_2$$

An estimate of the average number of runs batted in by a player with 17 homers and a batting average of 0.320 would be given by

$$\hat{\mu}_{Y|x^*} = -76.09 + 2.2237(17) + 371.9(0.320)$$
$$= 80.72$$

This is the value of a point estimate of $\mu_{Y|x_1 = 17, x_2 = 0.320}$, just as the value of $\bar{x}$ is an estimate of a population expectation $\mu$.

## Use of Minitab in Estimation and Prediction

The output from the Minitab subcommand PREDICT can be used with the REGRESS command to find a 95 percent confidence interval for $\mu_{Y|x^*}$. Exhibit 11.20 shows the output generated when the PREDICT subcommand was used with

**Exhibit 11.20**

```
MTB > NOTE MULTIPLE REGRESSION ESTIMATION AND PREDICTION
MTB > READ INTO C5-C10
MTB > NOTE DEPENDENT VARIABLE (Y) IS RBIS
      25 ROWS READ
 ROW    C5      C6     C7    C8    C9     C10

  1     449     87    175    24   118    0.390
  2     622     96    219    25   122    0.352
  3     528     87    180     0    40    0.341
  4     630     96    210     7    60    0.333
  .  .  .

MTB > NOTE DEPENDENT VARIABLE (Y) IS RBIS
MTB > NOTE INDEPENDENT VARIABLES X1,X2 ARE HOMERS AND BATTING AVERAGE
MTB > NAME  C8 'HOMERS' C9 'RBI' C10 'AVE'
MTB > BRIEF = 1
MTB > REGRESS C9 ON 2 XS IN C8 C10 RESIDS IN C11 PREDICTED IN C12;
SUBC> PREDICT FOR 17 0.320.

The regression equation is
RBI = - 76.1 + 2.22 HOMERS + 372 AVE

Predictor       Coef        Stdev      t-ratio
Constant       -76.09       41.37       -1.84
HOMERS          2.2237       0.2509      8.86
AVE           371.9        129.0         2.88

s = 13.42      R-sq = 79.2%     R-sq(adj) = 77.3%

Analysis of Variance

SOURCE        DF         SS          MS
Regression     2      15056.0      7528.0
Error         22       3960.1       180.0
Total         24      19016.2


     Fit  Stdev.Fit      95% C.I.           95% P.I.
    80.73      2.78   ( 74.96,  86.50)  ( 52.31, 109.15)
```

the data set for the 25 American League batters hitting 0.300 or better in 1980, for $x_1 = 17$ and $x_2 = 0.320$.

The values of $\hat{\mu}_{Y|x*}$ and $s_{\hat{\mu}_{Y|x*}}$, given as "Fit" and "Stdev.Fit" by Minitab, are 80.73 and 2.78, respectively. (The value of $\hat{\mu}_{Y|x*}$ estimated by Minitab differs by 0.01 from the value found previously because of roundoff error.) According to Equation 11.41, a 95 percent confidence interval is given by

$$80.73 \pm (2.78)t_{0.025,22} = 80.73 \pm 2.78(2.074) = 80.73 \pm 5.77$$

The interval is thus (74.96, 86.50). This result agrees with the one calculated by Minitab. Rounding the interval endpoints to the nearest integers, we have (75, 87) as an approximate 95 percent confidence interval for the average number of runs batted in by an American League batter with a season home run total of 17 and a batting average of 0.320.

As in the case of simple linear regression, it is possible to predict an individual value of $Y$ at $x_1 = x_1^*, \ldots, x_k = x_k^*$ using the multiple regression model. The value of the prediction $\hat{Y}_{x*}$ for particular values of the regressors is

$$\hat{Y}_{x*} = \hat{\beta}_0 + \hat{\beta}_1 x_1^* + \cdots + \hat{\beta}_k x_k^* \qquad \textbf{11.42}$$

exactly the same as the formula for estimating the average value. As in the simple linear regression case, the variance is larger for the prediction of an individual value than for the estimate of an average. The variance of $\hat{Y}_{x*}$ is estimated by

$$\widehat{\mathrm{Var}}(\hat{Y}_{x*}) = s_{\hat{\mu}_{Y|x*}}^2 + \hat{\sigma}^2 \qquad \textbf{11.43}$$

The standard deviation of $\hat{Y}_{x*}$ is thus estimated by

$$s_{\hat{Y}|x*} = \sqrt{s_{\hat{\mu}_{Y|x*}}^2 + \mathrm{MSE}} \qquad \textbf{11.44}$$

A $(1 - \alpha)100$ percent prediction interval for the individual value has endpoints given by

$$\hat{Y}_{x*} \pm (s_{\hat{Y}|x*})t_{\alpha/2,n-k-1} \qquad \textbf{11.45}$$

For the data of Example 11.1, the individual value of $Y$ predicted for $x_1 = 17$ and $x_2 = 0.320$ would be

$$\hat{Y}_{x*} = 80.72$$

Taking the value of the mean square for error from the ANOVA table in Exhibit 11.1, we have for the standard deviation

$$s_{\hat{Y}|x*} = \sqrt{(2.78)^2 + 180.0} = \sqrt{187.7284} = 13.70$$

Thus the endpoints of a 95 percent confidence interval for the individual value of $Y$ are

$$80.72 \pm 13.70t_{0.025,22} = 80.72 \pm 13.70(2.074)$$
$$= 80.72 \pm 28.42$$

The endpoints are (52.30, 109.14) or, rounding as before, (52, 109). The interval is identical to the 95 percent prediction interval (P.I.) calculated by Minitab in

Exhibit 11.20, except for roundoff error. The interval for the prediction of the individual value is wider (in this case substantially wider) than the interval for the estimate of the average value. The width of the latter is $87 - 75 = 12$, whereas the width of the former is $109 - 52 = 57$.

From Equations 11.44 and 11.45 we see that the interval for the individual prediction will always be wider than the interval for the estimate of the average value of $Y$ at $x_1 = x_1^*, \ldots, x_k = x_k^*$. The reason is exactly the same as the one given in Section 10.5 for the simple linear regression case. It also makes good intuitive sense, as more precision should be possible in the estimation of an average than in the prediction of an individual value.

## Exercises 11.5

**11.22** In exercise 11.3, $Y$ was the number of new resident students at a university, and $x_1$ was the number of junior college graduates and $x_2$ the number of high school graduates from the region in which the university was located. Use the information from that exercise to do the following.
  **a.** Estimate the average number of new resident students if $x_1 = 2.0$ and $x_2 = 6.0$. (All variables are measured in thousands of students.)
  **b.** Predict the actual number of new resident students for this year, given that there are 1600 junior college graduates and 5500 high school graduates this year.
  **c.** Find a 95 percent prediction interval for the prediction in part b.

**11.23** Use the data of exercise 11.4 to do the following.
  **a.** Estimate the average annual expenditures for a family in which the husband's income is $40,000 and the wife's income is $30,000.
  **b.** Find a 95 percent confidence interval for the estimate of part a.
  **c.** Predict a family's actual expenditures for a particular year, given that the husband has an income of $45,000 and the wife has an income of $22,000.
  **d.** Find a 95 percent prediction interval for the prediction in part c.

**11.24** Use the data of exercise 11.9 to do the following.
  **a.** Estimate the total number of coins minted in a year in which a billion cents, 100 million nickels, and 50 million dimes are minted.
  **b.** Given that 2.2 billion cents, 260 million nickels, and 300 million dimes were minted in 1961, predict the total number of coins minted in that year.

**11.25** Use the Minitab output for Example 11.3 to do the following.
  **a.** Estimate the average number of runs batted in by an American League batter such as Buddy Bell, who hit 17 home runs, batted 0.329, and had 161 hits.
  **b.** Predict the number of runs batted in by Bell in 1980, and find a 95 percent prediction interval for this prediction.
  **c.** Does the actual number of runs batted in by Bell fall in this interval?

**11.26** Use the data of exercise 11.14 to do the following.
  **a.** Estimate the average earnings per share in 1986 for a utility company that earned $3.20 per share and 14.0 percent on net worth and generated 20 percent of its power from nuclear sources in 1985.
  **b.** Given that in 1985 Savannah Electric and Power Company earned $2.90 per share and 13.8 percent on net worth and had no nuclear-generated power, predict this company's 1986 earnings per share.

**Summary**

The multiple regression model is a direct extension of the simple linear regression model. The basic idea is to describe how a dependent variable $Y$ is related to $k$ explanatory variables $x_1, x_2, \ldots, x_k$. The model is of the form

$$E(Y) = \beta_0 + \beta_1 x_1 + \beta_2 x_2 + \cdots + \beta_k x_k$$

that is, the average value of $Y$ is assumed to be a linear function of the regressors $x_1, x_2, \ldots, x_k$. The coefficients $\beta_0, \beta_1, \ldots, \beta_k$ are estimated from the data by means of a least squares procedure. Explicitly, if there are $n$ observations $(y_i, x_{i1}, \ldots, x_{ik})$,

$$\sum_{i=1}^{n} [y_i - (\beta_0 + \beta_1 x_{i1} + \cdots + \beta_k x_{ik})]^2$$

is minimized to yield the estimated regression function

$$\hat{y} = \hat{\beta}_0 + \hat{\beta}_1 x_1 + \cdots + \hat{\beta}_k x_k$$

For the multiple regression model with $k = 2$ regressors, the equation is

$$E(Y) = \beta_0 + \beta_1 x_1 + \beta_2 x_2$$

which represents a plane in three-dimensional space. The regression equation is the plane that best fits the observations $(y_i, x_{i1}, x_{i2})$, $i = 1, 2, \ldots, n$. The coefficient $\beta_1$ represents the true average change in the dependent variable $Y$ per unit change in $x_1$, with $x_2$ held constant. The interpretation of $\beta_2$ is similar (except that the roles of $x_1$ and $x_2$ are interchanged). Confidence intervals and tests for $\beta_1$ and $\beta_2$, which are based on Student's $t$ distribution with $n - 3$ degrees of freedom, depend on the following assumptions with respect to the error terms $\varepsilon_i$:

1    $E(\varepsilon_i) = 0$, $i = 1, 2, \ldots, n$
2    $\mathrm{Var}(\varepsilon_i) = \sigma^2$, $i = 1, 2, \ldots, n$
3    The $\varepsilon_i$ are normally and independently distributed.

The ANOVA table is based on the fundamental relationship

$$\mathrm{SST} = \mathrm{SSR} + \mathrm{SSE}$$

In the case where $k = 2$, $\mathrm{SSE}/(n - 3)$ is an unbiased estimator of $\sigma^2$. The $F$ statistic can be computed directly from the ANOVA table. The addition of another regressor $x_2$ to the simple linear model containing only the single regressor $x_1$ will always increase the value of the multiple regression coefficient

$$R^2 = \frac{\mathrm{SSR}}{\mathrm{SST}}$$

over that of the coefficient of determination $r^2$. In some cases, however, the increase may not be large enough to justify the increased complication of the model equation.

The residuals

$$y_i - \hat{y}_i = y_i - (\hat{\beta}_0 + \hat{\beta}_1 x_{i1} + \hat{\beta}_2 x_{i2}), \qquad i = 1, 2, \ldots, n$$

and the standardized residuals

$$\frac{y_i - \hat{y}_i}{s_{y_i - \hat{y}_i}}, \qquad i = 1, 2, \ldots, n$$

are important for several reasons. The plot of the standardized residuals versus the predicted values $\hat{y}_i$ and the normal plot of the standardized residuals are both useful in verifying the assumptions of the regression model. The first plot should be a random scatter if the model is appropriate for the data studied. The second plot should be linear if the normality assumption is valid. Both of the plots and the table of output from the REGRESS command are useful in detecting outliers —observations that represent extreme deviations from the others observed. Such observations should be examined carefully. A regression analysis may be changed substantially by deleting a single outlier. On the other hand, the outlier may be interesting in itself if it represents behavior that differs from the norm for significant reasons.

Determination of the regression equation, inference for the $\beta_i$, and construction of the ANOVA table for the general case where $k \geq 2$ are straightforward generalizations of the regressor model for $k = 2$. Inference for the $\beta_i$ is carried out using Student's $t$ distribution with $n - k - 1$ degrees of freedom. The overall $F$ test has $k$ and $n - k - 1$ degrees of freedom. The residual plots are directly analogous to those in the $k = 2$ case. Departures from model assumptions can be determined from these plots, as in the case where $k = 2$. Minitab can be used to carry out all substantial calculations and to construct the appropriate plots.

Polynomial regression is a special case of multiple regression in which it is assumed that

$$E(Y) = \beta_0 + \beta_1 x + \beta_2 x^2 + \cdots + \beta_k x^k$$

Here $x_1 = x, x_2 = x^2, \ldots, x_k = x^k$. This model is used to describe a dependent variable $Y$ that has a nonlinear expectation. The polynomial regression model is often applied to time series in which a single variable $Y_t$ is observed at times $t = 1, 2, \ldots, n$. Here $x_1 = t, x_2 = t^2, \ldots, x_k = t^k$. Polynomial regression is useful in describing the trend component—the long-run behavior of a time series. The projection of a polynomial trend into the future to predict values of $Y_t$ for time periods $t > n$ is a risky proposition. More advanced methods must be used to forecast future values of $Y$.

The regression equation is frequently used to estimate the average value of $Y$ or to predict an individual value of $Y$ for particular values of the regressor variables. The notation $x_1 = x_1^*, x_2 = x_2^*, \ldots, x_k = x_k^*$ is used, where the starred values represent the particular values of the regressors at which estimation or prediction is required.

error terms
estimator of $\mu_{Y|x^*}$
explanatory variables
$F$ test
general linear regression model
least squares plane
multiple regression coefficient

multiple regression model
normal equations
polynomial regression
regression equation
regressors
time series
trend component

NOBRIEF

# Chapter 12

# Analysis of Variance

## 12.1

**Introduction**

controls

Many applications require extension of the problem-solving methods introduced in Chapter 8 to $k \geqslant 2$ populations. For example, in a study of the effectiveness of two drugs in treating a specific illness, a medical researcher might decide to include a third group of individuals called **controls** who receive only a placebo. There would then be $k = 3$ populations to compare—those receiving drug A, those receiving drug B, and those receiving only the placebo. Similarly, researchers for a consumer group might want to compare the mileage of similarly priced six-cylinder compact cars made by American Motors, Chrysler, Ford, and General Motors. To do so, they might run five cars of each make over the same course with a fixed amount of gasoline and record the total mileage for each of the 20 cars. The true average number of miles per gallon for cars of each make might then be compared by testing the null hypothesis that the true average number of miles per gallon is the same for each make of car. Answering other inferential questions might involve making pairwise comparisons of the various makes of cars.

The analysis of variance (ANOVA) is a statistical technique used to compare the locations (specifically, the expectations) of $k \geqslant 2$ populations. The study of analysis of variance involves the investigation of very complex statistical models, which are interesting both statistically and mathematically. In this introductory chapter only two basic designs will be considered. The first is referred to as a *one-way classification* or a *completely randomized design*. The second is called a *two-way classification* or a *randomized block design*. The basic idea behind the term "analysis of variance" is that the total variability of all the observations can be separated into distinct portions, each of which can be assigned a particular source or cause. This decomposition of the variability permits statistical estimation and tests of hypotheses.

Suppose that we are interested in $k$ populations, from each of which we sample $n$ observations. (The assumption of equal sample size is made in order to simplify the explanation.) The observations are denoted by

$$Y_{ij}, \qquad i = 1, 2, \ldots, k; j = 1, 2, \ldots, n$$

where $Y_{ij}$ represents the $j$th observation from population $i$. The observations from a given population (fixed $i$) are considered to be a random sample from that population and thus independent. Observations from different populations are also assumed to be independent. A basic null hypothesis to test is

$$\mathrm{H}_0: \mu_1 = \mu_2 = \cdots = \mu_k$$

**analysis of variance**

that is, all the populations have the same expectation. The **analysis of variance** method used to test this null hypothesis is based on an $F$ statistic.

In many cases the samples from the $k$ populations are not of the same size. The notation

$$Y_{ij}, \qquad i = 1, 2, \ldots, k; j = 1, 2, \ldots, n_i$$

**completely randomized design**

indicates that there are $n_1$ observations from population 1, $n_2$ observations from population 2, . . . , $n_k$ observations from population $k$, and, in general, $n_i$ observations from the $i$th population. The samples from the populations are again considered random, and hence the $Y_{ij}$ are independent for fixed $i$. The observations from different populations are also assumed to be independent. This design is called the one-way classification or the **completely randomized design** with unequal sample sizes. The basic null hypothesis to be tested is the same as the one for the case of equal sample sizes.

The one-way classification might be used, for example, to analyze the statistics in Table 12.1 on the four divisions of the National Basketball Association. Table 12.1 gives the average number of points scored per game for each team in the NBA during the 1983–1984 season. The interesting question of whether the divisions are of equal strength could be addressed by testing the null hypothesis that the average points scored is the same for the four divisions. The same technique could be used to compare teams in the Eastern and Western Conferences —or to compare teams in the Midwest and Pacific Divisions, both of which are in the Western Conference. Similarly, teams in the Atlantic Division could be compared with all other teams in the NBA. The data in Table 12.1 will be considered later in the discussion of the completely randomized design with unequal sample size.

Comparisons of the expectations of pairs of populations and other more complex comparisons of population expectations are referred to as contrasts. In a drug testing experiment, for example, a comparison of the true average response of individuals receiving a drug (either A or B) with the response of those receiving

## Table 12.1

**Average Points Scored in the NBA (1983–1984)**

| Eastern Conference | | Western Conference | |
|---|---|---|---|
| *Atlantic Division* | | *Midwest Division* | |
| Boston Celtics | 112.1 | San Antonio Spurs | 120.3 |
| Philadelphia 76ers | 107.8 | Kansas City Kings | 110.0 |
| New York Knicks | 106.9 | Houston Rockets | 110.6 |
| Washington Bullets | 102.7 | Denver Nuggets | 123.7 |
| New Jersey Nets | 110.0 | Utah Jazz | 115.0 |
| | | Dallas Mavericks | 110.4 |
| | | | |
| *Central Division* | | *Pacific Division* | |
| Milwaukee Bucks | 105.7 | Phoenix Suns | 111.0 |
| Chicago Bulls | 103.7 | Los Angeles Lakers | 115.6 |
| Indiana Pacers | 104.5 | Portland Trail Blazers | 113.1 |
| Atlanta Hawks | 101.5 | Golden State Warriors | 109.9 |
| Cleveland Cavaliers | 102.3 | San Diego Clippers | 110.7 |
| Detroit Pistons | 117.1 | Seattle Supersonics | 108.1 |

*Source: Information Please Almanac* (Boston: Houghton Mifflin, 1985), p. 847.

the placebo (or control) treatment would be considered a contrast. Inference for such contrasts is based on Student's *t* distribution.

The basic concept of blocking was touched upon in Chapter 8 in the discussion of the method of paired comparisons, which involves comparing responses to two treatments using experimental units that are similar except with regard to the treatment received. The randomized block design extends this idea to $t \geqslant 2$ treatments. Blocks are defined so as to make the experimental units within a block as alike as possible except with regard to possible responses to the *t* treatments. One basic task is to determine whether there are true treatment differences when it is known that there are block differences. For example, in a study of salaries of faculty members at four different universities, we would not want to compare salaries of instructors with those of full professors. In this case blocks would be set up on the basis of professional rank—say, instructor, assistant professor, associate professor, and full professor. The treatments (in this case universities) would be compared after elimination of the known differences in pay levels for different ranks.

## 12.2

**The Completely Randomized Design with Equal Sample Sizes**

*k*-sample problem

First we will consider comparison of the true expectations of $k \geqslant 2$ populations, sometimes referred to as the **$k$-sample problem**. For simplicity of presentation, we will assume initially that an equal number of observations are randomly sampled from each population. These observations are denoted by

$$
\begin{array}{cccc}
Y_{11}, & Y_{12}, & \ldots, & Y_{1n} \\
Y_{21}, & Y_{22}, & \ldots, & Y_{2n} \\
\cdot & \cdot & \cdots & \cdot \\
Y_{k1}, & Y_{k2}, & \ldots, & Y_{kn}
\end{array}
\qquad \textbf{12.1}
$$

where $Y_{ij}$ represents the $j$th observation out of the $n$ randomly sampled observations from the $i$th population. Hence $Y_{12}$ would be the second observation from the first population. As the observations from a given population (fixed $i$) are considered to be a random sample from that population, the observations within a row of Equation 12.1 are independent. It is also assumed that observations from different populations (different rows of Equation 12.1) are independent. Hence all of the observations in the $k \times n$ table are independent. Within a row, however, all of the observations come from the same parent population.

In the completely randomized design, the observations are assumed to

**1**  come from normal populations;
**2**  come from populations with the same variance;
**3**  have possibly different expectations, $\mu_1, \mu_2, \ldots, \mu_k$.

These assumptions are expressed mathematically as follows:

$$
Y_{ij} \sim N(\mu_i, \sigma^2), \qquad i = 1, 2, \ldots, k; j = 1, 2, \ldots, n \qquad \textbf{12.2}
$$

This equation is equivalent to

$$
Y_{ij} = \mu_i + \varepsilon_{ij}, \qquad i = 1, 2, \ldots, k; j = 1, 2, \ldots, n \qquad \textbf{12.3}
$$

with the $\varepsilon_{ij}$ representing normally and independently distributed random variables, all with zero expectation and common variance. The assumptions with respect to the $\varepsilon_{ij}$ may be written mathematically as

$$
\varepsilon_{ij} \sim \text{NID}(0, \sigma^2), \qquad i = 1, 2, \ldots, k; j = 1, 2, \ldots, n \qquad \textbf{12.4}
$$

where N represents "normally," I represents "Independently," and D represents "distributed." The 0 means that $E(\varepsilon_{ij}) = 0$ for all pairs of indices $i$ and $j$, and $\sigma^2$ means that $\text{Var}(\varepsilon_{ij}) = \sigma^2$ for all such pairs. The parameters $\mu_1, \mu_2, \ldots, \mu_k$ are the expectations of the $k$ populations, about which inference is to be made.

Figure 12.1 illustrates density functions for the $k$ populations. The expectations of the populations are indicated by the $\mu_i$ values plotted. The initial hypotheses to be tested in the completely randomized design are

$$
\text{H}_0\colon \mu_1 = \mu_2 = \cdots = \mu_k
$$
$$
\text{versus} \quad \text{H}_1\colon \mu_i \neq \mu_l \text{ for some pair of indices } i \neq l \qquad \textbf{12.5}
$$

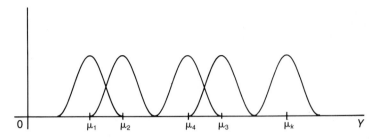

**Figure 12.1**

**Density Functions in the *k*-Sample Case**

The null hypothesis states that all of the $k$ populations have the same expectation. If this is true, then we know from Equation 12.2 that all of the $Y_{ij}$ observations have the same normal distribution and we are observing not $n$ observations from each of $k$ populations, but $nk$ observations, all from the same population.

There is an alternative form of the model for the completely randomized design. The random variable $Y_{ij}$ may be written as

$$Y_{ij} = \bar{\mu} + (\mu_i - \bar{\mu}) + \varepsilon_{ij}$$
$$= \bar{\mu} + \alpha_i + \varepsilon_{ij}$$

where, as before, $\varepsilon_{ij} \sim \text{NID}(0, \sigma^2)$. Defining $\bar{\mu}$ as

$$\bar{\mu} = \sum_{i=1}^{k} \frac{\mu_i}{k} \qquad\qquad \textbf{12.6}$$

we have

$$k\bar{\mu} = \sum_{i=1}^{k} \mu_i$$

from which it follows that

$$\sum \alpha_i = \sum (\mu_i - \bar{\mu}) = \sum \mu_i - k\bar{\mu} = 0$$

Hence the model for the $k$-sample problem given by Equations 12.2 through 12.4 is often expressed by

$$Y_{ij} = \bar{\mu} + \alpha_i + \varepsilon_{ij}, \qquad i = 1, 2, \ldots, k; j = 1, 2, \ldots, n$$

$$\text{with} \qquad \sum_{i=1}^{k} \alpha_i = 0 \qquad \text{and} \qquad \varepsilon_{ij} \sim \text{NID}(0, \sigma^2) \qquad \textbf{12.7}$$

The hypotheses of Expression 12.5 may be restated as

$$\text{H}_0\text{: } \alpha_i = 0, \quad i = 1, 2, \ldots, k \qquad \text{versus} \qquad \text{H}_1\text{: } \alpha_i \neq 0 \text{ for at least one } i$$
$$\textbf{12.8}$$

From Equation 12.7 we see that the observation $Y_{ij}$ has expectation

$$E(Y_{ij}) = \bar{\mu} + \alpha_i, \qquad i = 1, 2, \ldots, k; j = 1, 2, \ldots, n \qquad \textbf{12.9}$$

CHAPTER 12  **ANALYSIS OF VARIANCE**

**Table 12.2**

**ANOVA Table for the Completely Randomized Case with Equal Sample Sizes**

| Source of Variation | Degrees of Freedom | Sum of Squares | Mean Square | Expected Mean Square |
|---|---|---|---|---|
| Among populations or treatments | $k - 1$ | SSA | MSA $= $ SSA$/(k - 1)$ | $\sigma^2 + n \Sigma \alpha_i^2/(k - 1)$ |
| Error | $k(n - 1)$ | SSE | MSE $= $ SSE$/k(n - 1)$ | $\sigma^2$ |
| Total | $kn - 1$ | SST | | |

This expectation is composed of an overall mean $\bar{\mu}$, defined by Equation 12.6, which is common to all of the $k$ populations. The parameters $\alpha_i = (\mu_i - \bar{\mu})$ are differences or deviations from this common part $\bar{\mu}$ of the individual population expectations $\mu_i$. *If all of the $\mu_i$ are equal* (say to $\mu$), then we know from Equation 12.6 that $\bar{\mu} = \mu$. In that case all of the deviations $\alpha_i$ are zero, because

$$\alpha_i = \mu_i - \bar{\mu} = \mu - \mu = 0$$

Hence the null hypothesis in Expression 12.8 means that

$$E(Y_{ij}) = \bar{\mu}, \qquad i = 1, 2, \ldots, k; j = 1, 2, \ldots, n$$

that is, these expectations consist only of the common part $\bar{\mu}$.

The total variability of the observations in Equation 12.1 is measured by $\Sigma_i \Sigma_j (Y_{ij} - \bar{Y})^2$, where $\bar{Y} = \Sigma_i \Sigma_j Y_{ij}/nk$ is the mean of all of the observations. It can be shown that

$$\sum_{i=1}^{k} \sum_{j=1}^{n} (Y_{ij} - \bar{Y})^2 = n \sum_{i=1}^{k} (\bar{Y}_i - \bar{Y})^2 + \sum_{i=1}^{k} \sum_{j=1}^{n} (Y_{ij} - \bar{Y}_i)^2 \qquad \textbf{12.10}$$

The notation $\bar{Y}_i$ represents the average of the observations from the $i$th population; that is, $\bar{Y}_i = \Sigma_j Y_{ij}/n$. Equation 12.10 is represented by

$$\text{SST} = \text{SSA} + \text{SSE} \qquad \textbf{12.11}$$

SST
SSA
SSE

where **SST** represents the total sum of squares, **SSA** represents the sum of squares due to differences among populations or treatments, and **SSE** represents the sum of squares that is unexplained or said to be "due to error." As in simple and multiple regression, the decomposition given by Equation 12.11 is the basis for the ANOVA table, presented in Table 12.2.

This ANOVA table is quite similar to that given in Table 10.1 for the simple linear regression case. The total variation in the $Y_{ij}$ observations represented by SST is divided into two portions, one ascribed to differences among population means (SSA) and the other to error (SSE). For populations (or treatments) the number of degrees of freedom is $k - 1$, one less than the number of populations sampled. This is related to the fact that when the $\bar{Y}_i - \bar{Y}$ deviations are known for

$k - 1$ values of $i$, the remaining deviation is known as

$$\sum_{i=1}^{k} (\bar{Y}_i - \bar{Y}) = \sum_{i=1}^{k} \sum_{j=1}^{n} \frac{Y_{ij}}{n} - k \sum_{i=1}^{k} \sum_{j=1}^{n} \frac{Y_{ij}}{kn} = 0$$

The total number of degrees of freedom is $kn - 1$, one less than the total number of observations (as in the regression case). The degrees of freedom for error can be obtained by subtracting as follows:

$$\begin{aligned} \text{d.f. (total)} - \text{d.f. (treatments)} &= \text{d.f. (error)} \\ (kn - 1) - (k - 1) &= k(n - 1) \end{aligned}$$  **12.12**

**mean square among treatments**   The **mean square among treatments** (MSA)—that is, among populations—and the mean square for error (MSE) are obtained by dividing the appropriate sum of squares by the corresponding degrees of freedom:

$$\text{MSA} = \frac{\text{SSA}}{k - 1} \quad \text{and} \quad \text{MSE} = \frac{\text{SSE}}{k(n - 1)}$$  **12.13**

As in Table 10.1, it can be shown that the mean square for error (MSE) is an unbiased estimator of $\sigma^2$. That is,

$$E(\text{MSE}) = \sigma^2$$  **12.14**

It also can be shown that the expectation of the mean square among treatments is given by

$$E(\text{MSA}) = \sigma^2 + n \sum_{i=1}^{k} \frac{\alpha_i^2}{k - 1}$$  **12.15**

From Equation 12.14 we see that the mean square for error is an unbiased estimate of $\sigma^2$, *whatever the values of the* $\alpha_i$. On the other hand, the MSA is an unbiased estimator of $\sigma^2$ if and only if $\alpha_i = 0$ for all $i$—namely, if the null hypothesis of no difference in population expectations is true. Furthermore, it can be shown that given the model assumptions of Equation 12.7, the statistic MSA/MSE has an $F$ distribution with $k - 1$ and $k(n - 1)$ degrees of freedom under this null hypothesis. If some of the $\alpha_i$ are not zero, we see from Equation 12.15 that the expected value of MSA tends to be *larger* than $\sigma^2$. Hence, for an $\alpha$-level test, a reasonable critical region for the alternative hypotheses in Expressions 12.5 and 12.8 is

$$F = \frac{\text{MSA}}{\text{MSE}} \geq F_{\alpha}[k - 1, k(n - 1)]$$  **12.16**

**Example 12.1**

Table 12.3 gives per capita debt to the nearest dollar for each of five states randomly selected from each of three regions—the East, the Midwest, and the South. Comparing the levels of per capita debt among these regions is a $k$-sample problem, with $k = 3$ and $n = 5$.

**DOTPLOT**     Minitab has a useful command **DOTPLOT**, which can be used to display a plot of the observations of the per capita debt of the states by region. The Minitab

**Table 12.3**

---

**1981 Per Capita Debt by State**

| East | Per Capita Debt | Midwest | Per Capita Debt | South | Per Capita Debt |
|---|---|---|---|---|---|
| Connecticut | 1248 | Illinois | 550 | Alabama | 265 |
| Delaware | 1755 | Iowa | 185 | Georgia | 257 |
| New Hampshire | 976 | Kansas | 185 | Louisiana | 708 |
| New York | 1346 | Nebraska | 127 | Mississippi | 323 |
| Vermont | 1280 | Wisconsin | 520 | Virginia | 360 |

*Source:* U.S. Treasury Department, as reported in *The World Almanac 1983*, p. 116.

**Exhibit 12.1**

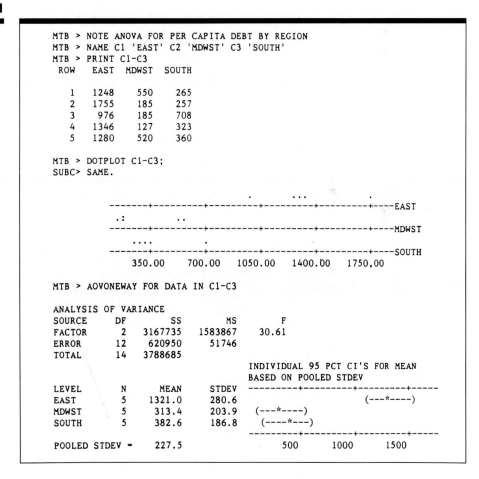

```
MTB > NOTE ANOVA FOR PER CAPITA DEBT BY REGION
MTB > NAME C1 'EAST' C2 'MDWST' C3 'SOUTH'
MTB > PRINT C1-C3
 ROW   EAST  MDWST  SOUTH

   1   1248    550    265
   2   1755    185    257
   3    976    185    708
   4   1346    127    323
   5   1280    520    360

MTB > DOTPLOT C1-C3;
SUBC> SAME.


                                .       ...              .
        -------+---------+---------+---------+---------+---------+----EAST
        .:           ..
        -------+---------+---------+---------+---------+---------+----MDWST
        ....         .
        -------+---------+---------+---------+---------+---------+----SOUTH
           350.00    700.00    1050.00   1400.00   1750.00

MTB > AOVONEWAY FOR DATA IN C1-C3

ANALYSIS OF VARIANCE
SOURCE     DF        SS        MS        F
FACTOR      2   3167735   1583867    30.61
ERROR      12    620950     51746
TOTAL      14   3788685
                                     INDIVIDUAL 95 PCT CI'S FOR MEAN
                                     BASED ON POOLED STDEV
LEVEL       N      MEAN     STDEV   ---------+---------+---------+-----
EAST        5    1321.0     280.6                        (---*----)
MDWST       5     313.4     203.9   (---*----)
SOUTH       5     382.6     186.8   (----*---)
                                    ---------+---------+---------+-----
POOLED STDEV =     227.5              500      1000      1500
```

command used to obtain the analysis of variance table in the $k$-sample situation is **AOVONEWAY**. The output from DOTPLOT and AOVONEWAY for the data in Table 12.3 is shown in Exhibit 12.1.

The plot indicates that per capita debt tends to be higher in eastern states than in the other two regions. The output from AOVONEWAY indicates that the average per capita debt in the three regions is given by

$$\bar{Y}_1 = 1321 \qquad \bar{Y}_2 = 313.4 \qquad \bar{Y}_3 = 382.6$$

The analysis of variance table gives $k - 1 = 2$ degrees of freedom for regions (denoted as FACTOR by Minitab), $k(n - 1) = 3(4) = 12$ degrees of freedom for error, and $nk - 1 = 5(3) - 1 = 14$ for total degrees of freedom. The corresponding sums of squares are SSA = 3,167,735, SSE = 620,950, and SST = 3,788,685. The mean squares are MSA = 1,583,867 and MSE = 51,746. The $F$ statistic was also computed by Minitab:

$$F = \frac{1,583,867}{51,746} = 30.61$$

For $\alpha = 0.01$, a critical region for the test of the hypothesis that average per capita debt is equal in the three regions is given by

$$F \geqslant F_{0.01}(2, 12) = 6.93$$

It is clear that the null hypothesis of equal per capita debt in the three regions should be soundly rejected.

---

It is frequently important to obtain $(1 - \alpha)100$ percent confidence intervals for the individual population expectations $\mu_i$, using the output from AOVONE-WAY. Arguments analogous to those of previous chapters can be used to show that the endpoints of such an interval are given by

$$\bar{Y}_i \pm \sqrt{\frac{\text{MSE}}{n}} \left( t_{\alpha/2, k(n-1)} \right) \qquad\qquad \textbf{12.17}$$

Note that, as usual, the degrees of freedom for the $t$ percentile correspond to the degrees of freedom for error. For the data of Example 12.1, endpoints of the intervals for $\mu_1$, $\mu_2$, and $\mu_3$, respectively, are given by

$$1321 \pm \sqrt{\frac{51,746}{5}} \left( t_{0.025, 12} \right) = 1321 \pm 221.7$$

$$313.4 \pm \sqrt{\frac{51,746}{5}} \left( t_{0.025, 12} \right) = 313.4 \pm 221.7$$

$$382.6 \pm \sqrt{\frac{51,746}{5}} \left( t_{0.025, 12} \right) = 382.6 \pm 221.7$$

These intervals are shown graphically in Exhibit 12.1.

An appropriate rule-of-thumb would be to reject the hypothesis that theoretical population means are equal if their corresponding confidence intervals do not overlap. For Example 12.1, this guideline implies that average per capita debt in the East differs from that in both the Midwest and the South. The AOVONEWAY output in Exhibit 12.1 indicates that per capita debt is substantially greater in the East than in the other two regions. There appears to be no significant difference between the Midwest and the South because the corresponding confidence intervals substantially overlap.

## Example 12.2

In William L. Hayes's book *Statistics for the Social Sciences*, Second Edition (New York: Holt, Rinehart and Winston, p. 767), he describes a situation in which 25 girls were assigned at random to each of four groups. The $k = 4$ groups, or treatments, represent four clubs with increasingly stringent membership requirements. Each girl was asked to indicate on a 12-point scale how interested she was in joining each club, with 1 representing least interest and 12 greatest interest. Histograms for the 25 observations for each group are given in Exhibit 12.2. Use of the AOVONEWAY command with these data yielded the Minitab output shown in Exhibit 12.3.

Let us first consider the analysis of variance table. We see that

$$\text{MSE} = \hat{\sigma}^2 = 2.95$$

is the value of the unbiased estimator of $\sigma^2$. For a test of the null hypothesis that there is no difference in true average scores of those assigned to the various clubs, Minitab calculated $F = 6.67$. For $\alpha = 0.01$, the critical region for the test of the null hypothesis is

$$F \geqslant F_{0.01}(3, 96) = 4.03$$

This result suggests that there is a difference among the girls' reactions to the clubs.

Using Expression 12.17 and the Minitab output, it is a straightforward process to find 95 percent confidence intervals for $\mu_1, \mu_2, \mu_3$, and $\mu_4$. The endpoints are given by

$$\bar{Y}_i \pm \sqrt{\frac{\text{MSE}}{25}} \, (t_{0.025,96})$$

Using $Z_{0.025}$ as an approximate value of $t_{0.025,96}$, we have

$$8.84 \pm \sqrt{\frac{2.95}{25}} \, (1.96) = 8.84 \pm 0.67$$

$$8.04 \pm \sqrt{\frac{2.95}{25}} \, (1.96) = 8.04 \pm 0.67$$

$$7.12 \pm \sqrt{\frac{2.95}{25}} \, (1.96) = 7.12 \pm 0.67$$

$$6.92 \pm \sqrt{\frac{2.95}{25}} \, (1.96) = 6.92 \pm 0.67$$

**Exhibit 12.2**

```
MTB > NOTE SELECTION OF CLUBS WITH INCREASING STANDARDS EXAMPLE
MTB > SET C1
C1
     6     6     7     7    .   .   .

MTB > SET C2
C2
     5     5     6     6    .   .   .

MTB > SET C3
C3
     4     4     4     5    .   .   .

MTB > SET C4
C4
     4     5     6     6    .   .   .

MTB > HIST C1                           MTB > HIST C3

Histogram of C1   N = 25                Histogram of C3   N = 25

Midpoint   Count                        Midpoint   Count
       6       2   **                          4       3   ***
       7       3   ***                         5       4   ****
       8       5   *****                        6       5   *****
       9       5   *****                        7       3   ***
      10       7   *******                      8       1   *
      11       3   ***                          9       4   ****
                                               10       4   ****
MTB > HIST C2                                   11       1   *

Histogram of C2   N = 25                MTB > HIST C4

Midpoint   Count                        Histogram of C4   N = 25
       5       2   **
       6       2   **                   Midpoint   Count
       7       6   ******                       4       1   *
       8       5   *****                        5       1   *
       9       5   *****                        6       8   ********
      10       3   ***                          7      10   **********
      11       2   **                           8       0
                                                9       4   ****
                                               10       1   *
```

**Exhibit 12.3**

```
MTB > AOVONEWAY C1-C4

ANALYSIS OF VARIANCE
SOURCE      DF        SS        MS        F
FACTOR       3     58.91     19.64     6.67
ERROR       96    282.80      2.95
TOTAL       99    341.71
                                       INDIVIDUAL 95 PCT CI'S FOR MEAN
                                       BASED ON POOLED STDEV
LEVEL        N      MEAN     STDEV    --------+---------+---------+------
C1          25     8.840     1.491                      (-----*------)
C2          25     8.040     1.670              (-----*------)
C3          25     7.120     2.205       (------*------)
C4          25     6.920     1.382    (------*------)
                                       --------+---------+---------+------
POOLED STDEV =     1.716                   7.0       8.0       9.0
```

as the endpoints of the respective confidence intervals. Thus the intervals for $\mu_1$, $\mu_2$, $\mu_3$, and $\mu_4$ are, respectively, (8.17, 9.51), (7.37, 8.71), (6.45, 7.79), and (6.25, 7.59).

The fact that their intervals do not overlap suggests that $\mu_1$ differs from $\mu_3$ and from $\mu_4$. This finding is shown graphically in the display of these confidence intervals in Exhibit 12.3. It appears that the girls preferred the club with the fewest requirements (club 1) over those with more stringent membership requirements (club 3 and club 4).

## Exercises 12.2

**12.1** The following data give the 1978 per capita energy consumption (in kilograms of coal equivalents) for five countries in each of the regions indicated.

| South America | Energy per Capita | Europe | Energy per Capita | Middle East | Energy per Capita |
|---|---|---|---|---|---|
| Brazil | 794 | Austria | 4048 | Iran | 1808 |
| Chile | 997 | France | 4368 | Israel | 2362 |
| Columbia | 700 | Greece | 1925 | Kuwait | 6771 |
| Peru | 649 | Italy | 3230 | Saudi Arabia | 1306 |
| Venezuela | 2989 | Sweden | 5954 | Syria | 968 |

*Source:* Statistical Office of the United Nations, *Statistical Yearbook*, as reported in *The Information Please Almanac* (Boston: Houghton Mifflin, 1982), pp. 115–116.

**a.** Use Minitab to create an ANOVA table for these data.
**b.** What is the value of an unbiased estimate for $\sigma^2$?
**c.** Test the null hypothesis that energy consumption per capita is the same in these regions. Use $\alpha = 0.05$.

**12.2** The following data give the actual number of seconds that had actually passed when three sets of 20 persons without watches thought that a 60-second interval had elapsed.

```
Set 1:  25  30  35  35  40  42  42  45  45   51
        53  53  60  65  67  68  68  70  75   90
Set 2:  30  45  45  45  47  50  50  50  50   55
        56  59  59  60  62  69  70  70  72   86
Set 3:  20  23  35  42  44  45  45  46  47   49
        51  54  62  65  70  70  70  80  89  138
```

*Source:* T. M. Smith and G. Iglewicz, "An Effective Classroom Technique for Comparison of Robust Estimators," *The American Statistician* 36 (1982): 166–167.

**a.** Construct an analysis of variance table for these data using Minitab.
**b.** Does it seem reasonable that $\mu_1 = \mu_2 = \mu_3$? (Use $\alpha = 0.05$.)
**c.** Does any group seem to be estimating 60 seconds accurately?

**12.3** A home builder wants to know the effect of type of structure on heating costs. Three types of structures are studied. A random sample of four homes of each of three types yields the following data on winter heating costs (in dollars).

| | Structure Type | | |
|---|---|---|---|
| Sample Home | 1 | 2 | 3 |
| 1 | 189 | 204 | 195 |
| 2 | 201 | 220 | 189 |
| 3 | 187 | 198 | 200 |
| 4 | 187 | 279 | 185 |

**a.** Construct an analysis of variance table for these data using Minitab.
**b.** Is there evidence that heating costs differ for the three types of structures? (Use $\alpha = 0.05$.)

**12.4** The following data give the divorce rate per 1000 persons in 1979 for five states in each of three regions.

| East | Divorce Rate | South | Divorce Rate | West | Divorce Rate |
|---|---|---|---|---|---|
| Connecticut | 4.5 | Arkansas | 9.3 | California | 6.1 |
| Massachusetts | 3.0 | Georgia | 6.5 | Colorado | 6.0 |
| New Jersey | 3.2 | Louisiana | 3.8 | Oregon | 7.0 |
| Pennsylvania | 3.4 | North Carolina | 4.9 | Utah | 5.6 |
| Vermont | 4.6 | Tennessee | 6.8 | Washington | 6.9 |

*Source:* U.S. Department of Health and Human Services, National Center for Health Statistics, as reported in *The Statistical Abstract of the United States*, 1981, p. 127.

**a.** Carry out parts a and b of exercise 12.2 for these data.
**b.** Does one region clearly appear to have a different divorce rate than another?

**12.5** Complete the following for the ANOVA model for the $k$-sample problem with equal $n$.
**a.** Using Equation 12.10, show that SSE $= (n - 1) \sum_{i=1}^{k} S_i^2$, where $S_i^2$ is the sample variance of the $n$ observations from the $i$th population.
**b.** Using the fact that $E(S_i^2) = \sigma^2$, show that $E(\text{SSE}) = k(n - 1)\sigma^2$.
**c.** Using parts a and b, show that $E(\text{MSE}) = \sigma^2$.

## 12.3

## The Completely Randomized Design with Unequal Sample Sizes

In many studies in which the expectations of $k \geqslant 2$ populations are compared, the samples from each population are not ultimately of equal size—even in cases where we attempt to maintain equal sample sizes. For example, suppose we decide to compare three teaching methods using three classes of students from the same age group. The teachers of the classes agree to each use one of the three teaching methods (that is, teacher 1 will use the first method, teacher 2 will use the second method, and teacher 3 will use the third method). The plan for the comparison is to give a common examination to all of the students in each class after two months of instruction. Even if the classes are initially of the same size, they may differ after two months because students have dropped out for one reason or another. Thus we need a way to analyze the $k$-sample problem when the samples are of unequal sizes.

unequal sample size

In the case of **unequal sample size**, the observations are denoted by

$$Y_{11}, \quad Y_{12}, \quad \ldots, \quad Y_{1n_1}$$
$$Y_{21}, \quad Y_{22}, \quad \ldots, \quad Y_{2n_2}$$
$$\vdots \qquad \vdots \qquad \ldots \qquad \vdots$$
$$Y_{k1}, \quad Y_{k2}, \quad \ldots, \quad Y_{kn_k}$$

12.18

where, again, $Y_{ij}$ represents the $j$th observation from the $i$th population. For the $i$th population there are $n_i$ observations. In the case of equal sample sizes, $n_i = n$ for $i = 1, 2, \ldots, k$.

The model assumptions are the same for the unequal sample size case as for the equal sample size case (except with regard to the unequal $n_i$ values). The $Y_{ij}$ are assumed to

1  come from normal populations;
2  come from populations with the same variance;
3  have possibly different expectations, $\mu_1, \mu_2, \ldots, \mu_k$.

These assumptions are expressed formally as

$$Y_{ij} \sim N(\mu_i, \sigma^2), \qquad i = 1, 2, \ldots, k; j = 1, 2, \ldots, n_i$$

12.19

or as

$$Y_{ij} = \mu_i + \varepsilon_{ij}, \qquad i = 1, 2, \ldots, k; j = 1, 2, \ldots, n_i$$

12.20

with

$$\varepsilon_{ij} \sim \text{NID}(0, \sigma^2), \qquad i = 1, 2, \ldots, k; j = 1, 2, \ldots, n_i$$

12.21

The first null and alternative hypotheses to test are exactly the same as those in the previous section—namely,

$$H_0: \mu_1 = \mu_2 = \cdots = \mu_k$$
$$\text{versus} \qquad H_1: \mu_i \neq \mu_l \text{ for some pair of indices } i \neq l$$

12.22

As before, the model for the completely randomized design may be presented alternatively as

$$Y_{ij} = \bar{\mu} + \alpha_i + \varepsilon_{ij}, \qquad i = 1, 2, \ldots, k; j = 1, 2, \ldots, n_i$$
$$\text{with} \quad \sum_{i=1}^{k} n_i \alpha_i = 0 \quad \text{and} \quad \varepsilon_{ij} \sim \text{NID}(0, \sigma^2)$$

12.23

In this case the overall mean, $\bar{\mu}$, is given by

$$\bar{\mu} = \frac{\sum_{i=1}^{k} n_i \mu_i}{N}$$

12.24

where $N = \Sigma_{i=1}^{k} n_i$ is the total number of observations. Here $\bar{\mu}$ is a weighted average of the population expectations $\mu_i$, where the weights are $n_i/N$, the proportion of observations coming from the $i$th population.

The hypotheses of Expression 12.22 can also be restated as

$$\text{H}_0: \alpha_i = 0, \quad i = 1, 2, \ldots, k \qquad \text{versus} \qquad \text{H}_1: \alpha_i \neq 0 \text{ for at least one } i$$

**12.25**

As before, the observation $Y_{ij}$ has expectation

$$E(Y_{ij}) = \bar{\mu} + \alpha_i, \qquad i = 1, 2, \ldots, k; j = 1, 2, \ldots, n_i \qquad \textbf{12.26}$$

The expectation of an observation from the $i$th population is composed of an overall mean, $\bar{\mu}$, plus a contribution $\alpha_i$ due to the $i$th population. If the null hypothesis in Expression 12.25 is true, then

$$E(Y_{ij}) = \bar{\mu}, \qquad i = 1, 2, \ldots, k; j = 1, 2, \ldots, n_i$$

that is, the expectations consist only of the common part $\bar{\mu}$ and hence all of the $Y_{ij}$ have a common distribution. Thus,

$$Y_{ij} \sim N(\bar{\mu}, \sigma^2), \qquad i = 1, 2, \ldots, k; j = 1, 2, \ldots, n_i$$

under this null hypothesis. The total variability of the observations is again partitioned into two portions by

$$\sum_{i=1}^{k} \sum_{j=1}^{n_i} (Y_{ij} - \bar{Y})^2 = \sum_{i=1}^{k} n_i (\bar{Y}_i - \bar{Y})^2 + \sum_{i=1}^{k} \sum_{j=1}^{n_i} (Y_{ij} - \bar{Y}_i)^2 \qquad \textbf{12.27}$$

or

$$\text{SST} = \text{SSA} + \text{SSE} \qquad \textbf{12.28}$$

Here

$$\bar{Y}_i = \sum_{j=1}^{n_i} \frac{Y_{ij}}{n_i}, \quad i = 1, 2, \ldots, k \qquad \text{and} \qquad \bar{Y} = \sum_{i=1}^{k} \sum_{j=1}^{n_i} \frac{Y_{ij}}{N} \qquad \textbf{12.29}$$

where $N = \Sigma_{i=1}^{k} n_i$. As before, $\bar{Y}_i$ represents the average of the observations from the $i$th population, $N$ is the total number of observations, and $\bar{Y}$ is the average of all the observations. Again SST represents the total sum of squares, SSA represents the sum of squares due to differences among populations or treatments, and SSE represents the sum of squares due to error. The decomposition is presented in the ANOVA table in Table 12.4.

Table 12.4 is very similar to Table 12.2 and reduces to that table in the case where $n_i = n$ for all $i$. The number of degrees of freedom for treatments or populations is $k - 1$, as before. The number of degrees of freedom for error is $N - k$. As before, we have

$$\text{d.f. (total)} = \text{d.f. (treatments)} + \text{d.f. (error)} \qquad \textbf{12.30}$$
$$N - 1 = k - 1 + N - k$$

The mean square among treatments and the mean square for error are once again

**Table 12.4**

**ANOVA Table for the Completely Randomized Case with Unequal Sample Sizes**

| Source | d.f. | SS | MS | EMS |
|---|---|---|---|---|
| Among populations or treatments | $k - 1$ | SSA | $\text{MSA} = \text{SSA}/(k - 1)$ | $\sigma^2 + \sum_{i=1}^{k} n_i \alpha_i^2 / (k - 1)$ |
| Error | $N - k$ | SSE | $\text{MSE} = \text{SSE}/(N - k)$ | $\sigma^2$ |
| Total | $N - 1$ | SST | | |

equal to the appropriate sums of squares divided by the corresponding degrees of freedom. That is,

$$\text{MSA} = \frac{\text{SSA}}{k - 1} \quad \text{and} \quad \text{MSE} = \frac{\text{SSE}}{N - k} \qquad \textbf{12.31}$$

As in Section 12.2, it can be shown that the mean square for error (MSE) is an unbiased estimate of $\sigma^2$; that is,

$$E(\text{MSE}) = \sigma^2 \qquad \textbf{12.32}$$

Similarly, the expected mean square among treatments is given by

$$E(\text{MSA}) = \sigma^2 + \sum_{i=1}^{k} \frac{n_i \alpha_i^2}{k - 1} \qquad \textbf{12.33}$$

If the null hypothesis of Expression 12.25 is correct (that is, if there is no difference among the population expectations), both MSE and MSA are unbiased estimates of $\sigma^2$. Under this hypothesis, MSA/MSE has an $F$ distribution with $k - 1$ and $N - k$ degrees of freedom. Using reasoning analogous to that of Section 12.2, we reject the null hypothesis of Expression 12.25 at significance level $\alpha$ if

$$F = \frac{\text{MSA}}{\text{MSE}} \geqslant F_\alpha(k - 1, N - k) \qquad \textbf{12.34}$$

**Example 12.3**

Returning to the data of Table 12.1 on the average number of points scored per game for the teams of the NBA for the 1983–1984 season, let us label the Atlantic Division 1, the Central Division 2, the Midwest Division 3, and the Pacific Division 4. The values of the $n_i$ are $n_1 = 5$ and $n_2 = n_3 = n_4 = 6$. With the observations $y_{1j}$, $y_{2j}$, $y_{3j}$, and $y_{4j}$ for $j = 1, 2, \ldots, n_i$ set in columns C1, C2, C3, and C4, respectively, use of the AOVONEWAY command yielded the Minitab output shown in Exhibit 12.4.

The ANOVA table was created using $N - 1 = 23 - 1 = 22$ total degrees of freedom, $k - 1 = 4 - 1 = 3$ degrees of freedom for regions (labeled as FACTOR by Minitab), and $N - k = 23 - 4 = 19$ degrees of freedom for error. To test the null hypothesis of no differences between the divisions, we use the $F$ statistic from the Minitab output, $F = 4.38$. From Equation 12.34 and Table IV

**Exhibit 12.4**

```
MTB > NOTE ANALYSIS OF VARIANCE FOR NBA DIVISIONS 1983-84
MTB > SET C1
C1
   112.1   107.8   106.9   102.7     .   .   .

MTB > END
MTB > SET C2
C2
   105.7   117.1   101.5   102.3     .   .   .

MTB > END
MTB > SET C3
C3
   120.3   110.0   110.6   123.7     .   .   .

MTB > END
MTB > SET C4
C4
   111.0   115.6   113.1   109.9     .   .   .

MTB > END
MTB > NAME C1 'ATL' C2 'CEN' C3 'MIDWT' C4 'PAC'
MTB > PRINT C1-C4
 ROW    ATL     CEN    MIDWT     PAC

   1   112.1   105.7   120.3    111.0
   2   107.8   117.1   110.0    115.6
   3   106.9   101.5   110.6    113.1
   4   102.7   102.3   123.7    109.9
   5   110.0   103.7   115.0    110.7
   6           104.5   110.4    108.1

MTB > AOVONEWAY C1-C4

ANALYSIS OF VARIANCE
SOURCE      DF       SS        MS         F
FACTOR       3     289.3      96.4      4.38
ERROR       19     418.3      22.0
TOTAL       22     707.6
                                  INDIVIDUAL 95 PCT CI'S FOR MEAN
                                  BASED ON POOLED STDEV
LEVEL       N      MEAN     STDEV  -------+---------+---------+-------
ATL         5     107.90     3.54         (--------*--------)
CEN         6     105.80     5.74    (-------*-------)
MIDWT       6     115.00     5.82                      (-------*-------)
PAC         6     111.40     2.62             (-------*------)
                                       -------+---------+---------+-------
POOLED STDEV =     4.69                105.0     110.0     115.0
```

of Appendix C we find that a rejection region for a 0.05-level test of the null hypothesis is

$$F \geq F_{0.05}(3, 19) = 3.13$$

Hence we should reject the hypothesis that all the teams in the divisions have the same average number of points per game.

A $(1 - \alpha)100$ percent confidence interval for $\mu_i$ in the unequal sample case is given by

$$\bar{Y}_i \pm \sqrt{\frac{\text{MSE}}{n_i}} \, (t_{\alpha/2, N-k}) \qquad\qquad \textbf{12.35}$$

This expression is completely analogous to Expression 12.17 for the equal sample size case and reduces to that expression if $n_i = n$ for all $i$. Endpoints of 95 percent confidence intervals for the data in Exhibit 12.4 are as follows:

$$\bar{y}_1 \pm \sqrt{\frac{\text{MSE}}{n_1}} \, (t_{0.025,19}) = 107.9 \pm 4.39 \qquad \bar{y}_2 \pm \sqrt{\frac{\text{MSE}}{n_2}} \, (t_{0.025,19}) = 105.8 \pm 4.01$$

$$\bar{y}_3 \pm \sqrt{\frac{\text{MSE}}{n_3}} \, (t_{0.025,19}) = 115 \pm 4.01 \qquad \bar{y}_4 \pm \sqrt{\frac{\text{MSE}}{n_4}} \, (t_{0.025,19}) = 111.4 \pm 4.01$$

As Exhibit 12.4 shows, there is no overlap between the 95 percent confidence intervals for the Central and Midwest Divisions, suggesting that there is in fact a difference between the two divisions in average number of points scored per game.

## Exercises 12.3

**12.6** We are to compare the mileage per gallon (mpg) of four types of standard-size cars. We have four cars of makes 1 and 4 and three cars of makes 2 and 3. The following measurements of mpg are made for the four types of cars:

| 1 | 2 | 3 | 4 |
|----|----|----|----|
| 15 | 9 | 18 | 12 |
| 19 | 14 | 19 | 15 |
| 23 | 13 | 26 | 13 |
| 19 | | | 20 |

Do not use Minitab for this problem.

**a.** Construct an analysis of variance table for these data. Determine the degrees of freedom for error.

**b.** Test $H_0: \mu_1 = \mu_2 = \mu_3 = \mu_4$ (all types of cars get equal mileage per gallon) versus the alternative that the null hypothesis is false. Use $\alpha = 0.05$.

**c.** Find confidence intervals for the theoretical means. What do you conclude from these intervals?

**12.7** The data on page 468 show the percentage change in first-quarter earnings between 1982 and 1983 for ten banks, six large corporations with over one billion dollars in sales per quarter, and six small corporations. Use Minitab as needed.

**a.** Construct an analysis of variance table for these data.

**b.** Test the null hypothesis $H_0: \mu_1 = \mu_2 = \mu_3$ (the percentage changes are equal for the three groups). Use $\alpha = 0.05$ and state the critical region.

**c.** Explain in words what your analysis indicates regarding earnings for these three groups.

| Ten Banks | Six Large Corporations | Six Small Corporations |
|:---:|:---:|:---:|
| 14.7 | 29.0 | −9.8 |
| 21.7 | −81.5 | 25.0 |
| 106.4 | 21.8 | −29.2 |
| 1.7 | −90.0 | 46.7 |
| 15.2 | −8.5 | 5.6 |
| −21.0 | −13.8 | −14.4 |
| 7.1 | | |
| 15.1 | | |
| 12.6 | | |
| 43.9 | | |

*Source: The New York Times, April 15, 1983*

**12.8** A bank wishes to determine whether the average balances held in three different types of checking accounts differ. Eight accounts of type 1, ten of type 2, and nine of type 3 are selected, and the balance in each is recorded to the nearest dollar as follows.

| 1 | 2 | 3 |
|:---:|:---:|:---:|
| $602 | $ 580 | $152 |
| 166 | 522 | 670 |
| 212 | 510 | 870 |
| 220 | 1010 | 208 |
| 416 | 920 | 216 |
| 527 | 1210 | 281 |
| 325 | 481 | 370 |
| 480 | 1100 | 377 |
| | 1080 | 281 |
| | 900 | |

Use Minitab as needed.

**a.** Construct an ANOVA table for these data.

**b.** Test $H_0$: $\mu_1 = \mu_2 = \mu_3$ (the average balances are the same) versus the alternative that $H_0$ is false. Use $\alpha = 0.05$.

**c.** In type 2 accounts, a $500 balance is required in order to receive a money-market interest return. The other accounts pay no interest. Does the average balance seem to be higher for type 2 accounts than for the other two types?

**12.9** The following table gives the grades on a common examination for five students taught by teaching method A, six taught by method B, and five taught by method C.

| A | B | C |
|:---:|:---:|:---:|
| 74 | 80 | 76 |
| 87 | 70 | 61 |
| 89 | 79 | 76 |
| 79 | 71 | 72 |
| 73 | 87 | 58 |
| | 81 | |

**a.** Test $H_0$: $\mu_1 = \mu_2 = \mu_3$ using $\alpha = 0.05$.

**b.** What conclusion would you draw concerning the effectiveness of these three methods of teaching?

## 12.4

**Contrasts**    Often it is of interest to compare certain pairs or other combinations of population means. For example, given the data of Example 12.1, we might want to compare the population mean for the East with the population mean for the Midwest. In that case the appropriate comparison is of the form

$$\mu_1 - \mu_2$$

Alternatively, we might want to compare the East with both the Midwest and the South. In this case the appropriate comparison is of the form

$$\mu_1 - \frac{\mu_2 + \mu_3}{2}$$

Such comparisons are known as contrasts.

---

**Definition 12.1** ▬▬▬▬▬▬▬▬▬▬▬▬▬▬▬▬▬▬▬▬▬▬▬▬▬▬▬▬

**contrast**
**linear combination**

A **contrast** of $\mu_1, \mu_2, \ldots, \mu_k$ is a **linear combination**

$$\sum_{i=1}^{k} c_i \mu_i$$

where the constants $c_i$ satisfy $\Sigma_{i=1}^{k} c_i = 0$.

---

In the first contrast above, $c_1 = 1$, $c_2 = -1$, and $c_3 = 0$. In the second contrast, $c_1 = 1$, $c_2 = -1/2$, and $c_3 = -1/2$. Note that a contrast is a parameter because the constants $c_i$ are known but the $\mu_i$ are unknown.

The natural estimator of a contrast, which is a linear combination of population expectations, is the corresponding linear combination of the sample means. Hence the estimator of the contrast in Definition 12.1 is

$$\sum_{i=1}^{k} c_i \bar{Y}_i \qquad\qquad \textbf{12.36}$$

For the debt data of Table 12.3, the point estimator of $\mu_1 - \mu_2$ is

$$\bar{Y}_1 - \bar{Y}_2 = 1321 - 313.4 = 1007.6$$

Similarly, the estimator of $\mu_1 - (\mu_2 + \mu_3)/2$ is

$$\bar{Y}_1 - \frac{\bar{Y}_2 + \bar{Y}_3}{2} = 1321 - \frac{313.4 + 382.6}{2} = 973$$

The estimate 1007.6 is a point estimate of the difference between average per capita debt in eastern states and that in midwestern states. The value 973 is a point estimate of the difference between average per capita debt in eastern states and that in midwestern and southern states taken together. These values are point estimates of the corresponding theoretical contrasts, just as $\bar{x}$ is a point estimate of $\mu$ in a sample from a single population.

Let us now consider properties of the estimator in Expression 12.36, assuming for the moment that $n$ observations are sampled from each population. The expectation of the estimated contrast is given by

$$E\left(\sum_{i=1}^{k} c_i \bar{Y}_i\right) = \sum_{i=1}^{k} c_i E(\bar{Y}_i) = \sum_{i=1}^{k} c_i \mu_i \qquad \text{12.37}$$

and the variance of the estimated contrast is given by

$$\text{Var}\left(\sum_{i=1}^{k} c_i \bar{Y}_i\right) = \sum_{i=1}^{k} c_i^2 \, \text{Var}(\bar{Y}_i) = \left(\frac{\sigma^2}{n}\right) \sum_{i=1}^{k} c_i^2 \qquad \text{12.38}$$

From Equation 12.37 we see that the sample contrast of Expression 12.36 is an unbiased estimate of the theoretical contrast of Definition 12.1. Assuming that the normality assumptions of Expression 12.2 concerning the $Y_{ij}$ are valid,

$$\frac{\sum_{i=1}^{h} c_i \bar{Y}_i - \sum_{i=1}^{h} c_i \mu_i}{\sqrt{\left(\frac{\sigma^2}{n}\right) \sum_{i=1}^{k} c_i^2}} = Z \qquad \text{12.39}$$

that is, the standardized sample contrast has a standard normal distribution. As $\sigma^2$ is not known, the unknown variance is replaced by the mean square for error from the ANOVA table. It can then be shown that

$$\frac{\sum_{i=1}^{k} c_i \bar{Y}_i - \sum_{i=1}^{k} c_i \mu_i}{\sqrt{\left(\frac{\text{MSE}}{n}\right) \sum_{i=1}^{k} c_i^2}} = t \qquad \text{12.40}$$

that is, the approximation of the standardized sample contrast has Student's $t$ distribution with $v = k(n - 1)$ degrees of freedom. Knowledge of this distribution permits us to make inferences about the theoretical contrast of Definition 12.1 based on the corresponding sample contrast of Expression 12.36.

Using the distributional result of Equation 12.40 and reasoning as we have previously, we find that the endpoints of a confidence interval for $\sum_{i=1}^{k} c_i \mu_i$ are given by

$$\sum_{i=1}^{k} c_i \bar{Y}_i \pm \sqrt{\left(\frac{\text{MSE}}{n}\right) \sum_{i=1}^{k} c_i^2} \, (t_{\alpha/2, k(n-1)}) \qquad \text{12.41}$$

## Example 12.4

Using the Minitab output on regional per capita debt (Exhibit 12.1), we find that the endpoints of 95 percent confidence intervals for the two contrasts $\mu_1 - \mu_2$ and

$\mu_1 - (\mu_2 + \mu_3)/2$ are, respectively,

$$\bar{y}_1 - \bar{y}_2 \pm \sqrt{\frac{\text{MSE}}{n}(c_1^2 + c_2^2)}\,(t_{0.025,12})$$

$$= 1007.6 \pm \sqrt{\left(\frac{51746}{5}\right)2}\,(2.179)$$

$$= 1007.6 \pm 313.5$$

and

$$\bar{y}_1 - \frac{\bar{y}_2 + \bar{y}_3}{2} \pm \sqrt{\left(\frac{51746}{5}\right)\left[1^2 + \left(-\frac{1}{2}\right)^2 + \left(-\frac{1}{2}\right)^2\right]}\,(t_{0.025,12})$$

$$= 973 \pm \sqrt{15523.8}\,(2.179)$$

$$= 973 \pm 271.5$$

Hence the interval (694.1, 1322.1) is a 95 percent confidence interval for $\mu_1 - \mu_2$. Similarly, (701.5, 1244.5) is a 95 percent confidence interval for $\mu_1 - (\mu_2 + \mu_3)/2$.

---

In a contrast, the null hypothesis that is typically tested is

$$\text{H}_0: \sum_{i=1}^{k} c_i \mu_i = 0 \qquad\qquad \textbf{12.42}$$

Table 12.5 gives standard alternatives to this null hypothesis. The test statistic used is

$$t = \frac{\displaystyle\sum_{i=1}^{k} c_i \bar{Y}_i}{\sqrt{\left(\dfrac{\text{MSE}}{n}\right)\displaystyle\sum_{i=1}^{k} c_i^2}} \qquad\qquad \textbf{12.43}$$

which is equivalent to Equation 12.40 with the theoretical contrast $\sum_{i=1}^{k} c_i \mu_i$ set equal to zero. See Table 12.5 for critical regions for the standard alternatives.

**Table 12.5**

**Critical Regions for Tests of Contrasts**

| Alternative | Critical Region |
|---|---|
| $\sum_{i=1}^{k} c_i \mu_i > 0$ | $t \geq t_{\alpha,k(n-1)}$ |
| $\sum_{i=1}^{k} c_i \mu_i < 0$ | $t \leq -t_{\alpha,k(n-1)}$ |
| $\sum_{i=1}^{k} c_i \mu_i = 0$ | $|t| \geq t_{\alpha/2,k(n-1)}$ |

## Example 12.5

In order to compare the degree of interest expressed by the girls in Example 12.2 in clubs with increasingly stringent membership requirements, we can test the null hypothesis that the club with the highest requirements attracts less interest than the other clubs. This null hypothesis can be stated as

$$H_0: \mu_4 - \frac{\mu_1 + \mu_2 + \mu_3}{3} = 0$$

and the alternative can be expressed as

$$H_1: \mu_4 - \frac{\mu_1 + \mu_2 + \mu_3}{3} < 0$$

The value of the $t$ statistic is given by

$$
\begin{aligned}
t &= \left( \bar{y}_4 - \frac{\bar{y}_1 + \bar{y}_2 + \bar{y}_3}{3} \right) \bigg/ \sqrt{\left( \frac{\text{MSE}}{25} \right) \left[ 1^2 + 3 \left( -\frac{1}{3} \right)^2 \right]} \\
&= \left( 6.92 - \frac{8.84 + 8.04 + 7.12}{3} \right) \bigg/ \sqrt{\left( \frac{2.95}{25} \right) \left( \frac{4}{3} \right)} \\
&= -2.72
\end{aligned}
$$

For an $\alpha = 0.01$ level test, we would reject $H_0$ in favor of $H_1$ if

$$t \leqslant -t_{0.01,96} \doteq -Z_{0.01} = -2.326$$

The computed $t$ value is clearly in the rejection region, and thus there is strong evidence for the validity of the hypothesis that the club with the most stringent requirements attracts less interest than the other clubs.

---

When the sample sizes are unequal (when they have the values $n_1, n_2, \ldots, n_k$), the estimate of the theoretical contrast is still $\Sigma_{i=1}^{k} c_i \bar{Y}_i$, with $\bar{Y}_i$ being the average of the $n_i$ observations from the $i$th population. The standardized $t$ statistic becomes

$$\frac{\displaystyle\sum_{i=1}^{k} c_i \bar{Y}_i - \sum_{i=1}^{k} c_i u_i}{\sqrt{\text{MSE} \displaystyle\sum_{i=1}^{k} \frac{c_i^2}{n_i}}} = t \qquad\qquad \textbf{12.44}$$

The number of degrees of freedom for the $t$ statistic is $N - k$, where $N = \Sigma_{i=1}^{k} n_i$. Endpoints of a $(1 - \alpha)100$ percent confidence interval for $\Sigma_{i=1}^{k} c_i \mu_i$ are given by

$$\sum_{i=1}^{k} c_i \bar{Y}_i \pm \sqrt{\text{MSE} \sum_{i=1}^{k} \frac{c_i^2}{n_i}} \, (t_{\alpha/2, N-k}) \qquad\qquad \textbf{12.45}$$

Tests of the null hypothesis

$$H_0: \sum_{i=1}^{k} c_i \mu_i = 0$$

are carried out using the $t$ statistic in Equation 12.44, substituting 0 for $\Sigma_{i=1}^{k} c_i \mu_i$. The critical regions for appropriate alternatives are those given in Table 12.5, with the degrees of freedom changed from $k(n - 1)$ to $N - k$.

## Example 12.6

For testing the null hypothesis that teams in the Eastern and Western Conferences of the NBA score equal numbers of points on average (using the data of Table 12.1), an appropriate contrast is $(\mu_1 + \mu_2)/2 - (\mu_3 + \mu_4)/2$. We find that

$$\frac{(107.9 + 105.8)/2 - (115.0 + 111.4)/2}{\sqrt{(22/4)(1/5 + 1/6 + 1/6 + 1/6)}} = -3.24$$

Against a two-sided alternative, for $\alpha = 0.05$ the critical region is

$$|t| \geqslant t_{0.025,19} \quad \text{or} \quad |t| \geqslant 2.093$$

As the value $t = -3.24$ lies in the critical region, there is evidence to reject the null hypothesis that teams in the Eastern and Western Conferences score equal numbers of points on average. The data suggest that the Western Conference teams score a higher number of points per game on average.

## Exercises 12.4

**12.10** The data below give the numbers of murders per 100,000 residents in selected states in three regions of the United States for 1980.

| Northeast | Rate | Rocky Mountain | Rate | South | Rate |
|-----------|------|----------------|------|-------|------|
| Connecticut | 4.7 | Colorado | 6.9 | Alabama | 13.2 |
| Maine | 2.8 | Idaho | 3.1 | Georgia | 13.8 |
| Massachusetts | 4.1 | Montana | 4.0 | Louisiana | 15.7 |
| New Hampshire | 2.5 | Utah | 3.8 | Mississippi | 14.5 |
| Vermont | 2.2 | Wyoming | 6.2 | South Carolina | 11.5 |

*Source:* 1980 Uniform Crime Reports, Federal Bureau of Investigation, as reported in *The World Almanac, 1983,* pp. 966–967.

a. Use AOVONEWAY to create an ANOVA table.
b. Find a 95 percent confidence interval for the contrast $\mu_1 - (\mu_2 + \mu_3)/2$ (using 1 to represent the Northeastern states, 2 to represent the Rocky Mountain states, and 3 to represent the states in the South).
c. Test the null hypothesis that murder rates are the same in the Rocky Mountain states and the Southern states against the alternative that murder rates are higher in the South. Use $\alpha = 0.05$.
d. Find a 95 percent confidence interval for $\mu_1 - \mu_3$.

**12.11** Use the data of Example 12.2 and the analysis of variance output in Exhibit 12.3 to do the following.
   **a.** Find a 95 percent confidence interval for $(\mu_1 + \mu_2)/2 - (\mu_3 + \mu_4)/2$.
   **b.** Test $H_0: (\mu_1 + \mu_2)/2 - (\mu_3 + \mu_4)/2 = 0$ versus the alternative that this contrast is not equal to zero. Use $\alpha = 0.05$.

**12.12 a.** Use the data from exercise 12.3 to test the null hypothesis that heating costs for type 2 homes are no different from those for type 1 and type 3 homes against the alternative that the cost of heating type 2 homes is greater. Use $\alpha = 0.05$.
   **b.** Use the same data to find a 90 percent confidence interval for $\mu_2 - \mu_1$.

**12.13 a.** Use the data of exercise 12.4 to find a 95 percent confidence interval for $\mu_1 - (\mu_2 + \mu_3)/2$, where 1 refers to the East, 2 to the South, and 3 to the West.
   **b.** Test $H_0: \mu_1 - (\mu_2 + \mu_3)/2 = 0$ versus $H_1: \mu_1 < (\mu_2 + \mu_3)/2$, using $\alpha = 0.05$.

**12.14 a.** Use the data in exercise 12.6 to find a 95 percent confidence interval for the contrast between the average mileage per gallon (mpg) for type 1 cars and that for the other types of cars.
   **b.** Test the null hypothesis that the mileage for type 1 and type 3 cars is the same against a two sided alternative. Use $\alpha = 0.10$.

**12.15 a.** Use the data in exercise 12.8 to find a 90 percent confidence interval for the difference between the true average balance in type 2 checking accounts and that in type 1 and type 3 accounts.
   **b.** Test the null hypothesis $H_0: \mu_1 = \mu_3$ versus a two-sided alternative, using $\alpha = 0.10$.

## 12.5

### The Randomized Block Design

In Section 12.2 the model for the completely randomized design was summarized in Equation 12.7 as

$$Y_{ij} = \bar{\mu} + \alpha_i + \varepsilon_{ij}, \qquad i = 1, 2, \ldots, k; j = 1, 2, \ldots, n$$

$$\text{with} \quad \varepsilon_{ij} \sim \text{NID}(0, \sigma^2) \quad \text{and} \quad \sum_{i=1}^{k} \alpha_i = 0 \qquad \text{12.46}$$

The expectation of $Y_{ij}$, the $i$th observation from the $j$th treatment (population), was given by

$$E(Y_{ij}) = \bar{\mu} + \alpha_i \qquad \text{12.47}$$

This expectation was considered to be composed of an overall effect ($\bar{\mu}$) plus an effect ($\alpha_i$) reflecting the fact that the observation is from the $i$th population. In this section the assumption about $Y_{ij}$ is that

$$Y_{ij} = \bar{\mu} + \alpha_i + \beta_j + \varepsilon_{ij}, \qquad i = 1, 2, \ldots, t; j = 1, 2, \ldots, b$$

$$\text{with} \quad \varepsilon_{ij} \sim \text{NID}(0, \sigma^2) \quad \text{and} \quad \sum_{i=1}^{t} \alpha_i = 0 \quad \text{and} \quad \sum_{j=1}^{b} \beta_j = 0$$

$$\text{12.48}$$

As before, $E(\varepsilon_{ij}) = 0$ and $\text{Var}(\varepsilon_{ij}) = \sigma^2$ for all pairs $(i, j)$. The observation $Y_{ij}$ is said to be the observation from block $j$ on treatment $i$. As Equation 12.48 indicates, it is assumed that there are $t$ different treatments and $b$ blocks. Hence the expectation of $Y_{ij}$ is

$$E(Y_{ij}) = \bar{\mu} + \alpha_i + \beta_j \qquad \textbf{12.49}$$

**block effect**   This expectation is composed additively of an overall effect ($\bar{\mu}$), a treatment effect ($\alpha_i$), and a **block effect** ($\beta_j$). Frequently we know that there is a difference in the expectations $E(Y_{ij})$ for different values of $j$—that is, the $\beta_j$ are not all zero. One task is to test the null hypothesis

$$H_0: \alpha_i = 0, \qquad i = 1, 2, \ldots, t \qquad \textbf{12.50}$$

which states that there are no treatment differences, although there may be nonzero $\beta_j$ values reflecting block differences.

Blocking was used implicitly in Example 8.9 of Chapter 8, where paired comparisons were employed to compare room usage at a university on Mondays and Wednesdays. The blocks in that case were the different hours of the day (9:00–10:00, 10:00–11:00, . . . , 5:00–6:00). It was known that there were substantial differences in room usage at different hours of the day. The paired comparisons procedure permitted comparison of room use on Monday and Wednesday (the treatment effects) given differences in room usage at different hours of the day. The basic idea was to use the differences in the number of classrooms in use on Monday and Wednesday for *each* of the nine scheduled hours.

**randomized block design**   The method of paired comparisons permits comparison of only two treatment responses. In **randomized block design** the number of treatment responses observed within a block is extended to $t \geqslant 2$. If the experimental units within a block are alike with regard to the blocking factor, any differences in treatment responses observed within a block should be attributable to the treatments.

As an illustration, consider comparing three methods of teaching algebra, given that the overall average performance of students in different schools is different. One way to compare teaching methods is to select five schools representing different overall ability levels, use the three teaching methods in three algebra classes in each school, and give a common final examination to all students in the classes involved in the experiment. The schools are the blocks in this experiment. Within a school (a block) the students have similar general academic levels, so differences in performance within a school can be attributed to the teaching methods. In this experiment the observation $Y_{ij}$ represents the average score on the final examination for students taught by method $i$ in school $j$. Here $i = 1, 2, 3$ and $j = 1, 2, 3, 4, 5$, so $t = 3$ and $b = 5$. An observation of each treatment is made within each block, so the total number of observations is $bt = 5(3) = 15$.

The observations in a randomized block situation can be represented by an array of the following type:

$$
\begin{array}{cccc}
Y_{11} & Y_{12} & \cdots & Y_{1b} \\
Y_{21} & Y_{22} & \cdots & Y_{2b} \\
Y_{i1} & Y_{i2} & \cdots & Y_{ib} \\
Y_{t1} & Y_{t2} & \cdots & Y_{tb}
\end{array}
$$

**12.51**

Each column of the array represents the observations in a block. The observation $y_{12}$ is the observation in block 2 on treatment 1. Clearly there are $t$ observations in each block, one in response to each of the treatments. As there are a total of $b$ blocks, there must be a total of $bt$ observations.

## Example 12.7

An article by Howard Warner and Carl M. Francolini in the *American Statistician* described two empirical studies carried out to determine the effectiveness of graphical forms. In these studies several map types were presented to subjects to determine the efficacy of different geographical forms. Four trials were made by each of eight subjects for each map type. The observation $Y_{ij}$ represents the response time (in ten-second units) of the $j$th subject on the $i$th trial for a particular map type. The results for eight subjects are presented in the table. A statistical

| | | | | Subject | | | | |
|---|---|---|---|---|---|---|---|---|
| Trial | 1 | 2 | 3 | 4 | 5 | 6 | 7 | 8 |
| 1 | 16 | 14 | 18 | 15 | 19 | 15 | 20 | 17 |
| 2 | 12 | 13 | 14 | 16 | 20 | 14 | 22 | 16 |
| 3 | 12 | 12 | 21 | 13 | 19 | 11 | 18 | 19 |
| 4 | 13 | 14 | 13 | 12 | 20 | 10 | 28 | 18 |

*Source:* H. Warner and C. M. Francolini, "An Empirical Enquiry Concerning Human Understanding of Two-Variable Color Maps," *American Statistician* 34 (1980): 89.

hypothesis of interest was $H_0$: $\alpha_i = 0$, $i = 1, 2, 3, 4$, which states that the response times for each trial are on average, the same. Here blocking was by subject, which makes sense, as some persons respond to a stimulus more quickly than do others. The treatments in this case are the trial numbers, so $t = 4$. The subjects are the blocks, so $b = 8$.

As in the $k$-sample situation, the total sum of squares in a randomized block design can be partitioned into individual sums of squares and each of these parts can be attributed to an individual factor or cause. It can be shown that

$$\sum_{i=1}^{t} \sum_{j=1}^{b} (Y_{ij} - \bar{Y})^2 = b \sum_{i=1}^{t} (\bar{Y}_{i.} - \bar{Y})^2 + t \sum_{j=1}^{b} (\bar{Y}_{.j} - \bar{Y})^2$$
$$+ \sum_{i=1}^{t} \sum_{j=1}^{b} (Y_{ij} - \bar{Y}_{i.} - \bar{Y}_{.j} + \bar{Y})^2 \qquad \textbf{12.52}$$

Here, the $i$th treatment mean is

$$\bar{Y}_{i.} = \sum_{j=1}^{b} \frac{Y_{ij}}{b}$$

the $j$th treatment mean is

$$\bar{Y}_{.j} = \sum_{i=1}^{t} \frac{Y_{ij}}{t}$$

and the overall mean is

$$\bar{Y} = \sum_{i=1}^{t} \sum_{j=1}^{b} \frac{Y_{ij}}{bt}$$

Expression 12.52 can be abbreviated as

$$\text{SST} = \text{SSA} + \text{SSB} + \text{SSE} \qquad \textbf{12.53}$$

where SST is the total sum of squares and SSA, SSB, and SSE are the sums of squares for treatments, blocks, and error, respectively. The sum of squares due to
**SSA** differences among treatments (**SSA**) is the sum of the squared deviations of the *treatment means* from the overall mean, multiplied by the constant $b$. The sum of squares for blocks (**SSB**) is the sum of the squared deviations of the *block means*
**SSB** from the overall mean, multiplied by the constant $t$. The sum of squares for error (SSE) has a less obvious form, but it can be thought of as the remaining portion of SST which is unexplained by the model given by Equation 12.48.

The decomposition of the total sum of squares (SST) is presented in the ANOVA table in Table 12.6. The degrees of freedom are partitioned as follows:

$$\text{d.f. (total)} = \text{d.f. (treatments)} + \text{d.f. (blocks)} + \text{d.f. (error)}$$
$$bt - 1 = (t - 1) + (b - 1) + (b - 1)(t - 1) \qquad \textbf{12.54}$$

**Table 12.6**

**ANOVA Table for the Randomized Block Design**

| Source | d.f. | SS | MS | EMS |
|--------|------|-----|-----|-----|
| Among Treatments | $t - 1$ | SSA | $\text{MSA} = \text{SSA}/(t - 1)$ | $\sigma^2 + b \sum_{i=1}^{t} \alpha_i^2/(t - 1)$ |
| Blocks | $b - 1$ | SSB | $\text{MSB} = \text{SSB}/(b - 1)$ | $\sigma^2 + t \sum_{j=1}^{b} \beta_j^2/(b - 1)$ |
| Error | $(b - 1)(t - 1)$ | SSE | $\text{MSE} = \text{SSE}/(b - 1)(t - 1)$ | $\sigma^2$ |
| Total | $tb - 1$ | SST | | |

It is easy to check that the left and right sides of Equation 12.54 are equal. As with the completely randomized design, the mean squares MSA, MSB, and MSE are found by dividing the appropriate sum of squares by the corresponding degrees of freedom. Expressions for the expected mean squares for the treatment, blocks, and error are given in the last column of Table 12.6. Again these are functions of the unknown parameters $\alpha_i$, $i = 1, 2, \ldots, t$; $\beta_j$, $j = 1, 2, \ldots, b$; and $\sigma^2$ and cannot be computed numerically. Note however that, as usual,

$$E(\text{MSE}) = \sigma^2 \qquad\qquad \textbf{12.55}$$

Thus the expected mean square for error depends only on $\sigma^2$ and not the values of the $\alpha_i$ or the $\beta_j$.

The expected mean square among treatments, given by

$$E(\text{MSA}) = \sigma^2 + b \sum_{i=1}^{t} \frac{\alpha_i^2}{t - 1} \qquad\qquad \textbf{12.56}$$

depends only on the treatment effects $\alpha_i$, $i = 1, 2, \ldots, t$ and $\sigma^2$, and *not* on the block effects $\beta_j$, $j = 1, 2, \ldots, b$. If the null hypothesis of no treatment differences given in Equation 12.50 is true, $E(\text{MSA}) = \sigma^2$, as all the $\alpha_i$ equal 0 under that null hypothesis. Then both MSA and MSE are unbiased estimates of $\sigma^2$. It can be further shown that, *under* $H_0$,

$$F = \frac{\text{MSA}}{\text{MSE}} \sim F[t - 1, (b - 1)(t - 1)] \qquad\qquad \textbf{12.57}$$

that is, the ratio of the mean square for treatments to the mean square for error has an $F$ distribution with $t - 1$ and $(b - 1)(t - 1)$ degrees of freedom. If $H_0$ is false, then $H_1$: $\alpha_i \neq 0$ for at least one value of $i$ is true, and the expected mean square among treatments will be *greater* than $\sigma^2$. Hence, using an $\alpha$ level test, we reject $H_0$ in favor of $H_1$ if

$$F = \frac{\text{MSA}}{\text{MSE}} \geqslant F_\alpha [t - 1, (b - 1)(t - 1)]$$

For reasons analogous to those given in Section 12.2 for the completely randomized design, a test of

$$H_0: \beta_j = 0, \quad j = 1, 2, \ldots, b \qquad \text{versus} \qquad H_1: H_0 \text{ false}$$

can be carried out using the critical region

$$F = \frac{\text{MSB}}{\text{MSE}} \geqslant F_\alpha [b - 1, (b - 1)(t - 1)]$$

## Example 12.8

In Exhibit 12.5, the 32 response time observations given in Example 12.7 were SET in C1 by blocks. The treatment (trial) numbers were SET in C2 and the block numbers in C3; thus column C2 consists of the trial numbers 1, 2, 3, 4 (in this order) repeated 8 times, and column C3 consists of the block numbers 1, 1, 1, 1, 2, 2, 2,

**Exhibit 12.5**

```
MTB > NOTE ANALYSIS OF RESPONSE TIME DATA (RANDOMIZED BLOCK)
MTB > SET C1
C1
    16    12    12    13    .    .    .

MTB > SET C2
C2
     1     2     3     4    .    .    .

MTB > SET C3
C3
     1     1     1     1    .    .    .

MTB > NAME C1 'SECONDS' NAME C2 'TRIAL' C3 'SUBJ'
MTB > PRINT C1-C3
 ROW   SECONDS   TRIAL    SUBJ

   1      16       1       1
   2      12       2       1
   3      12       3       1
   4      13       4       1
   5      14       1       2
   6      13       2       2
   7      12       3       2
   8      14       4       2
   9      18       1       3
  10      14       2       3
  11      21       3       3
  12      13       4       3
  13      15       1       4
  14      16       2       4
  15      13       3       4
  16      12       4       4
  17      19       1       5
  18      20       2       5
  19      19       3       5
  20      20       4       5
  21      15       1       6
  22      14       2       6
  23      11       3       6
  24      10       4       6
  25      20       1       7
  26      22       2       7
  27      18       3       7
  28      28       4       7
  29      17       1       8
  30      16       2       8
  31      19       3       8
  32      18       4       8
```

**TABLE**

**TWOWAY**

2, . . . , 8, 8, 8, 8. In Exhibit 12.6, the **TABLE** command was used with the subcommand MEAN to find the eight block (subject) means and the four treatment (trial) means and to compute the overall mean $\bar{y} = 16.062$. The **TWOWAY** command in Minitab was used to produce the required ANOVA table.

**Exhibit 12.6**

```
MTB > TABLE 'SUBJ' BY 'TRIAL';
SUBC> MEAN 'SECONDS'.
  ROWS: SUBJ      COLUMNS: TRIAL
            1         2        3        4      ALL

    1     16.000   12.000   12.000   13.000   13.250
    2     14.000   13.000   12.000   14.000   13.250
    3     18.000   14.000   21.000   13.000   16.500
    4     15.000   16.000   13.000   12.000   14.000
    5     19.000   20.000   19.000   20.000   19.500
    6     15.000   14.000   11.000   10.000   12.500
    7     20.000   22.000   18.000   28.000   22.000
    8     17.000   16.000   19.000   18.000   17.500
  ALL     16.750   15.875   15.625   16.000   16.062

  CELL CONTENTS --
          SECONDS:MEAN


MTB > TWOWAY AOV DATA IN C1 SUBSCRIPTS IN C2 C3

ANALYSIS OF VARIANCE   SECONDS

SOURCE        DF        SS         MS
TRIAL          3       5.62       1.87
SUBJ           7     328.37      46.91
ERROR         21     137.87       6.57
TOTAL         31     471.87
```

For these data we find that

$$F = \frac{\text{MSA}}{\text{MSE}} = \frac{1.87}{6.57} = 0.285$$

A critical region for a test of $H_0: \alpha_i = 0, i = 1, 2, 3, 4$ versus $H_1: H_0$ false is given by

$$F \geq F_{0.05}(3, 21) = 3.07$$

At the 5 percent significance level there is no evidence that reaction times differ as a result of trial number (that is, whether the subject is on the first trial, second trial, etc.). To carry out a test of the null hypothesis of $H_0: \beta_j = 0, j = 1, 2, \ldots, 6$ (that is, to test for block effects), we calculate $F = \text{MSB}/\text{MSE} = 46.91/6.57 = 7.14$. For $\alpha = 0.05$, the critical region for this test is

$$F = \frac{\text{MSB}}{\text{MSE}} \geq F_{0.05}(7, 21) = 2.49$$

Here $7.14 > 2.49$, so there is a significant difference in response times for different individuals. As noted in Example 12.7, it is not surprising that there are differences in response times due to blocks (individuals). When these differences are taken into account, however, there do not appear to be response differences due to treatments (trial number).

The expression for the estimated contrast of treatment means is analogous to Equation 12.36:

$$\sum_{i=1}^{t} c_i \bar{Y}_i \qquad \textbf{12.58}$$

where $\Sigma_{i=1}^{t} c_i = 0$. In order to find the expectation of the sample contrast of Expression 12.58, we find the expectation of $\bar{Y}_{i.}$:

$$\begin{aligned}
E(\bar{Y}_{i.}) &= E\left( \sum_{j=1}^{b} \frac{Y_{ij}}{b} \right) \\
&= \sum_{j=1}^{b} \frac{E(Y_{ij})}{b} \\
&= \sum_{j=1}^{b} \frac{\bar{\mu} + \alpha_i + \beta_j}{b} \\
&= \bar{\mu} + \alpha_i
\end{aligned}$$

(The last step above arises from the fact that $\Sigma_{j=1}^{b} \beta_j = 0$.) It then follows that

$$E\left( \sum_{i=1}^{t} c_i \bar{Y}_{i.} \right) = \sum_{i=1}^{t} c_i E(\bar{Y}_{i.}) = \sum_{i=1}^{t} c_i(\bar{\mu} + \alpha_i) = \sum_{i=1}^{t} c_i\alpha_i \qquad \textbf{12.59}$$

so the sample contrast is an unbiased estimator of $\Sigma_{i=1}^{t} c_i\alpha_i$, the corresponding linear combination of the *treatment* effects.

In randomized block design, both confidence intervals and tests of hypotheses for contrasts of the form $\Sigma_{i=1}^{t} c_i\alpha_i$ are based on the fact that

$$\frac{\displaystyle\sum_{i=1}^{t} c_i \bar{Y}_{i.} - \sum_{i=1}^{t} c_i\alpha_i}{\sqrt{\left( \dfrac{\text{MSE}}{b} \right)\left( \displaystyle\sum_{i=1}^{t} c_i^2 \right)}} = t \qquad \textbf{12.60}$$

that is, the approximation of the standardized sample contrast has the $t$ distribution with $(b - 1)(t - 1)$ degrees of freedom. The exact formula for the endpoints of

**Table 12.7**

| Critical Regions for Tests of Contrasts in the Randomized Block Situation | |
|---|---|
| Alternative | Critical Region |
| $\sum_{i=1}^{t} c_i\alpha_i > 0$ | $t \geqslant t_{\alpha,(b-1)(t-1)}$ |
| $\sum_{i=1}^{t} c_i\alpha_i < 0$ | $t \leqslant -t_{\alpha,(b-1)(t-1)}$ |
| $\sum_{i=1}^{t} c_i\alpha_i \neq 0$ | $\lvert t \rvert \geqslant t_{\alpha/2,(b-1)(t-1)}$ |

a confidence interval corresponds to Equation 12.41:

$$\sum_{i=1}^{t} c_i \bar{Y}_i \pm \sqrt{\left(\frac{\text{MSE}}{b}\right)\left(\sum_{i=1}^{t} c_i^2\right)}\ t_{\alpha/2,(b-1)(t-1)} \qquad \textbf{12.61}$$

The test statistic for testing the null hypothesis, $H_0: \sum_{i=1}^{t} c_i \alpha_i = 0$, is Expression 12.60 with $\sum_{i=1}^{t} c_i \alpha_i = 0$. The rejection regions for appropriate alternatives are given in Table 12.7.

## Example 12.9

A university admissions official wants to compare starting salaries for outstanding bachelor's level graduates in agriculture, engineering, the mathematical sciences, and the liberal arts. The starting salary of the university's top graduate in each of these areas is shown in the table, in dollars per month. Because salaries tend to

| | Year | | | | |
|---|---|---|---|---|---|
| Area | 1 | 2 | 3 | 4 | 5 |
| Agriculture | 1800 | 2000 | 2100 | 2300 | 2400 |
| Engineering | 2200 | 2600 | 2500 | 2600 | 2850 |
| Mathematical Sciences | 1900 | 2000 | 2200 | 2400 | 2500 |
| Liberal Arts | 1650 | 1750 | 1800 | 2100 | 2250 |

increase over time as a result of inflation, time is used as a blocking factor. The output generated by using the TABLE and TWOWAY commands with these data is presented in Exhibits 12.7 and 12.8.

We will test

$$H_0: \alpha_E - \frac{\alpha_A + \alpha_M + \alpha_{LA}}{3} = 0 \quad \text{versus} \quad H_1: \alpha_E - \frac{\alpha_A + \alpha_M + \alpha_{LA}}{3} > 0$$

The null hypothesis states that there is no difference between the average starting salary in engineering and the average of starting salaries in the other areas. The alternative hypothesis states that average engineering salaries are higher than the average of salaries in the other fields. Assuming a significance level of 0.05, we find the rejection region to be

$$t \geq t_{0.05,12} = 1.782$$

The calculated value of $t$ is

$$t = \left(2550 - \frac{2120 + 2200 + 2110}{3}\right) \Big/ \sqrt{\left(\frac{46604}{5}\right)\left(\frac{4}{3}\right)}$$

$$= \frac{406.67}{111.48} = 3.65$$

**Exhibit 12.7**

```
MTB > NOTE COMPARISON OF B.A./B.S. SALARIES OF OUTSTANDING GRADUATES
MTB > SET C1
C1
   1800    2000    2100    2300     .    .    .

MTB > END
MTB > SET C2
C2
    1     1     1     1     .    .    .

MTB > END
MTB > SET C3
C3
    1     2     3     4     .    .    .

MTB > END
MTB > NAME C1 'SALARY' NAME C2 'AREA' C3 'YEAR'
MTB > PRINT C1-C3
 ROW   SALARY    AREA    YEAR

   1    1800      1       1
   2    2000      1       2
   3    2100      1       3
   4    2300      1       4
   5    2400      1       5
   6    2200      2       1
   7    2600      2       2
   8    2500      2       3
   9    2600      2       4
  10    2850      2       5
  11    1900      3       1
  12    2000      3       2
  13    2200      3       3
  14    2400      3       4
  15    2500      3       5
  16    1650      4       1
  17    2750      4       2
  18    1800      4       3
  19    2100      4       4
  20    2250      4       5
```

The evidence clearly suggests that top graduates with engineering degrees receive higher starting salaries than do top graduates in the other fields. A point estimate for $\mu_E - (\mu_A + \mu_M + \mu_{LA})/3$ is given by

$$2550 - \frac{2120 + 2200 + 2110}{3} = 406.67$$

indicating that engineering graduates receive an additional \$406.67 per month. A 95 percent confidence interval for the difference between the starting salaries of engineers and the average starting salaries of graduates in other fields has endpoints given by

$$406.67 \pm \sqrt{\left(\frac{46604}{5}\right)\left(\frac{4}{3}\right)}\, t_{0.025,12} = 406.67 \pm 242.91$$

**Exhibit 12.8**

```
MTB > TABLE 'YEAR' BY 'AREA';
SUBC> MEAN 'SALARY'.
  ROWS: YEAR     COLUMNS: AREA
              1        2        3        4      ALL

     1    1800.0   2200.0   1900.0   1650.0   1887.5
     2    2000.0   2600.0   2000.0   2750.0   2337.5
     3    2100.0   2500.0   2200.0   1800.0   2150.0
     4    2300.0   2600.0   2400.0   2100.0   2350.0
     5    2400.0   2850.0   2500.0   2250.0   2500.0
   ALL    2120.0   2550.0   2200.0   2110.0   2245.0


   CELL CONTENTS --
           SALARY:MEAN


MTB > TWOWAY ANOVA FOR DATA IN C1 SUBSCRIPTS IN C2 C3

ANALYSIS OF VARIANCE   SALARY

SOURCE        DF        SS        MS
AREA           3     644500    214833
YEAR           4     885750    221437
ERROR         12     559250     46604
TOTAL         19    2089500
```

Hence the interval ($163.76, $649.58) is a 95 percent confidence for this initial monthly salary difference.

---

It should be emphasized that this chapter presents only a brief introduction to the analysis of variance. Only two basic designs have been discussed—the completely randomized design and the randomized block design. The subject of the analysis of variance is a very well developed one, and it remains interesting from both applied and theoretical points of view. The fundamental question is how to assign the variability of observed values to specific causes, and this issue is of importance to all scientific fields. Students who wish to study analysis of variance more deeply are encouraged to read the following references:

Dunn, Olive Jean, and Virginia Clark. *Applied Statistics: Analysis of Variance and Regression.* New York: John Wiley and Sons, 1974.

Neter, John, and William Wasserman. *Applied Linear Statistical Models.* Homewood, Illinois: Richard D. Irwin, 1974.

Ott, Lyman. *An Introduction to Statistical Methods and Data Analysis.* Boston: Duxbury Press, 1977.

**12.16** The data below represent the response times of eight subjects on four different trials of a scientific experiment.

|       |    |    |    | Subject |    |    |    |    |
|-------|----|----|----|----|----|----|----|----|
| Trial | 1  | 2  | 3  | 4  | 5  | 6  | 7  | 8  |
| 1     | 16 | 13 | 20 | 31 | 20 | 17 | 29 | 19 |
| 2     | 12 | 12 | 20 | 32 | 13 | 15 | 24 | 19 |
| 3     | 16 | 10 | 17 | 16 | 16 | 15 | 20 | 14 |
| 4     | 12 | 10 | 18 | 16 | 14 | 10 | 19 | 15 |

*Source:* H. Warner and C. M. Francolini, "An Empirical Enquiry Concerning Human Understanding of Two-Variable Color Maps," *American Statistician* 34 (1980): 89.

**a.** Use the TABLE and TWOWAY commands to find the subject and trial means and to construct an analysis of variance table.

**b.** Is there a significant effect ($\alpha = 0.05$) due to differences among subjects?

**c.** A reduction in mean response time in later trials suggests that learning is taking place. Do the data support this hypothesis? Test $H_0: (\alpha_1 + \alpha_2 + \alpha_3)/3 - \alpha_4 = 0$ versus $H_1: (\alpha_1 + \alpha_2 + \alpha_3)/3 > \alpha_4$. Use $\alpha = 0.05$.

**12.17** In an experiment based on a randomized block design, with four treatments in each of six blocks, the calculated $F$ value for a test of the equality of treatment means was 5. The value of SST was 1440, and the mean square for error was 24. Construct an ANOVA table for these data. *Note:* In the last column, $\sigma^2$, $\alpha_i$, and $\beta_j$ cannot be given numerical values because they are unknown parameters.

**12.18** The following is a partial analysis of variance table for a randomized block design.

| Source     | d.f. | SS  | MS  | EMS |
|------------|------|-----|-----|-----|
| Blocks     | 7    | 112 | ___ | ____ |
| Treatments | 5    | 66  | ___ | ____ |
| Error      | 35   | 70  | ___ | ____ |
| Total      | 47   | ___ |     |     |

**a.** Fill in the blanks in the ANOVA table.

**b.** What are the numbers of treatments, $t$, and blocks, $b$?

**c.** Given $\bar{y}_1 = 42$ and $\bar{y}_2 = 39$, test $H_0: \mu_1 = \mu_2$ versus a two-sided alternative.

**d.** Find a 95 percent confidence interval for $\mu_1 - \mu_2$, using the data of part c.

**12.19** A firm is interested in three ways of advertising a new product: TV advertising, newspaper ads, and store demonstrations. To test the effectiveness of these methods, each is tried in one of three stores in a block. The stores are assigned to blocks by size: very small, small, medium, and large. The data observed, sales per quarter for each of the stores (in thousands of dollars), are given in the table on page 486.

**a.** Use AOVONEWAY to test the null hypothesis $H_0: \mu_1 = \mu_2 = \mu_3$ for the three sales methods, with $\alpha = 0.05$.

**b.** Use TWOWAY to test the null hypothesis $H_0: \alpha_1 = \alpha_2 = \alpha_3$, where $\alpha_1$ is the effect of method 1 on sales, $\alpha_2$ is the effect of method 2, and $\alpha_3$ is the effect of method 3.

c. Compare the estimates of $\sigma^2$ for the analysis of variance methods used in parts a and b.

d. Is the blocking factor significant at the 0.05 level?

e. Find a 90 percent confidence interval for $\alpha_3 - (\alpha_1 + \alpha_2)/2$, using the randomized block design.

| Store Size | Sales Method | | |
|---|---|---|---|
| | 1 | 2 | 3 |
| Very small | 30 | 70 | 110 |
| Small | 50 | 80 | 160 |
| Medium | 60 | 100 | 180 |
| Large | 100 | 150 | 230 |

**12.20** Following are quarterly figures on sales (in thousands of pounds) of product X in eight cities in the United Kingdom.

| Sales (in thousands of pounds) | First Quarter | Second Quarter | Third Quarter | Fourth Quarter |
|---|---|---|---|---|
| Sheffield | 230 | 220 | 190 | 220 |
| Leeds | 280 | 260 | 220 | 340 |
| Edinburgh | 140 | 130 | 130 | 210 |
| Hull | 70 | 81 | 71 | 84 |
| Swansea | 62 | 66 | 62 | 77 |
| Plymouth | 41 | 44 | 33 | 50 |
| Luton | 23 | 27 | 23 | 27 |
| Bolton | 31 | 29 | 25 | 29 |

*Source:* A. S. C. Ehrenberg, "The Problem of Numeracy," *American Statistician* 35 (1981): 68.

a. Use TWOWAY to create an ANOVA table for these data.

b. Letting the cities be blocks, test whether there is a quarterly sales effect. Use $\alpha = 0.05$.

**12.21** The following leukemia cell counts were taken after 2, 4, and 12 hours from cultures in three different test tubes, A, B, and C.

| Time | Test Tube | | |
|---|---|---|---|
| | A | B | C |
| 2 hours | 5.55 | 5.16 | 5.46 |
| 4 hours | 5.58 | 5.18 | 5.22 |
| 12 hours | 12.16 | 2.83 | 2.51 |

A. O. Williams and M. C. Path, "Ultra-structural Changes in Murine Leukemia Cells Exposed to L-asparaginase in Vitro," *American Journal of Chemical Pathology* 54 (1970): 659.

a. Using a randomized block design, create the appropriate ANOVA table, omitting the EMS column.

**b.** Test the null hypothesis $H_0: \alpha_A = \alpha_B = \alpha_C$ (the average cell counts are equal in the three tubes). Use $\alpha = 0.05$.

**12.22** In the *American Statistician*, Charles J. Monlezun presented the following data from a hypothetical agricultural experiment. Factor A represents the brand of seed, and factor B represents the type of soil. The response observed is crop yield in bushels per acre.

| | Type of Soil (B) | | | |
|---|---|---|---|---|
| Brand of Seed (A) | 1 | 2 | 3 | 4 |
| 1 | 50 | 35 | 65 | 90 |
| 2 | 70 | 80 | 75 | 40 |
| 3 | 40 | 70 | 55 | 60 |

Charles J. Monlezun, "Two-Dimensional Plots for Interpreting Interaction in the Three-Factor Analysis of Variance," *American Statistician* 33, No. 2 (1979): 67.

**a.** Create an ANOVA table for these data using TWOWAY.
**b.** Which factor is a more natural choice for the blocking factor?
**c.** Test the null hypothesis that there is no difference among the treatments, using $\alpha = 0.05$.

## Summary

The basic idea of analysis of variance is to decompose the overall variability (expressed as the sum of the squares of the deviations of all observations from the overall average) into parts, each of which can be attributed to a particular cause. If an individual sum of squares is large enough, we can conclude that its cause is significant.

In the $k$-sample situation, $n_i$ observations are taken from each of $i = 1, 2, \ldots, k$ populations that are assumed to be normally distributed, with common variance $\sigma^2$ but possibly different means $\mu_1, \mu_2, \ldots, \mu_k$. The null hypothesis to be tested is

$$H_0: \mu_1 = \mu_2 = \cdots = \mu_k$$

that is, all the populations have the same expectation and hence a common distribution. The alternative hypothesis is

$$H_1: \mu_i \neq \mu_j \text{ for some values } i \neq j$$

If the $k$ populations represent responses to different treatments, the rejection of $H_0$ indicates that there is a significant treatment effect. This design is referred to as the completely randomized design.

The basic decomposition of the variability in the completely randomized design is of the form SST = SSA + SSE. The total variability of the observations (SST) is partitioned into two parts. The first is a sum of squares due to differences among treatments (SSA). It will tend to be large if there are true treatment differences. The second, the sum of squares for error (SSE), is the unexplained portion of the variability. Using the notation $N = \Sigma_{i=1}^{k} n_i$, two mean squares may be defined:

$$\text{MSA} = \frac{\text{SSA}}{k-1} \quad \text{and} \quad \frac{\text{MSE}}{N-k}$$

A test of the null and alternative hypotheses may be based on the $F$ statistic, $F = \text{MSA}/\text{MSE}$, where the values $k - 1$ and $N - k$ are the appropriate numerator and denominator degrees of freedom. In the case of equal sample sizes, these reduce to $k - 1$ and $k(n - 1)$, respectively.

Contrasts are linear combinations of the form

$$\sum_{i=1}^{k} c_i \mu_i$$

where $\sum_{i=1}^{k} c_i = 0$. For example, the contrast

$$\frac{\mu_1 + \mu_2 + \mu_3}{3} - \mu_4$$

would be used to compare the expectation of population 4 with the average of the expectations of populations 1, 2, and 3. The sample estimate of a contrast is given by

$$\sum_{i=1}^{k} c_i \bar{Y}_i$$

where the $\bar{Y}_i$ are the sample means for the observations from the $i$th population. Both estimation and hypothesis testing for contrasts are based on Student's $t$ distribution.

Blocking involves arranging experimental units that are similar with respect to the blocking factor into blocks of size $t$. The treatments are then randomly applied within each of the $b$ blocks. The total variability is partitioned into sums of squares for treatments, blocks, and error: $\text{SST} = \text{SSA} + \text{SSB} + \text{SSE}$. The $F$ statistic $F = \text{MSA}/\text{MSE}$ permits testing for the existence of an effect due to treatments in the face of existing block effects. Blocking is essentially an extension of the paired comparisons procedure introduced in Chapter 8, in which experimental units within a pair were selected to be as similar as possible with regard to extraneous factors (those not associated with the two treatments being compared). The paired comparisons procedure is an example of blocking in which there are only two units in each block. The basic idea of blocking is to reduce the amount of unexplained variability in order to make a test more sensitive to the existence of treatment differences. As in the completely randomized design, in the randomized block design inference for contrasts or comparisons of treatment effects is based on Student's $t$ distribution.

analysis of variance
block effect
completely randomized design
contrast
controls
$k$-sample problem
linear combination
mean square among treatments
  (MSA)

randomized block design
SSA
SSB
SSE
SST
unequal sample size

AOVONEWAY          TABLE          TWOWAY
DOTPLOT

# Appendix A

## A Review of Some Mathematical Notation and Topics

### A.1
**The Greek Alphabet**

Greek letters are used frequently in mathematics to denote algebraic quantities. Table A.1 presents the letters of the Greek alphabet in their lower- and upper-case forms, together with their English language names.

In statistics, particular Greek letters are commonly used to denote specific quantities. Knowledge of these standard meanings is helpful, particularly in reading journal articles in fields in which statistical reasoning is used. Some of the most common usages are given in Table A.2.

### A.2
**Summation Notation**

The Greek symbol $\Sigma$ is used to indicate the summation operation. Expressions such as

$$\sum_{i=1}^{n} \frac{x_i}{n} = \bar{x} \quad \text{and} \quad \sum_{i=1}^{n} \frac{(x_i - \bar{x})^2}{n - 1} = s^2$$

are found in every statistics textbook.

The values assigned to the subscript $i$ determine the range of the summation. The first value of $i$ is given below the $\Sigma$ sign, and the last value of $i$ is given above the $\Sigma$ sign. The sum is over all integral values of $i$ from the first to

**Table A.1**

**The Greek Alphabet**

| Greek Letter | English Name | Greek Letter | English Name |
|---|---|---|---|
| $\alpha$, A | Alpha | $\nu$, N | Nu |
| $\beta$, B | Beta | $\xi$, $\Xi$ | Xi |
| $\gamma$, $\Gamma$ | Gamma | $o$, O | Omicron |
| $\delta$, $\Delta$ | Delta | $\pi$, $\Pi$ | Pi |
| $\varepsilon$, E | Epsilon | $\varrho$, P | Rho |
| $\zeta$, Z | Zeta | $\sigma$, $\Sigma$ | Sigma |
| $\eta$, H | Eta | $\tau$, T | Tau |
| $\theta$, $\Theta$ | Theta | $\upsilon$, $\Upsilon$ | Upsilon |
| $\iota$, I | Iota | $\phi$, $\Phi$ | Phi |
| $\kappa$, K | Kappa | $\chi$, X | Chi |
| $\lambda$, $\Lambda$ | Lambda | $\psi$, $\Psi$ | Psi |
| $\mu$, M | Mu | $\omega$, $\Omega$ | Omega |

the last. Thus the expression $\sum_{i=1}^{n} x_i$ means the sum of the $n$ quantities $x_1$, $x_2$, ..., $x_n$. If $x_1 = 4$, $x_2 = 3$, $x_3 = 8$, $x_4 = 9$, $x_5 = 6$,

$$\sum_{i=1}^{5} x_i = x_1 + x_2 + x_3 + x_4 + x_5 = 4 + 3 + 8 + 9 + 6 = 30$$

Similarly, $\sum_{i=1}^{n} x_i/n$ represents the average of $n$ values $x_1$, $x_2$, ..., $x_n$, universally denoted by $\bar{x}$. In the case of the five numbers given above,

$$\bar{x} = \sum_{i=1}^{5} \frac{x_i}{5} = \frac{30}{5} = 6$$

The general meaning of the summation sign is stated formally in the following definition.

**Table A.2**

**Standard Statistical Meanings of Greek Letters**

| Letter | Statistical Meaning |
|---|---|
| $\alpha$ (alpha) | The probability of a Type I error |
| $\beta$ (beta) | The probability of a Type II error |
| $\theta$ (theta) | A general unknown population parameter |
| $\mu$ (mu) | The population expectation or mean |
| $\varrho$ (rho) | The theoretical correlation coefficient |
| $\sigma$ (sigma) | The population standard deviation |
| $\chi$ (chi) (as $\chi^2$) | An important statistical distribution called the chi-square distribution |

## Definition A.1 ▬▬▬▬▬▬

Let $f(i)$ represent a specific function of $i$. Then

$$\sum_{i=j}^{k} f(i) = f(j) + f(j+1) + f(j+2) + \cdots + f(k)$$

where $j$ and $k$ are integers such that $j \leqslant k$.

In this case the first value of $i$ is $j$ and the last value of $i$ is $k$, so the summation is over all integers from $i = j$ to $i = k$. The expression being summed is given by $f(i)$. Letting $f(i) = x_i^2$ and using the five values of $x_i$ given in the previous paragraph, we have

$$\sum_{i=1}^{5} x_i^2 = x_1^2 + x_2^2 + x_3^2 + x_4^2 + x_5^2 = 4^2 + 3^2 + 8^2 + 9^2 + 6^2$$
$$= 16 + 9 + 64 + 81 + 36 = 206$$

The expression

$$\sum_{i=1}^{n} \frac{(x_i - \bar{x})^2}{n-1}$$

represents the sum of the squares of the differences of each of $n$ values $x_i$ from their average $\bar{x}$, divided by one less than $n$. This quantity, called the sample variance, is usually denoted by $s^2$. For the five values given above, we have

$$s^2 = \sum_{i=1}^{5} \frac{(x_i - \bar{x})^2}{5-1}$$
$$= \frac{(4-6)^2 + (3-6)^2 + (8-6)^2 + (9-6)^2 + (6-6)^2}{4}$$
$$= \frac{4 + 9 + 4 + 9 + 0}{4} = 6.5$$

In this case, $f(i) = (x_i - \bar{x})^2/4$.

For the values $x_1 = 7$, $x_2 = 4$, $x_3 = 2$, $x_4 = 5$, $x_5 = 7$, and $x_6 = 11$,

$$\sum_{i=1}^{6} x_i = x_1 + x_2 + x_3 + x_4 + x_5 + x_6$$
$$= 7 + 4 + 2 + 5 + 7 + 11 = 36$$
$$\sum_{i=4}^{6} x_i = x_4 + x_5 + x_6 = 5 + 7 + 11 = 23$$
$$\sum_{i=1}^{6} x_i^3 = x_1^3 + x_2^3 + x_3^3 + x_4^3 + x_5^3 + x_6^3$$
$$= 7^3 + 4^3 + 2^3 + 5^3 + 7^3 + 11^3 = 2214$$

$$\sum_{i=3}^{5} \left( \frac{1}{x_i} \right) = \left( \frac{1}{x_3} \right) + \left( \frac{1}{x_4} \right) + \left( \frac{1}{x_5} \right) = \frac{1}{2} + \frac{1}{5} + \frac{1}{7} = \frac{59}{70}$$

$$\sum_{i=1}^{6} \left( \frac{x_i}{6} \right) = \bar{x} = \frac{36}{6} = 6$$

$$\sum_{i=1}^{6} (x_i - \bar{x}) = (7 - 6) + (4 - 6) + (2 - 6) + (5 - 6)$$
$$+ (7 - 6) + (11 - 6) = 0$$

$$\sum_{i=1}^{6} (x_i - \bar{x})^2 = 1^2 + (-2)^2 + (-4)^2 + (-1)^2 + 1^2 + 5^2 = 48$$

$$\sum_{i=1}^{6} \frac{(x_i - \bar{x})^2}{6 - 1} = s^2 = \frac{48}{5} = 9.6$$

$$\sum_{i=1}^{6} \bar{x} = \bar{x} + \bar{x} + \bar{x} + \bar{x} + \bar{x} + \bar{x} = 6\bar{x} = 36$$

$$\sum_{i=1}^{5} (x_{i+1} - x_i) = (x_2 - x_1) + (x_3 - x_2) + (x_4 - x_3) + (x_5 - x_4)$$
$$+ (x_6 - x_5)$$
$$= x_6 - x_1 = 11 - 7 = 4$$

We will now consider several properties of the summation symbol. Although here the sums are taken from $i = 1$ to $i = n$ because these are the limits typically used with sample data, the properties apply as well to other ranges of the index $i$.

---

**Property A.1**

For any constant $c$,

$$\sum_{i=1}^{n} c = cn$$

---

**Property A.2**

For any constant $c$,

$$\sum_{i=1}^{n} cx_i = c \sum_{i=1}^{n} x_i$$

---

**Property A.3**

$$\sum_{i=1}^{n} (x_i \pm y_i) = \sum_{i=1}^{n} x_i \pm \sum_{i=1}^{n} y_i$$

---

Property A.1 says that the value of the summation of $n$ repetitions of a constant $c$ is $cn$. Property A.2 states that a multiplicative constant $c$ may be factored from each term of a summation. Property A.3 states that if each term in a sum is itself a sum (or difference) of two values, the entire sum is equal to the sum (or difference) of the first values plus (or minus) the sum of the second values.

Let $x_1 = 7$, $x_2 = 4$, $x_3 = 2$, $x_4 = 5$, $x_5 = 7$, and $x_6 = 11$, as before, and let $y_1 = 1$, $y_2 = 2$, $y_3 = 3$, $y_4 = 4$, $y_5 = 5$, and $y_6 = 6$. Then

$$\sum_{i=1}^{6} y_i = 21$$

$$\sum_{i=1}^{6} 4x_i = 4 \sum_{i=1}^{6} x_i = 4(36) = 144$$

$$\sum_{i=1}^{6} (x_i + y_i) = 8 + 6 + 5 + 9 + 12 + 17 = 57$$

$$= \sum_{i=1}^{6} x_i + \sum_{i=1}^{6} y_i = 36 + 21 = 57$$

$$\sum_{i=1}^{6} (x_i - y_i) = 6 + 2 + (-1) + 1 + 2 + 5 = 15$$

$$= \sum_{i=1}^{6} x_i - \sum_{i=1}^{6} y_i = 36 - 21 = 15$$

$$\sum_{i=1}^{6} (x_i - \bar{x}) = \sum_{i=1}^{6} x_i - \sum_{i=1}^{6} \bar{x} = \sum_{i=1}^{6} x_i - 6\bar{x} = 36 - 6(6) = 0$$

$$\sum_{i=1}^{6} (x_i^2 - y_i^2) = \sum_{i=1}^{6} (x_i + y_i)(x_i - y_i)$$

$$= 8(6) + 6(2) + 5(-1) + 9(1) + 12(2) + 17(5) = 173$$

$$= \sum_{i=1}^{6} x_i^2 - \sum_{i=1}^{6} y_i^2 = 264 - 91 = 173$$

Two additional properties of the summation operation are important in statistics. The following two properties are valid for any set of numbers $x_1, x_2, \ldots, x_n$.

---

**Property A.4** ▬▬▬▬▬▬▬▬▬▬▬▬▬▬▬▬▬▬▬▬▬▬▬▬▬▬▬▬

$$\sum_{i=1}^{n} (x_i - \bar{x}) = 0$$

where $\bar{x}$ is the average of $x_1, x_2, \ldots, x_n$.

---

## Property A.5

$$\sum_{i=1}^{n} (x_i - \bar{x})^2 = \sum_{i=1}^{n} x_i^2 - n(\bar{x})^2 = \sum_{i=1}^{n} x_i^2 - \frac{\left(\sum_{i=1}^{n} x_i\right)^2}{n}$$

The first of these properties is proved by writing

$$\sum_{i=1}^{n} (x_i - \bar{x}) = \sum_{i=1}^{n} x_i - \sum_{i=1}^{n} \bar{x} = \sum_{i=1}^{n} x_i - n\bar{x} = \sum_{i=1}^{n} x_i - \sum_{i=1}^{n} x_i = 0$$

The reader should be able to justify each step. The proof of the second property is somewhat more complicated.

$$\sum_{i=1}^{n} (x_i - \bar{x})^2 = \sum_{i=1}^{n} [x_i^2 - 2\bar{x}x_i + (\bar{x})^2] \qquad \text{(Squaring)}$$

$$= \sum_{i=1}^{n} x_i^2 - \sum_{i=1}^{n} 2\bar{x}x_i + \sum_{i=1}^{n} (\bar{x})^2 \qquad \text{(Property A.3)}$$

$$= \sum_{i=1}^{n} x_i^2 - 2\bar{x} \sum_{i=1}^{n} x_i + n(\bar{x})^2 \qquad \text{(Properties A.2, A.1)}$$

$$= \sum_{i=1}^{n} x_i^2 - 2\bar{x}(n\bar{x}) + n(\bar{x})^2 \qquad \text{(Definition of } \bar{x})$$

$$= \sum_{i=1}^{n} x_i^2 - n(\bar{x})^2 \qquad \text{(Algebra)}$$

$$= \sum_{i=1}^{n} x_i^2 - n\left(\sum_{i=1}^{n} \frac{x_i}{n}\right)^2 \qquad \text{(Definition of } \bar{x})$$

$$= \sum_{i=1}^{n} x_i^2 - \frac{\left(\sum x_i\right)^2}{n} \qquad \text{(Algebra)}$$

## Exercises A.2

**A.1** Let $x_1 = 40$, $x_2 = 50$, $x_3 = 30$, $x_4 = 20$, and $x_5 = 10$. Find the values of the following:

**a.** $\Sigma_{i=1}^{5} x_i$     **c.** $\Sigma_{i=1}^{5} (x_i - \bar{x})$

**b.** $\bar{x}$         **d.** $\Sigma_{i=1}^{5} \bar{x}$

**A.2** Let $x_1 = 5$, $x_2 = 2$, $x_3 = 1$, $x_4 = 3$, and $x_5 = 1$ be the number of children living at home in five households.

**a.** Find $\bar{x}$, the average number of children living at home in these five households.

**b.** Find $\Sigma_{i=1}^{5}(x_i - \bar{x})^2$ and $s^2$, the sample variance for these five observations.

**A.3** Use the values of $x_i$ given in exercise A.2 and the values $y_1 = 3$, $y_2 = 6$, $y_3 = 1$, $y_4 = 2$, and $y_5 = 3$ to find the following:

**a.** $\sum_{i=1}^{5} y_i$          **e.** $\sum_{i=1}^{5} (y_i - \bar{y})^2$

**b.** $\sum_{i=1}^{5} (y_i - x_i)$    **f.** $s_y^2$

**c.** $\bar{y} - \bar{x}$          **g.** $\bar{d}$ for $d_i = y_i - x_i$

**d.** $\sum_{i=1}^{5} (y_i - \bar{y})$    **h.** $\sum_{i=1}^{5} (d_i - \bar{d})^2$ for $d_i$ as in part g.

**A.4** Let $x_i = i$, $i = 1, 2, \ldots, 6$ and $y_i = 1/i$, $i = 1, 2, \ldots, 6$. Find the following:

**a.** $\sum_{i=1}^{6} x_i$        **d.** $\sum_{i=1}^{6} (x_i - y_i)$

**b.** $\sum_{i=1}^{6} x_i y_i$      **e.** $\sum_{i=1}^{6} x_i^2$

**c.** $\sum_{i=1}^{6} x_i / y_i$     **f.** $\sum_{i=1}^{6} (x_i)^i$

**A.5** Let $x_1 = 2$, $x_2 = 4$, $x_3 = 6$, $x_4 = 8$ and $y_1 = 1$, $y_2 = 3$, $y_3 = 5$, $y_4 = 7$. Find the following:

**a.** $\sum_{i=1}^{4} (x_i - y_i)$     **c.** $\sum_{i=1}^{4} y_i / x_i$

**b.** $\sum_{i=1}^{4} (x_i + y_i)$     **d.** $\sum_{i=1}^{4} x_i / y_i$

**A.6** The following is a valid formula for the sum of the first $n$ integers:

$$\sum_{i=1}^{n} i = \frac{n(n+1)}{2}$$

**a.** Verify this formula for $n = 1, 2, 3, 4$, and 5 by finding the value of both sides of the given expression.

**b.** Find the value of the average of the first $n$ integers, using the formula.

**A.7** The following is a valid formula for the sum of the squares of the first $n$ integers:

$$\sum_{i=1}^{n} i^2 = \frac{n(n+1)(2n+1)}{6}$$

**a.** Verify this formula for $n = 1, 2, 3, 4$, and 5.

**b.** Find the value of

$$\sum_{i=1}^{n} \left(i - \frac{n+1}{2}\right)^2$$

using Property A.5 and the result of part b of exercise A.6.

**A.8** **a.** Is

$$\sum_{i=1}^{n} x_i^2 = \frac{\left(\sum_{i=1}^{n} x_i\right)^2}{n}$$

true for all possible values of $x_i$ and $n$? Why or why not?

**b.** Show that the relationship in part a is true for $x_i = c$, $i = 1, 2, \ldots, n$ for a constant $c$.

**c.** Using Property A.5, show that the relationship in part a can be true only in the situation specified in part b.

**A.9** Let $r$ be a number satisfying $|r| < 1$. Consider the finite geometric series

$$S_n = \sum_{i=1}^{n} r^i = 1 + r + r^2 + \cdots + r^n$$

**a.** Show that $(1 - r)S_n = 1 - r^{n+1}$, so $S_n = (1 - r^{n+1})/(1 - r)$.

**b.** As $n$ gets large $(n \to \infty)$, $r^n$ approaches zero. Using this fact, show that $S_n$ approaches $1/(1 - r)$ as $n \to \infty$.

**c.** Find the value of $S_n$ for $r = 1/2$ and the limiting value of $S_n$ as $n \to \infty$. What is the limiting value of $1/2 + (1/2)^2 + \cdots + (1/2)^n$ as $n \to \infty$?

## A.3

**The Equation of a Straight Line**

In many cases, a dependent variable $y$ can be described as being (at least approximately) linearly related to an independent variable $x$. A linear relationship exists whenever the graph of $y$ as a function of $x$ is a straight line. For example, the velocity of an object falling in a vacuum (acted on only by the force of gravity) is a linear function of the time that the object has been falling. The relationship between the Fahrenheit measurement of temperature and the Celsius measurement of temperature is another example of a linear relationship.

A linear function is determined completely by the slope of the line and the value of the function for $x = 0$. The slope and $y$-intercept of a line are indicated in Figure A.1. The slope $m$ gives the change in the dependent variable $y$ for a unit change in $x$. The value of the $y$-intercept is the height of the line above or below the $x$-axis when $x = 0$.

---

**Definition A.2** ▬▬▬▬▬▬▬▬▬▬▬▬▬▬▬▬▬▬▬▬▬▬▬▬▬▬▬▬▬▬

The **slope-intercept equation** of a line is given by

$$y = mx + b$$

Any function of this form, where $m$ and $b$ are constants, will graph as a straight line.

---

Consider the simple example $y = 2x + 3$. The slope of this line is $m = 2$, and the $y$-intercept is $b = 3$. The values of this linear function for certain values of $x$ are given below.

| $x$ | $-3$ | $-2$ | $-1$ | $0$ | $1$ | $2$ | $3$ |
|---|---|---|---|---|---|---|---|
| $y$ | $-3$ | $-1$ | $1$ | $3$ | $5$ | $7$ | $9$ |

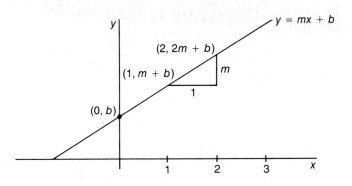

**Figure A.1**

Graph of $y = mx + b$

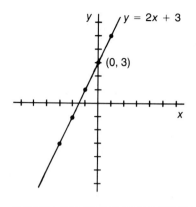

**Figure A.2**

Graph of $y = 2x + 3$

It is clear from these values that if $x$ increases by 1 unit, $y$ increases by 2 units. The value of the $y$-intercept is 3. A graph of this line is given in Figure A.2.

A linear function of $x$ is also fully determined by the slope of the line and a point $(x_0, y_0)$ that lies on the line.

**Definition A.3**

The **point-slope equation** of a line of slope $m$ passing through the point $(x_0, y_0)$ is given by

$$y = m(x - x_0) + y_0$$

This point-slope equation of a line can easily be transformed into the slope-intercept form, as $m(x - x_0) + y_0 = mx + (y_0 - mx_0)$.

Suppose a line with slope $-2$ passes through $(-1, 4)$. The equation of this line is given by

$$y = -2(x + 1) + 4 = -2x + 2$$

The table below shows various values of $y$ and corresponding values of $x$ for this linear function.

| $x$ | $-3$ | $-2$ | $-1$ | $0$ | $1$ | $2$ | $3$ |
|---|---|---|---|---|---|---|---|
| $y$ | 8 | 6 | 4 | 2 | 0 | $-2$ | $-4$ |

The line is plotted in Figure A.3.

A third method of defining a linear function of $x$ is to give two points, $(x_0, y_0)$ and $(x_1, y_1)$, that lie on the line. There is only one line passing through these two points.

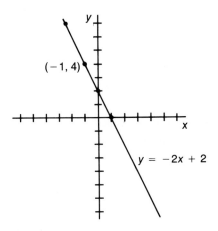

**Figure A.3**

Graph of $y = -2x + 2$

---

**Definition A.4** ▬▬▬▬▬▬▬▬▬▬▬▬▬▬▬▬▬▬▬▬▬▬▬

The equation of a line passing through $(x_0, y_0)$ and $(x_1, y_1)$ is

$$y = \left(\frac{y_1 - y_0}{x_1 - x_0}\right) x + \frac{x_1 y_0 - y_1 x_0}{x_1 - x_0}, \qquad x_1 \neq x_0$$

It is clear that the slope of such a line must be $m = (y_1 - y_0)/(x_1 - x_0)$, because if $x$ changes by $(x_1 - x_0)$ units, $y$ changes by $(y_1 - y_0)$ units. The intercept term $b = (x_1 y_0 - y_1 x_0)/(x_1 - x_0)$ is chosen so that when $x = x_0$, $y = y_0$ and when $x = x_1, y = y_1$. This fact may be verified by simple substitution into the equation given in Definition A.4.

Consider the relationship between the Fahrenheit ($y$) and Celsius ($x$) temperature scales. At $y = 32$, the freezing point of water, we have $x = 0$. At $y = 212$, the boiling point of water, we have $x = 100$. Hence the points $(0, 32)$ and $(100, 212)$ determine $y$ as a function of $x$. From Definition A.4 we have

$$m = \frac{212 - 32}{100 - 0} = \frac{180}{100} = \frac{9}{5}$$

and

$$b = \frac{100(32) - 212(0)}{100 - 0} = 32$$

Thus $y = (9/5)x + 32$ is the equation that gives Fahrenheit temperature as a linear function of Celsius temperature.

## Exercises A.3

**A.10** Find the equation of the line with $y$-intercept $-4$ and slope 2.

**A.11** A line has equation $y = 3x - 2$. What are the slope and $y$-intercept of this line?

**A.12** Find the equation of a line with slope 4 passing through the point (2, 3).

**A.13** The equation of a line is $y = -2(x - 4) + 2$. Find the slope of the line and the value of $x_0$, given that $(x_0, 2)$ lies on this line.

**A.14** Find the slope and the equation of the line passing through (2, 4) and (4, 9).

**A.15** What is the equation of the relationship between weight in pounds ($y$) and weight in ounces ($x$)?

**A.16** Find the Fahrenheit temperature corresponding to 25°C; to 5°C; to $-15$°C.

**A.17** If it is 0° Fahrenheit, what is the Celsius temperature?

**A.18** Suppose the fixed cost of producing $x$ units of a product is 1.5 (in thousands of dollars) and the variable cost is \$5.00 per unit. Express the cost $y$ (in thousands of dollars) as a linear function of $x$.

**A.19** Two lines, $y = mx + b$ and $y = m'x + b$, are perpendicular if and only if $mm' = -1$. Find the line perpendicular to the line in exercise A.12 passing through (2, 3).

**A.20** Two lines are parallel if they have the same slope. Find the line parallel to the line in exercise A.11 through $(-1, 4)$.

**A.21** Find the equation of the line intersecting the parabola $y = x^2$ at (0, 0) and (1, 1).

## A.4

## Factorial Notation and Binomial Coefficients

Factorial notation provides a convenient way of designating the product of all the positive integers from $k$ down to 1.

---

**Definition A.5** ▬▬▬

The product $k(k - 1)(k - 2) \cdots 3 \cdot 2 \cdot 1 = k!$ is called $k$ **factorial**.

---

For example,

$$1! = 1$$
$$2! = (2)1 = 2$$
$$3! = (3)(2)1 = 6$$
$$4! = (4)(3)(2)1 = 24$$
$$5! = (5)(4)(3)(2)1 = 120$$

and so forth.

Factorials are extremely useful for expressing binomial coefficients. The binomial coefficient $_nC_k$ or $\binom{n}{k}$ (read as "$n$ choose $k$") represents the number of distinct subsets of size $k$ that can be taken from a set $S$ of size $n$. Consider the set $S = \{A, B, C, D\}$, which has $n = 4$ elements. There are six subsets of size two, which may be listed as follows:

$$S_1 = \{A, B\} \quad S_2 = \{A, C\} \quad S_3 = \{A, D\}$$
$$S_4 = \{B, C\} \quad S_5 = \{B, D\} \quad S_6 = \{C, D\}$$

Hence, $_4C_2 = \binom{4}{2} = 6$.

The following general expression for the binomial coefficient is given in terms of factorial notation.

---

**Definition A.6** ▬▬▬▬▬▬▬▬▬▬▬▬▬▬▬▬▬▬

The number of subsets of size $k$ that can be taken from a set of size $n$ is

$$_nC_k = \binom{n}{k} = \frac{n!}{k!(n-k)!}$$

---

To check the validity of this definition for $n = 4$ and $k = 2$, we calculate

$$_4C_2 = \binom{4}{2} = \frac{4!}{2!2!} = \frac{24}{4} = 6$$

Some other examples of the binomial coefficient are shown below:

$$\binom{5}{1} = \frac{5!}{1!4!} = \frac{120}{24} = 5$$

$$\binom{5}{2} = \frac{5!}{2!3!} = \frac{120}{12} = 10$$

$$\binom{5}{3} = \frac{5!}{3!2!} = \frac{120}{12} = 10$$

$$\binom{5}{4} = \frac{5!}{4!1!} = \frac{120}{24} = 5$$

Following are several important properties of the binomial coefficient $\binom{n}{k}$.

---

**Property A.6** ▬▬▬▬▬▬▬▬▬▬▬▬▬▬▬▬▬▬

The value of 0! is defined to be 1.

---

Notice that $S$ has only one subset of size $n$—namely, the whole set $S$. Hence $\binom{n}{n} = 1$. As

$$\binom{n}{n} = \frac{n!}{n!0!}$$

by Definition A.6, 0! must be equal to 1, or else the definition would fail for $k = n$.

### Property A.7

The binomial coefficients $\binom{n}{k}$ and $\binom{n}{n-k}$ are equal.

Property A.7 must be valid for $k = 1, 2, \ldots, n - 1$, because for each subset of size $k$ chosen from a set of size $n$, there is a distinct subset of size $n - k$—namely, those elements not chosen. The converse is also true—for every subset of $n - k$ elements not chosen, there is a distinct subset of size $k$ that is chosen. In order for Property A.7 to be valid for $k = n$, $\binom{n}{n}$ must be equal to $\binom{n}{0}$. As

$$\binom{n}{n} = 1$$

$\binom{n}{0}$ must be equal to 1. The binomial coefficient

$$\binom{n}{0} = \frac{n!}{0!n!} = 1$$

counts the number of subsets of $S$ that have no elements. This single subset is called the empty set or null set and is denoted by $\varnothing$.

One important use of binomial coefficients is in the binomial theorem, which plays a central role in statistics. The binomial theorem is stated as follows:

### Binomial Theorem

$$\sum_{i=0}^{n} \binom{n}{i} x^i y^{n-i} = (x + y)^n$$

for any real values $x$ and $y$.

This theorem will not be proved here, but some simple cases will be illustrated. For $n = 2$,

$$\sum_{i=0}^{2} \binom{2}{i} x^i y^{2-i} = \binom{2}{0} y^2 + \binom{2}{1} xy + \binom{2}{2} x^2 = y^2 + 2xy + x^2$$

The latter expression is the well-known expansion of $(x + y)^2$. For $n = 3$,

$$\sum_{i=0}^{3} \binom{3}{i} x^i y^{3-i} = y^3 + 3xy^2 + 3x^2y + x^3 = (x + y)^3$$

For $n = 4$,

$$\sum_{i=0}^{4} \binom{4}{i} x^i y^{4-i} = y^4 + 4xy^3 + 6x^2y^2 + 4x^3y + x^4$$
$$= (x + y)^4$$

**Table A.3**

| $i$ | $P$(Exactly $i$ heads in 5 tosses) |
|---|---|
| 0 | 1/32 |
| 1 | 5/32 |
| 2 | 10/32 |
| 3 | 10/32 |
| 4 | 5/32 |
| 5 | 1/32 |

A major use of the binomial theorem is in the evaluation of certain sums. For example, substituting $x = y = 1$ into the theorem gives

$$\sum_{i=0}^{n} \binom{n}{i} = (1 + 1)^n = 2^n$$

The sum on the left counts the number of subsets of all sizes in a set of size $n$, as $i$ takes on the values 0, 1, 2, . . . , $n$. The number of these subsets, including the empty set, is $2^n$. For $n = 3$, there should be $2^3 = 8$ subsets. Let $S = \{A, B, C\}$. The eight subsets of $S$ are

|  |  |  |  |
|---|---|---|---|
|  | $\{A, B, C\}$ |  | (Size 3) |
| $\{A, B\}$ | $\{A, C\}$ | $\{B, C\}$ | (Size 2) |
| $\{A\}$ | $\{B\}$ | $\{C\}$ | (Size 1) |
|  | $\varnothing$ |  | (Size 0) |

Substituting $n = 9$ into the equation gives $2^9 = 512$ for the number of subsets (of all possible sizes) of the planets.

In the case of probability theory, $x = p$ and $y = q$, where $0 < p < 1$ and $q = 1 - p$. The binomial theorem then gives

$$\sum_{i=0}^{n} \binom{n}{i} p^i q^{n-i} = (p + q)^n = 1^n = 1 \qquad \text{A.1}$$

The $n + 1$ terms in Equation A.1 represent individual probabilities, which add up to one (as shown by the binomial theorem). In the particular case where $p = q = 1/2$, the expression $\binom{n}{i}(1/2)^n$ gives the individual probabilities. Thus Equation A.1 can be interpreted to mean

$$\sum_{i=0}^{n} P(\text{Exactly } i \text{ heads in } n \text{ tosses}) = 1$$

The probabilities for $n = 5$ are given in Table A.3. It is easy to check that the sum of these six probabilities is equal to one.

**Exercises A.4**

**A.22** Find the values of the following factorials:
   **a.** 8!    **c.** 0!
   **b.** 10!    **d.** 1!

**A.23** Find the values of the following binomial coefficients:

a. $\binom{6}{3}$    c. $\binom{8}{3}$

b. $\binom{7}{3}$    d. $\binom{6}{4}$

**A.24** A committee has 10 members. Find the number of possible subcommittees of size 3; of size 4; of size 5.

**A.25** Using the properties of the binomial coefficients, find the following:

a. $\binom{15}{12}$    c. $\binom{100}{0}$

b. $\binom{28}{26}$    d. $\binom{2000}{1999}$

**A.26** Find the values of $\binom{6}{k}$ for $k = 0, 1, 2, 3, 4, 5, 6$. Show that

$$\sum_{k=0}^{6} \binom{6}{k} = 2^6$$

**A.27** Use the binomial theorem to show that for any $n$,

$$\sum_{k=0}^{n} \binom{n}{k}(-1)^k = 0$$

Use the values of $\binom{6}{k}$ from the preceding exercise to illustrate this identity.

**A.28** Show that $\binom{n}{k} = \binom{n}{n-k}$ by using Definition A.6.

**A.29** The numbers of ways that the integers in $S = \{1, 2, \ldots, n\}$ may be listed is $n!$ For example, for $n = 3$, there are $3! = 6$ lists: 123, 132, 213, 231, 312, 321. Use this fact to answer the following questions:

a. In how many ways may all the teams in a ten-team conference be listed?

b. In how many ways may six people sit at a counter that has exactly six seats?

**A.30** For $n \geqslant 3$ it can be shown that

$$\left| e - \sum_{k=0}^{n} \frac{1}{k!} \right| \leqslant \frac{1}{(n+1)!}$$

Use this fact to estimate $e$ with an error of no more than $1/7!$

*Note:* $1/7! < 0.0002$.

**A.31** Using Definition A.6, show that

$$\binom{n}{k} + \binom{n}{k+1} = \binom{n+1}{k+1}$$

This relationship allows us to generate all of the binomial coefficients successively by using the following pattern, called Pascal's triangle. Each number, except the beginning and ending ones in a row, is found by adding the numbers above it to the left and right in the table.

```
                    1
                 1     1
              1     2     1
           1     3     3     1
        1     4     6     4     1
     1     5    10    10     5     1
  1     6    15    20    15     6     1
```

In the row beginning with 1    5, the binomial coefficients $\binom{5}{k}$, $k = 0, 1, 2, 3, 4, 5$ are found. In the row beginning with 1    $n$, the binomial coefficients $\binom{n}{k}$, $k = 0, 1, \ldots, n$ are found.

# Appendix B

# Elementary Commands in Minitab

## B.1

**Introduction**

The Minitab Statistical Computing System was developed at Pennsylvania State University. It has enjoyed widespread popularity as an important primary teaching device and data analysis tool in statistics since 1976, when the *Minitab Student Handbook* by Barbara F. Ryan, Brian L. Joiner, and Thomas A. Ryan, was first published. The second edition of the *Minitab Student Handbook* was published in 1985. That edition describes Release 5.1 of Minitab, which is upward-compatible with previous versions of Minitab (with a small number of exceptions). The system is widely used in the analysis of statistical data at introductory and more advanced levels in the academic world, government, and industry. The system is particularly effective in teaching statistics, partly because a relatively small amount of time is required to introduce a user to the system and to make Minitab accessible as a tool. The system has been designed so that those who are *not* computer professionals can easily use it to manipulate, display, and analyze numerical data. The commands in the system have understandable English-language names which suggest the operations to be performed. In addition, the output from most commands is in a form that permits straightforward interpretation. Subcommands used in conjunction with Minitab commands enhance the effectiveness and usefulness of the commands themselves.

Minitab may be used with most large computers in both the batch and interactive modes. It may also be used with microcomputers, including the DEC Professional 350, the Rainbow, the Fortune 32:16, and the IBM PC. The use of Minitab in the interactive mode is particularly effective for teaching data analysis, as the user gets responses to statistical commands immediately and hence can choose appropriate commands in light of current results.

The Minitab system produces a worksheet of rows and columns in which numeric and alphabetic data may be stored. In some computing systems there are 50 columns and 100 rows and hence 5000 locations on the worksheet. On other computing systems the number of locations available on the worksheet is much larger. The Minitab system itself will show the number of locations available on the worksheet in the form of a statement in the first few lines of output: STORAGE AVAILABLE 5000 (or whatever the appropriate number may be). The worksheet can be pictured as a matrix of the form indicated schematically in Table B.1.

Minitab commands consist of English-language names followed by column numbers, constants, or stored constants represented in algebraic form. There are some 200 such commands which can be used to carry out such operations as entering data, algebraically manipulating data entered in the worksheet, editing data, outputting data, and performing certain statistical calculations (frequently on columns). The English-language name is used by the computer to enter a "dictionary" of Minitab commands to find the appropriate operation to be executed. Only the first four letters in the name need be correctly spelled, as Minitab pays attention only to those letters and to the following column numbers and constants (real or stored).

Below is an example of a simple Minitab program.

NOTE THIS IS A SIMPLE EXAMPLE OF A MINITAB PROGRAM

SET THE FOLLOWING HEIGHTS IN C1

67, 67, 67, 68, 68, 69, 69, 69, 69, 69

69, 70, 70, 70, 70, 70, 71, 71, 71, 71

71, 71, 71, 71, 71, 72, 72, 72, 72, 72

72, 72, 72, 73, 73, 73, 73, 74, 74, 74

74, 74, 74, 74, 74, 75, 75, 76, 77, 78

END

PRINT C1

AVERAGE C1

HISTOGRAM C1

SET C2

  1 : 50

END

PLOT C1 VERSUS C2

STOP

**Table B.1**

**The Minitab Worksheet**

|          | Column 1 | Column 2 | $\cdots$ | Column 50 |
|----------|----------|----------|----------|-----------|
| Row 1    | *        | *        | $\cdots$ | *         |
| Row 2    | *        | *        | $\cdots$ | *         |
| .        | .        | .        | $\cdots$ | .         |
| .        | .        | .        | $\cdots$ | .         |
| .        | .        | .        | $\cdots$ | .         |
| Row 100  | *        | *        | $\cdots$ | *         |

The letters underlined here are the only ones in the command names to which the system responds. (The letters are not underlined in an actual program.) Hence the commands

PRINT C1     PRINTO C1

PRINS C1     PRINTER C1

would all have the same result—namely, the printing of the contents of column C1. The NOTE command is used only to include a remark in the program and in the Minitab output. The SET command is used to enter numbers in a particular column—in this case, the first one. The additional English words after SET may be omitted; that is, SET C1 would have the same result as SET THE FOLLOW-ING HEIGHTS IN C1. The system will put all the numbers on the lines following the SET command in column one (C1), until it encounters the END command. The PRINT command causes the values in C1 to be printed out, and the AVERAGE command causes the average of these values to be calculated and printed out. The HISTOGRAM command produces a histogram of the contents of C1. The second SET command followed by the line 1 : 50 causes the integers from 1 to 50 to be entered into C2. Again the END command signals the termination of the SET command. The PLOT command creates a plot of the corresponding entries of C1 and C2. The values in C1 are plotted on the vertical axis, and those in C2 are plotted on the horizontal axis. The STOP command ends execution of this Minitab program. The Minitab output from the execution of this program is shown in Exhibit B.1.

Some commands in Minitab can be used in conjunction with related commands called subcommands, which allow certain options or create additional output. If subcommands are used, the main command appears on a line by itself, followed by a semicolon. The subcommands are then placed on the following lines, one at a time. Each of these lines ends with a semicolon, except the final line, which ends with a period.

Following are some general facts about notation and procedures, which you should keep in mind as you read the descriptions of particular Minitab commands in the remaining sections.

```
MTB > NOTE THIS IS A SIMPLE EXAMPLE OF A MINITAB PROGRAM
MTB > SET THE FOLLOWING HEIGHTS IN C1
C1
    67     67     67     68     .    .    .

MTB > END
MTB > PRINT C1
C1
    67     67     67     68     68     69     69     69     69     69     69
    70     70     70     70     70     71     71     71     71     71     71
    71     71     71     72     72     72     72     72     72     72     72
    73     73     73     73     74     74     74     74     74     74     74
    74     75     75     76     77     78

MTB > MEAN C1
    MEAN     =        71.620
MTB > HISTOGRAM C1

Histogram of C1    N = 50

Midpoint    Count
       67       3   ***
       68       2   **
       69       6   ******
       70       5   *****
       71       9   *********
       72       8   ********
       73       4   ****
       74       8   ********
       75       2   **
       76       1   *
       77       1   *
       78       1   *


MTB > SET C2
C2
     1      2      3      4     .    .    .

MTB > END
MTB > PLOT C1 VERSUS C2

          -
          -                                                      *
     77.0+                                                       *
          -                                                      *
C1        -
          -                                              **
          -                                      ********
     73.5+
          -                                 ****
          -                            ********
          -
          -                   *********
     70.0+             *****
          -         ******
          -
          -     **
          -   ***
     66.5+
          -
           +---------+---------+---------+---------+---------+-C2
           0        10        20        30        40        50

MTB > STOP
```

1.      C is the representation for a column. In an actual Minitab program, a column is identified by a C followed directly by a number—for example, C2, C5, or C19.

2.      K is the representation for a constant. In an actual Minitab program, the constant may be a number, such as 3.14159, or a stored constant, which is identified by a K followed directly by a number—for example, K4, K8, or K10.

3.      E is the general representation for an expression that can be either a column or a constant.

4.      The bracket notation [ ] indicates that the enclosed argument is optional —it need not be included for the command to be executed.

5.      The notation C1–C5 is acceptable in Minitab as a replacement for C1, C2, C3, C4, C5. Generally CI–CJ can be used to represent the columns from CI to and including CJ, for integers $I < J$.

6.      Minitab worksheets may be stored for future use. Stored worksheets are called files, and they are named by the SAVE command. For example, if the command

         SAVE 'HEIGHTS'

were included at the end of the program in Exhibit B.1, that Minitab program would be saved by the system. If the program were needed again, the command

         RETRIEVE 'HEIGHTS'

could be used to restore the program to the worksheet. The system would restore the worksheet as it existed when SAVE was executed.

7.      Typically the only character groups recognized by Minitab on a command line (other than the first four letters of the command itself) are column numbers (such as C2), column names (such as 'LENGTH'), constants (such as 71.2), stored constants (such as K2), and file names (such as 'FILE'). Thus other English-language text may be used in a Minitab command to clarify the program. Symbols such as &, ∗, :, +, and ; should not be used on a command line, however, as these have particular meaning to the Minitab system.

## B.2

### Commands for Input of Numerical Values

In order to use the Minitab system, you must be able to enter numbers into the worksheet. One of the simplest of the input commands is the READ command. The READ command has the following form:

     READ THE FOLLOWING NUMBERS INTO C, C, . . . , C

This command will cause the numbers on subsequent lines of a Minitab program to be put successively into the first row, second row, third row, and so forth, until the system encounters the END command or another Minitab command. For example, the following lines in a Minitab program will cause five rows of data to be entered in C1, C2, C3, and C4 of the worksheet:

```
READ INTO Cl, C2, C3, C4
    1.0     2.0     3.0     4.0
    4.0     3.0     2.0     1.0
    1.0     1.0     1.0     1.0
   −2.0    −1.5    −1.0    −0.5
    3.0     2.0     1.0     0.0
END
```

If the first data line were

1.0   2.0   3.0   4.0   5.0

the last number, 5.0, would be ignored. If there are less than four numbers on any line following the READ command, an error message to that effect will be printed by the Minitab system.

Another input command, used to input numbers to a *single* column of the worksheet, is the SET command. The SET command has the following form:

SET THE FOLLOWING NUMBERS INTO C

This command will cause all the numbers on subsequent lines of the program to be read successively into the rows of the indicated column, until the system encounters an END command or another Minitab command. For example, the following lines in a Minitab program will cause ten numbers to be entered into the first ten rows of C2:

```
SET THE FOLLOWING NUMBERS IN C2
2, 3, 4, 5
6
7 8 9
10, 1
END
```

The numbers in C2 will be in the order 2, 3, 4, 5, 6, 7, 8, 9, 10, 1.

The numbers on a data line may be separated by a blank or a comma. If a SET or READ command refers to columns that already contain data, the existing data will be replaced by the most recent data.

There are several important points to note about the form of data lines.

**1**   The numbers on a line may or may not have decimal points. Scientific notation is also acceptable. Thus the following are all acceptable and equivalent:

421.2   4.212E2   4.212E+2   4.212+2   42120−2

**2**   The first four rows of a READ or SET command are printed out by Minitab for verification.

**3**   There must not be any recognizable Minitab commands in the data lines. Thus any NOTE commands should be placed before or after the data.

The READ and SET commands can be used in conjunction with files that contain data in an appropriate form. Assuming FILENAME is the name of an appropriate file, the following commands will cause the content of FILENAME to be entered into the worksheet:

READ NUMBERS FROM 'FILENAME' INTO C, C, . . . , C
SET NUMBERS FROM 'FILENAME' INTO C

The name of the appropriate file must be placed between single quotation marks. As conventions with regard to the naming of files vary among computer centers, you must learn the appropriate local conventions.

The LET command may also be used to enter data into the worksheet. The general form of this command is

LET E = (EXPRESSION)

Appropriate uses of the LET command are illustrated below:

LET C1 = C2+C3
LET C2 = 2*C1
LET K1 = 3.14159263
LET K2 = 2*K3+K4

The first of these LET commands assigns to the rows of C1 the sums of the corresponding elements in the rows of C2 and C3. The second LET command assigns to the rows of C2 twice the values of the elements currently in the corresponding rows of C1. The third LET command assigns to K1, a stored constant, a value approximating that of the constant $\pi$. The last LET command assigns to K2 a value equal to twice K3 plus K4. The LET command can be used to correct entries in the worksheet. For example, the command

LET C2(4) = 5.12

will replace the current value of the fourth row of column 2 by 5.12.

DELETE is another command that is useful for correcting data on the worksheet. The general form of the DELETE command is

DELETE ROWS K, K, . . . , K OF C, C, . . . , C

This command deletes the indicated rows of the named columns. Suppose the following values were in the first five rows of C1 and C2:

| C1 | C2 |
|----|----|
| 1  | 5  |
| 2  | 4  |
| 3  | 3  |
| 4  | 2  |
| 5  | 1  |

The command DELETE ROWS 2 AND 3 OF C1, C2 would leave three rows in

C1 and C2—namely,

| C1 | C2 |
|----|----|
| 1  | 5  |
| 4  | 2  |
| 5  | 1  |

The INSERT command can be used to place data into the rows of a column (or columns) of the worksheet. The INSERT command has the following form:[1]

INSERT THE FOLLOWING NUMBERS BETWEEN ROWS        &
K AND K OF COLUMNS C, C, . . . , C

All the numbers on the subsequent lines of the program will be inserted into the indicated columns, until the system encounters another Minitab command. For example, suppose that C1 and C2 contained the entries

| C1 | C2 |
|----|----|
| 1  | 0  |
| 2  | 2  |
| 6  | 10 |
| 7  | 12 |

and the Minitab program contained the lines

INSERT BETWEEN ROWS 2 AND 3 OF C1, C2

3  4

4  6

5  8

Upon execution of the INSERT command, the contents of C1 and C2 would become

| C1 | C2 |
|----|----|
| 1  | 0  |
| 2  | 2  |
| 3  | 4  |
| 4  | 6  |
| 5  | 8  |
| 6  | 10 |
| 7  | 12 |

The INSERT command can be used with a file, in which case the form of the command is

INSERT DATA FROM 'FILENAME' BETWEEN ROWS K        &
AND K OF COLUMNS C, C, . . . , C

---

[1]An ampersand at the end of a Minitab command indicates that the command continues on the next line.

If no row numbers are specified with the INSERT command, the data will be entered into the worksheet following the last filled row of the indicated columns. The form of the command is

INSERT DATA AT THE END OF C, C, . . . , C

The SET command can be used to insert the inegers from 1 to *n* in a column. For example, the SET command

SET C1
 1 : 10
END

will enter the integers 1, 2, . . . , 10 in the first ten rows of C1. Similarly, the following command will put the six integers 5, 6, 7, 8, 9, 10 into C5:

SET C5
 5 : 10
END

The SET command can also be used to input other forms of patterned data into the worksheet. The reader is referred to the *Minitab Student Handbook*, Second Edition, for details. The Minitab program in Exhibit B.2 illustrates the use of the READ, SET, LET, DELETE, and INSERT commands. The READ command causes the first ten positive integers to be entered (in increasing order) in C1 and the first ten positive odd integers (in increasing order) in C2. The LET command is then used to multiply each integer in C1 by 2 and to place the result—the first ten even integers—in C3. Then columns C1–C3 are printed. Next the DELETE command is used to delete rows 6 through 10 of C1 and C2. The abbreviated columns are then printed. The SET command is used to enter eight numerical values in C3, overwriting the previous contents, and to enter the integers from 1 to 8 in C4. Finally the INSERT command is used to insert a new row in C4 and C3 between the old rows numbered 7 and 8.

## B.3

**Commands for Output of Numerical Values**

One of the commands most frequently used in Minitab is the PRINT command. The PRINT command has the following form:

PRINT THE VALUES IN C, C, . . . , C

or

PRINT THE CONTENTS OF K, K, . . . , K

The effect of this command is to print the values that are currently in the indicated columns or currently stored as constants. The use of the PRINT command was illustrated in Exhibit B.1, where the 50 numbers in C1 were printed out. In Exhibit B.2 the PRINT command was used to print the contents of C1–C2, C1–C3, C3, and C4 C3. Note that the columns are printed out in the order in which they are listed in the PRINT command.

The contents of a single column are printed horizontally. In contrast, the contents of more than one column are printed vertically, with the appropriate row numbers listed on the left-hand side of the output. If columns to be printed jointly are of unequal length, blanks will be printed in those rows of a column that do not

**Exhibit B.2**

```
MTB > NOTE MINITAB PROGRAM FOR INPUT COMMANDS
MTB > READ INTO C1 C2
       10 ROWS READ
ROW    C1    C2

  1     1     1
  2     2     3
  3     3     5
  4     4     7
   .    .    .

MTB > END
MTB > PRINT C1-C2
ROW    C1    C2

  1     1     1
  2     2     3
  3     3     5
  4     4     7
  5     5     9
  6     6    11
  7     7    13
  8     8    15
  9     9    17
 10    10    19

MTB > LET C3 = C1*2
MTB > PRINT C1-C3
ROW    C1    C2    C3

  1     1     1     2
  2     2     3     4
  3     3     5     6
  4     4     7     8
  5     5     9    10
  6     6    11    12
  7     7    13    14
  8     8    15    16
  9     9    17    18
 10    10    19    20

MTB > DELETE ROWS 6:10 OF C1-C2
MTB > PRINT C1-C2
ROW    C1    C2

  1     1     1
  2     2     3
  3     3     5
  4     4     7
  5     5     9
```

```
MTB > SET C3
C3
   1.2    1.8    -4.2    3.5     .   .   .

MTB > END
MTB > PRINT C3
C3
   1.2    1.8    -4.2    3.5    -1.5    -2.2    -3.0    0.5

MTB > NOTE THE FOLLOWING SET COMMAND USES 1:8 AS INPUT
MTB > SET C4
C4
   1    2    3    4    .   .   .

MTB > END
MTB > PRINT C4 C3
 ROW    C4       C3

   1     1      1.2
   2     2      1.8
   3     3     -4.2
   4     4      3.5
   5     5     -1.5
   6     6     -2.2
   7     7     -3.0
   8     8      0.5

MTB > NOTE 7.5 4.0 WILL BE INSERTED AS INDICATED BY THE NEXT COMMAND
MTB > INSERT BETWEEN ROWS 7 AND 8 OF C4,C3
      1 ROWS READ
MTB > END
MTB > PRINT C4 C3
 ROW     C4       C3

   1     1.0     1.2
   2     2.0     1.8
   3     3.0    -4.2
   4     4.0     3.5
   5     5.0    -1.5
   6     6.0    -2.2
   7     7.0    -3.0
   8     7.5     4.0
   9     8.0     0.5
```

actually contain data. Whenever a single column is printed vertically, a column without values must also be printed.

The commands OW and OH are used to specify the height and width of the output that results from the PRINT command. The forms of these commands are

OW = K SPACES

OH = K LINES

For the OW command, K may be any number from 65 to 132. The OH command determines the number of lines per page (or, in the interactive mode, the number of lines per screen). If the number of lines is not specified by an OH command, the Minitab system will use a value of 60 lines (24 in the interactive mode).

```
MTB > NOTE MINITAB PROGRAM FOR OUTPUT COMMANDS
MTB > READ INTO C1-C5
       5 ROWS READ
 ROW    C1    C2    C3    C4    C5

   1     1     2     3     4     5
   2     6     7     8     9    10
   3    11    12    13    14    15
   4    16    17    18    19    20
   .  .  .

MTB > END
MTB > PRINT C1-C5
 ROW    C1    C2    C3    C4    C5

   1     1     2     3     4     5
   2     6     7     8     9    10
   3    11    12    13    14    15
   4    16    17    18    19    20
   5    21    22    23    24    25

MTB > WRITE THE VALUES IN C1-C5
  1  2  3  4  5
  6  7  8  9 10
 11 12 13 14 15
 16 17 18 19 20
 21 22 23 24 25
```

A second command that may be used to obtain data from the worksheet is the WRITE command. The WRITE command has the following form:

WRITE [TO 'FILENAME'] THE VALUES IN C, C, . . . , C

If the file name is omitted, the contents of the indicated columns will be printed out in compact form, as illustrated in Exhibit B.3. If the name of a file is included, it must appear between single quotation marks, as with the READ command. If a file name is used, the contents of the rows of the current worksheet become the rows of the file. The numbers in a row are separated by a single blank. Again, your computer center should be consulted regarding local conventions on the naming of files. The Minitab program in Exhibit B.3 illustrates the use of the PRINT and WRITE commands.

## B.4

## Commands for Arithmetic Operations and Functions

The basic arithmetic operations may be applied to columns of data in a worksheet or to stored constants. Following are the Minitab commands used for the operations of addition, subtraction, multiplication, division, and raising to a power:

ADD E TO E . . . TO E, PUT INTO E

SUBTRACT E FROM E, PUT INTO E

MULTIPLY E BY E . . . BY E, PUT INTO E

DIVIDE E BY E, PUT INTO E

RAISE E TO THE POWER E, PUT INTO E

In order for columns to be added, subtracted, multiplied, or divided, they must be the same length (that is, they must have the same number of entered numerical values). The results of any arithmetic operation may be put into one of the original columns, but then the original contents are erased.

Minitab commands may also be used to compute a number of frequently used functions, either for all entries in a column or for stored constants. The most commonly used of these commands are shown in Table B.2.

Three commands that are not as familiar as those listed in Table B.2 are illustrated in Exhibit B.4. The first is ROUND, which calculates the nearest integer for each of the numbers of a column. The second is PARSUM, which computes the partial sums of the elements in a column. The third is PARPRODUCT, which computes the partial products of the elements in a column. This latter command is useful in computing the values of $k!$

The first PRINT statement in Exhibit B.4 shows how the numbers 1.1 to 2.0 are rounded by Minitab. The original numbers are in C1, and the rounded versions are in C2. The second PRINT statement shows how PARSUM and PARPRODUCT operate on the integers 1, 2, . . . , 10 in C3. The values $\Sigma_{i=1}^{k} i$ and $k!$ for $k = 1, 2, . . . , 10$ appear in C4 and C5, respectively.

As indicated in Section B.2, the LET command may be used to perform additional operations on columns or stored constants. The arithmetic operators $+$,

## Table B.2

**Elementary Minitab Functions**

| Command | Name | Function |
|---|---|---|
| ABSOLUTE VALUE OF E, PUT INTO E | absolute value | $\lvert x \rvert$ |
| ANTILOG OF E, PUT INTO E | antilog | $\text{antilog}_{10}(x)$ |
| ACOS OF E, PUT INTO E | arccosine | $\arccos(x)$ |
| ASIN OF E, PUT INTO E | arcsine | $\arcsin(x)$ |
| ATAN OF E, PUT INTO E | arctangent | $\arctan(x)$ |
| COS OF E, PUT INTO E | cosine | $\cos(x)$ |
| EXP OF E, PUT INTO E | exponentiation | $e^x$ |
| LOGE OF E, PUT INTO E | logarithm (base $e$) | $\log_e(x)$ |
| LOGTEN OF E, PUT INTO E | logarithm (base 10) | $\log_{10}(x)$ |
| SIGNS OF E, PUT INTO E | signs | $\text{sgn}(x) \begin{pmatrix} -1 \text{ if } x < 0 \\ 0 \text{ if } x = 0 \\ 1 \text{ if } x > 0 \end{pmatrix}$ |
| SIN OF E, PUT INTO E | sine | $\sin(x)$ |
| SQRT OF E, PUT INTO E | square root | $\sqrt{x}$ |
| TAN OF E, PUT INTO E | tangent | $\tan(x)$ |

## Exhibit B.4

```
MTB > NOTE EXAMPLE MINITAB PROGRAM FOR ROUND, PARSUM, PARPROD
MTB > SET IN C1
C1
    1.1    1.2    1.3    1.4    .    .    .

MTB > ROUND C1 IN C2
MTB > PRINT C1 C2
 ROW    C1    C2

   1    1.1    1
   2    1.2    1
   3    1.3    1
   4    1.4    1
   5    1.5    1
   6    1.6    2
   7    1.7    2
   8    1.8    2
   9    1.9    2
  10    2.0    2

MTB > SET C3
C3
      1    2    3    4    .    .    .

MTB > END
MTB > PARSUMS C3 IN C4
MTB > PARPRODUCT C3 IN C5
MTB > PRINT C3-C5
 ROW    C3    C4        C5

   1     1     1         1
   2     2     3         2
   3     3     6         6
   4     4    10        24
   5     5    15       120
   6     6    21       720
   7     7    28      5040
   8     8    36     40320
   9     9    45    362880
  10    10    55   3628800
```

$-$, $*$, $/$, and $**$ (which represent addition, subtraction, multiplication, division, and exponentiation, respectively) and the functions described above (except for the PARSUM and PARPRODUCT commands) may be used with the LET command.

The Minitab output in Exhibit B.5 includes several examples of the LET command. In C2 the values $k\pi/10$ are generated for $k = 1, 2, \ldots, 20$. In C3 and C4 the sines and cosines of these values are generated. In C5 the values of $\sin^2(k\pi/10) + \cos^2(k\pi/10)$ are computed for $k = 1, 2, \ldots, 20$. As $\sin^2(x) + \cos^2(x) = 1$ for any $x$, these values are all 1, as shown in C5.

```
MTB > NOTE MINITAB PROGRAM USING THE LET COMMAND
MTB > SET C1
C1
      1     2     3     4    .    .    .

MTB > END
MTB > LET K1 = 3.14159263/10
MTB > LET C2 = K1*C1
MTB > LET C3 = SIN(C2)
MTB > LET C4 = COS(C2)
MTB > LET C5 = C3**2 + C4**2
MTB > PRINT C1-C5
 ROW     C1        C2        C3        C4     C5

   1      1     0.31416   0.30902   0.95106    1
   2      2     0.62832   0.58779   0.80902    1
   3      3     0.94248   0.80902   0.58779    1
   4      4     1.25664   0.95106   0.30902    1
   5      5     1.57080   1.00000   0.00000    1
   6      6     1.88495   0.95106  -0.30902    1
   7      7     2.19911   0.80902  -0.58778    1
   8      8     2.51327   0.58779  -0.80902    1
   9      9     2.82743   0.30902  -0.95106    1
  10     10     3.14159   0.00000  -1.00000    1
  11     11     3.45575  -0.30902  -0.95106    1
  12     12     3.76991  -0.58778  -0.80902    1
  13     13     4.08407  -0.80902  -0.58779    1
  14     14     4.39823  -0.95106  -0.30902    1
  15     15     4.71239  -1.00000  -0.00000    1
  16     16     5.02655  -0.95106   0.30902    1
  17     17     5.34070  -0.80902   0.58778    1
  18     18     5.65486  -0.58779   0.80902    1
  19     19     5.96902  -0.30902   0.95106    1
  20     20     6.28318  -0.00000   1.00000    1
```

## B.5

### Elementary Commands for Columns and Rows

A number of very simple but useful Minitab commands operate on individual columns or rows. The English-language names of these commands clearly describe the function performed. Several of these commands are listed in Table B.3.

Similar commands can be used to carry out an operation on all of the rows of specified columns and place the results in an indicated column. The forms of these commands are as follows:

| | |
|---|---|
| RCOUNT | OF C, C, . . . , C PUT IN C |
| RMAXIMUM | OF C, C, . . . , C PUT IN C |
| RMEAN | OF C, C, . . . , C PUT IN C |
| RMEDIAN | OF C, C, . . . , C PUT IN C |
| RMINIMUM | OF C, C, . . . , C PUT IN C |
| RN | OF C, C, . . . , C PUT IN C |

| | |
|---|---|
| RNMISS | OF C, C, . . . , C PUT IN C |
| RSSQ | OF C, C, . . . , C PUT IN C |
| RSUM | OF C, C, . . . , C PUT IN C |
| RSTDEV | OF C, C, . . . , C PUT IN C |

Exhibit B.6 shows the Minitab output generated when the elementary column operations listed above were performed on the integers from 1 to 10, which were generated in C1.

Another Minitab command that can be used with columns is the NAME command. This command allows a column to be assigned a name. The name can be any list of up to eight characters; the only restriction is that it cannot begin or end with a blank. In subsequent commands a column can be referred to either by its column number (for example, C2) or by its name. If the latter is used, the name must be enclosed in single quotation marks. Once the NAME command has been executed, Minitab will use the name to identify the column. This feature is particularly useful for labeling axes of plots, as will be demonstrated in Section B.7. The name assigned to a column remains assigned until the column is renamed by another NAME command. A NAME command has the following form:

NAME COLUMNS C 'NAME 1', C 'NAME 2', C 'NAME 3'

## Table B.3

**Elementary Minitab Commands for Columns**

| Command | Function |
|---|---|
| COUNT C [PUT IN K] | Counts the number of values entered in a column |
| MAXIMUM C [PUT IN K] | Finds the maximum value in a column |
| MEAN C [PUT IN K] | Calculates the mean of the values in a column |
| MEDIAN C [PUT IN K] | Calculates the median of the values in a column |
| MINIMUM C [PUT IN K] | Finds the minimum value in a column |
| N C [PUT IN K] | Finds the number of values present in a column |
| NMISS C [PUT IN K] | Finds the number of values missing from a column |
| SSQ C [PUT IN K] | Calculates the sum of squares of the values in a column |
| SUM C [PUT IN K] | Calculates the sum of the values in a column |
| STDEV C [PUT IN K] | Calculates the standard deviation of the values in a column |

```
MTB > NOTE MINITAB PROGRAM ILLUSTRATING COLUMN OPERATIONS
MTB > GENERATE 1 TO 10 IN C1
MTB > NAME C1 'TEN INT'
MTB > PRINT C1
TEN INT
       1      2      3      4      5      6      7      8      9     10

MTB > COUNT C1
   COUNT    =       10.000
MTB > MEAN C1
   MEAN     =        5.5000
MTB > MEDIAN C1
   MEDIAN   =        5.5000
MTB > SUM C1
   SUM      =       55.000
MTB > SSQ C1
   SSQ      =      385.00
MTB > STDEV C1
   ST.DEV.  =        3.0276
MTB > MAXIMUM C1
   MAXIMUM  =       10.000
MTB > MINIMUM C1
   MINIMUM  =        1.0000
MTB > N C1
   N        =       10.000
MTB > NMISS C1
   NMISSING= 0.000000000
```

In the Minitab output of Exhibit B.6, C1 is named TEN INT, an abbreviation for "the first TEN INTegers." When the command PRINT C1 was used with this column, the output was labeled TEN INT instead of C1.

The TALLY command is another command that can be used with an individual column (or columns). Its general form is

TALLY C, C, . . . , C

The TALLY command causes a frequency table to be printed for the observations in the columns specified. The TALLY command is used with five subcommands, which specify what is to be printed in the table. The subcommands are

COUNTS
PERCENTS
CUMCNTS (cumulative counts)
CUMPCTS (cumulative percents)
ALL (equivalent to all of the above subcommands)

When the TALLY command and the ALL subcommand were used with the height data of Section B.1, the output in Exhibit B.7 was generated.

```
MTB > NOTE EXAMPLE OF THE USE OF THE TALLY COMMAND
MTB > SET THE FOLLOWING HEIGHTS IN C1
C1
    67    67    67    68    .   .   .

MTB > NAME C1 'HEIGHTS'
MTB > TALLY C1;
SUBC> ALL.


HEIGHTS  COUNT  CUMCNT  PERCENT   CUMPCT
     67      3       3     6.00     6.00
     68      2       5     4.00    10.00
     69      6      11    12.00    22.00
     70      5      16    10.00    32.00
     71      9      25    18.00    50.00
     72      8      33    16.00    66.00
     73      4      37     8.00    74.00
     74      8      45    16.00    90.00
     75      2      47     4.00    94.00
     76      1      48     2.00    96.00
     77      1      49     2.00    98.00
     78      1      50     2.00   100.00
    N=      50
```

## B.6

**Commands for Editing the Worksheet**

Commands useful for editing and manipulating data include ORDER, which has the following form:

ORDER C, C, . . . , C PUT IN C, C, . . . , C

This command causes the data within each column indicated in the first list to be ordered by magnitude. The ordered data are then placed in the columns indicated in the second list. (The ORDER command technically is not in Release 5.1 of Minitab; it is in Release 82. Because of the upward compatibility of Release 5.1, however, it may still be used.) A similar command, SORT, has the following form:

SORT C [CARRY ALONG ROWS OF C, . . . C] PUT IN C,       &
[PUT CORRESPONDING ROWS IN C, . . . , C]

This command causes the values in the first column indicated to be ordered by magnitude. The corresponding rows of the other columns indicated are then sorted in exactly the same way as those in the first column were. Examples of the use of the ORDER and SORT commands are given in Exhibit B.8.

The COPY command may be used to copy data from one place on a worksheet to another. The general form of the COPY command is

COPY C, C, . . . , C  into C, C, . . . , C
COPY K, K, . . . , K  into K, K, . . . , K

```
MTB > NOTE EXAMPLE OF THE USE OF THE ORDER AND SORT COMMAND
MTB > SET C1
C1
      8    7    6    5    .    .    .

MTB > END
MTB > SET C2
C2
      1    2    3    4    .    .    .

MTB > END
MTB > ORDER C1 C2 PUT IN C3 C4
MTB > PRINT C1-C4
  ROW    C1    C2    C3    C4

   1     8     1     1     1
   2     7     2     2     2
   3     6     3     3     3
   4     5     4     4     4
   5     4     5     5     5
   6     3     6     6     6
   7     2     7     7     7
   8     1     8     8     8

MTB > NOTE EXAMPLE OF THE USE OF THE SORT COMMAND
MTB > SET C2
C2
      1    2    3    4    .    .    .

MTB > END
MTB > SORT C1 CARRYING ALONG C2 PUT IN C3 C4
MTB > PRINT C1-C4
  ROW    C1    C2    C3    C4

   1     8     1     1     8
   2     7     2     2     7
   3     6     3     3     6
   4     5     4     4     5
   5     4     5     5     4
   6     3     6     6     3
   7     2     7     7     2
   8     1     8     8     1
```

```
COPY C              into K, K, . . . , K
COPY K, K, . . . , K into C
```

The subcommands USE and OMIT permit portions of a data set to be moved from one location in a worksheet to another. Suppose the league (American League = 1, National League = 2), batting average, and number of home runs of eight batters had been put into C1–C3 and named LEAGUE, BA, and HR. The following command would put the data for the American League batters in C4–C5:

```
COPY C2 C3 INTO C4 C5;
      USE 'LEAGUE' = 1.
```

The worksheet would then appear as follows:

| C1 | C2 | C3 | C4 | C5 |
|----|-------|----|-------|----|
| 1 | 0.355 | 21 | 0.355 | 21 |
| 1 | 0.350 | 14 | 0.350 | 14 |
| 2 | 0.342 | 10 | 0.319 | 15 |
| 2 | 0.325 | 32 | 0.315 | 28 |
| 2 | 0.321 | 11 | | |
| 1 | 0.319 | 15 | | |
| 2 | 0.318 | 8 | | |
| 1 | 0.315 | 28 | | |

The USE subcommand can also be used to designate a set or range of values for a variable. For example, the commands

    COPY C2 C3 INTO C6 C7;
        USE 'HR' = 20:40.

would cause the following data from the set above to be transferred to columns C6–C7:

| C6 | C7 |
|-------|----|
| 0.355 | 21 |
| 0.325 | 32 |
| 0.315 | 28 |

That is, those batters with 20 to 40 home runs would be identified and their batting averages and numbers of home runs placed into C6 and C7.

The OMIT subcommand is the reverse of USE. Instead of specifying the rows to be copied, it gives the rows to be omitted. For example, use of the command

    COPY C2 C3 INTO C8–C9;
        OMIT 'LEAGUE' = 1.

with the above data will cause the batting averages and numbers of home runs of the National League hitters to be moved to columns C8 and C9. Similarly, the command

    COPY C2 C3 INTO C6 C7;
        OMIT 'HR' = 0:19.

will cause Minitab to list batting averages and numbers of home runs for all hitters who did *not* have between 0 and 19 home runs. Note that this command has the same effect as the first COPY command with the USE subcommand, which caused those batters with 20 to 40 home runs to be selected. Exhibit B.9 illustrates the use of the COPY command with the USE and OMIT subcommands for the data on the eight hitters.

Two other useful editing commands are STACK and UNSTACK. The general form of the STACK command is

STACK (E, . . . , E), . . . , (E, . . . , E) STORE IN (C, . . . , C)

Suppose columns C1–C4 had the following contents:

| C1 | C2 | C3 | C4 |
|----|----|----|----|
| 1  | 2  | 5  | 10 |
| 2  | 4  | 6  | 12 |
| 3  | 6  | 7  | 14 |
| 4  | 8  | 8  | 16 |

**Exhibit B.9**

```
MTB > NOTE EXAMPLE OF USE OF COPY COMMAND
MTB > SET C1
C1
    1    1    2    2    .    .    .

MTB > END
MTB > SET C2
C2
  0.355   0.350   0.342   0.325    .    .    .

MTB > END
MTB > SET C3
C3
     21    14    10    32    .    .    .

MTB > END
MTB > NAME C1 'LEAGUE' C2 'BA' C3 'HR'
MTB > COPY C2 C3 INTO C4 C5;
SUBC>   USE 'LEAGUE' = 1.
MTB > PRINT C1-C5
 ROW   LEAGUE       BA      HR        C4      C5

   1        1    0.355      21     0.355      21
   2        1    0.350      14     0.350      14
   3        2    0.342      10     0.319      15
   4        2    0.325      32     0.315      28
   5        2    0.321      11
   6        1    0.319      15
   7        2    0.318       8
   8        1    0.315      28

MTB > COPY C2 C3 INTO C6 C7;
SUBC>   USE 'HR' = 20:40.
MTB > PRINT C1-C3,C6-C7
 ROW   LEAGUE       BA      HR        C6      C7

   1        1    0.355      21     0.355      21
   2        1    0.350      14     0.325      32
   3        2    0.342      10     0.315      28
   4        2    0.325      32
   5        2    0.321      11
   6        1    0.319      15
   7        2    0.318       8
   8        1    0.315      28
```

```
MTB > COPY C2 C3 INTO C8 C9;
SUBC>    OMIT 'LEAGUE' = 1.
MTB > PRINT C1-C3,C8-C9
 ROW  LEAGUE       BA    HR       C8      C9

   1       1    0.355    21    0.342      10
   2       1    0.350    14    0.325      32
   3       2    0.342    10    0.321      11
   4       2    0.325    32    0.318       8
   5       2    0.321    11
   6       1    0.319    15
   7       2    0.318     8
   8       1    0.315    28

MTB > COPY C2 C3 INTO C10 C11;
SUBC>    OMIT 'HR' = 0:19.
MTB > PRINT C1-C3 C10-C11
 ROW  LEAGUE       BA    HR      C10     C11

   1       1    0.355    21    0.355      21
   2       1    0.350    14    0.325      32
   3       2    0.342    10    0.315      28
   4       ?    0.325    3?
   5       2    0.321    11
   6       1    0.319    15
   7       2    0.318     8
   8       1    0.315    28
```

To stack the data so that the contents of C5 and C6 were the integers 1, 2, . . . , 8 and 2, 4, . . . , 16, respectively, the following STACK command could be used:

STACK (C1, C2) (C3, C4) INTO (C5, C6);
SUBSCRIPTS C7.

The subcommand SUBSCRIPTS creates a new column indicating the columns from which the observations came.

The command UNSTACK reverses the operation of stacking. To restore the data stacked in C5 and C6 to their original form, the following command could be used:

UNSTACK (C5, C6) INTO (C8, C9);
SUBSCRIPTS C7.

Exhibit B.10 illustrates the use of the STACK and UNSTACK commands.

The LAG command is an editing command used in the creation of time series. It has the following form:

LAG K DATA IN C, PUT IN C

Assume that there are $n$ observations in the data column. This command causes the first observation in the data column to be put into row $K + 1$ of the indicated column, the second observation in the data column to be put into row $K + 2$ of

```
MTB > NOTE EXAMPLE OF USE OF STACK AND UNSTACK COMMANDS
MTB > SET C1
C1
    1     2     3     4

MTB > END
MTB > SET C2
C2
    2     4     6     8

MTB > END
MTB > SET C3
C3
    5     6     7     8

MTB > END
MTB > SET C4
C4
   10    12    14    16

MTB > END
MTB > PRINT C1-C4
 ROW   C1    C2    C3    C4

   1    1     2     5    10
   2    2     4     6    12
   3    3     6     7    14
   4    4     8     8    16

MTB > STACK (C1,C2) (C3,C4) INTO (C5,C6);
SUBC> SUBSCRIPTS C7.
MTB > PRINT C5,C6,C7
 ROW   C5    C6    C7

   1    1     2     1
   2    2     4     1
   3    3     6     1
   4    4     8     1
   5    5    10     2
   6    6    12     2
   7    7    14     2
   8    8    16     2

MTB > UNSTACK (C5,C6) INTO (C8,C9) (C10,C11);
SUBC> SUBSCRIPTS C7.
MTB > PRINT C8-C11
 ROW   C8    C9   C10   C11

   1    1     2     5    10
   2    2     4     6    12
   3    3     6     7    14
   4    4     8     8    16
```

the indicated column, and so forth, until the $(n - K)$th observation in the data column is put into the $n$th row of the indicated column. Asterisks are placed in rows $1, 2, \ldots, K$ of the indicated column. The output in Exhibit B.11 illustrates the use of the LAG command with lags of 1, 2, and 3 rows for the first ten positive integers in C1.

**Exhibit B.11**

```
MTB > NOTE EXAMPLE OF THE USE OF THE LAG COMMAND
MTB > SET C1
C1
      1    2    3    4    .    .    .

MTB > END
MTB > LAG 1 OF C1 PUT IN C2
MTB > LAG 2 OF C1 PUT IN C3
MTB > LAG 3 OF C1 PUT IN C4
MTB > PRINT C1-C4
  ROW    C1   C2   C3   C4

    1     1    *    *    *
    2     2    1    *    *
    3     3    2    1    *
    4     4    3    2    1
    5     5    4    3    2
    6     6    5    4    3
    7     7    6    5    4
    8     8    7    6    5
    9     9    8    7    6
   10    10    9    8    7
```

## B.7

### Commands for Plots and Displays

The Minitab system has several commands that can be used to make two-dimensional plots. The PLOT command has the following form:

PLOT C VERSUS C

Values in the first column following the word PLOT will be plotted on the vertical axis, and values in the second column will be plotted on the horizontal axis. In general, each point is plotted with the asterisk symbol *. If between two and nine points fall on a single plotting position, a numeral indicating the number of points with that value will be plotted. If more than nine points fall on a single position, the symbol + will be plotted.

Minitab will choose the scales for the axes, unless the user includes subcommands to specify the scales. The subcommands used with the PLOT command to specify the scales have the following forms:

XINCREMENT = K

XSTART AT K [END AT K]

YINCREMENT = K

YSTART AT K [END AT K]

The subcommand XINCREMENT gives the distance between the + marks on the horizontal axis. The subcommand XSTART specifies the first (and last) point on the horizontal axis.

Two other commands control the height and width of plots. These are

HEIGHT = K lines
WIDTH = K spaces

If the HEIGHT and WIDTH commands are not included, Minitab will use a standard plot size (19 lines high plus two lines for labels and 57 spaces wide plus 18 spaces for labels).

In Exhibit B.12, C1 and C2 give the sales and net income (in millions of dollars) of ten companies for a particular quarter. The Minitab command PLOT was used to plot sales on the horizontal axis versus net income on the vertical axis.

The same data were then re-plotted using the HEIGHT and WIDTH commands and the XSTART and YSTART subcommands with the PLOT command. The output appears in Exhibit B.13.

There are several variants of the PLOT command. One of these is the multiple plot command, MPLOT, which has the following form:

MPLOT C VS C   C VS C   C VS C

The first column in each pair is the one whose values are to be plotted on the vertical axis. The second column in each pair is the one whose values are to be plotted on the horizontal axis. The second column must be the same for all of the pairs. The first "vertical" column is plotted using the letter A, the second "vertical" column is plotted using the letter B, and so forth. To illustrate the use of MPLOT, another set of $y$-values was generated for the data of the previous example and put into C3. The output in Exhibit B.14 includes a multiple plot of the original $y$-values versus the original $x$-values and the new $y$-values versus the same $x$-values. The original $y$s are plotted with As and the new $y$s with Bs.

A second variant on the PLOT command is the LPLOT command, which produces a letter plot. The LPLOT command has the following form:

LPLOT C VS C USING TAGS IN C

The tags given in the last column of the command determine which letter is used to plot each $(x, y)$ pair. The correspondence is as follows:

| ... | −4 | −3 | −2 | −1 | 0 | 1 | 2 | 3 | 4 | ... | 25 | 26 | 27 | ... |
|-----|----|----|----|----|---|---|---|---|---|-----|----|----|----|-----|
|     | V  | W  | X  | Y  | Z | A | B | C | D | ... | Y  | Z  | A  | ... |

Hence if a 2 appears in the first row of the last column of an LPLOT command, the letter B will be used to plot the first $(x, y)$ point. An LPLOT is useful for distinguishing two different types of points on a two-dimensional plot. For example, if we designate 1 for male and 2 for female in the last column of an LPLOT command, the observations for the different genders are plotted as As and Bs and thus are immediately recognizable.

Although several other variants of PLOT are available, these will not be described, as PLOT, MPLOT, and LPLOT should be adequate for the requirements of an introductory statistics course. It should be mentioned, however, that the HEIGHT and WIDTH commands apply to *all* PLOT, MPLOT, and LPLOT

```
MTB > NOTE THIS IS AN EXAMPLE OF THE USE OF THE MINITAB PLOT COMMAND
MTB > SET C1
C1
   63.0   66.2   43.7   41.7     .     .     .

MTB > END
MTB > SET C2
C2
   4.507   3.745   5.977   0.347     .     .     .

MTB > END
MTB > NAME C1 'SALES' C2 'NET INC'
MTB > PRINT C1 C2
 ROW   SALES   NET INC

   1    63.0    4.507
   2    66.2    3.745
   3    43.7    5.977
   4    41.7    0.347
   5    27.5    0.587
   6    56.6    1.598
   7    96.7    6.509
   8    23.1    1.140
   9     7.5    0.142
  10    35.2    0.838

MTB > PLOT C2 VS C1

NET INC -
        -
        -                                                      *
    6.0+                            *
        -
        -
        -
        -                                      *
    4.0+  .
        -                                 *
        -
        -
        -
    2.0+
        -                          *
        -            *
        -        *       *
        -     *       *
    0.0+    *
        +---------+---------+---------+---------+---------+------SALES
        0        20        40        60        80       100
```

commands that follow them. The height and width of plots can be changed by
including new HEIGHT and WIDTH commands.

Several valuable graphical procedures are available for summarizing information about the values in a column. The most frequently used is HISTOGRAM.
The HISTOGRAM command has the following form:

HISTOGRAM C, C, . . . , C

**Exhibit B.13**

```
MTB > NOTE AN EXAMPLE OF PLOT COMMAND WITH SUBCOMMANDS
MTB > HEIGHT = 30
MTB > WIDTH = 40
MTB > PLOT 'NET INC' VS 'SALES';
SUBC> XSTART = 5 END = 100;
SUBC> YSTART = 0 END = 8.


            -
            -
     7.5+
            -
NET INC  -
            -                                         *
            -
     6.0+                        *
            -
            -
            -
            -
     4.5+                             *
            -
            -                              *
            -
     3.0+
            -
            -
            -
     1.5+                        *
            -        *
            -             *
            -          *
            -                   *
     0.0+   *
         --------+---------+---------+---------+SALES
               25        50        75       100
```

This command causes a histogram of each indicated column of data to be printed. Convenient midpoints for the classes are chosen by the system. If an observation falls on the boundary of a class, it is included in the class with the larger midpoint. An example of the use of the HISTOGRAM command was given in Exhibit B.1, which included a histogram of the observed heights of 50 male college students. For those data Minitab chose the integers 67, 68, . . . , 78 as the midpoints of twelve classes. The number of heights observed in each class was printed out, along with an asterisk for each observation in the class. In cases where the number of observations in a class is large (more than 50), an asterisk may be used to represent two or more observations. Minitab prints out a message stating the number of observations represented by an asterisk.

Two subcommands may be used with the HISTOGRAM command to specify the scale for the histogram. The subcommands are

INCREMENT = K

START = K [END WITH K]

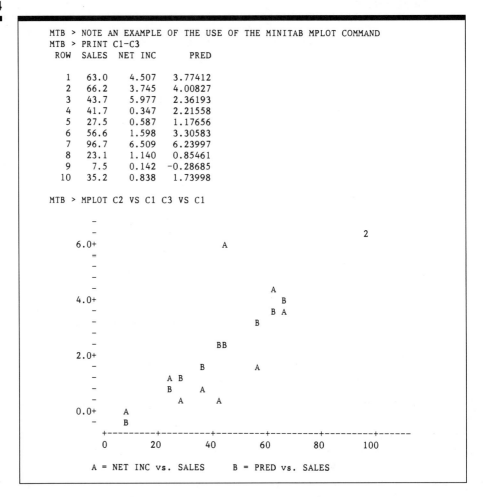

```
MTB > NOTE AN EXAMPLE OF THE USE OF THE MINITAB MPLOT COMMAND
MTB > PRINT C1-C3
 ROW   SALES  NET INC      PRED

   1    63.0    4.507     3.77412
   2    66.2    3.745     4.00827
   3    43.7    5.977     2.36193
   4    41.7    0.347     2.21558
   5    27.5    0.587     1.17656
   6    56.6    1.598     3.30583
   7    96.7    6.509     6.23997
   8    23.1    1.140     0.85461
   9     7.5    0.142    -0.28685
  10    35.2    0.838     1.73998

MTB > MPLOT C2 VS C1 C3 VS C1


      -
      -                                                         2
 6.0+                           A
      -
      -
      -
      -                                  A
 4.0+                                      B
      -                                    B A
      -                                  B
      -
      -                           BB
 2.0+
      -                     B         A
      -             A B
      -             B   A
      -               A     A
 0.0+       A
      -       B
      +---------+---------+---------+---------+---------+------
      0        20        40        60        80       100

      A = NET INC vs. SALES     B = PRED vs. SALES
```

The INCREMENT subcommand controls the length of a class interval. The START subcommand gives the midpoint of the first (last) interval. In the histogram of the 50 heights in Exhibit B.15, the INCREMENT and START subcommands were used to establish a first midpoint of 67 and a class interval of 2.

Included in the Minitab system are a number of commands taken from exploratory data analysis (EDA). Only two such commands will be described here —the STEM-AND-LEAF command and the BOXPLOT command. Further EDA commands are given in the *Minitab Student Handbook* and in *ABC's of EDA* by P. Velleman and D. Hoaglin (Boston: Duxbury Press, 1981), which fully describes this relatively new method of summarizing and analyzing data.

The STEM-AND-LEAF command produces a display similar to a histogram. The display is based on the idea that any numerical value in a sample can be represented by an initial part, called the stem, and a remaining part, called the

**Exhibit B.15**

```
MTB > NOTE THIS IS A SIMPLE EXAMPLE OF A MINITAB PROGRAM
MTB > SET THE FOLLOWING HEIGHTS IN C1
C1
   67    67    67    68    .    .    .

MTB > END
MTB > NOTE HISTOGRAM COMMAND WITH MIDPOINTS AND INTERVAL CHOSEN
MTB > HISTOGRAM C1;
SUBC> START = 67;
SUBC> INCREMENT = 2.

Histogram of C1    N = 50

Midpoint   Count
   67.00       3   ***
   69.00       8   ********
   71.00      14   **************
   73.00      12   ************
   75.00      10   **********
   77.00       2   **
   79.00       1   *
```

leaf. For example, the number 125 can be thought of as having a stem of 12 and a leaf of 5.

The STEM-AND-LEAF command has the following form:

STEM-AND-LEAF C, C, . . . , C

Each line in the stem-and-leaf display produced for the numerical values of a column has three parts, corresponding roughly to the class frequencies, class midpoints, and the asterisks found in each line of output of the HISTOGRAM command. The first number printed on each line is a cumulative frequency. If the line contains only observations less than the median of the sample, the cumulative frequency is the number of observations on that line plus the number of observations on *preceding* lines. If the line contains only observations greater than the median, the "cumulative frequency" is the number of observations on the current line plus those on *succeeding* lines. If the class contains the median of the sample, the number of observations in this class is printed in parentheses. The second part of the output gives the stem value for that line. The third part of the output gives the leaf digits for each of the values represented.

Exhibit B.16 shows the output generated when the STEM-AND-LEAF command was used with a data set of 100 observations. Frequently a given stem value is printed on more than one line. In this example each stem value (except 6) is printed on two lines. The leaf digits 0, 1, 2, 3, and 4 appear on the first line, and the leaf digits 5, 6, 7, 8, and 9 appear on the second line. Minitab also orders the leaf digits, making it easier to view the overall data set. For example, it is clear that the number 96 is the value that occurs most frequently in this sample.

Note that decimals are not used in a STEM-AND-LEAF display. The numbers 420, 42, 4.2, and 0.42 would all have a stem value of 4 and a leaf value

**Exhibit B.16**

```
MTB > NOTE EXAMPLE OF USE OF STEM-AND-LEAF COMMAND
MTB > PRINT C1
C1
    94.9   128.3    65.0    96.9   117.2   117.3   103.1    94.6
   101.2   108.7    86.6    99.5    94.0    80.8   111.7   106.8
    96.2    96.6    94.6   107.6   100.0    86.3   136.4   100.3
   125.1    89.6   117.6   125.4    88.1    84.5   107.6   108.7
   101.1   104.3   102.5    91.4    85.4   106.6    95.1   108.4
    99.3   105.5   107.2    83.9    96.1    86.4    81.7   104.3
    95.9    84.0    87.1    92.0   108.4    86.0    78.3   113.9
    96.5   104.6   101.9    88.9   102.7   108.7    95.3   112.6
   112.0    80.9    96.9    91.9   113.1   108.5   100.6    89.6
   118.3   103.6   106.4   109.1   106.3    79.6   102.1    99.5
   117.2    91.2   114.4   134.3   104.0    77.3    67.0   110.3
   104.1   115.8   107.1    82.0   112.3   121.1   110.6    96.9
   139.2   121.2   123.8   136.9

MTB > STEM-AND-LEAF C1

Stem-and-leaf of C1        N  = 100
Leaf Unit = 1.0

      2     6 57
      2     7
      5     7 789
     12     8 0012344
     22     8 5666678899
     30     9 11124444
     43     9 5556666666999
    (16)   10 0001112223344444
     41    10 5666677778888889
     25    11 001222334
     16    11 577778
     10    12 113
      7    12 558
      4    13 4
      3    13 669
```

of 2. If the leaf unit specified in the command were 2, a stem value of 4 and a leaf value of 2 would represent the number 420. If the leaf unit specified were 1, the same stem and leaf values would represent the number 42. Similarly, leaf units of 0.1 and 0.01 would represent the numbers 4.2 and 0.42, respectively. In the STEM-AND-LEAF output in Exhibit B.16, with a leaf unit of 1.0, there are, for example, four observations of 117.

The second graphical EDA display we will consider is BOXPLOT. Several terms associated with BOXPLOT are defined below.

---

**Definition B.1** ▬▬▬▬▬▬▬▬▬▬▬▬▬▬▬▬▬▬▬▬▬

The **lower hinge** is the first quartile of the sample. The **upper hinge** is the fourth quartile of the sample. *H*-spread is the difference between the upper hinge and the lower hinge.

---

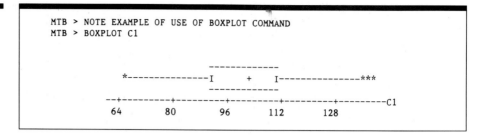

```
MTB > NOTE EXAMPLE OF USE OF BOXPLOT COMMAND
MTB > BOXPLOT C1


                          -------------
       *---------------I     +     I---------------***
                          -------------
       --+---------+---------+---------+---------+--------C1
        64        80        96       112       128
```

The lower hinge is denoted by $h_l$, the upper hinge by $h_u$, and the $H$-spread by $H$.

---

**Definition B.2** ▬▬▬▬▬▬▬▬▬▬▬▬▬▬▬▬▬▬▬▬▬▬▬▬▬▬▬▬▬▬

The **inner fences** are the two values located at $h_l - 1.5H$ and $h_u + 1.5H$. The **outer fences** are two two values located at $h_l - 3H$ and $h_u + 3H$.

---

**Definition B.3** ▬▬▬▬▬▬▬▬▬▬▬▬▬▬▬▬▬▬▬▬▬▬▬▬▬▬▬▬▬▬

The **adjacent values** are the two most extreme data values that are at least as large as $h_l - 1.5H$ and no more than $h_u + 1.5H$, respectively.

---

The BOXPLOT command has the following form:

BOXPLOT C

This command creates a plot that describes the values in the indicated column. The "middle" of these values is indicated by a box extending from the lower hinge to the upper hinge. The median of the set of values is marked by a $+$ which appears within the box. "Whiskers" extend from the hinges to the corresponding adjacent values. The values between the inner and outer fences on each side are potential outliers and are represented by asterisks. Values less than the lower outer fence or greater than the upper outer fence are probable outliers and are represented by zeros. Exhibit B.17 shows a BOXPLOT for the data previously generated to illustrate the STEM-AND-LEAF command.

## B.8

## Commands for Random Value Generation

One of the most useful functions of the Minitab system is its ability to generate random observations from many important discrete and continuous distributions. The basic command used for such simulations is the RANDOM command. Various subcommands may be used with the RANDOM command to define the distribution from which observations are to be simulated. A simple example is

```
MTB > NOTE EXAMPLE OF THE USE OF THE RANDOM COMMAND WITH THE BERNOULLI
MTB > NOTE SUBCOMMAND
MTB > BASE = 100
MTB > RANDOM 50 OBSERVATIONS IN C1;
SUBC>   BERNOULLI P = 0.300.
MTB > PRINT C1
C1
    0    1    0    0    0    0    0    0    0    0    1    0    0    0    0
    0    1    0    1    0    1    1    0    0    1    1    0    0    1    0
    0    1    0    0    0    0    0    0    1    0    1    0    0    0    0
    1    0    0    0    0

MTB > AVERAGE C1
    MEAN    =       0.26000
```

random sampling from a Bernoulli distribution. In this case we obtain the outcomes of a specified number of independent trials resulting in either failure or success, where the prescribed probability of a success is $p$. The form of this command is

> RANDOM K OBSERVATIONS IN C, C, . . . , C
> BERNOULLI P = K [SUCCESS = K FAILURE = K]

The effect of this command is to simulate K Bernoulli observations in each of the columns C, C, . . . , C. A success will be designated by a 1 and failure by a 0, unless other values are specified in the subcommand.

Consider the case of a batter who has a probability of 0.300 of getting a hit. Fifty at bats were simulated in the output in Exhibit B.18. The outcomes of the 50 trials were placed in C1, and this column was printed. The AVERAGE command was used to find the relative frequency of success (batting average) of the hitter in these 50 at bats. The output shows that the average is 0.260, corresponding to the 13 ones and 37 zeros in C1.

Note that one other command was used with RANDOM in Exhibit B.18: BASE = K. If this command is not used, the Minitab system will haphazardly start choosing "random observations" from a list. To obtain the same set of "random observations" on more than one execution of a simulation, you must use the BASE command, which directs that the first "random observations" be selected from a specific location in the list. If the value of BASE is kept the same, the selection will always begin at the same place in the list. The value specified with the BASE command should be a positive integer. If more than one RANDOM command appears in a program following a BASE command, the second command will begin reading from the list where the first command stopped, the third where the second stopped, and so forth.

The forms of the subcommands used for simulating observations from various important discrete distributions are as follows:

> INTEGER A = K        B = K
> BINOMIAL N = K       P = K

POISSON MU = K

DISCRETE VALUES IN C, PROBABILITIES IN C

Through use of the DISCRETE subcommand, random observations having values $x_1, x_2, \ldots, x_k$ with probabilities $p_1, p_2, \ldots, p_k$ may be selected from a discrete distribution. The $x$s and $p$s must be stored in the columns indicated by the DISCRETE subcommand before the RANDOM command is executed.

The forms of the subcommands used for simulating observations from continuous distributions are as follows:

NORMAL MU = K    SIGMA = K

UNIFORM A = K    B = K

The NORMAL subcommand permits simulation from a normal population with expectation defined by $\mu = K$ and standard deviation defined by $\sigma = K$. The UNIFORM subcommand permits simulation from a continuous uniform distribution on the interval (A, B) defined by $A = K$, $B = K$. Simulation is possible from other continuous distributions also. The reader is referred to the *Minitab Student Handbook*, Second Edition, for further details.

In the Minitab output in Exhibit B.19, random samples of size 25 are taken from the binomial distribution with $n = 20$ and $p = 0.8$, the discrete uniform distribution with $A = 1$ and $B = 37$, and the normal distribution with $\mu = 50$ and $\sigma = 10$. These observations are put into C1, C2, and C3, respectively, and printed. The discrete uniform distribution assigns equal probability to each of the integers from A to B, so each integer from 1 to 37 has a probability of 1/37 of being chosen to appear in C2.

## B.9

## Elementary Probability and Statistical Commands

Two Minitab commands—PDF and CDF—permit the generation of individual and cumulative probabilities for discrete random variables. Subcommands must be used with PDF and CDF to define the random variables to be used. The PDF command with the binomial random variable has the following form:

PDF FOR VALUES IN E [PUT RESULTS IN E]

BINOMIAL N = K    P = K

Suppose we want to know the probability that a 0.300 hitter will get five hits in his next ten at bats. The following two Minitab lines will produce the required probability:

PDF 5;

BINOMIAL N = 10    P = 0.300.

Unless the results are to be stored by Minitab, the PDF command will cause the requested probabilities to be printed. In response to the above command, the Minitab system would compute and print out the probability 0.1029.

```
MTB > BASE = 500
MTB > NOTE EXAMPLE OF THE USE OF THE RANDOM COMMAND IN BINOMIAL CASE
MTB > RANDOM 25 OBS IN C1;
SUBC> BINOMIAL N = 20 P = 0.8.
MTB > PRINT C1
C1
    17      15      16      15      17      16      19      16      15      14.     16
    16      18      16      16      16      13      15      14      15      18      17
    15      17      18

MTB > TALLY C1

        C1    COUNT
        13      1
        14      2
        15      6
        16      8
        17      4
        18      3
        19      1
        N=     25

MTB > NOTE EXAMPLE OF THE USE OF THE RANDOM COMMAND FOR INTEGERS
MTB > RANDOM 25 OBS IN C2;
SUBC> INTEGER A = 1 B = 37.
MTB > PRINT C2
C2
    24      34      37       5      14      25      27       4      12      12      20
    36      36      15      33      17      23      24       6       6      26      28
    34      33      11

MTB > NOTE EXAMPLE OF THE USE OF THE RANDOM COMMAND IN NORMAL CASE
MTB > RANDOM 25 OBS IN C3;
SUBC> NORMAL MU = 50 SIGMA = 10.
MTB > PRINT C3
C3
    58.1637   55.6039   52.3291   63.0065   48.0748   35.5793   54.5038
    60.2733   52.7998   39.0323   44.0700   31.7189   61.1261   48.6116
    41.2267   60.9676   49.8591   60.0639   66.0155   52.3777   41.3250
    48.3923   55.2734   59.5608   58.0307
```

If the PDF line includes no arguments, the entire distribution is printed. The form of the PDF command used with the Poisson distribution is particularly simple, as only one parameter, $\mu$, must be specified. To find all Poisson probabilities for $\mu = 4$, the following command and subcommand would be used:

PDF;

POISSON MU = 4.

The second command, CDF, causes Minitab to calculate the cumulative probabilities for discrete distributions. As with PDF, appropriate subcommands must be used to specify the distribution of interest. The general form of the CDF command for the binomial distribution is

CDF FOR VALUES IN E [PUT RESULTS IN E]

BINOMIAL N = K      P = K

Similarly, for the Poisson distribution CDF takes the form

CDF FOR VALUES IN E [PUT RESULTS IN E]
POISSON MU = K

Exhibit B.20 shows the output generated when the PDF and CDF commands were used to obtain the individual and cumulative probabilities for the binomial distribution with $n = 20$ and $p = 0.25$ and for the Poisson distribution with $\mu = 4$. Because probabilities smaller than 0.00005 are not printed out by these commands, no individual or cumulative probabilities are printed in the B(20, 0.25) output for values of X exceeding 13. Similarly, no individual or cumulative probabilities are printed in the Poisson ($\mu = 4$) output for values of X exceeding 14.

**Exhibit B.20**

```
MTB > NOTE EXAMPLE OF USE OF PDF AND CDF COMMANDS
MTB > NOTE BINOMIAL CASE
MTB > PDF;
SUBC> BINOMIAL N = 20 P = 0.25.

      BINOMIAL WITH N =   20  P = 0.250000
        K          P( X = K)
        0            0.0032
        1            0.0211
        2            0.0669
        3            0.1339
        4            0.1897
        5            0.2023
        6            0.1686
        7            0.1124
        8            0.0609
        9            0.0271
       10            0.0099
       11            0.0030
       12            0.0008
       13            0.0002
       14            0.0000
MTB > CDF;
SUBC> BINOMIAL N = 20 P = 0.25.

      BINOMIAL WITH N =   20  P = 0.250000
        K  P( X LESS OR = K)
        0            0.0032
        1            0.0243
        2            0.0913
        3            0.2252
        4            0.4148
        5            0.6172
        6            0.7858
        7            0.8982
        8            0.9591
        9            0.9861
       10            0.9961
       11            0.9991
       12            0.9998
```

```
MTB > NOTE POISSON CASE
MTB > PDF;
SUBC> POISSON MU = 4.

        POISSON WITH MEAN =    4.000
          K            P( X = K)
          0              0.0183
          1              0.0733
          2              0.1465
          3              0.1954
          4              0.1954
          5              0.1563
          6              0.1042
          7              0.0595
          8              0.0298
          9              0.0132
         10              0.0053
         11              0.0019
         12              0.0006
         13              0.0002
         14              0.0001
         15              0.0000
MTB > CDF;
SUBC> POISSON MU = 4.

        POISSON WITH MEAN =    4.000
          K   P( X LESS OR = K)
          0              0.0183
          1              0.0916
          2              0.2381
          3              0.4335
          4              0.6288
          5              0.7851
          6              0.8893
          7              0.9489
          8              0.9786
          9              0.9919
         10              0.9972
         11              0.9991
         12              0.9997
         13              0.9999
         14              1.0000
```

A simple but useful Minitab command called DESCRIBE gives elementary statistics for a column or columns of data. The DESCRIBE command has the form

DESCRIBE C, C, . . . , C

For each of the indicated columns, the DESCRIBE command calculates the number of values, the mean and the median, the 5 percent trimmed mean, the standard deviation $s$, the standard error of the mean $s/\sqrt{n}$, and the minimum, maximum, and first and third quartiles. Exhibit B.21 shows the output generated when the DESCRIBE command was used with the height data of Exhibit B.1.

**Exhibit B.21**

```
MTB > NOTE THIS IS AN EXAMPLE OF THE USE OF THE DESCRIBE COMMAND
MTB > SET THE FOLLOWING HEIGHTS IN C1
C1
    67    67    67    68    .    .    .

MTB > END
MTB > PRINT C1
C1
    67    67    67    68    68    69    69    69    69    69    69
    70    70    70    70    70    71    71    71    71    71    71
    71    71    71    72    72    72    72    72    72    72    72
    73    73    73    73    74    74    74    74    74    74    74
    74    75    75    76    77    78

MTB > DESCRIBE C1

                  N      MEAN    MEDIAN    TRMEAN    STDEV    SEMEAN
C1               50    71.620    71.500    71.568    2.531    0.358

                MIN       MAX        Q1        Q3
C1           67.000    78.000    70.000    74.000
```

The TINTERVAL and TTEST commands are useful for analyzing individual columns of data. The TINTERVAL command has the following form:

TINTERVAL WITH K PERCENT CONFIDENCE, DATA IN C

This command provides the count, mean, standard deviation, and standard error of the mean for the values in the indicated column, together with the endpoints of a confidence interval for $\mu$, based on the normal distribution. The stated confidence coefficient is used with the $t$-distribution to produce these endpoints.

The TTEST command and the ALTERNATIVE subcommand have the following form:

TTEST OF MU = K FOR C
ALTERNATIVE = K

This command causes the $t$ statistic, $(\bar{x} - \mu_0)/(s/\sqrt{n})$, to be computed. The alternative may be coded as $-1$, 0, or 1, to represent less than, unequal to, or greater than $\mu_0$. A $p$-value is computed for the indicated alternative. If the alternative is not specified, the unequal (0) alternative is assumed. Exhibit B.22 shows the output generated when the TINTERVAL and TTEST commands were used with the height data.

The CORRELATION command computes the Pearson correlation coefficient between all columns of data specified by the command. The command has the form

CORRELATION COEFFICIENTS BETWEEN C, C, . . . , C

The output of this command is the matrix of correlation coefficients between the columns specified. If some values are missing, the system calculates the correlation

## Exhibit B.22

```
MTB > NOTE EXAMPLE OF USE OF TINTERVAL AND TTEST COMMANDS
MTB > TINTERVAL WITH 90 PERCENT CONFIDENCE, DATA IN C1

              N       MEAN    STDEV   SE MEAN      90.0 PERCENT C.I.
C1           50      71.620   2.531    0.358    ( 71.020,   72.220)

MTB > TTEST OF MU = 70 DATA IN C1;
SUBC> ALTERNATIVE = 0.

TEST OF MU = 70.000 VS MU N.E. 70.000

              N       MEAN    STDEV   SE MEAN         T    P VALUE
C1           50      71.620   2.531    0.358        4.53    0.0000
```

coefficient between *pairs* of columns, using those rows that have no missing data. Exhibit B.23 shows the use of the CORRELATION command with data from *Introduction to Statistical Models in Geology*, by W. C. Krumbein and F. A. Graybill (New York: McGraw-Hill, 1965).

There are two Minitab commands used for the two-sample problem. The first is the TWOSAMPLE command, which has the following form and subcommands:

TWOSAMPLE T TEST [PERCENT CONF = K] DATA IN C AND C
ALTERNATIVE = K
POOLED PROCEDURE

Assume that there are $n_1$ observations in the first column and $n_2$ observations in the second column. The means are $\bar{x}_1$ and $\bar{x}_2$, the variances are $s_1^2$ and $s_2^2$, and the corresponding theoretical expectations are $\mu_1$ and $\mu_2$. The alternative specified in the subcommand ALTERNATIVE may be $-1$ or $1$, to correspond to $\mu_1 < \mu_2$ or $\mu_1 > \mu_2$, respectively. If the ALTERNATIVE subcommand is not used, a two-sided test is carried out. The output from TWOSAMPLE includes the values of $n_1$, $\bar{x}_1$, $s_1$, and $s_1/\sqrt{n_1}$ and $n_2$, $\bar{x}_2$, $s_2$, and $s_2/\sqrt{n_2}$. An estimate of the standard deviation of $\bar{x}_1 - \bar{x}_2$ is computed in the form of $s = (s_1^2/n_1 + s_2^2/n_2)^{1/2}$. The $t$ value, $t = (\bar{x}_1 - \bar{x}_2)/s$, is calculated. This statistic has a $t$ distribution, with an approximated value for the degrees of freedom under $H_0$. A $p$ value is computed for the appropriate alternative, using this distribution. Endpoints $\bar{x}_1 - \bar{x}_2 \pm st_{\alpha/2}$ are computed for a confidence interval for $\mu_1 - \mu_2$. Here $t_{\alpha/2}$ is the upper $(\alpha/2)$th percentile of this $t$ distribution. [The value of the confidence coefficient is $100(1 - \alpha)$.] Minitab computes the confidence interval if requested to do so on the command line.

The POOLED subcommand may be used along with the ALTERNATIVE subcommand for the two-sample problem. The assumption underlying the POOLED subcommand is that the populations from which the samples have been selected have a common variance $\sigma^2$. The value of $\sigma^2$ is estimated by $s_p^2 = [(n_1 - 1)s_1^2 + (n_2 - 1)s_2^2]/(n_1 + n_2 - 2)$, where $s_p^2$ is called the pooled

```
MTB > NOTE EXAMPLE OF USE OF CORRELATION COMMAND
MTB > READ INTO C1-C3
     12 ROWS READ
 ROW      C1      C2      C3

   1    12.0   0.870    1.69
   2     5.5   0.202    1.17
   3     4.5   0.203    1.17
   4     4.5   0.198    1.17
  .    .    .

MTB > END
MTB > PRINT C1-C3
 ROW      C1      C2      C3

   1    12.0   0.870    1.69
   2     5.5   0.202    1.17
   3     4.5   0.203    1.17
   4     4.5   0.198    1.17
   5    10.5   0.730    1.63
   6     4.5   0.510    1.59
   7     6.0   0.205    1.14
   8     4.5   0.670    1.92
   9     5.5   0.205    1.22
  10     6.0   0.271    1.71
  11     4.0   0.203    1.16
  12     6.0   0.264    1.37

MTB > CORRELATION BETWEEN C1,C2,C3

             C1        C2
 C2       0.722
 C3       0.398     0.803
```

estimate of $\sigma^2$. The standard deviation of $\bar{x}_1 - \bar{x}_2$ is estimated by $s_d = s_p(1/n_1 + 1/n_2)^{1/2}$. The $t$ value, $(\bar{x}_1 - \bar{x}_2)/s_d$, is assumed to have the $t$ distribution with $n_1 + n_2 - 2$ degrees of freedom under $H_0$. Appropriate endpoints of a confidence interval for $\mu_1 - \mu_2$ are computed, along with a $p$-value for the appropriate alternative.

Exhibit B.24 shows the output generated when the TWOSAMPLE command with $n_1 = 8$ and $n_2 = 10$ was used with some artificial data in C1 and C2. In the first application of TWOSAMPLE, alternative $-1$ was used without the POOLED subcommand. In the second application of TWOSAMPLE, the POOLED subcommand was used.

The second command used with data from two samples is the TWOT command. Its general form is

TWOT [K PERCENT CONFIDENCE] DATA IN C GROUPS IN C

The function of this command is to compare two independent samples stacked in a single column. The subcommands ALTERNATIVE and POOLED are used, just as with the TWOSAMPLE command. Exhibit B.25 shows the output generated when the data of the previous example were stacked in C3 with subscripts in C4.

```
MTB > NOTE EXAMPLES OF USE OF THE TWOSAMPLE COMMAND
MTB > SET C1
C1
    10    11    14     9    .    .    .

MTB > SET C2
C2
    12    10     8     9    .    .    .

MTB > PRINT C1-C2
  ROW   C1    C2

    1    10    12
    2    11    10
    3    14     8
    4     9     9
    5     8    15
    6     7    16
    7    15    18
    8    12    14
    9          12
   10          14

MTB > TWOSAMPLE T TEST, PERCENT CONF = 90, DATA IN C1,C2;
SUBC> ALTERNATIVE = -1.

TWOSAMPLE T FOR C1 VS C2
        N      MEAN    STDEV    SE MEAN
C1   8       10.75     2.82      1.0
C2  10       12.80     3.19      1.0

90 PCT CI FOR MU C1 - MU C2: (-4.5, 0.4)
TTEST MU C1 = MU C2 (VS LT): T=-1.45 P=0.084 DF=15.8

MTB > TWOSAMPLE T TEST, PERCENT CONF = 90, DATA IN C1,C2;
SUBC> ALTERNATIVE = -1;
SUBC> POOLED.

TWOSAMPLE T FOR C1 VS C2
        N      MEAN    STDEV    SE MEAN
C1   8       10.75     2.82      1.0
C2  10       12.80     3.19      1.0

90 PCT CI FOR MU C1 - MU C2: (-4.6, 0.5)
TTEST MU C1 = MU C2 (VS LT): T=-1.43 P=0.087 DF=16.0
```

## B.10

**Commands for Analysis of Variance and Regression**

One-way analysis of variance (ANOVA) calculations may be carried out using either the AOVONEWAY command or the ONEWAY command. The output from the two commands is quite similar.

The AOVONEWAY command has the following form:

AOVONEWAY FOR DATA IN C, C, . . . , C

```
MTB > NOTE EXAMPLE OF USE OF THE TWOT COMMAND
MTB > STACK C1,C2 INTO C3;
SUBC> SUBSCRIPTS C4.
MTB > NAME C3 'DATA' C4 'SUBSCRPT'
MTB > PRINT C3,C4
 ROW    DATA  SUBSCRPT

   1      10         1
   2      11         1
   3      14         1
   4       9         1
   5       8         1
   6       7         1
   7      15         1
   8      12         1
   9      12         2
  10      10         2
  11       8         2
  12       9         2
  13      15         2
  14      16         2
  15      18         2
  16      14         2
  17      12         2
  18      14         2

MTB > TWOT, PERCENT CONF = 90, DATA C3, SUBSCRIPTS C4;
SUBC> ALTERNATIVE = -1.

TWOSAMPLE T FOR DATA
SUBSCRPT    N       MEAN     STDEV    SE MEAN
1           8      10.75      2.82       1.0
2          10      12.80      3.19       1.0

90 PCT CI FOR MU 1 - MU 2: (-4.5, 0.4)
TTEST MU 1 = MU 2 (VS LT): T=-1.45 P=0.084 DF=15.8

MTB > TWOT, PERCENT CONF = 90, DATA C3, SUBSCRIPTS C4;
SUBC> ALTERNATIVE = -1;
SUBC> POOLED.

TWOSAMPLE T FOR DATA
SUBSCRPT    N       MEAN     STDEV    SE MEAN
1           8      10.75      2.82       1.0
2          10      12.80      3.19       1.0

90 PCT CI FOR MU 1 - MU 2: (-4.6, 0.5)
TTEST MU 1 = MU 2 (VS LT): T=-1.43 P=0.087 DF=16.0
```

A one-way analysis of variance is carried out under the assumption that the observations in each of the indicated columns are for a particular level of the treatments being compared. The numbers of observations of treatments need not be the same. Exhibit B.26 shows the output generated when the AOVONEWAY command was used with the following data on final exam scores in a statistics course for students from three different academic fields.

```
MTB > NOTE EXAMPLE OF THE USE OF THE AOVONEWAY COMMAND
MTB > SET C1
C1
    112     76     124      64     .    .    .

MTB > END
MTB > SET C2
C2
     84    100      56     108     .    .    .

MTB > END
MTB > SET C3
C3
     80     96      96      92     .    .    .

MTB > END
MTB > PRINT C1-C3
 ROW     C1     C2     C3

   1    112     84     80
   2     76    100     96
   3    124     56     96
   4     64    108     92
   5    132     96    116
   6    112     64
   7     88     92
   8    100    124
   9     80    136
  10            132

MTB > AOVONEWAY FOR DATA IN C1-C3

ANALYSIS OF VARIANCE
SOURCE      DF        SS       MS        F
FACTOR       2        36       18     0.03
ERROR       21     11482      547
TOTAL       23     11517
                                   INDIVIDUAL 95 PCT CI'S FOR MEAN
                                   BASED ON POOLED STDEV
LEVEL        N      MEAN    STDEV   -------+---------+---------+-------
C1           9     98.67    23.15       (----------*----------)
C2          10     99.20    26.92        (----------*----------)
C3           5     96.00    12.96   (--------------*--------------)
                                   -------+---------+---------+-------
POOLED STDEV =     23.38               84        98       112
```

| Agriculture | Liberal Arts | Home Economics |
|---|---|---|
| 112 | 84 | 80 |
| 76 | 100 | 96 |
| 124 | 56 | 96 |
| 64 | 108 | 92 |
| 132 | 96 | 116 |
| 112 | 64 | |
| 88 | 92 | |
| 100 | 124 | |
| 80 | 136 | |
| | 132 | |

The output from the AOVONEWAY command includes the analysis of variance table, the means and standard deviations by treatments, the square root of the mean square for error, and a plot of 95 percent confidence intervals for the true treatment means. An interpretation of this output is given in Chapter 12 of this text.

The ONEWAY command requires that all the data on each of the treatments appear in a single column. The treatment levels corresponding to the observations are given in another column. The ONEWAY command has the following form:

ONEWAY ANOVA FOR DATA IN C, SUBSCRIPTS IN C

The subscript column contains integers that specify the treatment level for the values in the data column. Customarily, all rows of the subscript column corresponding to observations at treatment level one contain a 1, all rows corresponding to observations at treatment level two contain a 2, and so forth. Any convenient integers may be used to identify the treatment levels. The data need not be in any particular order, so long as the treatment levels are appropriately identified. The output of the ONEWAY command for the final examination data is given in Exhibit B.27.

The ONEWAY command also can be used to obtain residuals and fitted values. For the one-way analysis of variance, the fitted values are the group means and the residuals are the differences between the observations and the corresponding group means. The form of the ONEWAY command used to obtain fitted

**Exhibit B.27**

```
MTB > NOTE EXAMPLE OF THE USE OF THE ONEWAY COMMAND
MTB > NOTE CREATION OF SUBSCRIPT COLUMN
MTB > JOIN C3 C2 C1 IN C1
MTB > SET C2
C2
    1   1   1   1   .   .   .

MTB > END
MTB > NAME C2 'COLLEGE'
MTB > ONEWAY ANOVA FOR DATA IN C1 SUBSCRIPTS IN C2

ANALYSIS OF VARIANCE ON C1
SOURCE      DF        SS        MS        F
COLLEGE      2        36        18      0.03
ERROR       21     11482       547
TOTAL       23     11517
                                    INDIVIDUAL 95 PCT CI'S FOR MEAN
                                    BASED ON POOLED STDEV
LEVEL        N      MEAN     STDEV   -------+---------+---------+-------
   1         9     98.67     23.15          (----------*----------)
   2        10     99.20     26.92          (----------*----------)
   3         5     96.00     12.96   (--------------*--------------)
                                    -------+---------+---------+-------
POOLED STDEV =     23.38            84        98        112
```

```
MTB > ONEWAY DATA C1 C2 RESIDS C3 FITTED VALUES C4

ANALYSIS OF VARIANCE ON C1
SOURCE      DF       SS        MS         F
COLLEGE      2       36        18      0.03
ERROR       21    11482       547
TOTAL       23    11517
                                      INDIVIDUAL 95 PCT CI'S FOR MEAN
                                      BASED ON POOLED STDEV
LEVEL        N     MEAN     STDEV   -------+---------+---------+-------
    1        9    98.67     23.15          (----------*----------)
    2       10    99.20     26.92         (----------*----------)
    3        5    96.00     12.96   (----------------*----------------)
                                      -------+---------+---------+-------
POOLED STDEV =   23.38                     84        98       112
MTB > NAME C4 'FITS' C3 'RESIDS'
MTB > PLOT C3 C4


RESIDS  -
        -                                          *      2
        -
   25+                                             *      *
        -        *
        -                                          2
        -                                                 *
        -
    0+           2                                 *      *
        -        *                                        2
        -                                          *
        -        *                                        *
        -                                          *
  -25+                                             *
        -
        -                                          *      *
        -
        -                                                 *
  -50+
        --+---------+---------+---------+---------+---------FITS
       95.90     96.60     97.30     98.00     98.70
```

values and residuals is

ONEWAY ANOVA FOR DATA IN C, LEVELS IN C,                    &
[RESIDS IN C [FITS IN C]]

Various useful plots can be generated using the residuals. These plots may be used to check the normality assumption or the equal variance assumption, as well as for other purposes. Exhibit B.28 shows the output generated when the ONEWAY command was used with the examination data to plot the residuals, stored in C3, versus the fitted values, stored in C4.

The TWOWAY analysis of variance command is very similar in form and output to the ONEWAY command. The command carries out an analysis of variance for a balanced design (that is, one in which each row and column has an equal number of observations). The TWOWAY command has the following form:

> TWOWAY ANOVA FOR DATA IN C, ROW LEVELS IN C,         &
> COLUMN LEVELS IN C

The output from the TWOWAY command presents the analysis of variance table. Exhibit B.29 is an example of the output generated by the TWOWAY command for a $3 \times 4$ situation in which there are two observations per cell. The data are synthetic data created for the purpose of illustrating the TWOWAY command. An interpretation of such output for the randomized block design is given in Chapter 12 of this text.

The REGRESS command is one of the most important and useful commands in Minitab. For simple linear regression the REGRESS command has the following form:

> REGRESS Y IN C ON 1 X IN C, [PUT STANDARD RESIDS       &
> IN C], [PUT PRED IN C]

The model used is $E(Y) = \beta_0 + \beta_1 X$. The first column mentioned gives the values of the dependent variable, and the second column mentioned gives the corresponding values of the independent variable. Additional columns may be specified for the storing of particular output from the regression. The first of these will be used to store the values of the standardized residuals, $(y_i - \hat{y}_i)/s_{(y_i - \hat{y}_i)}$, $i = 1, 2, \ldots, n$, after the REGRESS command is executed. The second of these will be used to store the predicted values, $\hat{y}_i = \hat{\beta}_0 + \hat{\beta}_1 x_i$, $i = 1, 2, \ldots, n$, where $\hat{\beta}_0$ and $\hat{\beta}_1$ are the intercept and the slope of the least squares line. The standardized residuals and the predicted values are useful for creating various plots which aid in determining the goodness-of-fit of the simple linear model and in verifying the assumptions of the simple linear model.

An example of the Minitab output from the REGRESS command for the simple linear regression case is given in Exhibit B.30. The data are mean risk scores for managers (in C2) in a given age group (in C1). The data come from an article entitled "The Relationship Between Age and Risk Taking Among Managers," by Victor Vroom and Bernd Pahl, in the *Journal of Applied Psychology* 55, 1971.

The first portion of the output is the regression equation, which in the simple linear case is the equation of the least squares line. In this case it is $\hat{y} = 0.632 - 0.0115x$. The next portion of the output gives the coefficients $\hat{\beta}_i$, the standard deviations of the coefficients $s_{\hat{\beta}_i}$ and the $t$ values $\hat{\beta}_i/s_{\hat{\beta}_i}$ for $i = 0, 1$. These $t$ values can be used to test the hypotheses $H_0: \beta_i = 0$ using a test with $n - 2$ degrees of freedom. The value of the square root of the mean square for error, $\sqrt{\text{MSE}}$, is calculated and printed out as $s = 0.07978$. The degrees of freedom, $(n - 2) = 13$, is printed out. The value of $R^2 = \text{SSR}/\text{SST}$, the quotient of the sum of squares for regression and the total sum of squares (corrected), is calculated and printed out as a percentage, 67.3. This value can also be written as $1 - (\text{SSE}/\text{SST})$, where SSE represents the sum of squares for error. The adjusted

```
MTB > NOTE EXAMPLE OF THE USE OF THE TWOWAY COMMAND
MTB > SET C1
C1
     3     2     5     7     .   .   .

MTB > END
MTB > NOTE ROW AND COLUMN SUBSCRIPTS
MTB > SET C2
C2
    1    1    2    2    .   .   .

MTB > END
MTB > SET C3
C3
    1    1    1    1    .   .   .

MTB > END
MTB > PRINT C1-C3
  ROW    C1    C2    C3

    1     3     1     1
    2     2     1     1
    3     5     2     1
    4     7     2     1
    5    11     3     1
    6    10     3     1
    7     5     1     2
    8     4     1     2
    9    10     2     2
   10    11     2     2
   11    15     3     2
   12    16     3     2
   13    12     1     3
   14    14     1     3
   15    15     2     3
   16    17     2     3
   17    20     3     3
   18    21     3     3
   19    14     1     4
   20    15     1     4
   21    21     2     4
   22    20     2     4
   23    26     3     4
   24    25     3     4

MTB > TWOWAY ANOVA FOR DATA IN C1, ROWS SUBS IN C2, COL SUBS IN C3

ANALYSIS OF VARIANCE   C1

SOURCE         DF        SS        MS
C2              2    351.583   175.792
C3              3    694.458   231.486
INTERACTION     6     12.417     2.069
ERROR          12     10.500     0.875
TOTAL          23   1068.958
```

## Exhibit B.30

```
MTB > NOTE EXAMPLE OF USE OF THE REGRESSION COMMAND
MTB > NOTE SIMPLE LINEAR REGRESSION CASE
MTB > SET C1
C1
     25     26     28     31     .   .   .

MTB > END
MTB > SET C2
C2
    0.42   0.46   0.32   0.35     .   .   .

MTB > END
MTB > NAME C1 'X' C2 'Y'
MTB > BRIEF = 3
MTB > REGRESS Y IN C2 ON 1 X IN C1 STANDARD RESIDS C3 PREDICTED C4

The regression equation is
Y = 0.632 - 0.0115 X

Predictor        Coef         Stdev      t-ratio
Constant       0.63168       0.08554       7.38
X             -0.011471      0.002220     -5.17

s = 0.07978    R-sq = 67.3%    R-sq(adj) = 64.7%

Analysis of Variance

SOURCE          DF          SS            MS
Regression       1       0.16995       0.16995
Error           13       0.08274       0.00636
Total           14       0.25269

Obs.       X        Y       Fit  Stdev.Fit  Residual  St.Resid
  1      25.0    0.4200    0.3449   0.0344    0.0751     1.04
  2      26.0    0.4600    0.3334   0.0326    0.1266     1.74
  3      28.0    0.3200    0.3105   0.0293    0.0095     0.13
  4      31.0    0.3500    0.2761   0.0250    0.0739     0.98
  5      32.0    0.1100    0.2646   0.0238   -0.1546    -2.03R
  6      33.0    0.2600    0.2531   0.0228    0.0069     0.09
  7      34.0    0.2500    0.2417   0.0219    0.0083     0.11
  8      35.0    0.1300    0.2302   0.0213   -0.1002    -1.30
  9      37.0    0.1200    0.2073   0.0206   -0.0873    -1.13
 10      38.0    0.1300    0.1958   0.0206   -0.0658    -0.85
 11      41.0    0.1200    0.1614   0.0221   -0.0414    -0.54
 12      43.0    0.1400    0.1384   0.0241    0.0016     0.02
 13      46.0    0.1700    0.1040   0.0281    0.0660     0.88
 14      55.0    0.0500    0.0008   0.0442    0.0492     0.74
 15      57.0    0.0100   -0.0222   0.0481    0.0322     0.51

R denotes an obs. with a large st. resid.
```

value of $R^2 = 1 - [(n - 1)/(n - 2)](SSE/SST)$ is also calculated and printed out as a percentage, 64.7.

The next portion of the output from the REGRESS command is the ANOVA (analysis of variance) table. The headings SOURCE, DF, SS, and MS stand for the source of the variation, the degrees of freedom, the sum of squares, and the mean square, respectively. Following the analysis of variance table is

```
MTB > NOTE USE OF THE PREDICT SUBCOMMAND WITH THE REGRESSION COMMAND
MTB > BRIEF = 1
MTB > REGRESS Y IN C2 ON 1 X IN C1 STANDARD RESIDS C3 PREDICTED C4;
SUBC> PREDICT X =40.

The regression equation is
Y = 0.632 - 0.0115 X

Predictor        Coef        Stdev      t-ratio
Constant      0.63168      0.08554         7.38
X            -0.011471     0.002220        -5.17

s = 0.07978     R-sq = 67.3%     R-sq(adj) = 64.7%

Analysis of Variance

SOURCE         DF          SS          MS
Regression      1       0.16995     0.16995
Error          13       0.08274     0.00636
Total          14       0.25269


    Fit  Stdev.Fit         95% C.I.            95% P.I.
 0.1728     0.0214   ( 0.1266, 0.2191)   (-0.0056, 0.3513)
```

another table with the headings Obs., X, Y, Fit, Stdev.Fit, Residual, and St.Resid. For each value of $i$, $x_i$, $y_i$, $\hat{y}_i = \hat{\beta}_0 + \hat{\beta}_1 x_i$, $s_{\hat{y}_i}$, $y_i - \hat{y}_i$, and $(y_i - \hat{y}_i)/s_{y_i - \hat{y}_i}$ are printed. These values represent, respectively, the observed $x$-value, the observed $y$-value, the value of the least squares equation at $x = x_i$, the standard deviation of this prediction, the residual $y_i - \hat{y}_i$, and the standardized residual for each point. See Chapter 10 for further description of these terms.

It is frequently important to estimate an average value of $Y$ for a prescribed level of $x$, say $x = x_0$. We can obtain this estimated value, $\hat{\beta}_0 + \hat{\beta}_1 x_0$, by using the simple subcommand PREDICT with the REGRESS command. Suppose we want to know what the average risk score is for a manager of age 40, based on the previous data. Use of the simple subcommand

PREDICT 40

following the REGRESS command produces the output shown in Exhibit B.31.

The PREDICT subcommand gives two 95 percent intervals. The first is for the average value of $Y$ at $x = x_0$ and has the endpoints

$$\hat{\beta}_0 + \hat{\beta}_1 x_0 \pm \sqrt{\text{MSE}} \sqrt{\frac{1}{n} + \frac{(x_0 - \bar{x})^2}{\Sigma(x_i - \bar{x})^2}}\,(t)$$

or

$$\hat{y} \pm s_{\hat{y}}(t)$$

where $s_{\hat{y}}$ is the standard deviation associated with the estimate $\hat{y}$ and $t$ represents $t_{0.025, n-2}$. The second is for the prediction of an individual value of $y$. This prediction interval is wider and has endpoints given by

$$\hat{y} \pm \sqrt{\text{MSE}} \sqrt{1 + \left(\frac{1}{n}\right) + \frac{(x_0 - \bar{x})^2}{\Sigma(x_i - \bar{x})^2}} \ (t)$$

or

$$\hat{y} \pm \sqrt{s_{\hat{y}}^2 + \text{MSE}} \ (t)$$

The 95 percent confidence and prediction intervals for the risk score for a 40-year-old manager were found by Minitab to be (0.1266, 0.2191) and (−0.0056, 0.3513).

To obtain multiple regression output, only a very simple modification of the REGRESS command is required. The number of regressors must be indicated, and the columns in which the values of these regressors are located must be identified. The modified command has the following form:

REGRESS Y IN C ON K XS IN C, C, . . . , C, [PUT STD RESIDS &
IN C], [PUT PRED IN C]

The general form of the model used is $E(Y) = \beta_0 + \beta_1 x_1 + \cdots + \beta_p x_p$. The multiple regression equation is of the form $\hat{y} = \hat{\beta}_0 + \hat{\beta}_1 x_1 + \hat{\beta}_2 x_2 + \cdots + \hat{\beta}_p x_p$, where $\hat{\beta}_i$ are estimates of the corresponding $\beta_i$, $i = 0, 1, 2, \ldots, p$. As an example, the mean risk scores for managers were used with the independent variables $x$ and $x^2$ to yield the Minitab output shown in Exhibit B.32.

The output of the REGRESS command for multiple regression is very similar to that for the simple linear case. The regression equation is given in Exhibit B.32 as

$$\hat{y} = 1.36 - 0.0495x + 0.000465x^2$$

The individual coefficients $\hat{\beta}_i$ can be used to test $H_0$: $\beta_i = 0$ for $i = 0, 1, 2, \ldots, p$, with $n - p - 1$ degrees of freedom ($n - 3 = 12$ in this example). The value of $s$ is still defined to be $\sqrt{\text{MSE}} = 0.06789$. The value of $R^2 = \text{SSR/SST} = 0.781$, and the adjusted value of $R^2$ is $1 - [(n - 1)/(n - p)](\text{SSE/SST}) = 0.745$. Note that $R^2$ has increased substantially with the inclusion of $x^2$. The analysis of variance table now has $p$ degrees of freedom for regression and $n - p - 1$ degrees of freedom for error. For this example the actual values are $p = 2$ and $n - p - 1 = n - 3 = 12$, respectively. The analysis of variance table is also decomposed into terms of the form $\text{SS}(\beta_1)$, $\text{SS}(\beta_2|\beta_1)$, $\text{SS}(\beta_3|\beta_1, \beta_2)$, . . . , $\text{SS}(\beta_p|\beta_1, \beta_2, \ldots, \beta_{p-1})$, each of which has 1 degree of freedom. The form of the last table in the output differs in two respects from the one generated in the simple linear case. First, only the values for the first regressor, $x_{i1}$, are listed. Second, the predicted values are of the form $\hat{y}_i = \hat{\beta}_0 + \hat{\beta}_1 x_{i1} + \hat{\beta}_2 x_{i2} + \cdots + \hat{\beta}_p x_{ip}$.

The PREDICT subcommand may be used as in the simple linear case; it has the form

PREDICT E, E, . . . , E

Additional information on the interpretation of multiple regression output may be found in Chapter 11 and in the *Minitab Student Handbook,* Second Edition.

## Exhibit B.32

```
MTB > NOTE EXAMPLE OF REGRESSION COMMAND FOR MULTIPLE REGRESSION
MTB > MULT C1 BY C1 IN C3
MTB > NAME C2 'Y' C1 'X' C3 'X*X'
MTB > REGRESS Y IN C2 ON 2 XS IN C1 C3 STANDARD RES C4 PREDICTED C5

The regression equation is
Y = 1.36 - 0.0495 X +0.000465 X*X

Predictor        Coef         Stdev      t-ratio
Constant        1.3644       0.3090        4.41
X              -0.04953      0.01572      -3.15
X*X             0.0004652    0.0001907     2.44


s = 0.06789     R-sq = 78.1%    R-sq(adj) = 74.5%

Analysis of Variance

SOURCE          DF          SS           MS
Regression       2      0.197387     0.098693
Error           12      0.055307     0.004609
Total           14      0.252693

SOURCE          DF        SEQ SS
X                1      0.169955
X*X              1      0.027432

Obs.       X          Y       Fit Stdev.Fit  Residual    St.Resid
  1      25.0     0.4200    0.4169   0.0415    0.0031        0.06
  2      26.0     0.4600    0.3911   0.0365    0.0689        1.20
  3      28.0     0.3200    0.3422   0.0281   -0.0222       -0.36
  4      31.0     0.3500    0.2760   0.0213    0.0740        1.15
  5      32.0     0.1100    0.2557   0.0206   -0.1457       -2.25R
  6      33.0     0.2600    0.2365   0.0206    0.0235        0.36
  7      34.0     0.2500    0.2181   0.0210    0.0319        0.49
  8      35.0     0.1300    0.2007   0.0218   -0.0707       -1.10
  9      37.0     0.1200    0.1686   0.0236   -0.0486       -0.76
 10      38.0     0.1300    0.1539   0.0246   -0.0239       -0.38
 11      41.0     0.1200    0.1156   0.0266    0.0044        0.07
 12      43.0     0.1400    0.0947   0.0272    0.0453        0.73
 13      46.0     0.1700    0.0703   0.0276    0.0997        1.61
 14      55.0     0.0500    0.0474   0.0422    0.0026        0.05
 15      57.0     0.0100    0.0525   0.0511   -0.0425       -0.95

R denotes an obs. with a large st. resid.

MTB > STOP
```

The amount of output generated by the REGRESS command can be controlled by using the BRIEF command. The form of this command is

BRIEF = K

K can have the value 1, 2, or 3. The larger the value of K, the more regression output is provided. The output is restricted as follows:

BRIEF = 1: Minitab prints the regression equation, table of coefficients, $s$, $R^2$, and the first portion of the ANOVA table.

BRIEF = 2: Minitab prints the above information, plus the second portion of the ANOVA table and the table of data, fitted values, standard deviations of the fitted values, residuals, and standardized residuals only for "unusual" observations (that is, those labeled X or R).

BRIEF = 3: Minitab prints essentially the same information as for BRIEF = 2, except that the full table of data, fitted values, standard deviations of the fitted values, residuals, and standardized residuals is printed.

## B.11

## Miscellaneous Commands

There are a number of Minitab commands that are used for special formatting, inputting, and outputting of data, including

```
BATCH
ERASE E, E, . . . , E
NEWPAGE
NOTE
RESTART
STOP
TSHARE
HEIGHT OF PLOTS IS K LINES
WIDTH OF PLOTS = K SPACES
OW = K SPACES
OH = K LINES
OUTFILE 'FILENAME'
```

The BATCH command makes Minitab suitable for "batch" use; TSHARE makes Minitab suitable for interactive use. Note that these commands do not cause the system to be in one mode or the other; they merely make its actions suitable for a particular mode.

The ERASE command permits the deletion of values in columns of the worksheet or stored constants. The NEWPAGE command causes the following output on a line printer to come at the beginning of a new page. (Unlike other commands, this command does not appear on the printed Minitab output.) The NOTE command allows the user of the Minitab system to write any desired comment or remark on a line in the program. This command is useful in documentation of Minitab programs. (Examples of the NOTE command can be seen in most of the exhibits in this Appendix.) The RESTART command causes the worksheet to be erased, allowing the user to begin a new Minitab program. The STOP command is the last command in a Minitab program; it terminates conversation with the system.

There are several commands that, when used with particular subcommands, will cause Minitab to accept input or generate output in FORTRAN format. Such commands include READ, SET, INSERT, PRINT, and WRITE. Each of these commands must be followed by a subcommand that gives a FORTRAN format specification. Consult the *Minitab Student Handbook* for further information on these procedures.

The HEIGHT and WIDTH commands allow the specification of the height and width of plots. These commands were discussed in Section B.7. All plots following HEIGHT and WIDTH commands will use the values specified, until these values are changed by other HEIGHT and/or WIDTH command(s).

There are several useful output commands, including the OW command, which permits determination of the width (in spaces) of Minitab output, and the OH command, which specifies the height (in lines). The OUTFILE command directs the Minitab system to place the output from Minitab into a specified file.

In addition, the symbols # and & have special meaning in Minitab. The Minitab system ignores anything on a line after the # symbol. The & symbol at the end of a Minitab line allows continuation of a command to the next line.

# Appendix C

# Statistical Tables

# Table I

**Cumulative Normal Distribution, $P(Z \leqslant z)$**

| z | .00 | .01 | .02 | .03 | .04 | .05 | .06 | .07 | .08 | .09 |
|---|---|---|---|---|---|---|---|---|---|---|
| .0 | .5000 | .5040 | .5080 | .5120 | .5160 | .5199 | .5239 | .5279 | .5319 | .5359 |
| .1 | .5398 | .5438 | .5478 | .5517 | .5557 | .5596 | .5636 | .5675 | .5714 | .5753 |
| .2 | .5793 | .5832 | .5871 | .5910 | .5948 | .5987 | .6026 | .6064 | .6103 | .6141 |
| .3 | .6179 | .6217 | .6255 | .6293 | .6331 | .6368 | .6406 | .6443 | .6480 | .6517 |
| .4 | .6554 | .6591 | .6628 | .6664 | .6700 | .6736 | .6772 | .6808 | .6844 | .6879 |
| .5 | .6915 | .6950 | .6985 | .7019 | .7054 | .7088 | .7123 | .7157 | .7190 | .7224 |
| 6 | .7257 | .7291 | .7324 | .7357 | .7389 | .7422 | .7454 | .7486 | .7517 | .7549 |
| .7 | .7580 | .7611 | .7642 | .7673 | .7704 | .7734 | .7764 | .7794 | .7823 | .7852 |
| .8 | .7881 | .7910 | .7939 | .7967 | .7995 | .8023 | .8051 | .8078 | .8106 | .8133 |
| .9 | .8159 | .8186 | .8212 | .8238 | .8264 | .8289 | .8315 | .8340 | .8365 | .8389 |
| 1.0 | .8413 | .8438 | .8461 | .8485 | .8508 | .8531 | .8554 | .8577 | .8599 | .8621 |
| 1.1 | .8643 | .8665 | .8686 | .8708 | .8729 | .8749 | .8770 | .8790 | .8810 | .8830 |
| 1.2 | .8849 | .8869 | .8888 | .8907 | .8925 | .8944 | .8962 | .8980 | .8997 | .9015 |
| 1.3 | .9032 | .9049 | .9066 | .9082 | .9099 | .9115 | .9131 | .9147 | .9162 | .9177 |
| 1.4 | .9192 | .9207 | .9222 | .9236 | .9251 | .9265 | .9279 | .9292 | .9306 | .9319 |
| 1.5 | .9332 | .9345 | .9357 | .9370 | .9382 | .9394 | .9406 | .9418 | .9429 | .9441 |
| 1.6 | .9452 | .9463 | .9474 | .9484 | .9495 | .9505 | .9515 | .9525 | .9535 | .9545 |
| 1.7 | .9554 | .9564 | .9573 | .9582 | .9591 | .9599 | .9608 | .9616 | .9625 | .9633 |
| 1.8 | .9641 | .9649 | .9656 | .9664 | .9671 | .9678 | .9686 | .9693 | .9699 | .9706 |
| 1.9 | .9713 | .9719 | .9726 | .9732 | .9738 | .9744 | .9750 | .9756 | .9761 | .9767 |
| 2.0 | .9772 | .9778 | .9783 | .9788 | .9793 | .9798 | .9803 | .9808 | .9812 | .9817 |
| 2.1 | .9821 | .9826 | .9830 | .9834 | .9838 | .9842 | .9846 | .9850 | .9854 | .9857 |
| 2.2 | .9861 | .9864 | .9868 | .9871 | .9875 | .9878 | .9881 | .9884 | .9887 | .9890 |
| 2.3 | .9893 | .9896 | .9898 | .9901 | .9904 | .9906 | .9909 | .9911 | .9913 | .9910 |
| 2.4 | .9918 | .9920 | .9922 | .9925 | .9927 | .9929 | .9931 | .9932 | .9934 | .9936 |
| 2.5 | .9938 | .9940 | .9941 | .9943 | .9945 | .9946 | .9948 | .9949 | .9951 | .9952 |
| 2.6 | .9953 | .9955 | .9956 | .9957 | .9959 | .9960 | .9961 | .9962 | .9963 | .9964 |
| 2.7 | .9965 | .9966 | .9967 | .9968 | .9969 | .9970 | .9971 | .9972 | .9973 | .9974 |
| 2.8 | .9974 | .9975 | .9976 | .9977 | .9977 | .9978 | .9979 | .9979 | .9980 | .9981 |
| 2.9 | .9981 | .9982 | .9982 | .9983 | .9984 | .9984 | .9985 | .9985 | .9986 | .9986 |
| 3.0 | .9987 | .9987 | .9987 | .9988 | .9988 | .9989 | .9989 | .9989 | .9990 | .9990 |
| 3.1 | .9990 | .9991 | .9991 | .9991 | .9992 | .9992 | .9992 | .9992 | .9993 | .9993 |
| 3.2 | .9993 | .9993 | .9994 | .9994 | .9994 | .9994 | .9994 | .9995 | .9995 | .9995 |
| 3.3 | .9995 | .9995 | .9995 | .9996 | .9996 | .9996 | .9996 | .9996 | .9996 | .9997 |
| 3.4 | .9997 | .9997 | .9997 | .9997 | .9997 | .9997 | .9997 | .9997 | .9997 | .9998 |

*Source:* E. S. Pearson and H. O. Hartley, eds. *Biometrica Tables for Statisticians.* 3rd ed. Vol. 1. Cambridge: Cambridge University Press, 1966. Adapted from Table 1 with permission of the *Biometrika* Trustees.

An entry in the table gives the area of probability $P(t > t_{\alpha,v}) = \alpha$, where $t$ has a Student's $t$ distribution with $v = $ degrees of freedom.

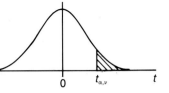

## Table II

**Student's $t$ Distribution**

| $v$ | $\alpha$ .10 | .05 | .025 | .01 | .005 |
|---|---|---|---|---|---|
| 1 | 3.078 | 6.314 | 12.706 | 31.821 | 63.657 |
| 2 | 1.886 | 2.920 | 4.303 | 6.965 | 9.925 |
| 3 | 1.638 | 2.353 | 3.182 | 4.541 | 5.841 |
| 4 | 1.533 | 2.132 | 2.776 | 3.747 | 4.604 |
| 5 | 1.476 | 2.015 | 2.571 | 3.365 | 4.032 |
| 6 | 1.440 | 1.943 | 2.447 | 3.143 | 3.707 |
| 7 | 1.415 | 1.895 | 2.365 | 2.998 | 3.499 |
| 8 | 1.397 | 1.860 | 2.306 | 2.896 | 3.355 |
| 9 | 1.383 | 1.833 | 2.262 | 2.821 | 3.250 |
| 10 | 1.372 | 1.812 | 2.228 | 2.764 | 3.169 |
| 11 | 1.363 | 1.796 | 2.201 | 2.718 | 3.106 |
| 12 | 1.356 | 1.782 | 2.179 | 2.681 | 3.055 |
| 13 | 1.350 | 1.771 | 2.160 | 2.650 | 3.012 |
| 14 | 1.345 | 1.761 | 2.145 | 2.624 | 2.977 |
| 15 | 1.341 | 1.753 | 2.131 | 2.602 | 2.947 |
| 16 | 1.337 | 1.746 | 2.120 | 2.583 | 2.921 |
| 17 | 1.333 | 1.740 | 2.110 | 2.567 | 2.898 |
| 18 | 1.330 | 1.734 | 2.101 | 2.552 | 2.878 |
| 19 | 1.328 | 1.729 | 2.093 | 2.539 | 2.861 |
| 20 | 1.325 | 1.725 | 2.086 | 2.528 | 2.845 |
| 21 | 1.323 | 1.721 | 2.080 | 2.518 | 2.831 |
| 22 | 1.321 | 1.717 | 2.074 | 2.508 | 2.819 |
| 23 | 1.319 | 1.714 | 2.069 | 2.500 | 2.807 |
| 24 | 1.318 | 1.711 | 2.064 | 2.492 | 2.797 |
| 25 | 1.315 | 1.708 | 2.060 | 2.485 | 2.787 |
| 26 | 1.315 | 1.706 | 2.056 | 2.479 | 2.779 |
| 27 | 1.314 | 1.703 | 2.052 | 2.473 | 2.771 |
| 28 | 1.313 | 1.702 | 2.048 | 2.467 | 2.763 |
| 29 | 1.311 | 1.699 | 2.045 | 2.462 | 2.756 |
| 30 | 1.310 | 1.697 | 2.042 | 2.457 | 2.750 |
| 40 | 1.303 | 1.684 | 2.021 | 2.423 | 2.704 |
| 60 | 1.296 | 1.671 | 2.000 | 2.390 | 2.660 |
| 120 | 1.289 | 1.658 | 1.980 | 2.358 | 2.617 |
| $\infty$ | 1.282 | 1.645 | 1.960 | 2.326 | 2.576 |

*Source:* E. S. Pearson and H. O. Hartley, eds. *Biometrika Tables for Statisticians.* 3rd ed. Vol. 1. Cambridge: Cambridge University Press, 1966. Adapted from Table 12 with permission of the *Biometrika* Trustees.

**TABLE II** 559

An entry in the table gives the area of probability $P(\chi^2 > \chi^2_{\alpha, v}) = \alpha$, where $\chi^2$ has a chi-square distribution with $v$ = degrees of freedom.

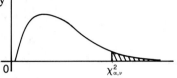

## Table III

**The Chi-Square Distribution**

| | | | $P$ | |
|---|---|---|---|---|
| $v$ | 0.995 | 0.990 | 0.975 | 0.950 |
| 1 | 0.0000393 | 0.0001571 | 0.0009821 | 0.0039321 |
| 2 | 0.0100251 | 0.0201007 | 0.0506356 | 0.102587 |
| 3 | 0.0717212 | 0.114832 | 0.215795 | 0.351846 |
| 4 | 0.206990 | 0.297110 | 0.484419 | 0.710721 |
| 5 | 0.411740 | 0.554300 | 0.831211 | 1.145476 |
| 6 | 0.675727 | 0.872085 | 1.237347 | 1.63539 |
| 7 | 0.989265 | 1.239043 | 1.68987 | 2.16735 |
| 8 | 1.344419 | 1.646482 | 2.17973 | 2.73264 |
| 9 | 1.734926 | 2.087912 | 2.70039 | 3.32511 |
| 10 | 2.15585 | 2.55821 | 3.24697 | 3.94030 |
| 11 | 2.60321 | 3.05347 | 3.81575 | 4.57481 |
| 12 | 3.07382 | 3.57056 | 4.40379 | 5.22603 |
| 13 | 3.56503 | 4.10691 | 5.00874 | 5.89186 |
| 14 | 4.07468 | 4.66043 | 5.62872 | 6.57063 |
| 15 | 4.60094 | 5.22935 | 6.26214 | 7.26094 |
| 16 | 5.14224 | 5.81221 | 6.90766 | 7.96164 |
| 17 | 5.69724 | 6.40776 | 7.56418 | 8.67176 |
| 18 | 6.26481 | 7.01491 | 8.23075 | 9.39046 |
| 19 | 6.84398 | 7.63273 | 8.90655 | 10.1170 |
| 20 | 7.43386 | 8.26040 | 9.59083 | 10.8508 |
| 21 | 8.03366 | 8.89720 | 10.28293 | 11.5913 |
| 22 | 8.64272 | 9.54249 | 10.9823 | 12.3380 |
| 23 | 9.26042 | 10.19567 | 11.6885 | 13.0905 |
| 24 | 9.88623 | 10.8564 | 12.4011 | 13.8484 |
| 25 | 10.5197 | 11.5240 | 13.1197 | 14.6114 |
| 26 | 11.1603 | 12.1981 | 13.8439 | 15.3791 |
| 27 | 11.8076 | 12.8786 | 14.5733 | 16.1513 |
| 28 | 12.4613 | 13.5648 | 15.3079 | 16.9279 |
| 29 | 13.1211 | 14.2565 | 16.0471 | 17.7083 |
| 30 | 13.7867 | 14.9535 | 16.7908 | 18.4926 |
| 40 | 20.7065 | 22.1643 | 24.4331 | 26.5093 |
| 50 | 27.9907 | 29.7067 | 32.3574 | 34.7642 |
| 60 | 35.5346 | 37.4848 | 40.4817 | 43.1879 |
| 70 | 43.2752 | 45.4418 | 48.7576 | 51.7393 |
| 80 | 51.1720 | 53.5400 | 57.1532 | 60.3915 |
| 90 | 59.1963 | 61.7541 | 65.6466 | 69.1260 |
| 100 | 67.3276 | 70.0648 | 74.2219 | 77.9295 |

*Source:* E. S. Pearson and H. O. Hartley, eds. *Biometrika Tables for Statisticians.* 3rd ed. Vol. 1. Cambridge: Cambridge University Press, 1966. Adapted from Table 8 with permission of the *Biometrika* Trustees.

|  | P | | |
|---|---|---|---|
| 0.050 | 0.025 | 0.010 | 0.005 |
| 3.84146 | 5.02389 | 6.63490 | 7.87944 |
| 5.99147 | 7.37776 | 9.21034 | 10.5966 |
| 7.81473 | 9.34840 | 11.3449 | 12.8381 |
| 9.48773 | 11.1433 | 13.2767 | 14.8602 |
| 11.0705 | 12.8325 | 15.0863 | 16.7496 |
| 12.5916 | 14.4494 | 16.8119 | 18.5476 |
| 14.0671 | 16.0128 | 18.4753 | 20.2777 |
| 15.5073 | 17.5346 | 20.0902 | 21.9550 |
| 16.9190 | 19.0228 | 21.6660 | 23.5893 |
| 18.3070 | 20.4831 | 23.2093 | 25.1882 |
| 19.6751 | 21.9200 | 24.7250 | 26.7569 |
| 21.0261 | 23.3367 | 26.2170 | 28.2995 |
| 22.3621 | 24.7356 | 27.6883 | 29.8194 |
| 23.6848 | 26.1190 | 29.1413 | 31.3193 |
| 24.9958 | 27.4884 | 30.5779 | 32.8013 |
| 26.2962 | 28.8454 | 31.9999 | 34.2672 |
| 27.5871 | 30.1910 | 33.4087 | 35.7185 |
| 28.8693 | 31.5264 | 34.8053 | 37.1564 |
| 30.1435 | 32.8523 | 36.1908 | 38.5822 |
| 31.4104 | 34.1696 | 37.5662 | 39.9968 |
| 32.6705 | 35.4789 | 38.9321 | 41.4010 |
| 33.9244 | 36.7807 | 40.2894 | 42.7956 |
| 35.1725 | 38.0757 | 41.6384 | 44.1813 |
| 36.4154 | 39.3641 | 42.9798 | 45.5585 |
| 37.6525 | 40.6465 | 44.3141 | 46.9278 |
| 38.8852 | 41.9232 | 45.6417 | 48.2899 |
| 40.1133 | 43.1944 | 46.9630 | 49.6449 |
| 41.3372 | 44.4607 | 48.2782 | 50.9933 |
| 42.5569 | 45.7222 | 49.5879 | 52.3356 |
| 43.7729 | 46.9792 | 50.8922 | 53.6720 |
| 55.7585 | 59.3417 | 63.6907 | 66.7659 |
| 67.5048 | 71.4202 | 76.1539 | 79.4900 |
| 79.0819 | 83.2976 | 88.3794 | 91.9517 |
| 90.5312 | 95.0231 | 100.425 | 104.215 |
| 101.879 | 106.629 | 112.329 | 116.321 |
| 113.145 | 118.136 | 124.116 | 128.299 |
| 124.342 | 129.561 | 135.807 | 140.169 |

**TABLE III**      **561**

## Table IV

**The *F* Distribution: Values of $F_{0.05}$**

| Horizontal Degrees of Freedom | Vertical Degrees of Freedom | | | | | | | | |
|---|---|---|---|---|---|---|---|---|---|
| | 1 | 2 | 3 | 4 | 5 | 6 | 7 | 8 | 9 |
| 1 | 161 | 200 | 216 | 225 | 230 | 234 | 237 | 239 | 241 |
| 2 | 18.5 | 19.0 | 19.2 | 19.2 | 19.3 | 19.3 | 19.4 | 19.4 | 19.4 |
| 3 | 10.1 | 9.55 | 9.28 | 9.12 | 9.01 | 8.94 | 8.89 | 8.85 | 8.81 |
| 4 | 7.71 | 6.94 | 6.59 | 6.39 | 6.26 | 6.16 | 6.09 | 6.04 | 6.00 |
| 5 | 6.61 | 5.79 | 5.41 | 5.19 | 5.05 | 4.95 | 4.88 | 4.82 | 4.77 |
| 6 | 5.99 | 5.14 | 4.76 | 4.53 | 4.39 | 4.28 | 4.21 | 4.15 | 4.10 |
| 7 | 5.59 | 4.74 | 4.35 | 4.12 | 3.97 | 3.87 | 3.79 | 3.73 | 3.68 |
| 8 | 5.32 | 4.46 | 4.07 | 3.84 | 3.69 | 3.58 | 3.50 | 3.44 | 3.39 |
| 9 | 5.12 | 4.26 | 3.86 | 3.63 | 3.48 | 3.37 | 3.29 | 2.23 | 3.18 |
| 10 | 4.96 | 4.10 | 3.71 | 3.48 | 3.33 | 3.22 | 3.14 | 3.07 | 3.02 |
| 11 | 4.84 | 3.98 | 3.59 | 3.36 | 3.20 | 3.09 | 3.01 | 2.95 | 2.90 |
| 12 | 4.75 | 3.89 | 3.49 | 3.26 | 3.11 | 3.00 | 2.91 | 2.85 | 2.80 |
| 13 | 4.67 | 3.81 | 3.41 | 3.18 | 3.03 | 2.92 | 2.83 | 2.77 | 2.71 |
| 14 | 4.60 | 3.74 | 3.34 | 3.11 | 2.96 | 2.85 | 2.76 | 2.70 | 2.65 |
| 15 | 4.54 | 3.68 | 3.29 | 3.06 | 2.90 | 2.79 | 2.71 | 2.64 | 2.59 |
| 16 | 4.49 | 3.63 | 3.24 | 3.01 | 2.85 | 2.74 | 2.66 | 2.59 | 2.54 |
| 17 | 4.45 | 3.59 | 3.20 | 2.96 | 2.81 | 2.70 | 2.61 | 2.55 | 2.49 |
| 18 | 4.41 | 3.55 | 3.16 | 2.93 | 2.77 | 2.66 | 2.58 | 2.51 | 2.46 |
| 19 | 4.38 | 3.52 | 3.13 | 2.90 | 2.74 | 2.63 | 2.54 | 2.48 | 2.42 |
| 20 | 4.35 | 3.49 | 3.10 | 2.87 | 2.71 | 2.60 | 2.51 | 2.45 | 2.39 |
| 21 | 4.32 | 3.47 | 3.07 | 2.84 | 2.68 | 2.57 | 2.49 | 2.42 | 2.37 |
| 22 | 4.30 | 3.44 | 3.05 | 2.82 | 2.66 | 2.55 | 2.46 | 2.40 | 2.34 |
| 23 | 4.28 | 3.42 | 3.03 | 2.80 | 2.64 | 2.53 | 2.44 | 2.37 | 2.32 |
| 24 | 4.26 | 3.40 | 3.01 | 2.78 | 2.62 | 2.51 | 2.42 | 2.36 | 2.30 |
| 25 | 4.24 | 3.39 | 2.99 | 2.76 | 2.60 | 2.49 | 2.40 | 2.34 | 2.28 |
| 30 | 4.17 | 3.32 | 2.92 | 2.69 | 2.53 | 2.42 | 2.33 | 2.27 | 2.21 |
| 40 | 4.08 | 3.23 | 2.84 | 2.61 | 2.45 | 2.34 | 2.25 | 2.18 | 2.12 |
| 60 | 4.00 | 3.15 | 2.76 | 2.53 | 2.37 | 2.25 | 2.17 | 2.10 | 2.04 |
| 120 | 3.92 | 3.07 | 2.68 | 2.45 | 2.29 | 2.18 | 2.09 | 2.02 | 1.96 |
| ∞ | 3.84 | 3.00 | 2.60 | 2.37 | 2.21 | 2.10 | 2.01 | 1.94 | 1.88 |

## Vertical Degrees of Freedom

| 10 | 12 | 15 | 20 | 24 | 30 | 40 | 60 | 120 | $\infty$ |
|------|------|------|------|------|------|------|------|------|------|
| 242 | 244 | 246 | 248 | 249 | 250 | 251 | 252 | 253 | 254 |
| 19.4 | 19.4 | 19.4 | 19.4 | 19.5 | 19.5 | 19.5 | 19.5 | 19.5 | 19.5 |
| 8.79 | 8.74 | 8.70 | 8.66 | 8.64 | 8.62 | 8.59 | 8.57 | 8.55 | 8.53 |
| 5.96 | 5.91 | 5.86 | 5.80 | 5.77 | 5.75 | 5.72 | 5.69 | 5.66 | 5.63 |
| 4.74 | 4.68 | 4.62 | 4.56 | 4.53 | 4.50 | 4.46 | 4.43 | 4.40 | 4.37 |
| 4.06 | 4.00 | 3.94 | 3.87 | 3.84 | 3.81 | 3.77 | 3.74 | 3.70 | 3.67 |
| 3.64 | 3.57 | 3.51 | 3.44 | 3.41 | 3.38 | 3.34 | 3.30 | 3.27 | 3.23 |
| 3.35 | 3.28 | 3.22 | 3.15 | 3.12 | 3.08 | 3.04 | 3.01 | 2.97 | 2.93 |
| 3.14 | 3.07 | 3.01 | 2.94 | 2.90 | 2.86 | 2.83 | 2.79 | 2.75 | 2.71 |
| 2.98 | 2.91 | 2.85 | 2.77 | 2.74 | 2.70 | 2.66 | 2.62 | 2.58 | 2.54 |
| 2.85 | 2.79 | 2.72 | 2.65 | 2.61 | 2.57 | 2.53 | 2.49 | 2.45 | 2.40 |
| 2.75 | 2.69 | 2.62 | 2.54 | 2.51 | 2.47 | 2.43 | 2.38 | 2.34 | 2.30 |
| 2.67 | 2.60 | 2.53 | 2.46 | 2.42 | 2.38 | 2.34 | 2.30 | 2.25 | 2.21 |
| 2.60 | 2.53 | 2.46 | 2.39 | 2.35 | 2.31 | 2.27 | 2.22 | 2.18 | 2.13 |
| 2.54 | 2.48 | 2.40 | 2.33 | 2.29 | 2.25 | 2.20 | 2.16 | 2.11 | 2.07 |
| 2.49 | 2.42 | 2.35 | 2.28 | 2.24 | 2.19 | 2.15 | 2.11 | 2.06 | 2.01 |
| 2.45 | 2.38 | 2.31 | 2.23 | 2.19 | 2.15 | 2.10 | 2.06 | 2.01 | 1.96 |
| 2.41 | 2.34 | 2.27 | 2.19 | 2.15 | 2.11 | 2.06 | 2.02 | 1.97 | 1.92 |
| 2.38 | 2.31 | 2.23 | 2.16 | 2.11 | 2.07 | 2.03 | 1.98 | 1.93 | 1.88 |
| 2.35 | 2.28 | 2.20 | 2.12 | 2.08 | 2.04 | 1.99 | 1.95 | 1.90 | 1.84 |
| 2.32 | 2.25 | 2.18 | 2.10 | 2.05 | 2.01 | 1.96 | 1.92 | 1.87 | 1.81 |
| 2.30 | 2.23 | 2.15 | 2.07 | 2.03 | 1.98 | 1.94 | 1.89 | 1.84 | 1.78 |
| 2.27 | 2.20 | 2.13 | 2.05 | 2.01 | 1.96 | 1.91 | 1.86 | 1.81 | 1.76 |
| 2.25 | 2.18 | 2.11 | 2.03 | 1.98 | 1.94 | 1.89 | 1.84 | 1.79 | 1.73 |
| 2.24 | 2.16 | 2.09 | 2.01 | 1.96 | 1.92 | 1.87 | 1.82 | 1.77 | 1.71 |
| 2.16 | 2.09 | 2.01 | 1.93 | 1.89 | 1.84 | 1.79 | 1.74 | 1.68 | 1.62 |
| 2.08 | 2.00 | 1.92 | 1.84 | 1.79 | 1.74 | 1.69 | 1.64 | 1.58 | 1.51 |
| 1.99 | 1.92 | 1.84 | 1.75 | 1.70 | 1.65 | 1.59 | 1.53 | 1.47 | 1.39 |
| 1.91 | 1.83 | 1.75 | 1.66 | 1.61 | 1.55 | 1.50 | 1.43 | 1.35 | 1.25 |
| 1.83 | 1.75 | 1.67 | 1.57 | 1.52 | 1.46 | 1.39 | 1.32 | 1.22 | 1.00 |

**TABLE IV**                                    563

## Table IV

| Horizontal Degrees of Freedom | Vertical Degrees of Freedom | | | | | | | | |
|---|---|---|---|---|---|---|---|---|---|
| | 1 | 2 | 3 | 4 | 5 | 6 | 7 | 8 | 9 |
| 1 | 4052 | 5000 | 5403 | 5625 | 5764 | 5859 | 5928 | 5982 | 6023 |
| 2 | 98.5 | 99.0 | 99.2 | 99.2 | 99.3 | 99.3 | 99.4 | 99.4 | 99.4 |
| 3 | 34.1 | 30.8 | 29.5 | 28.7 | 28.2 | 27.9 | 27.7 | 27.5 | 27.3 |
| 4 | 21.2 | 18.0 | 16.7 | 16.0 | 15.5 | 15.2 | 15.0 | 14.8 | 14.7 |
| 5 | 16.3 | 13.3 | 12.1 | 11.4 | 11.0 | 10.7 | 10.5 | 10.3 | 10.2 |
| 6 | 13.7 | 10.9 | 9.78 | 9.15 | 8.75 | 8.47 | 8.26 | 8.10 | 7.98 |
| 7 | 12.2 | 9.55 | 8.45 | 7.85 | 7.46 | 7.19 | 6.99 | 6.84 | 6.72 |
| 8 | 11.3 | 8.65 | 7.59 | 7.01 | 6.63 | 6.37 | 6.18 | 6.03 | 5.91 |
| 9 | 10.6 | 8.02 | 6.99 | 6.42 | 6.06 | 5.80 | 5.61 | 5.47 | 5.35 |
| 10 | 10.0 | 7.56 | 6.55 | 5.99 | 5.64 | 5.39 | 5.20 | 5.06 | 4.94 |
| 11 | 9.65 | 7.21 | 6.22 | 5.67 | 5.32 | 5.07 | 4.89 | 4.74 | 4.63 |
| 12 | 9.33 | 6.93 | 5.95 | 5.41 | 5.06 | 4.82 | 4.64 | 4.50 | 4.39 |
| 13 | 9.07 | 6.70 | 5.74 | 5.21 | 4.86 | 4.62 | 4.44 | 4.30 | 4.19 |
| 14 | 8.86 | 6.51 | 5.56 | 5.04 | 4.70 | 4.46 | 4.28 | 4.14 | 4.03 |
| 15 | 8.68 | 6.36 | 5.42 | 4.89 | 4.56 | 4.32 | 4.14 | 4.00 | 3.89 |
| 16 | 8.53 | 6.23 | 5.29 | 4.77 | 4.44 | 4.20 | 4.03 | 3.89 | 3.78 |
| 17 | 8.40 | 6.11 | 5.19 | 4.67 | 4.34 | 4.10 | 3.93 | 3.79 | 3.68 |
| 18 | 8.29 | 6.01 | 5.09 | 4.58 | 4.25 | 4.01 | 3.84 | 3.71 | 3.60 |
| 19 | 8.19 | 5.93 | 5.01 | 4.50 | 4.17 | 3.94 | 3.77 | 3.63 | 3.52 |
| 20 | 8.10 | 5.85 | 4.94 | 4.43 | 4.10 | 3.87 | 3.70 | 3.56 | 3.46 |
| 21 | 8.02 | 5.78 | 4.87 | 4.37 | 4.04 | 3.81 | 3.64 | 3.51 | 3.40 |
| 22 | 7.95 | 5.72 | 4.82 | 4.31 | 3.99 | 3.76 | 3.59 | 3.45 | 3.35 |
| 23 | 7.88 | 5.66 | 4.76 | 4.26 | 3.94 | 3.71 | 3.54 | 3.41 | 3.30 |
| 24 | 7.82 | 5.61 | 4.72 | 4.22 | 3.90 | 3.67 | 3.50 | 3.36 | 3.26 |
| 25 | 7.77 | 5.57 | 4.68 | 4.18 | 3.86 | 3.63 | 3.36 | 3.32 | 3.22 |
| 30 | 7.56 | 5.39 | 4.51 | 4.02 | 3.70 | 3.47 | 3.30 | 3.17 | 3.07 |
| 40 | 7.31 | 5.18 | 4.31 | 3.83 | 3.51 | 3.29 | 3.12 | 2.99 | 2.89 |
| 60 | 7.08 | 4.98 | 4.13 | 3.65 | 3.34 | 3.12 | 2.95 | 2.82 | 2.72 |
| 120 | 6.85 | 4.79 | 3.95 | 3.48 | 3.17 | 2.96 | 2.79 | 2.66 | 2.56 |
| ∞ | 6.63 | 4.61 | 3.78 | 3.32 | 3.02 | 2.80 | 2.64 | 2.51 | 2.41 |

## Vertical Degrees of Freedom

| 10 | 12 | 15 | 20 | 24 | 30 | 40 | 60 | 120 | ∞ |
|---|---|---|---|---|---|---|---|---|---|
| 6056 | 6106 | 6157 | 6209 | 6235 | 6261 | 6287 | 6313 | 6339 | 6366 |
| 99.4 | 99.4 | 99.4 | 99.4 | 99.5 | 99.5 | 99.5 | 99.5 | 99.5 | 99.5 |
| 27.2 | 27.1 | 26.9 | 26.7 | 26.6 | 26.5 | 26.4 | 26.3 | 26.2 | 26.1 |
| 14.5 | 14.4 | 14.2 | 14.0 | 13.9 | 13.8 | 13.7 | 13.7 | 13.6 | 13.5 |
| 10.1 | 9.89 | 9.72 | 9.55 | 9.47 | 9.38 | 9.29 | 9.20 | 9.11 | 9.02 |
| 7.87 | 7.72 | 7.56 | 7.40 | 7.31 | 7.23 | 7.14 | 7.06 | 6.97 | 6.88 |
| 6.62 | 6.47 | 6.31 | 6.16 | 6.07 | 5.99 | 5.91 | 5.82 | 5.74 | 5.65 |
| 5.81 | 5.67 | 5.52 | 5.36 | 5.28 | 5.20 | 5.12 | 5.03 | 4.95 | 4.86 |
| 5.26 | 5.11 | 4.96 | 4.81 | 4.73 | 4.65 | 4.57 | 4.48 | 4.40 | 4.31 |
| 4.85 | 4.71 | 4.56 | 4.41 | 4.33 | 4.25 | 4.17 | 4.08 | 4.00 | 3.91 |
| 4.54 | 4.40 | 4.25 | 4.10 | 4.02 | 3.94 | 3.86 | 3.78 | 3.69 | 3.60 |
| 4.30 | 4.16 | 4.01 | 3.86 | 3.78 | 3.70 | 3.62 | 3.54 | 3.45 | 3.36 |
| 4.10 | 3.96 | 3.82 | 3.66 | 3.59 | 3.51 | 3.43 | 3.34 | 3.25 | 3.17 |
| 3.94 | 3.80 | 3.66 | 3.51 | 3.43 | 3.35 | 3.27 | 3.18 | 3.09 | 3.00 |
| 3.80 | 3.67 | 3.52 | 3.37 | 3.29 | 3.21 | 3.13 | 3.05 | 2.96 | 2.87 |
| 3.69 | 3.55 | 3.41 | 3.26 | 3.18 | 3.10 | 3.02 | 2.93 | 2.84 | 2.75 |
| 3.59 | 3.46 | 3.31 | 3.16 | 3.08 | 3.00 | 2.92 | 2.83 | 2.75 | 2.65 |
| 3.51 | 3.37 | 3.23 | 3.08 | 3.00 | 2.92 | 2.84 | 2.75 | 2.66 | 2.57 |
| 3.43 | 3.30 | 3.15 | 3.00 | 2.92 | 2.84 | 2.76 | 2.67 | 2.58 | 2.49 |
| 3.37 | 3.23 | 3.09 | 2.94 | 2.86 | 2.78 | 2.69 | 2.61 | 2.52 | 2.42 |
| 3.31 | 3.17 | 3.03 | 2.88 | 2.80 | 2.72 | 2.64 | 2.55 | 2.46 | 2.36 |
| 3.26 | 3.12 | 2.98 | 2.83 | 2.75 | 2.67 | 2.58 | 2.50 | 2.40 | 2.31 |
| 3.21 | 3.07 | 2.93 | 2.78 | 2.70 | 2.62 | 2.54 | 2.45 | 2.35 | 2.26 |
| 3.17 | 3.03 | 2.89 | 2.74 | 2.66 | 2.58 | 2.48 | 2.40 | 2.31 | 2.21 |
| 3.13 | 2.99 | 2.85 | 2.70 | 2.62 | 2.53 | 2.45 | 2.36 | 2.27 | 2.17 |
| 2.98 | 2.84 | 2.70 | 2.55 | 2.47 | 2.39 | 2.30 | 2.21 | 2.11 | 2.01 |
| 2.80 | 2.66 | 2.52 | 2.37 | 2.29 | 2.20 | 2.11 | 2.02 | 1.92 | 1.80 |
| 2.63 | 2.50 | 2.35 | 2.20 | 2.12 | 2.03 | 1.94 | 1.84 | 1.73 | 1.60 |
| 2.47 | 2.34 | 2.19 | 2.03 | 1.95 | 1.86 | 1.76 | 1.66 | 1.53 | 1.38 |
| 2.32 | 2.18 | 2.04 | 1.88 | 1.79 | 1.70 | 1.59 | 1.47 | 1.32 | 1.00 |

**TABLE IV**                    **565**

# Answers to Selected Exercises

For those exercises in which part of the task was to engage in subjective interpretation or justification, in some cases only the objective portion of the answer is provided.

## CHAPTER 2

**Exercises 2.2**   **2.3**   **b.** Systematic sampling; $N = 50$, $k = 5$, $n = 10$
    **c.** No; convenience sampling
  **2.4**   No; fish of a given type tend to form schools that stick together. Hence the percentage of bass caught at a single location will not be a good estimate of the percentage of bass in the lake.
  **2.5**   The target population is families living in the school district; the sampled population is elementary-school children attending school in the district.

**Exercises 2.3**   **2.7**   **b.** $v_1 = 112$, $c = 7$, $k = 6$
    **c.** The third class

    **d.**
```
MTB > NOTE HISTOGRAM OF 50 WEIGHTS OF WOMEN
MTB > SET C1
C1
    115     128     147     120     .   .   .

MTB > END.
MTB > PRINT C1
C1
    115     128     147     120     126     121     126     126     136     133     128
    140     136     127     134     120     128     131     133     127     130     138
    125     129     128     128     135     128     136     137     115     118     129
    120     127     141     124     133     134     116     132     131     138     131
    132     126     128     109     127     142

MTB > NAME C1 'WEIGHTS'
MTB > HISTOGRAM 'WEIGHTS'

Histogram of WEIGHTS    N = 50

Midpoint    Count
    110       1    *
    115       3    ***
    120       5    *****
    125      10    **********
    130      15    ***************
    135      10    **********
    140       5    *****
    145       1    *
```

```
e.  MTB > NOTE HISTOGRAM OF 50 WEIGHTS OF WOMEN WITH GIVEN MIDPOINTS
    MTB > HISTOGRAM 'WEIGHTS';
    SUBC> START = 112;
    SUBC> INCREMENT = 7.

    Histogram of WEIGHTS   N = 50

    Midpoint   Count
      112.00     3   ***
      119.00     6   ******
      126.00    19   *******************
      133.00    15   ***************
      140.00     6   ******
      147.00     1   *
```

**2.8**  **a.**
```
         MTB > NOTE HISTOGRAM OF EXAM GRADE DATA OF 45 STUDENTS
         MTB > SET C1
         C1
             53    63    54    65      .    .    .

         MTB > END
         MTB > NAME C1 'GRADES'
         MTB > PRINT 'GRADES'
         GRADES
             53    63    54    65    64    76    74    61    59    53    71    78    89
             67    54    63    74    75    68    74    81    76    77    61    64    55
             74    68    68    74    64    78    79    82    73    94    88    73    72
             80    77    93    57    81    71

         MTB > HISTOGRAM 'GRADES';
         SUBC> START = 51;
         SUBC> INCREMENT = 7.

         Histogram of GRADES   N = 45

         Midpoint   Count
           51.00     4   ****
           58.00     5   *****
           65.00    10   **********
           72.00    11   ***********
           79.00    11   ***********
           86.00     2   **
           93.00     2   **
```

**b.**
```
    MTB > NOTE STEM-AND-LEAF DISPLAY FOR GRADES OF 45 STUDENTS
    MTB > STEM-AND-LEAF 'GRADES'

    Stem-and-leaf of GRADES    N  = 45
    Leaf Unit = 1.0

         4    5 3344
         7    5 579
        14    6 1133444
        19    6 57888
       (10)   7 1123344444
        16    7 56677889
         8    8 0112
         4    8 89
         2    9 34
```

**d.** 
```
MTB > NOTE OGIVE FOR GRADES OF 45 STUDENTS
MTB > SORT C1 IN C1
MTB > GENERATE 1 TO 45 IN C2
MTB > NAME C2 'CUMFREQ'
MTB > PLOT C2 C1
```

```
CUMFREQ -
        -
        -
        -
     45+                                                    *  *
        -                                          *       **
        -                                       *2
        -                                     2*
        -                                  *2
     30+                               ***
        -                             3
        -                          2 *
        -                         2*
        -                    3
     15+              **   *
        -           *2
        -        2  *
        -     * *   *
        -   * 2
      0+   *
        ------+---------+---------+---------+---------+---------+GRADES
            56.0      64.0      72.0      80.0      88.0      96.0
```

The fiftieth percentile is approximately 72.

**2.9** **a.** 
```
MTB > SET C1
C1
   6763    2599    8053    1190    .   .   .

MTB > END
MTB > NAME C1 'CIRC'
MTB > HISTOGRAM 'CIRC';
SUBC> START = 1000;
SUBC> INCREMENT = 2000.

Histogram of CIRC   N = 69

Midpoint   Count
    1000      40   ****************************************
    3000      11   ***********
    5000       8   ********
    7000       5   *****
    9000       1   *
   11000       2   **
   13000       0
   15000       0
   17000       2   **
```

The first class is the modal class; $M = 1000$.

**b.** 
```
MTB > NOTE HISTOGRAM OF CIRCULATION DATA FOR MAGAZINES WITH C = 1000
MTB > HISTOGRAM 'CIRC';
SUBC> START = 1500;
SUBC> INCREMENT = 1000.

Histogram of CIRC   N = 69
```

```
Midpoint   Count
   1500      40   *****************************************
   2500       9   *********
   3500       2   **
   4500       3   ***
   5500       5   *****
   6500       3   ***
   7500       2   **
   8500       1   *
   9500       0
  10500       2   **
  11500       0
  12500       0
  13500       0
  14500       0
  15500       0
  16500       0
  17500       2   **
```

The first class is the modal class; $M = 1500$.

**d.**

| Interval Number, $i$ | Endpoints | Midpoint, $v_i$ | Frequency, $F_i$ | Cumulative Frequency, $cF_i$ |
|---|---|---|---|---|
| 1 | $0 \leqslant x < 2000$ | 1000 | 40 | 40 |
| 2 | $2000 \leqslant x < 4000$ | 3000 | 11 | 51 |
| 3 | $4000 \leqslant x < 6000$ | 5000 | 8 | 59 |
| 4 | $6000 \leqslant x < 8000$ | 7000 | 5 | 64 |
| 5 | $8000 \leqslant x < 10000$ | 9000 | 1 | 65 |
| 6 | $10000 \leqslant x < 12000$ | 11000 | 2 | 67 |
| 7 | $12000 \leqslant x < 14000$ | 13000 | 0 | 67 |
| 8 | $14000 \leqslant x < 16000$ | 15000 | 0 | 67 |
| 9 | $16000 \leqslant x < 18000$ | 17000 | 2 | 69 |

**2.10  a.** Five classes

**b.**
```
MTB > NOTE HISTOGRAM FOR 25 "ONE-POUND" CONTAINERS
MTB > SET C1
C1
   0.9473   0.9775   0.9964   1.0077    .   .   .

MTB > END
MTB > NAME C1 'ONE-LB'
MTB > PRINT 'ONE-LB'
ONE-LB
   0.9473   0.9775   0.9964   1.0077   1.0182   0.9655   0.9788   0.9974
   1.0084   1.0225   0.9703   0.9861   1.0002   1.0102   1.0248   0.9757
   0.9887   1.0016   1.0132   1.0306   0.9770   0.9958   1.0058   1.0173
   1.0396

MTB > HISTOGRAM 'ONE-LB';
SUBC> START = 0.95;
SUBC> INCREMENT = 0.02.

Histogram of ONE-LB   N = 25

Midpoint   Count
  0.9500      1   *
  0.9700      6   ******
  0.9900      5   *****
  1.0100      9   *********
  1.0300      4   ****
```

**d.** MTB > NOTE STEM-AND-LEAF DISPLAY FOR "ONE-POUND" CONTAINERS
MTB > STEM-AND-LEAF 'ONE-LB'

```
Stem-and-leaf of ONE-LB    N = 25
Leaf Unit = 0.0010

    1    94  7
    1    95
    2    96  5
    7    97  05778
    9    98  68
   12    99  567
   (5)  100  01578
    8   101  0378
    4   102  24
    2   103  09
```

**2.11 a.** MTB > NOTE HISTOGRAM OF 1970–1980 PERCENTAGE CHANGE OF POPULATION BY STATE
MTB > SET C1
C1
    12.9    32.4    53.1    18.8    .   .   .

```
MTB > END
MTB > NAME C1 'PERCHG'
MTB > HISTOGRAM 'PERCHG';
SUBC> START = -5;
SUBC> INCREMENT = 10.

Histogram of PERCHG    N = 50

Midpoint    Count
   -5.0        2    **
    5.0       18    ******************
   15.0       15    ***************
   25.0        7    *******
   35.0        4    ****
   45.0        2    **
   55.0        1    *
   65.0        1    *
```

**2.12** Six, eight, ten, and ten classes

**2.14 a.** MTB > NOTE HISTOGRAM FOR NET WEIGHTS OF SUGAR PACKAGES
MTB > SET C1
C1
    42.2    40.2    42.7    40.5    .   .   .

```
MTB > END
MTB > NAME C1 'SUGARWT'
MTB > PRINT 'SUGARWT'
SUGARWT
    42.2    40.2    42.7    40.5    38.4    42.0    39.8    39.1    39.7    38.4    39.4
    40.0    38.3    42.2    41.6    40.9    39.7    37.2    38.9    41.3    40.6    41.9
    39.4    39.1    40.0    41.7    39.3    39.1    38.9    39.8    40.5    41.1    40.0
    42.6    41.5    37.6    39.4    37.4    39.8    38.5    38.7    40.3    40.3    40.1
    40.4    39.2    41.1    39.6

MTB > HISTOGRAM 'SUGARWT';
SUBC> START = 37.2;
SUBC> INCREMENT = 0.8.

Histogram of SUGARWT    N = 48
```

```
Midpoint   Count
 37.200      3   ***
 38.000      1   *
 38.800      9   *********
 39.600     14   **************
 40.400      8   ********
 41.200      6   ******
 42.000      5   *****
 42.800      2   **
```

**b.** `MTB > NOTE OGIVE FOR NET WEIGHTS OF SUGAR PACKAGES`
`MTB > SET C2`
`C2`
```
      1     2     3     4    .    .    .
```

`MTB > END`
`MTB > NAME C2 'CUMFREQ'`
`MTB > SORT C1 IN C1`
`MTB > PLOT C2 VS C1`

```
CUMFREQ -
        -                                                                      **
        -                                                              *  2
     45+-                                                          ** *
        -                                                      * * *
        -                                                  *  * *
        -                                             *2
     30+-                                           *2
        -                                        2*
        -                                      2  *
        -                                     2*
        -                                 2  *
     15+-                             ***
        -                          3
        -                      *  2
        -                   2*
        -       *  *      *
      0+- *
        --------+---------+---------+---------+---------+--------SUGARWT
             38.0      39.0      40.0      41.0      42.0
```

**2.15  a.** `MTB > NOTE HISTOGRAM OF ANNUAL RAINFALL IN 34 CITIES IN EL SALVADOR`
`MTB > SET C1`
`C1`
```
   1735   1936   2000   1973    .    .    .
```

`MTB > END`
`MTB > NAME C1 'RAINFALL'`
`MTB > PRINT 'RAINFALL'`
`RAINFALL`
```
   1735   1936   2000   1973   1750   1800   1750   2077   1920   1800   2050
   1830   1650   2200   2000   1770   1920   1770   2240   1620   1756   1650
   2250   1796   1890   1871   2063   2100   1918   1834   1780   1900   1976
   2296
```

`MTB > HISTOGRAM 'RAINFALL'`

`Histogram of RAINFALL    N = 34`

```
Midpoint    Count
   1600       1   *
   1700       3   ***
   1800      11   ***********
   1900       7   *******
   2000       4   ****
   2100       4   ****
   2200       2   **
   2300       2   **
```

**b.** MTB > NOTE STEM-AND-LEAF DISPLAY FOR RAINFALL DATA
MTB > STEM-AND-LEAF 'RAINFALL'

```
Stem-and-leaf of RAINFALL   N  = 34
Leaf Unit = 10

     1    16 2
     3    16 55
     4    17 3
    11    17 5557789
    15    18 0033
    17    18 79
    17    19 01223
    12    19 77
    10    20 00
     8    20 567
     5    21 0
     4    21
     4    22 04
     2    22 59
```

**c.** MTB > NOTE OGIVE FOR RAINFALL DATA
MTB > SORT C1 IN C1
MTB > SET C2
C2
```
    1     2     3     4    .   .   .
```

MTB > END
MTB > NAME C2 'CUMFREQ'
MTB > PLOT C2 VS C1

```
CUMFREQ -
        -                                                    *   *
        -                                                  *  *
   30+  -                                         *  *
        -                                         **
        -                                    2
        -                                    2
        -                               **
   20+  -                               2
        -                             **
        -                         *   *
        -                         *  *
        -                          2
   10+  -                       **
        -                       **
        -                      2
        -              *      *
        -             *  *
    0+  -
        --------+---------+---------+---------+---------+-------RAINFALL
             1650      1800      1950      2100      2250
```

The data set shows right skewness.

**Exercises 2.4**

**2.16** $\bar{x} = 128.98$, $\hat{m} = 128$

**2.17** $\bar{x} = 71 < \hat{m} = 73$; left skewness

**2.18** **a.** $\bar{x} = 3252.6$, $\hat{m} = 1783$; the sample median is a better measure of location because of the extreme right skewness of this data set.
**c.** $\bar{x} = 2814.1$; yes    **d.** $\hat{m} = 1734$; no

**2.19** **a.** $\bar{x} = 0.99826$, $\hat{m} = 1.0002$

**2.20** **a.** $\bar{x} = 538.08$, $\hat{m} = 536$

**2.21** $\bar{x} = 40.008$, $\hat{m} = 39.9$, $M = 39.6$

**2.22** **b.** $\bar{x} = 50.008$

**2.24** $\bar{x} = 2.5005$

**2.25** 68°F

**2.26** 30°C

**2.27** **a.** $\bar{x} = 12.195$, $\hat{m} = 7.985$

**b.**
```
MTB > NOTE HISTOGRAM FOR LENGTHS OF TIME AT CHECKOUT COUNTER
MTB > SET C1
C1
   10.41   17.79    3.99    3.94    .   .   .

MTB > END
MTB > NAME C1 'TIMES'
MTB > PRINT 'TIMES'
TIMES
   10.41   17.79    3.99    3.94    5.59    2.35   18.94   21.78    2.71
   69.61   12.44   12.48    8.59    6.65   45.95   14.96   13.98    1.33
   16.94    1.09    4.59    5.85    4.36    6.97   11.10    5.43    4.25
   10.34    4.49    2.68   19.67    5.94   18.53    1.99   37.71   13.33
    2.37   21.10   13.01    6.45   10.08   13.30    5.00    0.62    3.32
    2.28    7.38   15.42   40.83   19.86

MTB > HISTOGRAM 'TIMES'

Histogram of TIMES   N = 50

Midpoint   Count
       0      16   ****************
      10      21   *********************
      20       9   *********
      30       0
      40       2   **
      50       1   *
      60       0
      70       1   *
```

**2.29** $M = 0$

**2.30** **a.** $M = 1800$, $\hat{m} = 1895$, $\bar{x} = 1908$

**Exercises 2.5**

**2.31** **a.** $\bar{x}_1 = 40.6$, $\bar{x}_2 = 37.2$
**b.** $R_1 = 55$, $s_1^2 = 383.807$, $s_1 = 19.591$; $R_2 = 56$, $s_2^2 = 426.216$, $s_2 = 20.645$

**2.32** **a.** $s = 7.54$

**b.**
```
MTB > NOTE BOXPLOT FOR WEIGHTS OF 50 WOMEN
MTB > BOXPLOT 'WEIGHTS'
```

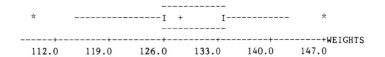

**2.33** **a.** $s = 10.40$

**b.** MTB > NOTE BOXPLOT FOR GRADES OF 45 STUDENTS
MTB > BOXPLOT 'GRADES'

**2.34** **a.** $\bar{x}_M = 69.409$, $s_M = 1.957$, $s_M^2 = 3.831$
**b.** $\bar{x}_F = 75.441$, $s_F = 2.542$, $s_F^2 = 6.462$

**c.** MTB > NOTE BOXPLOTS FOR MALE AND FEMALE LIFE EXPECTANCIES BY COUNTRY
MTB > BOXPLOT 'MALE'

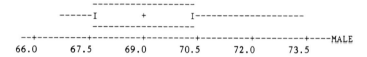

MTB > BOXPLOT 'FEMALE'

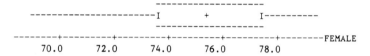

**d.** $\bar{x}_D = 6.032$, $s_D = 1.736$, $s_D^2 = 3.013$
**e.** Yes    **f.** No

**2.35** $s = 147.819$, $s^2 = 21850.5$

**2.36** $\bar{x} = 1.01$, $s = 0.01$

**2.38** **a.** MTB > NOTE BOXPLOT OF TIMES AT CHECKOUT COUNTER
MTB > BOXPLOT 'TIMES'

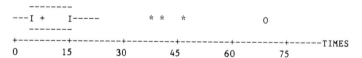

**b.** Yes, the data are skewed to the right.
**c.** 69.61 is an outlier.

**2.39** **a.** $\bar{x} = 1908.0$, $s = 176.0$

**b.** MTB > NOTE BOXPLOT FOR RAINFALL DATA IN 34 CITIES IN EL SALVADOR
MTB > BOXPLOT 'RAINFALL'

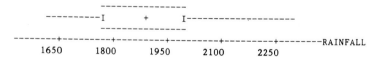

This plot indicates moderate right skewness.

**2.40** **a.** $\hat{m} = 143.5$, $Q_1 = 130$, $Q_3 = 160$

**b., c.**

```
MTB > NOTE USE OF DESCRIBE AND BOXPLOT COMMANDS USED WITH SUNFISH DATA
MTB > SET C1
C1
     81     97     97     102     .   .   .

MTB > NAME C1 'FISH'
MTB > PRINT 'FISH'
FISH
     81     97     97    102    102    104    112    112    119    120    122
    124    127    130    130    130    150    130    140    140    140    130
    130    130    127    137    142    145    140    160    160    140    140
    160    140    160    150    160    170    132    132    147    147    152
    152    155    157    160    168    170    170    170    150    170    170
    150    180    180    168    170    170    172    180    170

MTB > DESCRIBE 'FISH'

                N       MEAN    MEDIAN    TRMEAN     STDEV    SEMEAN
FISH           64     143.31    143.50    144.09     23.25      2.91

              MIN        MAX        Q1        Q3
FISH        81.00     180.00    130.00    160.00

MTB > BOXPLOT 'FISH'
```

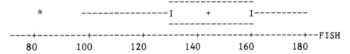

The value 81 is not within the inner fences; skewness to the left is indicated.

**2.41** **a., b.**

```
MTB > NOTE USE OF DESCRIBE, BOXPLOT AND HISTOGRAM COMMANDS FOR MICE DATA
MTB > SET C1
C1
    231    444    468     473     .   .   .

MTB > NAME C1 'MICE'
MTB > PRINT 'MICE'
MICE
    231    444    468    473    527    550    593    600    610    650    655
    660    715    720    752    785    832    838    859    891    896    904
    931    952    998    559    595    596    603    765    783    794    811
    856    870    883    897    975    978    991   1005   1023   1026   1053
    593    735    816    848    850   1046    500    591    713    751    778
    784    786    796

MTB > DESCRIBE 'MICE'

                N       MEAN    MEDIAN    TRMEAN     STDEV    SEMEAN
MICE           58      761.8     784.5     767.6     177.8      23.3

              MIN        MAX        Q1        Q3
MICE        231.0     1053.0     602.2     892.2
```

```
MTB > BOXPLOT 'MICE'


                                        ------------------
              -----------------------I          +          I----------
                                        ------------------
              --------+---------+---------+---------+---------+--------MICE
                    320       480       640       800       960
```

```
MTB > HISTOGRAM 'MICE'

Histogram of MICE   N = 58

Midpoint   Count
    200      1   *
    300      0
    400      1   *
    500      4   ****
    600     10   **********
    700      7   *******
    800     15   ***************
    900     10   **********
   1000      9   *********
   1100      1   *
```

The units of $\bar{x}$ and $s$ are days. Left skewness is indicated.

**c.** Yes

**2.42  a.** $\bar{x} = 12.332$, $s = 3.234$

**b.**
```
MTB > NOTE USE OF DESCRIBE, BOXPLOT AND HISTOGRAM COMMANDS
MTB > NOTE WITH RETURN ON EQUITY DATA FOR 19 NORTH CENTRAL
MTB > NOTE BANKS
MTB > SET C1
C1
   18.9   16.8   15.6   15.2   .   .   .

MTB > NAME C1 'RETURN'
MTB > PRINT 'RETURN'
RETURN
   18.9   16.8   15.6   15.2   14.5   14.4   13.5   13.5   12.4   12.4   11.5
   11.4   10.8   10.7   10.4    9.6    9.1    8.4    5.2

MTB > DESCRIBE 'RETURN'

                   N     MEAN   MEDIAN   TRMEAN    STDEV   SEMEAN
RETURN            19   12.332   12.400   12.365    3.234    0.742

                 MIN      MAX       Q1       Q3
RETURN         5.200   18.900   10.400   14.500

MTB > BOXPLOT 'RETURN'


                                  ------------------
              ---------------------I        +        I------------------
                                  ------------------
              +---------+---------+---------+---------+---------+------RETURN
            5.0       7.5      10.0      12.5      15.0      17.5

MTB > HISTOGRAM 'RETURN'

Histogram of RETURN   N = 19
```

```
Midpoint    Count
       6      1   *
       8      1   *
      10      5   *****
      12      4   ****
      14      4   ****
      16      3   ***
      18      1   *
```

The boxplot does not indicate either left or right skewness.


# CHAPTER 3

**Exercises 3.2**

**3.1**  **a.** $f(2) = 0.3921713, f(3) = 0.2281861, f(4) = 0.2084688,$
$f(5) = 0.1004861, f(6) = 0.0417451, f(7+) = 0.0289426$
**c.** $0.8288262$

**3.2**  $S = \{1, 2, 3\}, P(1) = P(2) = P(3) = 1/3$

**3.3**  $P(M) = P(F) = 4/13, P(T) = P(TH) = 2/13, P(W) = 1/13$

**3.5**  $P(k) = k/15$ for $k = 1, 2, 3, 4, 5$

**3.6**  **a.** $c = 12/25$
**b.** $P(k) = (1/k)(12/25) = 12/25, 6/25, 4/25, 3/25$ for $k = 1, 2, 3, 4,$ respectively

**3.7**  **a.** $S = \{0, 1\}$    **b.** $S = \{0, 1, 2\}$

**3.8**  **a.** 
```
MTB > NOTE HISTOGRAM FOR LEFT-MOST DIGITS OF DAM RESERVOIRS
MTB > SET C1
C1
      1    1    4    1    .    .    .

MTB > NAME C1 'LEFTDIG'
MTB > HISTOGRAM C1;
SUBC> START = 1;
SUBC> INCREMENT = 1.

Histogram of LEFTDIG    N = 70

Midpoint    Count
    1.00      25   *************************
    2.00      15   ***************
    3.00       7   *******
    4.00       8   ********
    5.00       2   **
    6.00       4   ****
    7.00       2   **
    8.00       3   ***
    9.00       4   ****
```

**Exercises 3.3**

**3.11**  $P(E_1) = 1/3, P(E_2) = 2/3, P(E_3) = 1/3$

**3.12**  $P(E_1) = 1/8, P(E_2) = 9/16, P(E_3) = 7/8, P(E_4) = 11/16$

**3.13**  **a.** $E_1 = \{1, 3, 5\}, E_2 = \{3, 4, 5\}, E_3 = \{1, 2, 3, 4\}$
**b.** $P(E_1) = 3/5, P(E_2) = 4/5, P(E_3) = 2/3$
**d.** $P(E_1 \cup E_2) = 13/15, P(E_1 \cup E_3) = 1, P(E_2 \cup E_3) = 1$
**e.** $P(\bar{E}_1) = 2/5, P(\bar{E}_2) = 1/5, P(\bar{E}_3) = 1/3$

**3.14**  **a.** $n(A \cap B) = 300$
**c.** $P(A \cup B) = 9/10, P(A \cap B) = 3/10, P(\bar{A}) = 3/10, P(\bar{B}) = 1/2$

**3.15**  **a.** $E_1 = \{2, 4, 6, 8\}, E_2 = \{2, 3, 5, 7\}, E_3 = \{4, 8\}$
**b.** $E_1 \cap E_2 = \{2\}, E_1 \cap E_3 = \{4, 8\}, E_2 \cap E_3 = \varnothing$

**c.** $P(E_1 \cap E_2) = 1/8$, $P(E_1 \cap E_3) = 1/4$, $P(E_2 \cap E_3) = 0$

**3.16** **a.** 2/3, 31/51, 14/51

    **b.** $P(\text{Odd}) = 26/51$, $P(\text{Even}) = 25/51$

**3.17** $P(E_1) = 8/13$, $P(E_2) = 4/13$, $P(E_1 \cup E_2) = 12/13$, $P(E_1 \cap E_2) = 0$

**3.18** **a.** $P(E_1) = 1/2$, $P(E_2) = 1/2$, $P(E_3) = 3/10$

    **b.** i. 1/2      ii. 9/10      iii. 7/10      iv. 7/10      v. 1/10

         vi. 1/10      vii. 1/10      viii. 0

**3.19** **a.** $P(E_1) = 3/5$, $P(E_2) = 7/10$, $P(E_3) = 2/5$

    **b.** i. 1      ii. 3/10      iii. 1      iv. 0      v. 7/10      vi. 2/5

**3.21** **a.** $P(k) = (k - 1)/36$, $k = 2, \ldots, 7$; $P(k) = (12 - k + 1)/36$, $k = 8, \ldots, 12$

**3.22** Three-fourths should display the dominant trait.

**Exercises 3.4**

**3.25** $P(E_1 \cup E_2) = 9/10$, $P(E_1 \cup E_3) = 7/10$, $P(E_2 \cup E_3) = 7/10$

**3.26** **a.** $P(E_1 \cup E_2) = 1$, $P(E_1 \cup E_3) = 1$, $P(E_2 \cup E_3) = 7/10$

    **b.** $P(\bar{E}_1) = 2/5$, $P(\bar{E}_2) = 3/10$, $P(\bar{E}_3) = 3/5$

**3.27** 5/6

**3.28** 15/16

**3.29** **a.** $n(\bar{A} \cap \bar{B}) = 20$, $n(A \cap \bar{B}) = 30$, $n(\bar{A} \cap B) = 80$, $n(A \cap B) = 270$

**3.30** **a.** 1/15     **b.** 7/15     **c.** 7/15

**3.31** **a.** 3/8     **b.** 2/3     **c.** 1/5     **d.** 3/8     **e.** 1/5     **f.** 2/3

**3.32** **a.** 3/4     **b.** 27/35     **c.** 3/5

**3.33** 0.35

**3.34** **a.** 16/31     **b.** 1/2     **c.** 379/744

**3.35** **a.** $13/42 = 0.310$     **b.** $20/63 = 0.317$

**3.36** **a.** 0.72     **b.** 0.08     **c.** 0.2

**3.37** 11/850, 22/425

**3.38** **a.** 5/18     **b.** 13/18     **c.** 1/3

**3.39** **a.** 1/2     **b.** 1/6     **c.** $1/[k(k + 1)]$     **d.** 1/10

**Exercises 3.5**

**3.40** **a.** $P(A \cap B) = 0.72$     **b.** $P(A \cup B) = 0.98$     **c.** $P(\bar{A} \cap \bar{B}) = 0.02$

**3.41** **a.** 0.49     **b.** 0.01     **c.** 0.5368

**3.42** **a.** Yes     **b.** No

**3.44** **a.** 0.9298     **b.** 0.0702

**3.45** **a.** $P(0) = 1/81$, $P(1) = 8/81$, $P(2) = 24/81$, $P(3) = 32/81$, $P(4) = 16/81$

**3.46** $P(0) = 0.0001$, $P(1) = 0.0036$, $P(2) = 0.0486$, $P(3) = 0.2916$, $P(4) = 0.6561$

**3.48** **a.** $P(1) = 1/6$     **b.** $P(2) = 5/36$     **c.** $P(x) = (1/6)(5/6)^{x-1}$

**3.49** $P(3) = 1/4$, $P(4) = 3/8$, $P(5) = 3/8$

**3.50** **a.** $P(1) = 6/24$, $P(2) = 11/24$, $P(3) = 6/24$     **b.** 17/24

**3.51** **a.** 1/8, 1/216, 1/27     **b.** 1/6     **c.** 5/6

**3.52** **a.** 8/27, 0.32768, 0.348678

    **b.** The probability appears to converge as $n$ increases (and actually converges to $e^{-1}$).

**3.53** $n = 4$

**3.55** **a.** Maximum probabilities are $k = 4$, 10, and 16, respectively.

    **b.** Maximum probabilities are at $x = 9$ and $x = 10$.

**3.56** **a.** $P(\text{two H in four tosses}) = 6/16$, $P(\text{three H in six tosses}) = 5/16$

**3.57** Smallest number of animals $= 13$

# CHAPTER 4

**Exercises 4.2**

**4.1** $p(3) = 0.10, p(4) = 0.20, p(5) = 0.40, p(6) = 0.30$

**4.2** $p(3) = 9/27, p(4) = 10/27, p(5) = 8/27$

**4.3** $p(1) = 12/25, p(2) = 6/25, p(3) = 4/25, p(4) = 3/25$

**4.4** $p(k) = (k - 1)/36, k = 2, \ldots, 7; p(k) = (13 - k)/36, k = 8, \ldots, 12$

**4.5** **c.** $p_X(0) = 1/16, p_X(1) = 4/16, p_X(2) = 6/16, p_X(3) = 4/16, p_X(4) = 1/16$; $Y$ has the same distribution as $X$; $p_W(\pm 4) = 1/16, p_W(\pm 2) = 4/16, p_W(0) = 6/16$

**4.7** $c = 1/21, p(x) = x/21, x = 1, \ldots, 6$

**4.8** **a.** $p(0) = p(5) = 1/32, p(1) = p(4) = 5/32, p(2) = p(3) = 10/32$

**4.9** **a.**
```
MTB > NOTE PDF FOR BINOMIAL DISTRIBUTION N = 11 P = 0.5
MTB > PDF;
SUBC>   BINOMIAL N = 11 P = 0.5.

      BINOMIAL WITH N =  11  P = 0.500000
           K          P( X = K)
           0           0.0005
           1           0.0054
           2           0.0269
           3           0.0806
           4           0.1611
           5           0.2256
           6           0.2256
           7           0.1611
           8           0.0806
           9           0.0269
          10           0.0054
          11           0.0005
```

**b.** $x = 5$ and $x = 6$ have the greatest probability.

**4.10** $p(x) = (1/2)^x, x = 1, 2, \ldots$

**4.11**
```
MTB > NOTE EXAMPLE OF SIMULATION
MTB > LET C2(1) = 1/6
MTB > LET C2(2) = 2/6
MTB > LET C2(3) = 3/6
MTB > SET C1
C1
    1    3    5

MTB > END
MTB > RANDOM 300 OBSERVATIONS INTO C3;
SUBC>   DISCRETE C1,C2.
MTB > HISTOGRAM C3;
SUBC>   START = 1;
SUBC>   INCREMENT = 2.

Histogram of C3   N = 300
Each * represents 5 obs.

Midpoint   Count
    1.00      38   ********
    3.00     100   ********************
    5.00     162   ********************************

MTB > TALLY C3;
SUBC>   PERCENTS.

        C3   PERCENT
         1     12.67
         3     33.33
         5     54.00
```

**4.14** **a.** $p(1) = 1/2, p(2) = 1/6, p(3) = 1/12$ **b.** $1 - 1/(n + 1)$
**4.15** $p(\text{Odd}) = 2/3, p(\text{Even}) = 1/3$

**Exercises 4.3**

**4.16** $\mu = 4.9, \sigma^2 = 0.89$
**4.17** $\mu = 107/27, \sigma^2 = 458/729$
**4.18** $\mu = 48/25, \sigma^2 = 696/625$
**4.19** $\mu = 7$
**4.20** **a.–c.** $E(X) = K1; \text{VAR}(X) = K2; \text{STDEV}(X) = K3$

```
MTB > NOTE COMPUTATION OF E(X),VAR(X),STDEV(X)
MTB > SET C1
C1
      58     16     23     34    .    .    .

MTB > END
MTB > NAME C1 'UNIV'
MTB > PRINT 'UNIV'
UNIV
      58     16     23     34    262    41    47    10    77    72    12
       9    154     66     62     52    42    32    27    54   119    96
      65     46     84     13     31     6    24    63    19   286   126
      16    133     43     43    178    13    61    18    76   147    14
      21     71     49     28     62     8

MTB > MEAN 'UNIV' PUT IN K1
   MEAN    =      62.180
MTB > SUBTRACT K1 FROM C1 IN C2
MTB > RAISE C2 TO POWER 2 IN C2
MTB > NOTE COMPUTATION OF VARIANCE
MTB > MEAN C2 PUT IN K2
   MEAN    =      3504.5
MTB > NOTE COMPUTATION OF STANDARD DEVIATION
MTB > LET K3 = SQRT(K2)
MTB > PRINT K3
K3        59.1992
```

**4.21** **a.** $\mu_X = 2, \sigma_X^2 = 1, \sigma_X = 1$

**b.**

| $y$ | 0 | 10 | 20 | 30 |
|------|-----|-----|-----|-----|
| $p(y)$ | 0.1 | 0.2 | 0.3 | 0.4 |

$\mu_Y = 20 = 10\mu_X, \sigma_Y^2 = 100 = (10)^2\sigma_X^2$

**4.22** On time for 27 classes; late for 18 classes; both have $\sigma^2 = 10.8$.
**4.23** **a.** $\mu_X = 90$ **b.** $\sigma_X^2 = 9$
**4.24** $(n + 1)/2$
**4.25** $\text{Var}(X) = 980/441$
**4.26** **a.** $p(-3) = 0.4, p(-2) = 0.3, p(-1) = 0.2, p(0) = 0.1$
**4.27** **a.** $\mu_X = 0, \sigma_X^2 = 4/3$ **b.** $\mu_Y = 10, \sigma_Y^2 = 4/3$

**Exercises 4.4**

**4.30** **a.** $1/5, 4/25, (1/5)(4/5)^{k-1}$ **b.** 5
**4.31** **a.** $p(x) = (0.01)(0.99)^{x-1}, x = 1, 2, \ldots$ **b.** $\mu_X = 100$ **c.** $(0.99)^{10}$
**4.32** **a.** $1/2, 1/4, (1/2)^k$ **b.** $2/3, 1/3$

**4.34**   MTB > NOTE POISSON DISTRIBUTION WITH E(X) = 1
MTB > PDF;
SUBC> POISSON MU = 1.

```
POISSON WITH MEAN =    1.000
    K          P( X = K)
    0            0.3679
    1            0.3679
    2            0.1839
    3            0.0613
    4            0.0153
    5            0.0031
    6            0.0005
    7            0.0001
    8            0.0000
```

**4.35**  0.4232, 0.3528, 0.2240

**4.36**  **a.**  MTB > NOTE POISSON DISTRIBUTION WITH E(X) = 4
MTB > PDF;
SUBC> POISSON MU = 4.

```
POISSON WITH MEAN =    4.000
    K          P( X = K)
    0            0.0183
    1            0.0733
    2            0.1465
    3            0.1954
    4            0.1954
    5            0.1563
    6            0.1042
    7            0.0595
    8            0.0298
    9            0.0132
   10            0.0053
   11            0.0019
   12            0.0006
   13            0.0002
   14            0.0001
   15            0.0000
```

     **b.**  0.0511

**4.37**   MTB > NOTE COMPARISON OF B(100,.01) AND POISSON WITH MU = 1
MTB > PDF;
SUBC> BINOMIAL N = 100 P = .01.

```
BINOMIAL WITH N = 100   P = 0.010000
    K          P( X = K)
    0            0.3660
    1            0.3697
    2            0.1849
    3            0.0610
    4            0.0149
    5            0.0029
    6            0.0005
    7            0.0001
    8            0.0000
```
MTB > PDF;
SUBC> POISSON MU = 1.

```
           POISSON WITH MEAN =    1.000
               K          P( X = K)
               0            0.3679
               1            0.3679
               2            0.1839
               3            0.0613
               4            0.0153
               5            0.0031
               6            0.0005
               7            0.0001
               8            0.0000
```

**4.38  a.** 4    **b.** 0.2381, 0.4335, 0.6288    **c.** 3 or 4

**4.39**  
```
MTB > NOTE SIMULATION OF 1000 OBSERVATIONS FROM POISSON, MU = 2.5
MTB > BASE = 1000
MTB > RANDOM 1000 OBS IN C1;
SUBC> POISSON MU = 2.5.
MTB > TALLY C1;
SUBC> PERCENTS.

               C1    PERCENT
               0       8.60
               1      21.50
               2      24.50
               3      19.40
               4      13.80
               5       7.80
               6       2.80
               7       1.20
               8       0.40

MTB > NOTE POISSON PROBABILITIES WITH MU = 2.5
MTB > PDF;
SUBC> POISSON MU = 2.5.

           POISSON WITH MEAN =    2.500
               K          P( X = K)
               0            0.0821
               1            0.2052
               2            0.2565
               3            0.2138
               4            0.1336
               5            0.0668
               6            0.0278
               7            0.0099
               8            0.0031
               9            0.0009
              10            0.0002
              11            0.0000
```

## Exercises 4.5

**4.42  a.** 0.5    **b.** 0.125    **c.** 0.125    **d.** 0.875    **e.** 0.875    **f.** 0  
**4.43  b.** 0.2, 0.2    **d.** $\mu = 0.5, m = 0.5$  
**4.44  a.** $1/(b - a)$    **b.** $(a + b)/2$  
**4.45  a.** $1/\theta$    **b.** 0.5    **c.** 0.75    **d.** $k$  
**4.47  b.** 3/4    **c.** 1/8    **d.** 1/8    **f.** $\mu = 1, m = 1$  
**4.48  a.** 4    **b.** 1/32, 1/8    **c.** 15/16, 3/4  
**4.49  b.** $(\sqrt{2} - 1)/\sqrt{2}$  

## Exercises 4.6

**4.50  a.** 0.7745    **b.** 0.2119    **c.** 0.0808    **d.** 0.1859    **e.** 0.3674    **f.** 0.025  
**4.51  a.** 0.9    **b.** 1.5    **c.** 1.96    **d.** 1.96    **e.** 1.645    **f.** 1.3

**4.52** **a.** 0.9192    **b.** 0.8643    **c.** 0.5416    **d.** 0.6826

**4.53** **a.** 87.45    **b.** 54.55

**4.54** **a.** 0.9876

      **b.** 0.9876; this number represents the probability that an observation is within 2.5 standard deviations of $\mu$ in any normal distribution.

**4.55** **a.** 0.6247   **b.** 0.0668    **c.** 0.3085   **d.** 0.6915    **e.** Zero

**4.56** 4.01 percent

**4.57** 2.28 percent

**4.58** 0.5

**4.61**
```
MTB > NOTE SIMULATION OF 50 OBSERVATIONS FROM N(100,225)
MTB > RANDOM 50 OBSERVATIONS IN C1;
SUBC> NORMAL MU = 100 SIGMA = 15.
MTB > HISTOGRAM C1

Histogram of C1   N = 50

Midpoint    Count
      60       1    *
      70       4    ****
      80       2    **
      90      11    ***********
     100       6    ******
     110      13    *************
     120      10    **********
     130       2    **
     140       1    *

MTB > NOTE NORMAL PLOT OF SIMULATED DATA
MTB > NSCORES C1 IN C2
MTB > NAME C1 'SIMNDATA'
MTB > NAME C2 'NSCORES'
MTB > PLOT C2 VERSUS C1
```

```
         -
NSCORES  -
         -                                                          *
         -                                                   *   *
    1.5+                                                 *  *
  .  -                                               ** *
         -                                         *2*
         -                                       *22
         -                                     *2*2
    0.0+                                *  * *3
         -                          2*2*
         -                        *4
         -                      ****
         -             *   *   *
   -1.5+           **
         -       *
         -    *
         -
         -
          ----+---------+---------+---------+---------+---------+--SIMNDATA
             60        75        90       105       120       135
```

**4.62** MTB > NOTE SIMULATION OF 25 OBSERVATIONS FROM U(0,1)
MTB > RANDOM 25 OBSERVATIONS IN C1;
SUBC> UNIFORM A = 0 B = 1.
MTB > HISTOGRAM C1

Histogram of C1    N = 25

| Midpoint | Count | |
|----------|-------|------|
| 0.0 | 1 | * |
| 0.1 | 2 | ** |
| 0.2 | 3 | *** |
| 0.3 | 2 | ** |
| 0.4 | 2 | ** |
| 0.5 | 1 | * |
| 0.6 | 2 | ** |
| 0.7 | 1 | * |
| 0.8 | 4 | **** |
| 0.9 | 3 | *** |
| 1.0 | 4 | **** |

MTB > NOTE NORMAL PLOT OF SIMULATED DATA
MTB > NSCORES C1 IN C2
MTB > NAME C1 'SIMUDATA'
MTB > NAME C2 'NSCORES'
MTB > PLOT C2 VERSUS C1

```
          -
NSCORES  -                                              *
          -
          -                                           *
    1.2+                                             *
          -                                       *  *
          -                                   **
          -                               **
          -                            *  *
    0.0+                        2      *
          -               *    *
          -           *   *
          -         *   *
          -       **
   -1.2+     *
          -    *
          -
          -  *
          -
          +---------+---------+---------+---------+---------+------SIMUDATA
        0.00      0.20      0.40      0.60      0.80      1.00
```

**4.64** MTB > NOTE NORMAL PLOT OF WEIGHTS OF 50 WOMEN
MTB > NSCORES C1 IN C2
MTB > NAME C2 'NSCORES'
MTB > PLOT C2 VS C1

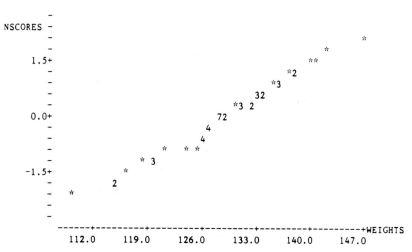

**4.65** MTB > NOTE NORMAL PLOT OF LIFE LENGTH DATA FOR 58 MICE
MTB > NSCORES C1 IN C2
MTB > NAME C2 'NSCORES'
MTB > PLOT C2 VERSUS C1

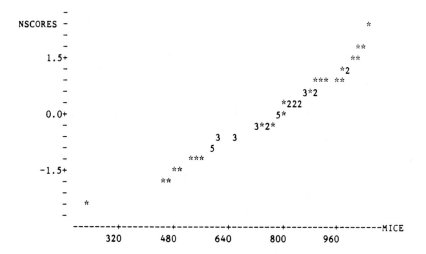

```
MTB > STEM-AND-LEAF 'MICE'

Stem-and-leaf of MICE       N  = 58
Leaf Unit = 10

         1      2 3
         1      2
         1      3
         1      3
         2      4 4
         4      4 67
         6      5 02
        13      5 5599999
        16      6 001
        19      6 556
        23      7 1123
       (10)     7 5567888899
        25      8 11334
        20      8 55578999
        12      9 03
        10      9 57799
         5     10 0224
         1     10 5
```

**Exercises 4.7**

**4.66 a.**

| $x$ | 0 | 1 |
|---|---|---|
| $p(x)$ | 1/2 | 1/2 |

| $y$ | 0 | 1 |
|---|---|---|
| $p(y)$ | 1/2 | 1/2 |

| $u$ | 0 | 1 |
|---|---|---|
| $p(u)$ | 1/2 | 1/2 |

| $v$ | 0 | 1 |
|---|---|---|
| $p(v)$ | 1/2 | 1/2 |

**b.** $X$, $Y$, $U$, and $V$ have the same marginal distributions.

**c.** The random variables must be independent.

**4.67 a.**

| $w$ \ $x$ | 1 | 2 | 3 | 4 |
|---|---|---|---|---|
| 1 | 4/16 | 1/16 | 1/16 | 1/16 |
| 2 | 0 | 3/16 | 1/16 | 1/16 |
| 3 | 0 | 0 | 2/16 | 1/16 |
| 4 | 0 | 0 | 0 | 1/16 |

**b.**

| $x$ | 1 | 2 | 3 | 4 |
|---|---|---|---|---|
| $p(x)$ | 1/4 | 1/4 | 1/4 | 1/4 |

| $w$ | 1 | 2 | 3 | 4 |
|---|---|---|---|---|
| $p(w)$ | 7/16 | 5/16 | 3/16 | 1/16 |

**4.68**

| $y$ \ $x$ | 1 | 2 |
|---|---|---|
| 1 | 0.3 | 0.3 |
| 2 | 0.2 | 0.2 |

**4.69 a.** $E(X) = 7/2$, $E(Y) = 7/2$
**b.** 7   **c.** 35

**4.70 a.** $E(X + Y) = \$32{,}000$   **b.** $E(X - Y) = \$8000$

**4.71 a.** 35/12   **b.** 35/6

**4.72 a.** $\sigma_X^2 + \sigma_Y^2$   **b.** $\sigma_X^2 + \sigma_Y^2$

**4.73** $\sigma_X^2 = (n^2 - 1)/12$

**4.74** $E(X) = 50$, $\text{Var}(X) = 25$

**4.75**    **a.** $4\sigma^2$    **b.** $2\sigma^2$

**4.76**    **a.** $E(X - Y) = 3$      **b.** $\text{Var}(X - Y) = 8$

**4.77**    **a.**

| $x$ | 0 | 1 | 2 | 3 |
|-----|---|---|---|---|
| $p(x)$ | 1/8 | 3/8 | 3/8 | 1/8 |

$E(X) = 3/2$

     **b.**

| $y$ | 0 | 1 | 2 | 3 |
|-----|---|---|---|---|
| $p(y)$ | 8/27 | 12/27 | 6/27 | 1/27 |

$E(Y) = 1$

     **c.** $\text{cov}(X, Y) = -1/2$

**4.78**    **a.** $E(XY) = 2030$      **b.** $\text{Var}(X + Y) = 185$

**4.80**    $\text{cov}(X, Y) = 0, \text{cov}(U, V) = -1/8$

# CHAPTER 5

**Exercises 5.2**

**5.1**    **a.** $E(\bar{X}) = 25$   **b.** $\text{Var}(\bar{X}) = 25/36$    **c.** 0.1151, 0.0082    **d.** 0.8767

**5.2**    0.0548

**5.3**    0.0013

**5.4**    **a.** 0.5    **b.** 0.9772    **c.** 0.9772    **d.** 0

**5.5**    **a.**

| $\bar{x}$ | 1 | 1.5 | 2 | 2.5 | 3 | 3.5 | 4 | 4.5 | 5 | 5.5 | 6 |
|-----|---|-----|---|-----|---|-----|---|-----|---|-----|---|
| $p(\bar{x})$ | 1/36 | 2/36 | 3/36 | 4/36 | 5/36 | 6/36 | 5/36 | 4/36 | 3/36 | 2/36 | 1/36 |

     **b.** $E(X) = E(\bar{X}) = 3.5$    **c.** $\text{Var}(X) = 35/12, \text{Var}(\bar{X}) = 35/24$

**5.6**    **a.**

| $\bar{x}$ | 1 | 1.5 | 2 | 2.5 | 3 | 3.5 | 4 |
|-----|---|-----|---|-----|---|-----|---|
| $p(\bar{x})$ | 1/16 | 2/16 | 3/16 | 4/16 | 3/16 | 2/16 | 1/16 |

     **b.** $E(X) = E(\bar{X}) = 2.5$    **c.** $\text{Var}(X) = 1.25, \text{Var}(\bar{X}) = 0.625$

**5.8**    **a.** 0.3372

     **b.**
```
MTB > NOTE HISTOGRAM
MTB > SET C1
C1
    734     121     404     646     .   .   .

MTB > END
MTB > NAME C1 'CORRECT'
MTB > PRINT C1
CORRECT
    734     121     404     646    1072     148     312     773      43    1102     111
    641     754     598      86    2138     150    1047     907     165     166       6
     94    1023     903     355     303    1378     202     343    1266

MTB > HISTOGRAM C1

Histogram of CORRECT    N = 31
```

```
Midpoint    Count
       0        4   ****
     200        7   *******
     400        5   *****
     600        3   ***
     800        3   ***
    1000        5   *****
    1200        2   **
    1400        1   *
    1600        0
    1800        0
    2000        0
    2200        1   *
```

**5.9**   **a., b.**

```
MTB > NOTE SIMULATION OF AVERAGES OF 16 U(0,1) OBSERVATIONS
MTB > BASE = 1000
MTB > RANDOM 100 OBSERVATIONS IN C1-C16;
SUBC> UNIFORM A = 0 B = 1.
MTB > ADD C1-C16 IN C17
MTB > DIVIDE C17 BY 16 IN C17
MTB > NAME C1 'UNIRAND'
MTB > NAME C17 'UNIMEANS'
MTB > NOTE HISTOGRAM OF 100 U(0,1) OBSERVATIONS
MTB > HISTOGRAM C1;
SUBC> START = .05;
SUBC> INCREMENT = .1.
```

```
Histogram of UNIRAND    N = 100

Midpoint    Count
   0.050        8   ********
   0.150       10   **********
   0.250       10   **********
   0.350       16   ****************
   0.450       10   **********
   0.550       10   **********
   0.650        9   *********
   0.750        7   *******
   0.850       10   **********
   0.950       10   **********
```

```
MTB > NOTE HISTOGRAM OF 100 MEANS OF 16 U(0,1) OBSERVATIONS
MTB > HISTOGRAM C17
```

```
Histogram of UNIMEANS    N = 100

Midpoint    Count
   0.36        3   ***
   0.40        9   *********
   0.44       22   **********************
   0.48       14   **************
   0.52       17   *****************
   0.56       23   ***********************
   0.60        7   *******
   0.64        4   ****
   0.68        1   *
```

**c.** $E(\bar{U}) = 0.5$, $\text{Var}(\bar{U}) = 1/192$

**Exercises 5.3**   **5.11**   (12.018, 12.982)
**5.12**   (980.4045, 980.8203)
**5.13**   (12.42, 17.84)

**5.14** **b.** (45.71, 51.92)

**5.15** **a.** (4.36, 4.94)     **b.** (4.40, 4.90)

**5.16** **a.** (36.82, 40.74)

**5.17** (48.440, 51.260)

**5.18** **a.** (32.370, 32.626)

    **b., c.**

```
MTB > NOTE HISTOGRAM OF NET WEIGHTS OF "TWO-POUND" PACKAGES
MTB > HISTOGRAM C1

Histogram of NETWT    N = 64

Midpoint   Count
    31.2     1    *
    31.4     0
    31.6     1    *
    31.8     2    **
    32.0    12    ************
    32.2     7    *******
    32.4    13    *************
    32.6     8    ********
    32.8     6    ******
    33.0     7    *******
    33.2     1    *
    33.4     3    ***
    33.6     2    **
    33.8     1    *
```

```
MTB > NOTE BOXPLOT OF NET WEIGHTS OF "TWO-POUND" PACKAGES
MTB > BOXPLOT 'NETWT'
```

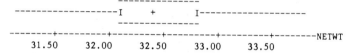

```
MTB > NOTE DESCRIBE COMMAND USED WITH NET WEIGHTS OF "TWO-POUND" PACKAGES
MTB > DESCRIBE 'NETWT'

              N      MEAN    MEDIAN    TRMEAN     STDEV    SEMEAN
NETWT        64    32.498    32.415    32.486     0.522     0.065

             MIN       MAX        Q1        Q3
NETWT     31.150    33.810    32.057    32.825
```

**5.19 a., b.**

```
MTB > SET C1
C1
  0.03   0.32   0.98   0.41    .   .   .

MTB > NAME C1 'COINS'
MTB > PRINT 'COINS'
COINS
  0.03   0.32   0.98   0.41   1.19   0.12   0.38   0.40   1.13   0.38   0.50
  0.23   1.20   1.03   0.14   0.25   1.09   0.00   0.88   1.16   0.50   0.28
  0.73   0.62   0.26   1.07   0.27   0.82   0.93   0.00   0.60   0.25   0.19
  0.52   1.16   0.07   1.35   0.06   0.47

MTB > DESCRIBE 'COINS'

               N      MEAN    MEDIAN    TRMEAN     STDEV    SEMEAN
COINS         39    0.5633    0.4700    0.5549    0.4104    0.0657

              MIN       MAX        Q1        Q3
COINS      0.0000    1.3500    0.2500    0.9800

MTB > NOTE DETERMINATION OF LARGE SAMPLE CONFIDENCE INTERVAL
MTB > STDEV C1 IN K1
   ST.DEV. =       0.41041
MTB > ZINTERVAL 95 PERCENT CONFIDENCE SIGMA = K1 DATA IN C1

THE ASSUMED SIGMA =0.410

               N      MEAN     STDEV   SE MEAN    95.0 PERCENT C.I.
COINS         39    0.5633    0.4104    0.0657   ( 0.4343,  0.6923)
```

**c.**
```
MTB > NOTE HISTOGRAM AND BOXPLOT OF COIN DATA
MTB > HISTOGRAM 'COINS';
SUBC> START = 0.2;
SUBC> INCREMENT = 0.2.

Histogram of COINS    N = 39
5 Obs. below the first class

Midpoint    Count
   0.200       9   *********
   0.400       6   ******
   0.600       5   *****
   0.800       3   ***
   1.000       5   *****
   1.200       5   *****
   1.400       1   *

MTB > BOXPLOT 'COINS'


                     ----------------------------
          ----------I          +            I----------------
                     ----------------------------
          +---------+---------+---------+---------+---------+------COINS
        0.00      0.25      0.50      0.75      1.00      1.25
```

**5.20 a., b.**

```
MTB > SET C1
C1
    176    1443     11     65    .    .    .

MTB > NAME C1 'CHECKS'
MTB > HISTOGRAM 'CHECKS'

Histogram of CHECKS    N = 50

Midpoint   Count
      0      45    **************************************************
   2000       2    **
   4000       1    *
   6000       0
   8000       1    *
  10000       0
  12000       0
  14000       0
  16000       0
  18000       1    *

MTB > BOXPLOT 'CHECKS'


             --
             +I* 00    0            0                        0
             --

        +---------+---------+---------+---------+---------+------CHECKS
        0       3500      7000     10500     14000     17500

MTB > STEM-AND-LEAF 'CHECKS'

Stem-and-leaf of CHECKS    N  = 50
Leaf Unit = 1000

   (47)    0 00000000000000000000000000000000000000000000011
     3     0 3
     2     0
     2     0
     2     0 8
     1     1
     1     1
     1     1
     1     1 7

MTB > DESCRIBE 'CHECKS'

                N     MEAN   MEDIAN   TRMEAN   STDEV   SEMEAN
CHECKS         50      738       83      180    2729      386

               MIN      MAX       Q1       Q3
CHECKS           5    17639       35      217
```

**c.**
```
MTB > NOTE CONFIDENCE INTERVAL FOR CHECK DATA
MTB > STDEV 'CHECKS' IN K1
    ST.DEV. =      2728.9
MTB > ZINTERVAL 95 PERCENT SIGMA = K1 DATA IN 'CHECKS'

THE ASSUMED SIGMA =2729

                N     MEAN    STDEV   SE MEAN   95.0 PERCENT C.I.
CHECKS         50      738     2729       386   (     -19,    1496)
```

**5.21** **a.** (50.64, 53.47)     **b.** (49.84, 54.28)
**5.22** **a.** $\mu = 4,\ \sigma^2 = 4$

## Exercises 5.4

**5.23** **a.** (0.642, 0.718)     **b.** (0.634, 0.726); the confidence interval lengthens.
**5.24** **a.** (0.479, 0.541)     **b.** No
**5.25** (0.7374, 0.7566), (0.6324, 0.6536)
**5.26** **a.** (0.524, 0.641)     **b.** (0.359, 0.476)     **c.** The intervals are of equal length.
**5.27** **a.** (0.375, 0.425)
**5.28** (0.657, 0.735)
**5.29** (0.78, 0.82)
**5.30** (0.81, 0.85)
**5.31** (0.577, 0.643)

## Exercises 5.5

**5.33** (45, 53)
**5.34** (10, 19)
**5.35** **a.** (36, 43)
**b.** MTB > NOTE HISTOGRAM FOR HOME RUNS OF NATIONAL LEAGUE CHAMPION (1919-81)
MTB > HISTOGRAM C1

```
Histogram of HRS    N = 63

Midpoint   Count
      10       1    *
      15       1    *
      20       1    *
      25       3    ***
      30      10    **********
      35       9    *********
      40      12    ************
      45      15    ***************
      50       9    *********
      55       2    **
```

**5.36** **a.** (47, 53)
**5.37** **a.** (49.3, 133.6)
**5.38** **a.** (32.33, 32.64)
**b.** The confidence interval based on normal theory is shorter.
**5.39** **a.** (51, 130)
**b.** The interval for $m$ is shorter than the one found in exercise 5.20, and the data are highly skewed.
**c.** The interval in part a of this exercise is preferred.

## Exercises 5.6

**5.40** Yes
**5.41** **a.** 62     **b.** 107
**5.42** 97
**5.43** 385
**5.44** 1537
**5.45** 2436
**5.46** $|p - \hat{p}| \leqslant 0.1$
**5.47** 984
**5.48** 1112

# CHAPTER 6

**Exercises 6.2**

**6.1**  **a.** 1/15  **b.** 3/5

**6.2**  **a.** 1/16  **b.** 70/81

**6.3**  **c.** 0.0755

**d.** 0.6769, 0.4049, 0.2061, 0.0913, 0.0355, 0.0036, 0.0002

**6.4**  **a.** $Y \leqslant 4$

**b.** 0.9147, 0.8334, 0.7108, 0.5501, 0.2018, 0.0170

**6.5**  **a.** 0.0668   **b.** 0.305

**6.6**  **a.**
```
MTB > NOTE SIMULATION OF TYPE I AND TYPE II ERRORS
MTB > BASE = 2000
MTB > NOTE TYPE I ERROR SIMULATION
MTB > RANDOM 1000 OBSERVATIONS IN C1;
SUBC> BINOMIAL N = 100 P = .5.
MTB > TALLY C1;
SUBC> CUMCNTS.
```

| C1 | CUMCNT |
|----|--------|
| 36 | 2 |
| 37 | 3 |
| 38 | 8 |
| 39 | 13 |
| 40 | 26 |
| 41 | 37 |
| 42 | 60 |
| 43 | 98 |
| 44 | 147 |
| 45 | 199 |
| 46 | 258 |
| 47 | 322 |
| 48 | 400 |
| 49 | 469 |
| 50 | 551 |
| 51 | 639 |
| 52 | 696 |
| 53 | 753 |
| 54 | 807 |
| 55 | 872 |
| 56 | 900 |
| 57 | 928 |
| 58 | 939 |
| 59 | 965 |
| 60 | 982 |
| 61 | 993 |
| 62 | 995 |
| 64 | 998 |
| 65 | 999 |
| 67 | 1000 |

Simulated $\alpha = 0.072$

**b.**
```
MTB > NOTE TYPE II ERROR SIMULATION
MTB > RANDOM 1000 OBSERVATIONS IN C2;
SUBC> BINOMIAL N = 100 P = .6.
MTB > TALLY C2;
SUBC> CUMCNTS.
```

| C2 | CUMCNT |
|----|--------|
| 45 | 3 |
| 46 | 5 |
| 47 | 8 |
| 48 | 13 |
| 49 | 22 |
| 50 | 32 |
| 51 | 43 |
| 52 | 62 |
| 53 | 95 |
| 54 | 133 |
| 55 | 178 |
| 56 | 236 |
| 57 | 314 |
| 58 | 391 |
| 59 | 471 |
| 60 | 553 |
| 61 | 626 |
| 62 | 711 |
| 63 | 770 |
| 64 | 815 |
| 65 | 868 |
| 66 | 901 |
| 67 | 938 |
| 68 | 961 |
| 69 | 974 |
| 70 | 981 |
| 71 | 987 |
| 72 | 992 |
| 73 | 995 |
| 74 | 999 |
| 76 | 1000 |

Simulated $\beta(0.6) = 0.314$

**6.7**   **a.** 0.0233     **b.** 0.0202, 0.0000

**6.8**   **a.** 0.0547     **b.** 0.8327, 0.6172, 0.3222, 0.0702, 0.0000

**6.9**   **a.** 0.0069     **c.** 0.0005

**6.10**  **a.** 0.083      **b.** 0.766 using simulation output

```
MTB > NOTE SIMULATION OF TYPE I AND II ERRORS
MTB > NOTE SIMULATION FOR TYPE I ERROR
MTB > BASE = 1000
MTB > RANDOM 1000 OBSERVATIONS IN C1;
SUBC> BINOMIAL N = 20 P = 0.05.
MTB > TALLY C1;
SUBC> CUMCNTS.
```

| C1 | CUMCNT |
|----|--------|
| 0 | 336 |
| 1 | 737 |
| 2 | 917 |
| 3 | 984 |
| 4 | 995 |
| 5 | 1000 |

```
MTB > NOTE SIMULATION FOR TYPE II ERROR
MTB > RANDOM 1000 OBSERVATIONS IN C2;
SUBC> BINOMIAL N = 20 P = .20.
MTB > TALLY C2;
SUBC> CUMCNTS.
```

|  C2 | CUMCNT |
|-----|--------|
|  0  |    7   |
|  1  |   75   |
|  2  |  234   |
|  3  |  413   |
|  4  |  614   |
|  5  |  794   |
|  6  |  906   |
|  7  |  970   |
|  8  |  989   |
|  9  |  999   |
| 10  | 1000   |

**Exercises 6.3**

**6.11** **a.** $Z \geqslant 1.645$　　**b.** $Z = 2.03$; reject $H_0$.
**c.** 0.3483, 0.0078　　**d.** $Z \geqslant 2.326$; retain $H_0$.

**6.12** $Z = -0.50$; retain $H_0$.

**6.13**
```
MTB > NOTE TEST OF AGE OF REPRESENTATIVES = 45
MTB > STDEV 'AGES' PUT IN K1
    ST.DEV. =        10.386
MTB > ZTEST OF MU = 45 SIGMA = K1 DATA 'AGES'

TEST OF MU = 45.00 VS MU N.E. 45.00
THE ASSUMED SIGMA = 10.4
```

|      |  N | MEAN  | STDEV | SE MEAN |  Z   | P VALUE |
|------|----|-------|-------|---------|------|---------|
| AGES | 43 | 48.81 | 10.39 |  1.58   | 2.41 |  0.016  |

Reject $H_0$.

**6.14** As the confidence interval does not contain 20, $H_0$: $\mu = 20$ is rejected.

**6.15** $Z = 0.94$; retain $H_0$.

**6.16**
```
MTB > NOTE TEST OF MU = 40 FOR HOME RUN LEADERS IN NATIONAL LEAGUE
MTB > STDEV 'HRS' PUT IN K1
    ST.DEV. =        9.4364
MTB > ZTEST OF MU = 40 SIGMA = K1 DATA 'HRS'

TEST OF MU = 40.00 VS MU N.E. 40.00
THE ASSUMED SIGMA = 9.44
```

|     |  N | MEAN  | STDEV | SE MEAN |   Z   | P VALUE |
|-----|----|-------|-------|---------|-------|---------|
| HRS | 63 | 38.78 |  9.44 |  1.19   | -1.03 |  0.30   |

Retain $H_0$.

**6.17** The confidence interval contains 50, so $H_0$: $\mu = 50$ is retained.

**6.19 a., b.**

```
MTB > NOTE TEST CF MU = 32 (OUNCES) FOR "TWO-POUND" PACKAGES
MTB > STDEV 'NETWT' PUT IN K1
   ST.DEV. =     0.52185
MTB > ZTEST OF MU = 32 SIGMA = K1 DATA 'NETWT'

TEST OF MU = 32.0000 VS MU N.E. 32.0000
THE ASSUMED SIGMA = 0.522

                N     MEAN    STDEV   SE MEAN      Z    P VALUE
NETWT          64   32.4978   0.5218   0.0652    7.63    0.0000
```

Reject $H_0$.

**6.20 a.** $c = \mu_0 - (\sigma/\sqrt{n})z_\alpha$

**b.** $\bar{X} < 4.306$; No, the observed value does not fall in this region.

**Exercises 6.4**

**6.21** $Z = 2$, $z_{0.05} = 1.645$; reject $H_0$.

**6.22** $Z = 1.92$; reject $H_0$; $p$-value $= 0.0274$.

**6.23** $Z = -1$; retain $H_0$: $p = 1/6$; $p$-value $= 0.3174$.

**6.24** $Z = -1.83$; retain $H_0$: $p = 3/4$.

**6.25 a.** $H_0$: $p = 0.5$

**b.** $Z = 2$; reject $H_0$ in favor of $H_1$: $p \neq 0.5$.      **c.** 0.0456

**6.26** $Z = -2.49$; reject $H_0$; $p$-value $= 0.0064$.

**6.27 a.** $H_0$: $p = 0.300$; $H_1$: $p < 0.300$      **b.** $Z = -1.22$; retain $H_0$.      **c.** 0.1112

**d.** 0.7852; this number is the probability of incorrectly stating the player is batting at least 0.300 when, in fact, his average is 0.280.

**6.28 a.** $H_0$: $p = 0.36$          **b.** $H_1$: $p > 0.36$

**c.** $Z = 2.64$; reject $H_0$.      **d.** 0.1660

**6.29 a.** $Z = 4.45$, $z_{0.05} = 1.645$; reject $H_0$.

**b.** Reject $H_0$ for both $\alpha = 0.01$ and $\alpha = 0.001$.

**6.30 a.** $Z = 8.34$, $z_{0.01} = 2.326$; reject $H_0$.      **b.** Yes

**Exercises 6.5**

**6.32 a.** $H_0$: $\mu = 18$; $H_1$: $\mu > 18$      **b.** $H_0$: $m = 18$; $H_1$: $m > 18$

**c.** $Z = 3.53$; reject $H_0$.      **d.** $Z = 2.83$; reject $H_0$.      **e.** Yes

**6.33** $Z = 2.16$; reject $H_0$.

**6.34** $Z = 0.90$; retain $H_0$.

**6.35** $Z = 0$; retain $H_0$.

**6.36** $Z = -0.43$; retain $H_0$.

**6.37** $Z = 1.62$; retain $H_0$.

**6.38 a.** $Z = 5$; reject $H_0$.      **b.** $Z = -1.75$; reject $H_0$.

**6.39 a.** $Z = -2.40$; reject $H_0$.      **b.** $Z = -2.39$; reject $H_0$.

**6.40** A 95 percent confidence interval is (166, 773); retain $H_0$: $m = 300$.

**6.41** A 95 percent confidence interval is (51, 130); retain $H_0$: $m = 100$.

# CHAPTER 7

**Exercises 7.1**

**7.1** **a.** MTB > SET C1
C1
```
      349     293     300     274     .   .   .
```

```
MTB > END.
MTB > PRINT C1
C1
      349     293     300     274     242     255     224     182     273     272     233
      214     242     206     235     195
```

```
MTB > NAME C1 'GF'
MTB > BOXPLOT 'GF'
```

```
                                   -----------------
                       -----------I      +      I----------------------
                                   -----------------
                    --+---------+---------+---------+---------+---------+----GF
                    175         210       245       280       315       350
```

MTB > HISTOGRAM 'GF'

Histogram of GF    N = 16

| Midpoint | Count |      |
|----------|-------|------|
| 180      | 1     | *    |
| 200      | 2     | **   |
| 220      | 2     | **   |
| 240      | 4     | **** |
| 260      | 1     | *    |
| 280      | 3     | ***  |
| 300      | 2     | **   |
| 320      | 0     |      |
| 340      | 1     | *    |

```
MTB > NOTE NORMAL PLOT OF GF
MTB > NSCORE C1 IN C2
MTB > NAME C2 'NSCORES'
MTB > PLOT C2 VS C1
```

```
           -                                                    *
   NSCORES -
           -
           -                                          *
      1.0+                                         *
           -                              *
           -                              *
           -                              *
           -                        *
      0.0+                    2
           -                *
           -                *
           -             *
           -          *
     -1.0+        *
           -     *
           -
           -
           -     *
         --+---------+---------+---------+---------+---------+----GF
         175        210       245       280       315       350
```

The normality assumption is justified.

**b.** 
```
MTB > SET C1
C1
   221     240     251     230      .    .    .

MTB > END.
MTB > PRINT C1
C1
   221     240     251     230     250     319     296     247     164     164     231
   238     273     248     275     342

MTB > NAME C1 'GA'
MTB > BOXPLOT 'GA'


                                        --------------
                          *       ---I    +    I-------------           *
                                        --------------
              ------+---------+---------+---------+---------+---------+GA
                   175       210       245       280       315       350

MTB > HISTOGRAM 'GA'

Histogram of GA    N = 16

Midpoint    Count
     160      2    **
     180      0
     200      0
     220      1    *
     240      6    ******
     260      2    **
     280      2    **
     300      1    *
     320      1    *
     340      1    *


MTB > NOTE NORMAL PLOT OF GA
MTB > NSCORE C1 IN C2
MTB > NAME C2 'NSCORES'
MTB > PLOT C2 VS C1

            -                                                        *
NSCORES  -
            -                                                  *
   1.0+                                               *
            -                                    *
            -                                  *
            -                            *
            -                          *
   0.0+                             2
            -                     *
            -                   *
            -               *
            -              *
  -1.0+            *
            -
            -    2
            -
            -
              ------+---------+---------+---------+---------+---------+GA
                   175       210       245       280       315       350
```

The normality assumption is reasonable.

**7.2**  **a.**
```
MTB > READ C1 C2
       18 ROWS READ
  ROW     C1     C2

    1     194   1008
    2     903   8834
    3     200   2164
    4     163   1239
      .    .    .

MTB > END.
MTB > PRINT C1 C2
  ROW     C1     C2

    1     194   1008
    2     903   8834
    3     200   2164
    4     163   1239
    5      69    684
    6     310   3879
    7     331   2689
    8      44    535
    9     518   5945
   10     396   3712
   11      74   1044
   12     169   2044
   13     123   2451
   14      60    661
   15      92   1569
   16     177   1942
   17     101   2038
   18     304   3623

MTB > NAME C1='ARTICLES', C2='PAGES'
MTB > BOXPLOT 'ARTICLES'
```

```
MTB > HISTOGRAM 'ARTICLES'

Histogram of ARTICLES    N = 18

Midpoint    Count
      0       1   *
    100       6   ******
    200       5   *****
    300       3   ***
    400       1   *
    500       1   *
    600       0
    700       0
    800       0
    900       1   *
```

```
MTB > NOTE NORMAL PLOT OF ARTICLES
MTB > NSCORE C1 IN C3
MTB > NAME C3 'NSCORES'
MTB > PLOT C3 VS C1
```

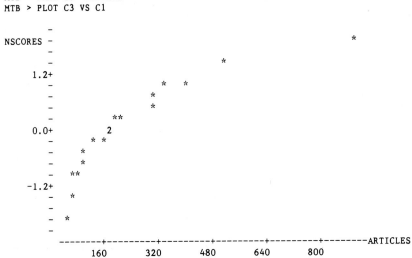

```
MTB > BOXPLOT 'PAGES'
```

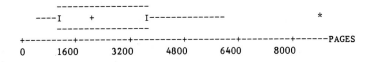

```
MTB > HISTOGRAM 'PAGES'

Histogram of PAGES    N = 18

Midpoint   Count
    1000      6    ******
    2000      6    ******
    3000      1    *
    4000      3    ***
    5000      0
    6000      1    *
    7000      0
    8000      0
    9000      1    *
```

```
MTB > NOTE NORMAL PLOT OF PAGES
MTB > NSCORE C2 IN C4
MTB > NAME C4 'NSCORES2'
MTB > PLOT C4 VS C2
```

```
          -                              .
NSCORES2-                                              *
          -
          -                        *
     1.2+
          -              **
          -              *
          -           *
          -         **
     0.0+        2
          -     * *
          -    *
          -   *
          -  * *
    -1.2+
          -  *
          -
          - *
          -
          +---------+---------+---------+---------+---------+------PAGES
          0        1600      3200      4800      6400      8000
```

**7.3**  **a.** 
```
MTB > READ C1-C3
     20 ROWS READ
  ROW    C1     C2     C3

    1    4.3    3.0    2.2
    2    5.0    4.1    3.7
    3    4.6    3.9    3.7
    4    4.3    3.1    3.1
     .    .    .

MTB > END.
MTB > PRINT C1-C3
  ROW    C1     C2     C3

    1    4.3    3.0    2.2
    2    5.0    4.1    3.7
    3    4.6    3.9    3.7
    4    4.3    3.1    3.1
    5    3.1    3.3    2.6
    6    4.8    2.9    2.2
    7    3.7    3.3    2.9
    8    5.4    3.9    2.8
    9    3.0    2.3    2.1
   10    4.9    4.1    3.7
   11    4.8    4.7    4.7
   12    4.4    4.2    3.5
   13    4.9    4.0    3.3
   14    5.1    4.6    3.4
   15    4.8    4.6    4.1
   16    4.2    3.8    3.3
   17    6.6    5.2    4.3
   18    3.6    3.1    2.1
   19    4.5    3.7    2.4
   20    4.6    3.8    3.8

MTB > NAME C1 = 'LEVEL0', C2 = 'LEVEL1', C3 = 'LEVEL2'
```

```
MTB > BOXPLOT 'LEVELO'


                                  ----------
                  **      ----------I   +  I-------              *
                                  ----------
              +---------+---------+---------+---------+---------+------LEVELO
            2.80      3.50      4.20      4.90      5.60      6.30

MTB > HISTOGRAM 'LEVELO'

Histogram of LEVELO   N = 20

Midpoint   Count
     3.0       2   **
     3.5       2   **
     4.0       1   *
     4.5       6   ******
     5.0       7   *******
     5.5       1   *
     6.0       0
     6.5       1   *

MTB > NOTE NORMAL PLOT OF LEVELO
MTB > NSCORE C1  IN    C4
MTB > NAME C4 'NSCORES'
MTB > PLOT C4 VS 'LEVELO'
```

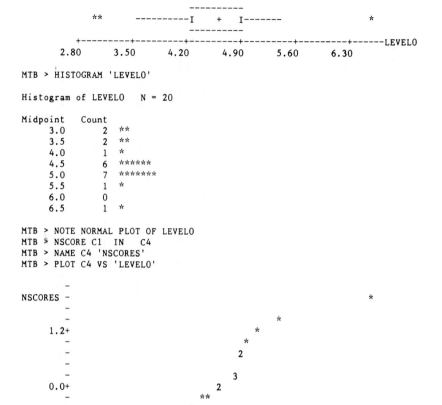

```
              +---------+---------+---------+---------+---------+------LEVELO
            2.80      3.50      4.20      4.90      5.60      6.30
```

```
MTB > BOXPLOT 'LEVEL1'


                                    -----------------
                    ---------------I       +       I-----------------
                                    -----------------
              ------+---------+---------+---------+---------+---------+LEVEL1
                  2.40      3.00      3.60      4.20      4.80      5.40


MTB > HISTOGRAM 'LEVEL1'

Histogram of LEVEL1    N = 20

Midpoint   Count
    2.4      1    *
    2.8      1    *
    3.2      5    *****
    3.6      1    *
    4.0      7    *******
    4.4      1    *
    4.8      3    ***
    5.2      1    *

MTB > NOTE NORMAL PLOT OF LEVEL1
MTB > NSCORE C2  IN   C5
MTB > NAME C5 'NSCORES1'
MTB > PLOT C5 VS 'LEVEL1'
```

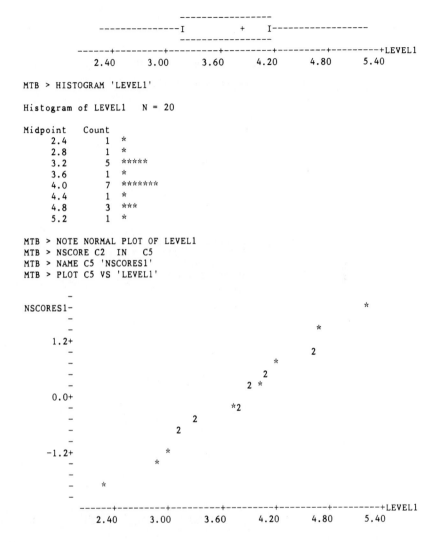

```
MTB > BOXPLOT 'LEVEL2'


                          --------------------------
                --------I               +       I-------------------
                          --------------------------
                +---------+---------+---------+---------+---------+------LEVEL2
              2.00      2.50      3.00      3.50      4.00      4.50

MTB > HISTOGRAM 'LEVEL2'

Histogram of LEVEL2   N = 20

Midpoint   Count
     2.0      2  **
     2.4      3  ***
     2.8      3  ***
     3.2      3  ***
     3.6      5  *****
     4.0      2  **
     4.4      1  *
     4.8      1  *

MTB > NOTE NORMAL PLOT OF LEVEL2
MTB > NSCORE C3  IN   C6
MTB > NAME C6 'NSCORES2'
MTB > PLOT C6 VS 'LEVEL2'
```

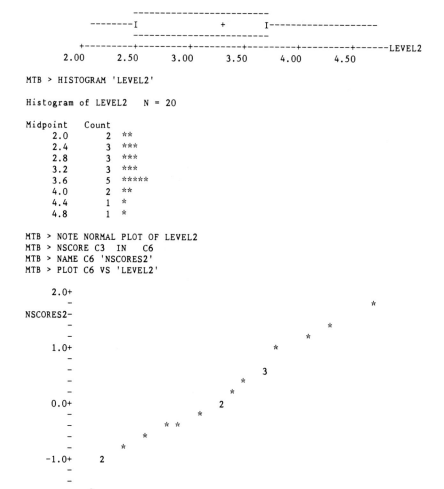

```
     2.0+
        -                                                           *
NSCORES2-
        -                                                      *
        -                                                 *
     1.0+                                       *
        -
        -                               3
        -                          *
        -                      *
     0.0+                2
        -             *
        -        *  *
        -      *
        -   *
    -1.0+   2
        -
        - 2
          +---------+---------+---------+---------+---------+------LEVEL2
        2.00      2.50      3.00      3.50      4.00      4.50
```

**c.** 6.6 is a possible outlier.

**d.**
```
MTB > READ C1-C3
      20 ROWS READ
   ROW     C1     C2     C3

     1    4.3    3.0    2.2
     2    5.0    4.1    3.7
     3    4.6    3.9    3.7
     4    4.3    3.1    3.1
     .     .      .

MTB > END.
MTB > LET C8=C1-C2
MTB > PRINT C1 C2 C8
   ROW     C1     C2          C8

     1    4.3    3.0     1.30000
     2    5.0    4.1     0.90000
     3    4.6    3.9     0.70000
     4    4.3    3.1     1.20000
     5    3.1    3.3    -0.20000
     6    4.8    2.9     1.90000
     7    3.7    3.3     0.40000
     8    5.4    3.9     1.50000
     9    3.0    2.3     0.70000
    10    4.9    4.1     0.80000
    11    4.8    4.7     0.10000
    12    4.4    4.2     0.20000
    13    4.9    4.0     0.90000
    14    5.1    4.6     0.50000
    15    4.8    4.6     0.20000
    16    4.2    3.8     0.40000
    17    6.6    5.2     1.40000
    18    3.6    3.1     0.50000
    19    4.5    3.7     0.80000
    20    4.6    3.8     0.80000
```

```
MTB > NAME C8 'DIFFER'
MTB > BOXPLOT 'DIFFER'
```

```
MTB > HISTOGRAM 'DIFFER'

Histogram of DIFFER    N = 20

Midpoint   Count
   -0.2      1    *
    0.0      0
    0.2      3    ***
    0.4      2    **
    0.6      2    **
    0.8      5    *****
    1.0      2    **
    1.2      1    *
    1.4      2    **
    1.6      1    *
    1.8      0
    2.0      1    *

MTB > NOTE NORMAL PLOT OF DIFFER
MTB > NSCORE C8  IN C9
MTB > NAME C9 'NSCORES'
MTB > PLOT C9 VS C8
```

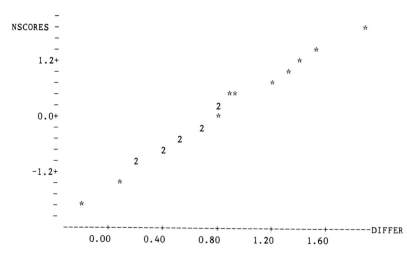

Yes, the normality assumption appears to be justified.

**7.4**
```
MTB > SET C1
C1
  0.390   0.352   0.341   0.333    .    .    .

MTB > END.
MTB > PRINT C1
C1
  0.390   0.352   0.341   0.333   0.331   0.329   0.326   0.321   0.320
  0.319   0.318   0.307   0.305   0.304   0.304   0.304   0.303   0.302
  0.302   0.302   0.301   0.300   0.300   0.300   0.300

MTB > NAME C1 'BA'
MTB > BOXPLOT 'BA'


                          -------------
                      -I +          I-------------                   *
                          -------------
                   ------+---------+---------+---------+---------+---------+--BA
                      0.300     0.320     0.340     0.360     0.380     0.400


MTB > HISTOGRAM 'BA'

Histogram of BA    N = 25

Midpoint    Count
   0.30       12    ************
   0.31        2    **
   0.32        4    ****
   0.33        4    ****
   0.34        1    *
   0.35        1    *
   0.36        0
   0.37        0
   0.38        0
   0.39        1    *


MTB > NOTE NORMAL PLOT OF BA
MTB > NSCORE C1 IN C2
MTB > NAME C2 'NSCORES'
MTB > PLOT C2 VS C1


        2.0+                                                        *
           -
NSCORES    -                                             *
           -
           -                                        *
        1.0+                                    **
           -                                  *
           -                             *  *
           -                          2
           -                        *
        0.0+                     **
           -                    3
           -                    *
           -                    3
           -
       -1.0+                   *
           -
           -                  4
           -
           ------+---------+---------+---------+---------+---------+--BA
              0.300     0.320     0.340     0.360     0.380     0.400
```

**7.5**
```
MTB > SET C1
C1
    69    57    83    82    .    .    .

MTB > END.
MTB > PRINT C1
C1
    69    57    83    82    99    75    58    78    66    61    71    70    68
    70    65    86    65    64    47    68    93    66    51    80    61    80
    62    61    63    62    89    84

MTB > NAME C1 'SCORE'
MTB > BOXPLOT 'SCORE'
```

```
                                 --------------------
                 ---------------I      +            I-------------------
                                 --------------------
                 ------+---------+---------+---------+---------+---------+SCORE
                      50        60        70        80        90       100
```

```
MTB > HISTOGRAM 'SCORE'

Histogram of SCORE    N = 32

Midpoint    Count
      45      1    *
      50      1    *
      55      1    *
      60      6    ******
      65      6    ******
      70      6    ******
      75      1    *
      80      4    ****
      85      3    ***
      90      1    *
      95      1    *
     100      1    *

MTB > NOTE NORMAL PLOT OF SCORE
MTB > NSCORE C1 IN C2
MTB > NAME C2 'NSCORES'
MTB > PLOT C2 VS C1
```

```
           -                                               *
  NSCORES  -                                          *
           -                                      *
     1.2+                                      *
           -                                 **
           -                            2  *
           -                     *   *
           -                 2*
     0.0+                 2*
           -             22
           -           **
           -          2
           -         3
    -1.2+        *
           -       *
           -     *
           -   *
           ------+---------+---------+---------+---------+---------+SCORE
                50        60        70        80        90       100
```

Yes, it is reasonable to hypothesize that the underyling distribution is normal.

**Exercises 7.2**

**7.6**  $t_{0.05,2} = 2.920$, $t_{0.05,5} = 2.015$, $t_{0.05,10} = 1.812$, $t_{0.05,20} = 1.725$, $Z_{0.05} = 1.645$

**7.7**  **a.** 0.01  **b.** 0.10  **c.** 0.90  **d.** 0.01  **e.** 0.01  **f.** 0.05

**7.8**  **a., b.**

```
MTB > SET C1
C1
    349    293    300    274    .    .    .

MTB > END.
MTB > PRINT C1
C1
    349    293    300    274    242    255    224    182    273    272    233
    214    242    206    235    195

MTB > TINTERVAL 95 PERCENT CONFIDENCE FOR DATA IN C1

              N      MEAN     STDEV   SE MEAN     95.0 PERCENT C.I.
C1           16     249.3      43.2      10.8   (  226.3,    272.3)

MTB > TINTERVAL 99 PERCENT CONFIDENCE FOR DATA IN C1

              N      MEAN     STDEV   SE MEAN     99.0 PERCENT C.I.
C1           16     249.3      43.2      10.8   (  217.5,    281.1)
```

**7.9**  **a., b.**

```
MTB > SET C1
C1
  0.056   0.068  -0.079   0.013    .    .    .

MTB > END.
MTB > PRINT C1
C1
  0.056   0.068  -0.079   0.013  -0.055  -0.071  -0.034  -0.122   0.030
 -0.045

MTB > TINTERVAL 95 PERCENT CONFIDENCE FOR DATA IN C1

              N      MEAN     STDEV   SE MEAN     95.0 PERCENT C.I.
C1           10   -0.0239    0.0628    0.0199   ( -0.0688,   0.0210)

MTB > TTEST OF MU=0  ALTERNATIVE=0   ON DATA IN C1

TEST OF MU = 0.0000 VS MU N.E. 0.0000

              N      MEAN     STDEV   SE MEAN         T    P VALUE
C1           10   -0.0239    0.0628    0.0199     -1.20       0.26
```

Retain $H_0$.

**7.10 a., b.**

```
MTB > SET C1
C1
    416    594   1192   1269    .    .    .

MTB > END.
MTB > PRINT C1
C1
    416    594   1192   1269   1453   1555   2065   2070   2438   2497   2595
   2845   2967   2999   3130   3162   3251   3283   3414   3467   3516   3729
   3963   4006   4388   5395   5520   5895   7059

MTB > NOTE NORMAL PLOT OF C1
MTB > NSCORE C1 IN C2
MTB > NAME C2 'NSCORES'
MTB > PLOT C2 VS C1
```

```
          -
NSCORES  -                                              *
          -                                        *
          -                                      *
     1.2+                                      *
          -                              *  *
          -                            **
          -                       2
          -                      2*
     0.0+                       *2
          -                  *  **
          -                  **
          -             2
          -       2
    -1.2+        *
          -        *
          -    *
          -   *
          -
         +---------+---------+---------+---------+---------+------C1
         0       1500      3000      4500      6000      7500
```

```
MTB > TINTERVAL 90 PERCENT CONFIDENCE FOR DATA IN C1

            N    MEAN   STDEV   SE MEAN    90.0 PERCENT C.I.
C1         29    3108    1553      288   (    2617,    3599)
```

Reject $H_0$.

**7.11 a., b.**

```
MTB > READ C1-C3
    20 ROWS READ
 ROW    C1     C2     C3

   1    4.3    3.0    2.2
   2    5.0    4.1    3.7
   3    4.6    3.9    3.7
   4    4.3    3.1    3.1
    .    .    .

MTB > END.
MTB > LET C8=C1-C2
MTB > PRINT C1 C2 C8
 ROW    C1     C2          C8

   1    4.3    3.0    1.30000
   2    5.0    4.1    0.90000
   3    4.6    3.9    0.70000
   4    4.3    3.1    1.20000
   5    3.1    3.3   -0.20000
   6    4.8    2.9    1.90000
   7    3.7    3.3    0.40000
   8    5.4    3.9    1.50000
   9    3.0    2.3    0.70000
  10    4.9    4.1    0.80000
  11    4.8    4.7    0.10000
  12    4.4    4.2    0.20000
  13    4.9    4.0    0.90000
  14    5.1    4.6    0.50000
  15    4.8    4.6    0.20000
  16    4.2    3.8    0.40000
  17    6.6    5.2    1.40000
  18    3.6    3.1    0.50000
  19    4.5    3.7    0.80000
  20    4.6    3.8    0.80000

MTB > TINTERVAL 95 PERCENT CONFIDENCE FOR DATA IN C8

            N      MEAN    STDEV   SE MEAN    95.0 PERCENT C.I.
 C8         20     0.750   0.522   0.117    ( 0.506,    0.994)

MTB > TTEST OF MU=0 ALTERNATIVE=+1 ON DATA IN C8

TEST OF MU = 0.000 VS MU G.T. 0.000

            N      MEAN    STDEV   SE MEAN      T     P VALUE
 C8         20     0.750   0.522   0.117      6.43    0.0000
```

Reject $H_0$.

**7.12** The $t$ statistic would be inappropriate for these data because of the failure of the normality assumption.

**7.13** **a., b.**

```
MTB > SET C1
C1
    20      23      35      42      .    .    .

MTB > END.
MTB > PRINT C1
C1
    20      23      35      42      44      45      45      46      47      49      51
    54      62      65      70      70      70      80      89     138

MTB > NOTE NORMAL PLOT OF C1
MTB > NSCORE C1 IN C2
MTB > NAME C2 'NSCORES'
MTB > PLOT C1 VS C2
```

```
        140+                                                            *
           -
C1         -
           -
           -
        105+
           -
           -                                                    *
           -                                            *
           -
         70+                                     3
           -                              *  *
           -                          *
           -                    ** * *
           -              * *   2
         35+        *
           -
           -  *      *
           -
           --------+---------+---------+---------+---------+--------NSCORES
              -1.40     -0.70      0.00      0.70      1.40
```

```
MTB > TINTERVAL 95 PERCENT CONFIDENCE FOR DATA IN C1

          N     MEAN    STDEV   SE MEAN    95.0 PERCENT C.I.
C1       20    57.25    25.88     5.79   (  45.13,   69.37)
```

The observation 138 is a good candidate for an outlier.

**c., d.**

```
MTB > SET C1
C1
   20    23    35    42    .    .    .

MTB > END.
MTB > PRINT C1
C1
   20    23    35    42    44    45    45    46    47    49    51    54    62
   65    70    70    70    80    89

MTB > NOTE NORMAL PLOT OF C1
MTB > NSCORE C1 IN C2
MTB > NAME C2 'NSCORES'
MTB > PLOT C1 VS C2

C1      -
        -                                                      *
        -
      80+                                               *
        -
        -                                         3
        -
        -                                    * *
      60+
        -                               *
        -                             *
        -                        * * *
        -              *   *   2
      40+
        -          *
        -
        -
        -      *
      20+    *
        --------+---------+---------+---------+---------+--------NSCORES
             -1.40     -0.70      0.00      0.70      1.40


MTB > TINTERVAL 95 PERCENT CONFIDENCE FOR DATA IN C1

          N      MEAN    STDEV   SE MEAN    95.0 PERCENT C.I.
C1       19     53.00    18.05     4.14    (  44.30,    61.70)
```

Yes, the normality assumption seems more reasonable now. The interval in
part b is longer than that in part d.

**7.14  a., b.**

```
MTB > NOTE DATA IS TIMES IN MINUTES OF 25 STUDENTS TO FINISH QUIZ
MTB > SET C1
C1
   29.6   31.6   32.0   29.5   .   .   .

MTB > END
MTB > PRINT C1
C1
   29.6   31.6   32.0   29.5   31.6   31.8   30.9   31.2   31.1   29.4   31.3
   32.8   31.2   35.0   30.1   33.1   31.9   29.0   34.7   35.1   30.3   31.9
   30.3   37.4   26.8
```

```
MTB > DESCRIBE C1

              N      MEAN    MEDIAN    TRMEAN     STDEV    SEMEAN
C1           25    31.584    31.300    31.539     2.245     0.449

            MIN       MAX        Q1        Q3
C1       26.800    37.400    30.200    32.400

MTB > HISTOGRAM C1

Histogram of C1   N = 25

Midpoint   Count
      27       1   *
      28       0
      29       3   ***
      30       4   ****
      31       5   *****
      32       6   ******
      33       2   **
      34       0
      35       3   ***
      36       0
      37       1   *

MTB > NOTE NORMAL PLOT OF C1
MTB > NSCORE C1 IN C2
MTB > NAME C2 'NSCORES'
MTB > PLOT C2 VS C1
```

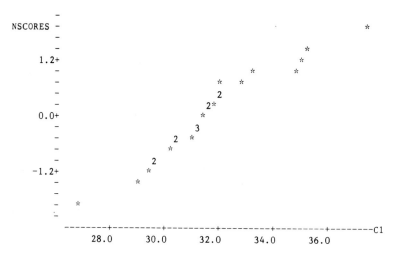

```
MTB > TTEST OF MU=30   ALTERNATIVE=+1 ON DATA IN C1

TEST OF MU = 30.000 VS MU G.T. 30.000

              N      MEAN     STDEV    SE MEAN         T    P VALUE
C1           25    31.584     2.245      0.449      3.53     0.0009
```

Reject $H_0$.

**7.15 a., b.**

```
MTB > SET C1
C1
   40.0    34.1    29.4    27.9     .    .    .

MTB > END.
MTB > PRINT C1
C1
   40.0    34.1    29.4    27.9    42.4    28.5    35.0    28.6    39.5    41.3    32.8
   36.1    42.9    35.4    29.1    34.0    36.7    31.5    29.7    31.1    26.9    40.7
   29.2    37.4    35.7

MTB > HISTOGRAM C1

Histogram of C1    N = 25

Midpoint    Count
      26        1   *
      28        3   ***
      30        4   ****
      32        3   ***
      34        3   ***
      36        4   ****
      38        1   *
      40        3   ***
      42        3   ***

MTB > NOTE NORMAL PLOT OF C1
MTB > NSCORE C1 IN C2
MTB > NAME C2 'NSCORES'
MTB > PLOT C2 VS C1


            -
  NSCORES  -                                                              *
            -
            -                                                          *
      1.2+                                                        *
            -                                                 *   *
            -                                            *       *
            -                                     *  *
            -                                  **
      0.0+                              **   *
            -                      *   *
            -                  *      *
            -              **
            -          *  *
     -1.2+           *
            -       *
            -
            -    *
            -
            --+---------+---------+---------+---------+---------+----C1
             27.0      30.0      33.0      36.0      39.0      42.0

MTB > TTEST OF MU=30  ALTERNATIVE=+1 ON DATA IN C1

TEST OF MU = 30.000 VS MU G.T. 30.000

            N      MEAN    STDEV    SE MEAN       T    P VALUE
C1         25    34.236    4.966      0.993    4.27     0.0001
```

Reject $H_0$.

**7.16  a.** $\bar{x} = 22.5$     **b.** Reject $H_0$.

**Exercises 7.3**

**7.18  a.**
```
MTB > SET C1
C1
    349     293     300     274    .    .    .

MTB > END.
MTB > PRINT C1
C1
    349     293     300     274     242     255     224     182     273     272     233
    214     242     206     235     195

MTB > NAME C1 'GF'
MTB > AVERAGE C1
    MEAN    =       249.31
MTB > MEDIAN C1
    MEDIAN =        242.00
MTB > WALSH OF C1 IN C2 INDICES IN C3,C4
MTB > MEDIAN C2
    MEDIAN =        247.75
MTB > SORT C1 IN C1
MTB > PICK ROWS 2 TO 15 OF C1 IN C5
MTB > AVERAGE C5
    MEAN    =       247.00


MTB > SET C1
C1
    221     240     251     230    .    .    .

MTB > END.
MTB > PRINT C1
C1
    221     240     251     230     250     319     296     247     164     164     231
    238     273     248     275     342

MTB > NAME C1 'GA'
MTB > AVERAGE C1
    MEAN    =       249.31
MTB > MEDIAN C1
    MEDIAN =        247.50
MTB > WALSH OF C1 IN C2 INDICES IN C3,C4
MTB > MEDIAN C2
    MEDIAN =        248.00
MTB > SORT C1 IN C1
MTB > PICK ROWS 2 TO 15 OF C1 IN C5
MTB > AVERAGE C5
    MEAN    =       248.79
```

**7.19 a.** 
```
MTB > SET C1
C1
    20      23      35      42      .    .    .

MTB > END.
MTB > PRINT C1
C1
    20      23      35      42      44      45      45      46      47      49      51
    54      62      65      70      70      70      80      89     138

MTB > AVERAGE C1
   MEAN     =       57.250
MTB > MEDIAN C1
   MEDIAN =        50.000
MTB > WALSH OF C1 IN C2 INDICES IN C3,C4
MTB > MEDIAN C2
   MEDIAN =        55.000
MTB > SORT C1 IN C1
MTB > PICK ROWS 2 TO 15 OF C1 IN C5
MTB > AVERAGE C5
   MEAN     =       48.429

MTB > NOTE CDF FOR BINOMIAL N = 20 P = 0.5
MTB > PRINT C1
C1
    20      23      35      42      44      45      45      46      47      49      51
    54      62      65      70      70      70      80      89     138

MTB > CDF;
SUBC> BINOMIAL N=20 P=0.5.

     BINOMIAL WITH N =  20   P = 0.500000
        K  P( X LESS OR = K)
         1         0.0000
         2         0.0002
         3         0.0013
         4         0.0059
         5         0.0207
         6         0.0577
         7         0.1316
         8         0.2517
         9         0.4119
        10         0.5881
        11         0.7483
        12         0.8684
        13         0.9423
        14         0.9793
        15         0.9941
        16         0.9987
        17         0.9998
        18         1.0000
```

**b.** $(X_{(6)}, X_{(15)})$ or $(45, 70)$

**7.20**  **a.** MTB > READ C1-C3
           20 ROWS READ
          ROW    C1    C2    C3

            1    4.3   3.0   2.2
            2    5.0   4.1   3.7
            3    4.6   3.9   3.7
            4    4.3   3.1   3.1
            .    .    .

```
MTB > END.
MTB > LET C4=C1-C2
MTB > PRINT C4
C4
   1.30000   0.90000   0.70000   1.20000  -0.20000   1.90000   0.40000
   1.50000   0.70000   0.80000   0.10000   0.20000   0.90000   0.50000
   0.20000   0.40000   1.40000   0.50000   0.80000   0.80000

MTB > AVERAGE C4
    MEAN    =     0.75000
MTB > MEDIAN C4
    MEDIAN  =     0.75000
MTB > WALSH OF C4 IN C5 INDICES C6,C7
MTB > MEDIAN C5
    MEDIAN  =     0.75000
MTB > SORT C4 IN C4
MTB > PICK ROWS 2 TO 19 OF C4 IN C4
MTB > PRINT C4
C4
   0.10000   0.20000   0.20000   0.40000   0.40000   0.50000   0.50000
   0.70000   0.70000   0.80000   0.80000   0.80000   0.90000   0.90000
   1.20000   1.30000   1.40000   1.50000

MTB > AVERAGE C4
    MEAN    =     0.73889
```

**7.21 a.** 
```
MTB > SET C1
C1
    61    59    76    50    .    .    .

MTB > END.
MTB > PRINT C1
C1
    61    59    76    50    61    54    57    45    41    40    74    75    64
    48    62    42    52    43    50    40

MTB > NSCORE C1 IN C5
MTB > NAME C2 'NSCORES'
MTB > PLOT C5 VS C1
```

```
     2.0+                                                          *
        -
C5      -
        -                                                     *
        -                                                     *
     1.0+                                              *
        -                                           *
        -                                      2
        -                                   *
        -                               *
     0.0+                        *    *
        -                    2
        -                 *
        -            *
        -         *
    -1.0+        *
        -        *
        -
        -    2
       ------+---------+---------+---------+---------+---------+---------+C1
          42.0      49.0      56.0      63.0      70.0      77.0
```

**b.**
```
MTB > SORT C1 IN C1
MTB > PRINT C1
C1
    40    40    41    42    43    45    48    50    50    52    54    57    59
    61    61    62    64    74    75    76

MTB > CDF;
SUBC> BINOMIAL N=20 P=0.5.

     BINOMIAL WITH N =  20   P = 0.500000
       K   P( X LESS OR = K)
       1         0.0000
       2         0.0002
       3         0.0013
       4         0.0059
       5         0.0207
       6         0.0577
       7         0.1316
       8         0.2517
       9         0.4119
      10         0.5881
      11         0.7483
      12         0.8684
      13         0.9423
      14         0.9793
      15         0.9941
      16         0.9987
      17         0.9998
      18         1.0000
MTB > TINTERVAL 95.86 PERCENT CONFIDENCE FOR DATA IN C1

             N      MEAN    STDEV   SE MEAN    95.9 PERCENT C.I.
C1          20     54.70    11.68     2.61   (  48.99,   60.41)
```

$(X_{(6)}, X_{(15)})$ or $(45, 61)$

**c.** The latter interval would be preferable because of the lack of normality in the data.

**7.22**
```
MTB > CDF;
SUBC> BINOMIAL N=24 P=0.5.

     BINOMIAL WITH N =  24   P = 0.500000
       K   P( X LESS OR = K)
       2         0.0000
       3         0.0001
       4         0.0008
       5         0.0033
       6         0.0113
       7         0.0320
       8         0.0758
       9         0.1537
      10         0.2706
      11         0.4194
      12         0.5806
      13         0.7294
      14         0.8463
      15         0.9242
      16         0.9680
      17         0.9887
      18         0.9967
      19         0.9992
      20         0.9999
      21         1.0000
```

**a.** 1.0000    **b.** 0.9998

**c.** The interval in part b is shorter and has the smaller confidence coefficient.

**7.24**  **a.** MTB > SET C1
C1
    57    61    57    57

MTB > END.
MTB > PRINT C1
C1
    57    61    57    57    58    57    61    54    68    51    49    64    50
    48    65    52    56    46    54    49

MTB > AVERAGE C1
    MEAN    =    55.700
MTB > MEDIAN C1
    MEDIAN =    56.500
MTB > WALSH OF C1 IN C2 INDICES IN C3,C4
MTB > MEDIAN C2
    MEDIAN =    55.500
MTB > SORT C1 IN C1
MTB > PICK ROWS 2 TO 19 OF C1 IN C5
MTB > AVERAGE C5
    MEAN    =    55.556

MTB > PRINT C1
C1
    46    48    49    49    50    51    52    54    54    56    57    57    57
    57    58    61    61    64    65    68

MTB > CDF;
SUBC> BINOMIAL N=20 P=0.5.

    BINOMIAL WITH N =   20   P = 0.500000
        K    P( X LESS OR = K)
        1         0.0000
        2         0.0002
        3         0.0013
        4         0.0059
        5         0.0207
        6         0.0577
        7         0.1316
        8         0.2517
        9         0.4119
       10         0.5881
       11         0.7483
       12         0.8684
       13         0.9423
       14         0.9793
       15         0.9941
       16         0.9987
       17         0.9998
       18         1.0000

**b.** $(X_{(7)}, X_{(14)})$ or (52, 57)

**7.25 a.**
```
MTB > SET C1
C1
     50    47    55    55    .    .    .

MTB > END.
MTB > PRINT C1
C1
     50    47    55    55    54    42    51    56    55    51    54    51    60
     62    43    55    56    61    52    69

MTB > AVERAGE C1
   MEAN      =        53.950
MTB > MEDIAN C1
   MEDIAN  =        54.500
MTB > WALSH OF C1 IN C2 INDICES IN C3,C4
MTB > MEDIAN C2
   MEDIAN  =        53.750
MTB > SORT C1 IN C1
MTB > PICK ROWS 2 TO 19 OF C1 IN C5
MTB > AVERAGE C5
   MEAN      =        53.778
MTB > PRINT C1
C1
     42    43    47    50    51    51    51    52    54    54    55    55    55
     55    56    56    60    61    62    69

MTB > CDF;
SUBC> BINOMIAL N=20 P=0.5.

         BINOMIAL WITH N =   20   P = 0.500000
           K   P( X LESS OR = K)
           1          0.0000
           2          0.0002
           3          0.0013
           4          0.0059
           5          0.0207
           6          0.0577
           7          0.1316
           8          0.2517
           9          0.4119
          10          0.5881
          11          0.7483
          12          0.8684
          13          0.9423
          14          0.9793
          15          0.9941
          16          0.9987
          17          0.9998
          18          1.0000
```

A 0.926 percent confidence interval is $(X_{(7)}, X_{(14)})$ or (51, 55).

**7.28 a.** $\hat{m} = 143.5$, mw $= 145.0$

**7.29 a.** $\bar{x} = 761.79$, $t_{58}(1) = 766.07$    **b.** $\hat{m} = 784.5$, mw $= 769$

**Exercises 7.4**

**7.30 a.** (0.00324, 0.2600)    **b.** (0.068, 0.332)

**7.31 a.** $(-0.0421, 0.1428)$

**7.32 a.** (0.1647, 0.3708); (0.2024, 0.4130)

**7.34** $S = 8$; rejection region (R.R.): $S \leqslant 5$ or $S \geqslant 15$; retain $H_0$.

**7.36 a.** $\alpha = 0.0414$    **b.** $\beta(0.4) = 0.8728$

**7.38** $S = 13$; R.R.: $S \geqslant 15$; retain $H_0$: $m = 49$.

**7.39** $S = 16$; R.R.: $S \geqslant 14$; reject $H_0$: $m = 4$.

**Exercises 7.5**

**7.40** **a.** 11.0705    **b.** 31.4104    **c.** 21.6660    **d.** 37.5662

**7.42** $\chi^2 = 31.054$; R.R.: $\chi^2 > \chi^2_{0.05,24} = 36.4154$; retain $H_0$.

**7.43** **a.** $\chi^2 = 35.745$; R.R.: $\chi^2 > \chi^2_{0.05,21} = 32.6705$; reject $H_0$.
     **b.** (1.569, 2.634)

**7.44** (9.693, 16.0733)

**7.45** **a.** $\chi^2 = 17.747$; R.R.: $\chi^2 < 2.70039$ or $\chi^2 > 19.0228$; retain $H_0$.
     **b.** For $\sigma$, (0.0432, 0.1146)

**7.46** **a.** (1232, 2100)
     **b.** $\chi^2 = 67.53$; R.R.: $\chi^2 > \chi^2_{0.05,28} = 41.3372$; reject $H_0: \sigma \leqslant 1000$.

**7.47** **a.** (1.629, 3.498)
     **b.** $\chi^2 = 53.76$; R.R.: $\chi^2 > \chi^2_{0.05,24} = 36.4154$; reject $H_0: \sigma \leqslant 1.5$.

# CHAPTER 8

**Exercises 8.2**

**8.1** **a.** $H_1: \mu_x \neq \mu_y$; $Z = 5.31$; reject $H_0$.    **b.** (0.531, 1.009)

**8.3** **a.** $H_1: \mu_{CAI} \neq \mu_{Traditional}$; $Z = -1.285$; R.R.: $|Z| \geqslant 1.96$; retain $H_0$.
     **b.** $H_1: \mu_{CAI} \neq \mu_{Traditional}$; $Z = 1.757$; retain $H_0$.

**8.5** **a.** $Z = 2.157$; reject $H_0$. $H_1$: The cars traveling from east to west are going faster than the cars traveling from west to east.
     **b.** (1.31, 9.69)

**Exercises 8.3**

**8.6** **a.** $t = -1.867 < -1.734 = -t_{0.05,18}$; reject $H_0$.
     **b.** $(-10.838, 0.638)$
     **c.** Yes, the confidence interval in part b contains zero. No, it does not contradict the decision in part a because the test in part a is one-tailed.

**8.8** **a.** 32.143
     **b.** $t = -1.893$; R.R.: $t \leqslant -t_{0.05,28} = -1.702$; reject $H_0$.
     **c.** $(-0.33, 8.33)$

**8.10** **a., b.**

```
MTB > SET C1
C1
  6291   7372   5969   8927   .   .   .

MTB > SET C2
C2
  8903   7706   7924   8483   .   .   .

MTB > PRINT C1 C2
 ROW     C1     C2

   1    6291   8903
   2    7372   7706
   3    5969   7924
   4    8927   8483
   5    7573   8773
   6    6705   8224
   7    6716   7855
   8    5529   7740
   9    6574
  10    6515
  11    7137
  12    6288
  13    6547
  14    7730
  15    7671
```

```
MTB > TWOSAMPLE T DATA IN C1 C2 ;
SUBC>  POOLED;
SUBC>  ALTERNATIVE -1.

TWOSAMPLE T FOR C1 VS C2
       N      MEAN    STDEV    SE MEAN
C1    15      6903      848        219
C2     8      8201      471        167

95 PCT CI FOR MU C1 - MU C2: (-1976, -621)
TTEST MU C1 = MU C2 (VS LT): T=-3.99 P=0.0003 DF=21.0

MTB > MANNWHITNEY DATA IN C1 C2

Mann-Whitney Confidence Interval and Test

C1          N = 15    MEDIAN =       6705.0
C2          N =  8    MEDIAN =       8074.0
POINT ESTIMATE FOR ETA1-ETA2 IS   -1343.0022
95.1  PCT C.I. FOR ETA1-ETA2 IS (    -1955,     -718)
W =    129.0
TEST OF ETA1 = ETA2  VS.  ETA1 N.E. ETA2 IS SIGNIFICANT AT  0.0011
```

Reject $H_0$: $\mu_x = \mu_y$; $t = -3.99$; R.R.: $t < -t_{0.05,21} = -1.721$

Reject $H_0$: $m_x = m_y$; $Z = -3.29$; R.R.: $Z < -Z_{0.05} = -1.645$

**8.11  a., b.**

```
MTB > SET C1
C1
  509.21   107.49   128.45   193.81      .   .   .

MTB > SET C2
C2
  1152.79    634.05    938.55   1302.29      .   .   .

MTB > PRINT C1 C2
  ROW       C1         C2

    1    509.21    1152.79
    2    107.49     634.05
    3    128.45     938.55
    4    193.81    1302.29
    5    272.13     734.11
    6    146.21     549.66
    7     33.46    1267.92
    8    349.01    1035.74

MTB > TWOSAMPLE T DATA IN C1 C2 ;
SUBC>  POOLED.

TWOSAMPLE T FOR C1 VS C2
       N      MEAN    STDEV    SE MEAN
C1     8       217      153         54
C2     8       952      288        102

95 PCT CI FOR MU C1 - MU C2: (-982, -487)
TTEST MU C1 = MU C2 (VS NE): T=-6.37 P=0.0000 DF=14.0

MTB > MANNWHITNEY DATA IN C1 C2
```

Mann-Whitney Confidence Interval and Test

```
C1          N =   8      MEDIAN =        170.01
C2          N =   8      MEDIAN =        987.14
POINT ESTIMATE FOR ETA1-ETA2 IS     -761.1514
95.9  PCT C.I. FOR ETA1-ETA2 IS (    -1030,      -440)
W =    36.0
TEST OF ETA1 = ETA2  VS.  ETA1 N.E. ETA2 IS SIGNIFICANT AT   0.0009
```

**8.13  a., b.**

```
MTB > SET C1
C1
  9358   9983   9724   8982   .   .   .

MTB > SET C2
C2
  7268   8996   8073   7613   .   .   .

MTB > PRINT C1 C2
  ROW      C1      C2

    1     9358    7268
    2     9983    8996
    3     9724    8073
    4     8982    7613
    5     9365    8458
    6     8747    6580
    7     7806    7819
    8             7266
    9             7720
   10             9392
   11             7800

MTB > TWOSAMPLE T DATA IN C1 C2 ;
SUBC>  POOLED.

TWOSAMPLE T FOR C1 VS C2
         N      MEAN     STDEV    SE MEAN
C1   7         9138      720       272
C2  11         7908      803       242

95 PCT CI FOR MU C1 - MU C2: (438, 2022)
TTEST MU C1 = MU C2 (VS NE): T=3.29 P=0.0046 DF=16.0

MTB > MANNWHITNEY DATA IN C1 C2

Mann-Whitney Confidence Interval and Test

C1          N =   7      MEDIAN =       9358.0
C2          N =  11      MEDIAN =       7800.0
POINT ESTIMATE FOR ETA1-ETA2 IS     1291.9980
95.4  PCT C.I. FOR ETA1-ETA2 IS (      362,     2097)
W =    94.0
TEST OF ETA1 = ETA2  VS.  ETA1 N.E. ETA2 IS SIGNIFICANT AT   0.0145
```

Both methods result in rejection of $H_0$: $\mu_x = \mu_y$. The tests give $p$-values of 0.0046 and 0.0145, respectively.

**Exercises 8.4**

**8.16  a.**
```
MTB > READ C1 C2
      9 ROWS READ
    ROW     C1      C2

     1      95      83
     2     133     133
     3     128     131
     4     107     107
      .   .   .


MTB > END
MTB > LET C3=C1-C2
MTB > PRINT C1-C3
    ROW     C1      C2      C3

     1      95      83      12
     2     133     133       0
     3     128     131      -3
     4     107     107       0
     5      95      83      12
     6     112      63      49
     7      86      21      65
     8      80      15      65
     9      46       3      43

MTB > TWOSAMPLE T 90 PERCENT CONFIDENCE  DATA IN C1 C2 ;
SUBC>   POOLED.

TWOSAMPLE T FOR C1 VS C2
        N      MEAN     STDEV    SE MEAN
C1  9         98.0      26.4       8.8
C2  9         71.0      49.2        16

90 PCT CI FOR MU C1 - MU C2: (-5.5, 60)
TTEST MU C1 = MU C2 (VS NE): T=1.45 P=0.17 DF=16.0

MTB > TINTERVAL WITH 90 PERCENT CONFIDENCE FOR C3

              N      MEAN     STDEV    SE MEAN    90.0 PERCENT C.I.
C3            9      27.00    28.36     9.45    (   9.41,    44.59)
```
$\bar{x} - \bar{y} = 27$ is a point estimate.

**b.**
```
MTB > READ C1 C2
      9 ROWS READ
    ROW     C1      C2

     1      95      83
     2     133     133
     3     128     131
     4     107     107
      .   .   .


MTB > END
MTB > LET C3=C1-C2
MTB > PRINT C1-C3
    ROW     C1      C2      C3

     1      95      83      12
     2     133     133       0
     3     128     131      -3
     4     107     107       0
     5      95      83      12
     6     112      63      49
     7      86      21      65
     8      80      15      65
     9      46       3      43
```

```
MTB > TWOSAMPLE T 90 PERCENT CONFIDENCE  DATA IN C1 C2 ;
SUBC>   POOLED.

TWOSAMPLE T FOR C1 VS C2
        N      MEAN    STDEV    SE MEAN
C1  9    98.0    26.4      8.8
C2  9    71.0    49.2      16

90 PCT CI FOR MU C1 - MU C2: (-5.5, 60)
TTEST MU C1 = MU C2 (VS NE): T=1.45 P=0.17 DF=16.0

MTB > TTEST MU = 0 DATA IN C3

TEST OF MU = 0.00 VS MU N.E.  0.00

            N      MEAN    STDEV    SE MEAN      T    P VALUE
C3          9     27.00    28.36      9.45    2.86     0.021
```

The single-sample test is appropriate: $t = 2.86$; R.R.: $|t| > t_{0.05,8} = 1.86$; reject $H_0$.

**8.18**
```
MTB > READ C1 C2
      10 ROWS READ
  ROW      C1       C2

    1    34.21    34.18
    2    22.18    20.98
    3    81.92    81.85
    4    66.71    66.67
    .     .   .

MTB > END
MTB > LET C3=C1-C2
MTB > PRINT C1-C3
  ROW      C1       C2        C3

    1    34.21    34.18   0.03000
    2    22.18    20.98   1.20000
    3    81.92    81.85   0.07001
    4    66.71    66.67   0.03999
    5    24.23    24.23   0.00000
    6    43.97    43.94   0.03000
    7    83.28    83.28   0.00000
    8    18.25    18.84  -0.59001
    9   260.60   264.32  -3.71997
   10    95.25    95.18   0.06999

MTB > TTEST DATA IN C3;
SUBC> ALTERNATIVE=-1.

TEST OF MU = 0.000 VS MU L.T.  0.000

            N      MEAN    STDEV    SE MEAN      T    P VALUE
C3         10    -0.287    1.283     0.406   -0.71      0.25
```

$H_0: \mu_{1979} = \mu_{1980}$ versus $H_1: \mu_{1980} < \mu_{1979}$;

$t = -0.71$; R.R.: $t < -t_{0.10,9} = -1.833$; retain $H_0$.

**8.20** **a., b.**

```
MTB > LET C3=C1-C2
MTB > PRINT C1-C3
 ROW      C1      C2      C3

   1    31261   24593    6668
   2    32775   28588    4187
   3    40092   34578    5514
   4    31948   16789   15159
   5    33684   27310    6374
   6    11703   11593     110
   7    13653   13560      93
   8    29000   23418    5582
   9    28278   24038    4240
  10    33197   24417    8780
  11    33084   26482    6602
  12    33121   25082    8039
  13    23164   23087      77
  14    30728   27473    3255
  15    10277   10906    -629
  16    21498   22840   -1342
  17    30042   23501    6541
  18    33306   26868    6438
  19    27280   24906    2374
  20    33531   26654    6877
  21    17022   15723    1299
  22    14823   15836   -1013
  23    28675   27164    1511
  24    33817   28770    5047
  25    17011   15819    1192
  26    23274   21943    1331
  27    23842   21748    2094

MTB > TWOSAMPLE T  DATA IN C1 C2 ;
SUBC>  POOLED.

TWOSAMPLE T FOR C1 VS C2
        N      MEAN     STDEV   SE MEAN
C1   27     26670      8016      1543
C2   27     22729      5783      1113

95 PCT CI FOR MU C1 - MU C2: (123, 7759)
TTEST MU C1 = MU C2 (VS NE): T=2.07 P=0.043 DF=52.0

MTB > TINTERVAL FOR C3
             N      MEAN     STDEV   SE MEAN    95.0 PERCENT C.I.
C3          27      3941      3752       722   (   2456,    5425)
```

**c.** The interval based on TINTERVAL is preferable, because it is based on the differences between male and female salaries within job classifications. The interval based on TWOSAMPLE T is based on data that compare male and female salaries but ignore job classifications.

**Exercises 8.5**

**8.21** **a.** $(-0.0414, 0.0653)$    **b.** $Z = 0.45$; retain $H_0$.

**8.23** **a.** $(-0.2580, 0.0462)$    **b.** $(-0.0958, 0.1931)$    **c.** $Z = 0.66$; retain $H_0$.

**8.25** **a.** $Z = 46.57$; reject $H_0$.    **b.** $(0.023, 0.025)$

**8.27** **a.** $Z = 4.98$; reject $H_0$ and conclude that the proportion decreased.
   **b.** $(0.022, 0.051)$

**Exercises 8.6**
   **8.31**  **a.** 4.35    **b.** 8.89    **c.** 10.9    **d.** 0.092
   **8.32**  **a.** 0.113  **b.** 0.230   **c.** 0.010   **d.** 0.118
   **8.35**  **a.** $F = 0.82$; R.R.: $F \leqslant 0.187$ or $F \geqslant 5.35$; retain $H_0$.
          **b.** (0.154, 4.394)
   **8.37**  **a.** $F = 0.64$; R.R.: $F \leqslant 0.239$ or $F \geqslant 3.54$; retain $H_0$.    **b.** (0.153, 2.27)
   **8.38**  $F = 3.52$; R.R.: $F \leqslant 0.26$ or $F \geqslant 3.79$; retain $H_0$.

# CHAPTER 9

**Exercises 9.1**
   **9.1**  **a.** Nominal    **b.** Ordinal    **c.** Ratio    **d.** Ordinal
          **e.** Ratio      **f.** Ratio      **g.** Nominal   **h.** Ordinal

**Exercises 9.2**
   **9.5**  $\chi^2 = 4.1$, $\chi^2_{0.05,5} = 11.07$; retain $H_0$: Die is fair.
   **9.7**  **a.** $\chi^2 = 13.75$, $\chi^2_{0.05,4} = 9.49$; reject $H_0$.
          **b.** $\chi^2 = 2.563$, $\chi^2_{0.05,4} = 9.49$; retain $H_0$.
   **9.9**  **a.** 20    **b.** $\chi^2 = 8.2$, $\chi^2_{0.05,8} = 15.51$; retain $H_0$.
   **9.11**  $\chi^2 = 8.04$, $\chi^2_{0.05,3} = 7.815$; reject $H_0$.

**Exercises 9.3**
   **9.13**  **a.** $\chi^2 = 47.58$; $x^2_{0.05,2} = 5.99$    **b.** Yes
   **9.15**  **a.** $\hat{E}_{11} = 15$, $\hat{E}_{12} = 15$, $\hat{E}_{21} = 45$, $\hat{E}_{22} = 45$
          **b.** $\chi^2 = 0.71$, $\chi^2_{0.05,1} = 3.84$; retain $H_0$: There is no difference in exam performance
            due to college of registration.
   **9.17**  $\chi^2 = 3304.37$, $\chi^2_{0.01,9} = 21.67$; reject $H_0$; there is a significant association between
         left and right eye acuity.
   **9.18**  **a.** $\chi^2 = 3.47$, $\chi^2_{0.05,1} = 3.84$; there is no significant association between the
          variables at $\alpha = 0.05$.

**Exercises 9.4**
   **9.20**  **a.** 13.53, 27.07, 27.07, 18.04, 9.02, 5.27
          **b.** $\chi^2 = 1.45$; $\chi^2_{0.05,5} = 11.07$; retain Poisson assumption.
          **c.** $\chi^2 = 1.41$; $\chi^2_{0.05,4} = 9.49$; retain Poisson assumption.
   **9.21**  $\bar{x} = 0.61$; $\chi^2 = 0.316$; $\chi^2_{0.05,2} = 5.99$; retain Poisson assumption.
   **9.23**
```
MTB > BASE = 1000
MTB > RANDOM 400 IN C1;
SUBC> BINOMIAL N = 10 P = 0.4.
MTB > TALLY C1

      C1   COUNT
       0     2
       1    16
       2    57
       3    68
       4   108
       5    88
       6    40
       7    12
       8     9
      N=   400
```

```
MTB > PDF;
SUBC> BINOMIAL N =10 P = 0.4.

    BINOMIAL WITH N =   10   P = 0.400000
      K          P( X = K)
      0           0.0060
      1           0.0403
      2           0.1209
      3           0.2150
      4           0.2508
      5           0.2007
      6           0.1115
      7           0.0425
      8           0.0106
      9           0.0016
     10           0.0001
```

Classes are 0–1, 2, 3, 4, 5, 6, 7–10. $\chi^2 = 7.169$, $\chi^2 \geq \chi^2_{0.05,6} = 12.59$; retain $H_0$.

**9.25** **a.**

| Class | $Z$ interval | Observations |
|---|---|---|
| $0 \leqslant x < 250$ | $-\infty < z < -0.22$ | 39 |
| $250 \leqslant x < 500$ | $-0.22 \leqslant z < 0.11$ | 14 |
| $500 \leqslant x < 750$ | $0.11 \leqslant z < 0.44$ | 4 |
| $750 \leqslant x < 1000$ | $0.44 \leqslant z < 0.77$ | 4 |
| $1000 \leqslant x < 1250$ | $0.77 \leqslant z < 1.10$ | 0 |
| $1250 < x$ | $1.10 < z < \infty$ | 6 |

$\chi^2 = 18.37$; $\chi^2_{0.05,3} = 7.815$; reject normality assumption.

**b.**
```
MTB > NSCORES C1 IN C2
MTB > NAME C2 'NSCORES'
MTB > PLOT C2 C1
```

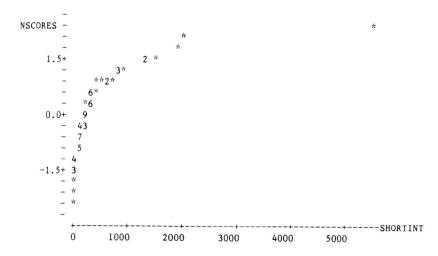

**9.26**

| Class | $Z$ interval | Observations |
|---|---|---|
| $x < 30$ | $-\infty < z < -0.93$ | 10 |
| $30 \leqslant x < 40$ | $-0.93 < z < 0.13$ | 20 |
| $40 \leqslant x < 50$ | $0.13 < z < 1.19$ | 27 |
| $50 < x$ | $1.19 < z$ | 6 |

$\chi^2 = 273$; $\chi^2_{0.05,1} = 3.841$; retain normality assumption.

# CHAPTER 10

## Exercises 10.1

**10.1** Intersection with $x$-axis is point $(-\alpha/\beta, 0)$; intersection with $y$-axis is point $(0, \alpha)$.

**10.3 a.** $y =$ husband's age, for example
**b.** $y =$ peak power demand on that day, for example

**10.4** Because $\alpha + \beta x_i$ is a constant

**10.5** MTB > PLOT 'RBIS' VERSUS 'HOMERS'

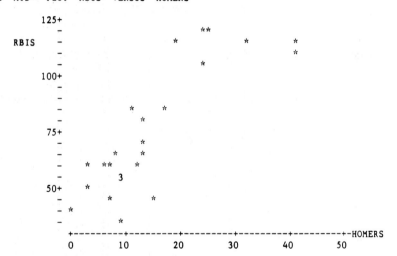

The two variables tend to increase together, although the relationship is not exactly linear.

**10.6 a.** $\alpha > 0$ is the fixed cost of production.
**b.** $\beta > 0$ is the variable cost of production.

## Exercises 10.2

**10.7 a.** $\hat{y} = 11.571 + 2.6786x$

**10.8 a.** $\hat{y} = 1.1 + 1.15x$ **b.** 1.15

**10.9 a.** $\hat{y} = 200 + 0.7x$

**10.11 a.** $\hat{y} = -2 + 2x$ **c.** $\hat{\alpha} = -2, \hat{\beta} = 2$

**10.12** $\hat{y} = -1.5 + 0.045x$

**10.15 a.** $\hat{y} = -4.643 + 0.875x$

**b.**
```
MTB > NOTE MULTIPLE PLOT OF Y AND YHAT VERSUS X
MTB > NOTE DATA IS VOTER REGISTRATION DATA
MTB > MPLOT C2 VS C1 C5 VS C1
```

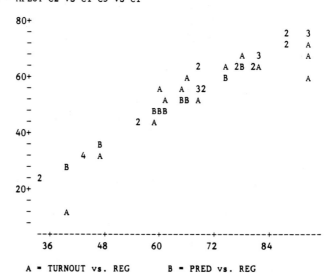

```
A = TURNOUT vs. REG        B = PRED vs. REG
```

**c.** 0.823

**Exercises 10.3**

**10.17 a.**

| Source | d.f. | SS | MS |
|---|---|---|---|
| Regression | 1 | 803.57 | 803.57 |
| Error | 5 | 10.43 | 2.09 |
| Total | 6 | 814.00 | |

**b.** $\hat{\sigma}^2 = 2.09$
**c.** $r^2 = 0.987$

**10.18 a.**

| Source | d.f. | SS | MS |
|---|---|---|---|
| Regression | 1 | 52.9 | 52.9 |
| Error | 3 | 5.1 | 1.7 |
| Total | 4 | 58.0 | |

**b.** $\hat{\sigma}^2 = 1.7$    **c.** $r^2 = 0.912$

**10.19 a.**

| Source | d.f. | SS | MS |
|---|---|---|---|
| Regression | 1 | 196000 | 196000 |
| Error | 25 | 4000 | 160 |
| Total | 26 | 200000 | |

**b.** 0.98    **c.** $\hat{\sigma}^2 = 160$

**10.21**

| Source | d.f. | SS | MS |
|---|---|---|---|
| Regression | 1 | 112 | 112 |
| Error | 5 | 4 | 0.8 |
| Total | 6 | 116 | |

$r^2 = 0.966$

**10.22**

| Source | d.f. | SS | MS |
|---|---|---|---|
| Regression | 1 | 202.5 | 202.5 |
| Error | 3 | 3.5 | 1.17 |
| Total | 4 | 206 | |

$r^2 = 0.983$

**10.23 a.** $\hat{y} = -25.56 + 0.788x$

**b.**

| Source | d.f. | SS | MS |
|---|---|---|---|
| Regression | 1 | 2622524 | 2622524 |
| Error | 8 | 43258 | 5407 |
| Total | 9 | 2665782 | |

**c.** $\hat{\sigma}^2 = 5407$    **d.** $r^2 = 0.984$

**10.24 b.**

| Source | d.f. | SS | MS |
|---|---|---|---|
| Regression | 1 | 4830.8 | 4830.8 |
| Error | 22 | 1035.8 | 47.1 |
| Total | 23 | 5866.6 | |

**c.** $\hat{\sigma}^2 = 47.1$    **d.** $r^2 = 0.823$

**Exercises 10.4**

**10.26 a.** (2.328, 3.030)    **b.** $t = 19.63$; $t_{0.025,5} = 2.571$; reject $H_0$.
**10.27 a.** (0.665, 1.635)    **b.** $t = 5.58$, $F = 31.12$; $t_{0.025,3} = 3.182$,
  $F_{0.05}(1, 3) = 10.13$; reject $H_0$.
**10.28 a.** (0.6588, 0.7412)
  **b.** $t = 0$; $t_{0.025,25} = 2.060$; retain $H_0$.
**10.30 a.** (1.57, 2.43)    **b.** $t = 11.83$, $F = 140$; $t_{0.025,5} = 2.571$,
  $F_{0.05}(1, 5) = 6.61$; reject $H_0$.
**10.31** (0.025, 0.065)
**10.32** (0.696, 1.054)
**10.34** (0.706, 0.871)

**Exercises 10.5**

**10.35 a.** 51.75    **b.** 51.75    **c.** $\bar{x} = 8$
**10.36 a.** 9.15    **b.** (7.696, 10.604)
**10.37 a.** (1928.8, 1971.2)    **b.** $\bar{x} = 2000$
**10.39** (5.32, 6.68)
**10.40 a.** 368.5    **b.** (190.4, 546.6)
**10.41 a.** 56.6 percent    **b.** 56.6 percent    **c.** (53.68, 59.52), (42.07, 71.13)
**10.43 a.** $\hat{y} = -468.6 + 20.128x$    **b.** $\hat{\sigma}^2 = 3260$; $r^2 = 0.717$; $s_\beta = 4.003$
  **c.** \$336.50    **d.** (\$294.7, \$378.4)

**Exercises 10.6**

**10.44 a.** Yes; Birmingham, AL, Minneapolis, MN. Both cities have a lower voter turnout than that predicted by the model.

**b.**
```
MTB > NOTE NORMAL PLOT OF THE STANDARDIZED RESIDUALS
MTB > NOTE DATA IS FROM VOTER TURNOUT EXAMPLE
MTB > NSCORES C4 IN C6
MTB > NAME C6 'NSCORES'
MTB > PLOT C6 C4
```

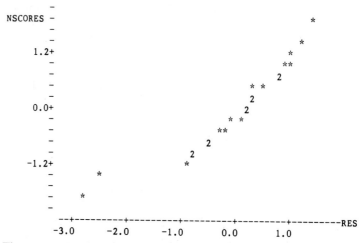

The two outliers in part a are indicated clearly on this plot.

**c.**
```
MTB > NOTE PLOT OF RESIDUALS VS PREDICTED VALUES
MTB > NOTE DATA IS FROM VOTER TURNOUT EXAMPLE
MTB > PLOT C4 C5
```

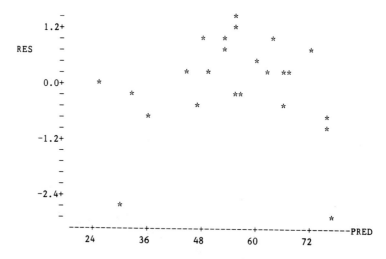

This plot shows a negative-positive-negative pattern of the residuals.

**10.46 a.** The fifth country (Canada)

**b.** MTB > NOTE MULTIPLE PLOT OF Y AND YHAT VERSUS X

MTB > MPLOT C2 VS C1 C4 VS C1

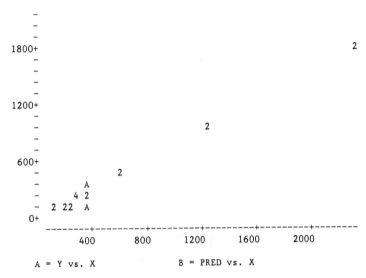

A = Y vs. X          B = PRED vs. X

**c.** MTB > NOTE NORMAL PLOT OF STANDARDIZED RESIDUALS

MTB > NSCORES C3 IN C5
MTB > NAME C5 'NSCORES'
MTB > PLOT C5 VS C3

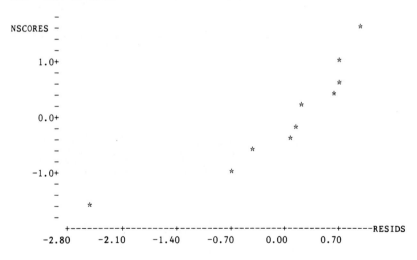

MTB > NOTE PLOT OF RESIDUALS VERSUS PREDICTED VALUES
MTB > PLOT C3 C4

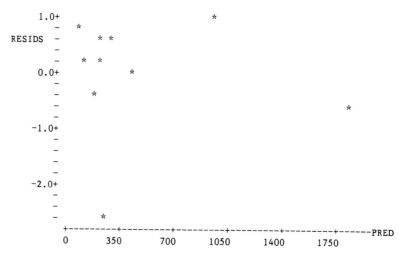

10.48  MTB > NOTE PLOT OF STANDARDIZED RESIDUALS VS THE PREDICTED VALUES
MTB > NOTE DATA IS NUMBER OF U.S. FARMS FROM 1880-1978
MTB > NOTE   RESIDUALS AND PREDICTIONS ARE FROM THE QUADRATIC MODEL
MTB > PLOT C4 C5

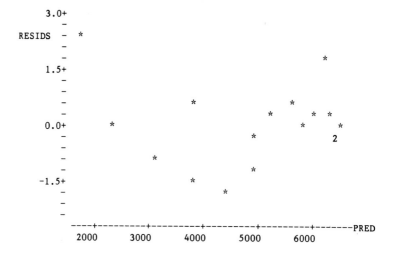

# CHAPTER 11

**Exercises 11.2**

**11.1** **a.** $(1.295, 4.705)$, $(-0.098, 3.098)$
 **b.** $t = 3.75$; R.R.: $|t| > 2.131$; reject $H_0$.
 **c.** \$33.00
**11.2** **a.** $(0.679, 8.921)$, $(-0.321, 1.179)$
 **b.** $t_{\beta_1} = 2$; R.R.: $|t| > 2.819$; retain $H_0$.
  $t_{\beta_2} = 3$; R.R.: $|t| > 2.819$; reject $H_0$.

**11.3**　**a.** $\hat{y} = 1.06 + 0.998x_1 + 0.216x_2$
　　**c.** $t_{\beta_1} = 2.75$; R.R.: $|t| > 2.12$; reject $H_0$.
　　　$t_{\beta_2} = 1.70$; R.R.: $|t| > 2.12$: retain $H_0$.
　　**d.** $(0.2293, 1.7663)$, $(-0.0526, 0.4846)$
**11.4**　**a.** $\hat{y} = 7.74 + 0.560x_1 + 0.676x_2$　**b.** $0.560$　**c.** $0.676$
　　**d.** $R^2 = 0.939$　**e.** $\hat{\sigma}^2 = 8.12$

　　**f.** MTB > NOTE PLOT OF STANDARDIZED RESIDUAL VS YHAT
　　　　MTB > PLOT C4 C5

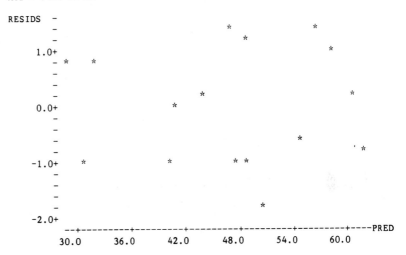

　　**g.** MTB > NOTE NORMAL PLOT OF STANDARDIZED RESIDUALS
　　　　MTB > NSCORES C4 IN C6
　　　　MTB > NAME C6 'NSCORES'
　　　　MTB > PLOT C4 C6

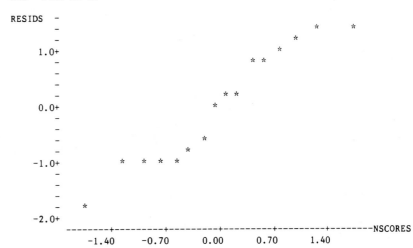

**11.6**　**a.** $\hat{y} = 222.66 + 3.1022x_1 - 613.5x_2$　**b.** $\hat{\beta}_1 = 3.1022$, $\hat{\beta}_2 = -613.5$; no
　　**c.** $R^2 = 0.797$

**d.** MTB > NOTE NORMAL PLOT OF STANDARDIZED RESIDUALS
MTB > NSCORES C21 IN C6
MTB > NAME C6 'NSCORES'
MTB > PLOT C21 C6

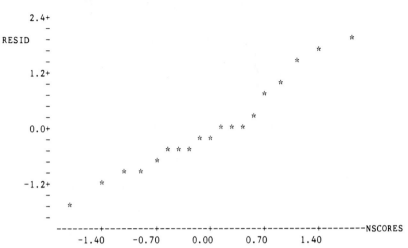

MTB > NOTE PLOT OF STANDARDIZED RESIDUALS VS PREDICTED VALUES

MTB > PLOT C21 C22

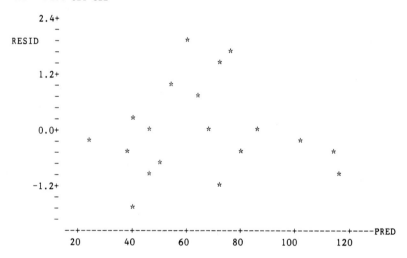

**11.7** **b.** $\hat{y} = 367.7 - 0.4265x_1 - 281x_2$; $R^2 = 0.02$
    **c.** $t_{\beta_1} = -0.47$; R.R.: $|t| > 2.201$; retain $H_0$.
       $t_{\beta_2} = -0.24$; R.R.: $|t| > 2.201$; retain $H_0$.
**11.9** **a.** $\hat{y} = 20.9 + 1.15x_1 + 1.27x_2$
    **b.** $t_{\beta_1} = 18.97$; R.R.: $|t| > 2.447$; reject $H_0$.
       $t_{\beta_2} = 3.10$; R.R.: $|t| > 2.447$; reject $H_0$.
    **c.** $R^2 = 0.994$
    **d.** 5.266 billion coins

**Exercises 11.3**

**11.11 a.**

| Source | d.f. | SS | MS |
|---|---|---|---|
| Regression | 3 | 1700 | 566.67 |
| Error | 14 | 300 | 21.43 |
| Total | 17 | 2000 | |

**b.** $F = 26.44$; $F_{0.05}(3, 14) = 3.34$; reject $H_0$.

**c.** $\hat{\sigma}^2 = 21.43$

**d.** R.R.: $|t| > 2.145$ for each test; hence each null hypothesis is rejected.

**e.** (12.69, 27.31)

**11.13 a.** $\hat{y} = 9.485 - 0.218x_1 + 2.097x_2 + 0.0709x_3$    **b.** $R^2 = 0.595$

**c.** $F = 4.41$; $F_{0.05}(3, 9) = 3.86$; reject $H_0$.

**11.14 a.** $\hat{y} = 4.55 + 0.245x_1 - 0.230x_2 - 0.0011x_3$

**b.** $R^2 = 0.71$; $\hat{\sigma}^2 = 0.04873$; $\hat{\sigma} = 0.2207$

**c.** $F = 13.9$; $F_{0.05}(3, 17) = 3.20$; reject $H_0$.

**d.** $t_{\beta_1} = 3.69$, $t_{\beta_2} = -5.66$, $t_{\beta_3} = -0.36$;
reject $H_0$: $\beta_1 = 0$ and $H_0$: $\beta_2 = 0$; retain $H_0$: $\beta_3 = 0$.

**f.** MTB > NOTE PLOT OF STANDARDIZED RESIDUALS VERSUS PREDICTED VALUES

MTB > PLOT C5 C6

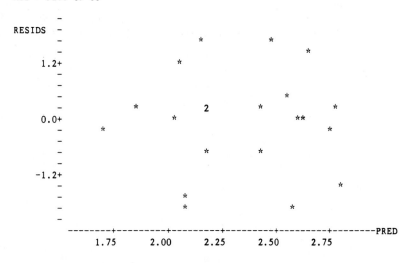

**g.** `MTB > NOTE NORMAL PLOT OF STANDARDIZED RESIDUALS`

```
MTB > NSCORES C5 IN C7
MTB > NAME C7 'NSCORES'
MTB > PLOT C5 C7
```

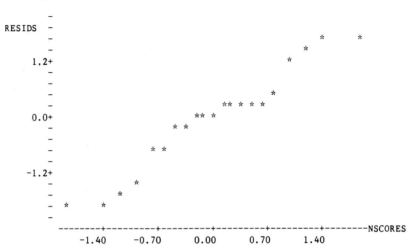

**11.15 a.** $\hat{y} = 92.3 + 2.75x_1 - 297x_2 + 0.234x_3$. $R^2 = 0.867$; $\hat{\sigma}^2 = 135.0$; $\hat{\sigma} = 11.62$. $F = 32.45$; $F_{0.05}(3, 15) = 3.29$; reject $H_0$. $t_{\hat{\beta}_1} = 7.32$; R.R.: $|t| > 2.131$, reject $H_0$. $t_{\hat{\beta}_2} = -1.22$; R.R.: $|t| > 2.131$, retain $H_0$. $t_{\hat{\beta}_3} = 2.79$; R.R.: $|t| > 2.131$; reject $H_0$. $\hat{\beta}_1$ and $\hat{\beta}_3$ are positive as expected, but $\hat{\beta}_2 < 0$.

```
MTB > NOTE PLOT OF STANDARDIZED RESIDUALS VS PREDICTED VALUES
MTB > NOTE NORMAL PLOT OF THE STANDARDIZED RESIDUALS
MTB > NAME C5 'RESIDS' C6 'PRED'
MTB > PLOT C5 C6
```

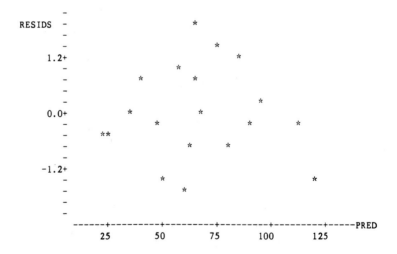

```
MTB > NOTE NORMAL PLOT OF THE STANDARDIZED RESIDUALS
MTB > NSCORES C5 IN C7
MTB > NAME C7 'NSCORES'
MTB > PLOT C5 C7
```

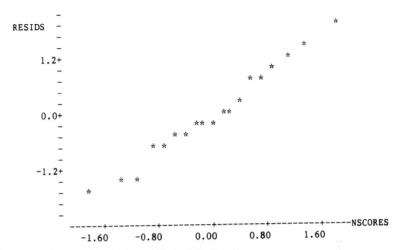

b. $(1.947, 3.547)$, $(-814.1, 220.7)$, $(0.055, 0.413)$

c. Only $\hat{\beta}_3$ falls into the confidence interval.

**Exercises 11.4**    **11.16 a.** $\hat{y} = -58.6 + 2.6513x - 0.0137x^2$

**b.**

| Source | d.f. | SS | MS |
|---|---|---|---|
| Regression | 2 | 5223.9 | 2612 |
| Error | 21 | 642.7 | 30.6 |
| Total | 23 | 5866.6 | |

**c.** $F = 85.4$; $F_{0.05}(2, 21) = 3.47$; reject $H_0$.

**d.** $t_{\beta_1} = 5.30$; R.R.: $|t| > t_{0.025,21} = 2.08$; reject $H_0$.
$t_{\beta_2} = -3.58$; R.R.: $|t| > 2.08$; reject $H_0$.

**e.** $R^2 = 0.890$; an increase of 6.7 percentage points

**f.**
```
MTB > NOTE NORMAL PLOT OF STANDARDIZED RESIDUALS FOR QUADRATIC MODEL
MTB > NOTE DATA IS VOTER TURNOUT DATA
MTB > NSCORES C4 IN C6
MTB > PLOT C6 C4
```

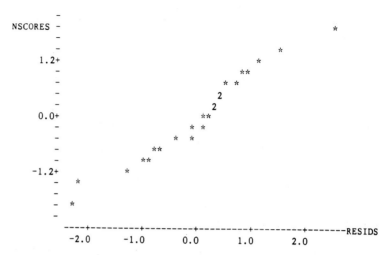

```
MTB > NOTE PLOT OF RESIDUALS VS PREDICTED VALUES FOR QUADRATIC MODEL
MTB > NOTE DATA IS VOTER TURNOUT DATA
MTB > NAME C4 'RESIDS' C5 'PRED'
MTB > PLOT C4 C5
```

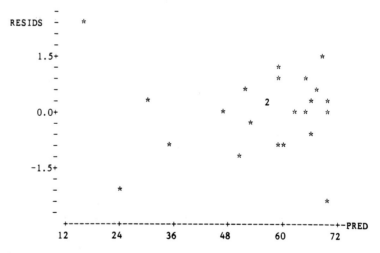

**11.17 a.** $\hat{y} = 49.9 - 13.4x + 1.17x^2$

**b.**

| Source | d.f. | SS | MS |
|---|---|---|---|
| Regression | 2 | 922.30 | 461.15 |
| Error | 29 | 203.75 | 7.03 |
| Total | 31 | 1126.05 | |

**c.** $F = 65.6$, $F_{0.05}(2, 29) = 3.33$; reject $H_0$.

**d.** $t_{\beta_1} = -5.32$; R.R.: $|t| \geqslant t_{0.025,29} = 2.045$; reject $H_0$.
$t_{\beta_2} = 3.26$; R.R.: $|t| \geqslant 2.045$; reject $H_0$.

**e.** $R^2 = 0.819$; an increase of 6.6 percentage points

**f.**
```
MTB > NSCORES C4 IN C6
MTB > NOTE NORMAL PLOT OF STANDARDIZED RESIDS
MTB > PLOT C6 C4
```

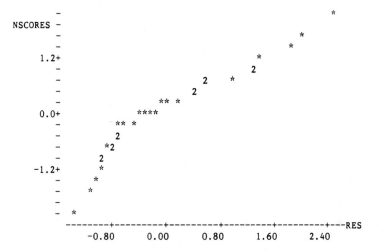

```
MTB > NOTE PLOT OF STANDARDIZED RESIDUALS VS PRED VALUES
MTB > PLOT C4 C5
```

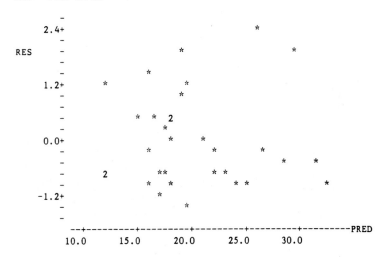

**11.19 a.**
```
MTB > NOTE PLOT OF 'MALTBEV' VS 'TIME'
MTB > PLOT C1 C2
```

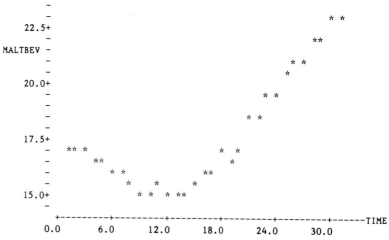

**b.** $\hat{y} = 17.6 - 0.422t + 0.0205t^2$

$\hat{y} = 18.5 - 0.741t = 0.0405t^2 - 0.00051t^3$

$R^2$ increases from 0.968 to 0.980; $\hat{\sigma}^2$ decreases from 0.24 to 0.153.

**11.20 a.** $\hat{y}_t = 1148.93 + 88.467t$

```
MTB > NOTE MULTIPLE PLOT OF Y AND YHAT VERSUS TIME
MTB > NOTE DATA IS ENERGY PRODUCTION
MTB > MPLOT C1 VS C2 C4 VS C2
```

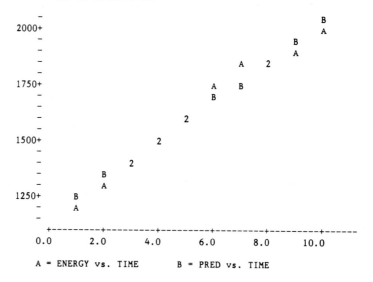

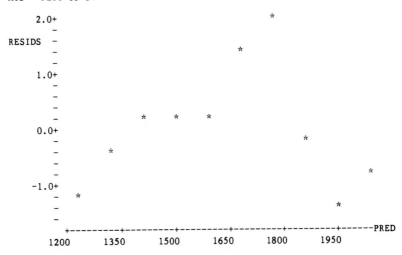

```
MTB > NOTE PLOT OF STANDARDIZED RESIDUALS VS PREDICTED VALUES
MTB > NOTE DATA IS ENERGY PRODUCTION
MTB > PLOT C3 C4
```

The residuals are negative, positive, and negative as time increases, suggesting the need for a quadratic term.

**11.20 b.** $\hat{y}_t = 1058.85 + 133.51t - 4.095t^2$; $R^2 = 0.989$

**Exercises 11.5**

**11.22 a.** 4.355 new students (in thousands)    **b.** 3.848 new students in thousands
**c.** (2.845, 4.851)
**11.24 a.** 1164.24 coins (millions)    **b.** 2915.77 coins (millions)
**11.26 a.** $2.09    **b.** $2.08

# CHAPTER 12

**Exercises 12.2**

**12.1 a.**

| Source | d.f. | SS | MS | EMS |
|--------|------|-----|-----|-----|
| Regions | 2 | 17,965,344 | 8,982,672 | $\sigma^2 + (5/2)\Sigma\alpha_i^2$ |
| Error | 12 | 35,175,824 | 2,931,318 | $\sigma^2$ |
| Total | 14 | 53,141,168 | | |

**b.** $\hat{\sigma}^2 = 2,931,318$
**c.** $F = 3.06$; R.R.: $F > F_{0.05}(2, 12) = 3.89$; retain $H_0$.

**12.3 a.**

| Source | d.f. | SS | MS | EMS |
|--------|------|-----|-----|-----|
| Structure type | 2 | 3018 | 1509 | $\sigma^2 + 2\Sigma\alpha_i^2$ |
| Error | 9 | 4377 | 486 | $\sigma^2$ |
| Total | 11 | 7395 | | |

**b.** $F = 3.10$; R.R.: $F > F_{0.05}(2, 9) = 4.26$; retain $H_0$.

**12.4 a.**

| Source | d.f. | SS | MS | EMS |
|---|---|---|---|---|
| Regions | 2 | 21.68 | 10.84 | $\sigma^2 + (5/2)\Sigma\alpha_i^2$ |
| Error | 12 | 21.23 | 1.77 | $\sigma^2$ |
| Total | 14 | 42.91 | | |

$F = 6.12$; R.R.: $F > 3.89$; reject $H_0$: $\mu_1 = \mu_2 = \mu_3$.

**b.** The divorce rate in the East appears to be lower than the rates in the other two regions.

**Exercises 12.3**

**12.6 a.**

| Source | d.f. | SS | MS | EMS |
|---|---|---|---|---|
| Make of car | 3 | 154.4 | 51.5 | $\sigma^2 + (4\alpha_1^2 + 3\alpha_2^2 + 3\alpha_3^2 + 4\alpha_4^2)/3$ |
| Error | 10 | 122.0 | 12.2 | $\sigma^2$ |
| Total | 13 | 276.4 | | |

**b.** $F = 4.22$; R.R.: $F > F_{0.05}(3, 10) = 3.71$; reject $H_0$.
**c.** Make 1: $19 \pm 3.89$; make 2: $12 \pm 4.49$; make 3: $21 \pm 4.49$; make 4: $15 \pm 3.89$

**12.8 a.**

| Source | d.f. | SS | MS | EMS |
|---|---|---|---|---|
| Account type | 2 | 1,312,240 | 656,120 | $\sigma^2 + (8\alpha_1^2 + 10\alpha_2^2 + 9\alpha_3^2)/2$ |
| Error | 24 | 1,342,895 | 55,954 | $\sigma^2$ |
| Total | 26 | 2,655,135 | | |

**b.** $F = 11.73$; R.R.: $F > F_{0.05}(2, 24) = 3.40$; reject $H_0$.
**c.** Yes, the average balance is higher in accounts that pay interest.

**Exercises 12.4**

**12.10 a.**

| Source | d.f. | SS | MS |
|---|---|---|---|
| Regions | 2 | 320.21 | 160.10 |
| Error | 12 | 25.32 | 2.11 |
| Total | 14 | 345.53 | |

**b.** $(-7.74, -4.28)$
**c.** $t = 9.73$; R.R.: $t > t_{0.05,12} = 1.782$; reject $H_0$.
**d.** $(-12.48, -8.48)$

**12.12 a.** $t = 2.49$; R.R.: $t > t_{0.05,9} = 1.833$; reject $H_0$.
**b.** $(5.67, 62.83)$

**12.14 a.** $(-1.62, 7.62)$
**b.** $t = 1.12$; R.R.: $|t| > t_{0.05,10} = 1.812$; retain $H_0$.

**Exercises 12.5**    **12.16 a.**  MTB > NOTE ANALYSIS OF RESPONSE TIME DATA (RANDOMIZED BLOCK)

```
MTB > SET C1
C1
    16    12    16    12   .   .   .

MTB > END
MTB > SET C2
C2
    1     2     3     4   .   .   .

MTB > END
MTB > SET C3
C3
    1     1     1     1   .   .   .

MTB > END
MTB > NAME C1 'SECONDS' C2 'TRIAL' C3 'SUBJECT'
MTB > PRINT C1-C3
```

| ROW | SECONDS | TRIAL | SUBJECT |
|---|---|---|---|
| 1 | 16 | 1 | 1 |
| 2 | 12 | 2 | 1 |
| 3 | 16 | 3 | 1 |
| 4 | 12 | 4 | 1 |
| 5 | 13 | 1 | 2 |
| 6 | 12 | 2 | 2 |
| 7 | 10 | 3 | 2 |
| 8 | 10 | 4 | 2 |
| 9 | 20 | 1 | 3 |
| 10 | 20 | 2 | 3 |
| 11 | 17 | 3 | 3 |
| 12 | 18 | 4 | 3 |
| 13 | 31 | 1 | 4 |
| 14 | 32 | 2 | 4 |
| 15 | 16 | 3 | 4 |
| 16 | 16 | 4 | 4 |
| 17 | 20 | 1 | 5 |
| 18 | 13 | 2 | 5 |
| 19 | 16 | 3 | 5 |
| 20 | 14 | 4 | 5 |
| 21 | 17 | 1 | 6 |
| 22 | 15 | 2 | 6 |
| 23 | 15 | 3 | 6 |
| 24 | 10 | 4 | 6 |
| 25 | 29 | 1 | 7 |
| 26 | 24 | 2 | 7 |
| 27 | 20 | 3 | 7 |
| 28 | 19 | 4 | 7 |
| 29 | 19 | 1 | 8 |
| 30 | 19 | 2 | 8 |
| 31 | 14 | 3 | 8 |
| 32 | 15 | 4 | 8 |

```
MTB > TABLE 'SUBJECT' BY 'TRIAL';
SUBC> MEAN 'SECONDS'.
 ROWS: SUBJECT       COLUMNS: TRIAL
                  1        2        3        4       ALL

         1     16.000   12.000   16.000   12.000   14.000
         2     13.000   12.000   10.000   10.000   11.250
         3     20.000   20.000   17.000   18.000   18.750
         4     31.000   32.000   16.000   16.000   23.750
         5     20.000   13.000   16.000   14.000   15.750
         6     17.000   15.000   15.000   10.000   14.250
         7     29.000   24.000   20.000   19.000   23.000
         8     19.000   19.000   14.000   15.000   16.750
       ALL     20.625   18.375   15.500   14.250   17.187


       CELL CONTENTS --
               SECONDS:MEAN

MTB > TWOWAY AOV DATA IN C1 SUBSCRIPTS IN C2 C3

ANALYSIS OF VARIANCE   SECONDS

       SOURCE       DF       SS       MS
       TRIAL         3      197.6    65.9
       SUBJECT       7      542.4    77.5
       ERROR        21      210.9    10.0
       TOTAL        31      950.9
```

**b.** $F = 7.75$; R.R.: $F > F_{0.05}(7, 21) = 2.49$; reject $H_0$; yes, there is a significant effect due to differences among subjects.

**c.** $t = 3.03$; R.R.: $t > t_{0.05,21} = 1.721$; reject $H_0$.

**12.18 a.**

| Source | d.f. | SS | MS | EMS |
|---|---|---|---|---|
| Blocks | 7 | 112 | 16.0 | $\sigma^2 + (3/4)\Sigma\beta_j^2$ |
| Treatments | 5 | 66 | 13.2 | $\sigma^2 + (4/3)\Sigma\alpha_i^2$ |
| Error | 35 | 70 | 2.0 | $\sigma^2$ |
| Total | 47 | 248 | | |

**b.** $t = 6$; $b = 8$

**c.** $t = 4.24$; R.R.: $|t| > t_{0.025,35} = 2.032$; reject $H_0$.

**d.** (1.563, 4.437)

**12.20 a.**

| Source | d.f. | SS | MS |
|---|---|---|---|
| Quarter | 3 | 5,132 | 1711 |
| City | 7 | 246,160 | 35166 |
| Error | 21 | 8,228 | 392 |
| Total | 31 | 259,520 | |

**b.** $F = 4.36$; R.R.: $F > F_{0.05}(3, 21) = 3.07$; reject $H_0$; there is a statistically significant quarterly effect.

**12.22 a.**

| Source | d.f. | SS | MS |
|---|---|---|---|
| Brand of seed | 2 | 204 | 102 |
| Soil | 3 | 242 | 81 |
| Error | 6 | 2846 | 474 |
| Total | 11 | 3292 | |

**b.** Type of soil is the natural blocking factor.

**c.** $F = 0.215$; R.R.: $F > F_{0.05}(2, 6) = 5.14$; retain $H_0$; there is no difference among brands of seeds.

# APPENDIX A

**Exercises A.2**

**A.1**  **a.** 150    **b.** 30    **c.** 0    **d.** 150

**A.2**  **a.** 2.4    **b.** 11.2; $s^2 = 2.8$

**A.3**  **a.** 15    **b.** 3    **c.** 0.6    **d.** 0
**e.** 14    **f.** 3.5    **g.** 0.6    **h.** 23.2

**A.4**  **a.** 21    **b.** 6    **c.** 91
**d.** 18.55    **e.** 91    **f.** 50,069

**A.5**  **a.** 4    **b.** 36    **c.** 71/24    **d.** 596/105

**A.6**  **b.** $(n + 1)/2$

**A.7**  **b.** $n(n^2 - 1)/12$

**Exercises A.3**

**A.10**  $y = 2x - 4$
**A.11**  $m = 3; b = -2$
**A.12**  $y = 4x - 5$
**A.13**  $m = -2; x_0 = 4$
**A.14**  $m = 2.5; y = 2.5x - 1$
**A.15**  $y = x/16$
**A.16**  77°F; 41°F; 5°F
**A.17**  $-160/9$°C
**A.18**  $y = 1.5 + 0.005x$
**A.19**  $y = -x/4 + 7/2$
**A.20**  $y = 3x + 7$
**A.21**  $y = x$

**Exercises A.4**

**A.22**  **a.** 40,320    **b.** 3,628,800    **c.** 1    **d.** 1
**A.23**  **a.** 20    **b.** 35    **c.** 56    **d.** 15
**A.24**  120; 210; 252
**A.25**  **a.** 455    **b.** 378    **c.** 1    **d.** 2000
**A.26**  1, 6, 15, 20, 15, 6, 1
**A.29**  **a.** $10! = 3,628,800$    **b.** $6! = 720$

# Index